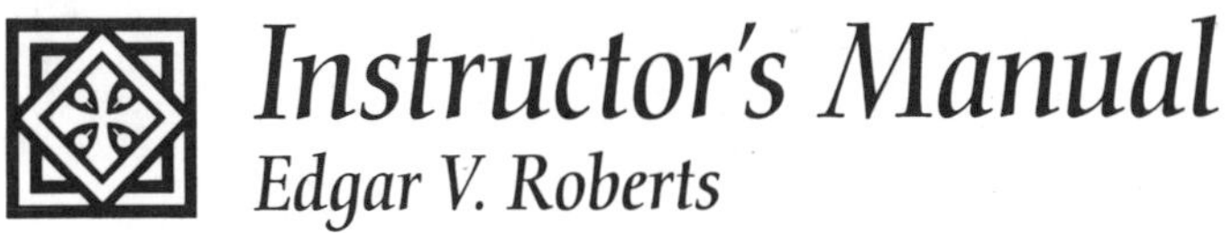

Instructor's Manual

Edgar V. Roberts

Literature

An Introduction to Reading and Writing

Sixth Edition

Edgar V. Roberts
Lehman College
City University of New York

Henry E. Jacobs

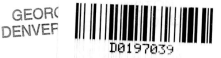

Prentice Hall ❖ Upper Saddle River, New Jersey 07458

PEARSON EDUCATION
Upper Saddle River, New Jersey 07458

10 9 8 7 6 5 4 3 2

ISBN-0-13-018402-0

Printed in the United States of America

Contents

■ Drama

■ Special Writing Topics about Literature

■ *This manual was designed and typeset by Jonathan Roberts on a Macintosh G4/450 computer, using Adobe InDesign software. The principal typeface family used is Adobe Nofret.*

To the Instructor

This manual is designed to help you in the practical tasks of teaching the various stories, poems, plays, and essay assignments in the fifth edition of *Literature: An Introduction to Reading and Writing*. For this reason, I encourage you to use the manual freely, in any way you wish, in classroom discussions. Above all, the conclusions in the manual should be used to encourage, never to dampen, student analysis. One problem encountered with questions in textbooks is that the questions are often mystifying. (I know that responses to many study questions take this approximate form: "What was on the author's mind on the day when he or she wrote the question?") I hope that this is not true of the study questions in the big book, but I have tried to make all the answers clear and unambiguous.

I do not claim perfection in these suggestions for discussion, nor do I expect that all instructors will find that they are adequate in all particulars. I have tried, however, to make the materials in the manual reliable both factually and logically. When there are points of varying interpretation I have offered possibilities for classroom discussion and disagreement.

For both the text and the manual, I would be grateful for suggestions for improvements and corrections of errors. Many people involved in the production of both text and manual have tried scrupulously to eliminate all mistakes. Please send both corrections of any mistakes you find, and suggestions for improvement (together with page numbers and locations of typographical errors) to me in care of Prentice Hall. If you have words of praise, these of course would be received with undying gratitude.

Thanks for assistance in the varying stages of the manual go to Carrie Brandon, Phil Miller, Joan Foley, and Virginia Livsey, all of Prentice Hall. I am grateful to Nanette Roberts for the helpful and penetrating advice she always gave me as long as she was able. I deeply mourn her untimely passing. I am especially grateful to Jonathan Roberts for his never-failing creativity in fashioning the manual's pleasing appearance.

— Edgar V. Roberts

Using This Manual

This manual is designed to help you in preparing to teach any of the works contained in the anthology, and also to help you in making assignments and in comparing individual works with other works. The chapters in the manual are therefore linked to the chapters of the big book Each of the manual chapters begins with introductory remarks and interpretive comments about the works (stories, poems, plays) within the chapter of the big book. These are then followed by detailed suggestions for discussion for every study question–question by question by question. Obviously our suggestions are not definitive but we offer them to give you a "launching pad" for your own classroom discussions. In addition, we have tried to be fairly complete in our answers, so that they might remind you of things that the classroom discussion might overlook or omit. Our goal in these suggestions for discussion is to provide you with as much assistance as possible.

In addition, to give you help in using the stories and poems in the *Stories for Additional Study* and *Poems for Additional Study* sections, we include brief general and thematic introductions and discussions of each of the works included there. In the "careers" chapters (11, 24, 31), we also provide a short working bibliography for further investigation and analysis.

Following the fiction section in the manual we provide a brief review of videotaped performances in *The American Short Story* series. Seven of the stories contained in the fiction section are included in this series ("I'm a Fool," "Paul's Case," "The Blue Hotel," "Barn Burning," "The Sky Is Gray," "Soldier's Home," and "The Jilting of Granny Weatherall").

Similarly, following the poetry section in the manual we provide a list of audiotapes available for 76 of the anthologized poets For the third section, however, on drama, we include references to available videotapes and audiotapes in our introductions in the manual.

Works for comparison. In this edition of the Instructor's Manual, a feature new in the fourth edition of the Manual is continued to help you in introducing comparisons of one work with others. This is the section entitled "Works for Comparison with . . . ." These "Works for Comparison" lists follow the "Writing topics" sections after each work discussed in the fiction and poetry sections (except for chapter 25). The works contained in the lists are all put there because they have points of comparison and contrast with the studied work. For example, the following entry appears for the story "Snow" by Robert Olen Butler (590):

WORKS FOR COMPARISON WITH BUTLER'S "SNOW"

Ozick, *The Shawl, 331*
Piercy, *Will We Work Together?,1185*
Salinas, *In a Farmhouse, 1193*
Tan, *Two Kinds, 226*

The listed works are parallel because all of them concern love, the effects of war, or the assimilation of immigrant people into American life. The circumstances of the works are different but are similar enough to encourage a vigorous discussion of comparisons and contrasts (text, Chapter 35, page 1979). This method of introducing works for comparison is an additional way of providing you with the help that is contained fully in the Thematic Table of Contents which immediately follows the comprehensive chapter-by-chapter Table of Contents. For your convenience, the text pages of the listed works offer you quick referral to the locations of the works in the big book.

FINDING LOCATIONS WITHIN THE MANUAL. The chapters in the manual are designed to be connected with the chapters in the text. In paginating the manual we have assumed that you will be beginning with a story, poem, or play in the big book, and that you will therefore find it easy to locate sections in the manual by reference to the pages in the big book. We have therefore used the page numbers from the big book as a running head along the top of each page of the manual (e.g., Text Pages 93–112; Text Pages 88–130, and so on). If you are teaching "The Concert Stages of Europe" by Jack Hodgins (396), for example, and are working up materials for the study questions following the story, the "Text Pages" number will direct you to the right spot in the manual. In this respect, the big book offers immediate and accurate access to the manual.

The page numbers of the manual itself are located at the bottom of each page.

Writing Assignments and Workshops

One of the central goals of the sixth edition of *Literature: An Introduction to Reading and Writing* is to help students learn to write about literature effectively. To this end, we discuss writing processes and strategies in every chapter. We encourage you to have your students read the relevant section(s) of the text before they undertake any writing assignments.

Discussions of prewriting and writing in the text presuppose in-class or out-of-class assignments that will generate fully developed essays of two to four pages. (Students frequently pad longer papers on a single work because, under the pressure of extending their thoughts to the prescribed number of pages, they begin to retell stories and plots, and therefore abandon their thematic development.) The prewriting and writing discussions focus on the movement from the formation of ideas to the finished essay. In the classroom, this process can be analyzed in stages.

Short developmental assignments. As a way of assigning writing as you lead your class in the analysis and discussion of the total writing process, you may wish to make daily assignments. To avoid overburdening yourself with mounds of papers to be examined in great detail, you might use the pass-fail option for your grades. You might also make the assignments no more lengthy than a single paragraph, which is an especially useful kind of assignment on most elements of literature. Such short assignments provide the advantages of constant writing and an ongoing monitoring of your students' skills. They can also, before class discussion, direct students to think about the material they are reading, thus leading to more productive and fruitful classes. Paragraph assignments can also serve as the building blocks for full-scale essays.

Writing assignments. Ideally, all assignments should be made in writing. This holds true for short paragraph assignments as well as full-scale essays. For a paragraph, a simple statement is probably enough, as long as your assignment is on a topic you have been studying with your students; e.g., *Write a paragraph about the character of Paul in Cather's "Paul's Case"* (assuming that Chapter 4, on Character, has been the subject of discussion). This same formulation may be employed with reference to any topic or element. These sorts of assignments might even be listed in the course syllabus. In full-scale essay assignments, however, you will usually want to explain the task in more detail (both in writing and in classroom discussion).

Sequencing assignments. In many instances, the sixth edition of *Literature: An Introduction to Reading and Writing* will be used in courses where your students have had little experience in writing about literature. You might therefore organize the writing assignments so that they begin with a rather easy (and obvious) goal such as those in the first few chapters, and then go on to tasks that are progressively more difficult. In initial assignments, you might give your students a fully developed central idea of your own devising, and ask them to produce an essay based on this idea. Such a procedure cuts short the floundering stages of prewriting and enables students to focus immediately on the mechanics of organizing, writing, and revising their essays. As the course progresses, and as your students become more familiar with the stages of composition, you can provide less direction. Ultimately, you may give your students complete control of their own writing, including the freedom to select details, develop the thesis, and generally create their own individual essays.

In-Class Writing Workshops

If time permits, in-class writing workshops should be incorporated into your course. These can be useful to help students improve their writing. Three types of workshops are especially helpful: outlining, rough-draft workshops, and post mortems.

Outlining. In this type of workshop, you can establish a sample thesis based on a work that the class has just discussed. Then you might ask your students to outline a possible essay, paragraph by paragraph. The resulting discussion can be particularly effective in teaching organization and the selection of supporting details.

Rough-draft workshops. Time permitting, all out-of-class essays might be submitted in two stages: rough draft and final form. You can go over rough drafts quickly, and advise students about obvious problems. To provide further help in the early drafting stages, an actual rough-draft workshop can be effective. The idea is to get students to read, analyze, criticize, and edit the developing essays of their peers. Of course, such rough drafts should be in readable condition if not in finished form. Students should be encouraged to treat the exercise seriously, since a competent job will obviously affect grades on the finished papers.

Mechanics. Students should be paired to exchange papers. Using a checklist like the sample on the following pages, which we encourage you to reproduce and distribute to your classes, students should go through the papers carefully. Each student of the pair should then explain whatever problems she or he found in the other's essay.

Post mortems. This type of workshop involves an in-class evaluation of several essays in final form. You can select student essays that demonstrate the strengths or weaknesses that you wish to discuss. Sample papers may be duplicated (xerographed, dittoed) or projected.

Sample Guidelines for Student Editors in Rough–Draft Workshops

Before you begin working on your partner's draft, please study the questions in these guidelines. Then read through the draft carefully, as if you were reading it aloud. When you discover trouble in understanding your partner's sentences, or in following his or her meaning or reasoning, or when you think one of the questions below might be helpful in making an improvement, make a marginal note so that you can find the problem again. After you finish your study of the draft, go over the trouble spots with your partner in light of the following fifteen questions. As you raise the issues with your partner, discuss how you may create improvements and modifications. Above all, don't do your partner's work. Ask questions; make suggestions; provide choices. In these ways you will be helping your partner make his or her own improvements.

1. Is the central idea clearly stated in the first paragraph?
2. Is the central idea followed and supported in the draft? Do all the paragraphs support the original idea, and do they hang together?
3. Does the draft have a strong and smooth introduction, and a conclusion that closes the essay without being abrupt, misleading, or irrelevant?
4. Does the writer avoid the trap of retelling the story, restating the ideas in the poem, or describing the actions of the play, while forgetting to make proper points in the essay?
5. Is the structure of the paper logical? Can you follow the thoughts and conclusions easily? Do the paragraphs follow each other logically?
6. Is there adequate transition between paragraphs?
7. Are the paragraphs correctly developed? Does each paragraph deal with one major thought or set of assertions? Should any paragraph be divided? How, and where?
8. Does the writer use enough quotation (but not too much) to support the central idea of the essay?
9. Does the writer avoid sentence problems? Check for the following:
    a. Sentences that are too long and confusing. Can they be broken into two or more shorter sentences?

Example: Cather creates an interesting and disturbing story in "Paul's Case" through the main character, Paul, an intelligent, sensitive, gifted, and potentially excellent person who has the misfortune to think himself beyond or above the usual demands of school, home, neighborhood, and law, thus illustrating either his bad luck or major flaws in his character, depending on how his character is interpreted.

Better: In "Paul's Case," Cather's interest and understanding are focused on her major character, Paul. Paul is pictured as an intelligent, sensitive, gifted, and potentially excellent person, but somehow he is unable to adjust to the world around him. Thus he fails at school, has difficulties at home, dislikes the neighborhood in which he lives, and finally breaks the law. The pathos of the story is that Paul, really a fine person, is not bad, but is primarily unlucky.

b. Run-on sentences or comma splices that link two complete sentences.

Example 1: *Cather's Paul is not bad but unlucky he steals money and spends it on a trip of enjoyment to New York.*

Example 2: *Cather's Paul is not bad but unlucky, he steals money and spends it on a trip of enjoyment to New York.*

Correction for both examples: *Cather's Paul is not bad but unlucky; he steals money and spends it on a trip of enjoyment to New York.*

c. Sentence fragments:

1. The result of groups of words missing a subject or verb (e.g., *This thought about a young woman who develops strength of character as a result of her responsibility.*)
2. The result of a word group beginning with a participle instead of a noun and finite verb (e.g., She is a lovely, aging woman. *Thinking about her past life and all the difficulties she has endured.*)
3. The result of the use of a dependent clause as a sentence (e.g., *Because the Duke of "My Last Duchess" knows that he has total power over the Count, his envoy, and his daughter.*)
4. The result of the use of an object of a preposition as the subject of a verb (e.g., *Within this character thinks sympathetically and understandingly of the problems her friend has encountered on the lonely farm.*)

d. Awkward or ill-written sentences.

e. Sentences that are confusing because of grammatical errors or misplaced modifiers.

f. Short, choppy sentences that might be more interestingly combined to make one or two longer sentences.

10. Does the writer avoid agreement problems? Do nouns and pronouns always match up?

Example: When *one* reads this story, *we* see that Phoenix Jackson is very old, and respect her greatly.

Do verbs and nouns agree as to number?

Example: A *person* in these conditions *are* disposed to be overly imaginative.

11. Does the writer avoid shifts in verb tenses?

Example: Phoenix *walks* through the woods and then *climbed* the steps of the hospital.

As a general principle, use the present tense exclusively when describing actions and speeches in any type of imaginative literature.

Example: The Prodigal Son *endures* great hardship for a long period, but when he *returns* home he is *welcomed* by his father, who *is delighted* to have him back.

See especially page 25–26 of the text for a detailed analysis and discussion of tense in the writing of essays about literary works.

12. Does the writer avoid excessive repetition of particular words, phrases, or sounds, particularly in close proximity? (Use the example of this question, which repeats *particularly* four words after *particular*, and then uses the word *proximity*, which also begins with the *p* sound.)

13. Does the writer use words that seem inappropriate or out of place? Is a uniform level of diction maintained?

14. Does the writer spell words correctly, and make proper use of capital letters?

15. Does the writer use punctuation correctly? In checking punctuation, pay careful attention to commas, semicolons, and colons.

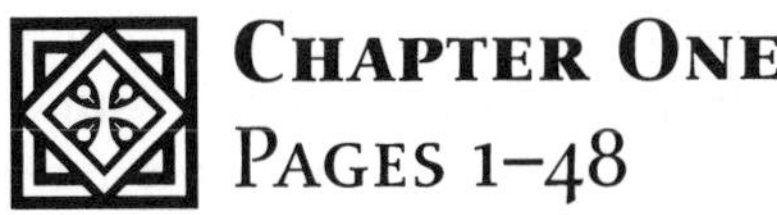

Chapter One
Pages 1–48

Introduction: Reading, Responding to, and Writing about Literature

Chapter 1 is a general introduction to literature and to the skills of writing about it. The chapter also includes one story which is used as the specimen for the various topics. In keeping with the introductory objectives, it proposes the most essential and basic of writing assignments: on likes and dislikes. All of these tasks may be somewhat imposing if taken in one large bite. You therefore may wish to assign pages 1–3 as a general introduction to the various genres, and then use "The Necklace" (4–11) as the basis of your introductory discussion about characteristics of literature generally and fiction specifically.

For emphasis on writing, pages 3-40 (including "The Necklace") make up a unit centered around the procedure of reading a literary work, making marginal annotations, keeping a journal of all responses, and then going through the prewriting and writing tasks of preparing an essay. Along with the description of this process, there is additional material on the characteristics of good writing. You may wish to coordinate these passages with the assignment on likes and dislikes on pages 40-48.

You might use the writing section as a separate introductory unit, but we also hope that you will find these sections a convenient reference point for your students throughout your course. We believe that the section offers basic advice for students no matter where they may be as thinkers and writers about literature.

Please note the special sections in this chapter. These are (1) *Writing by Hand, Typewriter, or Word Processor,* on page 22; (2) *Using the Present Tense of Verbs when Referring to Actions and Ideas,* on page 25; and (3) *Using the Names of Authors,* on page 36. These sections bring up points that need explaining when students first write on literary topics. You might wish to introduce and discuss them as a special group early in the semester, when you make your first assignments.

The first section of *Literature: An Introduction to Reading and Writing,* on pages 1–3, is designed to get students thinking about the nature of literature. Classroom discussion should produce many questions and provide the chance to relate the general principles to works in the anthology and also to works that students know from other sources. The paragraph on the power and value of literature (pages 1–2) is an attempt to express briefly some of the ideas about reading that students certainly know, but which they themselves may never have articulated.

The definition of genres on pages 2 and 3 is designed as a quick introduction to the types. In discussing it, you might wish to refer quickly to the story on pages 4–11 to illustrate the generic qualities that otherwise may remain abstract in the minds of your students. In any event, the use of "The Necklace" is virtually mandatory in the use of the first chapter. The marginal notations accompanying this story demonstrate how responses embody both assimilation of the factual details and initial observations about character, situation, and meaning generally. The story thus illustrates the first phase of studying a literary text.

Although students are familiar with the word "study," they may not fully understand what studying is in actuality. Study is to be contrasted with the act of simple reading, and hence the subject of study is introduced on pages 12–21. This section attempts to explain the need for a regularized set of steps to be followed, more or less in the order suggested, in the process of developing not just a familiarity with literary works but also an understanding of them. Obviously, the key to study is the reinforcement to learning provided by the methodical keeping of a journal-notebook. It is surprising to learn that students sometimes have no clear notion of what to include. The marginal notations in "The Necklace" provide one type of response, while the specimen journal entries on pages 12–13 give a sense of the responses and observations that can form the basis for further thought and writing. Students who dislike marking up pages of books might include both types in their notebooks.

Writing Essays on Literary Topics, *pages 15–29*

The writing component of the introduction, beginning on page 15, is a most important section for students. Because it assumes that students know "The Necklace," we stress once again that this story be assigned before the study of writing essays begins. The general definitions of an essay on page 15, for example, together with all the subsequent materials, will be meaningful only if students already have a good grasp of the story.

In the order of composition, once students have read the story assigned and begin to create their own essays, the discussion of "brainstorming" outlined on pages 17-21 is an essential first step. Sometimes students hesitate to commit their first thoughts to paper during this brainstorming stage. If hesitancy or self deprecation is a problem, it is important to disabuse students of these feelings. You might emphasize that once something—anything at all—is on paper, students may work with it and develop it as a part of the essay that they are shaping. The special section on page 22 is designed to stress the importance of getting something written, whether by hand, typewriter, or—especially for many of today's students—word processor. Even if students are uncomfortable with anything but a pencil or pen, however, it is worth emphasizing that writing is an essential aspect of thinking, because writing adds the dimension of vision to the process of thought.

Building on the brainstorming stage, and perhaps a part of it, is the process of establishing a central idea (pages 21–24). It is essential to the essay-writing process, because it enables students to focus their thoughts and to rewrite them in a clearly formed way.

The development of a central idea about a work is not a challenge that many students will have met before they get into your class. For this reason you may wish to devote a portion of classroom time to the discussion of thinking generally. A common misunderstanding you may need to overcome is that any kind of mental activity may be defined as thinking. Thus, the process of reasoning needed for developing a central idea should be distinguished from feeling, responding, daydreaming, planning a purchase (although such planning may involve some thinking), determining the day's activities, and so on. The process of abstract thinking will not come readily to the application of reading, however, unless the students can be shown that seemingly disparate details have some unifying, connecting theme. This process, involving the formulation of unifying themes in a work, is perhaps one of the major elements for you to stress in the initial stages of teaching writing about literary subjects.

The section from pages 24–27 concerns the mechanics of shaping an essay and of outlining. The central idea and thesis sentence separation, you will note, is an option presented as a way of dividing the thematic unity of an essay from the actual topics of the essay. Students often express nervousness about outlining. One of the most important assurances you can give them is therefore that a formal outline does not need to precede the writing of the essay. Instead, an outline is a constantly developing aspect of the composing process–one that can be provisionally established and then modified and reshaped as the student thinks and writes. Too often an outline is viewed as a preordained mold, into which the novice writer is expected to pour ideas. If the outline is used as a guide to thought and also as an incentive to develop further ideas, however, then it does not need to be such a frightening thing. This is not to say that outlines need to be neglected, but rather that they should be used for what they are–as an important part of the prewriting and freewriting processes leading to an advanced stage of composition–a means of giving shape to a writing process that is already well advanced.

The Two Demonstrative Student Essays (28 and 37). In this edition the two demonstrative essays are separated by the discussion entitled "Developing and Strengthening Your Essay Through Revision" beginning on page 29. The intention of presenting this discussion here is to emphasize the actual process of writing that should occur after a first draft: analysis, correction, revising, and rewriting. The first essay (28–29) is in an early but nevertheless acceptable stage. The second represents a rethinking and a revision in light of the discussion on revising which extends from pages 29 through 37. Our hope is that students will benefit from seeing how the same topic material may be reshaped and rewritten to fit a central idea. Accordingly, the second essay introduces the way in which students should include details in their essays. In paragraph 2, sentence 2, of the first essay, for example, the detail is simply reported:

> The walls are "drab," the furniture "threadbare," and the curtains "ugly."

In the second essay, this same material, in keeping with the connection of setting to character, is given a stronger thrust:

> Though everything is serviceable, she is dissatisfied with the "drab" walls, "threadbare" furniture, and "ugly" curtains.

A further discussion, stressing how the second essay keeps the central idea foremost, should provide the chances to make clear the ways in which students should emphasize their central ideas as they introduce materials into their essays.

Developing and Strengthening Your Essay Through Revision, *pages 29–37*

This section is a brief introduction to the standards by which student essays (and more broadly, all writing) are to be judged. It has been developed over a period of many years in response to innumerable student inquiries about why grades have not been higher on submitted work. Perhaps the greatest problem of students is that they summarize works rather than analyze them. Thus the suggested changing of the order in an essay from the order in the work, for example (29), is only an elementary device that may free students from the trap of retelling a story. Also, the thought that the potential audience will already know the literary work may also help students focus on their own ideas in preference to summarizing. The idea that literary material is to be used as evidence (29–30), in the writing of essays, is a way to help students break away from the narrative or logical order of the original.

For the section "Keep to your Point" beginning on page 31, we have introduced an unfocused paragraph, and then shown how, with the aid of the line drawings (31, 32), this paragraph may be focused in the light of the topic idea. Students would benefit from your pointing out to them the functional relationship of the underlined parts to the topic. Also, these underlined parts show that the writing of essays on literary topics should emphasize that the student writer take an interpretive, explanatory role with regard to his or her intended audience. There may be no other idea that is so important in the teaching of writing.

The final two parts of this writing section, "Checking the Development and Organization of Your Ideas" (33–34), and "Using Exact, Comprehensive, and Forceful Language" (34–36), are presented both as short-term and long-term goals. Because the need for accurate and forceful language will always be with everyone who ever takes up a pen or sits down in front of a word processor, you may wish to bring up the point whenever it becomes relevant as a result of student writing in your course. Indeed, many essential problems that students encounter as they write may be addressed by reference to a number of the subtopics in this section, which is presented as a guide and set of goals to which students may always go for help when they need to conceptualize and execute any writing task.

Responding to Literature: Likes and Dislikes, *pages 40–48*

The reason for this type of writing assignment is that too often responses are ignored while the business of analysis and thought goes forward. Therefore this discussion, coming here as the first actual writing assignment described for students in the big book, is intended to remind students that their responses are important and foremost. Additionally, this first exercise in response might be related to the section on reader-response criticism discussed in Chapter 33.

In relation to personal responses, it is important to consider the "de gustibus" argument that individual taste and opinion may take precedence over literary judgment. Thus we emphasize on pages 42–45 that responses of disliking may be modified upon thought to become the grounds for the broadened appreciation of literary works. We suggest that in teaching you might wish to stress this section as a reminder that the process of intellectual growth of students will be complemented by a corresponding development of taste. Of special note also is the list of possible reasons for liking a work (42) and in addition the recommended practice of keeping a journal record of responses. With regard to first impressions, it is most important to stress the words "informed" and "explained" (see pages 40–41). The journal should be used as an incentive to the need for students to comprehend all aspects of the work being studied. Responses based on an inaccurate reading will not be valid, and this point should be stressed for their benefit.

Sometimes, however, despite full understanding, a reader will not like a work. On page 45, we treat this possibility, emphasizing that disliking, as with liking, must be grounded both in proper information about the work and also in a clearly defined standard of response.

Writing about Responses: Likes and Dislikes, *pages 45–48*

This assignment is visualized as an exercise in how students respond to a literary text. It is not to be a full-scale analysis, nor is it to be a reasoned defense of the literary merit of the piece being studied. Rather, the writing is to be based on a simple response: What in the work provoked positive or negative reactions? Thus, of the types of responses for the body of an essay described on page 45 (and 42), the most common one will be a list of things liked. The demonstrative essay (46–47) illustrates an essay-length treatment along these lines. You might wish to read parts of the essay with your students to demonstrate how each of Mathilde's good qualities is developed at paragraph length. Perhaps the most important point to emphasize here is that the reasons for liking are developed beyond the simple description of an abstract response of approval.

The other possible ways to develop an essay about likes and dislikes are not illustrated in the demonstrative essay. You might discuss these with your students, noting that the second one described on page 46 is in effect a description of responses upon reading, and that the third and fourth possible essay developments are more fully considered on pages 40–45.

Questions for Guy de Maupassant, *The Necklace*, *pages 4–11*

Please note that in this edition the biographies precede the fiction selections, with the exception of this story, in which the biographical material is included in the footnote.

Questions for Study, together with Responses

(1) Describe the character of Mathilde. On balance, is she as negative as she seems at first? Why does Maupassant consider as "heroic" her efforts to help with the debt? How does her character create the situation that causes the financial penance the Loisels must undergo?

On balance, Mathilde is not negative, for in paragraphs 99–104, Maupassant describes the massive effort that she exerts to help pay the debt. The heroism that the speaker attributes to her suggests that readers are, finally, to admire her. The quality of character that is a first cause of the misfortune, however, is her refusal to accept the reality of her genteel poverty and her desire to use the borrowed necklace to appear prosperous.

(2) Are Mathilde's daydreams unusual for a woman of her station? How might a case be made that Maupassant fashions the ironic conclusion to demonstrate that Mathilde deserves her misfortune?

Her daydreams are not unusual. It is unlikely that Maupassant contrived the misfortune as a deserved punishment, particularly because Mathilde's good qualities are brought out as the story progresses. Also, the surprise ending indicates that the story is less concerned with showing how Mathilde gets her comeuppance than with evoking regret along with surprise. However, one might still claim that Mathilde deserves at least some acquaintance with reality, but certainly not the disaster that occurs. Thus Maupassant succeeds in directing sympathy toward Mathilde, together with whatever criticism she deserves because of her daydreams.

(3) What sort of person is Loisel? How does his character contribute to the financial disaster?

Loisel is a calm and complacent sort. He is satisfied with simple pleasures and is out of his depth at a formal social occasion. He is a hard, sincere worker, however, and sacrifices tirelessly for the sake of his integrity and honor. He contributes to the financial disaster by not insisting on confessing the loss of the necklace to Jeanne.

(4) Describe the relationship between Mathilde and Loisel as shown in their conversations. Does this relationship seem to be intimate, or is it less personal and more formal?

The conversations of Mathilde and Loisel in paragraphs 8–38 indicate that Mathilde pressures and manipulates Loisel. She seems to be less interested in him and in his needs than in her own. Loisel wants to please Mathilde, but is unable to deal with her on a personal level. More to attain his own composure than to give her pleasure, he buys her the dress and suggests that she borrow the jewels. There is no evidence in the story that the two have a warm and loving relationship.

(5) The speaker states that small things save or destroy people (paragraph 105). How does "The Necklace" bear out this idea? What role might fate play in this scheme of things, or is chance the more important governing influence?

The story bears out the idea, for any number of things could be cited as the cause of the disaster, none of them by themselves of major significance: (a) the invitation, (b) the new dress, (c) the borrowing of the necklace, (d) the hurrying away from the party (paragraphs 55–59), (e) the failure of Jeanne to tell Mathilde that the necklace is only a cheap imitation. In a discussion about whether the story emphasizes fate or chance, one should probably emphasize chance, for the idea of fate implies a more systematic pattern of opposition than the circumstances working against Mathilde.

(6) To what degree does Maupassant illustrate a view that might be described as "economic determinism" in the story? That is, how does he relate economic status to happiness and character fulfillment?

Maupassant introduces the idea of "the horrible life of the needy" in paragraph 98, and his description of what happens to Mathilde under these circumstances may be construed as an illustration of economic determinism. In addition, the fact that Jeanne Forestier is "always youthful, always beautiful, always attractive" can be read the same way inasmuch as Jeanne is "rich" (paragraph 6). The clear contrast, together with Maupassant's paragraph about "what would life have been like if she had not lost that necklace?" (paragraph 105), indicates that in this story at least Maupassant makes a connection between the economic condition of people and their happiness and character fulfillment. The discussion of economic determinism in Chapter 33 (p. 1833) might profitably be introduced here, at least briefly.

Writing Topics. The character of Mathilde. The structure of the story, including the surprise ending. The use of symbols. Economic issues. Tone and the irony of situation in the story.

Works for Comparison with "The Necklace"

Chopin, *The Story of an Hour*, 393
Glück, *Penelope's Song*, 979
Ibsen, *A Dollhouse*, 1793
Steinbeck, *The Chrysanthemums*, 447

Special Topics for Writing and Argument about Responses To Literature, *page 48*

(1) The first of these topics is designed to cause students to confront their own reading backgrounds. Some will have read a considerable amount, and will have a problem in picking and choosing from among the works they have read. Others (alas!) may not have been reading much, and therefore the option of discussing recent films or TV shows will be a convenient alternative for them. It might also make them think seriously of undertaking more future reading on their own.

(2) The second topic is designed to get students thinking about the state of a "finished" essay on the work they have just read. If they can bring out additional reasons for like or dislike, they will readily understand the ideas that writing is a process that develops in stages and that revision and rewriting are in effect never-ending. One is reminded of the idea that writing is not so much finished as abandoned–an important concept for students to assimilate.

(3) The third topic can be fruitful in helping students see writing from an author's position. Some students will be quite successful in developing their own paragraphs–which can sometimes blossom as complete stories. Not all students will be equal to the task, however, but even unsuccessful attempts can prove helpful for students in understanding the challenges facing writers of fiction.

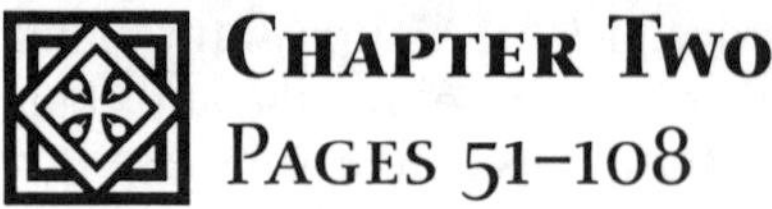

Chapter Two
Pages 51–108

Fiction: An Overview

The first part of this chapter, pages 51–63, is an introduction to the major characteristics and concepts of prose fiction. We therefore recommend that you assign it before any of the other fiction chapters. The aim of the section is a general, while also fairly complete, coverage of fiction. Thus, point of view is just briefly introduced here (58–60) so that students will have an overview of that topic as they study chapters such as plot, character, or symbolism. Should you not have time to use Chapter 5, which treats point of view in detail, you would still be assured that your students would know something about it from their introductory study here.

You may wish to expand upon the brief introductory explanations in this section. For example, a short definition and historical overview of narration and fiction is presented on 51–52, but you may wish to develop either of these topics in more depth. The same applies to the references to the beginnings of modern fiction (52–53) and to the development of the short story (53). The reproduction of *The Death of Socrates* (59), by David, should give students the chance to connect the narrative methods of art and fiction.

The key elements of fictional character (55–56), plot (56), structure (56–57), and theme (57) are all developed more fully in later chapters, so that here you need to be sure only that your students develop familiarity with the concepts. Still, there will be questions that need answers. We suggest that the five stories included in this chapter—"Neighbors," "An Old-Fashioned Story," "The Things They Carried," "Everyday Use," and "Taking Care"—may be used as references, because the problem in this introductory discussion will be maintaining concreteness.

The same will also hold true for your discussion of the major "tools" of fiction. Thus, narration (57), style (58), point of view (58–60), description (60), dialogue (60–61), and commentary (62) may all be discussed as they apply to the stories anthologized in the chapter, and may serve as reference points for discussions later in the school year. Tone and irony (61) and symbolism and allegory (61–62) are mentioned in reference to stories included earlier and later in the book. Hence your discussion should maintain concreteness through continued references to the relevant sections. Obviously, as your discussion progresses, students may introduce references to fictional and real-life incidents and characters that they have encountered in your course and elsewhere.

RAYMOND CARVER, *Neighbors*, *pages 63–67*

Suggestions for Discussing the Study Questions, page 67

(1) The speaker of "Neighbors" is an unnamed observer (third person limited). The speaker's attention is focused on Bill Miller, who is the major character, along with his wife Arlene.

(2) Carver's narrator introduces the Millers in the opening sentences: "Bill and Arlene Miller were a happy couple. But now and then they felt they alone among their circle had been passed by somehow, [. . .]" When their neighbors the Stones, who always seem to lead "a fuller and brighter life" (are such feelings anything more than normal?) leave for a ten-day trip, the Millers are asked to care for the vacant apartment and the Stones' cat. At this point the Millers' curiosity begins to consume their lives. Once the Stones entrust the Millers with their apartment, there are six scenes, or vignettes, all demonstrating the Millers' increasingly unstable behavior.

Although at first Bill's behavior the apartment of his neighbors seems normal enough, but in paragraph 16 he puts Harriet Stone's pills into his pocket and helps himself to some liquor, which can be construed as nothing else but theft. After this, each scene becomes progressively more detached and unreal, with the climax being in paragraphs 43–45, when Bill puts on Jim Stone's clothes and then Harriet's clothes. Arlene also shares this strange behavior, for when she goes next door to care for the cat she returns much later with a tale of "some pictures" (paragraph 61), which we assume are pornographic. The story does not so much end as stop, for Arlene has left the key within the Stones' apartment and therefore the Millers cannot get back in.

(3) The action of "Neighbors" justifies classifying it as minimalist and absurd. It is minimalist because there are no explanations—nothing but the simplest language and minimal descriptions of what is happening. It may also be considered absurdist because, even though the actions are connected to the lives of the Millers, they go beyond normality. In real life, most people in the house of a neighbor would find it natural to look about, take a book off a shelf, and look at wall

hangings. But could anyone regard the Miller's examination and use of the Stones' apartment as normal? Students may wish to consider the meaning of paragraph 55: "It's funny," she said. "You know—to go in someone's place like that." Does this statement, made by Arlene, justify the degree to which Bill and Arlene assume the identity of the absent Stones? Where does realism end and absurdity begin?

WRITING TOPICS. The characters of the Millers. Bill's absurdist actions in the apartment of the Stones. Is there a realistic basis for what the Millers do? Carver's style.

WORKS FOR COMPARISON WITH "NEIGHBORS"

Eliot, *Preludes*, 759
Field, *Icarus*, 987
Glaspell, *Trifles*, 1244, and *A Jury of Her Peers*, 202
Kincaid, *What I Have Been Doing Lately*, 148
Nemerov, *Life Cycle of Common Man*, 1179

LAURIE COLWIN, *An Old-Fashioned Story*, *pages 67–77*

The unusual part of this story is that it is not just about people meeting when they are young adults, and then falling in love. Instead it follows the young people from childhood, and it demonstrates that early emotions, particularly those of the point-of-view character, Elizabeth, are inimical to this outcome. The story concentrates on Elizabeth, who is a growing character and who develops from general rebellion concentrated on abhorring Nelson, whom we see at first as a do-gooder and a "rat, a suck-up, a traitor to all children." We follow many mix-ups in her life, including a failed love affair, and finally we see her realize she and Nelson are not very different, and never were.

Students may wish to discuss the phrase "old fashioned" in the title. Superficially, the story may be considered old fashioned because it is, finally, a love story. It is also old fashioned (and ironic) because the young couple, through their own understanding and not through compulsion, actually fulfill the "ardent hope" of their parents that they will "like each other well enough to marry" (paragraph 1).

Suggestions for Discussing the Study Questions, page 77

(1) The Rodkers and the Leopolds are bluebloods in the tradition of families who assume that alliances can be cemented by the marriages of their children. As a result, the parents always assume that Nelson and Elizabeth are intended for each other—an arrangement that secretly outrages Elizabeth, whose main characteristic is

her rebeliousness. She rebels in many ways, some of which are her selection of friends, her working at the stable, her setting up her own apartment, and her hoodwinking her parents. There are few social conventions that she does not flaunt, particularly her enticement of Nelson's brother James. The freedom she covets most is the desire to be herself, but, interestingly, this desire manifests itself in her feeling that the ultimate liberty is to read what she likes (paragraph 29).

(2) It is difficult to evaluate Nelson because for most of the story he is viewed objectively and dramatically, through the filter of Elizabeth's childhood and adolescent rebelliousness. Elizabeth dislikes Nelson for his apparent perfection, but uses him in the war she constantly wages against her parents. We learn most about him when he appears at Elizabeth's apartment just prior to Holly's New Year's Eve party, when we learn that he was just as much of a rebel as Elizabeth. He is, of course, superior to James, who, despite his spirit of free living, is ordinary, pompous and dull.

(3) The narrator is unnamed, and is therefore not a character in the story but a "fly on the wall" observer who explains Elizabeth and her attitudes from a limited omniscient point of view. We therefore learn about James and Nelson only as Elizabeth learns about them. A totally omniscient narrator would need to disclose information about the two young men as the story unfolds. By limiting attention to Elizabeth, Colwin is able to delay this knowledge until it is significant for the story development.

(4) The story has many amusing parts. A few are the belief that reading makes people lopsided (paragraph 23), Elizabeth's image that Nelson eats mashed potatoes with his hands (paragraph 11), and "A Mother's Ten Commandments" (paragraph 58). There are many other funny sections, to which students will draw attention.

(5) The concluding surprises are two, namely that Nelson believes that his "family is silly, stuffy, and rigid" (paragraph 107), and that Elizabeth and Nelson finally realize that they love each other, despite all Elizabeth's attempts to believe otherwise.

WRITING TOPICS. The character of Elizabeth, or of Nelson. The story's humor. Social satire in the story. Irony.

WORKS FOR COMPARISON WITH "AN OLD-FASHIONED STORY"

Butler, *Snow, 590*
Chekhov, *The Bear, 1625*
Henley, *Am I Blue, 1635*
Kauffmann, *The More the Merrier, 1255*
Viorst, *True Love, 1008*

Tim O'Brien, *The Things They Carried,* *pages 77-88*

This memorable story is set in the Vietnamese war, a war which is remote for many of today's students but which remains vivid with their parents. The story itself is unusual because of O'Brien's emphasis on the details of "the things they carried" and also because of the many characters who make themselves instantly real. In the story's brief length O'Brien successfully conveys the entire way of life of the men in the unnamed platoon. He does not make claims about the ugliness, dirt, and horror of the war, but lets detail accumulate to speak for itself.

Suggestions for Discussing the Study Questions, pages 88–89

(1) We learn about the life and thoughts of Lieutenant Jimmy Cross from the omniscient limited narration, which is alternated with detailed materials about what the men of the platoon carry on their patrols. Cross is therefore a centralizing, unifying character. He loves Martha, the girl back home, but he also realizes that concentrating on her has limited his leadership of his men. After Lavender is killed Kiowa believes that Cross is grieving over the death, when actually Cross is grieving "mostly" for "Martha, and for himself, because she belonged to another world" (paragraph 53). In addition to the unity provided by Cross, the story is unified by the many references to Lavender's death (both before and after) and by the many concentrated descriptions of the things the soldiers carry.

(2) The many repetitions about the weights, the need to carry things, and Lavender's death create the story's realism. The sometimes overwhelming detail literally transfers the experience of the men directly to readers, who cannot weigh the things but who nevertheless feel the heaviness of the burdens and also the threat of death that the men face each minute of every day.

(3) At first, Mitchell Sanders is not articulate or expansive in expressing the meaning and moral of the severed thumb. As much as he can do is to point to the dead man and say "There it *is*, man" (paragraph 37). Dobbins says that there is no moral. Later on (paragraph 75), the men consider the moral further. Students might wish to discuss what it means to repeat "there it is" as an "act of poise" and the further meaning of "you can't change what can't be changed."

(4) Paragraph 39 is skillfully detailed and is the central as well as the longest paragraph in the story. The men carry objects of all sorts, and also infections, parasites, and, literally, the soil of Vietnam itself, and they do so endlessly. Sometimes they die, as Lavender

dies. It is fair to say that the paragraph encapsulates the experiences of the men on constant patrol and in constant danger.

WRITING TOPICS. The character of Jimmy Cross. The frank dialogue among the men. The meaning and effect of the details about what the men carry.

WORKS FOR COMPARISON WITH "THE THINGS THEY CARRIED"

Forché, *Because One Is Always Forgotten, 1153*
Owen, *Dulce et Decorum Est, 810*
Ozick, *The Shawl, 331*
Seeger, *I Have a Rendezvous with Death, 1196*

ALICE WALKER, *Everyday Use,* *pages 89-95*

As a work of fiction, "Everyday Use" demonstrates a transition from one type of development to another. There is a mixture of narration and reflection in the first sixteen paragraphs, in which the narrator, Mrs. Johnson, describes herself while reflecting on the background and characteristics of her two daughters. At paragraph 17 the dramatic section of the story begins with the appearance of Dee and Hakim-a-Barber. After this time the story is reportorial and dramatic in nature, inasmuch as the subject is the dinner and also the requests (demands?) of Dee (Wangero) to secure the family artifacts. An answer to the issue about the use fiction makes of both narration and dialogue is that there should probably be a mixture of the two. Too much material like that at the beginning, which is mainly reflective, might cause readers to lose interest, but with the action and the dramatic dialogue together, along with Mrs. Johnson's observations, great interest is preserved.

Suggestions for Discussing the Study Questions, page 95

(1) Mrs. Johnson, the narrator, describes herself as a large and strong woman. She lives in the Georgia countryside, in a house that could be described as little more than a hovel. However, she is proud of her surroundings, and takes great care of the place both inside and out. She has not had an easy life, having been burned out of a previous house, and having also watched her younger daughter, Maggie, suffer severe burns in the fire. She is proud of her family history, knowing the past so well that she can even identify a patch of blue (Union?) cloth from the uniform "Great Grandpa Ezra" wore during the Civil War. She is also an acute observer, with great sensitivity for the wishes and feelings of both her daughters and with

a parent's wish to them both equally; hence she balks at giving Dee the quilts even though she readily gives Dee the butterchurn parts.

(2) The story provides many details about both Dee and Maggie. They seem as different as they can be, with Dee being the engaging and adventurous one, with tendencies to take up causes and enthusiasms, while Maggie is the shy, bashful, retiring homebody. Of the two, Dee is clearly attractive and proud of it, while Maggie is homely and scarred from burns, and is therefore withdrawn. Dee is more self-centered and self-absorbed, not at all realizing that Maggie, too, has feelings and also has a strong sense of family background. Maggie is generous, being willing to give up the quilts (paragraph 74) to her brash and somewhat thoughtless older sister, but perhaps her willingness is a submissive expectation of being down while Dee is at the top. However, Maggie also exhibits anger when Dee asks for the quilts (paragraph 57). In other words, Maggie is not totally submissive and retiring, and hence the two sisters are somewhat alike.

(3) Dee explains the change of her name to the Swahili-Black Muslim "Wangero" because she is persuaded that the name "Dee" was given to her by white oppressors (paragraph 27). This change provides her with a new sense of identity, according to her understanding, and it therefore gives her a distant perspective on her past, as though it is a collective set of artifacts and not something alive. She therefore regards the house as something to be photographed, and the things in the house as nothing more than centerpieces or wallhangings, which are by no means ever to be put to "everyday use."

(4) The phrase "everyday use" crystallizes the conflict in the story. It is tied up in the contrasting values of the two sisters, with Dee trying to participate in a new identity with a rejection of much of the past, while Maggie tries to accept the past and become a continuous part of it. Though the story exposes the pretentiousness of Dee's attitudes, it would seem to be suggesting a compromise–the African-American heritage is alive and present; creative people cannot build the future if they reject the past first, but they must accept it and develop from it. In short, people like Dee should put the past to work as a part of continuing, living consciousness.

Writing Topics. The problem of "everyday use" of the past. The narration of the story. A comparison of the two sisters.

Works for Comparison with "Everyday Use"

Molière, *Love Is the Doctor, 1605*
Olsen, *I Stand Here Ironing, 646*

Ondaatje, *Late Movies with Skyler,* 824
Wilder, *The Happy Journey to Trenton and Camden,* 1690

Joy Williams, *Taking Care,* *pages 95–102*

Some students may find elements of "Taking Care" depressing, such as the details about leukemia, the dead rabbit, and the songs on the death of children. The challenge of classroom discussion is hence the need to demonstrate the ways in which Jones, the protagonist, overcomes his discouraging surroundings through his love and the great strength of his character.

Suggestions for Discussing the Study Questions, page 102

(1) Answers about Jones's character should revolve about the way in which he accepts his role as a taker of care. As the story progresses, details about the life he is living become so oppressive that a weak person might be totally lost. But Jones is tenderly attentive and patient, and in no way does he even contemplate deserting his care for his wife and granddaughter. The issue of religious faith and possible dereliction is touched on in paragraph 9, but though Jones questions even the materials of his own sermon, there is no question about changing his call of service as a minister.

(2) Much of the story is told in the present tense, as though it is happening at the moment (see also page 248). The past tense is introduced only as a means of filling in the present narration. Such an emphasis on the present might be explained in a number of ways: (a) The present tense makes the story especially vivid. (b) The symbolic value of the story is enhanced by being told in the present, as though troubles like those of Jones are constant and continuous, not elements of the past. (c) In relationship to the story's end ("they enter the shining rooms"), the present tense connects the events to the future; in other words, because Jones's strength is established as a present characteristic, it suggests that this same strength will be his defense against future onslaughts.

(3) There are thirteen paragraphs in the story (is this figure significant?), some of them consisting of three to four hundred words. This emphasis on narration, and the almost total lack of dialogue, enables Williams to penetrate the mind of Jones. One might compare this method with stories like "Soldier's Home" by Hemingway (348) and "A Jury of Her Peers" by Glaspell (202), both of which utilize much dialogue. A writer's use of dialogue, dramatic and objective as it is, creates a barrier to further penetration of a character's mind.

With the extensive paragraphs developing Jones's character, however, Williams gives us something closer to his inner spirit.

(4) Some students might consider the story hopelessly depressing, but many students will be able, if they are in a confessional mood, to describe many similarly disheartening elements, perhaps in their own lives but certainly in the lives of people they know. Individual philosophies may get expressed, such as "you have to keep going on," "love and devotion give strength when everything seems to be going wrong," and so on. This story touches people on a deeply personal level.

WRITING TOPICS. Is "Taking Care" more like reality than fiction? Williams's use of the lengthy narrative paragraphs. The function of references to music and mythology in the story. Jones's relationship to the three women in his life. In what ways is "Taking Care" like "A Worn Path" (150) and "The Jilting of Granny Weatherall" (651)?

WORKS FOR COMPARISON WITH "TAKING CARE"

Atwood, *Variation on the Word Sleep*, 1124
Greenberg, *And Sarah Laughed*, 322
Purdy, *Poem*, 707
Ibsen, *A Dollhouse*, 1793

The Précis or Abridgment, *pages 102–107*

For teaching this section we suggest that a number of elements in the text might need emphasis and further exemplification. One important idea, stressed on page 102, is that a précis does not need to include everything. Students may needlessly lengthen their précis essays if they try to put in every detail from the story. Thus, the section on the need for selectivity (103) is also worthy of special mention, for in a précis the idea should be to make a brief rendering of the story, without any attempt at explanations. If you stress that the précis can be the basis of later interpretation, then the idea will become clear for the students. Perhaps the word "report" might help here, for a précis is in essence a simple report, like newspaper reports, of what happens in a story. The newspaper analogy is also helpful because reference to a news article as compared with an editorial might clarify the distinction between a précis and an analytical essay.

For study, the demonstrative essay (106) offers a good opportunity for the comparison of the original with the précis. Thus the first two paragraphs of the essay, containing 120 words, condenses 16 paragraphs, or, in bulk, close to forty per cent of the entire story.

With such a shortening, it is inevitable to omit details such as Mrs. Johnson's description of the television program, her description of butchering animals and cooking fresh meat, and her detailed reflections about her two daughters. In discussing the reasons for omitting such details, you can make a strong point both about essential actions in stories–a point worth making in its own right–and also about what students should include in planning and writing their essays.

Special Topics for Writing and Argument about Fiction, *pages 107–108*

(1) The first topic is designed to bring out a discussion of how an author may use narrative to penetrate a character and bring out innumerable traits (see also question 3, page 99). The point about Jones is that he does not so much undergo change as such in "Taking Care," but rather that he remains firm and constant amid the potentially destructive changes taking place around him.

(2) This issue is discussed earlier in this section of the manual, in the introductory paragraph to Walker's story.

(3) The stories demonstrate differing means of expressing love. "Taking Care" shows love as devotion, dedication, and sacrifice." An Old-Fashioned Story" shows how love—romantic love—may overcome apparent motives, feelings, and plans. One might also add that "An Old Fashioned Story" raises a question about freedom of will, inasmuch as the suddenness of the concluding affection overwhelms all of Elizabeth's previous thoughts and affirms the parental hopes about Elizabeth and Nelson.

(4) "The Things They Carried" might be considered by some as little more than a catalogue of military and personal effects. In fact, however, the story is unified by the platoon's typical actions, the threat of death as embodied in Lavender, and the concerns and feelings of Lieutenant Jimmy Cross. The unnamed narrator also furnishes constant understanding of the men and sympathy of the burdens of their wartime tasks.

(5) "Neighbors" can be seen as an argument about human character because of the freedom the Millers suddenly acquire to explore the Stones apartment once the Stones leave. An old saying has it that "Character is what you are when you are totally alone." Once Bill and Arlene are alone and unwatched (each one is separated from the other when exploring the Stones's apartment), their curiosity transforms them into peeping Toms and even burglars. The story only raises this basic issue of human character, for the closed door puts a

stop to anything even more weird than the Millers have already done (but irrationality and uncivilized behavior seem to be their basic characteristics, if they [and people generally?] are not checked).

(6) Students often filter this creative-writing topic through their experiences with historical movies and TV programs. One student visualized a pirate captain with a sense of Robin Hood's taking from the rich and giving to the poor. Another student created a behind-the-lines person directing people who are helping the wounded during the Civil War. A few suggestions like these will help students in creating original brief fictional works.

(7) The last topic is designed to get students into the library to use the reference room for standard works and to use the catalogue system for finding works about one of the writers in the chapter. It is most likely that students would find more materials about Hardy and Walker than the other writers, but they would also be successful with the others. The writing assignment should not be lengthy but rather brief, for it is an exercise, not an essay.

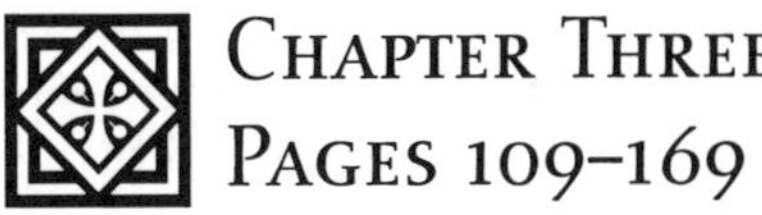

Chapter Three Pages 109–169

Plot and Structure: The Development and Organization of Stories

The first section of Chapter 3 is devoted to plot (109–110) and structure (111–14). The essential quality of plot is conflict, which creates doubt and tension, and therefore accounts for the major interest of each particular story. The discussion of structure makes available for students the formal five categories or stages. Discussion should make clear that these are necessary in any story, for without any of them a story would be unfinished. To borrow a phrase from Pope's "Essay on Criticism," the five elements may be considered as "Nature methodized." The discussion of "Formal and Actual Structure" (113–14) makes the point that the formal elements need not appear rigidly in the order 1, 2, 3, 4, 5 in the story, but that any story, no matter how it is organized, will display all the elements. They are natural and necessary for the reader's understanding, but authors may introduce them in light of particular artistic needs. It is the many variations on the pattern that make for the individuality and interest of fiction.

Stephen Crane, *The Blue Hotel,* *pages 114–33*

"The Blue Hotel," along with "The Open Boat" and "The Bride Comes to Yellow Sky," is one of Crane's better-known stories. It explores a situation that was real in frontier days and still real in many areas of life—violence precipitated by affronts to personal honor. Each of the major characters is amply portrayed, and except for the Cowboy they are also rounded. The Swede is guided by expectation, but he changes because he believes that he is above the forces of destruction he earlier fears. Scully is an entrepreneur who values his reputation above all else, but he changes because he consents to the fight of Johnnie with one of his guests. The Easterner is an observer, who does not tell the truth because he seems to have a strain of cowardice; however, he changes because he is the one whose discourse in paragraph 265 (132) indicates a strong sense of guilt about his role in the death of the Swede. The cowboy is bigoted, and is certainly not big on intelligence, as is indicated by his concluding statement in paragraph 266. He has listened to what the Easterner has told him, but he does not recognize that he has been involved in the death in any way (remember that it is he, Bill the Cowboy, who urges Johnnie to "kill" the Swede).

The demise of the unfortunate Swede is cast within Crane's framework of situational irony, made plain by the Easterner at the very end: People are involved in vast, unspoken conspiracies which they are unable to stop, even though a word at the right moment, which never comes, would halt impending disaster. The irony is that the agent of disaster is hardly even incidental in the generally destructive actions and reactions at work. In other words, in the face of such uncontrollable forces, people seem to be powerless.

Suggestions for Discussing the Study Questions, page 133

(1) The major conflict is between the Swede and the other characters. He sets himself apart at the story's exposition, and through his drunkenness, the card game, his fight with Johnnie, and his swift encounter with the gambler, he is always at odds. One might see him as a protagonist because he is a solitary person encountering difficulties–usually the role of the protagonist. Because we learn so little of him, however, he is not a good candidate for protagonist. The others stress his nationality primarily to preserve his separateness (note that the others are identified by trade or location, and that they are named; i.e., Bill the cowboy, Blanc the Easterner, Scully the hotel keeper, Johnnie the son of the hotel keeper). These distinctions do even more to stress that the Swede is an outsider.

(2) The Easterner's analysis in paragraph 90 (121) explains the Swede's uneasiness when he enters the hotel, but it does not explain his strange and aggressive behavior. There is a conflict in the story between the conventional expectations of violence on the frontier (which the Swede believes) and the beliefs of the Romper natives, who assume that their town is civilized. The story is hence not conventional; its realism brings out the individual causes of violence, even though this violence stems out of codes that might fit frontier expectations. The characters are individualized, then, but the results of the card game support the convention that the American West at the end of the nineteenth century was characterized by much mayhemThe irony of the story is that the Easterner is thus both

right and wrong about the dime-store novels. In effect the Swede becomes the victim of a self-fulfilling prophecy.

(3) The first seven numbered sections form a story with two parts. The first two sections comprise a short first part, with exposition and complication leading up to a minor crisis, climax, and dénouement (the Swede departs with Scully). The second part consists of sections 3–7, leading up to the fight (the climax) and the departure of the Swede. Section 8 is a short narrative in itself, which is climaxed by the stabbing and the vision of the dead Swede staring blankly at the cash register. Section 9 is the dénouement, and it summarizes and unites the action. The eighth section is brief because the story as a whole is more concerned with the motivations of the various characters than with the details of the murderous violence. The true facts about Johnnie's cheating are withheld until the end because of the story's point that pride and reputation (which Johnnie would have lost if he had admitted the Swede's claim that he had been cheating) are stronger causes for action—in this story, violence—than truth and the recognition of truth. Alas.

(4) The Easterner's analogy of grammar and human behavior (paragraph 265) takes a good amount of discussion, but it is unique in its placement of the gambler as an adverb, while the other characters—the Easterner, the Cowboy, Johnnie, and Scully—are parts of the main sentence. The analogy is particularly rewarding if one realizes that the various individuals, like actual parts of speech, follow laws of behavior, like laws of grammar, that they do not control. The analogy suggest that individuals are powerless to stop the forces of antagonism once they are set in motion. Discussion about these points can become quite interesting in an active class.

WRITING TOPICS. The outmoded concept of frontier lawlessness. The inevitability of conflict if people have no external restraints. The organization of the story, or of one of the major sections.

WORKS FOR COMPARISON WITH "THE BLUE HOTEL"

Dubus, *The Curse, 603*
Frost, *Acquainted with the Night, 1111*
Hughes, *Mulatto, 1663*

THOMAS HARDY, *The Three Strangers,* *pages 133–47*

This is one of the longer stories in the book, but students find it a likable one. It lends itself to an illuminating discussion of Hardy's narrative techniques, and also to stimulating give-and-take about

Hardy's views on law as represented by the hangman, on the one side, and the guests and the first and third strangers, on the other.

Suggestions for Discussing the Study Questions, page 147

(1) A case can be made that there are three levels of conflict in "The Three Strangers." Among the characters, there are many conflicts, most of them real or apparently real. Shepherd Fennel's wife argues with the Shepherd over the distribution of the good mead, and she expresses her ill will against the second stranger, the hangman, primarily because he represents a reduction in the household supply of mead. In addition, she is uneasy when the guests get too thirsty, again threatening her supply of mead. Just about everyone in the story develops antipathy against the hangman, first because of his personal manner, and second because of his expression of glee about his task of hanging Timothy Summers. The shepherds clearly abhor him because of his personality. There are also apparent conflicts, which the story resolves, between the guests and the first and third strangers.

On the level of legality, there is a conflict between the strict letter of law enforcement and the extenuating circumstances of the crime committed by Timothy Summers. There is little question which side Hardy directs us to take. He demonstrates that Summers, the first stranger, is personable, friendly, and daring, and without engaging in debate about the merits of the law, Hardy's comparative views of the hangman and Summers literally demand that readers take the side of extenuation, regardless of the reality of Summers' guilt.

The third level of conflict concerns the moral and ethical levels of the law. The law is the law, no doubt, but Hardy is introducing the issue of higher law–the spirit of law–which frequently comes into conflict with the strict letter of law. Because the hangman represents the law, which technically protects everyone, it would not be out of place for the shepherds to favor his views. But the circumstances, as with Jean Valjean and innumerable other victims of unjust persecution in both reality and literature, are such that the existing prosecution of law frequently does not protect people but instead attacks them.

(2) Hardy gives us many details about the natives of Higher Crowstairs because of the conflict between legal prosecution and extenuation of guilt. If there were not so much detail, the case for prosecution would be clear, but with the detail the case for extenuation gains validity. Hardy's references to planetary motion and biblical figures suggest that the issue is as old as humanity. Obviously,

many of the details are comic, such as the man who cannot serve as constable without his staff, and the slipping and sliding of the natives when searching for the third stranger. It is just such details that strengthen the need for understanding and compassion.

(3, 4) The identity of the first and third strangers is withheld until late in the story because of the need for showing their humanity and character as part of the story's argument. If the first stranger were named when he first appears, Hardy would be less able to give us a view of Summers' deserving nature. With the second stranger, the same delay also takes place because Hardy wants to make him seem obnoxious before telling us that this unlikable figure is the hangman. It is clear, however, that Hardy does not want any mystery to last too long about the second stranger.

WRITING TOPICS. The nature of the first and third strangers. Hardy's view of law, as expressed in the story. The symbolism of the planetary and biblical references. The reason for putting the story in the distant past (past, that is, even in Hardy's day). The dramatic presentation of the second stranger, the hangman.

WORKS FOR COMPARISON WITH "THE THREE STRANGERS"

Bierce, *An Occurrence at Owl Creek Bridge,* 257
Haines, *Little Cosmic Dust Poem,* 1156
Ibsen, *An Enemy of the People,* 1844
St. Luke, *The Parable of the Prodigal Son,* 445
Poe, *The Masque of the Red Death,* 541

JAMAICA KINCAID, *What I Have Been Doing Lately,* *pages 148–49*

"What I Have Been Doing Lately" is a brief and unsettling story, and it is also a memorable fantasy. It raises questions about the nature of reality. Even though we go through regular and almost ritualistic activities, are they real? In the world Kincaid creates, visitors ring doorbells and then vanish; the narrator begins a journey but does not go anywhere; she sees the planet Venus while walking north (perhaps suggesting a southern hemisphere?); on close inspection, distant beauty does not sustain itself; loved ones do not remain or are unreal, leaving one sad and bereft except to repeat the same regular routines. One is reminded of the Zen Master who claims that he had a dream about a butterfly, and now he doesn't know if he is a man dreaming about a butterfly or a butterfly dreaming about a man.

Suggestions for Discussing the Study Questions, page 150

(1) The story begins as though it were totally real, but then quickly goes into a dream or surreal level of description. In the second line of the first paragraph the altered level of reality is made plain by the sentence "Either it was drizzling or there was a lot of dust in the air [. . . .]" Once Kincaid establishes this dreamlike level, the story moves into its own plane of existence.

(2) The dream is based generally on realistic situations, but what matters is what Kincaid does with these situations. The narrator falls a long way into a hole, for example, but can then wish her way out of it and close the hole up. There are no futuristic elements in the story because the topic is not a future world but our everyday world and what we make of it. The details are therefore all modified from what we regard as normal reality

(3) The narrative becomes repetitive at ¶ 7, and also again at the very end, to illustrate, as if in a dream, the repetitive nature of life. The second sequence is different from the first in some specific changes in the activities. For example, in the second sequence the narrator's hands are drawn up and interlaced at the back of her neck. After she throws three stones at the monkey, the monkey finally catches the fourth stone and throws it back. When she walks her feet hurt, whereas earlier her walk produces no such discomfort. The second time she faces the water crossing, the activity suggests a Styx-like river which she pay to cross. All these variations indicate that life provides no lasting stability but only the need for constant change and adjustment.

(4) What makes the story is story is the narrative element and the central interest provided by the narrator. Certainly there is no conventional character development or change. There is also little if any plot development because there are no clearly established characters and no conflict. There is no question that the story is different from most of those we encounter.

WRITING TOPICS. The repetitive structure. The nature of the narrator. What conflicts, if any, are in the story? The story's level of reality/unreality.

WORKS FOR COMPARISON WITH "WHAT I HAVE BEEN DOING LATELY"

Bierce, *An Occurrence at Owl Creek Bridge*, 257
Carver, *Neighbors*, 63
Dickinson, *Some Keep the Sabbath*, 1076
Forster, *The Point of It*, 607

Eudora Welty, *A Worn Path,* *pages 150–55*

Phoenix, the main character of "A Worn Path," is a poor, aging black woman who is experiencing the onset of the afflictions of age (loss of memory, inflexible and arthritic joints, imaginings) while maintaining an indomitable spirit in the face of the hopeless nature of her own plight and that of her grandson. Students may need reminding of the intimate focus upon her character up to her appearance in the medical office, where she is seen objectively and dramatically.

As a narrative, the story is particularly interesting because exposition takes place from the beginning almost until the very end (paragraph 94, page 136). The complication is developing almost coincidentally, for the difficulties Phoenix experiences are also a part of the virtually impossible conditions of her life. The disclosure about her grandson (paragraphs 78–92) is an additional complication. The silence of Phoenix up to her speech (in paragraph 87) may be considered as the crisis, for her silence suggests that she may be unable to carry on after having come so far. The climax is her speech in paragraph 94, in which her recognition and determination are revealed. The resolution is her acceptance of the additional nickel and her retreat down the stairs to purchase a toy before returning home. The delay in the exposition about her grandson causes a reevaluation of the details prior to paragraph 91.

Suggestions for Discussing the Study Questions, pages 155–56

(1) The details of the sugar sacks and the rag establish Phoenix's poverty. Among other details that students might note in this regard are the untied tennis shoes and her charity-case status as revealed in the medical office. It is clear that her journey is along a *worn path,* and well worn at that, because she addresses the animals as acquaintances, closes her eyes when she balances on the log, and follows her feet rather than her mind to get to the medical office in Natchez. She seems accustomed to being alone because she is constantly speaking to herself. Her speech to animals and particularly her visualizing the boy suggest the debilitating effects of age. The nature of her speech (such as "I going to the store") indicates her lack of formal education.

(2) The plot is built up as a contrast between Phoenix, on one side, and the forces of poverty, natural obstacles, distance, age, and the illness of her grandson, on the other. One might also interpret the plot in terms of nobility and strength of character standing against forces of destructiveness. These forces are not malevolent, but are

shown rather to be a part of the natural course of things. Because there is no one actively attending to Phoenix and her grandson, her plight may be seen as reflecting the indifference and lack of concern of a social and political system which ignores the aged and ill, particularly among African Americans. The story, however, does not insist on the possible political-economic criticism, but instead reveals the pathos of Phoenix's situation.

(3) In considering the confrontation of Phoenix and the hunter, students might bring out her apparent earlier experiences with the arbitrary judgments and punishments that whites have made against blacks. The scene also suggests the young hunter's assumption about his own power and, in addition, Phoenix's belief that somehow all white people are aware of her misdeeds and are ready to punish her for them.

(4) Four possible responses to "A Worn Path" are given in the first sentence of this question. Only classroom discussion can bring out an examination of these and the other various responses that your students might have.

WRITING TOPICS. The topic of human strength as opposed to poverty, old age, or illness; or, the black-white conflict. The structuring of individual parts of the story, such as the early part describing the walk of Phoenix, the encounter with the dog and the hunter, or the episode in the medical office.

WORKS FOR COMPARISON WITH "A WORN PATH"

Porter, *The Jilting of Granny Weatherall, 651*
Hamod, *Leaves, 1158*
Keller, *Tea Party, 1266*

Tom Whitecloud, *Blue Winds Dancing, pages 156–60*

"Blue Winds Dancing" touches upon a recurrent problem among Native Americans—that of separation or assimilation. The story refers to the situation in the 1930s, but many of the circumstances remain unchanged today. In the story, the unnamed narrator's return to the reservation suggests a satisfactory resolution for him. If confinement on a reservation leads to want and boredom, however, and to the imitation by Indians of the worst vices of whites, the narrator's answer will not promote happiness for Native Americans who retreat from the prevailing economy and culture. There is no easy solution to the issues of how an entire people should respond to the uneasiness and lack of purpose that displacement creates, and of how they should find purposeful roles within their own culture and also within the white culture, but "Blue Winds Dancing," being a well-crafted and penetrating story, should raise consciousness on this issue.

Suggestions for Discussing the Study Questions, pages 160–61

(1) Paragraphs 1–11 comprise the first part of "Blue Winds Dancing." Exposition in this section consists of the information that fixes the narrator as a college student in California, yearning for home and questioning the value of continuing his studies. The complication occurs almost simultaneously as it becomes apparent that the speaker's nostalgia represents a deep-rooted rejection of the values he has been asked to accept at school. The case of claiming that this first section contains its own crisis and climax, as a miniature story almost in its own right, is that it works up to the narrator's decision to return. Thus the rest of the story is an enactment, or resolution, of that decision. More in conformity with the entire story, however, is the fact that the crisis and climax are reached later, in the narrator's fears about family acceptance and in his belief about the old woman under the ice.

(2) There is much in the first section about the narrator's attitudes. We learn that he is both homesick and "tired," that he has serious doubts about the values of the white culture, that he has a reverence for Nature, that he seeks a release from the pressure to achieve, that he resents the feelings of inferiority of his role as an Indian, that he values and prizes the personal closeness of life at home, and that he is willing to endure hardship because of his beliefs. He is rejecting civilization as a result of the personal, unhurried, aesthetic, and passive values of his home, together with a profound sense of identification with the home as a physical place. The major antagonist in the story is the set of values of the white culture, but there are also other antagonists, such as the cold and the sadistic threat of Denver Bob. There is also an inner conflict that develops when the narrator nears home. This conflict is manifested in self-doubt and worry about being received by family and tribe.

(3) The narrator deals with loneliness in paragraph 22, and there he seems to contrast his earlier loneliness (stemming out of his alienation from his surroundings) with the certitude he feels once he is among familiar things (even though he is alone). Student responses could become extensive, but whatever is said, a proper distinction between the words "alone" and "lonely" should be preserved, as the narrator makes this distinction in the story.

(4) Perceptive students will recognize the metaphorical nature of the dancing of the blue winds, perhaps revealing the feeling and sound of wind on a sunny day in winter. There is a synesthesia in the combining of color with dance. In answering the second part of this question, students may raise issues of practicality and things aesthetic: In a world devoted to work and acquisition, how can "unprofitable" values be maintained?

WRITING TOPICS. The plot as a conflict between Indian and white values, or between innocence and corruptibility. The structure of the formal elements in the story. The structure of the narrator's trip, which is marked not by American cities, but rather by the locations of Indian nations. The climax of the story, and what is brought to a head there.

WORKS FOR COMPARISON WITH "BLUE WINDS DANCING"

Hughes, *Mulatto, 1663*
Parédes, *The Hammon and the Beans, 415*
Wheatley, *On Being Brought from Africa, 1216*

Writing About the Plot of a Story, *pages 161–64*

This section emphasizes the plot as a laying out of the principal conflict within a story. The conflict and its ramifications may be most readily approached if it can be clearly defined, as in "The Blue Hotel." When the conflict is that between a person and forces ranged against him or her, students may find difficulty in defining and delimiting the forces. The demonstrative student essay, on Hardy's "The Three Strangers," should be particularly helpful here. If a student should try to define a plot in terms of abstract forces, such as "human indomitability versus overwhelming odds" (as in "A Worn Path") the job of definition would be particularly challenging, but the results might also be particularly rewarding.

An obstacle to overcome in the preparation of this essay is the tempting one that some students, while analyzing plot, may easily slip away from their central ideas, and instead use materials from the story not as exemplification but rather as a descriptive end in itself–in short, as a retelling of the story.

Writing About Structure in a Story, *pages 164–68*

The essay about structure is to be contrasted with the essay on plot. If assigned, it is most instructive to use the same story for both essays, as in the demonstrative essays on "The Three Strangers." Students should be reminded that the structure of a work depends on the arrangement and placement of materials, in addition to the basic plan of conflict with which the study of plot is concerned. The demonstrative essay, for example, describes the development of "The Three Strangers" as being arranged to bring out negative and positive responses, and also to create suspense. It is important to stress that this observation is designed to explain the actual placement of plot details–in other words, the structure. It might be convenient to explain the analysis of structure as the attempt to determine the rationale of the arrangement made by the author. Such an emphasis will enable students to provide critical discourse rather than uncritical data.

Special Topics for Writing and Argument about Plot and Structure, *pages 168–69*

The first three of these topics are designed to stress individual stories, treated according to plot (1) and structure (2 and 3). The problems to be overcome here are that while students write about the topics, they should emphasize the relationship of the subject to the technical matter at hand.

Topic 4 should introduce a comparative treatment of how authors utilize conflicts not only between characters but between ideals and values. In "Everyday Use" the conflict is between Dee and her mother, but on a more abstract level the conflict is between a tradition (Mrs. Johnson) and the abandonment of the tradition (Dee). In "Blue Winds Dancing" the conflict is more clearly between the values of Indians and the land, on the one hand, and those of whites and citification, on the other.

It seems clear that the subject of topic 5, Kincaid's "What I Have Been Doing Lately," could not be successful with precise and exact repetition. It therefore provides slight variations, which indeed are essential in showing both the sameness and the differences in life–close and mainly repetitive, but different.

Topic 6 is designed to start social and political discourse in your class. In such a discussion it is important to keep the text of "A Worn Path" foremost, or else students might create independent essays which, though interesting, would be tangential to the subject. Because Whitecloud's "Blue Winds Dancing" is also included in this chapter, and also because "The Blue Hotel" refers to people by nationality, the socio-political content of these stories might be introduced in relationship to "A Worn Path."

Topic 7 gives students the chance to create their own stories.

Under the cloak of anonymity, they may write about a conflict they know best (one of their own), even though they may find it easier to write about the conflicts of someone else. The point of the topic is that through their own creativity they may better understand the ways in which other story writers have met the problems of creating plot and structure.

Topic 8 is an optional exercise (as are all these special topic questions) designed to get students to use the library catalogue, to locate materials about Welty, and to pick and choose among the titles that they find. The resulting student writing should be a brief report, which may become more detailed as students include references to more than a few sources.

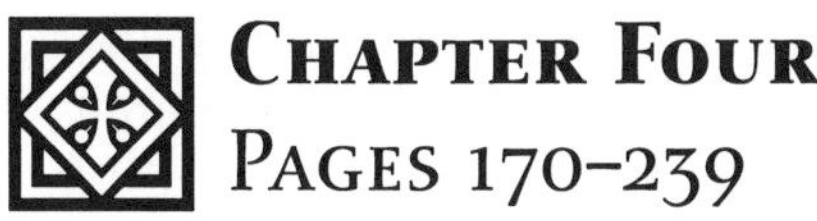

Chapter Four
Pages 170–239

Characters: The People in Fiction

One of the best ways to teach this section is to relate the materials directly to the experiences of your students. Hence, those characters in their lives whom they know well, such as brothers, sisters, close friends, and parents, are analogous to round characters in fiction. By contrast, flat characters tend to be those whom your students know less well, such as distant relatives and classmates who are no more than acquaintances.

To aid this discussion, the concepts *representative, static, stock,* and *stereotype* may also be seen as modes of defining flat characterizations. An interesting idea which often generates much thought and improved understanding concerns ourselves and the probable views that others hold of us. Most of us, in fact, seem to be round characters to the people we know and love, while we are simply flat to others whom we do not know (see question 4b, page 238).

In teaching the section on probability, the question of "How would a god (or demon, or fairy, or goblin, etc.) be expected to behave?" puts the creative act of fiction in a new light for many students (see page 176). The goal should be to encourage students to think about an author's presentation of character in the perspective of how they themselves would write in the same fictional mode.

To teach the various sorts of character, you might wish to use the following table as a basis of discussion:

ROUND CHARACTERS

- ❖ Major figures. How many are there? How many details do you learn about them? What do they do?
- ❖ Hero, heroine (antihero). Are these terms justified?
- ❖ Protagonist (central figure of interest in the plot) (also antagonist): What role do these major figures play?

- Dynamic quality. The capacity for change and growth. What changes do you observe? To what degree are the changes brought out by the interactions of characters and events?

FLAT CHARACTERS

- Minor characters. How many are there? What do they do? How are they important for your understanding of the major characters?
- Static quality. How limited are the static characters? How does the author use them? Why is it necessary for them, in relation to the major characters, to remain static?
- Stock, stereotype characters. How often do they appear? In what ways do they seem to have been stamped out of a mold?

WILLA CATHER, ***Paul's Case,*** *pages 177–90*

"Paul's Case," one of Cather's earliest and best-known stories, foreshadows later works in which outcast individuals are suppressed and destroyed (i.e., *My Mortal Enemy* [1926] and *Lucy Gayheart* [1935]). Another comparable work is *One of Ours* (1922, for which Cather received the Pulitzer Prize), which describes the life of a young man who, unlike Paul, successfully rises above his stultifying environment. In short, "Paul's Case" is similar to many Cather works in which the conflict is not so much one of persons versus persons–although Paul in this story experiences much antagonism–but is instead one of persons contesting against the society and the economic conditions which maintain it.

The plot of "Paul's Case" develops the opposition of Paul to his school, home, church school, and general environment. The story unfolds in two major parts: In the first, the crisis occurs in paragraph 36, when Paul loses the supports on which he previously relied, and the climax is in paragraphs 44–46, when Paul steals the money from the firm of Denny and Carson. If one regards the story after Paul's flight to New York as a second part, the crisis here is in paragraphs 58 and 59, when Paul learns that his escapade has been discovered, and the climax is in paragraph 64, when Paul makes his way to the ferry after obviously determining to commit suicide. A strong case could of course be made that the entire New York episode is a resolution of Paul's theft.

Suggestions for Discussing the Study Questions, page 190

(1) Paul is portrayed as a character marching to a different drummer. He is round because of his decisions to flee and to commit suicide, although a case could be made that his constant refusal to conform to the life around him has already marked the character changes that constitute fullness or roundness. His strengths are shown in paragraphs 15, 29, and 46, where his charm as an usher, his "vocation" for the theater, and his calmness in engineering the theft are described. His physical and psychological weaknesses are brought out particularly in paragraphs 2, 10, and 14, and also, more strongly, in paragraphs 44 and 64, where the sinister "thing in the corner" is described as being poised to destroy him. His weaknesses result from his lack of perspective about reality: He is unwilling to make any compromises whatever to live in accord with the world around him, and hence in the long run he loses everything, even though he believes that his brief taste of the elegant life was worth his sacrifice (paragraph 60). All his weaknesses are brought out in the city when he meets the young man, for it makes Paul realize the gap between the world he wants and the world he must spend his life in.

The word "case" in the title implies a problem in behavior, a clinical report. The subtitle provided by Cather, "A Study in Temperament," together with the observation of Paul's teachers that his is "a bad case" (paragraph 37) also suggests a clinical study. The fact is, however, that the narration is not purely clinical, for it is also sympathetic to Paul's position. The story is hence above all a story, despite the title.

(2) The speaker often views Paul dramatically, but at other times presents things almost as Paul himself would. It is clear, however, that the narrator clearly believes in Paul's value and in his worthiness, despite the difficulties that he experiences in his short and troubled existence. Although the speaker is sympathetic (she or he, too, cringes at the life on Cordelia Street, and seems frustrated because of the absence of any sympathetic ear), it is not clear that she or he understands Paul completely, and it is certain that she or he withholds approval of Paul. For example, although the narrator views Paul's theft of the money objectively, the word "spoils" (paragraph 57) indicates strong disapproval. Up through paragraph 37, the story of Paul takes place within the context of school, home, and extracurricular activity, but with paragraph 38, when Paul is on his way to New York after the theft, the focus is entirely on him. The shift indicates how Paul is now on his own and, except for the young

man from Yale, the world in which he moves is largely anonymous. Because of the speaker's belief in Paul's abilities, and because the speaker shows how Paul is increasingly unable to fit into society, the use of the word "design" at the end to describe Paul's death seems ironic.

(3) Paul's dread of an endless life of business and a perpetual residence in a home like that on Cordelia Street is brought out most fully in paragraph 59, where the terms "gray monotony" and "sickening vividness" describe the drabness and dullness that are so contrary to his hopes. It is the prospect of conforming endlessly to such a life that Paul dreads, and which he cannot face. By contrast, a period of imprisonment might at least have a termination, so that he could see to the end of that, where there might then be some hope.

The story portrays the life of business and Cordelia Street through Paul's perspective, and it reflects a harsh imposition of the sameness that he cannot bear. The school, for example, contains teachers who want him to be less noticeable and more conforming. In effect, the community offers Paul little that would enable him to exist and continue to function within it. Even the job of ushering, which Paul adores and where he comes alive, is tolerated by Paul's father because it brings him money, not joy and fulfillment. The life around Paul, and its suppression of him, is brought out to the fullest in paragraphs 27 through 37. Ironically, even some of the actors agree that Paul does not belong with them (paragraph 37).

WRITING TOPICS. The character of Paul. The stance of the narrator toward Paul. The structure of the story up to Paul's flight to New York. The structure after that.

WORKS FOR COMPARISON WITH "PAUL'S CASE"

Chopin, *The Story of an Hour, 393*
Henley, *Am I Blue, 1635*
Laurence, *The Loons, 408*
Nemerov, *Life Cycle of Common Man, 1179*
Roethke, *My Papa's Waltz, 831*

WILLIAM FAULKNER, *Barn Burning,* *pages 190–201*

Throughout Faulkner's extensive work about the special microcosm which he called Yoknapatawpha County, he treats life in the South as a symbol of humankind generally, emphasizing the decline of civilization and culture in the wake of the Civil War. Often he deals with degraded, sullen, and degenerate characters, and in this respect Abner Snopes of "Barn Burning" is typical. Abner is not violent but he is portrayed as an ex-horse-thief turned barn burner, and the loyalty he tries to exact from his son Sarty is one which excludes any allegiance to morality. Faulkner also uses the topic of the Snopes family in *The Hamlet* (1940), *The Town* (1957), and *The Mansion* (1960).

In "Barn Burning," Faulkner visualizes a "world in little" within the Snopes family. The dominant figure is Abner, the father. The members are the mother (Lonnie), the aunt (Lizzie), the older brother (elsewhere called Flem), the twin sisters, and Colonel Sartoris, or Sarty. The speaker discloses the habitual moving of the family in paragraphs 24 and 40. These constant removals have prevented the family from establishing roots, and they have also made the members dependent upon themselves and particularly upon Abner.

As a character, Abner is cold, hard, calculating, cruel, and contemptuous. The narrator speaks of his "wolflike independence" and "latent ravening ferocity" (paragraph 25). Abner is also manipulative, as is shown in his behavior in court at the beginning of the story. He shows great presumptuousness when he sues De Spain in protest against the costs for spoiling the rug (paragraph 70). That he is also callous and unthinking is shown in his treatment of his family and his work animals. He is not without some redeeming qualities, however, for his sociability is shown in the blacksmith's shop (paragraph 82). Also, his sense of family cohesiveness is shown in paragraph 27.

The central conflict in the story is between Sarty's commitment to truth and his allegiance to his father. There are lesser conflicts, such as that between the brothers (the older brother does not trust Sarty [paragraph 92]); between Abner and Lonnie, his wife; between Abner and Mr. Harris, Major De Spain, the justices, the black servant of the De Spains, and Mrs. De Spain; and also between Abner and the law generally. The major conflict is resolved when Abner directs his wife to restrain Sarty, indicating his judgment that Sarty's loyalty is to truth and honesty rather than to him.

Suggestions for Discussing the Study Questions, page 202

(1) Sarty is young, but has a strong sense of truth and justice, as shown in paragraphs 7, 29, and 92–103. For a time he supports his father, and therefore he seems to be taking on Abner's corrupt nature, but even then he wishes his father would reform. Sarty's wishes in this way indicate his desire to merge his family ties with his desire for justice (paragraph 69). At the end his commitment to justice predominates, and hence he warns De Spain and then runs away, not looking back (paragraph 108).

The speaker limits the narration to Sarty, so that most of what we learn is what Sarty himself sees and hears. Thus Abner is distant, remorseless, and unexplained because Sarty himself is not privy to any of Abner's plans, and it is only through Sarty's responses to the trial at the beginning of the story that we learn that Abner is charged with burning the Harris barn. Sarty knows this detail about his father, and he also knows his father's intention to burn the De Spain barn. It is these things to which he responds, for only the speaker knows the details about Abner's dishonorable "service" in the Civil War (see paragraphs 15, 27, and 107). Sarty is therefore round because he responds to the situations in the story, finally determining to follow "truth, justice" (paragraph 29), rather than accepting his father's advice to "stick to your own blood" (paragraph 29).

(2) The parallels between the Biblical Abner and Faulkner's Abner suggest that modern persons have lost the heroism of the past. Faulkner's Abner destroys rugs and barns, while the Biblical Abner leads armies. Both have great ability, but Faulkner's Abner is corrupted by selfishness and the desire for booty. Hence the story exposes Abner's corruption and disgrace. Faulkner introduces similar parallels elsewhere—in *Absalom, Absalom* (1936), for example, where the David-Absalom story is recast; in *Light in August* (1932), where there is a parallel with the crucifixion; and in *A Fable* (1954) which also introduces the parallel of the Passion.

(3) The time of "Barn Burning" is visualized as being somewhere between 1891 and 1895, and the scene is rural Mississippi. The date is given in paragraph 15, when the speaker explains how Abner Snopes got his limp.

(4) Sarty's mother and sisters are flat. The sisters are permitted to express very little personality, except, perhaps, for paragraph 50. The mother is constantly anxious and apprehensive, for good reason in light of the life of the family and of the contempt which Abner expresses for her. The aunt, Lizzie, is more individual, a trait shown in paragraph 98.

(5) At the climax, De Spain rides the horse and fires the shots. In this story, Faulkner does not disclose the results of the shooting because the point-of-view character, Sarty, is not in a position to learn about them. The mystery about the outcome is hence a direct result of Faulkner's use of a consistent point of view.

WRITING TOPICS. Sarty: his characteristics and his change. The consistencies and contradictions of Abner. Is Major De Spain round or flat, and why? The members of the Snopes family. The justices.

Works for Comparison with "Barn Burning"

Miller, *Death of a Salesman,* 1457
Roethke, *My Papa's Waltz,* 831
Tan, *Two Kinds,* 226
Walker, *Everyday Use,* 89

Susan Glaspell, *A Jury of Her Peers,* *pages 202–216*

During Susan Glaspell's writing career, which extended from 1914 to 1945, she wrote many plays, both short and long, together with a number of novels. "A Jury of Her Peers" is unique, because Glaspell wrote it in story form after having done it first as the short play *Trifles* (see page 1244) the year before. It is instructive to note, for example, that Martha Hale is the central figure in the narrative, whereas in the play she is major but not dominant. In addition, much information about Martha is introduced into the story easily and naturally because she is the focus of narrative attention, whereas in the play this material is less justifiable because Martha is only one person among many.

In "A Jury of Her Peers," the major character, about whom the story revolves, is Minnie Wright. But in the development of the story, the major acting and speaking character is Martha. She is the limited point-of-view character, and the narration and dialogue exist only because she is involved in them in some way. For example, paragraph 9 concerns Martha's feelings when she enters the Wright farmhouse. The men, who are technically the principal investigators of the murder, enter and leave, while Martha remains as the focus of our attention. We also realize that Martha is the major source of information about Minnie and about Wright, the dead husband. It is because of Martha's questions, observations, recollections, and responses that we develop sympathy for Minnie. For example, Martha justifies Minnie's housekeeping just as she also develops a justification for the murder. Not only is Martha sympathetic, but she is the major figure concealing and destroying the evidence that points conclusively to Minnie's guilt (see paragraphs 168–170, 228, and 291). She is, therefore, also the most important character in the story.

Suggestions for Discussing the Study Questions, page 216

(1) The story presents a unique example of how a major character who is absent from the action may be presented through the words of others. Minnie's traits emerge because Martha Hale remembers them, and also because discussions about the conditions of her

home and the murder of her husband bring them out. We learn from Martha's recollections that Minnie is a sensitive person, a lover of music–a cheerful sort who loves colorful clothes. We also learn that Minnie is capable of adjusting to a bad situation, and that she is also a realist in terms of her expectations (see paragraph 59, in which she shows her fear of Wright and also her certainty that she will never get the telephone with which she might have communicated with the outside world). Her work with her quilt shows that she is artistic and creative, and her birdcage demonstrates that her love of music has never diminished despite the grimness of her life with Wright. The murder indicates, however, how even her apparently total submissiveness can be overcome by her anger. The story makes clear that Wright's gratuitous cruelty in wringing the canary's neck is the final event in Minnie's developing hatred.

(2) Although Martha is the major character, Mrs. Peters is well portrayed. Both women are farmer's wives, and both have developed their present attitudes of sympathy to Minnie because of their own hard lives—Martha because she has been a close neighbor bringing up children on the farm, and Mrs. Peters because at one time she lived on a remote, distant homestead (paragraphs 254–255). Martha is the one whose mind we enter, and we learn about her regret and self-reproach at not having been closer to Minnie. It is clear that her support of Minnie comes about at least partly because of her feelings of guilt. Mrs. Peters is more objectively rendered. She is small, thin, and slightly fearful (paragraph 117). She has a shrinking manner, but is a shrewd observer, and understands Minnie's plight and also her murderous response, even though she does not admit these things directly. Mrs. Peters has great presence of mind (paragraphs 228–231, 237), but she is habitually self-minimizing (paragraph 162), and is customarily deferential to her husband, "the law" (paragraphs 145, 282–285). Martha is clearly the stronger of the two, and is the leader. Without Martha's initiative, the evidence in the kitchen would fall into the men's possession.

(3) Probably the two women do not voice their conclusions about Minnie as the murderer because their open discussion would change the nature of their obligations. As long as they say nothing, their knowledge remains a part of their own secret lives, which they keep private even (or especially) from their husbands. Thus their anger and indignation are their own, even at the end of the story. If they were to speak, they would presumably have to report their conclusions to their husbands. They draw these conclusions from

their observations of the half-finished tasks, the erratic sewing of the quilt, their own knowledge of knotting (as opposed to quilting), and the dead canary. They both create the rapid "cover-up" of the evidence at the end because they have formed a silent bond, not only with themselves, but also with Minnie Wright. This bond, together with their complete understanding of Minnie's plight, enables them to recognize a stronger obligation–to their feelings and to another woman–than to the letter of the law.

WRITING TOPICS. The character of Minnie. The issue of legality vs. personal bonding in the story. The character of Martha Hale, or of Mrs. Peters. The play (*Trifles*) contrasted with the story (see page 1244 for *Trifles*).

WORKS FOR COMPARISON WITH "A JURY OF HER PEERS"

Anonymous, *Barbara Allan, 1119*
Whur, *The First-Rate Wife, 809*
Keats, *La Belle Dame Sans Merci, 954*
Williams, *Taking Care, 95*

JOYCE CAROL OATES, *Shopping,* *pages 216–25*

The most recent of Oates's many achievements was her being granted an Honorary Doctor of Letters degree, in May, 2000, from Syracuse University, her undergraduate school.

"Shopping" highlights relationships between mother and daughter, and demonstrates how such relationships may be deeply strained, even when the mother and daughter are on a shopping excursion at the mall–a characteristically American activity. The women in your class will be naturally interested in the two women, and the men are not so far away from family life that they will not also be interested in the alienation that the story illustrates. Students may wish to refer to other works involving parent-child relationships, of which the thematic table of contents lists twenty-six entries.

Suggestions for Discussing the Study Questions, pages 225–26

(1) There is little that is unusual about either Mrs. Dietrich or Nola. What is important is the abundant detail about both of them, which indicates a changing or at least a modifying relationship. Dr. Johnson once, in discussing the relationship between a father and a son, stated that friction was inevitable since the father wished to keep control, while the son wished to become free. This analysis fits

here for mother and daughter. The occasion of the semester abroad is important not so much for itself as for the disputes it causes. Any other plan that Nola might describe would also introduce the same conflict. Paragraph 73 marks a feeling of resentment in Mrs. Dietrich—a new feeling resulting from her conclusion that Nola's attempted shoplifting was done in order to inflict hurt. Mrs. Dietrich's anger does not diminish her parental love, but it certainly does complicate it.

(2) The story is primarily about Mrs. Dietrich, inasmuch as the narration is focused on her. The women possess the differences that naturally, but regrettably, seem to develop between people when they are close together. A mother-daughter relationship does not preclude individuality, nor can it prevent anger. Ironically, the story's ending indicates that Mrs. Dietrich is inextricably a mother. Parents always wish to shield their children from hurt and embarrassment, right from birth through adolescence, adulthood, and old age (if parents live so long). The wish never dies. Mrs. Dietrich therefore finds reason for criticizing Nola at the same time she embraces her.

(3) Throughout the story Oates uses the names of fashionable stores and boutiques to be found at the typical American shopping mall. There is a good deal of criticism of the potential snobbishness and social inequality in these references. In the final paragraph, for example, Mrs. Dietrich recalls that she has never liked "that bulky L. L. Bean thing" her daughter is wearing. The vagabond woman represents a direct contrast to the comfortable middle to upper class world inhabited by Mrs. Dietrich and her daughter. Here is a variant on the classical theme "Et in Arcadia Ego"; right in the middle of life and prosperity, there is wretchedness, and, also, death. Despite the difficulties between mother and daughter, their difficulties pale in significance when measured against the problems of the vagabond woman.

(4) The present tense emphasizes the ongoing, constant nature of the conflicts between parents and children. The past tense narrative elements are introduced to show that present problems have their seeds in the past. The particular events in this story pertain, of course, only to Mrs. Dietrich and Nola, and they would be different for another mother and daughter. but the general problems in the relationship seem common.

(5) Paragraph 30 is remarkably perceptive and poignant about the enthusiasm of a marital relationship, with all the hopes for the future and with all the belief that a child will succeed where the

parents have failed. It is the combination of hope and expectation, mingled with disappointment and regret, that Oates succeeds in presenting here. Has there been a more penetrating and agonizing phrase than "Never before so happy, and never since"? Is Oates telling us that hopes for happiness are destined for disappointment? Is the pursuit of happiness never to reach its goal?

WRITING TOPICS. The character of Mrs. Dietrich. The character of Nola. The regret with which the story is tinged. The meaning of the vagabond woman. The story's attitude toward the socio-economic life of shopping malls.

WORKS FOR COMPARISON WITH "SHOPPING"

Colwin, *An Old Fashioned Story*, 67
Gilchrist, *Song of Songs*, 264
Halpern, *Summer in the Middle Class*, 1157
Lochhead, *The Choosing*, 1172
Olds, *The Planned Child*, 824
Olsen, *I Stand Here Ironing*, 646
Tan, *Two Kinds*, 226

AMY TAN, *Two Kinds*, *pages 226–233*

"Two Kinds" is a peculiarly American story—a tale of tensions between first and second generation immigrants and the problems of assimilation into American society. Attitudes have changed in recent times, with many writers emphasizing not the adjustments but instead the rights of immigrants to maintain their earlier ways of life. "Two Kinds," however, focuses on the second generation, represented by Jing Mei, who ardently wishes to establish her own identity apart from her mother, whose ardent wish is that her daughter, above all, must be obedient (paragraph 74).

Suggestions for Discussing the Study Questions, pages 233–34

(1) Jing-Mei's dominant characteristic is to make her own way as an independent person despite her origins as a Chinese-American. This leads her to the stubbornness, hardness, and even cruelty that she evidences in the story. The fact that she is telling the story at all, however, indicates the regret and shame she feels at the way she responded to her mother. Paragraph 79 is worth classroom discussion in this regard, particularly this sentence: "In the years that followed, I failed her so many times, each time asserting my own will, my right to fall short of expectations."

(2) Although the story concerns Jing-Mei's resistance to her mother, there is nothing especially unusual in the mother-daughter conflicts. Parents usually wish their children to excel, and try to push them into activities like chess, music, and athletics. Although parents are sometimes successful, many children normally put up great resistance to the pressure. The most extreme aspect of the conflict in "Two Kinds" is Jing-Mei's bitterness and renunciation brought out in paragraphs 75–77, for her resentment of the pressure is so great that she is willing to bring out the "worms and toads and slimy things crawling out of my chest."

(3) Jing-Mei's mother has had an immensely difficult life, having been dispossessed not only of her native country but also of her two earlier babies. In this respect she is sympathetic. It is natural that she would want to make up her losses through Jing-Mei. We are given only an objective view of the mother, however, even in paragraph 78, where her deepest feelings are described. Much is to be inferred from this paragraph. Although Jing-Mei does not express regret about the violence of her childhood feelings, her memories indicate that she has been emotionally reconciled.

(4) Details in the story indicate the ways in which American culture is reaching the first generation as represented by Jing-Mei's mother and father. These are the Ed Sullivan show and the high parental expectations for Jing-Mei: encouraging her to develop her talents and urging her to get high grades, to be popular, and to graduate from a good college. Ironically, all these high aims produce the reverse wishes in Jing-Mei, who sees her mother's aims not as encouragement but coercion. In Zabytko's "Home Soil" the parent-child connection is seen from the standpoint of the father, who does not understand his son. In Cisneros's "The House on Mango Street" the topic is not parent-child relationships but rather the economic deprivation of the narrator's homes, particularly the family house on Mango Street.

WRITING TOPICS. The character of Jing-Mei. Problems of first and second generant immigrants. The relationship between mother and daughter. Humor in the story.

WORKS FOR COMPARISON WITH "TWO KINDS"

Cisneros, *The House on Mango Street, 290*
Henley, *Am I Blue, 1635*
Hodgins, *The Concert Stages of Europe, 396*
Oats, *Shopping, 216*
Zabytko, *Home Soil, 511*

Writing About Characters, *pages 234–38*

A common problem in student essays about character is that emphasis is placed not on what characters are like but rather on what they do. Therefore, the most significant element, no matter what approach your students might select (from those suggested on pages 234–35), is that actions, comments, and speeches from the story should be introduced only if they reveal qualities of the character being studied. The story materials should never become an end in themselves, never a retelling of the story. Usually, the suggested organizations 1 and 3 (235) are the easiest types for students to apply. For example, a study of Abner of "Barn Burning" might be developed around the topics of ruthlessness, contempt, and anger—as traits—or around the campfire, the rug, and the attempted barn burning—as central incidents. Whenever it is possible in a story to perceive a "change" or "growth" of character, the second type would be in order. Thus an essay on Sarty of "Barn Burning," or on Mrs. Hale of "A Jury of Her Peers," could be organized to reflect the changes in these characters.

Special Topics for Writing and Argument about Character, *pages 238–39*

(1) This topic can prove extensive, but also quite interesting as methods of narration. Both Sarty and Paul are subjects of limited omniscient narrations, and the methods of revealing their characters may therefore be closely compared. Jing-Mei's mother, however, is viewed from the standpoint of the narrator, who is recollecting painful childhood memories. Sarty and Paul are of course the centers of their stories, whereas Jing-Mei, the narrator, is the principal subject of "Two Kinds."

(2) The second topic is designed so that students may concentrate on what it means for a character to undergo change. A philosophical issue to consider is whether change is really change, or whether change is the emergence of qualities that are already present in the individual. From the literary-structural standpoint, it is significant that the interaction of character and situation be introduced to show how character change or development occurs.

(3) In the discussion of character, the flat characters sometimes get left out. This question should therefore make clear that flat characters do have traits, and also play a vital role in the development of the story and also in the development of the major characters.

(4) All parts of the fourth question deal with problems connected with the various stories. In dealing with any of the prob-

lems, students should acquire a stronger understanding of the stories than they would otherwise do. Question 4b is a speculative assignment for those students who wish to consider the issues of character broadly.

(5) The characters to be discussed in relationship to the issue of circumstance and character are a child (Sarty), an adolescent (Jing-Mei), and an adult (Minnie Wright). The circumstances accordingly vary widely. We do not learn anything about the education of either Sarty or Jing-Mei, for example, but we do learn how they are being influenced by family. As preparation for this assignment, students might wish to consult Chapter 35, on comparison and contrast (p. 1979).

(6) Topic 6 provides students with the opportunity to do their own creative writing, basing their stories on their own lives, or on situations they might imagine themselves experiencing or having experienced.

(7) This library exercise is designed to introduce students to the world of Faulkner's fiction, particularly the Snopes family. Faulkner is one of America's unique writers because of this detailed world, a technique that many serious and popular writers have copied, particularly those (such as J. A. Jance and Sue Grafton) who feature recurring narrators.

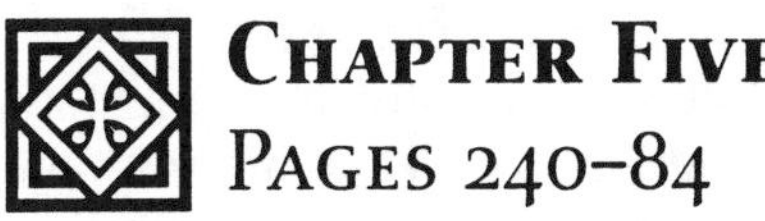

Chapter Five
Pages 240–84

Point of View: The Position or Stance of the Narrator or Speaker

Because point of view is likely a new concept and technique for students, you will need to emphasize its importance as a mode of presenting and authenticating narrative details. It is still somewhat of a revelation, however, that the author himself or herself is not the direct speaker of a story. Therefore the question "Do you mean the author's point of view?" should be addressed, for it will invariably be asked even after you have spent time in class explaining the meaning of the term. The question offers the chance to underscore the difference between point of view and opinions or ideas, a confusion which tends to persist even after much explanation.

The best way to reinforce the idea, of course, is to consider a number of stories and to determine the nature of the speaker in each of them. In addition, the sketch on page 242 should prove helpful in prompting a discussion about the unique ways in which speakers may perceive the things they describe. Once students see that the variation of point of view is a major way of explaining the unique and individualistic quality of much fiction, they will be well on their way to becoming capable, disciplined readers.

Sherwood Anderson, *I'm a Fool,* *pages 250–57*

"I'm a Fool" is a representative Anderson story, for the speaker, the major character, is trying to find his place in the world but because he lacks perspective and the capacity for adjustment he fails in what seems to be a major opportunity in his young life.

The plot develops out of a conflict between the narrator's actions and lies, on the one hand, and his valuation of truth, on the other. The narrator himself is thus both protagonist and antagonist. The crisis of the story is perhaps best seen as paragraph 44, in which the narrator explains his reason for lying to Lucy Wessen, and the climax is paragraph 45, in which he explains how he went "the whole hog" in his lies about his circumstances and background. Once he has lied, everything in the story follows naturally. It is not until later in the story (paragraph 62 ff) that he learns what his lies have cost him. However, the initial lying has damned his later realization about the potential importance of Lucy. Obviously, the value of the story is to maintain truth in all relationships. One might stress that the story does not get at the issues of apology and the admission of mistakes.

Suggestions for Discussing the Study Questions, page 257

(1) The point of view is first person, and the speaker is the unnamed narrator, a young man of considerable ability but little preparation for dealing with life's complications. We learn less about details of his life than of his attitudes, which are average and ill considered. His diction is characterized by plain, low, and slang words and phrases, suggesting that the style is to be taken as conversational rather than written. His speech contains frequent grammatical lapses, in keeping with the authentic manner of his normal speech. He shifts to the "you" phraseology in paragraphs 8 and 11–14 as an extension of his conversational style, thus associating himself intimately with the listener.

(2) Because the speaker increases in self-awareness and understanding in the story, he is round. He grows from a pleasant but average and cliché-ridden young man (see, for example, paragraph 10, where he derides the learning that may be obtained from universities and where he praises the value of simple experience) to a person who has developed insight into his mistakes and profound regret for them. Though he grows, however, he does not grow enough to admit his mistake to the young woman with whom he falls in love.

(3) Although Lucy and the narrator come from different walks of life, they seem enough alike to form an immediate infatuation and attachment (see especially paragraphs 55, 64, and 65). The story ends with the consequences of the narrator's lies, and hence the issue of family differences does not enter into any possible developing relationship. It would seem, however, that the narrator's family, though modest economically, is respectable enough to forestall objections. In addition, the speaker, though speaking colloquially in his narration, does not put Lucy off by his manner or speech habits during their meeting at the track and during their later conversations.

(4) A major aspect of the naturalistic style is the authenticity of the surroundings. The narrator's experiences as a swipe, the roister-

ing background of track life and post-track life in bars, and the activities with the Wessens–all give the impression of continued, verifiable reality. Obviously, the narrator's considerable knowledge about horses enables him to impress Lucy and her brother because they see the track and betting odds from their "horsy set" perspective as spectators and amateur bettors. They assume that the narrator's knowledge comes from experiences similar to theirs.

WRITING TOPICS. The story's point of view. The character of the narrator, and his reliability as a speaker. The effect of the narrator's self criticism upon the narration of the story. The reasons for the narrator's anger at himself. The nature of the narrator's speech. The character of Lucy.

WORKS FOR COMPARISON WITH "I'M A FOOL"

Butler, *Snow, 590*
Dickinson, *I Cannot Live with You, 1069*
Drayton, *Since There's No Help, 1146*
Piercy, *Will We Work Together? 1185*

AMBROSE BIERCE, *An Occurrence at Owl Creek Bridge,* *pages 257–63*

This story is of great interest because it is an early attempt to relate time and mental perception. It is mainly centered in the consciousness of the central character, Farquhar, except for the dramatically rendered section beginning with paragraph 8. Additionally, "An Occurrence at Owl Creek Bridge" is a fine suspense story, because as the narrator moves into Farquhar's mind the reader is led to believe, at least temporarily, in the actual escape. The story is therefore a virtuoso piece in the use of point of view.

Suggestions for Discussing the Study Questions, page 263

(1) The story takes place in northern Alabama during the Civil War. Union Forces are in control and martial law prevails; Therefore there are no civil rights, no safeguards for enemies of the Union, and no trials beyond those of a military court. From Section II, we infer that Farquhar, the main character, was lured or even entrapped into an attempt to blow up the bridge over the Owl Creek Bridge. He had tried to overcome the guard and then had been arrested, summarily tried, and condemned to death by hanging from the bridge which he had tried to destroy.

(2) In paragraph 5 the point of view shifts when Farquhar closes his eyes, thereby shutting off the outside world of his perceptions

and opening up the inner world of his imagination. Our attention is thus directed toward those things that he thinks he sees and experiences. First we learn of the apparent slowing of his watch, followed by his dream or belief that he is actually escaping (he has this extended perception once he is actually being hanged). In paragraph 37 the point of view becomes abruptly and cruelly dramatic. There is no more probing into Farquhar's mind because he is dead.

(3) The imagined time of Farquhar's escape is an entire day, from earliest daylight to night. That his escape is so lengthy is particularly interesting because his perceptions permit an enormous amount of imaginary action to take place within just a few seconds.

(4) Bierce is careful to point out that Farquhar is feeling "pain," that he is "suffocating," that there is "a sharp pain in his wrist," and that "his neck ached horribly; his brain was on fire" (paragraphs 18, 19). Also, Farquhar's "visible world" is wheeling "slowly round" (paragraph 21). These descriptions realistically describe the real pain of hanging that he is experiencing, even though he is also dreaming that he is making his escape.

(5) A major purpose of the movement into the present tense in paragraph 36 is to bring readers into the present moment, both in terms of the action and of Farquhar's perceptions. In addition, the present tense makes the situation of his escape dramatic and then it makes his death more poignant.

WRITING TOPICS. The compression of time within the story. Farquhar's realistic perceptions of pain. The shift in point of view in Section I of the story. The point of view of Section II.

WORKS FOR COMPARISON WITH "AN OCCURRENCE AT OWL CREEK BRIDGE"

Hawthorne, *Young Goodman Brown, 436*
Owen, *Dulce et Decorum Est, 810*
Ozick, *The Shawl, 331*
Sassoon, *Dreamers, 1195*
Seeger, *I Have a Rendezvous with Death, 1196*

ELLEN GILCHRIST, ***The Song of Songs,*** *pages 263–67*

"The Song of Songs" concerns the psychological aftereffects of adoption. Students may wish to discuss whether the story supports arguments for telling or not telling an adopted child about the adoption. To what degree are people entitled to know the entire truth about their parentage? If ignorance is bliss, is it folly to be wise?

If a person knows that he or she has been adopted, but does not know the identity of the original parents, will this uncertainty be psychologically destructive?

The plot of "The Song of Songs" (another title of the biblical "Song of Solomon") is the conflict between urges for life or death within the major character, Barrett Clare. The story takes place entirely on Christmas Day—a day on which Barrett is experiencing a crisis in her life. She has just learned who her biological mother really is, but is uncertain about how to contact her. After rising, preparing breakfast, and retiring to her room, she plays with the idea of suicide by putting the barrel of a gun into her mouth—an action she has taken many times before. This is the crisis of the story, which is interrupted by the climaxing phone call of Amanda, Barrett's mother, from Arkansas. The resolution is that Barrett immediately leaves for Arkansas with her young boy, Charles. The final paragraph powerfully describes the recognition, for the first time, of mother and child.

Suggestions for Discussing the Study Questions, page 267

(1, 2) "The Song of Songs" is a story with shifting points of view. Barrett is the center of attention throughout; hence the principal point of view may be considered as limited omniscient. In paragraph 22, however, the point of view focuses for one sentence on the thoughts of Charlie, Barrett's husband. He is thinking about "the soft little buns" of "Patsy," who, we assume, is a woman with whom he is having an affair. That the point of view shifts to provide this information is important for our understanding of why Barrett's marriage is failing. Generally, however, the prevailing limited omniscient point of view permits us to understand why Barrett feels totally alone, is deeply depressed, is seeing an analyst, and constantly toys with the gun and thinks of suicide. From paragraphs 27 to 42 the point of view changes to the dramatic with the telephone conversation between Barrett and her mother, and with the directions for the trip that Barrett gives to Charlie. The concluding point of view is also dramatic. The limited omniscient point of view permits us to share Barrett's thoughts directly, and the dramatic point of view demonstrates her resolution and her desire to be joined with her birth mother, Amanda.

The story's narrative voice, short as the story is, is close and sympathetic to Barrett. Barrett is religiously observant and writes poetry. She is greatly distressed with her life, at least partially because she knows that her husband has been cheating on her. She is financially but not psychologically secure. Her wealth is demonstrated by her fine house, expensive shoes, special china, original paintings, expensive gifts, and chartered airplane. Despite these outward signs of wealth, she is uncertain, and the story makes plain that her distress results from not knowing her biological parents. The degree of her disturbance is shown by her thought that blowing out her brains would mess up the Andrew Wyeth painting hanging in her room (paragraph 24). From this confusion and despair, her exultation at learning her identity brings about a shift in her outlook. Because the story focuses so tenaciously on Barrett's feelings, the conclusion represents a powerful and moving release. When she exclaims "I exist" in paragraph 38, we may presume that this outcry is her "song of songs."

(3) Christmas is considered a special family day even though there is nothing particularly religious about this Christmas day in the Clare household except for the beginning references to "Silent Night" and "For unto Us a Child Is Born." We may assume that Barrett's mother's name, Amanda (loving) suggests that the day will signify a new direction for Barrett, a genuine renewal.

(4) Clearly the story takes the position that the effects of adoption, on parent as well as child, are deleterious. Barrett has been destructively affected, and we learn, in paragraph 27, that Amanda has been equally distressed ever since giving Barrett away only five days after giving birth.

WRITING TOPICS. The character of Barrett Clare. The causes of her mental disturbance. The significance of knowing one's parentage. The story's point of view. The symbolism of Christmas morning and the gun.

WORKS FOR COMPARISON WITH "THE SONG OF SONGS"

cummings, *if there are any heavens, 1138*
Hayden, *Those Winter Sundays, 1161*
Oates, *Shopping, 216*
St. Luke, *The Parable of the Prodigal Son, 445*
Joy Williams, *Taking Care, 95*

SHIRLEY JACKSON, *The Lottery,* *pages 268–73*

In the forty years since "The Lottery" was written, it has justifiably become a classic. It skillfully withholds its grisly outcome until the final few paragraphs, and ends on a note of horror, even though many clues throughout the story anticipate this ending.

Suggestions for Discussing the Study Questions, page 273

(1) The point of view of "The Lottery" is the dramatic or third-person objective. The narrator seems to be a witness moving invisibly though the crowd, and thus is able to see and hear what is happening and how the townsfolk are responding. Sometimes the narrator seems close enough to people to hear and report what they say. At other times he or she is at a distance and thus simply reports actions and general reactions. In addition, the nameless narrator has a good supply of extra information about the background of the lottery and also about the activities of Messieurs Graves and Summers the night before. Consistent with the dramatic point of view, the speaker excludes from the narration any attempt to interpret the purpose of the lottery. By withholding knowledge in this way, Jackson builds up the suspense of the story.

(2) Either an omniscient or first-person point of view would need to include information about matters such as the hesitation of the two men (paragraph 4) and the tradition of the lottery (paragraph 5). In addition, an omniscient or limited omniscient speaker would probably need to personalize Tessie Hutchinson more than at present. Hence, either of these alternative points of view would make the conclusion more brutal if not more horrifying.

(3) Upon first reading, the conclusion is a definite surprise. However, there are many early hints about the outcome, such as the piles of stones (paragraph 2), the use of the black box (paragraph 5), the "sudden hush" (paragraph 19), the discussion of quitting the use of the lottery (paragraphs 31–34), and Tessie's anxiety (paragraph 44 and elsewhere). Upon reading the conclusion, students will see that these hints may be read as expressing double meaning. Thus, the conclusion of paragraph 1, in which lunch is mentioned, at first seems to suggest nothing more than ordinary activities on an ordinary day. On second reading, however, reference to lunch may be read as an indication of the callous insensibility of those who could return home after the stoning and sit down to eat as though nothing had happened.

(4) The ritual traces of the lottery are mentioned in paragraphs 5, 7, 13, 32, and 49. It would appear that elements such as the jingle (which was apparently supplied by Jackson's husband, the critic Stanley Hyman), and the former use of wood chips, suggest an earlier, more formalized procedure. Some common examples of anachronistic rituals might be touching wood, throwing salt over one's left shoulder, or fearing the path of a black cat. Students will un-

questionably be able to supply many other residual examples of superstitions.

(5) The story contains both horror and shock. The two are not mutually exclusive, for the surprise depends upon delaying the concluding information until the very end, and the horror is coincidental with the ritualized public murder.

WRITING TOPICS. The dramatic point of view in "The Lottery." The structure of the story. Hints about the purpose of the lottery drawing. The meaning—or lack of meaning—of the ritual.

WORKS FOR COMPARISON WITH "THE LOTTERY"

Dickey, *The Performance, 1142*
Dixon, *All Gone, 595*
Flannery O'Connor, *A Good Man Is Hard to Find, 635*
Poe, *The Black Cat, 545*
Quasímodo, *Auschwitz, 829*
Randall, *Ballad of Birmingham, 923*

LORRIE MOORE, *How to Become a Writer,* *pages 274–78*

Francie, the speaker of Moore's "How to Become a Writer," comments a number of times about how she has been told, by teachers and fellow students, that the plots of her stories are weak. Superficially, the same comment might be made about "How to Become a Writer." Therefore it is important to note that the story does indeed have a plot. One may perceive that the time lapse may be as much as seven or eight or more years, from high school to the period after college graduation. The period is that of the Vietnamese war (1965–1975), for Francie describes a brother who has served in Vietnam, has been wounded, and has returned home. Despite the episodic nature of "How to Become a Writer," and despite its lack of direct narrative presentation, the story also dramatizes a conflict. On the one hand, Francie adheres to the view that writing is an irresistible outgrowth of either nature or affliction (writing is "a lot like having polio" [paragraph 41])—the idea being that a writer is born, not made (*"poeta nascitur, non fit"*). On the other hand, the "how to" title seems committed to the opposing view that writing is a learned skill or science.

Suggestions for Discussing the Study Questions, page 278

(1) Unique about "How to Become a Writer" is its use of the second-person point of view—characteristic of a number of stories

in *Self Help*, the collection from which "How to Become a Writer" is selected—which is shown in the beginning words, "First, try," and which is sustained throughout. The speaker is Francie, a young writer herself. The dramatic situation is that she is giving advice to an unnamed listener about the right *cursus honorum* to follow in becoming a writer. It is clear, however, that the "you" is Francie's informal and indefinite way of referring to herself as much as to the listener. The story unfolds as though she is responding to the following question posed before the story opens: "How do you become a writer?" Under this aegis, Francie in effect ironically and comically describes what she herself has done. Anyone who has ever told someone else how to do something will have used the second person "you" in a similar way.

(2) The story's topic develops out of the proposition that people may actually *do* things to turn themselves into writers. In this debunking vein, Francie provides the advice that the potential writer should fail at something (paragraph 1), keep a journal (paragraph 15), write from experience (paragraph 19), jot down sayings from others or go to graduate school (paragraph 34), and dream up outlandish plots involving various types of mutilation (e.g., paragraphs 8, 32). While "suggestions" of this sort may sometimes be important, their effect is that the development of a writer is not logical but is, rather, irrational, and that there is no way of predicting or controlling the inner sparks of creative literary fire. To put a case, if one considers the story as argument, Moore's humor is a logical method of reducing to an absurdity the claim that writing may actually be taught. If one considers the advice as advice, the conclusion is that the budding writer should just live life as it happens, and then put to use everything that he or she has experienced. There is no other way.

(3) It is, of course, the humor that stands out in "How to Become a Writer." Moore introduces a number of comic comments and asides, such as "Some, you notice, are dumber than you" (paragraph 7), "watch how funny he can be, see what a really great sense of humor he can have" (paragraph 9), "These seem like important questions" (paragraph 11), "This is a quote from Shakespeare" (paragraph 16), and the puns on "Fishmeal" and "Liverworst" (paragraphs 17, 21). Francie's major comic *motif* is her constant variation of a story about couples who are destroyed or maimed in impossibly ludicrous ways.

It is within the context of such dire experiences that Moore's humor may be taken—comedy in a background of great concern and seriousness, however distant or removed it may be. The fact is that real-life writers have often experienced pain themselves. Thus Francie points out that she has "no words" to explain why her brother suffered a crippling wound in Vietnam (paragraph 22). In addition, in a number of places she indicates that she, too, has encountered personal grief, though she passes over it unceremoniously and unsentimentally: losing her boyfriend, being thought crazy, losing weight through anxiety, and becoming derelict about responsibility. This serious backdrop enables Moore to sustain her successfully comic tone in "How to Become a Writer."

Writing Topics. Is "How to Become a Writer" really a story? The use of the second-person point of view. Comedy and irony in the story. The nature of the "advice": could it work?

Works for Comparison with "How to Become a Writer"

Keats, *On First Looking Into Chapman's Homer, 777*
MacLeish, *Ars Poetica, 1022*
Olsen, *I Stand Here Ironing, 646*
Strand, *Eating Poetry, 740*

Writing About Point of View, *pages 278–83*

In the classroom use of this section, it is essential to emphasize that students are to write about point of view as a technique of narration. One of the most difficult aspects to get across to students is that a story's point of view is not about ideas and opinions, but rather about the narrative voice and the presentation of details (see the caveat on page 244). One of the best ways to bring out this fact, and hence also to provide students with the materials to be included in their essays, is to stress the various study questions dealing specifically with points of view of the stories and with the possibilities of approaching the material from other viewpoints. Once students have become familiar with the variations that might follow from differing points of view, they can undertake a specific assignment with confidence.

The demonstrative essay on "The Lottery" will repay careful reading because the details included in each paragraph support the topic sentence there. In classroom discussion, you might stress that any one of the aspects treated so briefly in this essay might be more deeply analyzed and exemplified as the basis for an entire essay. Thus, an essay might be devoted to (1) the characterizations and the means by which these are brought out in the story (2) the possibilities of telling the story from other points of view, and the consequent results as contrasted with the dramatic viewpoint used by Jackson, or (3) the control over detail in the story. Above all, students will need to be reminded that the immediate purpose of an essay on point of view is to help them not so much to analyze topics such as an author's symbols and ideas, but rather to study her or his narrative technique.

Special Topics for Writing and Argument about Point of View, *pages 283–84*

(1) Topic 1 is creative, with the emphasis to be placed on the ways of looking at life that might be brought out through the words of secondary or minor characters in the stories.

(2) Topic 2 should get students thinking concretely about other modes of narration than those used by the writer. An assumption of this assignment is that students may learn what the story is like by stressing alternative ways of presentation. It seems clear that the narrator of "A Worn Path" would view Brown more objectively and less sympathetically, while the narrator of An Occurrence at Owl Creek Bridge" might go into more detail about Brown's perceptions than Hawthorne does. The second narrator of "Luck" would likely be less sympathetic and even inimical toward Brown.

(3) Topic 3 may be an exercise not only in point of view, but in intellectual growth and tolerant understanding. Suppose, for example, a student as a child were playing with matches and started a fire in a closet. What would this child, now a mature person, be able to say from the point of view of a parent discovering the fire and punishing the child? (The author introduces this example because once, as a tiny tot, he nearly burned down the family home.)

(4) Topic 4 is speculative, although if examples from student experiences were to be introduced, the conclusions could be greatly strengthened. Students who experience difficulty in beginning the assignment might wish to launch their discourse by analyzing words from some of their friends, or from people with whom they have done business–assuming, of course, that names are not used and that all other circumstances are altered.

(5) The research component of this topic can be met if students use the reference section of their library. Of major concern is that they find additional material on point of view, and bring it to bear on the topic comparing "How to Become a Writer" and "I'm a Fool" (See Chapter 35, page 1979).

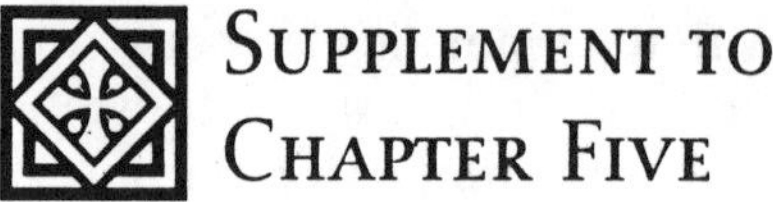

The Various Points of View in the Stories Included in the Sixth Edition

N. B. The following lists are intended to assist you in assigning essays on point of view in stories beyond those in the chapter, for purposes of special analysis, comparison, and variation of assignment.

I. First Person

A ◆ the narrator as a major mover

A & P
All Gone
Araby
The Black Cat
Blue Winds Dancing
The Cask of Amontillado
The Concert Stages of Europe
Everyday Use
First Confession
Home Soil
I'm a Fool
The Lesson
The Loons
Rape Fantasies
The Secret Sharer
Snow
The Sky is Gray
What I Have Been Doing Lately
The Yellow Wallpaper
Two Kinds

B ◆ the narrator as an observer and/or participant

The Fall of the House of Usher
The Hammon and the Beans
I Stand Here Ironing
Luck
The House on Mango Street
The Old Chief Mshlanga (*paragraphs 14–98*)
The Purloined Letter

C ◆ an unnamed narrator who is not a participant or an on-the-spot observer, but who reports all actions and speeches and who also establishes at least a degree of identity and individuality

The Masque of the Red Death
Neighbors
The Point of It
The Thimble
Unfinished Masterpieces

D ◆ first speaker introduces and quotes the first-person narrative of another.

Luck

E ◆ narrator speaks of herself in the third person.

The Old Chief Mshlanga (*paragraphs 1–13*)

II. Second Person

How to Become a Writer

III. Third Person

A ◆ **Limited Omniscient:** A major character is the principal focus of the narrative, together with responses and thoughts of this character.

And Sarah Laughed
Barn Burning
The Chrysanthemums
The Curse
The Found Boat
The Jilting of Granny Weatherall
A Jury of Her Peers
The Necklace
An Occurrence at Owl Creek Bridge
The Old Chief Mshlanga (*paragraphs 1–13*)
The Shawl
Shopping
The Song of Songs
The Story of an Hour
Taking Care
The Thimble
The Things They Carried
A Worn Path
Young Goodman Brown

B ◆ **Limited Dramatic:** a major character is the focus of the narrative, with few if any revelations of this character's thoughts.

The Portable Phonograph
The Fox and the Grapes
The Myth of Atalanta

C ◆ **Omniscient:** the All-Knowing Narrator

The Horse Dealer's Daughter
The Prodigal Son
The Three Strangers

D ◆ **Dramatic,** or **Objective**

The Lottery
The Blue Hotel

E ◆ Third Person Frame: The speaker introduces the third-person narrative of another.

The Prodigal Son

◆ Stories notable for special uses of points of view *(including stories already listed)*

Everyday Use *(first person and dramatic)*
Luck *(first person quotes a first-person speaker)*
The Old Chief Mshlanga *(speaker speaks of herself in the third person, then shifts to the first person)*
The Parable of the Prodigal Son *(narrator quotes a third-person narrative)*
The Yellow Wallpaper *(first-person narrator seems to be writing the story surreptitiously over an extended period of time)*

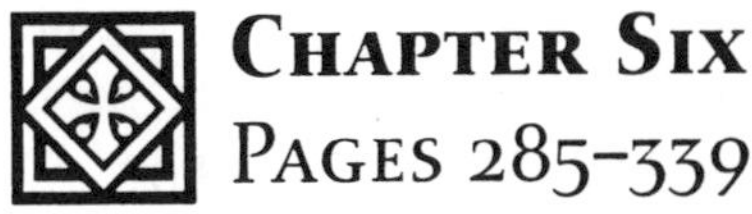

Chapter Six
Pages 285–339

Setting: The Background Of Place, Objects, and Culture in Stories

The goal of this chapter is to explain the importance of objects, place, and time in fiction. While the various aspects of setting may be defined and discussed abstractly, it is important that classroom discussion be directed toward the uses of setting in the stories you assign for your students. "The House on Mango Street," "The Portable Phonograph," "The Secret Sharer," "And Sarah Laughed," and "The Shawl" present abundant materials for the study of setting. None of these stories could be told without their references to physical locations. "The House on Mango Street" is actually about locations and the meaning of locations to the aims of the narrator and her family and to the ones whom they meet. Clark makes "The Portable Phonograph" inextricable from the grim post-cataclysmic world that he deftly sketches at the story's beginning. The shipboard location of "The Secret Sharer" serves first as a place of hiding and then as one of liberation. The isolation of the farm home in "And Sarah Laughed" emphasizes how the characters are isolated by deafness. Ozick's story is both literally and symbolically imprisoned within its concentration-camp confines.

Sandra Cisneros, *The House on Mango Street,* *pages 290–91*

The book titled *The House on Mango Street,* from which this story is selected, is not so much a collection of short stories as a series of brief vignettes or impressions about the life of the narrator, a young woman named Esperanza Cordero, and those living near the poor little house on Mango Street.

Suggestions for Discussing the Study Questions, page 291

(1) The speaker is responding to the insecurity of her family's poverty, and that her unhappiness with the houses she has lived in

results from shame. She therefore yearns for a house she can "point to" with pride (paragraph 11). She also yearns for release, and hence in a later impression (not anthologized here) entitled "Mango Says Goodbye Sometimes," she declares that the house on Mango Street is a "house I belong but do not belong to."

(2) The house is described in paragraph 5. The details demonstrate the impoverishment of Esperanza's family. The windows are small, the steps tiny, the brickwork crumbling, the rooms few, the bathroom a common one for all six members of the family, and the bedroom also a common one for the family.

(3) The eleven paragraphs comprising the story do not provide extensive details from which we may infer the narrator's character. But we do learn of the things that pain her, namely the squalor of earlier family residences, the embarrassment caused by the physical details of the house on Mango Street, the even greater embarrassment and shame deriving from the house on Loomis, and the ironic conclusion at the story's end (paragraph 11). The result is that the narrator is revealed a person of good power of observation, combined with strong feelings about her status and her wish to improve and to rise in the world.

Writing topics. Use of detail in the story. The implied comparison between the family's actual residences and the narrator's wished-for residences. The narrator's character, and her attitude toward her surroundings.

Works for Comparison with "The House on Mango Street"

Hughes, *Mulatto, 1663*
McKay, *The White City, 1177*
Parédes, *The Hammon and the Beans, 415*
Salinas, *In a Farmhouse, 1193*

Walter Van Tilburg Clark, *The Portable Phonograph,* *pages 292–96*

The central character in "The Portable Phonograph" is the "host," Dr. Jenkins. The speaker's giving him the title of "doctor" suggests that he is a medical doctor, although some students claim that he is a professor of literature since he thinks (paragraph 37) that he knows "all of Shelley by heart" (how many English professors would make such a claim?). He values literature and music most highly. His possession of the books, the phonograph, and the records, together with his management of his little cell, indicate a person of taste who is also practical enough to retain what he prizes most even under the worst conditions.

An interesting issue of interpretation arises in the reading of this story. If the protagonist of "The Portable Phonograph" is identified as the doctor, the antagonist might then readily be seen as the musician. If the story is viewed as a political tract or prognostication, the protagonist is civilization and the antagonist is warfare. Everyone in the story is then a victim of the antagonist; no one wins. Then too, the story may be read as a realistic portrayal of the precariousness of civilization. The protagonist would then again be the doctor and the music, while the musician would be the antagonist representing the force threatening the continuance of civilization. The story thus would be a parable about the need for eternal vigilance. In effect, the story ends during the crisis, and technically is unfinished. For this reason the resolution is Dr. Jenkins's recognition both of the threat and also of the need for continued watchfulness and preparedness.

The conclusion may require some attention. Even though the note for paragraph 15 (294) explains the nature of old-style wind-up phonographs, students in these days of compact-disk perfection may need some additional information so that the significance and uniqueness of the phonograph may be understood. A virtue of the old victrolas was that they operated without electric power, so that Dr. Jenkins and his group could listen to records any time they wished (despite the threat that the records were close to wearing out). In addition, students sometimes do not understand that the danger concluding the story is the musician. This uncertainty results from Clark's focusing of the point of view on Dr. Jenkins. What is described at the end is thus limited to what Dr. Jenkins can hear, and what he hears is vague and unclear. Clark's narrative technique therefore may need to be stressed and discussed.

Suggestions for Discussing the Study Questions, page 296

(1) The story is set in a bleak, cold, lifeless prairie that had once been a battleground. Heavy tanks have broken up the old pavement on the roads, and bombs have left large craters. The land has not yet regenerated itself, although there are "young trees trying again" (paragraph 1). The opening paragraphs convey a feeling of desperation and hopelessness, and an atmosphere of harshness.

(2) Adjectives such as *narrow, cold,* and *mute* have in common a quality of stillness, constriction, emptiness, and fragility. They con-

tribute to the impression of lifelessness and bleakness about the setting, and therefore characterize the world in which beauty and graciousness are no more than a dim memory.

(3) Dr. Jenkins's home is a *cell* (paragraph 3). The fire, dim as it is, is a kind of deception. The fire is *petty* and *acrid,* and the burning is *chary* (spare and meager), and is also *smoldering* (paragraph 4). Blankets are *old and dirty,* while the wrapping cord is home-made out of grass. Only a few utensils are mentioned, and those are of "tin," which in 1942 connoted cheapness and tawdriness. These details all suggest the spare, austere life lived by the few survivors in the story's devastated world.

(4) The men agree to hear Debussy's *Nocturne* for piano, primarily because it is selected by the musician (paragraph 44), whom they regard as an expert. The playing time of this piece, which is less well known than Debussy's three *Nocturnes* for orchestra and chorus, is about six minutes. Reactions of the listening men are described in paragraph 45. Three of the men perceive "tragically heightened recollection" while the musician listens more objectively, hearing "nothing" but what is there, but his response when the music ends indicates his heightened emotion and therefore his appreciation.

(5) After the group leaves, Dr. Jenkins hides all his valuables and rearranges his bed so that he may see any intruder, because he has heard noises outside and has seen a shadow indicating that the musician is waiting to enter his cell and steal the phonograph and the records. In effect, the doctor is being forced by the musician to return to a state of nature.

WRITING TOPICS. The setting of postwar devastation. The importance of scene, temperature, and darkness in the mood of the story. Setting and the characters of Dr. Jenkins and the musician. The setting as a symbol of destructive warfare. The use of artifacts. The integration of action and setting.

WORKS FOR COMPARISON WITH "THE PORTABLE PHONOGRAPH"

Nash, *Exit, Pursued by a Bear,* 791
Owen, *Anthem for Doomed Youth,* 750
Yeats, *The Second Coming,* 961
Zabytko, *Home Soil,* 511

JOSEPH CONRAD, *The Secret Sharer,* *pages 297–322*

"The Secret Sharer" deals with the issues of guilt and evil, on the one hand, and guilt and good, or at least good intentions, on the other. In many respects the story brings out the qualities of tragedy. A work demonstrating that a guilty action is also evil would be a clear illustration of how punishment should follow crime, and, according to Aristotle, there is nothing tragic about that. But what if the guilty action is done not maliciously but with benevolent motives, as in Leggatt's story in which the murder of the complaining seaman results in the saving of the ship and the preservation of the lives of everyone else on board? This issue, which is at the heart of tragedy, is the one that students find appealing about "The Secret Sharer," and for the most part they agree that Conrad's Captain is justified in hiding Leggatt even if this action makes the Captain an accomplice, after the fact, to the murder. The Captain in fact joins Leggatt in the "crime" and the concealment, and the Captain is not ambiguous about his judgment of Leggatt. Frequently, in fact, the Captain calls Leggatt his double. In legal parlance, the Captain's actions are tantamount to "jury nullification" because his "complicity" is extenuated by the unfairness of Leggatt's imprisonment and impending punishment.

Students reading "The Secret Sharer," however, are not members of a jury, but readers of a story which involves all the complexities of life and all the difficult choices that people constantly face. These issues of "The Secret Sharer" are also treated in Glaspell's "A Jury of Her Peers" (202) and *Trifles* (1244) in which the two principal characters together cover up the crime committed by Minnie Wright, who is guilty by legal standards and therefore deserving of punishment. Another immediately comparable work is Hardy's "The Three Strangers" (133), in which a fugitive escaping punishment is hidden by people of the countryside, who believe that his crime is justifiable. Here we have not just one or two people involved in a coverup, but an entire community.

Other works in the anthology also involve degrees of crime and the results. In some of the works the "perpetrator" is punished not only by others ("An Occurrence at Owl Creek Bridge" [257] and "Revolutionary Petunias" [1212]), but also by themselves (*Mulatto* [1663] and "Paul's Case" [177]). In each of these four works we get to know the persons who die, and in none of the works are the persons evil. They are at worst ambiguous, and as a result readers can understand and sympathize with them, for their actions result rather from predicament and dilemma than from evil, as with Oedipus in Sophocles' *Oedipus the King* (1305). A similar action occurs in Ibsen's *An Enemy of the People* (1844), in which Dr. Stockmann's "crime" is to disobey an official directive while he pursues what he considers to be a greater good. His punishment is of course that he loses his job—far short of the death and mutilation suffered by the other characters.

The issue of crime and punishment in other works collected in *Literature: An Introduction to Reading and Writing* is extensive. A difficult issue occurs when crime or evil is committed during warfare, as in Hardy's "The Man He Killed" (673) and Zabytko's "Home Soil" (511). To what degree must a person involved in official killing feel guilt, or is a sense of guilt inevitable regardless of wartime justification? A less difficult issue occurs when criminals are not punished even though they are both evil and guilty, as in Dixon's "All Gone" (595) and Dubus's "The Curse" (603). Such people, who are basically anonymous in the two stories, are agents of evil and are worthy of our condemnation In Faulkner's "Barn Burning" (190) and Flannery O'Connor's "A Good Man Is Hard to Find" (635) we see, up close, violent characters who are both guilty and evil. The consequence is that Abner Snopes and the major evildoers in "A Good Man Is Hard to Find" are difficult for most readers to understand and judge. Interestingly "crime" is treated lightly and satirically in Hardy's "The Ruined Maid" (702) and Eliot's "Macavity, the Mystery Cat" (861), primarily because the "crimes" described in these poems are shown to be no crimes at all.

Suggestions for Discussing the Study Questions, page 322

(1, 4) In the section marked "The Publisher to the Reader" prefacing Swift's *Gulliver's Travels*, the speaker remarks about "innumerable Passages relating to the Winds and Tides, as well as the Variations and Bearings in the several Voyages; together with the minute Descriptions of the Management of the Ship in Storms, in the Style of Sailors [. . .]." In the same section, the speaker mentions that "There is an Air of Truth apparent through the whole [. . .]." Swift's analysis seems appropriate for a consideration of the early passages in "The Secret Sharer." Conrad's use of detail here and throughout the story establishes a pattern. Conrad continues the pattern in the Captain's description of the ship's interior, which permits the concealment of Leggatt, and in the Captain's description of how he is able to free the ship when it is in danger of foundering near Koh Ring.

(2, 3, 5) Most of the issues raised in these study questions are considered above and also in the demonstrative essay.

Writing topics. The importance of the story's location at a far-distant place. The scene on ocean and the importance of nearby land. The character of the captain, of Leggatt, of the Captain of the *Sephora*. The function of the crew in the story. Conrad's use of shipboard detail.

WORKS FOR COMPARISON WITH "THE SECRET SHARER"

Glaspell, "A Jury of Her Peers," *202*, and *Trifles, 1244*
Hardy, "The Three Strangers," *133*
Ibsen, *An Enemy of the People, 1844*
St. Luke, "The Parable of the Prodigal Son," *445*
Sophocles, *Oedipus the King, 1305*

JOANNE GREENBERG, *And Sarah Laughed,* *pages 322–31*

The time sequence in this story is particularly interesting because it begins at a central point of time, in effect *in medias res* or in the middle of things, then moves backward in retrospect, and finally moves forward. The point occurs when Sarah's son Abel and his new bride come home and create a new challenge for Sarah, who has the gift of hearing but whose family is deaf. Prior to this point, Sarah has made the difficult adjustment to her family's inability to hear and speak. The story's early paragraphs indicate how she learns to live with the deaf, first with her husband (Matthew) and then with her children (Abel, Rutherford, Lindsay, and Franklin Delano). We learn that she has taught her children to read her lips, and that at one point she put cotton in her ears to make her sympathetic to living without sound (paragraph 14). We also realize that this situation limits the connections that her family can have with the outside world (paragraph 25).

Once Janice appears with Abel, however, beginning with paragraph 32, Sarah is forced into a new situation requiring her adjustment, namely the use of sign language for the deaf. This new situation causes her to conclude that her life "had suddenly become . . . strange to her" (paragraph 35) because she finds "something obscene" about the signing gestures (paragraph 59). From this point the story's movement involves Sarah's realization that her family's happiness requires her assent to sign language and her involvement with it. The concluding paragraphs dramatically portray the power of her reconciliation and the love her family can give her through their only means of communication.

Suggestions for Discussing the Study questions, page 331

(1) Sarah is characterized as a plain, serious, and decent woman who as a farm wife takes great pride in her personal circumstances and surroundings. Her concern for the appearance of the farm shows an almost compulsive need to make things "clean and orderly" (paragraph 2). But she also has a great capacity for adjustment, as is shown in her acceptance of her husband's deafness and her ability to communicate with him through his reading her lips. Even so, she is starved for communication and exchanges notes with her friend, Luita (paragraph 8). This characteristic is her strongest, and the conflict she endures because of it is complex. Her adjustment to deafness gives her a certain amount of power over her family, and their wish to learn signs demonstrates a degree of individuality that involves her letting them go. But there is a great, yearning hunger for expression, and Sarah's acceptance of that shows her love and her power of adaptation.

(2) Outside, the farm of Sarah and Matthew is in an almost painterly setting, covered with a blue and silent sky that is crossed with passing birds and bordered by a garden and a row of poplar trees. There is an orchard and a grape arbor. Inside everything is in order, and Sarah has developed a routine for serving meals to her family, including the preparation of "surprise" desserts like the shortcake she serves at the climax of the story (paragraphs 62–68). These details are included to demonstrate that the life of Sarah and her family is economically adequate but no more. The need is not for improved economic circumstances, but for communication, and it is this need that brings out her tears in paragraph 64. In addition, the farm is a location that separates the people from the outside world. People are distant, and thus not communicative, just as the deafness of Sarah's family isolates them—and also somewhat alienates them—from her.

(3) The fact of Matthew's deafness is not disclosed until the middle of paragraph 7. This delay enables readers to identify Sarah's life as involving the adjustment to normal life situations, such as the appearance of her son with his new bride. Abel's congenital deafness is made more poignant because Sarah does not realize it until the infant boy has been unable to hear the "madhouse of bells, horns, screaming sirens" of the fire engines racing to a nearby fire (paragraph 21). Her response is to cry bitterly and uncontrollably (paragraph 23).

(4) We realize that Sarah has adjusted to the deafness of her family and has been reconciled to it for twenty-five years. Janice's enthusiasm for signs has, in effect, rendered Sarah "the deaf one"

(paragraph 64). We may judge Sarah's responses as being a mixture of jealousy, a loss of power, and an unwillingness to change habits fixed over her lifetime. Because such negative impulses are not in her character they constitute a crisis in her life. Sarah's first responses are grief and frustration, but her love for her family enables her to become reconciled and to accept the challenge of change. The title, derived from the Book of Genesis, suggests a parallel with the Biblical Sarah (Genesis 18:9–15), who laughed—probably in ironic disbelief—when she learned that she was destined to have a child in her old age. Students may wish to discuss the parallel situations of the two Sarahs, together with the effects of their responses.

WRITING TOPICS. The character of Sarah. The relationship of the farm surroundings to the life of Sarah and Matthew and their family. Problems that deafness (or other disability) creates for people within families.

WORKS FOR COMPARISON WITH "AND SARAH LAUGHED"

Piercy, *Will We Work Together?, 1185*
Pound, *The River-Merchant's Wife, 1188*
Walker, *Everyday Use, 89*

CYNTHIA OZICK, *The Shawl,* *pages 331–34*

"The Shawl" is noteworthy because of its scrupulous control of its limited point of view, with the point-of-view character being the mother of a starving infant during the Holocaust. There is nothing in the story about the political conditions in Germany's Third Reich, which developed a policy of mass extermination of Jews, yet, within just a few pages, the story provides an inside view of the horror as it affected those who were the victims of this unspeakable policy. Students need to be reminded that the story requires great attention, for the details are not described objectively, but rather appear as they have been filtered through the suffering eyes and mind of the major figure, Rosa.

Suggestions for Discussing the Study Questions, pages 334–35

(1) The details of the setting, important as they are, are not laid out according to any plan or scheme. We learn in the first four paragraphs that Rosa, along with her young daughter Stella and her infant daughter Magda, have been on a forced march, and that spectators have lined up along the way as the marching Jews have gone by. With paragraph 5 the scene shifts to the confines of a Nazi extermination camp, which is not named. Ultimately, a German

guard throws Magda against an electrically charged fence of this camp, and kills her by this action. Ozick presents these details as the major character, Rosa, perceives them—not as she sees them and remembers them in outline, but as she receives impressions about them. The result is that we experience the setting as it affects Rosa. Unless she perceives it, it is not included in the story.

(2) The details in paragraph 15 heighten the story's irony. Outside the fence, one may see sun, butterflies, "placid, mellow" light, green meadows, dandelions, violets, and tiger lilies. The irony is that the world outside is the way things should be, as contrasted with the horrors which result from the political and military domination that turns life into hell for Rosa and the other prisoners, and that destroys the innocent child, Magda.

(3) The center of narrative interest in the story is Rosa, the mother, who hides Magda within the shawl. She has been arrested by the Nazis and imprisoned because she is Jewish (paragraph 2). She has been so maltreated that she is losing touch with reality. For example, she hears voices in the surrounding fence, and also feels that she has become light as air. Her response to hunger is probably realistic, however, for with no food to satisfy her "ravenous" appetite she learns to "drink the taste of a finger in one's mouth" (paragraph 5), and at the story's end she has become like her lost infant, Magda, as she drinks "Magda's shawl until it dried" (paragraph 16).

(4) The brutal details of paragraph 15 reveal the horror of life in the extermination camps. A short description of World War II and some of the facts of the Anti-Semitic policies of the Nazis may need explaining now that the war has been over for more than half a century. The story itself, however, provides a telling description of what the effects of these policies were, as the victims themselves were forced to experience them.

Writing topics. The setting of the story, as it was and as Rosa experiences it. The relationship of Rosa to her daughter Stella. The story's use of details about physical condition. Responses to various actions in the story.

Works for Comparison with "The Shawl"

Writing About Setting, *pages 335–39*

The problem to confront in teaching this section is that of moving from the abstract descriptions of possible essays to the specific topics about which students will be writing. The most approachable topic on setting for most students will hence be the first one (336), on setting and action. With your guidance, students will quickly be able to determine this relationship and apply it to whatever topic you assign or they select. If you assign some of the other types, you may need to ask specific questions about stories to get your students to express their observations about the uses of setting. Types 4 and 5 will be the most difficult of the five listed (336). The sample essay, based on Conrad's "The Secret Sharer," is an illustration mainlyof the first type.

Special Topics for Writing and Argument about Setting, *page 339*

(1) Topic 1 should emphasize the qualities of character brought out by adversity. One may presume that if the Doctor and the Musician had met during civilized times of prosperity, they would have had great rapport and friendship, because they have similar interests.

(2) Topic 2 could become extensive if all five characters are chosen for discussion. It might therefore be reserved for assignment as the finishing writing task for a unit, or for an extended paper. The black-and-white reproductions of the Boucher and Hopper paintings (286, 287) are intended to give artistic students the chance to relate art to literature. That these paintings graphically show differences of character perception might be especially useful in developing comparisons and contrasts between Sarah and either Miss Brill or Mrs. Johnson.

(3) Topic 3 is designed to get students thinking about the integration of environment and character, in this respect exploring the ways in which time and place almost literally seem to govern our natures. In any event, both "The House on Mango Street" and "The Secret Sharer" would not be possible in their present forms without the integration of action, place, and character that we find in the stories.

(4) Topic 4 requires a creative transplanting. More important than the transposition, however, is the analysis of the process that students might carry out, and their understanding of the various stories which they are studying.

(5) Topic 5 is focused on the creative writing of a scene, but it might become a short-short story if a student wishes. Direction *a* focuses on the artistic connection between feelings, actions, and moods to conditions of light and atmosphere. Direction *b* might stem directly from

a life-experience, so that one student might describe how a television program or a toy causes an argument, while another student might write about how the return of something found (say a set of car keys, or a book) brings about a new friendship. Whatever topic the student may choose, the important thing is to emphasize the relationship of setting to character and action.

(6) Students may wish to locate more than two books on Conrad for this topic. The main goal of the student searches should be to establish the concreteness of Conrad's imagination, for without the solid basis in apparent reality, Conrad's sometimes abstract ideas could not achieve the credibility they need for success. In the early part of *Heart of Darkness,* for example, Conrad's first and unnamed narrator states that Marlow, the major narrator, presents tales that are comparable with the misty haloes that sometimes surround the moon. Comparably, we learn in "The Secret Sharer" that "In this breathless pause at the threshold of a long passage we seemed to be measuring our fitness for a long and arduous enterprise, the appointed task of both our existences to be carried out, far from all human eyes, with only sky and sea for spectators and for judges" (298). With such an objective, the apparent reality of Conrad's narratives is essential.

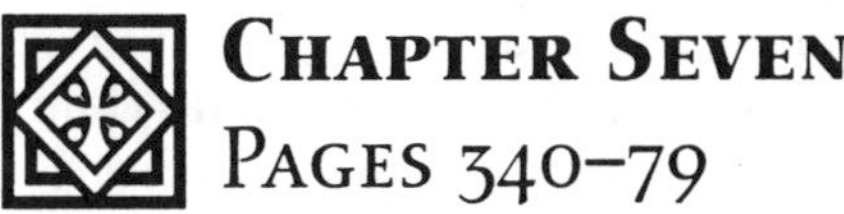

CHAPTER SEVEN
PAGES 340–79

Style: The Words That Tell the Story

In teaching this section, you may find that students need assistance in understanding the examples. Thus, for instance, the passage from Munro's "The Found Boat," on page 341 (and also on page 436) may need in-class reading and analysis, with the use of the blackboard to illustrate the "they . . . them . . . their" sentences. Students may inquire what prevents these repeated patterns from becoming "boring," and you may need to respond that the sentences are of unequal length and content, and that therefore they illustrate the principle of variety–an important standard of excellence in style.

A good teaching approach, once you have covered the various concepts to your satisfaction, is to go to a story you have already read and discussed, and pick a passage at random for analysis. If you intermingle student comment with your own insights, such an impromptu consideration can build confidence in students about approaching their own analyses of style.

ERNEST HEMINGWAY, *Soldier's Home,* *pages 348–53*

The plot of "Soldier's Home" involves Krebs as the protagonist in conflict with the abstract antagonism of peacetime adjustment. Obviously, those around him expect him to have been unchanged by the war. They therefore assume that he can begin life again as though nothing has happened. The crisis of the story is his conversation with his mother, and the climax is his promise to be a good boy for his "Mummy" (paragraph 86). This portion of the story indicates that his disaffection is approaching total alienation, a condition that he rejects. The resolution, in his decision to go to Kansas City, and in his going to watch his sister play ball, suggests a compromise with his disaffection. Although he will continue to feel like an outsider, in other words, he will keep his reservations to himself, and will fit in, at least externally, with life at home.

In class, students may raise questions about Hemingway's meaning in the story. There is no ready-made, easy answer, except to respond by analyzing the difficulties, real and imagined, that Krebs experiences after returning to the ordinary home town of his childhood after living through the bitter fighting in France during the First World War. Hemingway is using Krebs to pose basic questions about life: Can people get back to everyday, ordinary normality after going through the worst possible experience that they can ever face, and if they can, what prevents them from doubting the value of such a life?

Suggestions for Discussing the Study Questions, pages 352–53

(1) See page 343 of the text for a discussion about Hemingway's mixing of general and specific language, as shown in paragraphs 6 and 7 of the story. You might also wish to treat the question as it pertains to paragraphs 4, 11, 15, 16, and 95, where Hemingway uses a number of unspecific words to get at the uneasiness of Krebs as he attempts to adjust to life after the war.

(2) Generally, Hemingway uses short, almost clipped sentences, although, as in paragraphs 5 and 6, some of the sentences are fairly long and involved. Most of the words are short, but because of the topic of Krebs's difficulties a number of abstract words are introduced, such as *elaborately, actualities, reaction, apocryphal, exaggeration, complicated, consequences,* and *interesting*. But Hemingway's sentences are not necessarily uncomplicated. In paragraph 15, for example, one might notice that the following sentence is complex even though short: "But the world they were in was not the world he was in." The last sentence in paragraph 5, involving the "who" constructions, is as complex as any to be found anywhere. Once the section of the story involving dialogue commences (paragraph 17), the words are short and specific, in keeping with the tensions within the family and also with the general inarticulateness of the speakers.

(3) In this story Hemingway is not describing actions as much as Krebs's displacement from battlefield to home. The details are therefore not extensive, being confined to no more than are essential and elemental (e.g., "he was sleeping late in bed," and so on). Some of the repetitious phrases and sentences sound almost childish, so easy are they (e.g., "He learned that in the army." [paragraph 13]). Hemingway introduces adjectives and adverbs only sparingly, in keeping with the spare nature of Krebs's life at home. The descriptions are only minimal, and are not vivid. There are no details about the battles that Krebs experienced, for example, and we learn no more about them than that he was there.

(4) It is difficult to establish Krebs's true character because he is almost totally subdued and passive during the story. The only aspect of his life that seems to excite him is his encounter with books about the war, and this, we remind ourselves, is all in his past. Nevertheless he does undergo a change because of his decision to go to Kansas City (paragraph 95). Although he is neither deeply analytical nor articulate, he is trying to adjust to life back home. His adjustment for most of the story, however, takes the form of a general lassitude and a period of taking stock about his experiences during the war and also about his home and family. His integrity is shown in his good relationship with his sister and also in his regrets about the lies he has told. His integrity is additionally shown in his dissatisfaction with the thoughts about forming romantic attachments because of the additional lies he might have to tell and also because of the politics of establishing a love relationship.

Krebs is handicapped because he does not truly articulate his feelings. Most likely, however, he does not adjust quickly to the pattern of hometown life because he feels so changed by his war experience. He has gained a perspective that enables him to determine that many "lies" are essential for the habits of normal life, and he has likely concluded that the result of these lies is dissolution and war. He does not go to work immediately because he is unsure of what role he can honestly assume in the postwar world. In disavowing love for his mother (paragraph 73), he seems gratuitously cruel, but his remarks seem designed not to hurt her but rather to indicate his general unease and unhappiness.

WRITING TOPICS. The conversational style of Hemingway's characters. The words used by the narrator to describe Krebs's feelings. The importance of the family in Krebs's thoughts. The difficulties of postwar adjustment as seen in Krebs. The structure of the story.

WORKS FOR COMPARISON WITH "SOLDIER'S HOME"

Hardy, *The Man He Killed, 673*
Northrup, *Wahbegan, 1180*
Tan, *Two Kinds, 226*
Zabytko, *Home Soil, 511*

ALICE MUNRO, *The Found Boat,* *pages 353–59*

Like many of Munro's stories, "The Found Boat" is set in Munro's imaginary small town of Jubilee, which is visualized as being in western Ontario, near her own home town of Wingham. The story's plot may be seen as the conflicts or contrasts that young people experience at their time of growing sexual desires. The "Truth or Dare" game, for example, permits the young people to objectivize their private sexual wishes in a mixed friendly setting. Similarly, the discovery and repair of the boat offers the chance for companionship under the guise of cooperative effort. The high point of the sexual by-play is the collective decision to strip and run to the river, and Clayton's ejection of water from his mouth onto Eva's breasts. At the story's end, it seems that the girls will try to resume their lives as they were before, although their giggling suggests both their heightened emotions and their awareness that they are moving toward adulthood.

In teaching the story, you may discover that the emphasis on budding sexuality comes as a surprise to many students who believe that the first half is more about the boat than the young people. It hence becomes necessary to study the first part of the story to demonstrate the many details of boy–girl relationships established there. You may wish to refer to pages 341 and 346 for further discussions of Munro's style in "The Found Boat."

Suggestions for Discussing the Study Questions, page 360

(1) The descriptive passages of "The Found Boat" are specific and accurate, but most of them introduce an element of human response and involvement. Paragraph 10, for example, demonstrates this movement from description to character. Also, paragraph 1 is less focused on details about the spring flood than on the reactions it produces in young and old.

(2) The level of diction among the boys is generally low, with contractions and interjections (paragraph 4), profanity (paragraphs 7, 8), and grammatical mistakes (paragraph 22). Eva's language is more at a middle level, as is Carol's, although Carol indulges in slang in paragraph 55, and Eva uses an insulting slang term in paragraph 12.

(3) Paragraph 10 suggests that Eva's imagination is strong, and that she yearns for magical worlds of romance. When she becomes the point-of-view character, the style is elevated to complement her brief romantic reflection. Her taunting of the boys in paragraph 12 is comically contrasted with paragraph 10.

(4) The last paragraph emphasizes the actions of the girls in getting out of the water and in bursting out in giggles. The action verbs and participles are *giggle, slapping, splashing, set about developing, showed, snort, start up, make, bend over, grab,* and *had.* Some of these are neutral,

but many are graphic and vivid. The verb *snort,* which usually is used in reference to animals, is a perfect choice to describe the giggles.

(5) There are many details of setting in "The Found Boat." The lifestyle and artifacts of the people of Jubilee indicate a poor or working-class environment in the days before electronic entertainment. The town is graphically portrayed, as is shown in paragraph 47, where the recovery of winter's detritus is described. If the story is considered symbolically as an awakening of sexuality, the cold flood and the promise of warm water suggests the developing maturity of the major characters.

WRITING TOPICS. The style of the descriptive passages. The use of colloquialisms and slang. The relationship of style to character. The style in a paragraph (such as the last one).

WORKS FOR COMPARISON WITH "THE FOUND BOAT"

Henley, *Am I Blue, 1635*
Joyce, *Araby, 495*
Olds, *35/10, 1024*
Soto, *Oranges, 1203*

FRANK O'CONNOR, *First Confession,* *pages 360–65*

"First Confession" is both comic and good natured, mildly satiric but also affectionately tolerant. Students may claim to see antireligious sentiment in it, because the sternness and rigidity of the father, the sister, and Mrs. Ryan are subject to O'Connor's satiric thrusts. A consideration of the amused but understanding priest, however, will support the contention that the story treats its religious topic understandingly and sympathetically.

The conflict of the plot may be variously described: punishment versus forgiveness, anger versus toleration, rigidity versus understanding, or the letter of the law versus the spirit of the law. The complication begins simultaneously with the exposition, for we learn right at the start that the narrator has been subjected to home "troubles" and pressures. One might make a case that the story presents a series of mounting crises, namely the family squabble, the fear of hell as described by Mrs. Ryan, the narrator's hesitancy to go to confession, and the farcical actions in the church. The climax is the confession itself, which sets all the narrator's apprehensions aside, and the dénouement is a genuine *exodos*, in which the narrator and his sister walk away from the church toward home.

Perhaps in keeping with O'Connor's experiences in the theater, the story is arranged in easily marked scenes that progress logically. The story is thus a virtual case study in the simultaneity of plot and structure. Paragraphs 1–3 describe the home troubles; paragraphs 4–7 introduce religious instruction and the intensification of the possibilities of punishment; paragraphs 8–16 develop the initial agonies faced by the narrator about confession; paragraphs 17–33 are a first stage of confession involving the farcical actions in the confessional and in the aisle, climaxed by Jackie's developing composure about his "sinfulness"; the confession itself (the climax) is described in paragraphs 34–58; and the resolution extends from paragraphs 59 to 77.

Suggestions for Discussing the Study Questions, page 365

(1) Jackie is open and frank, sharing some of his amusement as an adult about his childhood feelings. He seems to be speaking rather than writing, and it is not clear that he has any specific listener in mind beyond his anonymous audience. He is a perceptive narrator, successfully transmitting his feelings of anger and indignation against his sister, his being bemused by Mrs. Ryan, his apprehensiveness about the state of his soul as he has learned to judge it in the punishment-driven household, and his fondness for the understanding and friendly priest. Words like *fastidious, mortified,* and *indignant* suggest his familiarity with a high level of diction. Jackie is also inventive as a speaker, using combinations like *heart-scalded* and *a religious woman like that, you wouldn't think she'd bother about a thing like a half-crown.* There are a number of Irish idioms and phrases, particularly in the dialogue, such as *Was it the priest gave them to you?, Begore ("by God"),* and *Jay (gee).*

(2) Jackie is the constant focus of attention in the story, which concerns his life at the age of seven, the traditional age of first confession and communion. A possible shortcoming in Jackie's character, noticed by a number of students, is that he has apparently not grown out of his antagonisms toward either his sister specifically or women generally. Some of his remarks (see, for example, paragraphs 17, 33) are more appropriate for an immature than for a mature person.

(3) Despite Jackie's fears about communion, the priest makes sure that the confession is "good" because he brings out all Jackie's guilt feelings. There is little question that the priest's religion wins the day in this story.

(4) That childish divisions within a family extend also to the adults is probably not unusual. Jackie's lashing out with the knife

at Nora and kicking his grandmother in the shins may be extreme, but Jackie is a small boy, and boys of that age generally hit before thinking. Students may wish to discuss whether the family is to any degree dysfunctional.

(5) The story is amusing and entertaining, and one does not need to be especially religious to appreciate the religious basis of the humor. Thus, we may laugh at Jackie's embarrassment at his grandmother's habits, his interest in Mrs. Ryan's half-crown (the equivalent of a large amount of money today), the priest's prediction about how someone will go after Nora with a knife and not miss, and Nora's bewilderment after Jackie's "first confession." In discussing the causes of laughter, students should note the relationship of situations such as these to the Bergsonian principles of rigidity and incongruity. Thus Jackie in the communion class should be considering the state of his soul, but instead he demonstrates a little boy's concern for Mrs. Ryan's money (in this way fitting his rigidly childish perspective into a situation requiring thought and fear). In addition, sober and proper behavior is expected in a confessional; Jackie's antics, so clearly out of place, are funny.

WRITING TOPICS. Mrs. Ryan as viewed by Jackie. Jackie as a narrator and a character. The apparent religious views of Jackie as shown in his attitudes toward Nora, Mrs. Ryan, and the priest. The humor in the story. The plot. The structure.

WORKS FOR COMPARISON WITH "FIRST CONFESSION"

Dickinson, *Some Keep the Sabbath Going to Church*, 1076
Joyce, *Araby*, 495
Zabytko, *Home Soil*, 511
Zimmer, *The Day Zimmer Lost Religion*, 1220

MARK TWAIN, *Luck*, *pages 366–68*

The story moves forward in fairly easy order. The exposition is in paragraphs 1–9; the complication in paragraphs 10–13; the crisis in paragraph 14. The climax occurs in paragraph 14, when Scoresby's blundering charge breaks the Russian ranks. The resolution (paragraphs 15, 16) emphasizes that "the best thing . . . that can befall a man is to be born lucky." In this way Twain ties together both the title and the resolution of the story.

Because there are two narrators, you might wish your class to consider their characteristics. The first narrator is fairly straightforward and not particularly noteworthy, while the second is much more conversational in manner and denunciatory in tone. He emerges as an individual.

Suggestions for Discussing the Study Questions, page 369

(1) From the example of this story, Twain includes only enough detail to make his concluding point clear, that "Scoresby's an absolute fool." He does not provide specifics about the "certain line of stock questions" on Caesar's *Gallic Wars,* but he gives only the general detail that the narrator drilled Scoresby on them. In the battle description (paragraphs 14–16) the narrator is not interested in detail for its own sake, but gives only enough to show that Scoresby turns blunders into triumphs.

(2) Examples of humor in the story are the titles of Scoresby (paragraph 1), the fortuitous passing of the exams in Caesar and math (paragraphs 6, 8), the grown men crying (paragraph 12), and the clumsy victory in battle (paragraphs 14–16). Despite the truism that too much analysis chills humor, a study of any of these passages will show that the comic response is integrated with Twain's arrangements of words.

(3) After the *look, and look, and look* phrase in paragraph 1, the language is elevated in an effort to inflate Scoresby as a recognized giant. Twain's obvious purpose is to use the rest of the story as an anti-climax to deflate Scoresby.

(4) The story about Scoresby is told within a narrative frame. An unnamed narrator (the "authorial voice") introduces the situation of confidential revelation in paragraphs 1–4. The second narrator, the clergyman, tells the story itself. This shift in point of view, from the unknowing narrator to the knowing counselor and friend (who is "a man of strict veracity" with a good "judgment of men" [paragraph 4]), is designed to authenticate the revelations about Scoresby's blundering career. The explanation of how Scoresby passed his exams, for example, depends on the clergyman's having been an instructor at Woolwich Academy and therefore having been familiar with the types of test questions usually asked (paragraph 5). In short, the clergyman narrator learns everything that he tells, first, because he was an observer and major mover, and, second, because he was an on-the-spot participant and observer.

WRITING TOPICS. Twain's stylistic purpose in the battle description, or in the opening paragraph. The ways in which Twain's style creates amusement and laughter. The differences in style between the two narrators.

WORKS FOR COMPARISON WITH "LUCK"

Cummings, *next to of course god america i,* 1012
Field, *Icarus,* 987
Parker, *Penelope,* 980
Piercy, *A Work of Artifice,* 792

JOHN UPDIKE, ***A & P,*** *pages 369–73*

"A & P" is readily accessible to most students, with the possible exception of those for whom English is a second language. For them you might wish to focus on study question 1, on the topic of Sammy's diction (page 373). It is significant to stress his disregard of grammar at the opening, and his greater care at the end. Even the concluding word, *hereafter,* is notable in the context of his narration, for it is not of the same wordstock as most of the language he uses.

Suggestions for Discussing the Study Questions, pages 373–74

(1) From Sammy's language we learn that he has a strong sense of his own identity. His anger at the "witch" in paragraph 1, for example, indicates an awareness of his own worth when he is taken to task for what he thinks is an inadvertent mistake. His first response to Stokesie, *"Darling," I said, "Hold me tight"* (paragraph 8), indicates a sense of humor, camaraderie, and capacity for enjoyment. Throughout the story, which is presented in a spoken rather than written style as though Sammy is speaking to a sympathetic and friendly listener, Sammy talks himself alive as a person of perception, sensitivity, and understanding. He does, however, violate strict grammatical rules. He switches tenses constantly (see, for example, the beginning of paragraph 12), and utilizes slang expressions (*gunk* in paragraph 12, *juggled* in paragraph 5), inexact modifiers (*kind of* in paragraph 32 and elsewhere), colloquial phrases (*they all three of them* in paragraph 5, *but never quite makes it* in paragraph 2), misplaced modifiers (*Walking in the A & P ... I suppose ...* in paragraph 4). That Sammy also correctly uses a possessive before a gerund (*His repeating this struck me as funny* in paragraph 15), together with other passages of correct English, suggests that his violations of standard English are deliberate.

(2) The exposition occurs simultaneously with the movement of the girls in the store. The essential character to learn about is the narrator, Sammy, and we find out much about him from his accurate and fascinated description of the girls' appearance, and from his observation of Stokesie and Stokesie's expression of doubt about the propriety of the girls' wearing swimming suits in the store (para-

graph 9). As further exposition, the basis of the conflict is explained in paragraph 10, in which Sammy describes the Massachusetts town as a rather staid, respectable place. The conflict is thus created out of the contrast between the town's superconservative expectations of propriety the out-of-place swimsuits of the girls.

The idea of fictional exposition is thus illustrated here, with enough material being introduced to make the conflict clear, but no more. The essential fact is that a story is not a sociological treatise; obviously a good deal more could be said about the town and about Lengel as one of the "pillars of society." With a fuller treatment along these lines, however, the narrative elements of the story would be obscured. In other words, exposition is to be judged only in its relationship to story.

(3) Sammy's observations, such as "two crescents of white" (paragraph 1), suggest his extensive experience as a "girl watcher." He has also watched older women, as is indicated by his disparaging comments about some of the less pleasant physical characteristics of aging. His remarks reflect his taste for youth and beauty, but also his own limited understanding of life as a boy of nineteen. His estimation of female intelligence in paragraph 2 about a "buzz like a bee in a glass jar" and his expressed lack of certainty about how girls' minds work indicate, under the guise of minimizing women, a lack of experience with women on an adult level. His gesture to quit his job is at odds with his patronizing estimate of women, for it shows more respect than he actually expresses.

(4) Sammy makes his sudden decision to quit for reasons that he does not articulate. Probably, however, his thinking (paragraph 21) is based on fears that he might eventually develop into a carbon copy of Lengel if he does not begin asserting himself on matters of principle. His explanation to himself is summed up in paragraph 31 with his observation that it would be "fatal" not to go through with his gesture. In other words, his sense of identity is on the line and he must maintain his integrity in his own eyes even if the girls know nothing about his action. He realizes that the world will be hard for him "hereafter" because people like Lengel may always be gaining economic or arbitrary power over him, and therefore he may feel future pressure to suppress his integrity.

WRITING TOPICS. A précis of "A & P." The plot and/or structure of the story. The character of Sammy. The theme of the story.

Works for Comparison with "A & P"

Anderson, *I'm a Fool*, 250
Faulkner, *Barn Burning*, 190
Henley, *Am I Blue*, 1635

Writing About Style, *pages 374–78*

Because writing about style must begin with the analysis of detail, the in-class work with style may be profitably developed from the "Questions for Discovering Ideas" on page 374. If you select a passage from any story, and show how the questions may produce materials that may be fitted into an essay, students may be guided to see that they, too, with these questions as analytical guides, may be able to produce materials suitable for their essays. Because the story chosen for analysis in the sample essay deals with only two paragraphs from Twain's "Luck," you may choose other paragraphs from this story as the basis of essay assignments in addition to any parts of the other stories, as you wish. You might also omit the two passages from "The Found Boat," on which there are illustrative commentaries. The demonstrative essay may be longer than essays your students may write, but it is presented as an example showing how a number of aspects of style may be connected by a major central idea. Here the classroom reading of the essay, together with comments, would clarify the writing task for your students.

Special Topics for Writing and Argument about Style, *pages 378–79*

(1) Topic 1 is designed to explore differences between two major speakers within the same story. Although there is less material from the first speaker than from the second, students should be able to develop enough details for a solid essay.

(2) Topic 2 is set up to permit students to explain the qualities of Hemingway's style through a contrast with the styles to be found in other stories. The contrasts are fairly obvious, particularly for Whitecloud (more articulateness) and Updike (detail and also slang). With a Faulknerian approach, there would probably be more detail about the father, and the story might end with Krebs leaving for Kansas City rather than going to the ball field to watch the sister play.

(3) Topic 3 gets at essential details about both "Soldier's Home" and "Luck." Obviously, Hemingway's portrait of Krebs is dramatic; Hemingway does not intend a full analysis of Krebs's uneasiness

and alienation and therefore he leaves the job of interpreting to the reader. Similarly, Twain is trying to present Scoresby dramatically, and the narrator's comments represent his opinions and nothing more. With both stories, details like those presented by Munro and Crane would uncover subtleties and create ambiguities that neither Hemingway nor Twain wishes to create. The style of "The Found Boat" and "The Blue Hotel" would therefore not be appropriate for either "Luck" or "Soldier's Home."

(4) Topic 4 is designed, like all the creative-writing assignments, to help students in their critical understanding because of their hands-on experiences as writers. Once students have finished their sketches, they may be surprised to discover that they have made many unconscious word choices. An interesting variant on the assignment is therefore to ask for a revision, and then to ask students to describe their conscious choices as they make their changes.

(5) The idea of topic 5 is to cause students to think seriously about the adequacy of the portraiture and the probability of the actions in the stories. "The Found Boat" (page 353) may be interpreted as a story about youthful sexuality; "The Yellow Wallpaper" (page 617) about mental deterioration in light of negative circumstances of life. Students may therefore find "The Found Boat" more immediately congenial as a writing topic, although some may be less inhibited in discussing "The Yellow Wallpaper." Of the two stories, "The Yellow Wallpaper" is likely to involve political as well as psychological discussions.

(6) Topic 6 is, like both earlier and later research topics, is designed to familiarize students with the library catalogue system. Since students need find only one book touching on the Hemingway style, the summary they produce might become fairly extensive. By selecting no more than a small number of examples, however, they can keep their reports brief. Obviously, the assignment may be augmented for a longer report.

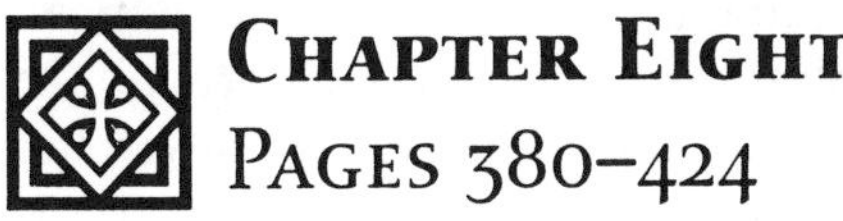

Chapter Eight
Pages 380–424

Tone: The Expression of Attitude in Fiction

The aim of this chapter is to introduce tone as a broad concept that includes literally everything that can make up a story. Tone begins with an attitude, and a study of tone should attempt to define and delimit the attitude. But then–this point is most important–the writer considering tone should analyze and explain how attitudes are rendered and made real. Hence students need reminding that to study tone is to consider how the story itself provides evidence of the author's awareness of the interdependence of speaker, character, circumstance, language, probability of action, and appropriateness of setting, together with evidence of how the author apparently views both audience and self–as nearly as these complex elements may be judged.

Margaret Atwood, *Rape Fantasies,* *pages 387–93*

"Rape Fantasies," excerpted from Atwood's 1977 volume entitled *Dancing Girls,* is noteworthy because of its "working-girl" speaker, whose manner is both individual and optimistic. In her imagination she turns constantly to conversation and sympathy as a civilized and sympathetic method of blunting the edge of potential violence. If one assumes, with her, that all persons have a similar bent, her concluding questions have great validity.

The plot of "Rape Fantasies" stems out of the reality and unreality of rape. Estelle provides continuity as the imagining protagonist, and the conflict results from her various ways of overcoming the rapists who are the antagonists. The crisis, if one may call it that, occurs when Estelle raises questions about the limits of sociability (paragraph 43), and the climax and resolution consist of her perplexity in the concluding paragraph. From the standpoint of actual rape, of course, there is no resolution, for the story treats an ongoing problem.

Suggestions for Discussing the Study Questions, page 393

(1) The comic elements in Estelle's various rape fantasies de-

velop out of her humanizing of the rapists of her imagination. By making the brutal situation normal and conversational through the everyday, matter-of fact way of describing it, Estelle provokes smiles and chuckles rather than horror. The rapists seem human, with ordinary human problems, and hence they may be approached through understanding and conversation. This contrast between the real and the imaginary provides the comedy of the story.

(2) Estelle's fantasies have in common that she is in control, and yet is involved with the rapists on a human level. Atwood controls the story's tone by the personalization and domestication of the experiences. Estelle has not had experience with violence, and thus does not permit violence in her imagination (paragraph 24). She is intelligent, pleasant, and comic, not analytical. Her background is that of an office worker, not of a criminologist, sociologist, or psychologist.

(3) The tone is intimate, conversational, personal, and chatty. This affects our perception of Estelle as being bright but superficial—vivid, lifelike, and comic (paragraphs 18, 23). Though Estelle is potentially analytical, Atwood confines her powers to the analysis of a misplayed hand at bridge (a misuse of the weak club opening, paragraph 3).

(4) From the extensive consideration of the subject matter we may conclude that Atwood is serious. The actual subject material she presents, however, keeps away from the dark side of rape—an aspect of life that most people find unbearable to face. Perhaps Atwood's symbol of the need for protection of women like Estelle is that the setting/location of the story, where Estelle is speaking to an unnamed listener about her fantasies, is the "nice place" where all the waiters know her and will protect her from molestation (paragraph 43). The true violence and brutality of rape, in short, are unreal for her.

(5) The women around the bridge table deflect the seriousness by considering rape not as a problem of violence, but rather as an everyday matter, prompted by the article that Chrissy has read. The article speaks about the fantasizing aspects of rape, not about the horror or pain of it (as Estelle rightly observes, paragraph 24).

WRITING TOPICS. The character of Estelle. The light, comic treatment of a serious topic. The tone of the story.

WORKS FOR COMPARISON WITH "RAPE FANTASIES"

Browning, *My Last Duchess, 695*
Chekhov, *The Bear, 1625*
Dubus, *The Curse, 603*
Joyce, *Araby, 495*

KATE CHOPIN, *The Story of an Hour,* *pages 393–95*

Though brief, "The Story of an Hour" is a minor masterpiece of irony. The heroine's feelings are known only to herself, and those around her totally misunderstand her responses and feelings. Her death, to them, seems like a supreme act of wifely devotion, even though we as readers learn that it is not the shock of "joy" that kills her, but rather the shock of sudden and supreme disappointment.

Chopin's plot for the story is built up out of Louise's conflicting roles of bereavement and liberation. Louise herself, the protagonist, feels identified with liberation, while all the others in the story assume the status of antagonists because they project upon her the role of grieving widow. The crisis and climax both occur, almost simultaneously (in paragraph 21) when Brently Mallard enters the house and Louise falls dead of a heart attack upon seeing him. One might make a case that the climax has been already established by Brently's having escaped the train crash, for it has been stated right at the beginning of the story that Louise's heart is weak (paragraph 1), and therefore any sudden shock would kill her. The resolution is of course the reassertion of male dominance, as expressed by the doctors.

Suggestions for Discussing the Study Questions, page 395

(1) Louise's husband is portrayed as a good man, who always looked on her with love (paragraph 12). He himself has done nothing to justify her relief at the news of his death. Indeed, he, like Louise, is more acted upon than acting, but then, it is the traditional married state itself that has been giving her pressure. The context of the story, emphasizing as it does the onrush of Louise's feelings, guides our perceptions of her. She does not create the feelings, but rather they overwhelm her as she retires to her room.

(2) The details in paragraph 5 are more appropriate for love and joy than for grief. Words like "aquiver," "delicious," "singing," and "twittering" all create an ironic perspective on Louise's grief, and it is these words that make possible her sense of relief, which would have been almost unbearably cruel and insensitive if the author had created a backdrop of darkness and sobriety.

(3) The narrator's attitude toward marriage is one of disapproval, not because of the human affections that are brought out by the institution, but because of the control it gives men over women (see paragraphs 14 and 23). The relief that Louise finds in discovering newly found freedom (paragraphs 11–16) is an aspect of tone that stresses her previously unspoken dissatisfaction with her inferior status as a deferential wife.

(4) Both Josephine and Richards have great concern for Louise, and do everything they can for her. The irony is that they do not and cannot comprehend Louise's true feelings, and thus they are concrete embodiments of the traditional and expected views on marriage.

(5) The key phrase in the last paragraph is "of joy that kills." The irony is that the doctors assume that Louise's death is caused by a heart failure brought about by seeing her husband alive. They are right, but we know that the failure is caused by Louise's sudden and unexpected realization that her freedom was illusory. The doctors hence exhibit a comic shortsightedness brought about by their own masculine vanity.

Writing Topics. Irony in the story. The presentation of Louise's character. The plot of the story.

Works for Comparison with "The Story of an Hour"

Gilman, *The Yellow Wallpaper, 617*
Glaspell, *A Jury of Her Peers, 202,* and *Trifles, 1244*
Hardy, *The Workbox, 814*
Pastan, *Marks, 1184*

Jack Hodgins, *The Concert Stages of Europe,* *pages 395–408*

"The Concert Stages of Europe" is obviously to be compared with Amy Tan's "Two Kinds" (page 226). Both develop out of family situations and center on the narrator, who learns the piano upon compulsion but who is unable to fulfill the hopes of loving but obtrusive parents. A major difference is that "Two Kinds" concerns an immigrant family and is serious about the mother-daughter relationship while "The Concert Stages of Europe" is about a well-settled family in the Canadian Pacific northwest and is more light-hearted about the oppositions.

Some students may question the meaning of paragraph 21, in which Clay states that "the country had convinced me it wanted me to grow up and get killed fighting Germans and Japanese," and describes the "coils of barbed wire along the beach." Students may need reminding that such preparations are realistic indications of the state of affairs along the Canadian Pacific during World War II, when there were fears that North America might have been invaded by the Japanese.

Suggestions for Discussing the Study Questions, page 408

(1) Clay concentrates not so much on his learning the piano as on his difficulties and embarrassment. Thus we hear about the German Shepherd who regularly greets him before his lesson and seems to

threaten his capacity for fathering the next generation. His wretched experience with Richy Ryder occupies paragraphs 70–99, and Ryder's embarrassing interview is climaxed with Clay's statement that maybe he won't be anything when he grows up. It is of course anyone's guess how good a pianist Clay might have become if he had developed the motivation to become a performer, but it is certain that the experience of the competition dashes his sense of worth and self-esteem, and that, indeed, is the point of the story's final scene.

(2) There are many comic portions of the story, involving single sentences, impossible ambition, and farcical action. The tone is set when we learn that Cornelia Horncastle's mother will not miss a "Ma Perkins" episode while her daughter practices on the cardboard keyboard. (*Ma Perkins* was a popular radio daytime soap opera for many years.) The idea that Clay's ambition was to be a Finn is uproarious, as is the greeting he receives from the German Shepherd (paragraph 34) and his description of his own awkward growth (paragraph 49). Despite the self-deprecating humor, however, Clay's self-awareness forestalls any negative reader reactions.

(3) The story is serious, despite the bungling of the lessons and the disastrous recital, because the issue of growth and development itself is vitally serious. Clay's sense of his own future is vague and relatively stupid (being a Finn, being nothing) , but because his ideas are those of a child and early teenager they need not be taken seriously. His ideas are in fact part of the story's humor.

(4) Attention to Cornelia Horncastle both begins and ends the story, like a frame. She is the first in the neighborhood to learn the piano, and always exceeds Clay's capacities, even in gaining more votes within the neighborhood. At the story's end, however, we learn that she has renounced the piano. The concert stages of Europe, it seems, are neither for her nor Clay, and she and Clay are similar in this respect. Cornelia is somewhat like Nelson in Colwin's "An Old Fashioned Story" (page 67), for both seem to be perfect while they reject their seemingly infallible roles.

Writing topics. The character of Clay, the speaker. Elements of farce in the story. Growth: the gap between the dream and the reality in "The Concert Stages of Europe."

Works for Comparison with "The Concert Stages of Europe"

Colwin, *An Old-Fashioned Story, 67*
Levine, *A Theory of Prosody, 866*
Tan, *Two Kinds, 226*
Williams, *The Glass Menagerie, 1703*

Margaret Laurence, *The Loons,* *pages 408–14*

In this story, the loons symbolize the loss that occurs inevitably with the changes in culture and civilization. The focus is on Piquette Tonnerre, the daughter of Indian "halfbreeds"—part Cree and part French Canadian. The plot concerns the loss of whatever past glory the Indians might have had, a loss that is symbolized by the degradation of nature and the disappearance of the loons from the lake where Vanessa and her family have a summer home.

Suggestions for Discussing the Study Questions, pages 414–415

(1) The story is told by a first-person participant-observer who, we learn, is named Vanessa MacLeod. She is a good observer and indicates strong feelings about what happens to her. It is important that Vanessa and Piquette be approximately the same age because of Vanessa's attitudes toward Piquette. These attitudes change and become more understanding in the course of the story—a naturally occurring set of changes in a growing and developing person like Vanessa, but less easy to introduce if the narrator were to be constant and unchanging.

(2) Piquette is at first pictured as an unattractive, sullen, profane, and aggressive child with a tubercular affliction in her legs (paragraphs 1–49). As a young woman, she is flamboyant, loud, and embarrassing to Vanessa (paragraphs 50–63). After she marries and has two children, Vanessa loses contact with her, but Vanessa is told the end of the story by Mrs. MacLeod, her mother. Piquette marries, has two children, ceases to care for her appearance, and eventually dies in a fire (paragraph 70). In other words, her life is brutish, nasty, and short, and she exhibits only remote stirrings of character to indicate that she is capable of kindness and nobility (paragraphs 58, 76). The poignancy of Piquette's character is brought out by Vanessa in paragraph 61: "For the merest instant, then, I saw her. I really did see her, for the first and only time in all the years we had both lived in the same town. Her defiant face, momentarily, became unguarded and unmasked, and in her eyes there was a terrifying hope." This perceptive and disturbing paragraph brings out the sense of what Piquette might have been. Our attitudes toward Piquette hinge upon our understanding of the waste and loss that her life represents.

(3) The story depends in crucial places on the natural, wild setting of the lake. Accordingly, a study of the descriptions in paragraphs 1, 6, 16, 17, 36–45, 72–73 repays careful study, for these paragraphs describe the natural areas, before and after degradation, that

are symbols of the changes that leave Piquette with no natural heritage and no ability to flourish. For example, the same changes that overwhelm the natural beauty of the lake (paragraphs 72–73), and destroy the habitat of the loons, have truncated the good qualities that under better circumstances would have enabled Piquette to become a mature, kind, and productive adult.

WRITING TOPICS. The story's first-person point of view. The character of the narrator. The story's connection between Piquette and environmental degradation. The symbolism of the loons.

WORKS FOR COMPARISON WITH "THE LOONS"

Bishop, *One Art, 909*
Lessing, *The Old Chief Mshlanga, 628*
Parédes, *The Hammon and the Beans, 415*
Song, *Lost Sister, 1202*
Whitman, *Full of Life Now, 1216*

AMERICO PARÉDES, *The Hammon and the Beans,* *pages 415–18*

"The Hammon and the Beans," first published in *The Texas Observer* in 1963, is a poignant story about the death of the narrator's playmate, but in broader social and economic perspective it is also a portrayal of the plight of poor immigrants. One of the noteworthy aspects of the story is the narrator. He is apparently an adult recalling events that occurred in the 1920s. His advanced age at the time of his narration might be expected to produce understanding and perspective, but such a perspective is not apparent. Instead, the narrator recalls the events and responses only as they occurred to him as a child. The narrations in Joyce's "Araby" (page 430) and Frank O'Connor's "First Confession" (page 307) are similar.

Suggestions for Discussing the Study Questions, pages 418–19

(1) Parédes locates the grandfather's house near the fort, introducing the military and political background of a border town during the turbulence of early twentieth-century Mexico. Thus, the connection of the children with the soldiers is natural, and Chonita's dependence on them for food is logical. The dirty yellow of the narrator's home suggests that even the Mexican-Americans who are better off do not enjoy a luxurious existence. The shack in which Chonita lives with her family indicates their poverty (paragraph 12).

(2) Chonita is flat because she is a child and makes no choices. She does come to life, however, and seems real and lovable. She is

described as a *scrawny little girl of about nine* (paragraph 14) who has a dramatic flair (paragraphs 16–17). Her behavior suggests great persistence (paragraph 7), along with incipient craving for recognition as a performer. She is also representative of her class of Mexican-Americans, for her death symbolizes the results of poverty and neglect. Dr. Zapata is in effect Parédes's *raisonneur*, or presenter, of these ideas (paragraphs 23–42).

(3) For Parédes's use of situational irony as a response to this question, please see the text, page 382. For further explanation of tone, one might consider the pathos exhibited in the sorry plight of Chonita as she receives a scolding before being given food (paragraph 11). Here the technique is the narrator's straightforward description, with no accompanying analysis or discussion. Dr. Zapata expresses indignation at Chonita's death. Parédes provides enough details for the doctor to substantiate his anger (paragraphs 21–33).

(4) That Dr. Zapata is a physician, thinker, and a caring person makes his anger credible. His declaration that he is not a political revolutionary is also consistent with his concern for the personal plight of persons like Chonita.

(5) The story is concerned with the problem of cultural assimilation (the attitudes expressed toward the soldiers), poverty (particularly that of Chonita and her family), inadequate health care (her death), and the Mexican revolutionary movements led by Villa and Zapata. In this political and economic context, Chonita's life and death are an example of what may happen on a broader scale to children raised in neglect.

(6) The women of Bryant's song are lovely and happy, but Chonita still wears her rags and speaks her pitiful English, even while the narrator describes his vision of her as a butterfly (paragraph 46). Though the narrator does not express his or her own feelings, it is logical that he or she would feel at least some indignation about Chonita's untimely death.

Writing Topics. Dr. Zapata and the story's tone. The tone and the economic and political situation. The irony in the education provided for the children of the town. The tone of the conclusion.

Works for Comparison with "The Hammon and the Beans"

Cisneros, *The House on Mango Street*, 290
Laurence, *The Loons*, 408
Randall, *Ballad of Birmingham*, 923
Villanueva, *Day-Long Day*, 1210
Whitecloud, *Blue Winds Dancing*, 156

Writing About Tone, *pages 419–24*

In presenting writing tasks about tone in fiction, you will need to emphasize that the study of tone requires an analysis of how attitudes are shaped and controlled, not merely the identification of the attitudes themselves. This point needs constant stressing. Because there is a sample student essay on Chopin's "The Story of an Hour" (page 421), you might assign this story beforehand, and use it as the reference point for your classroom discussion. Thus, in determining the tone of this story, you might stress how the reader's perspective is shaped by the way in which Chopin limits the point of view and thus withholds essential knowledge from all the characters surrounding Louise.

The types of essays you choose to emphasize will be governed by what you might assign. With tone, however, it is probably good to go into detail about the particular plan to be followed. It is not out of order, either, to lead a general discussion of the story you have chosen, without dealing with the specifics of tone in the story. Such a coverage liberates many students to consider tone without needing also to create their own interpretations from scratch. Obviously, students who wish to maintain their own readings are always free to do so.

As further aid to students for this assignment, you might wish to set up paragraph-length exercises on particular spots in, say, "The Story of an Hour." The benefit of these written exercises is that you can immediately address yourself to encouraging good approaches and correcting misperceived ones.

Special Topics for Writing and Argument about Tone, *page 424*

(1) The first of these topics should get at the relative condition of powerlessness of the various female characters. Louise and Mathilde are both to be judged as traditional housewives who are confined to this station in life. Piquette is similarly handicapped, and, moreover, has the additional difficulty of being a member of a minority. The most independent character is Phoenix, but she is being constrained by both poverty and age. A feminist consideration should get at the relationships of these characters to the politics of marriage and economics. Age is not as important an issue because it is outside the area of politics except as Phoenix's poverty makes her dependent on "charity" for the continued medication of her grandson.

(2) The idea of the topic 2 is to relate the conversational or narra-

tive style of the speaker to the ways in which we as readers perceive it. Thus, in "I Stand Here Ironing" and "The Concert Stages of Europe" we are led to understanding by the ways in which the narrators admit their own shortcomings. Similarly, we are impressed with the insights of the narrator of "Everyday Use" and also understand the limitations of the narrator of "First Confession." Students might write on two stories, or three or more, for a comparison-contrast essay (page 1979), should they wish.

(3) Estelle's attitude is conditioned by her expectation, or hope, that she would always be able to control the situation of rape. She is not vicious herself, and she expects humanity and even kindness of others. Therefore she is able to speak of rape as though it is an avenue toward friendship and even love. Obviously her attitude is shaped by her failure to understand the anger, hurt, guilt, rage, and viciousness of real-life rapists.

(4) In "The Hammon and the Beans" the children learn about the tradition of Marion, the "Swamp Fox," as quoted from Bryant's poem. Obviously the tradition of the American Revolutionary War is of concern to all United States citizens, but the irony, as the story makes clear, is that the Mexican-American children are not taught anything about their own history and literature. Therefore they become alienated from their own ethnic traditions.

(5) Topic 5 is perhaps more difficult to think about than to do. Students discover that the situation that they imagine (if indeed they exert a strong power of imagination) will govern their descriptions and word choices, so that irony is not as hard to bring out as it at first might seem. If they try to bring out verbal irony, of course, that will take more experimentation and experience.

(6) Because the *MLA International Bibliography* has become comprehensive and definitive, students should become familiar with it, and should go to it whenever they encounter a research situation in literary studies. Sometimes a problem occurs when students make a good list of works and then discover that their college libraries are lacking some of the items.

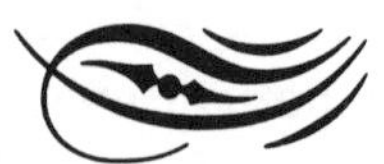

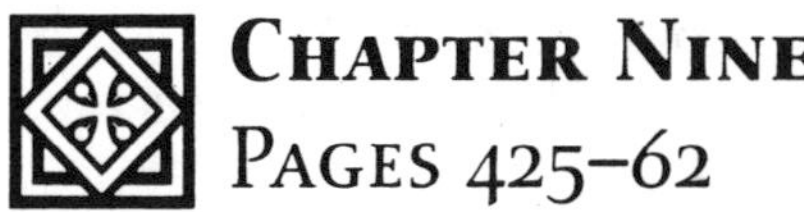

Chapter Nine
Pages 425–62

Symbolism and Allegory: Keys to Extended Meaning

This chapter aims to help students develop a working knowledge of these fundamental characteristics of literature. In teaching the subject, you may encounter uneasiness about symbols or allegorical patterns. For this reason you may wish to discuss a number of stories with the sole aim of determining whether and why certain elements and actions may be taken symbolically or allegorically. It is a revelation for students to realize that picking out symbols may not be as impossible as it first seems. As long as they realize that they must make a good case for what they choose, they will soon be adept at discussing symbolism and allegory. Even so, the greatest temptation students face is to locate symbols and allegories that are not really there. If you keep stressing the need for explanations, however, this tendency may be controlled and creatively shaped.

Aesop, *The Fox and the Grapes,* *page 431*

"The Fox and the Grapes" is one of Aesop's best known fables. Because it has given us the phrase "sour grapes," you might begin by asking if any of your students knows the meaning of the phrase. From there it is natural to stress that the fable is applicable to the general attitude of people toward the unattainable.

Suggestions for Discussing the Study Questions, page 431

(1) The fox exhibits normal traits: He needs to satisfy his hunger, and knows that he can get the grapes only by leaping for them. He is also normal enough to maintain his own self-esteem by denigrating the prize when he fails. These traits are essential to Aesop's moral, because the fable genre depends not on exceptional but on average or normal human character.

(2) The plot develops from consists of develops out of the desire the fox has for the grapes in conflict with his inability to get them. The resolution is his minimizing the reward he cannot gain.

(3) Obviously the fox's claim is a rationalization. Students may miss the moral that human beings should not justify their own shortcomings by resorting to distortions and lies. Aesop is stressing the need to recognize the truth both about oneself and also about the world outside.

(4) The fable as a genre features animals with human traits who carry on a brief action illustrating truths about human beings. The use of animals as protagonists (and antagonists also) enables the fabulist to concentrate on the topic without complications.

WRITING TOPICS. The fox and the grapes as a symbol. The nature of the fable as a genre. The nature of the action in the fable.

WORKS FOR COMPARISON WITH "THE FOX AND THE GRAPES"

Anderson, *I'm a Fool, 250*
Faulkner, *Barn Burning, 190*
Frost, *The Oven Bird, 1110*
Swift, *A Description of the Morning, 832*

ANONYMOUS, *The Myth of Atalanta,* *pages 432–33*

Even so straightforward an account of a mythical life as the story of Atalanta demonstrates just how important the understanding of myths really is. The study of myths rewards great scrutiny. It is possible, for example, to determine extensive meaning in every action and situation in a typical myth. Such meanings are suggested by the third question (page 453), which suggests eight topics of the Atalanta myth; each of these can serve as the basis of extensive interpretation and meaning. The most famous modern version of the Atalanta myth is Swinburne's poetic drama *Atalanta in Calydon* (1865), which deals with the episode of the Calydonian Boar and Atalanta's infatuation with Meleager.

Suggestions for Discussing the Study Questions, page 433

(1) Atalanta has abilities that make her equal if not superior to men. She is a superb athlete and hunter, and leads a life of adventure (some accounts indicate that she actually did sail with Jason on the expedition of the Argonauts). She tries to preserve her independence by challenging potential husbands to a footrace, killing them if they lose.

(2) Atalanta vows to shun men because of a warning by the Oracle at Delphi. According to the Oracle, marriage would change her character totally. Needless to say, marriage would also inhibit the

freedom she has enjoyed in pursuing her own way of life. It would seem that this awareness of her loss of freedom constitutes the principal meaning of the myth. The hatred of men that is mentioned in the retelling of the myth (paragraph 4) may be an expression of the idea that men and women have different interests, with women usually sacrificing theirs to serve those of men. That Milanion defeats Atalanta in their footrace suggests that the security represented by gold is, mythically, the most usual way in which men overcome women. It is difficult to interpret the metamorphosis of the lovers into lion and lioness, but a strong suggestion is that uncontrolled passion does not lead to stability and is, further, a violation of divine propriety.

(3) The symbolic meanings of the various actions in the myth may be these:

a. Atalanta's name defines her invincibility. This meaning suggests the power of women, and the need for men to become even more powerful if love, birth, and family—in short, society—are to be established and maintained.

b. The golden apples symbolize the power of men to confer home and consequent stability so that women may be confined to their role of wife and mother.

c. The chopping off of the heads of losing runners obviously symbolizes the idea that "only the brave deserve the fair" (a phrase from Dryden's "Alexander's Feast"). A modern scientific interpretation of the destruction of the inferior suitors is that the victorious ones win the right of maintaining the strength of the human gene pool.

d. The father's abandonment the infant Atalanta represents an ancient way of maintaining property (usually a woman gave her goods and titles to the man who married her) and also a means of controlling population and inheritance through reducing the numbers of women. That Atalanta was reared outside the home is a common element in many ancient stories (see, for example, the accounts of Moses, Oedipus, and Romulus and Remus).

e. Presumably Atalanta hides the birth of Parthenopaeus, and exposes him to die, as a way of forestalling attempts by the family of Meleager to force her to return to their kingdom to bring up the child. In this respect, her abandonment of the infant is another phase of her desire to maintain her independent way of life.

f. Atalanta's rejection of the centaur, Hylaeus, symbolizes one of the means, along with the foot-race challenge, by which women control their own lives. Appropriately, Milanion wins the favor of

Atalanta by protecting her when the rejected centaur attacks her. The myth therefore suggests another means by which men win women—through protection and, if necessary, sacrifice.

g. Atalanta presumably loses the race not through a lack of speed and power, but through a desire for the security represented by the apples. See also 3b.

h. The lovemaking in the holy grotto of Cybele, the Great Mother of Gods, represents a violation of holy ordinances. The underlying reasons for which promiscuous love was made taboo were likely economic. The offspring resulting from promiscuity would have tenuous claims to titles and inheritances. One might remember that the social structure in ancient Greece was tribal, and that therefore clear claims to parentage were essential in maintaining the social order.

WRITING TOPICS. The character of Atalanta. The symbolic or mythic meaning of her behavior. The importance of divine guidance on human affairs.

WORKS FOR COMPARISON WITH THE MYTH OF ATALANTA

cummings, *she being Brand / -new, 819*
Marvell, *To His Coy Mistress, 1023*
Rukeyser, *Looking at Each Other, 794*
Shakespeare, *A Midsummer Night's Dream, 1544*

ANITA SCOTT COLEMAN, *Unfinished Masterpieces,* *pages 433–35*

Coleman's work has gone largely unrecognized. The publication in 1999, however, of *The Crisis Reader*, edited by Sondra Kathryn Wilson (New York: Modern Library), in which "Unfinished Masterpieces" is included, should create greater interest in her writing.

Suggestions for Discussing the Study Questions, page 436

(1) The speaker points out Dora's ability as an artist and sculptor, and William's clear ability as a story-teller and raconteur. The implication of the story is that economic and racial conditions of life prevented both characters from developing their talents and therefore from making artistic contributions equal to their native abilities. In fact, William boasts of never having worked at anything for anyone. Both characters are hence "unfinished masterpieces" because of the deprivation that both experienced.

(2) Both Dora and William may be seen as symbols of blacks, and also of people generally, who have been denied the rights and opportunities to develop their skills and their humanity.

(3) The speaker speaks formally, with words such as "retrospective," "limpid," "disarray," and "sobriquet," to name just a few. The tone of the story is neither angry nor bitter, but regretful and, at the story's end, hopeful. The speaker's goal is clearly to elevate the potential of Dora Johns and William Williams and to assert that these two characters possessed innate abilities common to human beings. In no way does the speaker denigrate Dora and William as examples to demonstrate the validity of political rhetoric and political or even revolutionary proposals. Although a political cause is implicit in the story, the story itself emphasizes the potential and dignity of the major characters. Therefore her concluding emphasis is on "the widely opened door where white and black, rich and poor, of whatever caste or creed may enter and find comfort and ease and food and drink."

WRITING TOPICS. How are the characters in this story "unfinished"? In what ways are the characters symbolic?

WORKS FOR COMPARISON WITH "UNFINISHED MASTERPIECES"

Bambara, *The Lesson, 470*
Laurence, *The Loons, 408*
Parédes, *The Hammon and the Beans, 415*
Updike, *Perfection Wasted, 1210*

NATHANIEL HAWTHORNE, *Young Goodman Brown,* *pages 436–45*

In "Young Goodman Brown," the protagonist is the title character. The antagonist is ostensibly the devil, the spirit resembling his father (paragraph 13), although the antagonist might also be Brown's destructive sense of guilt—his projection of his own sinfulness upon others and his consequent damnation of them. The central conflict of the story, which seems lost even before it begins, is within Brown himself: an inner war of love and trust versus suspicion and distrust. The resolution occurs after Brown's climactic denial in paragraph 68. Brown's life is changed after this because his faith in others has been shattered, and therefore he alienates everyone around him.

Suggestions for Discussing the Study Questions, page 445

(1) The undeniable reality of the story is that Brown's journey is a dream, or nightmare. In psychological terms, Brown may be schizophrenic, because his view of others is distorted by his nightmarish convictions. It is probably best, however, to stress that his gloom results from religious fanaticism.

(2) Brown is a round character. Beginning as a seemingly good husband with a high estimate of the local minister (paragraph 21), his change into a foreboding, gloomy spirit marks a total alteration of character—for the worse, of course.

(3) The demonstrative essay (page 459) discusses the topic of symbolism in "Young Goodman Brown." There are additional symbols, such as the withering twigs (paragraph 38) and the fire (paragraph 53), to name two. The symbols suggest death and hell. Ironically, though Brown disavows the devil (paragraph 68), his preoccupation with these diabolical symbols governs his character and behavior.

(4) In Salem, the details of setting seem normal and ordinary: The threshold, street, church, meeting house, bed, pulpit, and grave are all a part of the town. The forest setting is provided with seemingly ordinary trees and a path which becomes increasingly unusual and symbolic. The woodland meeting place is characterized by the realistic details of the "dark wall of the forest," the altarlike rock, the blazing pines, the dense foliage, and the vague and sinful hymn, all bathed in red light. One can justify the forest setting as symbolic because it is a focus of Brown's preoccupation with sin, and because there the devil-like figure describes his awesome power (paragraphs 63–65).

(5) If one views the story allegorically, religious faith may be viewed as both constructive and destructive, and therefore the allegorical journey suggests the moral laxness and ambiguity into which people sometimes fall. The lesser characters belong both to Brown's journey into evil and also to his later life. Thus Deacon Gookin and Goody Cloyse meet Brown on the street as he returns to Salem (paragraph 70), and therefore they embody again the theme of Brown's hatred of hypocrisy. At this point the narrator presents these characters as virtuous, however, and in this way Hawthorne emphasizes Brown's distorted vision. Ironically—and irony of situation is a major aspect of this story—Brown becomes evil while pursuing good and supposed godliness. For these reasons together with a number of others, the forest journey justifies the claim that it is allegorical.

WRITING TOPICS. The story as allegory. The network of symbols. Setting and Brown's character. Brown as a symbol.

WORKS FOR COMPARISON WITH "YOUNG GOODMAN BROWN"

Blake, *The Tyger*, 754
Jeffers, *The Answer*, 1167
St. Luke, *The Parable of the Prodigal Son*, 445
Wright, *A Blessing*, 711

The Gospel of St. Luke 15:11–32, *The Parable of the Prodigal Son,* pages 445–46

Luke's story of the Prodigal Son is told in the words of Jesus. You may therefore wish to claim particular respect for the text, because some students may take offense at scripture being interpreted out of the context of their own churches. As long as the limits of the discussion are made clear, however, most students take a lively interest in a literary approach to the work.

Suggestions for Discussing the Study Questions, pages 446–47

(1) The Prodigal Son is self-indulgent and improvident, but he is introspective and has the courage to admit his mistake and to confess unworthiness. He is round because he grows to recognize and admit his error. It is necessary that he also be representative of many human beings, because the religious promise of the parable is intended for all believers.

(2) The plot grows out of the conflict (contrast) between the forgiving parent and the headstrong son. The antagonism against the son is also his self-caused poverty and his recognition that he has ruined his life. The religious point of the parable is the father's speech (verses 31, 32), which he makes in response to the angry words of his other son. This older son represents the traditional "eye for an eye" punishment, and he therefore is to be contrasted with the all-forgiving father.

(3) The resolution is the father's acceptance of the Prodigal Son and his explanation of why he has rejoiced at his Son's return. There is no "they lived happily ever after" conclusion, because the parable highlights the character of the father, not the life of the son. This point is worth stressing as a means of illustrating the nature of the parable as a genre.

(4) The structure of the parable may be described in this way, according to the verse numbers: 11–13, exposition; 14–16, complication; 17–19, crisis; 20, climax; 21–32, resolution. These parts coincide with the development of the plot, except that the resolution takes up more than half the entire parable. It would not be incorrect, in fact, to consider the resolution as a second story that might be entitled "The Angry Older Brother," for this section has its own brief plot development with its resolution in the father's explanation. In purely technical terms, the Older Brother's anger might be considered a second complication of the parable, except that the resolution of the Prodigal Son's story has already occurred. It is best to think of

the parable as a form, therefore, in which the structure is governed more by idea or theology than by plot.

(5) The point of view is limited omniscient in verses 12–21, with emphasis on the Prodigal Son. In verses 22–32 the point of view is dramatic, featuring the conversation of the older son and the father. In these last eleven verses, the Prodigal Son does not appear. This shift coincides with the shift in the structure of the parable.

(6) The parable as a form contains many characteristics of fiction: i.e., plot, character development, description, dialogue, and a relatively consistent point of view. The principal difference is that in the parable genre, literary characteristics are less important than theme and theology.

WRITING TOPICS. The Prodigal Son as a symbol. The parable as it allegorizes the possibility of forgiveness and a second chance. The shift in point of view in the parable.

WORKS FOR COMPARISON WITH "THE PRODIGAL SON"

Greenberg, *And Sarah Laughed*, 322
Hayden, *Those Winter Sundays*, 1161
Miller, *Death of a Salesman*, 1457
Roethke, *My Papa's Waltz*, 831

JOHN STEINBECK, *The Chrysanthemums*, *pages* 447–54

In teaching Steinbeck's "The Chrysanthemums," you may encounter an initial difficulty that students have in determining what has happened. Here a stress on symbolism in the story may prove fruitful as explanation, for the "dark speck" on the road (paragraph 108) is of course the pile of earth in which Elisa has earlier placed the chrysanthemum shoots. Sometimes students claim to dislike Elisa, but if they can see the story as one about a difficult personal relationship, they can be persuaded to care about her and thus to find the story interesting. As always, understanding can overcome aversion.

Suggestions for Discussing the Study Questions, page 454

(1) For the most part, the narrator observes Elisa dramatically, and utilizes omniscience only in paragraphs 108, 109, and possibly also in 110. The advantage of this mostly dramatic rendering is that the reader is left to infer the nature of Elisa's elation and therefore the extent of her great disappointment. Steinbeck, by thus directing the reader's sympathy and understanding, creates a memorable character and a powerful story.

(2) The setting (paragraph 1) is symbolic because it complements

Elisa's isolation as a woman. The time of the year is December, when things have ceased growing, and the foothills around the valley prevent the sun (a universal symbol of growth, intelligence, and fertility) from reaching the farm. Conditions at the Allen ranch suggest that everything is finished and put away, with nothing more to do. These aspects of the setting are clearly designed to symbolize the bleak prospects for Elisa.

(3) Elisa's solitude may be taken to symbolize the isolation of women—or of anyone—cut off from free and voluntary communication with others. She is wearing clothes that mask and hide her femininity, such as the large apron, the gloves, and the hat. This clothing—worth discussing in detail—symbolizes Elisa's suppressed life on the ranch. A similar instance of such symbolism stemming from the isolation of rural life is Minnie Wright in Glaspell's "A Jury of Her Peers" (page 202).

(4) The central symbol of the story, the chrysanthemums, is stressed in paragraphs 6, 8, 12, 27, 50–71 (especially 71), and 108–109. These flowers symbolize Elisa's strong sexual and nurturing power. Her connection with dirt, which she handles skillfully, symbolizes an earth-mother force. Her description of proper care of the buds in paragraph 71 suggests her love and satisfaction in growing things. Because she has no children on whom to bestow this talent, she transfers her force to the flowers.

(5) In the washing and dressing scene (paragraphs 93–98) Elisa wishes to make herself pretty and sexually attractive. The pumice is a normal means of sloughing off dead skin cells and uncovering live ones. For this reason it is a symbolic means of causing her sexuality to emerge, just as her care with her dress indicates her desire to be attractive.

(6) Elisa's responses, including her foreknowledge, her hurt, her anger, and her private despair, are described in paragraphs 108–121. The dumped flowers symbolize the rejection of her creative and sexual desires.

WRITING TOPICS. The symbolism of: (a) The chrysanthemums. (b) The setting. (c) The washing scene. Elisa's plight and the role of women within a rural setting.

WORKS FOR COMPARISON WITH "THE CHRYSANTHEMUMS"

Anonymous, *The Myth of Atalanta*, 432
Atwood, *Variation on the Word Sleep*, 1124
Dickinson, *Wild Nights—Wild Nights!*, 1078
Glaspell, *A Jury of Her Peers*, 202

Michel Tremblay, *The Thimble,* *pages 454–56*

"The Thimble," brief as it is, brings out more discussion from students than many longer works. Of particular interest is the story's unreal, dreamlike fabric. How does the woman appear? Where has she been before? Why is she carrying a thimble? What is magic about it? Why doesn't Bobby Stone take it at once and then throw it away? When it is forbidden him, why does he then want it, and why is he willing to kill for it? Why does the mysterious woman slow down so that he may overtake her? Can the story be read to say that any evil act is in effect the same as the destruction of all life? Students will raise these and other questions, for the story is deeply thought-provoking.

Suggestions for Discussing the Study Questions, page 456

(1) The introductory remark about a catastrophe gets the reader interested and looking for the conditions that can be called catastrophic. This opening sentence is like the opening sentence in O'Connor's "First Confession" (page 363), which contain a hint about the final outcome. Usually, in fiction, any hints about the outcome are avoided in order to build up suspense and interest. The catastrophe is the squashing of the entire universe—certainly no small matter. Although many elements of the narrative are realistic, the sequencing is unreal and dreamlike. An additional question might be, in light of the story's conclusion, whether "catastrophe" is an understatement.

(2) The woman says that she has locked the entire universe in the thimble. The next day Bobby throws the thimble in the garbage but then retrieves it to sew a loose button. Granted the story itself, nothing else would work as well as the thimble, but if a slightly different conclusion were made, just about any object would work because the symbolism is contextual.

(3) Students will be interested in considering questions like desiring and gaining forbidden objects (paragraph 7) and the anticlimactic feelings once goals have been attained. When Bobby puts the thimble on his little finger he squashes the entire universe. This outcome might seem absurd to many students until they realize that recent scientific theory holds that the universe was created originally as a *singularity*; that is, that the universe as we know it today expanded from an infinitely small point. Students might be asked if this hypothesis is any more difficult to understand than the idea that the universe can be contained within a thimble.

(4) Both "The Fox and the Grapes" and "The Thimble" are brief allegories about desire, temptation, and the rationalization that comes with rejection. Tremblay goes beyond Aesop by concluding his allegory on the note of the destruction of the universe.

WRITING TOPICS. "The Thimble" as an allegory: an allegory about what? The logic, or lack of logic, of the narrative. To what degree is Bobby visualized as a realistic or unrealistic character?

WORKS FOR COMPARISON WITH "THE THIMBLE"

Blake, *The Tyger*, 754
Dryden, *A Song for St. Cecilia's Day*, 1012
Hawthorne, *Young Goodman Brown*, 436
Hopkins, *God's Grandeur*, 863

Writing About Symbolism or Allegory, *pages 456–61*

By the time you work on this section you will already have been discussing the symbolism and allegory in a number of stories, and therefore an assignment will not come as a surprise to your students. The biggest problem they will likely ask about is what to say once they have identified a thing, character, situation, or response as a symbol, or once they have identified a narrative (or part of a narrative) as an allegory. Here the schemes on pages 458 and 459 might be introduced as aids for the development of subtopics for essays. You might wish to encourage students to develop their own tables or graphs.

As you teach the various ways to structure possible essays, you might wish to use some of the stories in this chapter. Certainly the demonstrative essay (page 459) offers an approach for an essay based on a number of separate symbols. This structure is easiest for most students. You might also use the symbolism of the flowers in Steinbeck's "The Chrysanthemums." This story is a fine example for showing the extent to which a symbol may pervade an entire story. It also illustrates the relationship of symbol to character.

Special Topics for Writing and Argument about Symbolism and Allegory, *page 462*

(1) Topic 2 is essentially a comparison-contrast assignment (see Chapter 35, page 1979). Most of the symbolism is contextual; the symbolism of the thimble would be uncertain out of its context in Tremblay's allegory, for example, and equally uncertain would be the symbolism of the flowers and the boat in the other two stories. The additional questions are suggestions for students in the development of their essays.

(2) Topic 2 is designed to start a discussion about persuasion in literature. The point that students should aim for is that religious and moral ideas, which are abstract, are best understood through the concrete medium of symbolism (and allegory). Human minds being what they are, in other words, a specific and concrete approach is better than abstract discussion. Symbolism and allegory provide the "objective correlative" to anchor moral and religious ideas.

(3) Topic 3 may surprise students who know the gospel parables separately, but who have never considered them as a group. The likeliest way for students to begin is to establish the moral or theological purposes of two, three, or more of the parables. Then, with this as the basis of comparison, they may consider aspects such as length, amount of detail, explanations within the Biblical text, and so on.

(4) The material about male-female relationships in "The Myth of Atalanta" should be clear to most students. What should be emphasized about this assignment, therefore, is that the Atalanta story is virtually as old as Western civilization. Some students might wish to make much of this truth.

(5) Students find this topic challenging and particular instructive. If a student is living away from home, perhaps a dog, a cat, or a particular street or store might prove to be the central contextual symbol in that student's story about characters back home. One student developed the symbol of the family doing the dishes after the evening meal. Another wrote about auto trips that the family took together. The point is that anything, even something seemingly unimportant, can be made symbolic if the writer gives it proper emphasis and importance.

(6) Topic 6 might cause students to raise questions about the various universal symbols they live with in daily life. Sometimes students respond to "images," since these are made important in aspects of life such as politics, advertising, religion, and social issues. The suggestions about the flag, water, and the explosion should also prompt students to develop these or other universal symbols.

(7) Topic 7 is designed not only for students to use the library's catalogue system, but also to use tables of contents and indices of the books they retrieve. You might wish to have students concentrate particularly on Hawthorne's symbolism, without having them relate the symbolism to Hawthorne's life.

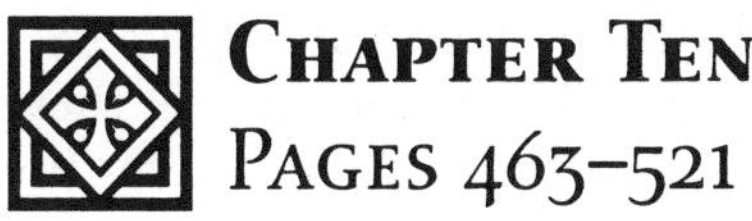

Chapter Ten
Pages 463–521

Idea or Theme: The Meaning and the Message in Fiction

This chapter introduces students to the words *idea* and *theme*, and to the means by which these words are made significant in fiction. The earlier chapters have actually been, in their ways, introductions to the use of fiction as idea. Thus *point of view* (Chapter 5) is a means by which authors dramatize ideas and make them authentic, and *symbolism* (Chapter 9) is a concrete means of rendering ideas. In addition, if you have discussed poetry, you may also wish to consider Chapter 23 in conjunction with your discussions about ideas.

Teaching this chapter will involve a good deal of discussion about what exactly is meant by the word *idea*. Related words that might lend clarification are *concept, thought, opinion, belief,* and *meaning*. *Conception, interpretation, motif, analysis,* and *explication* might also arise, together with others that your students might contribute. What is most important is that ideas should be expressed as sentences or assertions, for stories are genuinely dramatic renderings in narrative form of a moving idea. Thus the complete sentence, or assertion, as a form (page 463) should be stressed as an initial stage in the perceptions of ideas.

Toni Cade Bambara, *The Lesson,* *pages 470–75*

Not only does the story feature the guided dialogue of the children, but it also reflects the grievous setting of their lives and homes. One of the children, Flyboy, states that he doesn't "even have a home" (paragraph 21), although Sylvia suggests that this may be one of his habitual lies to gain sympathy. Sylvia, with Sugar and Junior (sister, brother, or cousins?) are living with Aunt Gretchen (paragraph 1), while the mothers live "in a la-de-da apartment up the block having a good ole time." Students may debate the meaning of this, but it would appear that the mothers are earning money through prostitution. With Sugar, Sylvia goes to a nearby store to terrorize "West Indian kids and take their hair ribbons and their money too" (paragraph 2). When the children go out to play, they must do so in locations which are soiled with human waste. These details, together with the dialogue during the excursion, make "The Lesson" not only a tightly knit story, but also encourage the most vigorous classroom discussion.

Suggestions for Discussing the Study Questions, page 475

(1) The socio-political underpinning of the story is focused in Miss Moore, who is a "cousin, mostly" who moved north along with Sylvia's family, and who now lives on the same block as the family. Miss Moore, who has attended college, says that "it was only right that she should take responsibility for the young ones' education" (paragraph 1). According to Sylvia, Miss Moore is always contriving "boring ass things" for the children to do (i.e., informal but guided educational tours), and we may assume that the excursion to F. A. O. Schwarz, the quintessential toy store on Fifth Avenue in Manhattan, is one of these "things." As a teacher, Miss Moore employs the Socratic method, and her aim is to demonstrate a situation, and then get the children to draw conclusions from it. Thus, as the children observe the toys, especially a toy fiberglass sail boat selling "at one thousand one hundred ninety-five dollars" (paragraph 25), their responses dramatize the economic inequality represented by the price. The response of Sugar, Sylvia's friend and roommate, is representative: "I think . . . that this not much of a democracy if you ask me. Equal chance to pursue happiness means an equal crack at the dough, don't it?" (paragraph 51). All the dialogue, from paragraph 11 to the story's end, builds up to these conclusions.

(2) While the views encouraged by Miss Moore are analytical, Sylvia, the narrator, represents a more pragmatic response to the situation being experienced by her family. Miss Moore entrusts Sylvia with five dollars to pay the taxi driver, but Sylvia pockets four of the dollars, saving money by beginning the walk home at the story's end. She is able to analyze the situation as well as Sugar (see paragraph 44, where she raises questions about those whose lifestyle permits conspicuous consumption, and paragraph 58, where she resolves to "think this day through"), but she adds touches of anger and combativeness to her attitude, as when she declares "ain't nobody gonna beat me at nuthin" at the story's conclusion.

(3) Sylvia's speech is conversational, as though it has been transcribed from an oral presentation. One may conclude that the story is being told orally because many spoken idioms of Black English

appear, such as "Sugar done swiped" (paragraph 2), "like we a bunch of retards" (paragraph 2), "Don't nobody want to go for my plan" (paragraph 3), "We all walkin on tiptoe" (paragraph 41), and so on. Although Sylvia's speech is colloquial, she has a remarkable flair for language, as in paragraph 40, where she states "the rest of us tumble in like a glued-together jigsaw done all wrong."

(4) These paragraphs contain the mathematical and economic analysis undergirding the impoverishment of the children in the story and their families. There are suggestions here of political analysis and resulting political action, even though the story does not go beyond the comparative prices of necessities and luxuries. Paragraph 50, spoken by Miss Moore, seems to summarize the story's ideas: "Imagine for a minute what kind of society it is in which some people can spend on a toy what it would cost to feed a family of six or seven." It would be difficult to imagine that the children would forget such an analysis and comparison, because they have seen and coveted the expensive toys, and will not forget them and their extravagant prices.

WRITING TOPICS: The narrator's speech. The character of Miss Moore. What is the "lesson"? How successfully does the story make its point about inequality?

WORKS FOR COMPARISON WITH "THE LESSON"

Brooks, *We Real Cool*, 858
Durem, *I Know I'm not Sufficiently Obscure*, 758
Hughes, *Harlem: A Dream Deferred*, 787
McKay, *White City*, 1177
Sanchez, *right on, white america*, 1193

ERNEST J. GAINES, *The Sky Is Gray*, *pages 475–94*

"The Sky Is Gray" demonstrates a number of ideas. From the viewpoint of the child, the narrator, it dramatizes the problems that African-Americans face as a minority group: poverty, hunger, hardship, and systematic discrimination. It also dramatizes most of the views and solutions that have been raised about racial problems in the United States: passivity, denial, religious refuge, and militancy. The elderly couple who shelter and feed the narrator and his mother demonstrate the idea that kindness and compassion are values that transcend political problems and solutions. Because the story contains so many perspectives, it should provoke extensive and thoughtful discussion among students.

Suggestions for Discussing the Study Questions, pages 494–95

(1) By using the eight-year old child as the narrator, Gaines establishes a disinterested, innocent voice, who is able to report what he says and hears, but who is unsophisticated and who cannot therefore provide extensive commentary. A more mature narrator would feel compelled, in the light of the difficulties experienced by the boy and his mother, to explain, make comments, and generally become political or philosophical. The child, however, experiences things directly and reports them directly.

(2) The killing and eating of the birds is to be taken as a literal illustration that the impoverished and almost starving family needs the birds for food. James is unwilling to kill the creatures because he senses their innocence and inability to protect thémselves, but his mother forces him to do so on the grounds that he, as an eight-year old, needs to grow and therefore needs to do some of the unpleasant tasks required for maturity (paragraph 82). One might say that a major evil of poverty and hunger is that it forces people to act against their own wishes. Hence poverty demeans and enslaves the people who suffer it.

(3) After an introductory section about the life of the boy James and his family, the major action of "The Sky Is Gray" is the trip that James and his mother take to Bayonne to get treatment for James's toothache, together with the delay, pain, and kindness they find. In this way the story dramatizes a major example of their poverty and inequality. The delays in the dentist's office permit the exposition of the views of the minister and the young man, the negative experiences both outside in the sleet and inside in the hardware store and the café, and the positive experience with the elderly couple in their little store.

(4) The discussion in the waiting room brings out the young man's militancy and the minister's endurance. After the minister leaves, the high point of this conflict is reached in paragraphs 220–230, particularly the young man's question to the nearby lady, "Name me one right that you have. One right, granted by the Constitution, that you can exercise in Bayonne." It is such radicalism, the story suggests, that may become a wave of the future. Certainly the young boy, James, immediately identifies with the young man's character and ideas (paragraph 185). That the minister strikes the young man demonstrates that anger and misunderstanding keep people apart even when they should be allies (paragraphs 165–170). The young man's turning the other cheek therefore does not deter the minister from using force, but rather encourages it.

(5) The elderly couple in the little store, Helena and Ernest ("Alnest"), represent kindness and compassion. Helena recognizes that Octavia, James's mother, is a woman of spirit and pride, and therefore she does not phone the superior dentist. Helena wants to pursue her kindness to the point of giving Octavia an oversize portion of salt meat, but Octavia, insisting on her dignity, refuses it, accepting only the smaller portion. One may read this incident to say that African Americans want no special favors, but only opportunity and fair treatment.

WRITING TOPICS. The meaning of the elderly couple in the store. The meaning of the discussion and conflict in the dentist's office. The dialect of the speaker. The character of the mother, Octavia.

WORKS FOR COMPARISON WITH "THE SKY IS GRAY"

Brooks, *Primer for Blacks, 1128*
Hughes, *Harlem: A Dream Deferred, 787*
Hughes, *Mulatto, 1663*
Parédes, *The Hammon and the Beans, 415*
Whitecloud, *Blue Winds Dancing, 156*

JAMES JOYCE, *Araby*, *pages 495–99*

Much of Joyce's work has been called "fictionalized autobiography," a quality shown in "Araby," one of the stories in *Dubliners*. As a young child, Joyce lived on North Richmond Street, just like the narrator of the story. The bazaar which the narrator attends actually did take place in Dublin, from May 14 to 19, 1894, when Joyce was the same age as the narrator. It was called "Araby in Dublin," and was advertised as a "Grand Oriental Fete."

Students may wonder why the narrator expresses unexplained chagrin about himself at the end. This question cannot be easily answered without a discussion of the reasons for the narrator's sense of guilt about his youthful feelings of love.

Suggestions for Discussing the Study Questions, page 499

(1) The principal idea of "Araby" is that youthful love is childish and foolish, but that it is also normal, overpowering, and creative. Ideally, memories like those the speaker is describing about his infatuation for Mangan's sister should be a cause for fondness, mingled perhaps with amusement. Much of the speaker's memory exhibits just such beauty. If the experience of the childhood "crush" produces unhappiness at the time it occurs, a mature understanding should be able to filter out and eliminate the childhood misgivings to achieve a celebration of time past. The speaker, however, does

not indicate that this process has taken place, and hence Joyce is presenting a portrait of a narrator who is still a victim of childhood inhibitions.

(2) Before the narrator goes to Araby, this bazaar symbolizes for him his adoration of Mangan's sister and also an "Eastern enchantment" (paragraph 12) of mystic fulfillment of love. At the end it symbolizes unreality and unreachable hope which has been dashed by his adolescent lack of power and by the drunken and passive-aggressive uncle.

(3) From the first paragraph one might discover a good deal of submerged hostility toward home. For example, it is significant and also amusing that the speaker chooses the phrase "set the boys free" about the school, for these words are appropriate to a release from prison. The speaker almost literally endows the houses with a life that encourages decency, but which does not develop humanness and love. *Blind* is a normal word for a dead-end street, but it also is appropriate for a social group with no understanding of human impulses. The relationship of the first and last paragraphs is subtle but real, for the speaker demonstrates anger not only against himself, as at the end, but also against the culture out of which he came, as at the beginning.

(4) The narrator is an adult telling about events that occurred specifically to him when he was an early adolescent. If one considers the story as fictionalized autobiography, the time of the events can be determined as 1893–1894, with the narrator therefore being a boy of eleven or twelve. It is difficult to determine the age of the narrator at the time of the narration, except to note that he is not yet mature himself, for he still evidences embarrassment at his childhood feelings (see, for example, the end of paragraph 4). The effect of the age differential is to create detachment, if not total objectivity, about the events. The narrator, for example, seems distant enough from the prayerful "O Love" sequence to share the scene with readers despite the fact that it is amusing (paragraph 6; one might assume that the narrator does not realize that the action is amusing). For comparison, similar uses of point of view may be found in Frank O'Connor's "First Confession" (page 363) and Parédes's "The Hammon and the Beans" (page 415).

Writing Topics. The point of view in "Araby." The ideas about love and inhibition. Setting and idea. The symbolism of the fair. The development of ideas. The idea of childhood love. The dead priest as a symbol.

Works for Comparison with "Araby"

Chekhov, *The Bear,* 1625
Keats, *La Belle Dame Sans Merci,* 954
O'Connor, *First Confession,* 363
Soto, *Oranges,* 1203

D.H. Lawrence, *The Horse Dealer's Daughter,* pages 499–510

"The Horse Dealer's Daughter" is typical of Lawrence's stories about the power of sexuality in life. Both main characters, Mabel Pervin and Dr. Jack Fergusson, have reached an impasse in their lives by themselves, and can go in new directions only when they realize their sexual needs. Despite their obvious reluctance and inexperience with their emotions, both Fergusson and Mabel realize that they need each other. This realization gives them both confidence and doubt at the same time (see paragraphs 142, 150, 152, 158, 159, and 191). From paragraph 142 to the end, Lawrence takes great pains to emphasize their ambiguous feelings. As they approach change and growth, in other words, they also become apprehensive. Character development is not without cost.

Suggestions for Discussing the Study Questions, pages 510–11

(1) By beginning the story with the breakup of the Pervin household, Lawrence stresses the idea that a central force is necessary for stability, and that instability and pain result once such force is gone (he could also be illustrating the need for young adults to establish their own ways of life independently of family ties). Some adjectives describing the scene are *desolate, desultory, dreary, strange, sullen-looking,* and *impassive,* all from paragraphs 2 and 3. These adjectives underscore the instability and pain being experienced by the brothers and sister in the disintegrating Pervin family.

(2) In paragraph 7, Joe Pervin, the eldest of the family, is compared to the massive draft horses. These are slow but strong (having a "slumbrous strength" [paragraph 6]), and are in harness, as Joe will be once he marries the daughter of the steward of the nearby estate. In paragraph 20, Joe is also compared to horses because of his appearance when walking and speaking. In addition, another brother, Fred Henry (paragraph 11), is compared to horses, for he is under the control "of the situations of life," even though he masters horses easily. Because the horses, though strong, need the external control of reins, the idea seems to be that those without love are without the strength they need to guide their own destinies.

(3) Mabel is "rather short, sullen looking" with a face of "impassive fixity" (paragraph 3). We are to understand that she has felt the loss of her mother deeply, but has appreciated the power of being mistress of the household for the following ten years. She has developed no friendships with either women or men (paragraphs 95–97), and treats her brothers with contempt (paragraph 96). At the beginning of the story, she has nowhere to go, and has made no plans. Lawrence's speaker stresses that she has reached the end (paragraph 98). Apparently she does not want even temporary residence with her sister Lucy (paragraph 12). Her dilemma is that she does not know where to turn.

(4) In paragraph 103 the speaker notes "some mystical element" that touches Fergusson as he looks at Mabel in the cemetery. This power is further explained in paragraph 104 as having the strength of a drug. When Jack sees Mabel attempting to kill herself, he does not feel alarm, but fears the possibility that he might "lose her altogether" (paragraph 108). These two examples suggest that he is slowly realizing his emotional tie with her. The idea is apparently that love may develop even when (perhaps *especially* when) the individuals involved do not realize what is happening to them.

(5) Fergusson's rescue of Mabel is described in paragraphs 110–115. The setting is wetness, dankness, muckiness, and a foul smell (the smell is mentioned a number of times). To determine how this setting reinforces mood and idea, one must conclude that Lawrence, by the rescue, is suggesting that even though unpleasantness is necessary in life, and though at times the environment is ugly and threatening, there can nevertheless be good results.

(6) In paragraph 150, Lawrence's narrator emphasizes Fergusson's lack of intention about Mabel, and thus the story brings out the idea that love is irresistible and overwhelming. To live without love leads people, literally, to the dead end in which both Mabel and Jack find themselves in the first part of the story. Therefore, the discovery of love is a power that cannot be resisted, for without love there is no life.

(7) The reason for which Lawrence emphasizes the ambiguity of love is that he is not espousing any easy answers: All problems will continue, including many of the personal reservations that people have about each other and themselves. Love, however, is the Lawrentian basis of life. The demonstrative essay (page 518) deals further with this idea.

WRITING TOPICS. The idea about the barrenness of a loveless

life as exemplified in the three brothers. The ideas represented by the horses and the harness. Lawrence's complex ideas about love as shown by the pond. The meaning of the wet, soggy, musty clothing in relationship to love.

Works for Comparison with "The Horse Dealer's Daughter"

Colwin, *An Old-Fashioned Story, 67*
Frost, *A Line-Storm Song, 1106*
Henley, *Am I Blue, 1635*
Joyce, *Araby, 495*

Irene Zabytko, *Home Soil, pages 511–515*

"Home Soil" centers upon the experiences and the guilt of a Ukrainian American, the narrator, and his son, Bohdan. The narrator committed a war crime in Ukraine during World War II, and he still replays "that scene in . . . [his] mind almost forty years after it happened" (paragraph 33). His son Bohdan, who has lost his Ukrainian roots (he prefers to be called "Bob" rather than "Bohdan" [paragraph 4]), has undergone some similar but undisclosed experience in the Vietnamese War.

The story itself takes place on a Sunday, the first section being in church (paragraph 1–36) and the second at the narrator's home. The parallel experiences of father and son reach a climax in paragraph 36, when the narrator speaks of the impossibility of finding inner peace even though he is leading a totally peaceful and successful life. The son's tears (paragraphs 40–42) show that he feels the same loss of inner peace. Interestingly, there is no solution to the existence of guilt. As much as the narrator can say is "I don't die. Instead I go to the garden" (paragraph 37), an action that suggests the irrevocability of inhuman actions and the permanence of guilt.

Suggestions for Discussing the Study Questions, pages 515–16

(1) The narrator is living in Chicago, and is doing well financially because he owns a restaurant and an apartment building. We learn that he, as a young Ukrainian during the Nazi occupation of Ukraine after the 1941 invasion, participated in the Holocaust. He wrote pro-German propaganda and especially, on one occasion, forced a group of Jews into a cattle car to be taken to an extermination camp (paragraphs 31–36). This event remains fixed in his mind because even though he was young at the time he participated in an inexcusable atrocity.

(2) The question about the exercise of power during warfare has been constant as long as there has been war. The narrator confesses that "I enjoyed that power, until it seeped into my veins and poisoned my soul" (paragraph 33). Those who have been responsible for the deaths of others, even though they can lead outwardly normal lives afterward, can never escape the memory of the past. The narrator hence wishes that he had sought the family of the Jewish girl so that he could have confessed his responsibility to them. Even the thought that they might have condemned him is the only hope of absolution that he could ever hope for.

(3) The complexity of the story is indicated by the tears of the narrator's son, Bohdan. The two, father and son, have obviously had parallel experiences with wartime atrocities, although we do not learn the precise nature of what Bohdan has been through. In light of the story's first-person point of view, we cannot learn what Bohdan has done because Bohdan does not speak to the narrator about his experiences. The parallel is made complete in paragraph 30, when the narrator observes that Bohdan may never tell him what happened in Vietnam. The narrator then confesses, "I never told anyone either." Some ideas that underlie this commonness of wartime experience are that fighting is never over, that people are called upon in warfare to engage in hostilities that produce death, that they can never forget that they have caused death even though they may find excuses for their actions, and that people and governments never learn from past experience to avoid the future guilt that state warfare creates in its citizens who participate in war.

(4) This statement suggests that maybe the narrator knows what it takes to crush someone's skull, and that in the story he has not told everything about his wartime experiences in Ukraine. There is a layer here, in other words, of something more sinister than the wartime action to which he confesses in paragraphs 31–36.

WRITING TOPICS. The ideas about warfare brought out in the story. The character of the speaker. The guilt that is disturbing Bohdan. The apparent success of the narrator's new life in the United States.

WORKS FOR COMPARISON WITH "HOME SOIL"

Forché, *Because One Is Always Forgotten*, 1153
Georgakas, *Hiroshima Crewman*, 1154
Hardy, *The Man He Killed*, 673
Northrup, *Ogichidag*, 677
Northrup, *Wahbegan*, 1180
Ozick, *The Shawl*, 331

(especially interesting, for example, is the patching of the outside wall), the beginning of the plowing, and the trip to the blacksmith-wheelwright. All of this is authentic Americana. Topics to discuss are the view of Abner Snopes and his articulation of his ideas of justice, his behavior in the trial scenes, and his preparations to burn the barn; the scornfully gratuitous maltreatment of the rug; the way Sarty learns about his father's background; the treatment of Sarty's character; and the concluding scene in daylight the day after the burning of the De Spain barn.

■ **Gaines, *The Sky Is Gray*** (1980). *Host,* Henry Fonda. *Screenplay,* Charles Fuller. *Producer,* Whitney Green. *Director,* Stan Lathan. *Starring* Olivia Cole *and* James Bond III. Text, page 475.

Granted the length of "The Sky Is Gray," this intelligently selective teleplay effectively supplements the story. Particularly strong are the scenes of the killing of the birds, the bus going to town, the dialogue in the waiting room, Olivia's thanking Helena, and Olivia's final advice to James. The waiting-room scene successfully conveys the story's conflict between passive and radical thinking, but because the film shows less hurtful violence than the story, it somewhat abates the story's underlying anger. Discussion might begin with the effect of the street scenes being filmed in sunshine rather than in sleet or rain, particularly because of the story's title.

■ **Hemingway, *Soldier's Home*** (1976). *Host,* Colleen Dewhurst. *Screenplay,* Robert Geller. *Producer,* David Appleton. *Director,* Robert Young. *Starring* Robert Backus *and* Nancy Marchand. Text, page 348.

Quite interesting in this film is the opening footage of World War I scenes and the posing group of young men, showing the transition from life to photograph. The part about the photograph is authentically derived from Hemingway's story. The costuming is particularly noteworthy, and the vintage automobiles give authenticity to the setting. For discussion, one might query why the production shows Krebs making a pass at the girl, and also why the friend seems angry. Other topics might include the comparative importance of Krebs's sister, the confrontation with his mother, and the concluding scene in which he leaves town. Perhaps most important are the ways in which story and film versions bring out Krebs's sense of alienation and disaffection with life in the small town after the action and excitement of the War. Does the line quoted by Colleen Dewhurst, about how to keep young men on the farm "after they've seen Par-ee," explain Krebs's feelings?

■ **Porter, *The Jilting of Granny Weatherall*** (1980). *Host,* Henry Fonda. *Screenplay,* Corinne Jacker. *Producer,* Robert Geller. *Director,* Randa Haines. *Starring* Geraldine Fitzgerald and Lois Smith. Text, page 651.

Of great interest in this film are the scenes and artifacts of the farm of Granny Weatherall. It is doubtful that many of today's students have seen a butterchurn, a wind-up floor-standing Victrola, or a "scratch" cake (in this age of premixed cake batter), or have seen how to lift a hen to recover eggs. The scenes reflect a period of the 1920s, although a 1937 Ford is driven in, and the farm has benefited from the introduction of Rural Electrification (earlier than it reached many farms). Topics to discuss are why Granny's early liveliness is followed so quickly by her quick failure and demise, her philosophy of work, the way in which her recollections are introduced as dialogue rather than memory, the two males around the farm, her visions of George and Hapsy, and the effectiveness of her dying moments and the receding figures of her loved ones.

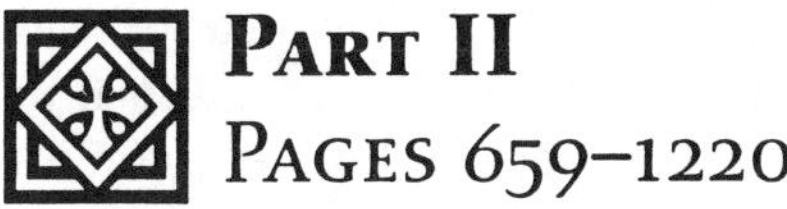

Part II
Pages 659–1220

Poetry

Coverage of the Manual

We provide information and suggestions for every poem in the sixth edition of *Literature: An Introduction to Reading and Writing* except for some of the poems that are discussed extensively in the text. For each poem with study questions in a chapter, we provide a brief overview and introduction, some observations on teaching, the answers to the study questions, and one or more suggested topics for writing. For poems without questions in the text, such as those in *Chapter 25: Poems for Additional Study,* we provide brief observations that might serve as the basis for classroom discussion, and for *Chapter 24: Three Poetic Careers: William Wordsworth, Emily Dickinson, and Robert Frost,* we provide questions together with suggestions for discussion. You may use as much or as little of the material here as you like; it is not our intention to tell you how to teach poetry. All the following material simply suggests some approaches; others are equally valid and rewarding. As with the rest of the manual, the material is designed to help rather than to prescribe.

Using the Chapters in the Poetry section of the Text

We do not expect you to use every poem in a chapter or even every chapter. The material in any given chapter may be taught using only a few of the included poems, or even poems from other chapters or from the "Poems for Additional Study" section. Nor do we expect that you will use the chapters in sequence; the text is designed so that the chapters may be taught in almost any order and number. To ensure that such a reordering of material will not confuse students, we have provided many cross-references and a glossary of literary terms. In addition, we repeat crucial information and guidelines where such material will be helpful.

Organization of Each Poetry Chapter

Although there is much variation, each chapter in the poetry section follows the same general plan. Each begins with an introduction to the aspect of poetry under consideration. This material may be assigned as outside reading and reviewed in class or not, as time permits. Along with this introduction, or at its close, a poem (or several poems) may be discussed in detail.

In each chapter, the introductory material is followed by poems for study that may be used to illustrate the characteristics and issues raised in the introduction. The number of these poems may vary; in addition, most chapters include much variety so that you may select poems that you prefer.

The poems in each chapter are followed by a discussion of writing. This section treats prewriting activities and strategies, questions for discovering ideas, formulations of central ideas, the identification of supporting details, and suggestions for organization. It also provides a demonstrative student essay and a brief commentary, followed by a number of topics for writing, including research exercises and many creative-writing assignments. The demonstrative essays deal with one of the poems in the chapter. For chapters in which you are not assigning an essay or a writing exercise, you may wish to omit the writing section. The demonstrative essays, however, might still serve as examples of how to treat the topics of the various chapters.

Texts and Titles of Poems

The texts for all poems are drawn from standard editions or standard anthologies. Where a poet has provided a title, it has been included. Untitled poems are identified in the text, index, and manual by their first lines. Poems that are often identified by number, such as Shakespeare's Sonnets or Donne's Holy Sonnets, carry both the numbers and the first lines as titles (in the Thematic Index, titles are shortened to the major key words).

Spelling and Punctuation

Many poems from the Renaissance and the late medieval period of the popular ballad were spelled originally in ways that are classed as "old spelling." Sometimes the old spelling includes letters used in outdated ways, such as *j* for *i*, *v* for *u*, and *u* for *v*. In the interests of providing a uniform text, and to avoid making reading any more complex than it needs to be, we have silently modernized these old spellings. American poetry is reproduced with American spelling; British poetry retains some of the qualities of British spelling, such as *honour*, or *centre*. Punctuation is left as is in the texts we have used. Interested readers may note that the punctuation in many of Shakespeare's sonnets is derived from the 1609 text. Ben Jonson's "Drink to Me, Only, with Thine Eyes," includes commas that we might not prefer today. In all cases, we have avoided extensive editorial intervention, and have sought to present the poems in the best versions available.

Glosses and Notes

The poems in the text feature both side glosses and (when necessary) explanatory notes. In the side glosses, we attempt to find a reasonable middle ground between glossing all "hard" words and glossing only foreign or obsolete words. Our aim is to be as helpful and as unobtrusive as possible. Students will still benefit if they read all poems with a dictionary close by and if they check out words that are not immediately clear. We use the explanatory notes to give various kinds of relevant information, including extended definitions, explanations of allusions, and identification of many historical, mythological, and literary figures and events. Occasionally, we use the notes to explain a possible meaning of a difficult phrase or line; for these occasions, we try to give a straightforward (rather than interpretive) reading. Also, in the interests of helping clarify a reading, we use the explanatory notes to change syntax, adding words in brackets when necessary, so that students may see a difficult line laid out in easy order.

Suggestions for Teaching Poetry

There are many helpful strategies for teaching poetry. One effective way is to begin by reading aloud; you or a student might read the poem aloud, sentence by sentence. The class may discuss (or you may ask questions about) the sense and the effect of each sentence. Questions about specific topics, such as those included following the poems, will allow students to see how the poem's ideas are presented, and these questions may provide data about the poem that you can put together, along with the class, to develop a larger view.

Analysis of this type can be followed by synthesis: A set of questions designed to allow the class to pull the whole poem back together into a coherent moment of experience, thought, and emotion. Again, by using questions and allowing responses (or insisting on them), you give your students the chance to follow your methods and thereby to learn the process of interpretation and understanding. At the close of discussion, you might have a student (perhaps the same student) read the poem aloud again. Let us hope that this second reading will reflect the intervening process of discovery and experience.

As in the guide for the fiction section, we have included the "Works for Comparison . . ." lists at the end of each selection in Chapters 13–23. These, it is hoped, will furnish an abundance of topics for study, discussion, and writing.

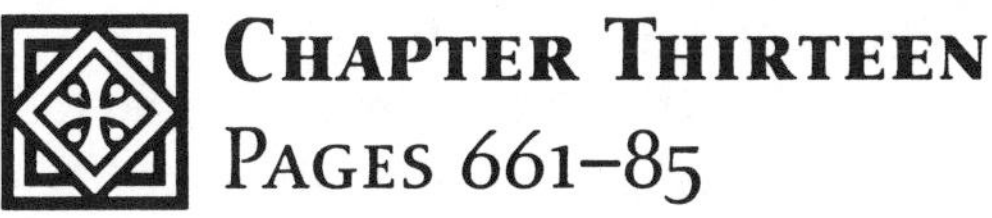

Chapter Thirteen Pages 661–85

Meeting Poetry: An Overview

This chapter introduces students to poetry and to the processes of analysis, interpretation, and explication. The opening pages raise some issues that you may want to discuss briefly in class. The high point of this opening material is the set of four reading objectives (667–68) that can be used at any stage in the study of poetry, to be augmented by specific topics as students become more informed and adept.

The chapter contains poetry that many students will be at least partly familiar with already, and this knowledge should help set them at ease. Indeed, many students may think that they already understand most of these poems, at least to some degree. Further reading and classroom discussion should help these students clarify and reappraise the understanding they already possess.

Early in the chapter, a number of poems are discussed in some detail. In your classroom discussion of these poems, you may wish to go over the explanations, and use these to illustrate the processes of reading, learning about details, analyzing them, and discovering meanings and relationships—all of which constitute the heart of reading poetry.

Lisel Mueller, *Hope*, *pages 661–62*

Suggestions for Discussing the Study Questions, page 662

(1, 3) The first two stanzas provide meaning for hope by illustrating various locations and actions where hope may be found. When hope hovers in dark corners, it is presumably hoping for light. When hope is asleep, it will soon be awake. When it is locked into dandelion heads, Nature itself allows it to burst forth to carry abroad the seed of new growth. Essentially, hope is seen as both omnipresent and ubiquitous, and it is both figuratively and literally identical with existence itself. To adapt words of Thomas Jefferson, just as human beings have been given the inseparable gifts of life and liberty, so have we also be given the gift of hope, and none of these gifts can be disjoined.

(2) Hope is therefore an indestructible "singular gift" of life. Hope as a "serum" is a little more problematic, but one may assume that if hope is a serum, it is an antitoxin against hatred and suspicion. Therefore it enables people to have faith in each other, thus preventing betrayal.

(4) The concluding line may represent a certain modesty on the part of the poet. When we speak, we speak about what we know, and what we plan to do. Hope is thus a corollary of speech, and of poetry. Implicit in all poetry is hence the expression of hope, if only we can detect where hope appears. In this sense, hope is "trying to speak."

WRITING TOPICS. The meaning of hope, as expressed in the poem. The relationship of hope and common objects. The importance of hope in human relationships.

WORKS FOR COMPARISON WITH "HOPE"

Frost, *Choose Something Like a Star, 1114*
Chief Dan George, *The Beauty of the Trees, 1154*
Levertov, *Of Being, 736*
Whitman, *Full of Life Now, 1216*
Wilbur, *Year's End, 958*

BILLY COLLINS, *Schoolsville, page 663*

The questions about this poem are treated on page 664. Question 4, requiring a comparison of Roethke's "Dolor" (738) and the Collins poem, might bring out that the realistic details in "Dolor" point toward a mood of dreariness, while the realistically based but also fanciful details in "Schoolsville" are shaped to create that amusement which we find in recognizing allusions and exaggerations. One might remark that adding "-ville" at the end of a word creates a slang expression indicating qualities and making observations about the word. Thus, "to be from Joysville" is to be happy, and to be from "Schoolsville" is to be imbued with the knowledge and customs of educational institutions.

WRITING TOPICS. The tone of the poem. The transition between reality and fantasy. The imagery.

WORKS FOR COMPARISON WITH "SCHOOLSVILLE"

Smith, *Not Waving But Drowning, 1201*
Stanton, *Childhood, 710*
Strand, *Eating Poetry, 740*

Robert Herrick, *Here a Pretty Baby Lies*, *page 664*

See page 665 for a brief discussion of this poem.

Anonymous, *Sir Patrick Spens*, *pages 668–69*

See page 670 for a brief discussion of this poem.

Writing topics. The use and omission of detail in the ballad form. The motivations of the various characters. Why is Sir Patrick Spens sent to sea at a dangerous time?

Works for Comparison with "Sir Patrick Spens"

Dickey, *The Performance*, 1142
Dickinson, *Because I Could Not Stop for Death*, 671
Lowell, *Patterns*, 1174

Emily Dickinson, *Because I Could Not Stop for Death*, *pages 671–72*

This poem presents an extraordinary perspective on death and the process of dying. It can be taught almost as a story, dealing with the narrative details in the order in which they occur. In the 1980s, composer John Adams set this text to music in his work "Harmonium," which was nominated for a Grammy award in 1985.

Suggestions for Discussing the Study Questions, page 672

(1) The speaker is characterized as having been preoccupied with her own self-importance. She was therefore too busy to stop for anything, as though the hustle-and-bustle of life ruled out anything new or different. There is a note of self-directed irony or mockery here. In the last stanza, we discover that the speaker is long dead, and that she is speaking from a perspective that has stretched out time. She also has given up her commitment to being busy, for she asserts (line 22) that her life in eternity has felt short to her.

(2) Death is characterized as gracious and polite; the key words in this portrait are "kindly" (line 2) and "civility" (line 8). This characterization is unconventional, for Death is not accompanied by pain, war, and sickness—Death is not the "grim reaper"—but rather Death is seen as a quiet, pleasant, and normal force that extends life into another dimension.

(3, 4) The carriage might be considered a hearse, the house a grave or vault. More abstractly, the carriage and the house suggest a movement from earth to heaven, in whatever conveyances take people there. On its journey to the grave, the carriage passes a school, children playing at recess, fields of grain, and the setting sun. The sun passing Death and the speaker in the carriage apparently suggests the ending of the speaker's time on earth. In any event, lines 12 and 13 together indicate movement away from earthly perspective to a more heavenly one.

WRITING TOPICS. The attitude toward death in the poem. The characterization of Death. The comparison between life and death.

WORKS FOR COMPARISON WITH
"BECAUSE I COULD NOT STOP FOR DEATH"

Justice, *On the Death of Friends in Childhood, 1018*
Poe, *The Masque of the Red Death, 541*
Ransom, *Bells for John Whiteside's Daughter, 1189*

ROBERT FRANCIS, *Catch,* *page 672*

This is a most engaging poem, particularly for those persons in your class who have had experience with any sort of baseball and softball. Many students find it fascinating to compare throwing a ball and understanding a poem.

Suggestions for Discussing the Study Questions, page 672

(1) The double meaning of the poem's diction is made clear in the very first line, where we learn that two boys are "tossing a poem" with each other. Once this language is established, readers are on guard to continue the comparison of throwing baseballs and understanding poems.

(2) Those who have ever played catch will recognize the aptness of the description. Although a game of catch usually begins with the two participants throwing the ball easily back and forth, it quickly changes to the sorts of activities described in the poem from lines 2–11. If students recognize the need for variety in throwing baseballs in a game of catch, they will need to recognize also the need for variety in poetry.

(3) The key to the entire comparison is that a game introduces skills of baseball. The skills of reading and understanding are analogous to the baseball skills that players exhibit even when practicing (and perhaps especially when practicing) in a game of catch.

WRITING TOPICS. The poem's comparison between poetry and baseball. The aptness of the poet's description of a typical game of catch. The meaning of "a pretty one plump in his hands" (line 11).

WORKS FOR COMPARISON WITH "CATCH"

Herbert, *Easter Wings, 907*
Keats, *On First Looking Into Chapman's Homer, 777*
Lux, *The Voice You Hear when You Read Silently, 763*
Wordsworth, *Scorn not the Sonnet, 1059*

ROBERT FROST, *Stopping by Woods on a Snowy Evening,* *page 673*

Frost's poem dramatizes a number of alternatives that students may not readily see: life versus death, action versus contemplation, involvement versus withdrawal. Life, action, and involvement are embodied in "promises"; death, contemplation, and withdrawal in the dark, cold, silent woods and the snowfall. In teaching the poem, you can open some of these darker and less accessible ideas through questions that focus on speaker, setting, and situation.

"Stopping by Woods on a Snowy Evening" is one of those set to music by Randall Thompson in his 1941 work *Frostiana* for chorus and piano. Along with "The Road Not Taken" (1109), it is one of the best known of Frost's poems.

Suggestions for Discussing the Study Questions, page 673

(1–4) The speaker is in familiar territory; he is riding through the woods during an evening snowfall and has stopped to watch them "fill up with snow." There is nothing particularly noteworthy in the speaker's decision to stop, for falling snow is lovely to watch. On a deeper level, however, the stopping may signify a reluctance to move forward, a fear of the future, and so on. The speaker apparently feels embarrassed by the stopping, for he notes that the "little horse" *must* be taking exception to the action. The speaker seems to be projecting onto the horse his own ideas that we must be busy every second of our lives. In addition, the speaker has a sense of invading someone else's property, for the "though" of line 2 suggests that he would not stop if the owner were present to observe him. Some commentators have asserted that the house in the village is a church, and that therefore the woody area belongs to God. The implications of this reading raise many speculations in a classroom full of students with varying religious convictions.

(5) In the last stanza, the alternatives are brought into sharp contrast: the woods vs. the promises and the miles. The speaker opts for responsibility, involvement, and action; all this is embodied in the single word "but" in line 14.

(6) Technically, the poem lends itself to classroom consider-

ations of sound and rhyme (see Chapter 19). Alliteration on the *s* and *w* sounds (lines 11–12) reinforces the silence and the sweep of the wind. The sounds are comforting and attractive; they seemingly invite withdrawal. The rhyme scheme is *a a b a, b b c b, c c d c, d d d d,* and it links or interlocks each stanza with the next. To end the poem, Frost uses the same rhyming sound throughout the last stanza and repeats the last line.

WRITING TOPICS. The implications of the setting and the situation. The alternative attitudes or courses of action implied in the poem. The effects produced through sound, rhyme, and meter.

WORKS FOR COMPARISON WITH "STOPPING BY WOODS ON A SNOWY EVENING"

Hemingway, *Soldier's Home, 348*
Herbert, *The Collar, 950*
Wordsworth, *Expostulation and Reply, 1054*

THOMAS HARDY, *The Man He Killed,* *pages 673–74*

The questions on page 610 are considered in the demonstrative student essays on pages 680 and 683–84. With regard to question 5, both "The Man He Killed" and "The Death of the Ball Turret Gunner" alike describe the deaths of men in war. Jarrell's poem is told first-person by the dead man, who describes how his awakening in life corresponds to a death-dealing nightmare, while Hardy's poem is told by the man who killed an enemy in battle. Both alike are antiwar poems, but Jarrell's reveals war's senseless brutality while Hardy treats its anomalous breakdown of normal human relationships.

WRITING TOPICS. The poem's irony. The speaker's character. His diction, and his probable situation. Hardy's view of warfare as manifested in the poem.

WORKS FOR COMPARISON WITH "THE MAN HE KILLED"

O'Brien, *The Things They Carried, 77*
Seeger, *I Have a Rendezvous with Death, 1196*
Whitman, *Reconciliation, 905*

JOY HARJO, *Eagle Poem,* *pages 674–75*

This poem is a prayer, emphasizing the identification of the human spirit with a universal spirit, symbolized by the soaring eagle (line 10). Of particular interest is the way in which the speaker cites the importance of the physical universe. Thus the four elements of sky, earth, sun, and moon are stressed as means of achieving the sacred, as are eagle's wings, which sweep hearts clean "with sacred wings."

Suggestions for Discussing the Study Questions, page 675

(1) What it means to open one's whole self is not easily understood, and would probably receive as many answers as there are students in class. Essentially, however, the idea is to forget daily cares and presuppositions, and to allow the mind to become receptive rather than active. Lines 4–9 build to the image of "circles of motion," also repeated in line 21; that is, to permit transcendent and unifying elements of the universe to reach one's spirit.

(2) Notice that the speaker does not say "the eagle," but rather "eagle," as though the bird is an individual, not a species. The idea is that the world and the universe are alive, not dead, and that all things in it are beings that make life sacred. Eagle makes a circle high in the blue sky (line 11), a symbol of continuity and perfection because a circle has no beginning and no ending, and therefore is infinite like the universe.

(3) The repeated phrase emphasizes the conclusion. Harjo echoes the concluding line from the "Healing Prayer from the Beautyway Chant" (1120), using the word to mean healing, repose, health, and perfection.

WRITING TOPICS. "Eagle Poem" as a prayer. Eagle as a symbol. The world as the means through which spiritual repose is reached

WORKS FOR COMPARISON WITH "EAGLE POEM"

Anonymous, *Healing Prayer from the Beautyway Chant, 1120*
Williams (Joy), *Taking Care, 95*
Wordsworth, *The Prelude, Book I, lines 301–474, 1040*

A.E. HOUSMAN, *Loveliest of Trees,* *page 675*

This lyric, from *The Shropshire Lad,* may be Housman's most famous. It has been memorized by many students, and has been read at many interpretive reading competitions. Some readers have queried the meaning of "white" in line 4, and "snow" in line 12, and also, the age of the speaker has been questioned. But the season of cherry blossoms should not occasion doubt, and the correct subtraction of twenty from threescore years and ten makes the speaker's age unequivocal. The poem is in the "carpe diem" tradition, although the movement toward life is vitality and appreciation, not seduction.

Suggestions for Discussing the Study Questions, pages 675–76

(1) The time of year is spring, when the cherry trees are filled with spring blossoms. The speaker is twenty years old, for the math he performs indicates that he has fifty springs more to live, granted that he will fill out the traditional seventy years suggested in Psalms 90:10. Because he has fifty remaining, he has already lived twenty years of his allotted time.

(2) Even though the speaker is young, he has lived long enough to acknowledge the speed with which time passes. The words "only" (line 7) and "little" (line 10) indicate his perspective, for both words suggest shrinkage and diminution.

(3) The idea about time, beauty, and life is that these things pass quickly. The seasonal setting—spring and the Easter season—suggests that even at the beginning there is an awareness that things will eventually end. Because of this fact, people should celebrate their existence when they are able, and "see the cherry hung with snow" now in the light of inevitable change and impermanence. If life is not lived now, it will be lost.

WRITING TOPICS. The speaker's age, and his resolution about life. The meaning of the references to "white" and "snow." Reasons for enjoying life now, as expressed in the poem.

WORKS FOR COMPARISON WITH "LOVELIEST OF TREES"

Frost, *Birches, 1107*
Kennedy, *Old Men Pitching Horseshoes, 956*
Stevens, *The Emperor of Ice-Cream, 1206*

RANDALL JARRELL, *The Death of the Ball Turret Gunner,* *page 676*

This poem is one of the many anti-war poems that were created by people who participated in the major wars of the twentieth century. When the airplane was developed in World War II as a strategic means of delivering powerful bombs to targets on land and sea, the traditional area of warfare was extended from the ground to the air, and many young men died not only in aerial combat but in bombing formations. The speaker of "The Death of the Ball Turret Gunner" is one of the young men who died.

Suggestions for Discussing the Study Questions, page 676

(1) The topic of the poem is the violent death of a gunner on a World War II bomber, imagined as being told by the dead gunner himself, who represents all young men who have been killed in

war. He has been hit by enemy anti-aircraft fire on a high-altitude bombing mission, presumably over Europe, and has been pulverized within his gun turret.

(2) The opening comparison draws a parallel between the fetus in a mother's womb and the gunner. Thus the "wet fur" in line 2, a reference to the collar of a flight jacket, also suggests fetal hair. Expanding the metaphor, the poet suggests that the gunner is representative of young men who are killed in war before they ever have a chance to live.

(3) The nature of gun turrets is explained in the note (676). The gunner's death is horrible, highlighted by the closing image of his splattered remains—all traces of his identity in life ("me")—being washed "out of the turret with a hose."

WRITING TOPICS. The tone. The accuracy with which the fate of the Gunner is portrayed. The anti-war theme.

WORKS FOR COMPARISON WITH "THE DEATH OF THE BALL TURRET GUNNER"

Eberhardt, *The Fury of Aerial Bombardment, 732*
Forché, *Because One Is Always Forgotten, 1153*
Gay, *Let Us Take the Road, 781*
Georgakas, *Hiroshima Crewman, 1154*

LOUIS MACNEICE, *Snow,* *pages 676–77*

"Snow" repays careful study, for the circumstances of the snow against the window pane develops powerful significance by the poem's end.

Suggestions for Discussing the Study Questions, page 677

(1) The speaker is apparently inside a room, watching the snow accumulate outside against the window pane, before which is standing a bouquet of pink roses. The roses are warm and colorful, and signify human relations and love. The snow, on the other hand, is cold; if it were to penetrate the glass, it would kill the roses. The scene is important because it represents so well the slender difference between the cold, hostile universe and the delicate fragility of civilization.

(2) Words expressing the nature of snow are *spawning, incompatible, suddener, incorrigibly plural, various,* and *gay*. These words are all abstract and impressionistic, in keeping with the speaker's idea that nothing is simple in the world (universe), and that human beings are unable to explain and define the diversity of life.

(3) This is a puzzling line that students may enjoy speculating about. Briefly, the glass may be interpreted symbolically to indicate the cumulative history of humankind, the many ways of life, discoveries, customs, and institutions that enable us to continue our civilization against great odds. On the other hand, some students might claim that the glass symbolizes the ways in which our civilization separates us from our roots in the natural world. Good discussing.

(4) Between Frost and MacNeice, Frost is more precise in his visualization of the outdoor scene, and his speaker speculates briefly and then continues his tasks. MacNeice sees things from inside, and speculates about the difficulty and sometimes the irrationality of life—the good and the bad, the civilized and the uncivilized, which MacNeice characterizes as "more spiteful and gay than one supposes."

WRITING TOPICS. The symbolism of the snow and the roses. The speaker's ideas about the worlds inside and outside. The use of abstract and impressionistic words.

WORKS FOR COMPARISON WITH "SNOW"

Frost, *Stopping by Woods on a Snowy Evening, 673*
Hopkins, *Spring, 761*
Whitecloud, *Blue Winds Dancing, 156*

JIM NORTHRUP, *Ogichidag*, *page 677*

Today's students may need some explanation of the wars cited in the poem, from World War I ("WW One," line 3) to some future war (line 21). You may thus need to assist students in answering the first study question.

Suggestions for Discussing the Study Questions, page 678

(1) In the first World War, chlorine gas was used by the German armies in Ypres, in Belgium. Guadalcanal is a Pacific Island which was the location of fierce fighting between Japanese and American forces in 1943. The North African campaign was chiefly between German and allied forces (led by the German General Rommel and the British General Montgomery) in 1943. The Battle of the Bulge occurred in Belgium during the winter of 1944–45. The Korean War, between North Korea and United Nations forces (principally American), occupied the first years of the 1950s. The "Cuban Missile Crisis," which was caused by the attempt to introduce Russian missiles into Cuba, occurred in 1962. The Vietnamese War (of which Da Nang

was a part) lasted from 1965 to 1975. The poem, in short, covers all the major wars in which the United States was engaged during the twentieth century.

(2) The speaker states that he learned about the battles second hand from old men, uncles, and cousins. Then he experienced battle first hand because of his participation in the fighting at Da Nang. The method of acquiring information is thus personal. The speaker concludes the poem in this immediate way by referring to wars in which his son might be engaged.

(3) There is a progression of information in the poem, developing from the words of "old men" (line 2) to himself and his son. The question about what the son might experience is significant because it involves a continuous interaction among men with personal and family ties. The poem thus closes on a note of dread and apprehension.

WRITING TOPICS. The relationship between the poem's structure and the references to various wars and battles. The character of the speaker. The importance of the conclusion.

WORKS FOR COMPARISON WITH "OGICHIDAG"

Georgakas, *Hiroshima Crewman, 1154*
Hardy, *The Man He Killed, 673*
Owen, *Dulce et Decorum Est, 810*
Sassoon, *Dreamers, 1195*
Weigl, *Song of Napalm, 1215*

NAOMI SHIHAB NYE, *Where Children Live*, *page 678*

This poem is unique in many ways because it views children with "secret smiles" (line 20). It is filled with details that in life might give a harried parent fits, but in the poem's context the memory of children overshadows the chaos they usually create with the detritus of their play.

Suggestions for Discussing the Study Questions, page 678

(1) "Where Children Live" introduces a number of images of "pleasant rumpledness," such as lost shoes, chipped trucks, "bottle rockets, and whistles, / Anything whizzing and spectacular, brilliantly short-lived" (lines 12–13).

(2) This poem is about children as children themselves go about creating their own identities. Adults may try to impose their visions, and give children "swings, leafy plants, slow-motion back and

forth" (line 10), but children do their own things and make their own messes, so that they imprint their characteristics on the locations where they have been playing.

(3) The poem is unique in creating sentiment, without being sentimental, about a subject that very easily may go over the edge.

WRITING TOPICS. Images of childhood play. The poem's tone. The speaker: a parent or a detached observer?

WORKS FOR COMPARISON WITH "WHERE CHILDREN LIVE"

Frost, *Nothing Gold Can Stay*, 1111
Gilchrist, *Song of Songs*, 264
Schnackenberg, *Paperweight*, 1195
Whitman, *Full of Life Now*, 1216

WILLIAM SHAKESPEARE, *Sonnet 55: Not Marble,* *page 679*

This is one of the most memorable of Shakespeare's sonnets, treating the theme of how only art can confer eternal life upon human beings. The speaker addresses a loved one and determines that the poem itself is so strong an artifact that the listener will continue to live in it, "and dwell in lovers' eyes" (line 14).

Suggestions for Discussing the Study Questions, page 679

(1) The speaker addresses a listener who is deeply respected and loved. We do not learn much about the "you," except that the relationship with the speaker is a close one. The "you" and "your" pronoun referring to the unnamed listener occurs six times in the poem.

(2) The powers of destruction mentioned in the poem are "sluttish time," "wasteful war," "broils," "Mars his sword," "war's quick fire," "death," "all-oblivious enmity," and the collective forgetfulness of "all posterity." The speaker claims that his own poem ("powerful rhyme," line 2) will survive all destruction, because even though people, buildings, and institutions perish, the language will live on, and the poem is important enough to attract endless future interest.

(3) The "living record of your memory" of line 8 refers to the poem itself, Sonnet 55. The idea is that even though the listener is unknown to readers, the "living record" still exists and the listener also therefore exists.

(4) The subject of the poem is the impermanence of civilizations which may decay and which may be destroyed by war, as contrasted with the survival of a literate culture which may exist long after the lost civilizations in which it was produced. The theme of the

poem is that love, art, and things of the mind confer universality and longevity, while specifics may be lost.

WRITING TOPICS. The poem's use of images of destruction. The speaker's confidence in the durability of his poem. The character of the speaker.

WORKS FOR COMPARISON WITH "NOT MARBLE"

Hass, *Museum, 915*
Keats, *Ode on a Grecian Urn, 1018*
Shelley, *Ode to the West Wind, 877*
Wordsworth, *On the Extinction of the Venetian Republic, 1058*

Writing a Paraphrase of a Poem, *pages 679–81*

This section explains how to paraphrase poetry and to suggest some reasons why paraphrasing can be useful. In teaching paraphrasing, you might stress that a paraphrase is always reductive. Indeed, paraphrasing can heighten students' awareness of the skill with which the original poem has been put together. All the poems in the chapter are good candidates for an exercise in paraphrasing, and this skill will be useful as students continue to study poetry. The demonstrative paraphrase and the commentary (680–81) provide an example and a bit more guidance for students.

Writing an Explication of a Poem, *pages 681–85*

The explication essay is useful, particularly if it is assigned along with the paraphrase, because it highlights the general skills of reading. You might remind students that they can sharpen their analytical abilities as they progress in the course, and that they should therefore be able to write more extensive explications. However, even as they enlarge their knowledge and skill, they will always find it necessary to relate individual parts (which they may discuss at length) to the entirety of the poem. Interestingly, therefore, all the later assignments, circularly, should turn back to the explication essay, because this type always requires general understanding. The ultimate goal is wholeness of interpretation, and the explication will always have a part in this goal.

The demonstrative student essay (683–84) demonstrates an important aspect of explication; that is, the writer should select notable aspects of the poem, and stress these in the discussion. The essay treats what are seemingly the most important aspects of the poem, namely the speaker, the colloquial language, and the similarity of the speaker to the man he killed. In these ways, the writer of an explication deals with those elements that the poem itself invites the writer to consider.

Special Topics for Writing and Argument about the Nature of Poetry, *page 685*

(1) This subject can be as detailed as you wish students to make it. There are more than 400 poems in the text from which to select, on many separate subjects. Before beginning classroom study of poetry, it would be interesting to ask students about the topics they consider most suitable for poetry, and then, after you have considered poetry for a time, ask the same question. If students are able to suggest "additional subject matter," you may be able to refer them to already-existing poems that deal with it. In addition, you might ask students making such suggestions to try writing their own poems on the topics.

(2) The topic of compression is an interesting one. The poems suggested for illustration, "The Man He Killed" "Snow," "Catch," and "Stopping by Woods," all offer wide avenues of further development. The aim should be to have students expand on the poems, suggesting how much detail is crystallized or encapsulated by the poems, and speculating about how much inessential detail is left out. A prose poem, or extensive paraphrase, might bring out the compressed nature of poetry, particularly if students permit themselves to include many details about, say, fighting in World War I for Hardy's poem, the interests of the speaker in "Snow," about the possible responsibilities involving the rider of the sleigh in Frost's poem, or about playing catch and reading poems in Francis's poem.

(3) A common thread in the three war poems is the death of men in combat. Two of the poems treat death individually ("Ball Turret Gunner" and "The Man He Killed"). The third ("Ogichidag") treats the subject more distantly. Each poem is unique in that one is specifically about the man who is killed; the second is about the man who does the killing; and the third is about the general experience of going to war.

(4) The "creative-writing" poetry assignment is designed to get students to explore, at both first and second hands, the essential connection between speaker, attitude, and situation. The differing situations, involving differing presuppositions, will create entirely different poems. There are many later such assignments for students to write poems of their own. In these, and in this assignment, the

second half, in which students turn critics and analyze their own creative needs and responses, is most essential. To the degree that the students can reflect upon their own creative experiences, they will become more skilled as disciplined readers.

(5) This assignment is designed to connect the experience of poetry with the personal experience of students, and, in addition, to demonstrate the theoretical basis of reader-response readings. Of great importance, therefore, is the last sentence of the assignment: Students should use their own experience to get into the poem or poems, and should stress the poetry first and their experience second.

(6) This assignment should prove a happy one for many students, particularly if they can visualize a responsive child to whom they may present their descriptions. Some students enjoy creating a dialogue, or even a short scene, on the topic. The goal should be to enable students to state more than they think they know on the topic.

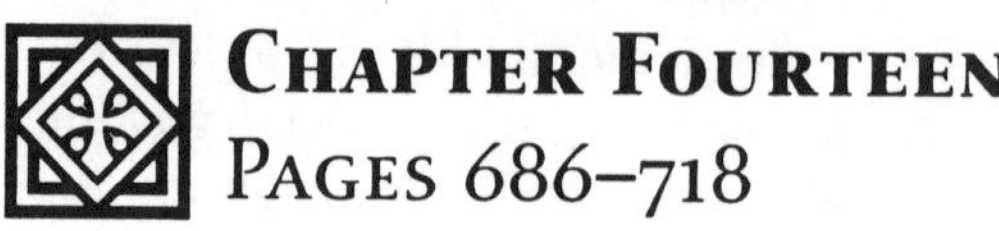

Chapter Fourteen
Pages 686–718

Character and Setting: Who, What, Where, and When in Poetry

This chapter demonstrates the importance and interrelationships of character, situation, and setting in poetry. Unlike fiction, poetry usually does not trace the growth of a character through all the interactions and changes that bring about roundness and development. Rather, in poetry, characters are at a crisis or climax, making a decision, reflecting about the past, or pointing in a new direction. Place and situation (*what, where, when*), then, are significant because of the bearing they have upon characters (*who, whom, whose*) at important moments and crossroads in their lives.

As a practical consideration, it is important to emphasize that there is a difference between the poet and the speaker; students have a strong tendency to conflate the two. Poems like "The Passionate Shepherd" (705) and "The Nymph's Reply" (707) are ideal to make the distinction, because Marlowe was certainly not a shepherd and Raleigh was not a nymph. Once students understand that the speaker of a poem is no less fictional and no less a character than the narrator of a short story, they will be better able to understand poetry and discuss it in class.

With regard to setting in poetry, students find it easy to describe the places, periods, and artifacts that are mentioned. Indeed, some may be able to provide actual sketches. It is harder to get them to recognize how character and attitude are shaped by the objective surroundings described in poems. You may therefore find it essential to emphasize that the setting is vital because the poet introduces it to clarify and develop the responses, attitudes, and thoughts of the various characters and listeners who people the lines of poetry.

Western Wind, When Will Thou Blow?, *page 687*

The speaker of this poem speaks about love and warm spring days (nurtured by the misty fertilizing spring rains), so that he and his love may celebrate their affection in his bed. The loved one is absent, and the weather is presumably still cold, but the speaker's yearning is strong and his hopes are high.

WRITING TOPICS. The situation of the speaker. The poem as a celebration of desire. The connection between season and love.

WORKS FOR COMPARISON WITH "WESTERN WIND"

Burns, *A Red, Red Rose*, 763
Frost, *A Line Storm Song*, 1106
Haines, *Little Cosmic Dust Poem*, 1156

***Bonny George Campbell**, page 688*

This poem illustrates the swiftness of narration and the inclusion of speech to be found in traditional ballads. The repetition (e.g., *toom home, Saddled, and bridled*) is one of the characteristics of the ballad form. Additionally, the poem focuses attention upon the reality of the permanent, unchangeable absence of the leader of the family. The version included here is assembled from the various states included in the Child collection of ballads.

Suggestions for Discussing the Study Questions, page 688

(1) The three characters in the poem are Campbell, his mother, and his wife. None is described in any detail. Although we may conclude that the family is well-off and perhaps noble, details do not seem to matter; the poem focuses only on the climax of a series of actions.

(2) Bonny George Campbell is clearly dead, having ridden away to an unspecified battle—probably a border skirmish. He has been killed, and his horse returns home without him. We may infer that his comrades, too, were also killed, because if they had survived they would have brought the corpse home. The ballad leaves us to imagine these events, first of all, because our discovery deepens our awareness and our involvement with the poem, and second, because the ballad is a short form, at its best when it touches the main details without superfluous explanations.

(3) The quotation marks indicate a speaker, most likely Campbell's wife, although some observers have suggested that the speaker may be Campbell's ghost (because of the unbuilt barn). If the wife is indeed the speaker, all her major supports of life are gone with Campbell's death.

WRITING TOPICS. The effect of the reader's emotional detachment. The riderless horse. The repetition of the "never came he" refrain.

Works for Comparison with "Bonny George Campbell"

Anonymous, *Sir Patrick Spens, 668*
Dickinson, *The Bustle in a House, 1068*
Dixon, *All Gone, 595*
Tennyson, *The Passing of Arthur, 880*

Ben Jonson, *Drink to Me, Only, with Thine Eyes,* *page 690*

This song is Jonson's most famous because of the lovely music to which it is sung. Those who have sung both stanzas, however, may be unaware of the wit and complexity of Jonson's handling of the dramatic situation.

Suggestions for Discussing the Study Questions, page 690

(1) The speaker is a young swain who demonstrates great wit because he shows the capacity for merging compliment with irony. He also shows a working familiarity with ancient mythology, and we may therefore conclude that his level of education is high.

(2) Before the poem the situation was this: The speaker had sent the lady a "rosy wreath" (line 9), which she sent back to him (line 14) in apparent rejection of his offer of love. He has decided to try again, and hence he is writing the poem to make the lady really take notice of him.

(3) The tone of the second stanza is particularly important. A strong case may be made that the speaker is demonstrating his ingenuity rather than simply complimenting his lady. He succeeds in complimenting her breath (stating that it is comparable to that of the rose), but he also qualifies his reasons for sending the wreath (line 10). It is clear that he wishes to draw attention to his own wit, but also to cause the lady to observe that he is persistent in his attention.

Writing topics. The situation of the poem. The tone of the second stanza. The nature of the speaker's compliments.

Works for Comparison with "Drink to Me, Only"

Donne, *A Valediction: Forbidding Mourning, 784*
Wakoski, *Inside Out, 798*
Waller, *Go, Lovely Rose, 1213*

Ben Jonson, *To the Reader,* *page 691*

The voice here is a persona that Jonson employs in much of his poetry: the positive-minded critic who tells his readers how his poems should be read.

MATTHEW ARNOLD, *Dover Beach*, *pages 693–94*

"Dover Beach" is Arnold's best-known poem, for many reasons, not the least of which is the powerful conclusion. Arnold perceived a loss of absolute religious faith in his time, and hence he stressed the need for an intensive search to recover absolutes—an indefinite time of searching, inquiry, and what he called "criticism." "Dover Beach" reflects the loss of faith, while at the same time it stresses the need for integrity.

Arnold's speaker is unnamed. He (most likely) is an educated, thoughtful person, fully attuned to the intellectual (and particularly the religious) currents of the time. The speech begins as a kind of soliloquy, but by the middle of the first stanza the speaker is addressing another person, someone dear enough to be called "love" in the last stanza.

Suggestions for Discussing the Study Questions, page 694

(1) Words used in establishing the setting include "sea," "moon," "straits," "cliffs of England," "window," "night," and "pebbles." The time is evening, the place a room overlooking the sea and the beach. Because the night is clear and moonlit, one can see all the way across the English Channel to the French coast. The reference to the withdrawal of the Sea of Faith places the poem in the mid-nineteenth century, when European Protestantism in particular was reeling under the combined effects of scientific developments and the application of new scholarly techniques and discoveries to Biblical texts and religious teachings.

(2) The speaker and the listener are in a room in Dover overlooking the English Channel directly across from France. They can see the sea and the cliffs, and also the moon-blanched land, and can also see a light on the French coast. They can hear the constantly pounding surf.

(3) The speaker's eye moves from distant (the sea and the French coast) to near (the English shore), and finally to the room and to the situation of the two persons in the room.

(4) To Sophocles, the speaker says, the Aegean was a reminder of the "ebb and flow / Of human misery" (rather like Wordsworth's "still, sad music of humanity" in the "Tintern Abbey" lines). By comparing Sophocles's thoughts to the present, the speaker suggests the timeless and inevitable unhappiness of the human condition.

(5) The faith that remains is personal fidelity, based on love between people. Nothing else is sure; the beauty, joy, and other

human experiences which we wish were certitudes—all these are illusory. The private world of the little room assumes the full weight of human life and freedom. Therefore, what remains is the commitment that individuals make to fidelity, and this commitment enables people to conquer all that is vulnerable and transient.

WRITING TOPICS. Structure and setting. The importance of location and philosophy on the speaker's thoughts about life. The pounding surf and the influence of its sound. The faith that remains amidst uncertainty.

WORKS FOR COMPARISON WITH "DOVER BEACH"

Frost, *Misgiving, 1111*
Frost, *The Silken Tent, 1112*
Williams (Joy), *Taking Care, 95*
Wordsworth, *Lines Composed a Few Miles above Tintern Abbey, 1044*
Zimmer, *The Day Zimmer Lost Religion, 1220*

WILLIAM BLAKE, *London*, *page 695*

Blake was distressed because he believed that the human spirit was being suppressed by custom and politics. His idea was that humanity could flower if institutions could be redirected or at even eliminated. The poem may be considered revolutionary because it stresses the need to correct the misery the speaker describes. Those who are degraded should be healthy and wholesome. By contrast, we are reminded of privilege, soldiers, and palaces, all of them aspects of oppressive authority. *Songs of Experience*, from which "London" is taken, was a collection of poems on this basic theme. Blake published the work in 1794 (the French Revolution was only five years old at the time) with his own engravings.

Suggestions for Discussing the Study Questions, page 695

(1) London represents a fallen world. Every person the speaker observes has been blighted or plagued, and the midnight streets heighten the darkness, misery, and danger.

(2) The speaker mentions cries, both of adults and children, public pronouncements, the cry of the Chimney Sweep, the sigh of the Soldier, and the curses of young prostitutes. These are sounds of sorrow, rage, poverty, and debasement; they symbolize the political degradation of human beings.

(3) *Chartered* suggests the privilege of those who can hire the river Thames itself for their use and whose lives contrast with the misery

of the poor. It also suggests that all of this is *charted* (i.e. mapped), and thus the city itself has violated natural beauty by creating artificial streets, and by consigning even the river to commerce and ownership. *Marks* in line 4 means permanent marring of people's faces by grief; in line 3 it simply means *observe.* In stanza four the reiteration of the *bl* sound gives each word emphasis, as does the position of this sound in stressed syllables.

(4) The poem purports to be based on the personal observation of the speaker, the "I" who has observed these abuses and horrors. Having made these observations, the speaker is qualified to speak from experience. The inclusion of the poem in *Songs of Experience* is therefore natural.

WRITING TOPICS. The use of actions and sounds as setting, The destructiveness of the political system on human character. The relationship of the setting to the mood of indignation.

WORKS FOR COMPARISON WITH "LONDON"

Halpern, *Summer in the Middle Class, 1157*
Sandburg, *Chicago, 1194*
William Carlos Williams, *Landscape with the Fall of Icarus, 990*

ROBERT BROWNING, *My Last Duchess,* *pages 695–97*

(*See the demonstrative student essay on pages 715–17.*) Although Browning did not invent the dramatic monologue, he specialized in it and made his poems in the form memorable. The Duke and his most recent Duchess are portrayed in the poem (discussed in the sample essay) as widely diverging characters. Students sometimes assert that the Duchess must have been guilty of something more than inappropriate smiles or blushes. They usually suspect infidelity. If this point arises, it can be an effective point of discussion, because it leads naturally to the characteristics of both Duchess and Duke.

WRITING TOPICS. The character of the Duke. The place of his wealth in his view of others. The symbolism of the works of art. The picture the poem leaves us of the Duchess: Could she have ever done anything right to satisfy the Duke?

WORKS FOR COMPARISON WITH "MY LAST DUCHESS"

Anonymous, *Lord Randal, 1121*
Eliot, *Eyes That Last I Saw in Tears, 786*
Steinbeck, *The Chrysanthemums, 447*

WILLIAM COWPER, *The Poplar Field,* *page 697*

In many respects this poem has a modern ring. The speaker meditates on the cutting of trees, or forests, that once gave shade, comfort, and visual beauty. We presume that the cutting was done in the name of progress and economy, although this motivation is not made clear. What is clear is that the trees, and the accompanying personal and aesthetic benefits, have been taken away.

Suggestions for Discussing the Study Questions, page 698

(1) The speaker is observant and meditative. The past twelve years, which have seen the loss of the trees, remind him of a future time in which he himself will be the subject of death, and also in which human beings will be gone, with all the "pleasures of man."

(2) The blackbird, a symbol of the beauteous sounds that the speaker once heard when near the poplar trees, has been displaced. The bird has not been destroyed, however, but has been forced to flee to a "retreat" where "hazels afford him a screen from the heat." The speaker obviously cares because of the loss of one aspect of natural beauty.

(3) The loss of the trees causes the speaker to meditate on "the perishing pleasures of man," including himself. As the trees are cut, so also will be cut the life of humanity.

WRITING TOPICS. The nature of the speaker. The importance of the passage of time in the poem. The awareness of ecology in the poem.

WORKS FOR COMPARISON WITH "THE POPLAR FIELD"

Frost, *The Oven Bird, 1110*
Ibsen, *An Enemy of the People, 1844*
Laurence, *Loons, 408*
Longfellow, *Song of the Sea, 867*
Wright, *A Blessing, 711*

LOUISE GLÜCK, *Snowdrops,* *page 698*

Students might find this poem initially quite difficult because of the fact that it does not provide specifics about why the speaker finds an identification with the coldness of snowdrops (snowflakes?). One way to treat this problem is to imagine that the listener knows all the details, and then to imagine that there is a great closeness with the speaker. The poem can then be seen as the concluding part of a more extensive private conversation, in which the speaker describes her conclusions and resolutions, despite her misgivings.

Suggestions for Discussing the Study Questions, page 698

(1, 2) With a remote echo of Thoreau's *Walden* ("how I lived"), the speaker describes her earlier condition impressionistically rather than graphically. We as readers are not privy to the specifics of the coldness of spirit the speaker describes. For understanding the poem, we need to know no more than that the coldness has existed. For this reason the reader is able to concentrate on the speaker's analogy of snowdrops with her feelings. Actual snowdrops are cold, and, according to the speaker, can make one understand despair because their life is so brief. Thus winter "should have meaning for you (the listener? also the reader?)," who, we may presume, understands or may even have experienced cold feelings of despair. If we move from snowdrops to the speaker, we are hearing the agonized speech of a person who has likened her existence to snow; life is brief like snow, and therefore the speaker "did not expect to survive, [. . .] to waken again." Because snow, when melted, however, creates new growth, the speaker states that she has resolved to face life, even though she is "afraid." But with the analogy of the creative power of snowdrops to strengthen her resolve, she is willing to "risk joy" even though there are raw winds in "the new world." There are no guarantees of joy or pleasure, but the attempt to live joyfully is a necessary goal, for even the cold of depression contains the possibility of fulfillment and satisfaction, and also the comfort of rejoining the "you" of the poem in friendship and communication.

(3) Many modern poems do not have capitalized first lines, and so one might say simply that the poem follows modern convention. More importantly, however, the lines in this poem do not have initial capitalization because of the confessional nature of the subject matter. We presume that the speaker is speaking not formally but confidentially, without the need for formal structures like capitalization and meter. The style, in other words, fits the subject.

WRITING TOPICS. What has the speaker resolved to do? Why? Who is the listener of the poem, the "you" of lines 1, 3, and 12?

WORKS FOR COMPARISON WITH "SNOWDROPS"

Henley, *Am I Blue, 1635*
Lawrence, *The Horse Dealer's Daughter, 500*
MacEwen, *Dark Pines Under Water, 1176*
Ridler, *Nothing Is Lost, 830*
Sarton, *The Phoenix Again, 993*
Shakespeare, *Sonnet 29: When in Disgrace with Fortune and Men's Eyes, 1198*

Thomas Gray, *Elegy Written in a Country Churchyard,* *pages 698–701*

Gray's "Elegy" is one of the major lyrics of the eighteenth century, and one of the representative poems of the "graveyard school" of poetry, a major theme of which was the need for living a sensible, good life in view of the inevitability of death. As a biographical note, you might point out that Gray himself was the only one of his parents' twelve children to grow to adulthood. A concern with death and how to take life is therefore not an unexpected aspect of his art.

Suggestions for Discussing the Study Questions, page 702

(1) The time of day of the poem is twilight. The cattle are heading back to the barn to be milked, the farmer is returning from the fields, the sun is setting, and the curfew bell is ringing from the church tower. For much of the poem, the speaker seems to be addressing no one in particular, but in line 37 he does address "ye proud," and in line 93 he seems to speak to a buried person (see question 4).

(2) The people buried in the church graveyard are humble, rural folk. Yet the speaker asserts that they are not contemptible because of their simplicity; instead he emphasizes their "useful toil" and "homely joys," pointing out that death is the great leveler, and that "the paths of glory lead but to the grave." Some of those buried here might have made great rulers, musicians, defenders of human rights, or poets. But the speaker balances the missed opportunities for good buried here by pointing out that the people never had the chance to do evil either. In short, the churchyard is the occasion of reflection on the need for goodness and piety, and the inevitability of death is cause for people to live their lives to their fullest potential.

(3) The setting (the rural landscape with its animal sounds, the churchyard and cemetery, the closing of day and the tolling of the bell) establishes immediately a mood of intensity, heightened by the approach of night with its overtones of dying. Times of passage and change (dawn, nightfall, festivals marking changes of season) are often viewed as moments when the natural and supernatural are most open to one another.

(4) The "thee" of line 93 is the author of the "frail memorial . . . erected high" which in unlettered fashion attempts to record and honor those buried here. He was the natural poet, a loner, lover of nature and its beauties, one not quite at home in life, perhaps "crazed with care, or crossed in hopeless love" (line 108). He too has died, and is buried here.

WRITING TOPICS. Time of day and the passage of time. The setting in the graveyard. The effect on life of the presence of death and the dead in cemeteries.

POEMS FOR COMPARISON WITH GRAY'S "ELEGY"

Dickinson, *Safe in Their Alabaster Chambers, 1075*
Donne, *Death Be Not Proud, 1145*
Pinsky, *Dying, 826*
Ransom, *Bells for John Whiteside's Daughter, 1189*
Thomas, *A Refusal to Mourn, 1209*

THOMAS HARDY, *The Ruined Maid*, *page 702*

"The Ruined Maid" represents Hardy's mastery, within a short compass, of deeply felt dramatic situations. His long experience as a novelist had sharpened his skill at perceiving human interactions, a capacity he also exhibits with great skill in, for example, "The Workbox" (814). In "The Ruined Maid," he captures the brazenness and vitality of the young woman who has been "ruined."

Suggestions for Discussing the Study Questions, page 703

(1) The relationship between the speaker and "'melia" (Amelia) has been long-standing, for the first speaker tells us in stanzas 2–5 about how poor and ordinary Amelia had been before she "left us" (line 5). It is clear that Amelia has been gone from the farming community for a considerable time, and that in the interval she has gone into keeping with a wealthy man. Hence she has been "ruined" by conventional social standards even though she is also now well dressed and prosperous. It would be unreasonable to assume that she is not bragging about her new life. We may presume that the first, unnamed, speaker has not heard anything about Amelia because the society in which both live is not literate and for this reason people are not informed about people who no longer are present and nearby.

(2) Amelia is aware of her situation of being "ruined" but she has easily come to terms with it because she is doing so well financially. She has not shed all her previous colloquialisms, as may be seen in her concluding sentence "You ain't ruined" (line 23).

(3) "Ruined" has the double meaning of (1) an actual ruined reputation, and (2) the benefits that come from an increase in financial circumstances. Hardy is not using the poem to attack conventional moral judgments, but he certainly is raising the issue of whether strict morality might have too great a cost, particularly in view of the descriptions in stanzas 4 and 5 of Amelia's ill condition, both

physically and psychologically, before leaving the farm. The poem is satirical, but not satire, and it does thumb its nose to strict morality.

WRITING TOPICS. Hardy's poetic use of dialogue. Amelia's condition before and after leaving the farm. Elements of satire and humor in the poem. The effect of the concluding lines.

WORKS FOR COMPARISON WITH "THE RUINED MAID"

Eliot, *Macavity, the Mystery Cat, 861*
Parker, *Résumé, 1184*
Stevens, *The Emperor of Ice Cream, 1206*
Whitecloud, *Blue Winds Dancing, 156*

THOMAS HARDY, *Channel Firing,* *pages 703–704*

Readers might expect a poem about warfare, written immediately before World War I and "spoken" by a skeleton, to be thoroughly depressing. Surprisingly, this poem is rather amusing until we stop and think about its implications; then it becomes depressing indeed. The references to the locations of Stourton Tower, Camelot, and Stonehenge expands the poem's time frame from the immediate present back through history (Stourton Tower) and legend (Camelot) to the dim past of prehistoric Britain (Stonehenge). Because these places are all gone, the implication is that our present civilization, too, may vanish if warfare continues and if red war continues to get redder.

Suggestions for Discussing the Study Questions, page 704

(1) The speaker is a skeleton who has been long buried in the local churchyard. The noise of guns, being fired out at sea in distant target practice, has awakened him, along with all the other skeletons in the cemetery. (This is a play on the idea that a noise can be so loud it would waken the dead.)

(2) The *your* of line 1 could refer to us, the listeners, who support the existence of armaments with our resources, or to the Naval Commanders who direct the guns. The "our" is all the dead in the church and churchyard coffins.

(3) The guns have awakened the speaker and his companions. The mistake—and the joke—is that the speaker thinks that Judgment Day has come.

(4) The other three voices are God, another skeleton, and Parson Thirdly. Their traits are revealed through the qualities of their individual speeches. God is scornful, ironic, and amused, but he nevertheless he is not without compassion. The other skeleton, unnamed, is disillusioned. Parson Thirdly is regretful about his life of

piety, and wishes he had enjoyed himself when he was alive rather than preaching for forty years.

(5) This question is a good one for both writing and discussion. Essentially, the poem suggests that humanity may be powerless to stop war, for human beings are indifferent to suffering and ignore those who try to do good. There is a restlessness or madness driving us to war, and we may not be able to stop this drive until we have "rest eternal" (line 24).

WRITING TOPICS. The dramatic situation. The vision of human character. The traits of God as presented by Hardy. The other corpses. The poem's structure. The effect of the concluding references.

WORKS FOR COMPARISON WITH "CHANNEL FIRING"

Eberhart, *Fury of Aerial Bombardment, 731*
Georgakas, *Hiroshima Crewman, 1154*
Nash, *Exit, Pursued by a Bear, 791*
Yeats, *The Second Coming, 961*

C. DAY LEWIS, *Song,* *pages 704–705*

Obviously, this poem is to be compared with the two poems by Marlowe (705) and Raleigh (707) elsewhere in the chapter. Marlowe was of course, followed by Raleigh and, later, by Lewis.

Suggestions for Discussing the Study Questions, page 705

(1, 2) Lewis's poem parodies Marlowe's "The Passionate Shepherd." It reflects the conditions of contemporary life, complete with poverty and pollution, thus being like Raleigh's "The Nymph's Reply" (707).

(3) The speaker—a man—invites the listener—a woman—to share the pleasures that "chance employment" might provide. The life that he offers is meager and uncertain, full of care, pain, toil, and hunger.

(4) Lewis's diction underscores the ironic uncertainty of modern life. Phrases like "dainties on the docks" and "a wreath of wrinkles" undercut the pastoral, Arcadian assumptions of Marlowe's poem. Instead of "having" summer frocks or "hearing" madrigals, as in Marlowe, Lewis's speaker offers only the chance to "read" about dresses and the "hope" to hear songs. The "chance employment" suggests the difficulty of modern persons who depend on wages which may be lost in a time of layoffs.

WRITING TOPICS. The view of modern life. Human relationships in the light of modern insecurities. The political implications of Lewis's poem.

WORKS FOR COMPARISON WITH LEWIS'S "SONG"

Dickinson, *I Cannot Live with You*, 1069
Keats, *La Belle Dame Sans Merci*, 954
Marlowe, *The Passionate Shepherd to His Love*, 705
Raleigh, *The Nymph's Reply to the Shepherd*, 707
Soto, *Oranges*, 1203

CHRISTOPHER MARLOWE, *The Passionate Shepherd to His Love*, *page 705*

This is an ideal poem for the speaker–listener relationship since both are named in the title.

Suggestions for Discussing the Study Questions, page 706

(1, 2) The title identifies the speaker as the "passionate shepherd" and the listener as "his love." The poem is a speech of persuasion in which the shepherd asks the lady to join him in love. Since the speaker is trying to persuade, we may assume that the lady has resisted his advances up to this point.

(3) The shepherd offers the lady a world of "valleys, groves, hills, and fields" where they can watch "shepherds feed their flocks" and listen to "melodious birds sing madrigals." In this Arcadian, ideal world, the young "dance and sing" each "May morning." The world being offered is therefore one of total "delights."

(4) In portraying the idealized world, the shepherd almost ignores the reality of everyday life. He does slip, however, when he mentions "cold" in line 15—his only acknowledgment that spring and May are not eternal.

WRITING TOPICS. The relationship of the shepherd and his lady. The shepherd's view of the natural and artificial world. The nature of reality/unreality in the poem.

WORKS FOR COMPARISON WITH "THE PASSIONATE SHEPHERD"

Raleigh (707) *and* Lewis (704)
Donne, *The Good Morrow*, 1144
Frost, *A Line Storm Song*, 1106
Lawrence, *The Horse Dealer's Daughter*, 500

MARGE PIERCY, *Wellfleet Sabbath*, *page 706*

Marge Piercy is well known as a novelist, and in addition to her many novels she has published a number collections of poetry. Three of her poems may be found elsewhere in the anthology ("The

Secretary Chant," "Will We Work Together?" and "A Work of Artifice" 1185, 1185, 792).

Suggestions for Discussing the Study Questions, page 706

(1, 2) While elsewhere one may note tones of irony or even anger, and also tentativeness, in Piercy's poems, here the dominant mood is one of satisfaction. Among words for the outdoors that suggest calm and serenity are "softly feathered," "sailing free," "purrs and rolls over," and "fresh clean night," for these indicate a metaphorical aura of benign Nature and domesticity. One need look no further than the fourth stanza for the same interior mood. Dinner candles flicker between the phlox (a bouquet) and the roast chicken, illumined also by shining red wine. The key word is "Shekinah" (see the note, page 706) suggesting that the divinity manifesting itself in the external world (of the summer day in Wellfleet) is also present in the internal world of the Sabbath where the presence of divinity is being celebrated.

(3) The speaker is apparently in a dining room, just before the Sabbath meal, and everything seems orderly and calm. No specific person is being addressed, and the reader is therefore invited to share the serenity of the moment. The original insights provided by the poet's metaphors (such as the water being gray like a dove, and the sky being barred like the sand after the tide is out) indicate that both speaker and reader may view life with wonder and love.

Writing topics. The poem's observations about the external and internal world. How does the poet achieve a reverential mood? The relationship of the mood to animals and objects like hawks, doves, sparrows, chicken, balloons, and cats.

Works for Comparison with "Wellfleet Sabbath"

Dickinson, *This World Is Not Conclusion, 1078*
Harjo, *Eagle Poem, 674*
O'Connor, *First Confession, 363*
Warren, *Heart of Autumn, 1214*

Al Purdy, *Poem*, *page 707*

Al Purdy's "Poem" is short and poignant, the offering of a brief speech to a dying person—summarizing the meaning of the relationship between the two, and stating the inevitable fact that whatever love people may have had in life, in death they must be forever alone. The poem shows a speaker of great strength and great tenderness.

Suggestions for Discussing the Study Questions, page 707

(1) In this dramatic monologue the speaker is at the bedside of a dearly loved one who is presumably dying. It is clear that the relationship is close, and has been long-lasting. Ultimately, the poem deals with the need for closeness, touch, and constancy.

(2) The speaker is healthy and is undertaking a vigil. He exhibits care, understanding, and patience. In addition he is reconciled to the fact that not only his loved one, but he and all people, must die—the "darknesses / to come later which all of us must endure alone" (lines 7–9).

WRITING TOPICS. The dramatic situation of the poem. The relationship of the speaker to the listener. The speaker's thoughts about approaching death: what can a well person do in the face of the inevitability of dying?

WORKS FOR COMPARISON WITH PURDY'S "POEM"

Dickinson, *This World Is Not Conclusion, 1078*
Dixon, *All Gone, 595*
Dryden, *To the Memory of Mr. Oldham, 911*
Justice, *On the Death of Friends in Childhood, 1018*
Joy Williams, *Taking Care, 95*

SIR WALTER RALEIGH, *The Nymph's Reply to the Shepherd, pages 707–708*

This poem was intended as a reply to Marlowe's poem, and students enjoy making the comparison. Marlowe's shepherd is passionate, supplicating, and sly; he knows that spring and youth do not last, but he avoids dwelling on this detail. Raleigh's nymph is honest, realistic, and cynical; she ruthlessly exposes the flaws in the shepherd's argument.

Suggestions for Discussing the Study Questions, page 708

(1) As in Marlowe's poem, the speaker and the listener are identified in the title. The speaker is the "nymph" pursued by the shepherd; the listener is the shepherd, although he may not wish to listen to the end. Raleigh's poem imitates the situation, rhythm, rhyming words, and stanza form of Marlowe's poem. Both offer six four-line stanzas, and rhyme on the word "love" at the beginning and end.

(2) The nymph's rejection of love is based on her realistic awareness of love and the world, as contrasted with the ideal and nonrealistic world portrayed by Marlowe's shepherd. Time consumes all; flowers fade; storms rage; the world is full of cares.

(3) A parody is an imitation of an artistic form for purposes of ridicule (either the form or the topic of the original). Because Raleigh uses the same form as Marlowe, and introduces many of the same details (but with an opposite view), the poem qualifies as a parody. In this respect, it is also a refutation of the unrealistic, head-in-the sand views of life that may do more harm to relationships than the more realistic view of the nymph.

(4) The nymph's refutation may be schematized in a logical pattern: 1. If A, then B. 2. Not A. 3. Therefore, not B. The 1 is "if the world were young, etc., then I would live with you" (brought out in stanza 1). The 2 is all the negative detail in stanzas 2–5. The 3 is the final stanza, in which she draws the conclusion of the previous stanzas. The world is not eternally young and pleasant, and therefore she rejects the shepherd; in fact, however, even if the world were perfect, she does not concede to the shepherd that he would be her choice ("my mind *might* move," line 24).

WRITING TOPICS. The speaker's argument, schematized and considered. The character of the speaker. The connection between the natural world and human activity. The dramatic situation of the poem.

WORKS FOR COMPARISON WITH "THE NYMPH'S REPLY"

Drayton, *Since There's No Help, 1048*
Queen Elizabeth I, *On Monsieur's Departure, 796*
Shakespeare, *My Mistress' Eyes, 767*
Wyatt, *I Find No Peace, 800*

CHRISTINA ROSSETTI, *A Christmas Carol,* *pages 708-709*

This poem is also one of the famous Christmas hymns, with music by Gustav Holst (1874–1934) whose best-known orchestral composition is *The Planets* (1914–1916). You may be fortunate enough to have students who know the tune of *A Christmas Carol* and who also have the bravery to sing it. Note that most hymnals that include "A Christmas Carol" omit the third stanza. Some hymnals, also, contain changes in the text written by modern editors.

Suggestions for Discussing the Study Questions, page 709

(1) The time is Christmas day, here shown as in the coldest depths of winter, the place allegedly Bethlehem. Yet Rossetti is describing an English winter (frozen ground, snow falls, ice stony hard, etc.). The bitterness and bleakness contrast with the warmth and glory of the event.

(2) The location—stable, manger, adoring Magi, shepherds, and animals—is part of the story of Jesus' birth as presented in the Biblical books of Matthew and Luke, and as legend has embroidered it. The simplicity is essential, theologically, to present the human vulnerability of the God/Man and yet to remind readers (most of whom, at least in Rossetti's day, would have known Christian teaching) that the person born in such poverty was the King of Kings.

(3) Both angels and the mother are present to love and honor the child (stanza 4). They stress human involvement in the event, and therefore prepare us for the speaker's own poverty and humanity in the final stanza.

(4) The speaker considers the gifts (gold, frankincense, myrrh, and, presumably, a lamb), which were offered by poor and rich alike. Being "poor," she opts for the gift of herself. Since the heart is both the traditional location of emotions and also the center of one's whole being, her gift is total; no one could offer more.

WRITING TOPICS. Winter and warmth. Historical and legendary scenes of the birth. The connection between the speaker's adoration and the scene she describes. The structure of the poem, leading to the climactic last line.

WORKS FOR COMPARISON WITH "A CHRISTMAS CAROL"

Crashaw, *On Our Crucified Lord,* 758
Donne, *A Hymn to God the Father,* 1145
Hopkins, *God's Grandeur,* 863
Wordsworth, *It Is a Beauteous Evening, Calm and Free,* 1058

JANE SHORE, *A Letter Sent to Summer,* *pages 709–710*

This poem could only have been written by a poet living in a temperate zone. It surely represents a mood that people experiencing winter have often felt. On certain cold, snowy, windy days, the yearning for summer occurs, even allowing for some of the summer's unpleasant aspects. "A Letter Sent to Summer" is notable for its negative as well as positive details about summer, and for this reason it avoids the excessive romanticizing often found in popular songs, such as "White Christmas" and "Autumn in New York," that extol the various seasons.

Suggestions for Discussing the Study Questions, page 710

(1) The speaker is obviously a creative person who evidences strong powers of observation. Line 14, for example, assumes that the "hapless rabbit" is hibernating and therefore also wishes the

summer to come so that "Desire" may "return." The speaker also evidences a sense of humor, as shown in the many inventive images (such as inviting summer to "wallpaper" her bedroom, and describing winter's snow as "buckets of whitewash").

(2) Summer, to the speaker, means a return of natural pleasantness, as shown in the friendly "baskets of flowers" that summer leaves, just "like an old friend." The bugs and monsoons, in addition to plums and the rose, show that the speaker's views are balanced, and that she recognizes summer's negative as well as positive aspects. Despite these, warm weather and summer provide the incentive for the speaker toward action, unlike winter, which causes her to "curl back into . . . [her] blizzard of linens" (line 19).

(3) The phrase "always snowing" suggests an admission that the speaker's moods correspond to the seasons. She admits to a permanent degree of lassitude or even depression (she says "it is always snowing" inside her head), particularly in winter, but that this feeling is lessened by the sights and flora of summer.

WRITING TOPICS. The positive and negative images of summer. The speaker's sense that summer is an antidote to negative moods. The various personifications of summer in the poem.

WORKS FOR COMPARISON WITH "A LETTER SENT TO SUMMER"

Berry, *Weeks of Deep Snow, 1126*
Keats, *To Autumn, 788*
Oliver, *Wild Geese, 957*
Shelley, *Ode to the West Wind, 877*

MAURA STANTON, *Childhood,* *pages 710–11*

This poem is based on a fancy that "all the world's turned upside down." The phrase is commonly applied to situations in which the unexpected and unusual happens. (When the British surrendered to American forces in 1783, for example, a band played "All the World's Turned Upside Down" to observe the occasion.) In the poem, the speaker assumes that gravity is somehow suspended and that therefore her world is governed by life on the ceiling. If one grants this fanciful supposition, what would the world down on the floor, where gravity applies, be like?

Suggestions for Discussing the Study Questions, page 711

(1) The first four lines describe a normal enough type of daydream in which the speaker admits to imagining that she could walk on the ceiling of her house all by herself. Perhaps not everyone

has had such a daydream, but most people have had, at one time or another, similar wild fancies that are fun to pursue to their logical extensions.

(2) The world as seen from the ceiling is accurate and well imagined. The lines "I liked to walk across the swirling plaster / Into the parts of the house I couldn't see" (lines 10–11), for example, are applicable to walkers in a house whether on the floor or on the ceiling. The rooms described from above (lines 13–17) contain the normal clutter of a house that is lived in by a normal family.

(3) Line 20 is a pivoting line that shifts the poem from its fanciful base toward a consideration of serious issues. In light of the title, the subject seems to be growth. As a child one accepts all the circumstances and situations of living in the family, but as one gets older, one becomes more distant and disconnected from childhood. If we accept such a proposition about the purpose of the final thirteen lines, the line "How do I ever get back to the real house" takes on a serious and almost plaintive tone.

(4) The speaker is obviously brilliant and imaginative. She is also expressing the concerns of a young person growing out of childhood, moving out of the confines of home, and trying to become established in life. A change in the line "I strive to look down" to "I strive to look back" clarifies the idea that the poem reflects a transition from childhood to adulthood. Of course, the line "I strive to look down" is infinitely better because it is so vibrantly consistent with the concept and imagery of the poem.

WRITING TOPICS. The meaning of living on the ceiling. The shift that line 20 brings about in the poem. The accuracy of life on the floor, as seen from the ceiling. The meaning of the title.

WORKS FOR COMPARISON WITH "CHILDHOOD"

Carver, *Neighbors, 63*
Collins, *Schoolsville, 663*
Frost, *Nothing Gold Can Stay, 1111*
Hall, *Scenic View, 1156*
Strand, *Eating Poetry, 740*
Olds, *35/10, 1024*

JAMES WRIGHT, *A Blessing,* *pages 711–12*

Wright's "A Blessing" demonstrates a flat, common portrayal of experience. The skill of the poem is its restraint in the rendering of action, and its sudden, climactic expansiveness at the end. In this respect "A Blessing" may be compared with Virginia Scott's "Snow" (939).

Suggestions for Discussing the Study Questions, page 712

(1) The two ponies have come out of the woods, as if to welcome the two representatives of another order of beings (the speaker and friend). The present tense gives the poem immediacy, so that the greeting appears to be happening before the speaker's eyes.

(2) The setting is specific: The event is located in place and time, moving from physical concreteness into the speaker's more intense but less easily described feelings of satisfaction and happiness.

(3) The realization which overtakes the speaker is that of the kinship, perhaps even the "oneness," of living things. Filled with love for the animals, the speaker delights in the feel of the pony. At that point the speaker realizes that, could he or she transcend the human body and its limitations, the true expression at the moment could only be a transformation into a burst of blossoms.

(4) The first 21 lines are essential because they allow the reader to share, verbally, the speaker's experience. The care with which the landscape is drawn, the description of events in the present tense, the shift from what the ponies do to how the speaker is responding—all this gives an immediacy which sets the stage for the speaker's concluding revelation.

WRITING TOPICS. The importance of the details about natural setting. The structure leading up to the last lines. The significance of twilight and darkness in connecting speaker, animals, and natural scene.

WORKS FOR COMPARISON WITH "A BLESSING"

Harjo, *Eagle Poem, 674*
Hopkins, *Pied Beauty, 1165*
Wordsworth, *My Heart Leaps Up, 1035*

Writing About Character and Setting in Poetry, *pages 712–17*

An essay stemming from this chapter should emphasize the interactions of character with time, place, and circumstance. Traits are not brought out over an extended time, as in fiction, but rather the immediate circumstances and traits merge to create attitudes or decisions. In Purdy's "Poem," for example, the life full of living together has already taken place between the speaker and the listener, and the speaker is now exhibiting loving traits combined with sorrowful perceptiveness about life's shortness and approaching death.

Similarly, the demonstrative student essay (715–17) illustrates the treatment of a character in the midst of a situation. The Duke's various traits are brought out because of what he tells us about his past, and his evil nature is clearly brought out in the way he is speaking to the envoy of the Count. It is the interactions of character and circumstance, in this way, that should be emphasized.

Special Topics for Writing and Argument about Character and Setting in Poetry, PAGES 717–18

(1) Topic 1 requires the comparison of three poems that fall together naturally because of authorial intention—a rare circumstance in the study of literature. Making the comparisons is in a great sense the attempt to show how the later poems follow Marlowe's original in form, detail, and development.

(2) The poems by Arnold, Blake, Cowper, Hardy, and Shore are, respectively, philosophical, political, ecological, and somewhat whimsical. They all center upon responses to change. Blake's, however, seems to point toward political changes. Arnold emphasizes how individuals should use the past in order to move into the future. Cowper treats a present change in the context of permanent change. Hardy demonstrates that adaptation can improve circumstances although some persons would consider the adaptation immoral. Shore deals with the subtle but nevertheless real connections between mood and circumstance.

(3) Students may express embarrassment about trying to create an autobiographical poem. For this reason they might be glad to resort to the anonymity of a using a third person, even if they themselves are still the subject. What is important here is that they use details about events and places as a means of developing the topic of character: qualities, responses, resolutions, and decisions.

(4) All four of the poems base their religious conclusions upon a concrete situation, from twilight near the water to ponies in a field. It is difficult to determine what students will conclude as a result of their analyses, but the connection between the reality of place and the vitality of religious experience should be stressed with all the poems.

(5) Students should be able to find a good many works about Browning. You might want to limit them to relating what they discover to a limited number of poems like, for example, "My Last Duchess," "The Bishop Orders His Tomb at St. Praxed's Church," "Porphyria's Lover," and "Soliloquy of a Spanish Cloister." Certainly the longer dramatic dialogues would be beyond the scope of this library and writing exercise.

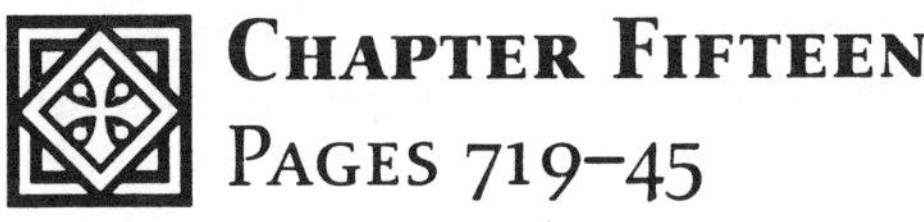

Chapter Fifteen
Pages 719–45

Words: The Building Blocks of Poetry

This chapter introduces students to the importance of individual words and of word order in poetry. In teaching the concepts, you can stress the relatively heavy load that each individual word must carry in a poem. In teaching denotation and connotation (725–28), you may want to call on your students to provide more examples of words that have acquired negative or positive connotations. The analysis of advertisements, both printed and dramatized on television, can be a gold mine for strongly connotative words.

The discussion of diction (719–24) may also be expanded in the classroom with a call for student examples. This can be especially effective with jargon and slang. A good illustrative field here is computer jargon, which is quickly moving into "mainstream" English. Jargon is especially important in discussing the poems by Reed and Eberhart.

In teaching syntax (724–25), your problem may well be how to stop. It is unlikely that many students will have thought much about syntax beyond their awareness of the differences between declarative and interrogative sentences. For examples, you might select the line "Yet morning smiles the busy race to cheer / And new-born pleasure brings to happier men" from Gray's "Sonnet on the Death of Richard West" (733), and ask students to lay it out in an order more in line with today's speech ("Yet morning smiles to cheer the busy race [of human beings] / And brings new-born pleasure to happier men"). The examples in the discussion about parallelism and repetition should be sufficient for establishing the relationship of syntax to rhetorical patterns.

Robert Graves, *The Naked and the Nude,* *pages 726–27*

This poem, discussed briefly on pages 727–28, dramatically shows the impact of denotation and connotation, not only on language and poetry, but also on human behavior. The first study question (727) invites the student to associate *naked* with its origin in Old English, and *nude,* with the elevation and tendency toward abstraction of many words that have come to our language from French and Latin. This point may be buttressed with the examination of English-Latinate pairs of words like *live* and *reside, hearty* and *cordial, will* and *testament, house* and *mansion, cow* and *beef,* and *think* and *ponder.*

WRITING TOPICS. Denotation and connotation in the poem. The importance of word selection in conveying the right meaning. The nature of the speaker.

WORKS FOR COMPARISON WITH "THE NAKED AND THE NUDE"

Keats, *Ode on a Grecian Urn, 1018*
MacLeish, *Ars Poetica, 676*
Strand, *Eating Poetry, 740*
Webb, *Poetics Against the Angel of Death, 929*

WILLIAM BLAKE, *The Lamb,* *page 728*

This poem is useful for discussing the effects of simple diction and repetition in creating tone and meaning. The childlike diction reinforces the simplicity of the speaker and the listener, and emphasizes through connotation the poem's portrayal of a Creator with loving and mild attributes. The first stanza asks the poem's central question four times: "who made thee?" The diction implies an answer; words like *lamb, delight, softest, wooly, tender,* and *rejoice* suggest a loving and cherishing creator. The second stanza answers the question, equating God with both the lamb and the child (lines 13–18). The English composer John Tavener has composed a fine *a capella* anthem to Blake's poem.

Suggestions for Discussing the Study Questions, page 729

(1) The speaker is a child and the listener a lamb (line 20); they are linked in their mildness, simplicity, and symbolic value as alternate images of the Creator (Jesus as a child and the Lamb of God, the *agnus dei*).

(2) The repetition (the rhetorical device *anaphora*) stresses the speaker's innocent, childlike qualities and makes the structure of the poem simple and clear.

(3) The diction is neutral and concrete, in keeping with the speaker's childlike character, and appropriate for the concept of a beneficent and peaceful God.

(4) The Creator, like the lamb and the child, is meek and mild, loving and gentle, simple and caring. The words all connote the most direct, least complicated view of God that is possible.

(5) Blake's idea of God in this poem from *The Songs of Innocence* is that God is a God of peace and love, not the God of Donne's "Batter My Heart" (731) who is an active warrior ready to break down the barriers that people erect through their spiritual impiety, negligence, and defiance.

WRITING TOPICS. The effect of diction and repetition in the poem. The image of the creator. The speaker's character. Good poems for comparison are listed immediately above in the discussion of Donne's "Batter my Heart."

WORKS FOR COMPARISON WITH "THE LAMB"

Frost, *Misgiving, 1111*
Herbert, *Virtue, 916*
Hopkins, *God's Grandeur, 863*
St. Luke, *The Parable of the Prodigal Son, 445*
Zimmer, *The Day Zimmer Lost Religion, 1220*

ROBERT BURNS, *Green Grow the Rashes, O,* *pages 729–30*

This poem is one of Burns's most famous. It is included here for this reason and also because of its use of dialect. With only a few side notes, students can recognize the words that otherwise might be obscure (such as *han'* and *war'ly*), and they can readily appreciate the relationship between the rhythmical lines and the content.

Suggestions for Discussing the Study Questions, page 730

(1) The speaker is an individual who is celebrating his love of women. He is unabashed in his pronouncements but there is no reason to take his remarks as anything but serious, despite his use of hyperbole in praising women.

(2) The speaker claims that he has spent his "sweetest hours" among "the lasses." He also seeks to corroborate his attitude by claiming that the "wisest man the war'l e'er saw" was also a person who "dearly loved the lasses." He is uncomplimentary toward sober people who might sneer at his pronouncements (lines 17–18).

(3) There are two Biblical versions of God's creation of humankind. In the first (Genesis 1:27), men and women are created simultaneously. In the second and more recognized version (Genesis 2:20–23), God fashions woman out of one of the man's ribs. Because of Burns's stanza 5, in which man is only the work of Nature's apprentice hand, with woman being the presumed product of Nature's master hand, it is likely that people in 1787 would have felt shocked if not outraged. One might also note that Burns's speaker attributes the creation of humankind not to God but to "Nature."

WRITING TOPICS. Burns's use of Scottish dialect. The speaker's reasons for praising women. The nature of the speaker.

WORKS FOR COMPARISON WITH "GREEN GROW THE RASHES, O"

Butler, *Snow*, 590
cummings, *she being Brand*, 819
Pastan, *The Suitor*, 981
Rückert, *If You Love for the Sake of Beauty*, 766
Rukeyser, *Looking at Each Other*, 794

LEWIS CARROLL, *Jabberwocky*, *pages 730–31*

This poem shows that we can understand poetry to some extent without knowing the meanings of all the words. Like Alice, we can get the drift without being able to pin down the exact meaning of any lines. To make the poem as clear as it is, Carroll depends on the suggestions that sounds create for meaning. More importantly, however, he uses key words to give us the essential idea (such as "Beware," "sword," "through and through," and "dead"), and he also scrupulously observes the proper syntax, so that we may construct meanings for some of the nonce words. Ironically, some words that Carroll made up for this poem have entered the language to such an extent that computerized spell-checkers do not flag them as misspelled.

Suggestions for Discussing the Study Questions, page 731

(1) The "tale" of this short, ballad-like poem is that an unnamed hero goes forth, defeats the monstrous Jabberwock, and returns home victorious.

(2) The unpacking exercise can work very well in class, especially if you ask the students to prepare something in writing beforehand. When you make the assignment, you might ask the students to consider how they can tell what part of speech (noun, verb, adjective) a specific word is supposed to be. The answer, of course, is that Carroll's syntax defines the role of each portmanteau word absolutely. Here are some of the more obvious unpackings you might offer as examples: *slithy* = slippery + slithering + lively + lithe; *toves* = toads + doves; *gimble* = gambol + nimble; *manxome* = maximum + noxious + fearsome; *galumphing* = galloping + lumbering + lump; *chortle* = chuckle + snort ("Chortle" has become a standard word.)

WRITING TOPICS. Why "Jabberwocky" works, despite the made-up words. How the ballad-narrative tradition helps us understand the poem.

WORKS FOR COMPARISON WITH "JABBERWOCKY"

Hall, *Scenic View*, 1156
Strand, *Eating Poetry*, 740
Swift, *A Riddle (The Vowels)*, 1207
Plath, *Metaphors*, 793

JOHN DONNE, *Holy Sonnet 14: Batter My Heart, Three-Personed God,* *pages 731–32*

This sonnet is a meditation on the speaker's sinfulness and his desire that God purify him. Of great interest are Donne's verbs of violence—the metaphor being that the speaker's soul is like a fortress, or a woman "betrothed" to another man; paradoxically, neither will be free and pure unless God defeats them. The central quatrains are based on traditional metaphors. In lines 5–8, the speaker compares himself to a town captured by evil forces, the governor (Reason) having failed to defend it for the king (*You*, God).

Suggestions for Discussing the Study Questions, page 732

(1) The "three-personed God" is the Trinity; the active verbs in the first quatrain suggest that God is a being with awesome, overwhelming power.

(2) *Knock* and *break* can be associated with God the Father, *breathe* and *blow* with the Holy Spirit (*spiritus* = spirit, breath, wind, blowing), and *shine* and *burn* with God the Son (the pun lurking here is the traditional play on *son* and *sun*).

(3) The effect of the altered word order is to throw emphasis on the *me* as the object of the verb *defend* and, similarly, to put *fain* into a position of stress so that the speaker may show that his will is to love God, but that his character is such that he is weak, and cannot follow his own will without the control of God.

(4) In lines 9–14 the speaker becomes the bride, Satan the *enemy* to whom the speaker is engaged, and Christ the bridegroom who must "break that knot again." The couplet states the clinching paradox; the speaker will never be *free* of sin unless God enthralls him and he will never be *chaste* (cleansed of sin) unless God ravishes him. *Enthrall* means both *enslave* and *captivate; ravish* means both *seize by force* and *fill with joy*. Spiritually, of course, both suggest their opposites; to be enthralled or ravished by God implies freedom from sin and absolute purity.

WRITING TOPICS. The way that the diction creates a specific image of God in this poem. The speaker's conceptualization of his own spiritual state. The use of sexual imagery.

WORKS FOR COMPARISON WITH "BATTER MY HEART"

Blake, *The Tyger*, 754
Herbert, *Love (III)*, 1162
Swenson, *Question*, 12007
Wordsworth, *My Heart Leaps Up*, 1035

RICHARD EBERHART, *The Fury of Aerial Bombardment*, *page* 732

Eberhart's poem, like Hardy's "Channel Firing" (703), uses the occasion of war to consider questions about God and humanity. In class, you might begin by asking your students to describe the differences they see between the first three stanzas and the last.

Suggestions for Discussing the Study Questions, pages 732-33

(1) The speaker, as we discover in the last stanza, is a military instructor ("late in school"); the "you" can be the reader, an unspecified person who might be present, or humanity in general.

(2) The diction of the first three stanzas is general and abstract. The speaker asks unanswerable questions: Why does humanity continue to wage war? Why doesn't God put a stop to it? Is humanity stupid? Is God indifferent? Is warfare the only "eternal truth"?

(3) In the last stanza, the speaker shifts to specific and concrete terms and names: *Van Wettering, Averill, list, lever, pawl.* He also shifts from abstract considerations ("infinite space," "eternal truth") to specific facts: the names of young soldiers who have "gone to early death" (notice the ironic contrast between the "*early* death" and "*late* in school"). This shift does not answer the earlier questions, but it does focus the poem and bring it to an effective conclusion. The jargon in this closing stanza works perfectly; it provides the concreteness of objects and weaponry even if we cannot identify the objects.

(4) Both poems bring out strong anti-war sentiments. Hardy vividly brings out the character of a scoffing, jesting God and also the disillusioned Parson Thirdly, while Eberhart does not develop any characters. Both poems raise the same questions, though Eberhart attributes war more to God than to humankind, unlike Hardy's attribution of war to nations striving to make "red war yet redder." A thorough comparison could become fairly extensive. One might also compare Reed's poem, "The Naming of Parts" (736) as another anti-war poem with a teacher-student similarity to "The Fury of Aerial Bombardment," but with a less ironic and bitter tone.

WRITING TOPICS. The tone of the last stanza. The view of God, and the questions about God. The view of humankind. The specific names.

WORKS FOR COMPARISON WITH
"THE FURY OF AERIAL BOMBARDMENT"

Crane, *Do Not Weep, Maiden*, 1137
Dickinson, *My Triumph Lasted Till the Drums*, 1074
Hardy, *Channel Firing*, 703
Seeger, *I Have a Rendezvous with Death*, 1196
Weigl, *Song of Napalm*, 1215

THOMAS GRAY, *Sonnet on the Death of Richard West*, *page 733*

This poem was Gray's poetic response to the death of his good friend, Richard West, in 1742. It is notable here primarily because Wordsworth used it as the basis for criticizing the diction of the previous age while defending his own concept of poetic diction. For today's students the poem is of interest because of the diction and also because of Gray's relatively unfamiliar syntax.

Suggestions for Discussing the Study Questions, page 733

(1) A good case can be made that the speaker's subject is himself. It is only in the thirteenth line that the subject ("him that cannot hear") is mentioned, but for the rest of the poem the speaker concentrates on his own responses and makes no effort to praise the dead friend.

(2) See the special discussion (723–24) for a discussion of the concept of decorum and poetic diction. Gray's phrases all have an element of accuracy about them, as with "redd'ning Phoebus," which refers to the ruddy appearance of the sun when it first rises. Certainly the phrases are not common, and their use keeps the references distant from the reader rather than immediate.

(3) The characteristic of these lines is that objects and modifiers are not placed in the order that students today are accustomed to seeing. Thus, line 6 may be inverted to read "These eyes do require a different object." Similar rearrangements may be carried out with the other lines. Students may ask why the poet has written such lines. The obvious answer, of course, is that Gray assumed that his audience had been schooled in Latin, and that the use of Latinate syntax in English elevated English to the level of Latin.

(4) The revolution in language that Wordsworth sought to carry out required that poetry should contain words that were to be middle, not high, and that they should be appropriate for both prose and poetry. By this standard many of Gray's lines fell short. The lines Wordsworth noted contain none of the elaborate phrases, such

as "smiling mornings," to which he objected. Students may want to debate the issues Wordsworth raised; likely they will agree with Wordsworth.

WRITING TOPICS. The meaning of many of Gray's phrases. The reasons for Wordsworth's objections. The topic of the poem.

WORKS FOR COMPARISON WITH "SONNET ON THE DEATH OF RICHARD WEST"

cummings, *Buffalo Bill's Defunct, 910*
Dryden, *To the Memory of Mr. Oldham, 911*
Robinson, *Richard Cory, 737*
Whitman, *Dirge for Two Veterans, 1217*

CAROLYN KIZER, *Night Sounds,* *page 734*

To portray the loneliness of failed love, the poem fuses images of the nightscape with the speaker's feelings. The central images are visual and auditory. The moonlight is cold, disturbing, and a "map of personal desolation." The night sounds (lines *2–6*: "voices," "weeping," "love-cries") stress the speaker's isolation. She alters the "history" of the relationship (lines *10–17*), seeking comfort in the lover's restlessness and abstraction, but the attempt fails in the memory of joyous sexuality (lines *18–19*). The speaker is left with the sounds of other "distant voices" and "a dog's hollow cadence."

Suggestions for Discussing the Study Questions, page 734

(1) The poem is confessional, with the speaker, a woman, baring her soul, expressing the terror that comes to her at night, and lamenting the loss of her love and the onset of loneliness, admitting that she is altering "our history" to justify the breakup by stating that her loved one, even when things were good, was always "withholding something."

(2) The "you" of the poem is the departed husband, or lover. The speaker closes with reminiscences of "lovely times" when *no* was met with affirmation. In the present time, however, she contrasts her fear with lost love, her cries with no answers, her silence with only distant voices.

(3) The words all suggest that the speaker's circumstances have changed, and that everything she now experiences is "tinged" with weeping and nightmares, terror or sentimental reliving of a better past.

(4) The use of participles indicates ongoing situations of the past and the present. The participles "coaxing," "withholding," "try-

ing," and "feigning" are all in the past, descriptive of the imperfections of the relationship. The participles "living" and "weeping" are participles of the speaker's present condition, both indicating the difficulties she is now experiencing.

WRITING TOPICS. The poem as a confession. The speaker's character. The relationship of the past to the present.

WORKS FOR COMPARISON WITH "NIGHT SOUNDS"

Atwood, *Variation on the Word Sleep, 1124*
Dickinson, *I Cannot Live with You, 1069*
Dixon, *All Gone, 595*
Rossetti, *Echo, 892*

MAXINE KUMIN, *Hello, Hello Henry, page 735*

This poem by the Pulitzer Prize winner is one of a series featuring the character of the speaker's country neighbor, Henry Manley. Henry is a person out of the past: individualistic, cantankerous, stubborn, slow to change, and generally representing the lifestyle of a vanished time. Kumin's poems about Henry contain a mood of mild amusement mingled with genuine respect and affection.

Suggestions for Discussing the Study Questions, page 735

(1, 2) The language is studiously specific. The result is that the poem seems to be about the real world, the outside one affected by world leaders like Stalin, Roosevelt, and Churchill (the "Big Three"), and the local one lived in by the likes of Henry, who slowly have been assimilating the artifacts and conveniences of the twentieth century. The implication is that the more real of the worlds is the one that ordinary people, like Henry and the speaker, inhabit. Because world politics are remote, and unreachable, a reasonable response is interest in the activities of real, ordinary folks.

(3) The speaker is unidentified (the authorial voice?), but is a reasonable, observant sort, whom we may presume to be a woman, also wishing for her own identity and space. The third stanza indicates her desire for privacy and individuality, and also suggests why she is friendly and sympathetic to Henry.

(4) The listener is apparently someone with whom the speaker has been involved. She has tried to sever her connection with him, but he still calls her and lets the phone ring all afternoon, an action which she regards as a "summons" (line 15). The listener's response indicates her strong wish to be herself and to be free.

WRITING TOPICS. Kumin's use of specific language. The nature of

Henry's character and circumstances. The meaning of the telephone to Henry and to the speaker.

WORKS FOR COMPARISON WITH "HELLO, HELLO HENRY"

Dickinson, *The Soul Selects Her Own Society*, 1076
Halpern, *Summer in the Middle Class*, 1157
Nemerov, *Life Cycle of Common Man*, 1179
Sexton, *To a Friend Whose Work Has Come to Triumph*, 989

DENISE LEVERTOV, *Of Being*, *page 736*

Levertov's diction in "Of Being" should occasion considerable classroom discussion. As the poem begins, we learn that the speaker is experiencing great satisfaction and "happiness," although we do not know why. As the poem develops we learn that the natural scene around her has occasioned the happiness. Students may wish to describe similar experiences of their own.

Suggestions for Discussing the Study Questions, page 736

(1) The speaker feels happy, but also knows that her happiness is temporary, dependent on good circumstances and a good mood. The change is inevitable, with the loss of mood and the imposition of difficulties. Hence, "this happiness / Is provisional."

(2) In a mood of happiness and satisfaction, the difficulties mentioned in lines 3 and 4 seem distant and unimportant (at least temporarily), even though they are still within the speaker's consciousness. We may assume that the verbal noun "Being" in the title takes into account both good and bad circumstances. Life is neither all good nor all bad; it is a mixture of both.

(3) "Peripheral vision" refers to the nature of the speaker's consciousness, in which apparently pressing problems become less pressing, just as when we focus on an object in front of us, other objects beside us, though present, are not of immediate concern. "Ineluctable" refers to the elements introduced in lines 7–12; under the right circumstances they force themselves to become major parts of the speaker's concerns. The "blue leaves," "flood of stillness," and "lake of sky" are all examples of synesthesia (i.e., leaves are green; stillness does not rush about like a flood; lakes contain water, not the sky). They seem true within the speaker's reflections on the scene around her, and their merging together seems part of the great "mystery" of existence. Under the mystical mood described by the speaker, everything in the natural world, and also in her immediate sphere of activity, is one–a blending of the earth and sky. (We may

take "dance" as symbolic of human activity, "kneel" as symbolic of worshipful activity.)

(4) The colon implies that more is to come, that life continues even though it is a mystery that human beings cannot comprehend. A period would indicate more definiteness than the poet intends in the poem.

WRITING TOPICS. Levertov's diction: concrete or abstract? The poem's use of synesthesia. What does "provisional" mean within the poem?

WORKS FOR COMPARISON WITH "OF BEING"

Anonymous (Navajo), *Healing Prayer, 1120*
Twichell, *Blurry Cow, 1209*
Updike, *On the Way to Delphi, 995*
Wordsworth, *My Heart Leaps Up, 1035*

HENRY REED, *Naming of Parts,* *pages 736-37*

Reed's ironic anti-war poem, which balances the parts of a weapon against an altogether different set of parts in nature, works well in class. The two sets of parts named in the poem are pieces of a weapon and objects in nature, such as the Japonica, the branches, blossoms, and the early bees. In addition, an overtone in the speaker's meditations is that he is also thinking about the parts of a woman. The ideas explored here are neither profound nor cosmic; the poem suggests that young men in spring would prefer to follow their natural instincts rather than listen to boring military lectures. Some students may not immediately perceive the poem's ambiguity. The contrast between the lecture and the out-of-doors is fairly easily understood, but the application to lovemaking may not be perceived quite as readily.

Suggestions for Discussing the Study Questions, page 737

(1) The two voices that we hear in the poem are the instructor's lecture and the recruit's musings about nature and the garden. Ask your students to establish exactly when (or where) one voice stops and the other begins in each stanza.

(2) The setting is apparently a lecture room in which recruits are attending a weapons lecture as a part of their basic training. A group leader is likely standing in front of a drawing which lays out the parts of a rifle, which he is explaining. He does not, however, have an actual gun as his example, and things are dull. It is a lovely spring day, there are nearby gardens, and one thoroughly bored

recruit's mind keeps slipping away from the lecture to consider the burgeoning fertility of the spring.

(3, 4) The recruit "slides" one set of words into another in his mind as he picks up words and phrases from the lecture and applies them to the garden and also to himself in the sense of sexual activity. Phrases like "easing the spring," "point of balance," and "rapidly backwards and forwards" do not require an exhaustive explanation to determine that they may refer equally to the operations of firearms and sexual parts.

WRITING TOPICS. Ambiguity in the poem. The setting. The tone, particularly about war and also about young people. The organization.

WORKS FOR COMPARISON WITH "NAMING OF PARTS"

Atwood, *Rape Fantasies, 387*
cummings, *she being Brand / -new, 819*
Herrick, *Upon Julia's Voice, 863*
Wakoski, *Inside Out, 798*

EDWIN ARLINGTON ROBINSON, *Richard Cory,* *pages 737–38*

This poem contrasts what seems with what is, and it reaches a powerful climax in the final line. Students may be interested in being reminded (or being told) that Paul Simon made a musical adaptation of "Richard Cory" in 1966 (compiled in Simon & Garfunkel's *Collected Works,* Columbia, C3K 45322).

Suggestions for Discussing the Study Questions, page 738

(1) All these words are used in plain, everyday activities of location and eating, and they therefore locate the speaker and fellow admirers of Richard Cory as ordinary people whose lives never seem to rise to any high level of achievement.

(2) Richard Cory may echo "Richard Coeur de Lion," the noble English king of the middle ages. Also, *Richard* suggests riches and accomplishments. *Gentleman* is a word suggesting high, noble birth and elegant manners and accomplishments.

(3) The word choices of "sole to crown" and "imperially slim" put Cory into an elevated class, whereas the contrasting phrases would be appropriate for ordinary persons.

(4) The repetition of *And* at the beginning of six of the lines keeps the poem moving rapidly, driving us on from line to line, and suggests that all Richard Cory's qualities are connected.

(5) The positive characteristics were his physical appearance,

manner of dress, gentle speech, and the ability to speak directly to people while maintaining his power to impress them.

WRITING TOPICS. The characterization of the speaker. Contrasts between appearance and reality.

WORKS FOR COMPARISON WITH "RICHARD CORY"

Bishop, *One Art, 909*
Dickinson, *One Need Not Be a Chamber, 1075*
Frost, *Acquainted with the Night, 1111*
Lee, *A Final Thing, 1170*
Updike, *Perfection Wasted, 993*

THEODORE ROETHKE, *Dolor,* *page 738*

In this poem, Roethke combines general and abstract words for sadness or grief with concrete and specific words that describe the details of day-to-day life in the offices or institutions of the modern world, in this way asserting that lives lived in such places are empty and unhappy. In a discussion of the poem, it is useful to let your students separate the two classes of words and let them see that the specific-concrete terms define and focus the general-abstract ones.

Suggestions for Discussing the Study Questions, page 738

(1) "Dolor" refers to pain, suffering, and grief. Words generally related are *sadness, misery, desolation,* and *pathos.* The details objectifying the word are made objective through a linkage with concrete and specific words and images, such as *pencils, pad, paper-weight, dust, nails,* and *pale hour.* The linkage is done with the object and an aspect of dolor. *Misery,* for example, is linked to "manila folders and mucilage," just as *sadness* is associated with "pencils." One may compare this aspect of the poem with Eliot's detail in "The Love Song of J. Alfred Prufrock" about measuring out one's life in coffee spoons (1147). A contrast might be Billy Collins's "Schoolsville" (663), particularly the detail about chalk dust (line 5).

(2) The poem resembles a sonnet although it is not rhymed and is not molded into any dominant rhythmical pattern. Unity is achieved through rhythmical cadence groups and alliteration (e.g., *misery of manila ... mucilage*). The most notable break with the sonnet form is that there are thirteen lines rather than fourteen. One might claim that thirteen, often considered an unlucky number, is appropriate for the poem's ideas and tone.

(3) Although the poem is not specific about the institutions characterized by dolor, we may assume that Roethke is referring to places

such as business offices, reception rooms, administrative offices, schools, and anywhere else where business is carried out and where files are kept. All such places have in common a certain sameness in which procedure takes precedence over life and spontaneity.

(4) For a discussion of this question, see page 724 in the text.

WRITING TOPICS. Specific–general and concrete–abstract words. The meaning of dolor. The tone of the poem. The structure.

WORKS FOR COMPARISON WITH "DOLOR"

Eliot, *The Love Song of J. Alfred Prufrock,* 1147
Collins, *Schoolsville,* 663
Piercy, *The Secretary Chant,* 1185

STEPHEN SPENDER, *I Think Continually of Those Who Were Truly Great,* 739

This poem is the subject of the demonstrative student essay on pages 742–44, in which the questions are addressed.

WRITING TOPICS. The use of abstract words in the poem. The definition of what it means to be "truly" great. The poem's tone. Its organization.

WORKS FOR COMPARISON WITH "I THINK CONTINUALLY"

Birney, *Can. Lit.,* 1126
Keats, *On First Looking into Chapman's Homer,* 777
Larkin, *Next, Please,* 1021
Williams (Joy), *Taking Care,* 95

WALLACE STEVENS, *Disillusionment of Ten O'Clock,* *pages* 739–40

The poem contrasts the colorless lives and imaginations of the townspeople of an unidentified town (the white nightgowns) with the vivid and exotic life and imagination of the drunken sailor. In teaching the poem, you might begin by discussing this contrast.

Suggestions for Discussing the Study Questions, page 740

(1) The time of the poem is evening, as indicated by *nightgown* and *dream.*

(2) Stevens's strategy in lines 3–11 is negative; he tells us that the townspeople *do not* have the experience or imagination to dream of anything beyond their own average lives, nor do they have the flair to wear anything green, purple, yellow, multi-colored, or ringed; instead, they wear only their white nightgowns.

(3) The people in the sleeping town are contrasted in lines 12–15 with the "old sailor" who has what the townspeople lack: the extensive experience which has supplied his imagination with some of the wonders contained in the world, so that his dreams are rich even though he is old.

(4, 5) All the vivid colors, bizarre images, lace socks, beaded ceintures, baboons and periwinkles disassociated from the townspeople in these lines are ultimately linked to the old drunken sailor who dreams of catching tigers in *red weather*. The lace and beaded ceintures suggest finery (wealth, a sense of fine living, exotic foreign places, different ways of life, a different mentality, and a broad outlook on the world). The baboons hint at distant ports and jungles, and the periwinkles evoke the sea.

(6) The disillusionment of the title may refer to the absence of illusions (dreams, imagination) or to the poet's revelation that the people in white nightgowns lack any imaginative life.

WRITING TOPICS. The dominant tone of the poem. The contrast between the people in white nightgowns and the drunken sailor. Stevens's use of color and connotative words.

WORKS FOR COMPARISON WITH "DISILLUSIONMENT OF TEN O'CLOCK"

Lightman, *In Computers, 1171*
McHugh, *Lines, 1177*
Shelley, *Ozymandias, 925*
C. K. Williams, *Dimensions, 834*

MARK STRAND, *Eating Poetry,* *page 740*

Usually writers indicate the acquisition of learning and poetry by referring to difficult and tiring actions like "burning the midnight oil" and "hitting the books." "Eating Poetry" is unique, however, because it emphasizes the pleasure and joy of learning. Indeed, the poem is an intellectual romp, just like the dogs coming up the stairs (line 9) to devour more poems. Poetic allusion in the poem may be seen in the phrase "eyeballs roll," an overstatement to indicate the throes of passion which is used by Pope in "Eloisa to Abelard." In addition, the phrase "bookish dark" (line 18) recalls Frost's "pillared dark" in the poem "Come In." In Frost, the pillared dark is like an invitation to come in and change the speaker's life. Here Strand uses the phrase similarly, for the "bookish dark" has effected such a change in the ebullient speaker.

Suggestions for Discussing the Study Questions, page 741

(1) Obvious indications that the poem is not to be taken literally are the ink running from the corners of the speaker's mouth and the eating of poetry. The image developed in the poem is that the speaker has been emptying the shelves of books in the way dogs would empty shelves of dog food.

(2) The serious topic undergirding the poem is suggested by line 2, "There is no happiness like mine," and line 16, "I am a new man." These lines clearly suggest that learning is accompanied with joy.

(3) With the exceptions noted in question 2, almost all the words indicate the comic topic. The sad eyes, the poems being gone, the rolling eyeballs, the stamping of the librarian's feet, the licking of the hand, the screaming–all are clearly a part of the poem's comic scene.

WRITING TOPICS. What does it mean to be "eating poetry"? The contrast between the poem's comic mode and its serious intent.

WORKS FOR COMPARISON WITH "EATING POETRY"

Bradstreet, *The Author to Her Book, 818*
Keats, *On First Looking into Chapman's Homer, 777*
Levine, *Theory of Prosody, 866*
Moore, *How to Become a Writer, 274*
Nash, *Very Like a Whale, 868*

Writing About Diction and Syntax in Poetry, *pages 741-45*

This assignment might prove difficult for those students who are not used to thinking about words and the possibilities of various shades of meaning among them. The material here should help solve at least part of the problem. The opening discussion considers ways to begin this sort of investigation, to discover ideas, and to formulate a central idea for an essay. In preparing your students to write an essay about words, you might wish to take them through the investigative and thesis-formation processes in class, using the model of a specific poem. You could then have them write about that poem or any other in the text. The demonstrative essay on "I Think Continually" (742–44) illustrates many of the principles and processes discussed in the chapter. These are highlighted once again in the commentary on the essay (744–45).

Special Topics for Writing and Arguement about the Words of Poetry, *page 745*

(1) This topic, requiring the analysis of four separate poems, can be difficult unless the students can lay out their materials so that they can see them at a glance. For this, separate sets of cards, or separate columns, are necessary. Ask students to study Chapter 35, on the Extended Comparison-Contrast Essay (1979), for ideas about how to develop their essays without making their papers too long.

(2) The key to understanding the portmanteau words in "Jabberwocky" is that Carroll puts everything in normal syntactic order. There are enough words from our normal word stock to make the made-up words meaningful. The suggestions for discussing "Jabberwocky" in this manual should help students discuss the sounds of the new words.

(3) Some subjects for topic 2 are discussed here at the Suggestions for Discussion about "Richard Cory" (739). A more extensive and systematic comparison and contrast (Chapter 35) would be necessary for a full essay.

(4) Using all four poems might create a long essay set out in four parts. It might therefore be better to ask students to analyze just one of these poems, or perhaps two in a comparison-contrast essay.

(5) To write the short poems suggested in the third writing topic, students will need to exert their imaginations energetically. Yet today, with all the television and film fare analyzing crime from the standpoint of criminals, they may have precedents for seeing things in that way. What is important is that they are able to explain why different choices of words, both favorable and unfavorable, stem naturally out of the differences in approach to the particular "crime" they write about.

(6) There should be little difficulty in finding library books about either Robinson or Carroll. You may wish to anticipate your students, if you make this assignment, by placing some of the materials on reserve. Because students have likely not discussed poetic diction as such, in the past, it is important that they be careful in using quotation marks and in crediting their sources properly.

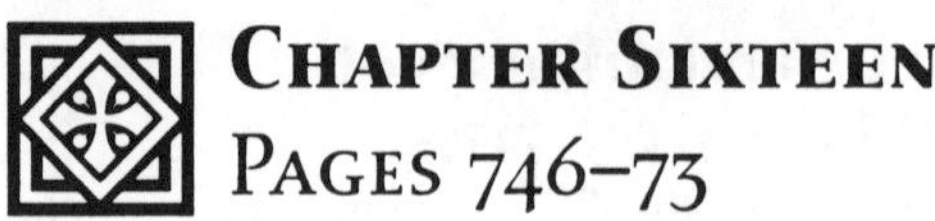

Chapter Sixteen
Pages 746–73

Imagery: The Poem's Link to the Senses

This introductory section acquaints students with the various types of images—visual, auditory, olfactory, gustatory, tactile, kinetic, and kinesthetic—all of which account for the appeal and validity of poetry. Real images in a poem lend reality to the poem's assertions. The logic of understanding imagery is this: Readers have seen many of the same things that poets describe (sun, moon, stars, ocean), and have also perceived many similar things (roses, boats, fish, sweethearts, boats, singers, songs, jewels, hair, and so on). Therefore, references to these things create a bond of perception authenticating the presuppositions, responses, attitudes, thoughts, and ideas of poetry. The use of the black-and-white reproduction of the Herkomer painting (748), which was exhibited in Washington's National Gallery in the Spring of 1997, may help as a visual demonstration of the relationship between the viewer-reader and the artist-poet's depictions of the world.

John Masefield, *Cargoes*, *pages 748–49*

"Cargoes" is a fascinating image-picture, analogous to a triptych in art, in which things are almost graphically rendered in poetry. Students respond readily to the language. Indeed, the poem's great value is that its diction, being so real itself, leads naturally into a general discussion of degrees of reality as represented by language.

Suggestions for Discussing the Study Questions, page 749

(1) Stanza 1 provides images which are exotic and splendid. They represent color and oriental grandeur, as well as the values of a world now long gone. All the objects are appropriate to Solomon's time, whether as gifts to amuse the court or as building materials. They evoke the nostalgia with which we view this lost world. Stanza 2 and its images are closer to our world. Stanza 3 shows us what it has all been for—so that a dirty coastal ship can carry fuel and

cheap products for sale in the modern world. Gone are the splendor, the color, and the beauty; utility and trade are all.

(2) The images are mainly visual. Almost all suggest colors and textures, though some also suggest aromas (*cedarwood, cinnamon*) and some suggest smells (*smoke stack, coal*). The blazing colors of stanza 2 are preceded by somewhat less color in stanza 1 and followed abruptly by an almost unrelieved gray-brown-black palette of color in stanza 3. There is little stress on auditory images, except that one may imagine the apes chattering and the peacocks calling.

(3) The use of the participles intensifies the impression that the poem is a word, or image, picture. It is not a description of action but a verbal rendering, almost like a painting of ships. *Rowing* suggests human action, and one visualizes the unified motions of men and oars; *dipping* suggests flight, like that of a bird; *butting* suggests struggle, and the determined action of a stubborn and tough animal like a mule or a goat.

(4) The supposition is possibly accurate, but Masefield obscures that line of thought by his choice of verbals and word pictures.

WRITING TOPICS. Masefield's images of sight. The relationship of image to mood. The allusiveness of the imagery.

WORKS FOR COMPARISON WITH "CARGOES"

Lightman, *In Computers, 1171*
Nemerov, *Life Cycle of Common Man, 1078*
Page, *Photos of a Salt Mine, 764*
Pound, *In a Station of the Metro, 766*
Stevens, *Disillusionment of Ten O'Clock, 739*

WILFRED OWEN, *Anthem for Doomed Youth, page 750*

Wilfred Owen was killed in France in 1918, a week before the Armistice that ended World War I. Today he is considered one of the foremost anti-war poets. Benjamin Britten set "What Passing Bells" for tenor and orchestra in his 1962 *War Requiem*. The band "10,000 Maniacs" recorded a version of this work, along with *Dulce et Decorum Est*, on *Hope Chest* (Elektra 9-60962-2).

Suggestions for Discussing the Study Questions, page 750

(1) The predominant images in the octave are those of sound. Lines 1, 4, 5, 6, and 8 refer to sounds of peace, while 2, 3, and 7 ironically displace these peaceful sounds with sounds of war. Thus the "passing-bells" are not bells but gunfire, and the prayers ("orisons") are made up of rapidly rattling rifles. In line 8, the sound of bugles

from "sad shires" suggests the solemnity of military burials. In the last six lines the images are primarily visual—held candles, shining eyes, pale brows, flowers, and the repeated drawing of window shades. It is as though a cease-fire calm had descended.

(2) The contrast and tone are set in the first line, where the image of the death of cattle stands for the death of men in combat. The image suggests that the men are not valued as human beings. Similarly, the metaphorical comparisons of rifle fire to prayers, and the wailing of shells to the sounds of demented choirs, underline the monstrous lack of dignity with which these men died.

(3) There is a progression of images in the poem, all having to do with those who are left behind—family, sweethearts, parents. The "holy glimmers of good-byes" suggests how light from altar candles shines in the tear-filled eyes of those who mourn. The grief of sweethearts is suggested by the "pallor of girls' brows." The consolations of philosophy and the privacy of grief are brought out by the "tenderness of patient minds" and the "drawing-down of blinds." All the images share in depicting the unutterable grief of those whose loved ones are now dead.

WRITING TOPICS. The auditory images. Images conducive to sorrow. The use of irony or ironic reversal in the images.

WORKS FOR COMPARISON WITH "ANTHEM FOR DOOMED YOUTH"

Jarrell, *The Death of the Ball Turret Gunner, 676*
Northrup, *Ogichidag 677*
O'Brien, *The Things They Carried, 77*
Owen, *Dulce et Decorum Est, 810*
Seeger, *I have a Rendezvous with Death, 1196*
Zabytko, *Home Soil, 511*

ELIZABETH BISHOP, *The Fish,* *pages 751–53*

With its stress on vivid details and flat, scrupulously plain diction, "The Fish" has been a particular favorite among lovers of Nature and the environment. It was so often requested for anthologies that by the early 1970s Bishop did not grant permission for it to be printed, on the grounds that she wanted readers to learn the wider range of her poetry.

Suggestions for Discussing the Study Questions, page 753

(1) The actions imaged in the poem are (a) the catching of the fish and holding him out of the water by the speaker, (b) the fish's absolute passivity (line 7), (c) the movement of his gills as he breathes,

(d) the speaker's careful observation of this trophy, (e) the fish's tiny eye movements, (f) the expansion of the speaker's sense of triumph, (g) the development of the rainbow colors in the boat, and (h) the release of the fish. The images are both ordinary and unusual, since it is the internal motion (the growth of the sense of victory) which pulls the reader into the poem's movement and excitement.

(2) The fish is very ugly. It is described in such detail to give us a sense of its identity and therefore its value.

(3) The fish has been caught before and has, on five previous occasions, broken the line and gotten away. It is a fish of almost legendary prowess in the battle with its human enemies.

(4) The rainbow is a floating oil stain, but to the speaker it represents the shimmering excitement of victory.

(5) The action is abrupt, but in the light of the fish's unusual passivity (a fish hooked and pulled out of water fights and wiggles desperately) and its almost Olympian refusal to meet its captor's eye, release is the only appropriate act. Letting the fish go signifies both the speaker's respect for this old fighter and the speaker's realization that to have caught the fish is victory and achievement enough.

WRITING TOPICS. The fish and the rainbow as symbols. The kinesthetic images. Images of endurance and indomitability.

WORKS FOR COMPARISON WITH "THE FISH"

Evans, *The Iceberg Seven-eighths Under,* 786
Momaday, *The Bear,* 1179
Stern, *Burying an Animal on the Way to New York,* 1206
Whitecloud, *Blue Winds Dancing,* 156
Wright, *A Blessing,* 711

WILLIAM BLAKE, *The Tyger,* *pages* 754–55

"The Tyger" is one of Blake's best-known poems, to be contrasted with "The Lamb" (728). The large predator as a symbol of evil is readily understood; our tradition abounds with fearsome images of wolves, foxes, bears, and so on. Some students today, newly enlightened and firmly aware of the ecological need for the preservation of the predator-prey relationship and also of the endangered state of the world's predators, regret Blake's choice. In all other respects, however, Blake's poem is timely.

Suggestions for Discussing the Study Questions, 755

(1) *Burning* suggests heat, brightness, danger, and the capacity to spread and engulf all. The fire is bright at night and, like everything

else, seems more dangerous then. That night has "forests" makes it all the more wild and dangerous.

(2) Creation is a kinesthetic image; other such images include burning, flying, seizing, twisting, hammering, and grasping. These images, including that of the blacksmith, suggest powerful muscularity.

(3) The question posed in the poem is whether God is the source of both good (the lamb) and evil (the tyger) in the world, and the poem therefore raises the issue of how an allegedly all-powerful and beneficent creator permits evil at all.

(4) The word "could" suggests the simple ability to do something, while the word "dare" implies a willingness to accept a challenge to perform an action without a primary concern about the outcome.

WRITING TOPICS. The meaning the tyger and the lamb. The kinesthetic imagery of creativity. Darkness and night as images.

WORKS FOR COMPARISON WITH "THE TYGER"

Dickinson, *To Hear an Oriole Sing,* 859
Laurence, *The Loons,* 408
Oliver, *Ghosts,* 1182
Tennyson, *The Eagle,* 899

ELIZABETH BARRETT BROWNING, *Sonnets from the Portuguese,* No. 14, *pages* 755–56

"If Thou Must Love Me" is to be compared with Rückert's "If You Love for the Sake of Beauty" (766), which Barrett Browning knew and which has been included in this edition for comparison.

Suggestions for Discussing the Study Questions, page 756

(1) The speaker is female, as is indicated in line 3. The poem itself may be considered as a part of a previous discussion in which her suitor has stated that he loves her for a variety of reasons, such as her smile, her appearance, her gentle speech, and her ability to set him at "pleasant ease" (line 6).

(2, 3) The speaker refers mainly to kinetic images as possible causes for loving, such as her speech, her expressiveness, and her putting people at their ease. In addition the kinetic image of "wiping my cheeks dry" might also be a cause for loving inasmuch as the suitor might love her because he consoles her. None of these is an actual cause for being in love because they might all end, and with this ending might also come the suitor's love. Most important, therefore, is the need of love "for love's sake," which can go on "through love's eternity" because such transcendent love does not depend on temporary advantages and on "hands, lips, eyes" (to quote Donne's "A Valediction: Forbidding Mourning").

WRITING TOPICS. What images of impermanent things are denied as a cause for love? The nature of the speaker. Who is the listener, and what is his role in the speaker's train of thought?

WORKS FOR COMPARISON WITH "IF THOU MUST LOVE ME"

Atwood, *Variation on the Word Sleep, 1124*
Butler, *Snow, 590*
Donne, *A Valediction: Forbidding Mourning, 784*
Rückert, *If You Love for the Sake of Beauty, 766*
Shakespeare, *Let Me Not to the Marriage of True Minds, 903*

SAMUEL TAYLOR COLERIDGE, *Kubla Khan,* *pages 756–57*

This poem is a virtuoso piece in every major respect, even though we have only a fragment of a much longer work that Coleridge was in the process of writing. We can only regret that the fatal knock on the door, which drove the rest of it from his mind, did not occur several hours later. As "Kubla Khan" exists, however, it possesses its own unity, being a perfect representation of the Romantic theory of inspired composition that attributed the source of creativity to a "penetralium [penetralia] of mystery," to use Keats's phrase. Of particular note is the indulgence in sound. Lines 17–24 form a unit that illustrates the device of onomatopoeia, and so also do lines 25–28.

Suggestions for Discussing the Study Questions, page 757

(1) Many of the imagined scenes are panoramic, especially those in stanzas one and two. They could be sketched or visualized, although the sounds of the mighty fountain would be missing, and they are essential to a full sense of the excitement and splendor of the scene. The damsel with the dulcimer is a close-up image, as is that of the wailing woman. The romantic setting of the poem is a fictitious and exotic locale (Xanadu), complete with palace, deep caverns, a sacred river, gardens, incense, and greenery.

(2) The auditory images convey excitement, sorrow, danger, and supernatural involvement in the action of the poem.

(3) The poem does not seem unfinished, although the abrupt switch at line 37 from landscape description to the far more simple, human, and quiet image of the damsel points in a new direction that Coleridge did not complete. Yet, as an argument for completion, one might note that Coleridge's speaker is asserting that inspiration, whether it be from a vision or from the milk of Paradise, is essential

to the development of creative energy like that which shaped Khan's palace and its gardens and landscapes.

(4) "Miracle" and "rare" suggest wonder and scarcity, something widely out of the ordinary, and therefore remarkable. Sun and ice together appear to be contradictory, but to combine them as sources of pleasure suggests a mysterious union, beyond everyday reality.

(5) To the speaker, the magical union is represented by the image of the singing maid; she is an incentive to him to aspire to goals that he has not yet seen but has only imagined. The poem concludes with the image of a group of persons, who are in awe of the person of inspiration, who dance around the speaker three times to protect themselves through ritual. The kinesthetic images recall the earlier images of motion, but here they have brought the movement into human terms.

WRITING TOPICS. The visual imagery. Images appropriate to natural scenery. The effect on the poem of auditory imagery and onomatopoeia. The image of the Abyssinian maid and the speaker.

WORKS FOR COMPARISON WITH "KUBLA KHAN"

Dickinson, *I Died for Beauty, 1070*
Keats, *Ode on a Grecian Urn, 1018*
MacLeish, *Ars Poetica, 676*
Shakespeare, *Not Marble, 679*

RICHARD CRASHAW, *On Our Crucified Lord, Naked and Bloody,* *page 758*

Characteristic of seventeenth-century religious poetry, the sanguinary imagery here is heavily allusive. In addition to Mark 15:24 and 15:17, interested readers may also see John 20:23 and Matthew 27:28. In lines 2–4, the image refers to the Roman soldier who speared Christ in the side after he had died (John 20:34 alone includes this detail).

Suggestions for Discussing the Study Questions, page 758

(1) The poem is built on contradiction and irony: The idea is that the speaker wishes that Jesus would not have been beaten and crucified, but unless he had been so treated, he would not have risen. Then, however, there would be no Christian religion, and the speaker would not be worshipping him. In the first line, therefore, the speaker refers to the clothing taken away from Jesus before the scourging, and asserts his wish that the Lord could have been left naked rather than undergoing crucifixion. The speaker laments the

crucifixion personally, though he worships the divinity that Christ assumed through it.

(2) These words refer to the horrors of the flagellation and crucifixion of Jesus. "This garment" in line two refers to the blood which covered his body as a result of the thorns, sticks, fists, whips, and sword. "Thee with Thyself" (line 3) refers to the Lord's own blood which covered his body, which itself becomes a garment. To consider blood in this way is ironic and contradictory, since it would neither warm, protect, nor conceal. But the speaker asserts that Jesus is so rare a being that no human garment could be fine enough to clothe him except for his own blood.

(3) Although the emphasis on blood may seem excessive, the concern is appropriate to the Christian tradition which has always seen the blood of Christ as life-giving.

WRITING TOPICS. The double meaning of *robe* and *garment*. Color imagery. Allusiveness. Images as causes of worship.

WORKS FOR COMPARISON WITH "ON OUR CRUCIFIED LORD"

Herbert, *Easter Wings, 907*
Hopkins, *Pied Beauty, 1165*
Williams (Joy), *Taking Care, 95*
Wordsworth, *It Is a Beauteous Evening, Calm and Free, 1058*

RAY DUREM, *I Know I'm Not Sufficiently Obscure,* *pages 758–59*

In this poem Durem's speaker grants that he does not write poetry that is intellectual and replete with poetic ornament such as imagery, but rather he believes in the *Poet Engagé*—the poet who expresses outrage and advocates change.

Suggestions for Discussing the Study Questions, page 759

(1, 2) The "you" of these lines is a group of conventional poets and critics who, in the speaker's eyes, write poetry—and write about it—as though poetry should be removed from life, with no political purpose. In addition, the speaker's words criticize imagery that in his eyes creates obscurity rather than meaning. The fact is, however, that the speaker does indeed express himself through imagery, such as the woman of line 9 and the soldier of lines 13–15.

(3) The references in these lines are to a "lavender word," a black soldier, and "an autumn leaf." The first and third are often indicative of peace, even though a "lavender" word suggests that the speaker might be accusing traditional poets of effeminacy. The "lavender word for lynch" thus creates a jarring contrast between two tradi-

tions. At the end, the visual image of the body in the tree indicates the speaker's idea that poetry should lead to political action. The specifics of political oppression may have changed since 1962, the year in which "I Know I'm Not Sufficiently Obscure" was published, but social inequality and bigotry persist. Thus, Durem's speaker mentions "rebellion" twice, with the clear implication that poets should become involved in the battle for social justice.

WRITING TOPICS. Visual images. Images rendering sensations of heat. The images of cutting, rending, and plowing.

POEMS FOR COMPARISON WITH "I KNOW I'M NOT SUFFICIENTLY OBSCURE"

Hughes, *Harlem, 787*
Ibsen, *An Enemy of the People, 1844*
Lorde, *Every Traveler Has One Vermont Poem, 1173*
Rich, *Diving into the Wreck, 1190*
Shelley, *Ode to the West Wind, 877*
Walker, *Revolutionary Petunias, 1212*

T. S. ELIOT, *Preludes*, *pages 759–60*

This poem reflects Eliot's early poetry in the imagist tradition. Eliot presents little vignettes almost cinematically, as though he had selected them through the process of montage. Because these vignettes represent the reverse side of life, the anti-heroic nature of modern urban existence, they cause "Preludes" somewhat to resemble the view of city life presented by Swift in "A Description of the Morning" (793).

Suggestions for Discussing the Study Questions, page 760

(1) The images of evening in stanza one are derived from locations just outside buildings. In the second stanza the early morning images move into the thousands of furnished rooms in which urbanized human beings spend their lives. The third stanza focuses on one of these rooms in the morning, and a woman in the room is dozing before getting up to begin the day.

(2) We may presume that the "you" is female because of the image of the curled papers in the hair. The images associated with this woman are "sordid," and a terribly damnatory statement is that her "soul" is "constituted" out of a thousand such images; in other words, the negative pictures of life are more prominent than the positive. The things she sees are the shutters, the gutters, soiled hands, and the yellow soles of feet. There is nothing pretty or idealistic here.

(3) The identity represented by "his" is not clear. We may as-

sume that a general person is intended, one of the representative ones who live in one of the thousand furnished rooms, one of the faceless persons in the crowd. The meaning of "blackened street" seems to be that there is much that is bad in the urban environment (it is "blackened"), but that it too needs to be active. There is a direction in the impatience to "assume the world," but it is all in the anti-heroic direction.

(4) There are not many references to the human body. The feet are muddy, the hand is raising a dingy shade, the hair is rolled with papers, the soles of feet are yellow, and the fingers are short and square. Images of the urban scene are more abundant. Both are equally discouraging about the development of humankind.

(5) The idea of stanza five is that there is a power somewhere which may be able to make sense out of the urban images, who through suffering may be able to redeem the people who are consigned to the dreariness of the city. The last stanza moves from this hope to final resignation. Have your beer, wipe the foam away, and have a good time, because the world goes on in its own way despite the best anyone can do. This idea is not dissimilar to the *carpe diem* tradition, but it provides a twist on the theme because of the poem's emphasis on dreariness, not on mortality.

WRITING TOPICS. A characterization of the urban images. The development of the poem's stanzas. The meaning of the concluding unnumbered stanzas.

WORKS FOR COMPARISON WITH "PRELUDES"

Ginsberg, *A Supermarket in California, 913*
Swift, *A Description of the Morning, 832*
Kennedy, *Old Men Pitching Horseshoes, 956*
William Carlos Williams, *The Red Wheelbarrow, 1218*

GEORGE HERBERT, *The Pulley, page 761*

"The Pulley" is an excellent poem for the illustration of imagery because of its graphic title and emblematic comparison of mechanics and salvation. Students who are artistic may be able to draw a sketch of a pulley for the benefit of your class. If any students of physics know about the mechanical advantage of pulleys, you may be able to call on them to furnish the literal basis of the image.

Suggestions for Discussing the Study Questions, page 761

(1) The dramatic scene of the poem is apparently The Garden of Eden or somewhere on earth at the time of the Creation. God

is deciding what blessings to bestow. God decides to withhold rest or repose, fearing that we human beings will otherwise have all we need and will have no reason for divine reliance. Herbert may be thinking of the frequent Biblical references to the need for rest (e.g., Lamentations 5:5; Revelation 14:11), and particularly to Matthew 11:28 ("Come unto me, all ye who labor and are heavy laden, and I will give you rest.").

(2) These blessings include strength, beauty, wisdom, honor, and pleasure. All are blessings because they give joy and happiness as corollaries of living.

(3) Herbert is building the poem on the faith that God accepts humankind unconditionally; his phrase "repining restlessness" (line 17) describes the anxiety prior to this acceptance. Herbert emphasizes "weary" and "weariness" here as the accompanying condition of the search. Weariness is a recurring Biblical word and concept. See, for example, Isaiah 28:12 ("give rest to the weary").

(4) The dominant image of the pulley is unusual and ingenious, but it is also brilliantly right. When we realize that pulleys are mechanical devices, that they hold exceedingly firm, and that they sustain and lift great weights, we may see the appropriateness of the image.

WRITING TOPICS. The image of blessings as part of a liquid. Allusiveness. The metaphor of the pulley (how does it connect the various parts of the poem?).

WORKS FOR COMPARISON WITH "THE PULLEY"

Donne, *A Hymn to God the Father, 1145*
Hopkins, *God's Grandeur, 863*
Porter, *The Jilting of Granny Weatherall, 651*
St. Luke, *The Parable of the Prodigal Son, 445*

GERARD MANLEY HOPKINS, *Spring, pages 761–62*

"Spring" is a poem of celebration—celebration of the time of year, the existence of the world and the universe, the glorious sounds of English words, and the Resurrection. Like "Kubla Khan," it is a virtuoso piece of sound. Even students who are not particularly perceptive about sounds can appreciate the repeating segments, as in patterns like "weeds, wheels," "long and lovely and lush," and "strikes like lightnings," to quote just a few of the many ringing examples.

Suggestions for Discussing the Study Questions, page 762

(1) Images supportive of the beauty of spring include lushly

growing weeds, bird songs, blue skies, and leaves and flowers. Except for the weeds, they are not unexpected. What seems unusual is the language of movement in which the speaker expresses them.

(2) Imagery of motion is the thrush song "like lightnings," the leaves brushing "the descending blue," the blue being in "a rush," and the lambs racing. These are dynamic images, suggesting that the speaker is surrounded by a season of moving color and sound.

(3) This pristine beauty is like Eden before the fall, and is equally at risk because of sin (line 12). But for now it is all new and lovely.

(4) For many readers, the references to Christ, and the assertion that this Edenic world is worthy of him, may make the poem seem nothing more than an intellectual exercise. But the loveliness of the first eleven lines is fully accessible to all who respond to color, movement, and word painting.

WRITING TOPICS. Images of nature. Visual images. Images of motion. Allusiveness.

WORKS FOR COMPARISON WITH "SPRING"

Herbert, *Easter Wings, 907*
Housman, *Loveliest of Trees, 675*
Keats, *To Autumn, 788*
Oliver, *Wild Geese, 957*
Whitman, *A Noiseless Patient Spider, 958*

DENISE LEVERTOV, *A Time Past,* *pages 762–63*

This poem is a confessional one, involving the recollection of past times of happiness and present times of memory and sadness. The concluding image, of the wood waiting somewhere to be burnt, is especially strong, and jarring, for it shows a note of bitterness amidst the poem's previous sadness.

Suggestions for Discussing the Study Questions, page 763

(1) The visual imagery of the poem combines the manufactured (the two different sets of steps, and the wood of the first) and the natural (dew, quiet, the absence of birds, crickets, falling leaves, a breeze). A tactile image associated with the steps is the splinters, which the speaker still feels in her hands.

(2) The "old wooden steps" are a predominating image in the poem. They represent "a time past" of memories when life was new and love was ardent. That the steps have been "replaced with granite" indicates a loss of the good memories. The granite in the steps makes for a solid stairway, but it has none of the past associations.

From the poem's context, we are also to infer that granite suggests the granite of a gravestone.

(3) The speaker denies recollecting any other sounds because she concentrated so much on her husband's "cheerful, unafraid, youthful, 'I love you too,'" in response to her statement of love (line 7).

WRITING TOPICS. What is the relationship of the steps to "time past. Tactile images in the poem. The relationship of the final image to the rest of the poem.

WORKS FOR COMPARISON WITH "A TIME PAST"

Dickinson, *I Cannot Live with You, 1069*
Kizer, *Night Sounds, 734*
Piercy, *Will We Work Together, 1185*
Whitman, *Full of Life Now, 1216*

THOMAS LUX, *The Voice You Hear When You Read Silently,* *pages 763–64*

This is a very challenging poem, but also a rewarding one. The opening lines should be enough to get students started on rich avenues of thought. It might prove interesting to ask students what they think of the poet's use of "skull" (line 13) and "barn" (line 18). Some might think the words are rather "low," but might rethink their responses in light of the poem's development.

Suggestions for Discussing the Study Questions, page 764

(1) A constellation is of course a gathering together of stars, and it may also be understood to refer to a collection or gathering together of ideas. The two images here, that of a constellation (vastness, brilliance) and a barn (familiarity, drabness) are brought together in lines 20–31 to demonstrate how images expand far beyond immediately predictable limits. Particularly in lines 27–31, the speaker demonstrates the specific visual, tactile, and olfactory images that constellate from the initial impetus provided by the single image "barn."

(2) The voice we hear when we read silently is indeed silent as far as the outside world is concerned, but the words on a page sound mightily within our minds. Thus we have the paradox, on which the poem is built, that silent words are really loud words.

(3) A cathedral is a large church, the official chair from which a religious leader delivers wisdom and authority. The image indicates that our own wisdom and authority come from ourselves, from our own minds, as they are guided by all the literature we have read and all the experience and feelings we have ever had. Thus the "dark

cathedral" of our skulls is not only the receiver of wisdom through our individual acts of reading silently, but it is also the "chair" from which we deliver our own wisdom to the world.

WRITING TOPICS. Describe the mental operations the poet refers to in the poem. Expand on an image of your own choosing, in a way similar to the poem's lines 24–31. The meaning of the reference to the "cathedral / of your skull."

WORKS FOR COMPARISON WITH "THE VOICE YOU HEAR WHEN YOU READ SILENTLY"

Bradstreet, *The Author to Her Book, 818*
Collins, *Sonnet, 910*
Hass, *Museum, 915*
Moore, *How to Become a Writer, 274*

P. K. PAGE, *Photos of a Salt Mine,* *pages 764–66*

This is a most unusual poem, not the sort one ordinarily expects to find. The image of the camera filter pervades the lines, with the suggestion that, even though photos do not lie, a skillful cameraman can put scenes in such a light, and in such poses, as to make things seem better than they actually are. This truth makes for the poem's irony and its attack on the exploitation of workers. In addition, traditionally at least, a "salt mine," as in "back to the salt mine" has always indicated particularly difficult and dangerous work, even if the phrase no longer has such a specific meaning.

Suggestions for Discussing the Study Questions, page 766

(1) In camera work, filters are used to enable the photographer to bring out aspects of certain scenes. Thus, one type of filter may make things seem pretty, but another may bring out harshness of contrast. In the first 47 lines "innocence" has acted as the filter, minimizing faults and highlighting beauties.

(2) The beautiful things suggested by the images of the second question are those of a high mountain, clear in the air, and glistening jewels such as "rubies and opals." These images are in keeping with the opening idea that the photos show the innocence and idealization of work in the mine.

(3) In the last nine lines the filter is "not innocence but guilt," and it emphasizes the smallness and insignificance of the "strangely lit" workers. Climaxing this view, the speaker describes the scene as one resembling "Dante's vision of the nether hell," exposing the guilt of exploitation and the hellish working conditions.

(4) The images of motion are all distant. The first images are positive enough: sweeping up the salt, making love in fine sheets resembling the whiteness of salt, climbing in the mining excavation, and creating a magical cave resembling that of Aladdin from the Arabian Nights. Once the filter changes to guilt, the motions are those of pin-like figures dancing (like marionettes), struggling, and being locked into the "black inferno of the rock."

WRITING TOPICS. The perspectives of the poem and the changing views of the scene. The meaning of the reference to a "salt mine."

WORKS FOR COMPARISON WITH "PHOTOS OF A SALT MINE"

Dickinson, *Safe in Their Alabaster Chambers, 1075*
Frost, *Mending Wall, 1106*
Hall, *Scenic View, 1156*
Nemerov, *Life Cycle of Common Man, 1179*

EZRA POUND, *In a Station of the Metro,* *page 766*

This poem, an example of poems of the "Imagist School" that heavily influenced modern sensibility and taste in poetry, is an experiment because it does not embody traditional form or even traditional grammar. The impression, the image, is what Pound expresses, on the supposition that poetry exists in the transference of mood from the poet to the reader through the creation and apprehension of strong and direct images.

Suggestions for Discussing the Study Questions, page 766

(1) The image of the petals is complex: Are they part of a full blossom? Have they dropped off the flower? Are they sticking temporarily to the wet bough? Do they suggest that, even in rain and clouds, some remnants of beauty are still visible in human experience? If they were petals on a sunny tree they would be positive and less ambivalent.

(2) Another aspect of ambivalence is the word "apparition," which is usually a ghostly figure, but which may be simply an unexpected sight.

(3) Short as the poem is, it is still a poem because it works entirely in images, not logical development. It is, in effect, in the tradition of the Japanese *haiku* (*see page 816*).

WRITING TOPICS. The poem as image. Imagery and mood.

WORKS FOR COMPARISON WITH "IN A STATION OF THE METRO"

Kennedy, *Old Men Pitching Horseshoes, 956*
McHugh, *Lines, 1177*
William Carlos Williams, *The Dance, 930*

FRIEDRICH RÜCKERT, *If You Love for the Sake of Beauty,* *pages 766–67*

This brief poem was a favorite of the composer Gustav Mahler (*1860-1911*) who set it to music as one of his five *Rückert Lieder* in 1901. It is easily laid out as a set of logical/emotional propositions, and readers enjoy discussing the nature of the relationship between the speaker and the listener, and also discussing the various reasons for which people join together in love relationships and marriage.

Suggestions for Discussing the Study Questions, page 767

(1) The poem's hypothetical situation is that the speaker is speaking to a lover or suitor who has been offering reasons for loving the speaker. In this respect the poem is like Elizabeth Barrett Browning's "If Thou Must Love Me" (755) and Shakespeare's "Shall I Compare Thee to a Summer's Day" (794).

(2) Lines 2, 4, and 6 present images of bright golden hair, the rebirth of spring, and rich and clear pearls. The speaker uses these images to point out her or his limitations, for she or he could never sustain the listener's love for reasons of beauty, youth, and wealth in lines 1, 3, and 5.

(3) The final two lines, particularly the last, climax the previous six because the speaker settles on love alone as the cause of loving, not the previous causes, which have been rejected.

WRITING TOPICS. The images used in rejecting the reasons for love as expressed in lines 1, 3, and 5. The relationship of speaker and listener.

WORKS FOR COMPARISON WITH "IF YOU LOVE . . ."

Elizabeth Barrett Browning, *If Thou Must Love Me, 755*
Haines, *Little Cosmic Dust Poem, 1156*
Shakespeare, *Let Me Not to the Marriage of True Minds, 903*
Wakoski, *Inside Out, 798*

WILLIAM SHAKESPEARE, *Sonnet 130: My Mistress' Eyes Are Nothing Like the Sun,* *page 767*

This sonnet, from the 1609 edition of the sonnets, is one of those (numbered from 126 to 152) which supposedly refer to a "dark lady," about whom there have been many attempts at identification. More to the point of the sonnet is that in it Shakespeare openly ridicules some of the sonnet conventions that the English inherited from the Italian (Petrarchan) tradition. Students may be interested to note that the popular singer Sting entitled one of his records "Nothing Like the Sun."

Suggestions for Discussing the Study Questions, page 767

(1) The speaker makes the following comparisons: eyes to the sun, lips to coral, breasts to snow, hair to wires, cheeks to roses, breath to perfume, voice to music, and walk to the progress of a goddess. Then he concludes that no part of the lady can properly be compared to the object chosen. The negative comparisons are visual, olfactory, auditory, and kinesthetic.

(2) Shakespeare is mocking a style of hyperbolic comparison and rhetoric popular in his time. The point he makes by puncturing this particular balloon is that a human woman, who "when she walks, treads on the ground," is, for a real lover of flesh and blood, better than any remote and non-existent ideal.

(3) The images are not insulting because so many of the comparisons are preceded by "if . . . be . . . then" and so on, although in current English (but not in Shakespeare's English) the word *reeks* carries unfortunate connotations. The point is quite the contrary, for the conclusion stresses that the mistress has attributes which are rare.

(4) Although there is a good mixture of images in the poem, the poet relies most heavily upon visual images, such as ordinary and un-sunlike eyes, lips unlike red coral, dun rather than white breasts, black wires for hair, and so on.

(5) The point made about love poetry is that it usually concerns the speaker's enthusiasm about a loved one rather than any objective descriptions. The idea is that a relationship built upon reality and the recognition of truth is more solid and enduring than one in which the lover pedestalizes the woman (a modern word, but an old situation).

WRITING TOPICS. The nature of the images. The reversal of convention in Shakespeare's images. Humor and seriousness as a result of the images.

WORKS FOR COMPARISON FOR "MY MISTRESS' EYES . . ."

Bradstreet, *To My Dear and Loving Husband, 1128*
Poe, *Annabel Lee, 869*
Wyatt, *I Find No Peace, 800*

DAVID WOJAHN, *"It's Only Rock and Roll But I Like It": The Fall of Saigon,* *page 768*

"'It's Only Rock and Roll But I Like It'" is one of the powerful poems from the Vietnamese War era. The images, both of vision and sound, are vivid and graphic. The title is taken from the title song of an album by The Rolling Stones (CBS disk CK 40493). It may be difficult to determine just exactly what the lyrics are, but one might question Wojahn's "indeed" in line 7. The words sound more like this: "I know it's only Rock and Roll, but I like it; like it, yes I do."

Suggestions for Discussing the Study Questions, page 768

(1) The poem records an actual historical event, the final evacuation of Americans as they are lifted by helicopter from the roof of the United States Embassy in Saigon (now Ho Chi Minh City) in 1975. The poem itself explains the major actions. The Saigonese man clinging to the airborne skis is clearly afraid of being killed if he remains behind, and he is willing to risk his life by holding on to the landing apparatus.

Incidentally, the well-known photo showing Vietnamese climbing a stairway to board a waiting helicopter does not show the top of the U.S. Embassy in Saigon. Instead the photo shows the top of a nearby hotel.

(2) The three major images of sound are the noise of the helicopter, the music of The Rolling Stones, and the fists of the marine beating time on the fuselage. These images of sound are to be contrasted with the great seriousness of the military evacuation. Images of sight are plentiful, and, as the speaker says, "The camera gets / It all." Some of the sights the poem refers to are the arabesques of dust, the bonfires of official records, the helicopter straining to lift off, and the pathetic Saigonese holding on but then "giving way."

(3) The title is little more than a major line in a popular rock and roll song. The content of the poem concerns life and death. The apparent lack of concern of the marine beating time to the music is the irony in the poem.

(4) The images are about personal concerns. There is nothing said about the purpose of the war or about the political reasons for the withdrawal. The actual scene is one of "artful / Mayhem" of the lost war and the evacuation. The clear implication is that the war is irrelevant to the personal interests of those involved in the evacuation.

WRITING TOPICS. The poem's irony. The imagery of sight and

sound in the poem. The contrast between the poem's title and the subject matter.

WORKS FOR COMPARISON WITH " 'IT'S ONLY ROCK AND ROLL' "

Hardy, *In Time of 'The Breaking of Nations'*, 950
Jarrell, *Death of the Ball-Turret Gunner*, 676
Northrup, *Wahbegan*, 1180
Yeats, *The Second Coming*, 961

Writing About Imagery, *pages 768–72*

This section provides guidance for students who otherwise might not know what to do with an assignment on imagery. Of course, the major principle is that students deal with what they find in the poem they are studying, and then develop their essays in the light of their findings. Thus, for example, the poem "Cargoes" may be the basis of a type 1 essay (769) stressing images of sight, just as a major image of sight may be discussed in "In a Station of the Metro." Also appropriate for type 1 would be Shakespeare's Sonnet 130. "Cargoes" is an obvious example connecting images and mood, and "The Tyger" could be the subject of a similar essay. For type 3, the text (770) cites six poems which might be applicable.

Special Topics for Writing and Argument about Imagery in Poetry, *pages 772–73*

(1) The images in "I Have a Rendezvous with Death" (1196) are ones of gentleness in which the narrator imagines himself participating. The images of home in "Anthem for Doomed Youth" are those of the people back home expressing silent and helpless grief to the news of battlefield death. The deaths of the poets of course have nothing to do with the poems as such, but the poems take on a special poignancy in light that the deaths actually occurred.

(2) For the second writing direction, it would be best for students to lay out their observations in parallel columns, from which they might extract the details and conclusions they wish to bring out in their essays. In addition, students might profitably consult the second part of Chapter 35, on the Extended Comparison-Contrast essay (1983), for developing an approach to this topic.

(3) Suggestions for the essay on Eliot's "Preludes" may be developed from the answers responding to the study questions. Comparative poems might be Swift's "A Description of the Morning" (832), or Roethke's "Dolor" (738).

(4) Before attempting this topic, students should read Chapter 35, on comparison and contrast (1979). Because Rückert's poem antedated Browning's, it is worth considering the ways in which Browning adapted and changed "If You Love for the Sake of Beauty" for her own unique poem.

(5) The fifth direction gives a number of possibilities for short poems, to which students may add after consultation. As with most creative-writing assignments, it is best for students simply to write the poems, and turn critics of themselves only after they have completed a fairly advanced draft of their work.

(6) This assignment requires that students be able to work with the painting's images. Although the black-and-white minimizes much detail, the painting's principal images are clear (e.g., the tired couple, the long road, the emptiness of the distance ahead). These images may be contrasted with the view of spring in Hopkins's poem and the very brief but depressing observation of people walking in the train station in "In a Station of the Metro."

(7) The object of this assignment is to enable students to see that even the smallest college and university libraries have an absolute plethora of materials on Shakespeare. The writing assignment may be both or either/or.

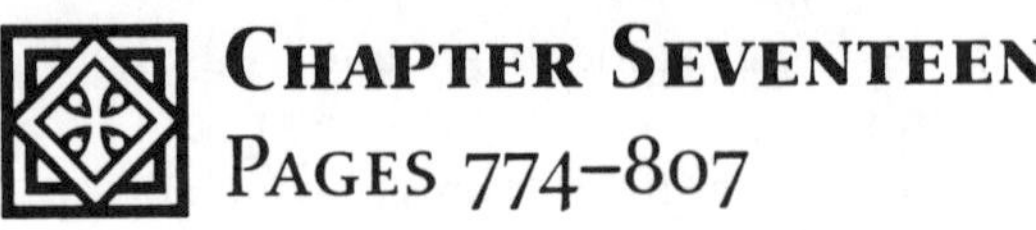

Chapter Seventeen
Pages 774–807

Figures of Speech, or Metaphorical Language: A Source of Depth and Range in Poetry

This chapter introduces students first to the concepts of metaphor and simile, and second, to a number of other figures of speech essential in poetry. Most students are familiar with similes, and can usually pick one out when they see one, but they have difficulty recognizing metaphors. Thus the use of many examples, together with accompanying explanations, will be fruitful.

The other figures are often omitted by instructors who in a one-semester course are pressed for time. Because it is important that students know at least some of the figures, however, we have structured this introductory section so that you may assign as many of the figures as you think important or for which you have time. Each of the discussions is self-contained: Students may benefit from as many of them as you assign. The "other" figures, with pages, are these:

Thus, for example, if you wish to assign paradox, personification, and the pun only, there should be no confusion about either the location or the extent of the discussions.

John Keats, *On First Looking into Chapman's Homer,* *page* 777

Students may be interested to learn that Keats had trained not as a poet or writer, but as an apothecary-surgeon. In the year of this poem, 1816, he received his license to practice, but he gave it up to pursue a life of reading, thinking, and writing. The excitement he describes in this poem explains that decision. One of the rhetorical figures usually associated with Keats is *synesthesia,* the metaphorical mingling of references to different senses. In line 7 of this poem, the word "serene" is both a political and ecological metaphor, referring both to clear air and the majesty of Homer's poetry. To "breathe its pure serene," by synesthesia, equates breathing with reading and also with understanding.

Keats uses the metaphors of *demesne* and *discovery* to indicate that he is experiencing the power of the ancient poet Homer. The unknown, in short, is becoming known. Students may testify to the universality of Keats's discovery by bringing out some of their own experiences with learning something for the first time. The metaphor of "travell'd" suggests that literature, like travel, takes us to new places, with all the acquisition of knowledge and experience that seeing new places implies. Keats uses the metaphors of "realms of gold" "goodly states and kingdoms," and "western islands," to illustrate the metaphor.

The similes in lines 9–10 and 11–14 convey the thrill of being the first person to see an unknown planet or an unknown ocean. With that thrill comes the awareness that the universe is larger and more amazing than had been dreamed. Keats has found exactly the right similes for this enlarged sense of the world. The metaphor of *a new planet swims* suggests that the planet is active, engaged in its own purpose in the universe. The other words, as metaphors or similes, would suggest a vaguer, less purposeful mission. The comparison of course is apt, since the vehicle is the power of Homer, who in *The Iliad* and *The Odyssey* was an intentional and deliberate poet.

Writing topics. Keats's similes of discovery. The value of reading as expressed in the metaphor of Homer's territory as a ruler. The metaphor of fealty and the condition of the writer.

Works for Comparison with "On First Looking Into Chapman's Homer"

Shakespeare, *Not Marble,* 679
Shelley, *Ode to the West Wind,* 877
Strand, *Eating Poetry,* 740

John Keats, *Bright Star,* *pages 779–80*

This is a personal poem in which Keats's speaker describes the wish to be a "steadfast" lover like the "bright star" which is a distant witness to the earth's waters and snows (i.e., the changing seasons). The most steadfast star that we know in the northern hemisphere is of course the North Star, or the Pole Star, and we may presume that this is the star that Keats has in mind for his metaphor of stability and permanence.

Suggestions for Discussing the Study Questions, page 780

(1) The topic is the speaker's love. The comparison of speaker and star is the implicit one that the speaker, being human and therefore changeable, is as impermanent as the waters and snows. The contrast with the star is that the speaker wants to remain close to his love ("pillowed upon my fair love's ripening breast" [line 10]) and not remain aloof in "lone splendor" (line 2).

(2) The qualities the speaker attributes to the star are steadfastness (line 1), patience (line 4), sleeplessness (line 4), and attentiveness ("gazing," line 7). He assigns to the star the role of guard or watcher, thus suggesting that the star is like a divine presence, neither slumbering nor sleeping because of eternal guardianship over the children of God.

(3) The words "forever" and "ever," combined with the attribution of the star's being "steadfast," provide a backdrop of permanence for the speaker's love, which he wishes would remain forever firm and steady. Granted the comparative permanence of the stars, the choice of the star as subject is quite appropriate.

Writing topics. The use of the star as a metaphor for a lover. The comparison of universal permanence and human impermanence. The character of the poem's speaker.

Works for Comparison with "Bright Star"

Anonymous, *Western Wind, 687*
Colwin, *An Old-Fashioned Story, 67*
Frost, *The Silken Tent, 1112*
Shakespeare, *Let Me Not to the Marriage of True Minds, 903*

John Gay, *Let Us Take the Road,* *page 781*

The questions on page 781 are discussed immediately following. You may wish to amplify some of the points, like the work of the alchemists. In addition, the first-line word *road* referred to grand theft that occurred on the open highways of eighteenth century England. Even today we still use the phrase "highway robbery," which originated in this aspect of eighteenth-century life. The song is sung by the gang of thieves to the music of Handel's march from the 1711 opera *Rinaldo*, and, in its time, the music became more closely associated with *The Beggar's Opera* than with the original opera. In fact, when Handel revived *Rinaldo* after *The Beggar's Opera*, he had to compose a new march to replace the old one because he thought people would have accused him of plagiarizing the music for "Let Us Take the Road."

Writing topics. The imagery appropriate to thievery in the poem. The use of puns. The use of rhyme.

Works for Comparison with "Let Us Take the Road"

Cohen, *'The killers that run . . .'*, 1134
Crane, *Do Not Weep, Maiden, for War Is Kind*, 1137
Hardy, *The Man He Killed*, 673

Robert Burns, *A Red, Red Rose*, *pages 783–84*

Burns wrote this poem for the *Scots Musical Museum*, which was a collection of old and new Scots songs in the eighteenth-century traditions of William Thomson's *Orpheus Caledonius* and the poems of the elder Allan Ramsay. Students can understand the poem with a minimum of annotation, for the diction is not overburdened with localisms, and the sentiments and expressions are clear and easy.

Suggestions for Discussing the Study Questions, page 784

(1) The initial two similes of the poem, and much of the rest of the speaker's language, are commonplace. The speaker is obviously male, an energetic and fanciful man who does not mind exaggerating a bit in the interests of wooing his sweetheart and impressing his listeners. His situation is that he is declaring his love for his "bonnie lass" (line 5), vowing his love's continuation, bidding her good bye, and promising to return. The charm of the poem lies in its evident sincerity and boldness, even if the language is unexceptional. This situation is like that in Donne's "A Valediction: Forbidding Mourning" (784), except that Burns's speaker does not have the wit or sophistication of Donne's speaker.

(2) Burns's first stanza is a brief general statement to whoever may be near, including the speaker's lass. In stanza two, and in the remainder of the poem, the speaker addresses the lass directly, explaining to her that even though he must travel, she will always

be foremost in his thoughts because he attributes to her the beauty of both flowers and music.

(3) The speaker asserts that seas must dry and rocks must melt before his love will end. These are both figures of overstatement, and they suggest a strong commitment. More serious as a figure is the metaphor of the "sands o' life," which compares life to an hour glass which will eventually run out of sand. Though the concluding metaphor of lengthy travel (we might remember that at the time a trip of ten thousand miles might have taken three or four years) is also hyperbolic, the sands metaphor suggests that the speaker, underneath his exaggerations, is not without his serious side.

WRITING TOPICS. The rose as a simile. Structure. Overstatement. A comparison with Donne's "Valediction."

WORKS FOR COMPARISON WITH "A RED, RED ROSE"

Dickinson, *Wild Nights – Wild Nights, 1078*
Frost, *A Line Storm Song, 1105*
Haines, *Little Cosmic Dust Poem, 1156*
Wyatt, *I Find No Peace, 800*

JOHN DONNE, *A Valediction: Forbidding Mourning,* *pages 784–85*

It is impossible to date this poem, and hence all we can do is surmise that it may have been inspired by an occasion of a trip, when the poet found a need to answer objections that might have been raised to his going. Students brought up in the jet age may wonder why a trip should be a cause of consternation or grief. They might need reminding that even a short trip in the days of horse and sail would require an absence of at least several weeks, and perhaps several months. More to the point here is the extensive use of metaphorical language, together with the renowned concluding metaphysical conceit, or simile, about the relationship of lovers to a geometric compass. It is of course important to explore this simile in some detail, for whenever students of literature refer to the "metaphysical conceit" they invariably turn to this poem and this comparison.

Suggestions for Discussing the Study Questions, page 785

(1) The situation of the poem is a valediction, literally, a saying of farewell. The speaker is speaking to his lady, to whom he is married or affianced, and who has apparently been "mourning" at the prospect of the speaker's departure. The poem is developed as a

set of statements and arguments to distract the listener from crying and mourning.

(2) The first two stanzas form a simile developing the following idea: *Let us part the way virtuous persons die, quietly and easily.* The phrases "tear-floods" and "sigh-tempests" are designed to tease the listener out of weeping, and then to emphasize the remaining parts of the poem, which are quite serious.

(3) The simile of dying men sets a serious tone, and makes clear that the parting is genuinely painful, both for speaker and listener.

(4) The metaphor of stanza three refers to parting and disruptions: Earthquakes destroy earth and the dwellings on it. Trepidation of the spheres disrupts the smooth, circular movements of heavenly bodies. Both these metaphorical equations may be considered less harmful than the parting of lovers because they are distant, inanimate, and non-feeling. To pursue the metaphors, however, we may conclude that these cosmic movements do no permanent harm, and that they are therefore "innocent." How, in comparison, can the smaller parting of lovers do any harm?

(5) The basis for the speaker's claim in lines 13–20 is that the love of ordinary lovers ("sublunary," line 13) is only physical, and that for this reason they cannot retain their love at a distance. By contrast, the love of the speaker and the listener is not just a physical love, but is also an interaction of minds; therefore a separation of the physical does not imply a separation of the mental.

(6) The subject of the simile about metallurgy begun in line 17 is the refining of gold, in which all dross and impurities are removed and only the purest and most valuable gold remains. The speaker also refers to the malleability of gold to suggest that even when lovers are apart they are still united, just like a sheet of delicate gold foil (line 24). This metaphor supports the conviction that this love is deep and lasting.

WRITING TOPICS. The apparent dramatic situation occasioning the poem. The extended simile of the compass. The concept of love as evidenced in the poem. The cosmological metaphors.

WORKS FOR COMPARISON WITH "A VALEDICTION: FORBIDDING MOURNING"

Burns, *A Red, Red Rose,* 783
Haines, *Little Cosmic Dust Poem,* 1156
Waller, *Go Lovely Rose,* 1213

T. S. Eliot, *Eyes That Last I Saw in Tears,* *page 786*

This poem is not one of Eliot's reputation poems (such as *Prufrock, The Waste Land, Preludes,* etc.), but it is unusual in his work because it is considered to be personal, likely a reflection of the pain he apparently experienced in his marriage.

Suggestions for Discussing the Study Questions, page 786

(1) The word *eyes* as a synecdoche stands for a person who was obviously in close communication and in an intimate relationship with the speaker. The word *tears* as an instance of metonymy is a substitute for the emotions of grief and sorrow.

(2) The tears result from "division," in other words, a rupture of the relationship. The meaning of eyes outlasting tears is apparently that people cannot sustain deep emotion. Eventually they go on to do other things, and, though they do not forget causes of sorrow, the emotions become less painful. The eyes holding "us in derision" (line 15) do so perhaps because hurt feelings can lead to anger. Perhaps, also, the speaker is here expressing guilt for having caused the tears. The meaning of the eyes being of "decision" (line 9) suggests that the grieving person has made personal choices that will lead to a new way of life. It is in the nature of these references that they cannot be expressed too specifically.

(3) The "eyes but not the tears" is paradoxical because the speaker seems to be remembering the eyes, without tears, as in a "golden dream;" that is, he thinks of the person as she was *before* the "division" occurred. The paradox is that the relationship seems over, but the fond memory is not. The "affliction," about which the speaker remarks in lines 6 and 7, is apparent inability to close off the memory.

(4) The entire poem might be considered a paradox because of the complex awareness of the speaker; he sees a "golden vision" but knows it is a dream; he knows of the tears but cannot see them when he recalls the eyes; he looks forward to less division in death than he experienced in life, but expects that ultimately all human beings ("us") will be held "in derision" by persons for whom all former arguments are now irrelevant. He would like reconciliation but knows that there can be none.

(5) The references to the two kingdoms of death are obscure and likely allusive. They may be explained perhaps as allusions to classical states of dreaming and death. Thus Homer (*Odyssey,* 19: 562) explains that an ivory gate opening to the region of dreams permits the issue of false dreams, while a gate of polished horn is the entry

way of true dreams predicting the future. Death is viewed not as an end but a continuation of consciousness. The kingdom of death, ruled by Hades, was reached through an entrance, or door.

WRITING TOPICS. The personal topic matter. Paradox and contradiction. The meaning of "eyes" and "tears."

WORKS FOR COMPARISON WITH "EYES THAT LAST I SAW IN TEARS"

Anonymous, *Barbara Allan, 1119*
Dickinson, *I Cannot Live with You, 1069*
Minty, *Conjoined, 790*

ABBIE HUSTON EVANS, *The Iceberg Seven-eighths Under,* *pages 786–87*

Suggestions for Discussing the Study Questions, page 787

(1) Evans uses the iceberg as a metaphor to explain the vastness of the universe that always remains hidden from view, no matter how well new instrumentation penetrates the universe. Scientists have explained much of the universe as "dark matter," and they have learned about "black holes" at the centers of galaxies. Astronomers have even used the Hubble Space Telescope to examine objects that extend as much as 12,000,000,000 light years in space, or, in other words, objects as they appeared near the time of the origin of the universe as we know it. Despite these advances, "We know incredibly much and incredibly little." There is so much to know that still "goes secret, sunken, nigh-submerged." The invisible part of the iceberg thus is an apt metaphor for the status of human knowledge about the universe.

(2) The "We" of the poem is described in the metaphors of (perhaps) insects ("wrapped in the envelope of gossamer air"), a mote (i.e., a mite, an indescribably small thing), a "chaff-cloud of great suns," and benighted individuals attempting to see in no more light than can be provided by the gibbous (hunchbacked) moon.

(3) The metaphor of darkness is prevalent in the poem, but despite the darkness of our knowledge it is able to "dazzle" because "We know incredibly much" even if we also know "incredibly little." In other words, Evans does not tell us that our knowledge is nil, but rather that it pales into insignificance because of so much that we do not still know. One is reminded of Sir Isaac Newton's metaphor explaining his career. Newton said that he reminded himself of a small boy gathering pebbles on an incredibly vast shoreline. He knew something, but there was still an infinity of knowledge to learn.

WRITING TOPICS. The meaning of the metaphor of the iceberg. Metaphors that reveal the state of human knowledge. How successfully does the poem explain the limitations science?

WORKS FOR COMPARISON WITH
"THE ICEBERG SEVEN-EIGHTHS UNDER"

Aldiss, *Flight 063*, 985
Dryden, *A Song for St. Cecilia's Day*, 1012
Sexton, *To a Friend Whose Work Has Come to Triumph*, 989

LANGSTON HUGHES, *Harlem*, *page 787*

This is perhaps Hughes's best known poem, principally because of the memorable second line, which was used by Lorraine Hansberry for her play *A Raisin in the Sun* in 1959.

Suggestions for Discussing the Study Questions, page 787

(1) The idea is that the goals and ideals as defined in the Declaration of Independence and the Constitution enunciated a great dream that has never been equally applied to African Americans. See also Hughes's poem "Let America Be America Again," in which the line "It never was America to me" is repeated almost as a refrain (866).

(2) The initial question (line 1) is answered by additional questions from lines 2 through 7. The interval of two lines offers one answer—namely that blacks will do nothing. The final line, however, resumes the predominant structure of questioning. This concluding line, 11, because of the implied answer that an explosion will be forthcoming, is one of the most powerful in all of Hughes's writing.

(3) The similes all refer to things spoiling and rotting, with those in lines 4 and 6 being particularly bitter and ironic. The last comparison (line 11) suggests how deferring a dream is like nurturing the fuse of a powerful explosive.

(4) The shift to the metaphor in line 11 involves a change from similarity to actuality. The idea is that the suppression of African Americans is creating not an *impression* of explosive hostility, but is creating *real* explosive hostility.

WRITING TOPICS. The negative metaphorical language in the poem. The power of the language as symbols. The structure of rhetorical questions in the poem. The meaning of the final line.

Works for Comparison with "Harlem"

Baraka, *Ka 'Ba*, 1125
Durem, *I Know I'm Not Sufficiently Obscure*, 758
Lorde, *Every Traveler Has One Vermont Poem*, 1173
Randall, *Ballad of Birmingham*, 923

John Keats, *To Autumn*, page 788

Because this poem is so successful and so lovely, readers may sometimes be oblivious to the many figures that Keats employs. Indeed, the poem is loved by many persons who would wonder if knowledge of the figures can add anything to their appreciation. The fact remains, however, that Keats created the figures as an integral part of the poem, and therefore to understand them is one way of following the processes of his poetic art.

Suggestions for Discussing the Study Questions, pages 788–89

(1) In the first stanza, Autumn is personified in his prime, actively "conspiring" with his "close bosom-friend," the sun, to "load" and set budding all growing things. Here is Autumn the busy, active producer of the copious harvest. In the second stanza, Autumn is a laborer who sometimes forgets the task of gleaning and making cider, and sits down instead to doze in the midst of the work day. The change suggests the passage of time: The actions of stanza one produce the crops, stanza two is concerned with reaping them and the resulting fatigue.

(2) The poem progresses in accord with qualities or powers given to Autumn. In stanza one Autumn is an internal force, expanding and making the world grow. In two, Autumn is manifested in human beings, replete and satisfied in the security of the harvest. In three, Autumn is a bringer of sounds and evening songs, all heard through the air illuminated by the rosy sun. There is a twist on convention here, for autumn in the tradition of pastoral poetry is a time of decline which leads to the death of winter. Keats's emphasis on the fruitfulness of the season therefore illustrates the security provided by Autumn as personified as the grower and harvester.

(3) Keats uses both synecdoche and metonymy in each of these two stanzas. Specifically, however, the metonyms in stanza one are the thatch-eaves, which represent the people who live in the houses so protected, and the clammy cells of line 11, which, because they are the location of honey, stand for the honey itself and the sweetness of the season. In stanza two, synecdoches are *hair* (line 15), which

figuratively represents the dust of harvested grain and therefore the grain itself; *laden head* (line 20), which represents the persons working in the autumnal harvest both as laborers and as planners of the season; and *oozings* (line 22), representing specifically cider but generally the substances made from the year's produce. These figures give insights into the intricacy of growth, harvest, and manufacture, and also along with the personification of autumn, the intention of Nature and life to nurture human beings.

(4) The metaphors throughout the poem suggest ripeness, harvest, rest, and beauty after labor. The trees are loaded with apples; the machinery (cider press, reaping hook) is that which is used at the time of harvest; the light is red and mellow—rosy—and is seen over plains of cut grain; and the sounds are those of twilight and night–not threatening but restful.

WRITING TOPICS. The structure of the poem. Metonymy and synecdoche. Metaphors of ripeness and fullness. Personification and apostrophe.

WORKS FOR COMPARISON WITH "TO AUTUMN"

Shore, *A Letter Sent to Summer, 709*
Snodgrass, *These Trees Stand, 1201*
Twichell, *Blurry Cow, 1209*
Wordsworth, *Daffodils (I Wandered Lonely), 1048*
Wordsworth, *Lines Written in Early Spring, 1048*

JANE KENYON, *Portrait of a figure Near Water*, *page 789*

The poem is dramatic until line 17: A woman has just fled in anger from an argument of some sort. She settles herself and is able to think about her own value. In line 17 we learn that her action has been part of a logical argument being made by the speaker about the value of water as a calming substance to end anger. Rhetorically, therefore, the action of the first sixteen lines is what Rhetoricians call an *enthymeme*; that is, a narrative or illustration used to support a logical proposition.

Suggestions for Discussing the Study Questions, page 789

(1) We cannot know the specifics of the "rebuke" the woman has received, nor can we know her age. We therefore presume that she is an adult and has just left the scene of a vigorous altercation which was climaxed by insults against her. The location is obviously a farm, for she flees from a house or other place into the barn.

(2) The barn is old and it roof is sagging, indicating its age and the many people who have worked there in the past. "Tilted" indicates that the barn swallow is angled against the beams, and it is also a word describing medieval combat. "Amphorae" is a plural Greek word for large containers. To call a metal milk can an *amphora* suggests that arguments have existed from the beginning of humanity, and that people have fled scenes of rage and anger just as long.

(3) The metaphor of anger as an inner arsonist emphasizes the destructiveness of anger. The water in the stone trough contains "calm" for persons like the protagonist. The suggestion is clearly that water is a lustration for the spirit, creating calm just as it initiates a new life during the ceremony of baptism.

WRITING TOPICS. The poem's action. The poem as an argument illustrating the calm of water. The implications of anger being an "inner arsonist."

WORKS FOR COMPARISON WITH "PORTRAIT OF A FIGURE NEAR WATER"

Butler, *Snow, 590*
Harjo, *Eagle Poem, 674*
Herbert, *Love (III), 1162*
Wordsworth, *My Heart Leaps Up, 1035*

HENRY KING, *Sic Vita,* *page 790*

"Sic Vita" is virtually a tabular arrangement of metaphorical language, and is memorable for this reason.

Suggestions for Discussing the Study Questions, page 790

(1) There are six similes in lines 1–6, ranging from the objects in the night sky to drops of dew on leaves and grass. All are comparisons from nature, and all describe motions which come to an end.

(2) In lines 7 and 8, human life is presented as light, so that night comes to represent death. Human light or life is borrowed, and can and will be called in for payment; that is, death. The source from which life is borrowed is God or Nature.

(3) Lines 9–12 are not logically essential, but without them, lines 7 and 8 would have to bear the weight of the poem, and the balance would be skewed. By adding these lines, King not only underscores his point, but does so in rhythms which give the poem stateliness, importance, and closure.

(4) The poem emphasizes the mutability and brevity of human existence, but similes like that of the falling star and the rippling

of water suggest that life is also beautiful, desirable, and admirable, despite its shortness.

WRITING TOPICS. The philosophy of the poem. The development of the similes. Borrowed light in relationship to life.

WORKS FOR COMPARISON WITH "SIC VITA"

Frost, *Misgiving, 1111*
Jeffers, *The Answer, 1167*
St. Luke, *The Parable of the Prodigal Son, 445*
Wordsworth, *It Is a Beauteous Evening, 1058*

JUDITH MINTY, *Conjoined,* *page 790*

Alert students will notice the irony in the poem's subtitle, "a marriage poem." Like Eliot's "Prufrock" (1147), which is supposed to be a love song but ironically has nothing to do with love, this poem's subtitle suggests a celebration about marriage, but instead expresses great misgiving if not hostility.

Suggestions for Discussing the Study Questions, pages 790–91

(1) The "us" and "we" of lines 10 and 11 refer to the speaker and the spouse, those who have just been married. If the poem were to be taken as an interior monologue, then the plural first-person pronouns could refer to the body and soul of one person (since to cut them apart might kill [line 13]), but husband/wife is more plausible. The paradoxical subordination-freedom idea of love and marriage in this poem may be compared with that in Wyatt's "I Find No Peace" (800).

(2) In the figures of the onion, the twins, and the calves, the three were intended to be separate, but instead they are freaks of nature, monstrous accidents that allowed them to live but to live abnormally. The speaker suggests that this situation is like marriage. In lines 12–13, the speaker suggests that freedom (divorce, separation) might kill one partner, as it sometimes kills a Siamese twin. Note that the one who might not survive is not specified. The metaphor thus represents a recognition of reality and both a reluctant concession and a decision to adjust.

(3) An increasing number of men now "slice onions," but men, more often in charge of power and money, usually lay out the grounds of a relationship. Hence it is often asserted that women must be alert to hidden dynamics (body language, looks) to protect themselves emotionally, while men may be more direct and less subtle.

WRITING TOPICS. The irony of the subtitle. The view of the marriage bond. The figures of the onion, the Siamese Twins, and the calves.

WORKS FOR COMPARISON WITH "CONJOINED"

Broumas, *Circe*, 978
Keats, *La Belle Dame Sans Merci*, 954
Lawrence, *The Horse Dealer's Daughter*, 500

OGDEN NASH, *Exit, Pursued by a Bear*, *pages 791–92*

"Exit, Pursued by a Bear" is more serious than one usually expects Nash's poetry to be, expressing, as it does, the destructiveness of a nuclear war. At the poem's end, the *fireball* refers to the explosion of a nuclear bomb. The idea is that nuclear war has no limits; once it begins, because of the politics of escalation, it must go on and on until there is nothing left. Some students may claim that the easing of East-West tensions make obsolete the dangers that Nash warns about in the poem. If such a claim is put forward, it should occasion energetic discussion.

The source of the idea about animals overrunning places of former wealth is Fitzgerald's translation of *The Rubaiyat of Omar Khayyam*, which Nash directly echoes in lines 17 and 21 (please see the explanatory notes on pages 791 and 792).

Suggestions for Discussing the Study Questions, page 792

(1) The allusion to Shakespeare's stage direction as the title of the poem creates the emphasis of irony and understatement. The bear of course refers to the bear that roars at and then eats up Antigonus in *The Winter's Tale* (III.3.58), and it can also refer to the danger added to the world by the proliferation of nuclear weaponry by potentially hostile countries.

(2) The interior location is one of extreme wealth—likely a private home as evidenced by the artifacts contained there, all suggested by the identifying names as metonyms. The home is now vacant, for the owners are presumed to have been killed as a result of warfare.

(3) Because the building is no longer maintained, animals have gained entry and now use the artifacts for their lairs. The situation has apparently lasted for a long time, for mold has had a chance to grow on the rare and expensive books (line 15).

(4) One paradox in the poem is that the collector's items, usually not used by people because of their value, are used indiscriminately by animals once the people are gone. Another paradox is that the

people who took such good care of the collector's items did not take enough care to negotiate for their ultimate security—the elimination of the nuclear threat.

WRITING TOPICS. The use of the names of museum pieces and collector's items as metonyms. Setting. Allusion. Paradoxes.

WORKS FOR COMPARISON WITH "EXIT, PURSUED BY A BEAR"

Hardy, *Channel Firing, 703*
Quasimodo, *Auschwitz, 829*
Whitman, *Beat! Beat! Drums!, 1216*
Yeats, *The Second Coming, 961*

MARGE PIERCY, *A Work of Artifice,* *pages 792–93*

This poem embodies a deeply effective metaphor which is straightforwardly detailed and applied, and a tone that one student described as "controlled fury."

Suggestions for Discussing the Study Questions, page 793

(1) The bonsai tree—a major metaphor of the poem—is a tree that has been traditionally cultivated, particularly in Japan, to remain small, even though it is otherwise capable of reaching great height. For the first sixteen lines, the apparent subject of the poem seems to be the tree itself, though after this it is clear that the subject is really women. The metaphor is apt granted the poem's view that traditional attitudes toward women do not encourage their development. A full growth ("eighty feet tall," line 3) could result only from equality of opportunity.

(2) In lines 12–16, the gardener's song represents society persuading women to be content with being dwarfed and feeling fortunate when and if they find "a pot to grow in" (a home) and a singing gardener (a husband). Note the implication that it is the gardener (i.e., the controlling class of males) that does both the stunting and the brainwashing.

(3) At line 17 the poem switches to a number of metaphors on the topic of women dwarfed in their growth. Thus distorted, they are concerned with their personal appearance (curlers), they have allowed their minds and abilities to become "crippled," and they occupy themselves only with love ("the hands you love to touch," the last line of a commercial for Woodbury soap). The metaphor of the bound feet (an old Chinese practice of stunting the feet of women) powerfully depicts the traditionally unnatural treatment of women.

WRITING TOPICS. The bonsai tree as metaphor. Piercy's critique of women's traditional roles. Irony in the last lines.

WORKS FOR COMPARISON WITH "A WORK OF ARTIFICE"

Browning, *My Last Duchess, 695*
Chopin, *The Story of an Hour, 393*
Hacker, *Sonnet Ending With a Film Subtitle, 1155*
Rukeyser, *Myth, 995*
Steinbeck, *The Chrysanthemums, 447*

SYLVIA PLATH, *Metaphors*, *page 793*

A posthumous recipient of the 1981 Pulitzer Prize in Poetry, Plath wrote highly personal, revelatory poems. "Metaphors" is one of her happier efforts.

Suggestions for Discussing the Study Questions, pages 793-94

(1) The major clue that the speaker is a woman, and a pregnant one, is line 7 ("I'm ... a cow in calf"), but the entire poem makes this conclusion certain.

(2) The nine syllables are the nine months of pregnancy. The pregnant woman is a riddle because (a) even today there is much unknown about pregnancy, and (b) traditionally, the results of pregnancy are not known until birth. The poem is a riddle because one has to determine the identity and condition of the speaker.

(3) The metaphors suggest size, ripeness, increase, and wealth. They all suggest normal feelings of pregnancy, especially the expectant mother's awareness that she cannot get off the train she is on (line 9). Some of the metaphors—the melon and tendrils, the elephant—are funny, for however big she might feel, a pregnant woman is not elephantine. None of the metaphors are shocking or demeaning; indeed, the speaker's sense of herself as having "fine timbers" or being a "fat purse" conveys her self-satisfaction.

(4) The aspect of early pregnancy suggested by the green apple metaphor is morning sickness, while the metaphor of the stage shows the speaker's awareness that she is the means by which the human race continues itself. The train metaphor conveys the speaker's sense that she is being carried along by forces beyond her control.

WRITING TOPICS. The metaphors of ripeness. The "difficulty" of the riddle. The humor. The seriousness.

Works for Comparison with "Metaphors"

Clifton, *homage to my hips, 819*
Parker, *Penelope, 980*
Porter, *The Jilting of Granny Weatherall, 651*
Swenson, *Women, 926*

Muriel Rukeyser, *Looking at Each Other, page 794*

This poem is notable for its strong expression of intimacy. It clearly describes sexual experiences, but does so impressionistically and psychologically, not graphically.

Suggestions for Discussing the Study Questions, pages 794-95

(1) There are two possibilities about the listener of this poem. The first and more likely listener is the speaker's partner or lover. The second is a close friend or confidante. In either case, the speaker assumes a closeness and confidentiality that excludes any casual listener.

(2) The poem is devoted to the device of anaphora; that is, deliberate repetition for rhetorical effect. The obvious repetitions are the words "Yes, we," with slight variations, and then there is a repetition of "each other" and "together." In addition, the sentence structures are also repeated throughout. One can hardly imagine a more thoroughgoing use of the rhetorical device of anaphora.

(3) If repetition is inadvertent it is awkward and it detracts from the ideas being expressed. In "Looking at Each Other," however, the repetition lends considerable weight to the emotional ties that the speaker is describing.

Writing topics. The poem's expression of closeness between two people. The use of anaphora, or repetition. The reason for the concluding line repeating the opening line.

Works for Comparison with "Looking at Each Other"

Bogan, *Women, 1127*
Hacker, *Sonnet Ending With a Film Subtitle, 1155*
Hope, *Advice to Young Ladies, 1163*

William Shakespeare, *Sonnet 18: Shall I Compare Thee to a Summer's Day?, page 795*

About this sonnet there is little that one can say except that it is one of the foremost poems in the language. The last two lines climax the poem's argument. Here the speaker asserts that the poem will endure as long as human life endures, and that as long as people can see (to read) the sonnet will give life to the woman the speaker is addressing. It is the immortality of art that the speaker exalts over life's transience.

Suggestions for Discussing the Study Questions, page 795

(1) A possible dramatic situation is that the speaker has been challenged by his lady to develop an elaborate comparison, and that the poem is his response. He then is speaking directly to her. It is possible that laughter might be sought early in the poem because the speaker is demonstrating his ingenuity. However, the poem grows more thoughtful and contemplative as it develops. The concluding words of line 8, for example, speak of "nature's changing course," and Death intrudes upon the argument in line 11. What begins as a virtuoso piece therefore becomes a sober discussion of the inevitability of death.

(2) The development in lines 1–8 asserts that natural beauty fades and dies. This assertion is essential to the point of the last six lines—that only art can give immortality.

(3) At line 9, the speaker begins asserting that, unlike natural objects, the lady's summer (i.e., the beauty of her disposition) cannot fade, and that even Death (line 11) cannot claim her as long as she is the subject of the "lines" of the poem. Here the speaker is complimenting the power of his own poetry as well as the beauty of the lady.

(4) The last two lines are related to the previous twelve because they all concern the value of the lady and the nature of time. "This" refers to the sonnet itself, and the giving of life is the immortality that is conferred by subsequent generations of readers, who will always remember the sonnet and the lady and therefore create a continuous collective mind of living memory.

WRITING TOPICS. The metaphor of summer and the brevity of beauty. The seriousness of the poem. The poem as a dramatic utterance. The immortality conferred by art.

WORKS FOR COMPARISON WITH "SHALL I COMPARE THEE TO A SUMMER'S DAY?"

cummings, *buffalo bill's defunct*, 910
Keats, *Ode on a Grecian Urn*, 1018
Phyllis Webb, *Poetics Against the Angel of Death*, 929
Wordsworth, *Ode: Intimations of Immortality*, 1049

William Shakespeare, *Sonnet 30: When to the Sessions of Sweet Silent Thought,* pages 795–96

This is one of those sonnets, beginning with "when," that Edward Hubler praises on the ground that the "when" subordinate clause requires a logical development and an integrated couplet (*The Sense of Shakespeare's Sonnets,* 1952). To this interesting idea you might add that Shakespeare in the sonnets is fond of integrating connected systems of imagery as the basis of his metaphors and similes.

Please see the demonstrative student essay (804–805) for a consideration of the issues raised in the study questions on page 796.

Elizabeth Tudor, Queen Elizabeth I, *On Monsieur's Departure,* page 796

Through history, students know of Queen Elizabeth as a patron of Shakespeare and his theater company. Because few have ever studied any of Elizabeth's writings, this poem will therefore open a window of the private person who here expresses especially complex feelings about the contradictions between her public and private circumstances.

Suggestions for Discussing the Study Questions, page 797

(1, 2) The departure is the occasion for the meditation that is the poem, which is a personal consideration of the speaker's relationship with the departing man. Ordinarily, the poem implies, a departure (usually for a long period of time) gives those left behind the publicly sanctioned opportunity for sorrow and grief. That privilege, which is given to ordinary persons as a matter of right, is not given to the speaker, whose position denies her the customary sadness of a departure. Thus she begins the poem "I grieve and dare not show my discontent," and continues to discuss these antithetic circumstances throughout the poem. It is clear that the royal speaker is obligated to hide her feelings because of her elevated political status, which she considers a condition of life which only the "end of things" (line 12) and death (line 18) can ever stop. Ironically, because of obvious political dangers involved in revealing her feelings publicly, the speaker's supreme royal power weakens her in matters of the heart.

(3) The simile of the shadow in lines 7–10 demonstrates the closeness of the speaker with the departing man. The two are virtually one, as her shadow is always indelibly with her, but the private person who is the speaker is agonized by the need for suppressing her private feelings.

(4) The paradoxes in lines 5 and 15 arise from the speaker's consciousness of her public and private circumstances. Her public status requires that she be "not" in love, that she publicly "freeze," and that she be publicly "cruel" (inasmuch as she cannot admit her feelings). Her private status requires that she be ("am") in love, that she be "burned" with her love, and that she "love, and so be kind."

WRITING TOPICS. The nature of the speaker: What does she mean by "I am soft and made of melting snow"? The poem's use of paradoxes. The private-public contradictions described in the poem.

WORKS FOR COMPARISON WITH "ON MONSIEUR'S DEPARTURE"

Dickinson, *I Cannot Live with You, 1069*
Dixon, *All Gone, 595*
Minty, *Conjoined, 790*
Wyatt, *I Find No Peace, 800*

MONA VAN DUYN, *Earth Tremors Felt in Missouri*, *page* 797

Suggestions for Discussing the Study Questions, page 797

(1, 2, 4) The situation of the poem, between a (presumably) female speaker and a (presumably) male listener, demonstrates the intimate and confessional nature of the circumstances. The "quake last night," which the speaker refers to in line 1, may involve a personal problem, or else a problem in the attitude of the listener toward the speaker—we are not told the exact circumstances. But a problem was expressed, and to the speaker it has assumed the magnitude of "earth tremors felt in Missouri." Depending on the location of the speaker and listener, Missouri may be as far as half-way across the country. Personal circumstances, in other words, become earth shaking, and what might seem to be no more than a "pebble" to the outside world has planetary importance, even going so far as to comprehend "the sun." Ordinary, everyday life thus becomes large. This elevation of the personal to the virtually cosmic is reminiscent of the relationships described by Donne in a number of his love poems, most notably in "The Good Morrow" (1144), "The Canonization" (946), and "A Valediction: Forbidding Mourning" (784). The idea underlying the metaphor in both Van Duyn and Donne is that personal affairs are not small for the people involved, but are so great that any disturbance at all has life-changing implications. Donne emphasizes the positive nature of these conditions; Van Duyn emphasizes the danger in them.

(3) "Ordeal" and "woebegone" are words describing the difficulties in a relationship such as that exemplified by the speaker and the listener. Life is not smooth, but instead is an ordeal that sometimes fills the two participants with sadness, regret, and all the other negative feelings that flesh is heir to.

WRITING TOPICS. The circumstances implied in the phrase "quake last night." The dominant metaphor of the poem. The structure of the poem as a sonnet.

WORKS FOR COMPARISON WITH "EARTH TREMORS FELT IN MISSOURI"

Donne *(poems in paragraph 1, 2, 4)*
Haines, *Little Cosmic Dust Poem, 1156*
Marvell, *To His Coy Mistress, 1023*
Wakoski, *Inside Out, 798*

DIANE WAKOSKI, *Inside Out,* *page 798*

Wakoski is a poet of great imagination and insight, and "Inside Out" exhibits her originality to the highest degree. The speaker is a woman speaking to a man who is apparently a painter. She talks of a most personal and intimate relationship. For example, the two share knowledge of domestic details such as screen doors, Kool-Aid, and a commonly owned cat. We may conclude that the two have been living together and have developed this bond of common knowledge and shared experience. There is humor here, together with a keen understanding of both the depth and the limitation possible in the relations of women and men.

Suggestions for Discussing the Study Questions, pages 798–99

(1) The details of the listener's anatomy are the eye (line 1), the mind containing "old songs" (line 11), hands (line 11), mouth (line 15) and veins (line 20). The title, taken with these details, suggests that people who are close together genuinely do become part of each other. There is also a paradoxical reversal here of sexual roles: As the act of love involves the male's being within the female, the condition of love also involves the female's being metaphorically within the male. In this way, the poem concerns the closeness and oneness of human intimacy.

(2) The eye and the veins suggest through synecdoche the mind and emotions of the "you," while the paintings and the old hat may be transferred as metonyms to refer to the "you's" accomplishments and personal habits.

(3) These examples are all highly fanciful. Their precise meaning may not be possible to determine unless the reader exerts the kind of playful application intended by the poet. Hence the tire prints would give pain, and by transfer suggest not physical pain but rather emotional annoyance at responsibilities taking the couple away from their own personal world. Similarly, the mouth containing ground-up pigments transfers by synesthesia to taste and therefore to ideas about art. The ostrich feather which is used like a brush to paint on the moon suggests showiness and flamboyance but also delicacy of touch, and therefore the feather transfers to something like a vivid imagination. The moon and the mouth are appropriate to romantic moods. In the context, transfer by synæsthesia suggests that the speaker's thoughts become inspiration for the "you" who is the painter.

(4) In lines 19–24, the speaker denies the possibility that she can or should remain within the "you" for "too long." The idea is that individuals, even in an intimate relationship, must have their own identities. The paradox is that lovers must be close, but cannot be too close, on the principle of "too much of a good thing." The silver bullet therefore suggests this need for separateness and individuality as well as union.

(5) The paradox of lines 1 and 2 is that a red carpet is for royalty, while a butter server is used by a servant. Apparently without irony, the speaker thus indicates the duality of her relationship with the "you."

Writing topics. Personal intimacy. The uses of 1–paradox, 2–synecdoche, 3–metonymy, 4–synæsthesia. The playfulness of the poem. The difficulty of the references.

Works for Comparison with "Inside Out"

Donne, *The Sun Rising, 860*
Kizer, *Night Sounds, 734*
Lawrence, *The Horse Dealer's Daughter, 500*
Rukuyser, *Looking at Each Other, 794*

Walt Whitman, *Facing West from California's Shores,* *page 799*

This poem is characteristic of Whitman in most respects except that it is short. It lists the countries near the "shores of my Western sea," and is inclusive of the macrocosm-microcosm habits of Whitman's thought. The poem is especially interesting because it is built on a series of paradoxes which seem quite personal.

Suggestions for Discussing the Study Questions, page 799

(1) The paradox underlying the poem is that the speaker searches for something but does not find it, but even if he should find it he would never know his success because he characterizes himself as a seeker, on a continual quest. Thus the travels westward from our continent will prove rewarding in themselves, but they will not grant him the fruit of his search. His search, in short, is more significant than reaching his goal.

(2) The phrases are paradoxical because they are all, on the surface, contradictory. They describe situations that are unfinished, but the nature of the speaker's life is that his journeys will never be complete, his circle will never be joined, and his childhood will never end no matter how old he becomes. The underlying idea is that life is a continuum from birth onwards, and that goals constantly change, recede, and are redefined.

(3) The word "unfound" may be considered as a the poem's major theme because it summarizes the idea of the search. As a general principle, even if something is not found—say a cure for a supposedly incurable disease—that lack of success does not deny that the cure may nevertheless exist. The poem's theme is therefore that one's search cannot end as long as one is alive, even if we never reach where we started for so long ago.

WRITING TOPICS. The poem's paradoxes. The concept that meaning is the quest rather than the goal. The poem's geography. The character of the speaker

WORKS FOR COMPARISON WITH
"FACING WEST FROM CALIFORNIA'S SHORES"

Lightman, *In Computers, 1171*
Pollitt, *Archaeology, 1187*
Porter, *The Jilting of Granny Weatherall, 651*
Yeats, *The Wild Swans at Coole, 1219*

WILLIAM WORDSWORTH, *London, 1802,* *pages 799–800*

This is one of Wordsworth's political sonnets. Although he does not refer specifically to any corrupt politicians, his references make clear that politicians and the English public alike are subject to his anger, and to his assertions that there is a need to discover new and thoughtful leadership.

Suggestions for Discussing the Study Questions, page 800

(1) At the time Wordsworth wrote this poem, Milton had been

established as one of the great English voices. His most famous poem, *Paradise Lost*, had been acclaimed as the greatest of English epics. Wordsworth's apostrophe to Milton therefore has the effect of appealing to one of the greatest figures in the English tradition. It is likely that Wordsworth is thinking as much of Milton's connection with the causes of freedom developed during the revolution and interregnum (1642–1660) as of *Paradise Lost*.

(2) His claim is that the church (*altar*), the military (*sword*), the intelligentsia (*pen*), home and family life (*fireside*), and the legal establishment (*hall and bower*) have all lost the sense of meaning and direction that is their heritage (*have forfeited their ancient English dower*).

(3) The overstatement (hyperbole) of the *fen / Of stagnant waters* and the broad brush leveled against the institutions described in question 2 are clearly designed to show Wordsworth's sense of alarm, not to describe each individual in the country. Wordsworth therefore dramatizes his point that the country needs new thinkers, and new guidance, in the tradition established by Milton.

(4) The claims Wordsworth makes for Milton is that the great epic poet was a special person, in tune with God and Nature, but that he was also a person who lived in "life's common way." Therefore he combined the intelligence and compassion necessary in a national leader. The metonyms of *soul* and *heart* refer to Milton's spirituality and humanity.

Writing topics. Wordsworth's use of hyperbole or metonymy (or both). Wordsworth's judgment of Milton. The qualities of leadership as envisaged in the sonnet. Wordsworth's voice in the sonnet.

Works for Comparison with "London, 1802"

Blake, *London*, 695
Sandburg, *Chicago*, 1194
Shelley, *Ode to the West Wind*, 877

Sir Thomas Wyatt, *I Find No Peace*, *page 800*

This poem is one of the most famous for exploring the figure of paradox. It is by no means easy, and beginning students especially may need to be guided closely, line-by-line, in an examination of the ideas. It would be difficult within a fourteen-line limit to bring out more of the conflicting states that people in love sometimes experience. The poem should be placed in the context that love is often considered the solution of all problems, the "happily-ever-after" idea of a life without difficulty and doubt. The speaker is aware, however, of all his future needs for adjustment, and therefore his apprehension is the cause of the many paradoxes in the poem.

Suggestions for Discussing the Study Questions, page 801

(1) The speaker reflects on the paradoxical nature of his love. On the one hand, he wants to love deeply, but on the other he approaches the situation of love expecting that it will change his life completely. Thus, he describes both anticipation and trepidation. In expressing these opposing feelings, he brings in a number of metaphors and similes, such as those of peace and war (line 1), burning and freezing (line 2), flying like a bird (line 3), and wealth and poverty (line 4). All these paradoxical metaphors, if well considered, are successful in bringing out the contrary states of the speaker's feelings.

(2) A count reveals fifteen separate paradoxes in the poem. Lines 5 and 6 provide just one paradox, but lines 9 and 12 each give us two. The total effect of the paradoxes is to stress the conflicting emotions elicited by love. The point is made about as strongly as it can be, from the global paradoxes in lines 1–4 to the more political and personal ones in lines 5–8. The logic of turning the love of another to hate for oneself (line 11) is difficult to follow unless the line refers to the speaker's inability to express his love or to pursue it successfully. The assertion that the speaker's "delight" causes all the "strife" (line 14) is easier to follow. We may suppose that the speaker had established a regular way of life which has been upset by the changes required and anticipated by his having fallen in love.

(3) Wyatt's many paradoxes in this personal poem are the expression of a person who cannot communicate all his feelings with the loved one. The poem implies that the love may be forbidden in some way, or that the speaker has not yet had the opportunity to speak extensively with the loved one. Presumably, in a courtship in which the two lovers have unlimited freedom of expression, all the feelings might be aired, but in a courtship hemmed in by custom and inhibition, the speaker's expressions seem perfectly natural.

WRITING TOPICS. The effect of the first line. The number and nature of the poem's paradoxes. Possible reasons for the heavy reliance on paradox in the poem.

WORKS FOR COMPARISON WITH "I FIND NO PEACE"

Eliot, *Eyes that Last I Saw in Tears, 786*
Elizabeth Tudor, Queen Elizabeth I,
On Monsieur's Departure, 796

Keats, *La Belle Dame Sans Merci*, 954
Piercy, *Will We Work Together?*, 1185

Writing About Figures of Speech, *pages 801–806*

It is unlikely that you would want to assign full-length essays on a number of separate figures. Rather, we presume that writing assignments will be confined to just one major figure, such as metaphors or similes. With the other figures, as well, it is probably best to use just one figure per writing assignment. For these reasons, we have envisaged a paragraph-length treatment as shown in the paragraph-length demonstrative essay on page 804. Because of its brevity, such a paragraph could be done for in-class writing exercises, just as it might also be a model for examination questions.

The more common assignments will likely concern metaphors and similes. Accordingly, we have supplied a number of suggestions for development (803). Most students will probably model their essays on No. 1, with perhaps some reinforcement from No. 2, as is shown in the demonstrative essay beginning on page 804. The third type of essay, because it attempts to select characteristic metaphors, may be most useful if students study more than a single poem by a particular author (see Chapter 25, or consult the index under the names of individual poets, for such materials). The fourth development, in addition to being a study of metaphor generally, also brings in tone.

The second demonstrative essay (804–805) is useful as a guide to any of the suggested writing topics for this chapter because, throughout, it stresses the topic of metaphor. In such an essay it is easy to get diverted from the rhetorical figures and begin a general discussion. Students should concentrate on the assigned topic of this or any essay.

Special Topics for Writing and Argument about Figures of Speech in Poetry, *pages 806–807*

(1) Topic 1 can be readily done by those with a compass at hand. If students have left this equipment at home, however, a blackboard drawing, or a duplicated drawing, might serve as well. An interesting question is whether Donne himself, in writing the poem, had a compass in front of him, and worked out his extended simile as he changed the positions of the instrument.

(2) Topic 2 depends on the figures selected by the student. In developing the essay, students should pay particular attention to

the meaning of the word "effective." You might suggest clarifying words such as *clear, forceful, thought-provoking, emphatic, appropriate,* and so on.

(3) Topic 3 lists a series of topics, which might be used for shorter or longer essays. The topics could be made concrete if students were to use any of the study questions for the various poems. Of all these special writing topics, this one might require the greatest guidance from you, either in class or in individual conference.

(4) Topic 4 is designed to get students into the act of developing their own rhetorical figures in poems of their own. For this assignment, it is more important that they concentrate on their governing metaphor or simile than that they worry about the absolute best word choices and rhythms (this could, of course, come later). An important part of the exercise is the section in which students write about how they, as poets, decided to develop their poems.

(5) Cuddon's book is a particularly helpful and complete guide for students to know about, particularly for terms like the ones included in this chapter. You might want to have students augment their use of Cuddon with other library references.

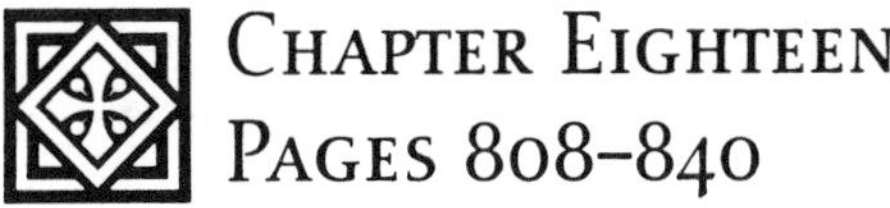

CHAPTER EIGHTEEN PAGES 808–840

Tone: The Creation of Attitude in Poetry

Tone is both easy and difficult. It is easy because the beginning and ending of a discussion of tone is the formulation of attitudes present in a poem, or a statement about the appropriateness of diction, imagery, or metaphor to the content. Usually these judgments are readily described.

It is difficult, however, because a full discussion requires not only the formulation of an attitude but also the analysis of how the poem permits the reader to draw conclusions. Thus, any investigation of tone is complex, requiring students to show the interaction of poet, material, reader, situation, word choice, fairness, completeness of development, truthfulness, and structure, together with anything else that might have a bearing on the proper interpretation of attitudes. When you ask students to describe the dominant tone in a poem, they may respond by saying "irony," "humor," "phoniness," "indignation," "pathos," or a number of other descriptive terms. The problem for them then becomes explaining the means by which the poem enables them to make these assessments. The reproduction of Léger's *The City* is included as a graphic complement to the study of literary tone, for Léger's arrangements, distortions, and partial views demonstrate the control he exerts to communicate a negative attitude toward city life.

CORNELIUS WHUR, *The First-Rate Wife*, *page 809*

The commentary on the poem (810) addresses the issues in the study questions.

WRITING TOPICS. The nature of the speaker. The tone with respect to women and men. How good (bad) is the poem?

WORKS FOR COMPARISON WITH "THE FIRST-RATE WIFE"

Atwood, *Variation on the Word Sleep, 1124*
Bradstreet, *To My Dear and Loving Husband, 1128*
Browning, *My Last Duchess, 695*
Waller, *Go, Lovely Rose, 1213*

WILFRED OWEN, *Dulce et Decorum Est,* *pages 810–11*

The text (811–12) deals with the subjects of the study questions on page 811.

WRITING TOPICS. The tone of the speaker toward the listener. Attitudes about warfare. The irony of the title.

WORKS FOR COMPARISON WITH "DULCE ET DECORUM EST"

Eberhart, *Fury of Aerial Bombardment, 732*
Hardy, *In Time of 'The Breaking of Nations,' 950*
Hemingway, *Soldier's Home, 348*
Jarrell, *Death of the Ball-Turret Gunner, 676*

THOMAS HARDY, *The Workbox,* *pages 814–15*

See page 815 for a brief discussion of "The Workbox."

Suggestions for Discussing the Study Questions, page 815

(1) The speaker is mainly the husband, a village cabinet-maker. The tone develops here as much in the rhyme scheme and rhythm used—variations on the ballad form—as in other devices. Here the poem tells a story, and though there is no refrain there is a parallelism of actions or words stressing the poem's concerns (e.g., "look white," line 21; "wan," line 37; face held or turned aside, lines 22 and 38; the intimate address of "little wife" and "my dear," lines 1 and 21). Thus the form suggests that a significant drama will occur, and that the poet wants us to be attentive, for much is suggested and not made explicit.

(2) The dialogue in lines 21–40 indicates that the wife knew the dead man, John, and had established a close relationship with him. She denies the previous connection because she had never told her husband about it before. She hence is covering up an earlier lie. The last stanza (lines 37–40) insinuates that in some way she had knowledge of the causes of John's death. The mystery is preserved about the death (lines 12 and 40) so that the irony of the poem may be maintained.

(3) The irony of the little workbox is that it is in effect a miniature coffin, and what the husband meant as a gift of love becomes its opposite—an occasion for pain each time the wife begins to sew.

(4) A more sinister possibility, of course, is that the husband knows the full story, or more likely that he suspects it, and has deliberately fashioned the workbox either as a test or as a punishment for his "little wife." The deeper irony is therefore that the husband,

by his suspicions, is probably destroying forever any possibility of future truth and intimacy with his wife. The wife's rejection of the husband's suggestion that she is "shocked" is also ironic. Whether she makes the denial to preserve her mystery or to defend herself from further probing is part of the poem's intriguing ambiguity.

(5) The opening speech of the narrator establishes the dramatic situation of the poem. Of the narrator's concluding four lines, the first two are dramatic, and the last two (lines 39–40) indicate his own conclusion about the wife. These lines could possibly be eliminated because they are not consistent with the objective viewpoint of the rest of the poem. Better lines would be descriptive ones, more like lines 37 and 38.

WRITING TOPICS. The use of irony in "The Workbox." The problematic nature of the wife's relationship with the dead man. The irony of situation. The role of the narrator.

WORKS FOR COMPARISON WITH "THE WORKBOX"

Browning (Elizabeth Barrett), *How Do I Love Thee, 1130*
Browning (Robert), *My Last Duchess, 695*
Glaspell, *A Jury of Her Peers, 202*
Ibsen, *A Dollhouse, 1793*

ALEXANDER POPE, *Epigram from the French, page 816*

Suggestions for Discussing the Study Questions, page 816

(1–3) This epigram may also be described as a squib, lampoon, or barb because of its shortness. The rhetorical structure in lines 2 and 4 is *chiasmus* or antimetabole: *poet, fool; fool, poet*. The characteristics of satire are the qualities of (a) attack, and (b) humor. Insult alone is not enough to create interest in such a poem, but with the wit shown in the speaker's attack, the poem captures the involvement and assent necessary for successful satire.

WRITING TOPICS. The speaker's nature. The speaker's attitude toward the listener. The poem as a brief example of satire.

WORKS FOR COMPARISON WITH "EPIGRAM FROM THE FRENCH"

Graves, *The Naked and the Nude, 726*
Moore, *How to Become a Writer, 274*
Nash, *Very Like a Whale, 868*

Alexander Pope, *Epigram, Engraved on the Collar of a Dog which I gave to His Royal Highness,* page 816

Suggestions for Discussing the Study Questions, page 817

(1–2) This barb is an even more brief illustration of satiric technique, yet it accomplishes much within this shorter space. Students who have had acting experience might be able to mimic the superciliousness of the speaker, and thereby demonstrate the skill with which Pope has brought this canine to life. Here, satire is illustrated *within* the speaker himself or herself: The speaker embodies the attitudes being satirized.

Writing topics. The speaker as subject of satire. The use of satire to attack attitudes. The dramatic situation.

Works for Comparison with "Epigram, Engraved on the Collar of a Dog"

Colwin, *An Old-Fashioned Story,* 67
Lochhead, *The Choosing,* 1172
Salinas, *In a Farmhouse in America,* 1193

Anne Bradstreet, *The Author to Her Book,* page 818

Anne Bradstreet's brother-in-law had arranged for publication of her manuscript poems in 1650, and did so without her knowledge and corrections (see lines 3–6). The volume, entitled *The Tenth Muse,* was the first poetic publication in England by anyone living in colonial America. Apparently a second and corrected edition was considered in about 1666, and "The Author to Her Book" was composed in this expectation as a prefatory poem. The new edition did not appear, however, until after Bradstreet's death in 1678.

Suggestions for Discussing the Study Questions, page 818

(1) The tone of the speaker's references to her friends eager to publish her work is one of both disapproval and disavowal, but at the same time she acknowledges their fidelity by labeling them "true" (line 3). The negative aspect of the tone is governed by the words "snatched," "less wise," and "exposed," all of which are ambiguous.

(2) The speaker's excuse for issuing the poems is stated in lines 11–12, where she talks of amending "blemishes"; that is, she wishes to have her reputation depend upon corrected and accurate copies of the poetry. The tone is conducive to humor because of the continuing metaphor of the child. Thus, the images of washing off spots, stretching joints, and improving clothing are all comic. The

concluding application of the metaphor, in effect equating the birth of the poems with the birth of a bastard, is amusing. Thus the tone throughout makes the collection of poems—the "book"—seem like an external object, to be laughed about by both poet and reader.

(3) The author's portrayal of herself is not unconventional: She declares herself as being both a busy and harried but also affectionate mother, trying to amend the appearance of a difficult child, thereby encouraging an amused response. Along with amusement, however, the details are arranged to promote understanding and sympathy.

(4) In dealing with the metaphor of the bastard child (lines 11–18), a metaphor appropriate for a female voice, the speaker demonstrates a degree of self-deprecation (she also says that the book is "ill-formed," suggesting shame). The metaphor is also developed elsewhere in the poem (e.g., lines 8, 22–23, among others).

WRITING TOPICS. The speaker's attitude toward herself and to her work. The attitude toward the well-meaning friends. The tone of the metaphor of the bastard child.

WORKS FOR COMPARISON WITH "THE AUTHOR TO HER BOOK"

Dickinson, *I Died for Beauty*, 1070
Keats, *On First Looking Into Chapman's Homer*, 777
Moore, *How to Become a Writer*, 274

LUCILLE CLIFTON, *homage to my hips*, *page 819*

This is a poem that surprises by its frankness. The line lengths are uneven and free, perhaps suggesting a swaying, dancelike motion. The structural development is also free and spontaneous. In lines 1, 5, 8, 11, and 12, new units begin with the phrase *these hips*. Elsewhere, the structure is governed by the repetition of *they*. These structures all suggest movement. The freedom and informality suggested by the motion is also complemented by the poem's lack of capitalization.

Suggestions for Discussing the Study Questions, page 819

(1) The topic of the speaker's hips is not the usual subject material of poetry. The attitude expressed here is not only that the speaker speaks freely about her hips, but demonstrates total delight in them, without embarrassment but with pride and the memory of delight and power.

(2) These words reflect a union between mentality and physicality. The hips are free, not enslaved, and do their own bidding. The speaker's philosophy is to move with the hips, and in no way to restrain the life, involvement, and memory that they bring.

(3) Words like *free, mighty, magic,* and *spin* often belong to other contexts, such as those of politics, power, incantation, and physical mechanics. Because they are put into the context of hips, they take on new meaning, and therefore produce smiles and laughter. This is a happy poem.

WRITING TOPICS. The poem's subject. The function of varying lines and absence of capitalization. The relationship of diction to the poem's tone.

WORKS FOR COMPARISON WITH "HOMAGE TO MY HIPS"

cummings, *she being Brand / -new, 819*
Gardner, *At a Summer Hotel, 862*
Wakoski, *Inside Out, 798*

E. E. CUMMINGS, *she being Brand / -new, pages 819–20*

This poem is characteristic of cummings in many ways. It demonstrates his use of popular material, in this case the breaking in of a new car. It also shows his frankness, sexual explicitness, and sense of fun, together with his poetic arrangement of poetry as unusual arrangement on the page. Modern students, accustomed to cars with self-starters, may not know that in 1926, the date of the poem, cars were started with a hand-crank (lines 9–10), gears did not always engage smoothly when the foot clutch was released (line 12), and the spark and choke were worked by levers (line 16) that were moved up and down, to be held in place on a heavily notched dial.

Suggestions for Discussing the Study Questions, page 820

(1) The sexual *double entendre* of the poem depends on the equation of "breaking in" a new car and a first experience with sex. Once this premise is admitted, most students are adept at determining the extensive double meanings in the poem. The excitement and discovery invariably cause students to remark that the poem is fun, although this aspect of the poem should probably not be emphasized if there are students who express any dismay about it.

(2) cummings's spacing and alignment assist in the visualization of the experiences both of sex and of driving a new car. The slowness caused by the specific line ["again slo – wly; bare, ly nudg. ing (my"] is appropriate to the tentative nature of testing new apparatus. Similarly, the run-together word "greasedlightning" suggests that once working, things may move smoothly. Need we be more explicit with regard to the double meaning?

(3) The poem is better called "frank," "open," or "happy" rather

than "bawdy" or "off color." The narration of the poem—the difficulty of breaking in the car—preserves a surface innocence. The frankness develops from the verbal irony and ambiguity.

WRITING TOPICS. The poem's frankness and joy. The *double entendre.* The spacing, alignment, and punctuation, and their effect on the tone.

WORKS FOR COMPARISON WITH "SHE BEING BRAND / -NEW"

Anonymous, *Western Wind, 687*
Burns, *Green Grow the Rashes, O, 729*
Herrick, *To the Virgins, to Make Much of Time, 1016*
Munro, *The Found Boat, 353*

MARI EVANS, *I Am a Black Woman,* *page 821*

Evans's open-form poem celebrates the power and strength of the black woman in the context of centuries of racial hatred, suppression, and war.

Suggestions for Discussing the Study Questions, page 822

(1) The arpeggio suggests that the tears are continuous, like ascending and descending musical chords, because of the hurts suffered by African Americans from their beginnings in America to the present time. The bitterness caused by life for the black woman is implied in the phrase "written in a minor key." This image connects the speaker's tears and her "humming in the night" over her sorrows.

(2) The long history of poverty and destruction is evoked by the images of death and birth (lines 10–12) and the four allusions to lynching and war (lines 13–20). To indicate her fear and regret, the speaker uses the words "screaming," "Nat's swinging body in a rain of tears," and "anguish."

(3) The speaker asserts the constructive power of the black woman; key terms are *strong, tall, defying, impervious, indestructible,* and *renewed.* This assertiveness makes the poem optimistic, although her character alone cannot change the details that she brings out in the earlier part of the poem.

WRITING TOPICS. The image of music in the poem. The character of the speaker.

WORKS FOR COMPARISON WITH "I AM A BLACK WOMAN"

Clisneros, *The House on Mango Street, 290*
Brooks, *Primer for Blacks, 1128*
Sanchez, *right on: white america, 1193*

LANGSTON HUGHES, *Theme for English B, pages 822–23*

"Theme for English B" is an original and witty poem in which Hughes dramatizes the need for everyone to recognize people for what they are, not for the groups in which they have been born or to which they belong. The poem itself is sufficient to demonstrate the truth of Hughes's assertions. It is a superior effort, and on its face it belies those who might want to claim that people like the speaker are inferior.

Suggestions for Discussing the Study Questions, page 823

(1) The speaker asserts his equality with his instructor and, by extension, with all those who may claim superiority to him. He stresses that he has ordinary likes and needs, and that his capacities are like those of everyone else. Thus, even though he lives at the Y, his rights, and his character, make him the equal of those who live in mansions.

(2) Ordinarily, in a course like English B, responses to assignments are prose essays. That the speaker composes a poem rather than an essay is a mark of boldness and confidence, more of a challenge than a response to an essay. The poem therefore is an aspect of the speaker's assertion of equality.

(3) All the words in lines 21–24 are short and simple. There is nothing elaborate about them, and therefore we can conclude that the speaker is asserting his ability to present ideas directly. His description of his likes makes him just like anyone else. There is no evasion or ambiguity about what he says, no assertion that he is superior. He simply puts forward his desires and tastes as a matter of fact, just as anyone else would.

(4) In lines 27–40 the speaker indicates that, granted his assertion of equality, he has the right to his own identity and privacy, and also to claim the ability to teach the instructor just as the instructor teaches him. The idea is that just as this understanding exists among all persons, it should exist between him and his instructor. The only reservation the speaker makes is in line 40, when he says that the instructor is "somewhat more free," as a white, than he, as a black.

WRITING TOPICS. The character of the speaker. The connection that the speaker establishes with his reader, the teacher.

WORKS FOR COMPARISON WITH "THEME FOR ENGLISH B"

Angelou, *My Arkansas*, 1119
Bontemps, *A Black Man Talks of Reaping*, 1128
McKay, *The White City*, 1177

X. J. KENNEDY, *John While Swimming in the Ocean*, *page 823*

This poem is selected from the poet's volume *Brats*. Perhaps this title is a fitting commentary on the unfortunate protagonist. One may compare "John While Swimming" with the satiric barbs of Pope (816).

Suggestions for Discussing the Study Questions, page 823

(1) The idea of a person's putting suntan lotion on the backs of sharks is ridiculous, and actually attempting to do it is impossible on the surface (not to mention under water).

(2) *Ocean* and *lotion* as rhymes are trochaic, and rhythmically they complement a comic mood. Also, the comparative sizes of *ocean* and *lotion* are so distinct that the juxtaposing of the two in rhyme causes the humor of anticlimax. To rhyme *John's* with *bronze* is unusual and good, and in the context marvelously funny.

(3) A characterization of the poem's attitude toward beach culture would be disapproval, at the very least.

WRITING TOPICS. The poem's use of rhyme. The ludicrous nature of the action. The poem in relation to Pope's short satiric poems (745).

WORKS FOR COMPARISON WITH "JOHN WHILE SWIMMING IN THE OCEAN"

Dickey, *The Performance*, 1142
cummings, *Buffalo Bill's Defunct*, 910
Walker, *Revolutionary Petunias*, 1212

SHARON OLDS, *The Planned Child*, *page 824*

See the demonstrative student essay (837–38) for a discussion of the issues brought out in the study questions on page 824.

WRITING TOPICS. The nature of the speaker. The speaker's reconciliation to her anger at being a "planned child." Unusual topic matter in the poem.

WORKS FOR COMPARISON WITH "THE PLANNED CHILD"

Gilchrist, *Song of Songs*, 264
Hayden, *Those Winter Sundays*, 1161
Wagner, *The Boxes*, 1211

MICHAEL ONDAATJE, *Late Movies with Skyler*, *pages 824–26*

This poem by the Academy Award winner is a short narrative about the relationship of life to a major form of art. Films make for a short respite in which it is possible to share laughter and establish friendship and intimacy, and also to strengthen oneself to face the future.

Suggestions for Discussing the Study Questions, page 826

(1) The old movies bring back the past for the speaker, who claims that they had a moral influence on them. Although he speaks ironically, he nevertheless admits that he had seen one of the films, *The Prisoner of Zenda,* three times when he was young. The commercials seem to provide the speaker and Skyler with the opportunity to have a time of "privacy," in which they can attend to a number of needs, including Skyler's playing on the guitar.

(2) Skyler is a friend, a younger brother, or the son of the speaker. He has come home after working in a logging camp in Canada, on Vancouver Island, under primitive conditions, and his means of recovering is funny just as it would be quite agonizing for a man. The speaker has a close and brotherly relationship with Skyler, although he seems to have reservations about the directions in which Skyler is pointing his life. Clearly, the contrast between the real life of Vancouver Island, Montreal, or the Maritimes, and the movie life of riding off "into the sunset," is affecting the speaker.

(3) The speaker presents a wry view of life characterized by words and phrases such as *terrible, staggering, get rid of crabs, bending over in agony, no doubt influenced me morally,* and *urinate under the trees.* The humor suggests that a strong bond exists between Skyler and the speaker, a bond developed from shared experiences and conversations.

(4) The last four lines describe the gap between fantasy, represented by the late movies, and reality, represented by the future that Skyler must face. The phrase *absolutely nothing /to do for the rest of their lives* brings home the fact that the *perfect* world of the film must end, not only because it is impossible but also because it does not exist. For the Skylers of the world, leaving the late movies means going on to a new and uncertain life of responsibility and work.

WRITING TOPICS. The relationship between Skyler and the speaker. The poem's humor. The contrast between life in the movies and real life.

WORKS FOR COMPARISON WITH "LATE MOVIES WITH SKYLER"

Coleridge, *Kubla Khan, 756*
Dickinson, *I Died for Beauty, 1070*
Keats, *Ode to a Nightingale, 918*
Stanton, *Childhood, 710*

ROBERT PINSKY, *Dying,* *page 826*

This poem by the three-time American poet laureate is entitled "Dying" but actually is about how things change and develop, climaxing in the final image of restless life persisting in the face of overwhelming odds.

Suggestions for Discussing the Study Questions, page 826

(1, 2, 3) The first two tercets introduce death from the standpoint of a child experiencing the deaths of neighboring animals. These concrete examples are complemented by references to language about death and to the reality of death. The provisional conclusion of this development is line 12: "The different pace makes the difference absolute." Yes, death is inflicted upon all at its own pace, so that it is true that "everyone is" dying, but each death is unique and individual, and not collective. Tercets 5–8 constitute a new section introducing references to the universality of death which, ironically, has an insistent life of its own, causing life processes to continue in human beings even after they are dead. This image brings up the brevity of life, which the speaker considers in tercet 9, the most uplifting part of the poem. The moth reflecting the light of a flame symbolizes the continuity of life, the "bright soul" which persists despite all the myriad ways in which death literally swallows living beings just as larger predators consume moths. The "bored and impatient" phrase in line 27 emphasizes that life, even though it might continue somehow as a "beating" entity (line 26), is not magically transformed. Life is life, in all its commoness and impatience. It is undeniable that the poem dwells on some of the morbid and detailed aspects of death, but the final lines are optimistic. Because each life is unique, life itself is also important and "bright" despite death's monstrous voraciousness.

WRITING TOPICS. The development of the poem's references to death. The meaning of the life-in-death images of nails and whiskers. The emotional effect of the final tercet in relationship to the poem's cumulative details about death.

WORKS FOR COMPARISON WITH "DYING"

Forster, *The Point of It*, 607
Frost, *Something Like a Star*, 1114
King, *Sic Vita*, 790
Whitman, *Full of Life Now*, 1216

ALEXANDER POPE, *from* **Epilogue to the Satires, Dialogue I,** *pages 827–28*

Because of the ways in which "An Essay on Man" is contrasted with Voltaire's *Candide*, Pope is often denigrated as an apostle of the idea that everything is for the best in this best of all possible worlds. This denigration, first of all, results from a misreading of his idea that "Whatever is, is right," which would be better construed as "Whatever is, is, and it won't change, so we had better do the best we can with what we are given." Second, the faulty interpretation ignores the fact that Pope was a satirist during his entire poetic career. The fragment contained here, from Dialogue I of the *Epilogue to the Satires*, is a self-contained unit illustrating the scope of Pope's satire, and the concluding line should dispel the misinterpretations from which Pope often suffers.

Suggestions for Discussing the Study Questions, page 828

(1) In light of the fact that Pope often uses the dialogue form in his satires, the designation *P* may be construed as a representation of Pope's own views. The final couplet surely is a personal statement, at least a statement of Pope's own sense of outrage at some of the actions he satirizes in the poem.

(2) Pope's satire is couched in general terms in this excerpt, but elsewhere he used generalized names to refer to reprehensible qualities. He skated a fine line in his satire, for if he named names, those who were not named would feel absolved. If he did not name names, people could claim that they were not intended for criticism. Here, Pope criticizes the importation of continental customs as opposed to English ones, corruption in "soldier, churchman, man in power" (line 161), and the public admiration of people who were noted not for their virtue but for their outrageousness.

(3) The tone of the excerpt rises from the opening to line 160, "That 'not to be corrupted is the shame.'" From there it sustains a strong level of invective, climaxing with line 170, "'Nothing is sacred now but villainy.'"

(4) Students might enjoy discussing this question, and might bring in copies of some of current tabloid publications which thrive on scandal and misdeeds. The question about these publications is whether people read them to revile the actions they describe, or to enjoy sharing the experiences. Lively discussion, in any event, should result.

WRITING TOPICS. The objects of Pope's satiric criticism. The tone of the satiric excerpt. The voice of the satirist in the poem.

WORKS FOR COMPARISON WITH POPE'S "EPILOGUE"

Eliot, *The Love Song of J. Alfred Prufrock*, 1147
Lightman, *In Computers*, 1171

Swift, *A Description of the Morning*, 832
C. K. Williams, *Dimensions*, 834

Salvatore Quasímodo, *Auschwitz*, *pages 829–30*

(*Please see the explanatory notes on pages 829 and 830.*) The poem "Auschwitz" (and Berkenau) is a searching and agonized poem in which the speaker describes a visit, with his "love," to the camp and attempts to explain its meaning. But answers are not easily found. The use of the imagery of transformations is hence appropriate, for those who are living must find meaning out of the hundreds of thousands of deaths that took place in the Auschwitz gas chambers.

Suggestions for Discussing the Study Questions, page 830

(1) The first ten lines describe negative images of rust, tangled fencing, rain, funeral cold, and general lifelessness, all of which produce a sense of depression, "hurt," and hopelessness. The concluding six lines have shifted away from the depressing images in the poem to a positive resolution: "never from the pit of ashes / to show itself [i.e., the horror, the atrocities] again." These lines supply at least some answer to the question about "the meaning of our destiny" posed in lines 9 and 10.

(2) These lines, 13 and 14, affirm the need for life in the light of "every No" that took place at the camp. In other words, the contemplation of the many exterminations at Auschwitz makes the speaker firmly resolved to take the actions that prevent such atrocities in the future. From death, in other words, there must arise life.

(3) The references to ancient myths of transformation, particularly to the stories of Alpheus and Arethusa (which Milton refers to in his elegy "Lycidas," where they also signify the continuation of life despite the reality of death), are intended to bolster the speaker's thoughts and also those of his listener. The specific transformations in lines 25–43 are those of the dead who have gone back into the earth. Many of the personal possessions of the victims, testifying to the reality of their suffering, are still displayed at the camp (lines 37–40). This visual testimony, in the speaker's judgment, should create a transformation of the people who visit the camp, a transformation through which people dedicate themselves not to military coercion but rather to ethical and political solutions of problems.

Writing topics. The use of realistic, physical imagery in the poem. The meaning of the transformation myths described in the poem. The sense of resolution in the concluding six lines.

WORKS FOR COMPARISON WITH "AUSCHWITZ"

Cohen, *'The killers that run . . .',* 1134
Forché, *Because One Is Always Forgotten,* 1153
Layton, *Rhine Boat Trip,* 1169
Ozick, *The Shawl,* 331
Zabytko, *Home Soil,* 511

ANNE RIDLER, *Nothing Is Lost,* *pages 830–31*

This provocative poem may be regarded dramatically, for the speaker is addressing her father, who died ten years previously. This situation prompts her to consider that the words of a person now dead still have the life that they had when the dead person wrote them. The poem stems from this situation.

Suggestions for Discussing the Study Questions, page 831

(1) The statement that "nothing dies" is challenging because according to ordinary observation, everything dies. The words indicate that the speaker might be introducing ideas about the soul's immortality, and that therefore the poem might be a religious one. But the speaker in fact brings in references to a variety of ways, both physical and social, by which individuals pass on their genes and their habits from one generation to the next. Thus the dead "are about us always, though unguessed" (line 5).

(2) In human beings, the connections among generations, from the very beginning ("Adam," line 20) to the present ("the new born," line 21) and, by implication, to the future, are propagated by love because of the emotional attachments coincident to sexual reproduction. Love is the key, for without knowing it we are part of a "chain of love" (the phrase is from Pope's "An Essay on Man") that transcends our own brief moment of life. Thus even our eye color may be seen as a perpetuation of the eye color of our first ancestors, Adam and Eve (the speaker does not mention Eve). In the sense of the speaker's view of the continuity and universality of life, it is indeed true that "all in love survive" (line 26).

(3) Those who believe in their own uniqueness and originality might find comfort in the poem because today's people are inheritors of a vast tradition to which they are in a position to contribute. Few people who claim to be individualistic would claim that they have begun life from scratch, and that they have invented the wheel all by themselves. If individuality is understood correctly, persons claiming to be unique will be persuaded that uniqueness requires a

deeply considered definition. The final lines put this idea in perspective: Our life is "only a tiny portion" (line 32) of a much vaster life, and we are, as it were, on the crest of an iceberg, supported by "deep supporting multitudes below" (line 35).

WRITING TOPICS. The tone of the poem, pessimistic or optimistic? What situation causes the speaker to begin writing? How does the iceberg image at the poem's end crystallize the previous ideas?

WORKS FOR COMPARISON WITH "NOTHING IS LOST"

Evans, *The Iceberg Seven-eighths Under,* 786
Forster, *The Point of It,* 607
Levertov, *Of Being,* 736
Whitman, *Full of Life Now,* 1216
Wilbur, *Year's End,* 958

THEODORE ROETHKE, *My Papa's Waltz,* *pages 831–32*

As is brought out in question 4, "My Papa's Waltz" might arouse a certain amount of controversy among students. One view is that the speaker considers the "waltzing" father as a pleasant association of childhood. Another view is that the experiences were not pleasant at all. Students may find justification in the poem to take either position. An attempt to achieve a balance is made in the following answers.

Suggestions for Discussing the Study Questions, page 832

(1) The opening description of the father is conducive to the speaker's boyhood sense of ambiguity and anxiety. The phrases "like death" and "such waltzing" are opposed; either one or the other is inappropriate, or else the speaker is being ironic. In the context of "like death," however, the term "waltzing" is likely an understatement. The tone then suggests apprehension and anxiety, although the assertion that the father's whiskey breath could make "a small boy dizzy" is a tempering (but not a temperance) overstatement.

(2) The "waltz" is an understatement describing a drunkenly boisterous mock dance done by the speaker's father, with the speaker as a boy being the partner. The tone of the description suggests the mixture of emotions conveyed in the opening stanza. The roughness and grossness of the father is brought out in the references to his battered knuckle, his lack of coordination, the scraping his buckle gives the speaker's ear, the tattoo on the boy's head, and the dirt-caked palm. The lack of control is made mildly amusing by the sliding of the pans and the frowning mother. The potential pain and

fright that might be experienced by the boy are mitigated by the light iambic trimeter and the trochaic rhyme of lines 10 and 12.

(3) "Countenance" is an instance of overstatement in line 7 because the word is inconsistent with the diction in the rest of the poem. In context, and along with the use of "unfrown," the word "countenance" suggests the mother's annoyance and disapproval but not outright anger or fear.

(4) The tone of the speaker's treatment of the father suggests the speaker's sense of powerlessness accompanying his memory. Whatever pain he experienced is not mentioned in the poem, even though the descriptions indicate that he would have felt at least some (such as having time beat out on his head, his right ear scraping the buckle). Thus the speaker's recollection emphasizes that he is attempting to understand and reconcile himself to his memory of his father, with the less pleasant aspects being diminished. In any event, it is unlikely that any person would remember with fondness the experience of having someone beating on his or her head.

Writing topics. The attitude towards the father. Overstatement and understatement. The speaker's attitude toward the memory. The function of rhythm and structure.

Works for Comparison with "My Papa's Waltz"

cummings, *if there are any heavens, 1138*
Hamod, *Leaves, 1158*
Hayden, *Those Winter Sundays, 1161*
Olds, *The Planned Child, 824*

Jonathan Swift, *A Description of the Morning,* *pages 832–33*

During the period from 1701–1714, Swift lived in England as a special envoy of the Irish church and also as a writer for the Tory government. This poem was one of many satiric pieces that he wrote during the time.

Answers to the Study Questions, page 833

(1) All the images are anti-heroic, being derived from seamy and unromantic aspects of life, such as the lazy apprentice, the dirty kennel's edge, and the noisy charcoal seller. "Betty" has spent the night with her master, and rushes to her own bed to "discompose" it so that those around her will believe that she spent her night innocently. Mention of "his lordship" is sarcastic; the lord symbolizes form without substance.

(2) The previous references are to adults, who are the main

inhabitants of this antiheroic world. By introducing the reference to schoolboys, who are not yet part of this world, Swift attains comprehensiveness, for the boys are reluctant to learn their lessons, but also, symbolically, move reluctantly forward into the adult world that Swift satirizes.

(4) The anti-heroic subject matter cast within heroic couplets emphasizes Swift's satiric view of London in the morning, and it also underscores his satiric dispraise of false appearances (the indebted lord) and the criminal prison keeper. The satiric basis of the poem is the discrepancy between pretentiousness and reality.

WRITING TOPICS. The negative images of life in the poem. The use of realism in the poem's satire. The satiric use of the schoolboys lagging with satchels in their hands.

WORKS FOR COMPARISON WITH
"A DESCRIPTION OF THE MORNING"

Collins, *Schoolsville, 663*
cummings, *next to of course god, 1012*
Field, *Icarus, 987*
Nemerov, *Life Cycle of Common Man, 1179*

DAVID WAGONER, *My Physics Teacher,* *pages 833–34*

This poem farcically but affectionately treats the memory of the speaker's physics teacher who tried but always failed to illustrate various scientific ideas. The poem's comedy stems from the failures of the demonstrations. An implied idea in the poem is that much in the universe does not yield itself to demonstration, despite all our efforts at understanding and our attempts at verbal formulations.

Answers to the Study Questions, page 834

(1) The teacher "believed in a World of Laws, where problems had answers." He therefore assumed that his classroom demonstrations would work to illustrate the truth and the validity of scientific principles. The speaker is clearly amused; he was amused at the time and he is still amused, not at the proposition that problems have answers, but at the inability of a human being to demonstrate the proposition infallibly.

(2) The demonstrations are comic and farcical because they do not work as they are supposed to. The failures of demonstration do not alter the validity of the scientific principles they were designed to illustrate. Treating the bumbling teacher's staggering actions as "his only uncontestable demonstration" is riotously farci-

cal, particularly the image of his putting "One foot forever into the wastebasket" (line 21).

WRITING TOPICS. The difficulty of illustrating scientific ideas. The drama of the classroom as shown in the poem. The poem's humor.

WORKS FOR COMPARISON WITH "MY PHYSICS TEACHER"

Aldiss, *Flight 063, 985*
Haines, *Little Cosmic Dust Poem, 1156*
Lightman, *In Computers, 1171*
Ortiz, *Story of How a Wall Stands, 1183*

C. K. WILLIAMS, *Dimensions,* *page 834*

The realistic basis for the poem is the hypothesis that there are other worlds in the universe that might resemble our own. Sometimes such remote worlds are considered utopias, where things approach perfection. The poem, however, envisages a world that is unendurable. The irony of the poem stems from the realization that the worse world is really our own.

Suggestions for Discussing the Study Questions, pages 834–35

(1) The poem is ironic because the world "somewhere else" is descriptive of much that exists in our own world. Thus, the contrast of the other world and our own ironically describes the present world in light of the "unendurable" other world. The irony is situational, but because other worlds and other dimensions are added in this poem, it is also cosmic.

(2) The title "Dimensions" suggests that one could connect the two worlds—our own and the other—time by time, character by character, event by event, and history by history. As one world is, so is the other. The opening line therefore is ironic because it could mean two things: (a) that there is another world that is unendurable, unlike our own, which is endurable, and (b) that there is another world, like our own, which is unendurable too. The second stanza is ironic because it gives a true picture of affairs just as it also disparages the situation. In contrast to the other world, "we know where we stand" could mean that our standing is (a) great, or (b) miserable.

(3) The concluding lines are not clear for they are suggestive more than descriptive. Going "over the border" thus might mean that some people get insights into the nature of our national and international politics, and they see things as they are and not as they are described in press releases. As a result of their thought and

insights, they are scarred because criticizing the status quo often creates harmful backlashes against those who do the criticizing.

WRITING TOPICS. The meaning of the "world somewhere else." The poem's use of irony. The tone of the poem, as manifested in the imagery of the third stanza.

WORKS FOR COMPARISON WITH "DIMENSIONS"

Hall, *Scenic View*, 1156
Stanton, *Childhood*, 710
Lochhead, *The Choosing*, 1172
Stevens, *Disillusionment of Ten O'Clock*, 739

Writing About Tone in Poetry, *pages 835–39*

In this section students need reminding that tone can be a slippery topic if they do no more than describe the attitudes they find in the poem. Always, it is important to emphasize that to write about tone is to explain how the attitudes are built up. Just to determine and describe the attitudes is not enough.

Therefore, the strategies for organizing ideas suggested on pages 835–37 may be stressed as providing ways for students to explore tone. The demonstrative essay on pages 837–38 illustrates that the approaches are by no means mutually exclusive. Thus a discussion of tone emphasizing the poem's situation will invariably include a section on diction, as the demonstrative essay does in paragraph 5. Probably the best thing to stress in teaching is that students should be prepared to adapt their approaches for their essays to the circumstances of the poems on which they will write. Once students are forewarned, they should be able to control their handling of tone in poetry.

Special Topics for Writing and Argument about Tone in Poetry, *pages 839–40*

(1) These poems all share the topic of love, though they treat it very differently. In "homage to my hips" the stress is on the physical leading to the ecstatic; in "she being Brand / –new" the stress is on merry sexuality; in "The Workbox" on secrecy, surreptitiousness, suspicion, and unhappiness; and in "The First-Rate Wife" on (unwitting) pompousness and condescension.

(2) From a feminist viewpoint (1960), three of the poems assume that women will be in an inferior position, while one celebrates the

physical power of women. Students will want to offer their own ideas about how to judge the poems as a result of these assumptions.

(3) a. "My Papa's Waltz" has aroused differences of interpretation. You might consult the discussion in this manual as a point of departure for your students.

b. Here the task is to use a critical biography to help interpret poems. It is always possible that reading a work in a vacuum may produce misinterpretations. The works will therefore be instructive in the interconnection of literature with the author's life and times.

(4) The task of writing poetry should underline for students the absolute need for imagination and thought in the molding of just the right tone for a poem. An additional idea: There are always elections going on either nationally or locally during fall semesters. As an exercise for students preparing to write a poem emphasizing tone, you might assign a political speech or political controversy, and ask for an analysis of the tone of the various office-seekers. By way of criticism, students might write short poems as either corrective or corroborative ways of treating the topics being brought up in the campaigns.

(5) Léger's painting (insert 3) should probably be discussed by the class as a group (or by small groups interested in working on this question) before anyone undertakes to write. The poems referred to in the question have mainly negative views of city life for comparison with the painting. "Chicago" is the only one of these poems that presents city life at all sympathetically.

(6) All the mentioned attitudes are to be found in the Quasimodo poem, but the development of a sense of resolution and firmness is probably the major attitude that emerges. This development governs the structure of the poem, from the negative images at the outset to the transformational myths introduced as the poem progresses.

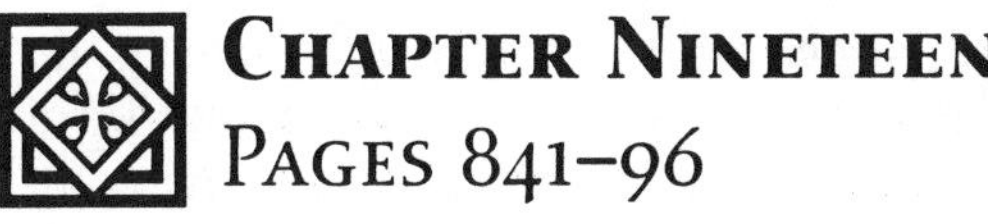

Prosody: Sound, Rhythm, and Rhyme in Poetry

Students may not need everything in this section to carry on a competent discussion of prosody. Some students can easily perceive light and heavy stresses and also the distinctions between sound and spelling; they may therefore produce good essays with no further instruction. Many students have difficulty, however, and therefore they may need to go back to basics about the syllable (844) and also about segments (843–44). Many students quickly recognize both regular and rhetorical substitutions. If they have difficulty, however, you may wish to have them study the section on these matters (849). Also, the section on the various feet and types of measures is longer than you perhaps will have time for in a one-semester course. As a result, the most essential material on the two-syllable feet (845–47) will serve most students first becoming acquainted with prosody. If students become genuinely interested in the complexities of rhythm, they may profit from pages 847–48, including the box in which the less common meters are described.

With the caesura, you may encounter surprise again about the role of pause and spacing in the development of meaning and rhythm. Most students understand junctures and use them properly. The problem comes when they are first asked to systematize their knowledge, and then to determine the effect of juncture or caesura in poetic rhythm. Punctuation is a great help here, for students will usually pause naturally at a comma or period. The problem will come in the determination of where internal open junctures and caesuras coincide. It may take much practice for many students to perceive caesurae occurring in these circumstances. Here, as elsewhere, practice, together with your supervision, will help.

A very basic and important idea which students should establish is the distinction between pronunciation and spelling (844). Some students, even against their own hearing, will identify sounds on visual rather than spoken evidence. It is therefore good to select a poem or short passage and have the class analyze the written words for the sounds themselves. Some students might truly believe that the < s > in *sure, silver,* and *resemblance* spell out the same sound. You will need to raise consciousness about the differences in these and in other words. Sometimes students have a special problem with digraphs, identifying the < t > in *the* with the < t > in *type,* the < t > in *thick,* or the < t > in *Betty.* The principle of the differences is not difficult, but it is often difficult for students to distinguish between what they see and what they hear.

Because rhyme is the aspect of poetry with which students are most familiar, the technical material in this chapter is limited and straightforward, and should be relatively easy to teach. Brief in-class explanations of exact rhyme, rising and falling rhyme, and slant and eye rhyme might be helpful. The section on rhyme schemes (857–58) is more demanding since it presupposes that students already understand the concepts and applications of meter. You might allow your students to define rhyme schemes simply by reference to the sounds (i.e., *abab, cdcd,* etc.). If you do use the whole formulation in class, be sure to remind students to look for the dominant meter and not to be misled by variant lines.

As exercises in segments, the following nonce sentences might prove useful for your students. You may add to these as you wish, or omit them. Students sometimes enjoy creating exemplifying lines of their own.

Vowel Sounds

He sees deep fields of green freezing peas.

Palely made cakes are aided by savory flavors.

Swift Camilla skims the pillowed plinths.

The fresh fellow offended Ted's sense of method.

Afterward, a lanky lad ambled by with angular ankles.

Often he saw faults that caused awe.

She told of opposing foes openly loading goalposts.

Puny new tunes are few in the pews on Tuesdays.

The stupidly foolish troupe coolly sat on stools.

I find the sky quite high in my mind's eye on the ninth of July.

He announced, avowed, and avouched that he found
the brows of cows to weigh one ounce.

His foible was joining in toil, not to foil but to spoil.

Consonant Sounds

The beau in the bed was bored with his beard and his billboard.

The dark darter daringly dashed from the den
to the dappled dawn.

The kiln cooked while the king courageously counseled quiet.

The pen pals panted palpably and probably panicked.

His task was tasting tangy but tart tangerines.

The game was to glide gallantly in galloping galoshes.

The ocean shore shifted the nation's passions.

Azure closures measure beige rouges.

Chinese chimpanzees chirp cheerfully in chimneys.

George generally enjoyed judging jellies and jams.

With special skill, Smith smashed several small smelt.

Zebras and zephyrs zigzagged in the zoo zones.

Phil fancied fabulous financial finds following
funny but fantastic failures.

Vales of vexatious vampires vanish in vapors of vinegar.

He was thumped and throttled thoroughly by the
thin but thriving thresher.

In the withering weather, the other brother with no bother
then went to bathe the feather.

Nervous neighbors never need nice new nutrition.

Mobilized manufacturers modestly make moccasins.

Red railroad ramps recede roaringly and raucously.

Limber and loose loops loom locally, linking linnets to limes.

GWENDOLYN BROOKS, *We Real Cool*, *pages 858–59*

Winner of the Pulitzer Prize for Poetry in 1950, Gwendolyn Brooks in later years has stressed the topic of race. "We Real Cool," with its strong pathos, is a part of this emphasis.

Suggestions for Discussing the Study Questions, page 859

(1) The major idea of the poem is that an aimless existence leads nowhere. The speakers are young men whose life pattern is based on diversionary and fruitless activity. They do not mention any obligation toward constructive service, but speak glowingly of enjoyable but destructive habits, which they describe as "cool." The last sentence

is a climax because it recognizes the outcome of the way of life depicted in the poem. The poet's attitude is clear because of the poem's situational irony: The opportunities for those who waste their lives at the Golden Shovel should be improved in all respects.

(2) The rhythmical stresses on all syllables are strong. The absence of weak stresses, making the poem totally strong-stressed, is achieved because all the words are of one syllable, and because there are no definite or indefinite articles, and no prepositions. Thus, every word counts as a subject, verb, object, or predicate adjective or adverb.

WRITING TOPICS. The use of strong stress in the poem. The relationship between the metrical beat and the main idea.

WORKS FOR COMPARISON WITH "WE REAL COOL"

Baraka, *Ka'Ba, 1125*
Evans, *I Am a Black Woman, 821*
Hughes, *Mulatto, 1663*

EMILY DICKINSON, *To Hear an Oriole Sing,* *page 859*

This poem beautifully illustrates Dickinson's power of compactness and dramatic expression. It contains, in little, the substance of an extensive aesthetic discussion and argument. Though the topic is the song of an oriole, the bird has little to do with the poem after the first line. Rather, the subject expands to the subject of beauty and how we perceive it.

Suggestions for Discussing the Study Questions, pages 859–60

(1) In classroom discussion, it helps to identify the speaker and the listener, and their positions, as quickly as possible. The listener ("The Skeptic") argues that the "Tune is in the Tree" (line 13). The speaker, who presents an aesthetic theory in fifteen lines, asserts that the tune (music, poetry, art) is "In Thee!" (the ear of the listener, the mind of the perceiver). Simply put, this poem exemplifies the adage that "beauty is in the eye of the beholder." Those who are interested may wish to relate the poem to Bishop Berkeley's ideas about perception and understanding, but too extensive a discussion along these lines would create a course in philosophy rather than literature.

(2) The poem is written in triplets, rhyming *aaa, bbb, ccc,* and so on. The rhymes coincide with the various shifts in topic and situation. Only the rhymes in the fifth stanza are exact throughout; the rest contain at least one slant rhyme (the fourth contains two).

(3) Only the rhymes in the fifth stanza are exact. The rest contain at least one slant rhyme, with the fourth containing two. The slant

rhymes emphasize and illustrate the various things that people might consider beautiful. If the slant rhymes work at all as rhyme, it is because our ears (eyes, imaginations, perceptions) make them work.

(4) The rhymes are developed according to a pattern of contrast or reinforcement. The first variation ("divine"), for example, is ironic, particularly because it is preceded by the word "only," as if divine things are less important than common ones (or is the entire world to be considered as a miracle?). The final stanza emphasizes the speaker's position, and hence this stanza is the only one with exact rhymes.

WRITING TOPICS. The rhymes. The degree to which the rhymes of the poem reflect and reinforce the poem's theme.

WORKS FOR COMPARISON WITH "TO HEAR AN ORIOLE SING"

Engels, *Naming the Animals, 1153*
Hall, *Whip-poor-will, 1015*
Momaday, *The Bear, 1179*

JOHN DONNE, *The Sun Rising,* *page 860*

In this poem Donne treats the idea that the microcosm (two lovers) are in effect the macrocosm (the entire world) because the lovers are in tune with universal forces. Love is all-powerful and all-consuming. Many of Donne's love poems treat this small-large equation, thus creating an "everywhere" in which his lovers can expand.

Suggestions for Discussing the Study Questions, page 861

(1) The speaker is a clever and ingenious fellow who is complaining about being awakened by the sun, and who therefore devises this poem to complain about it. The very idea of calling the sun a "busy old fool" who is "unruly" is evidence of his humor.

(2) The speaker and his beloved (in bed) have been wakened by the sun (the "Busy old fool"). The speaker talks directly to the personified sun and asks the sun to "go chide" (i.e., get things moving) with the public world (school boys, apprentices, huntsmen, farmers) since the speaker's love has created a private world detached from time. The speaker treats the listener, the sun, as an equal, and that is one of the poem's jokes.

(3) The poem's major metaphor is summarized in line 21: "She'is all States, and all Princes, I." Once this metaphor is expressed, the solar (the sun warms the world by warming us), seasonal ("no season knows"), geographical ("the Indias of spice and Mine"), and political ("Princes do but play us") metaphors follow as though Donne is

focusing the entire universe on the lovers. Donne pulls more and more of the cosmos into their bed.

(4) The rhyme pattern is *abba cdcd ee*, an interlocking scheme that culminates in the concluding rhyming couplet. The metrical pattern is iambic, but there are many variants in the pattern. The opening line, for example, begins with a trochee, which creates an explosive opening and appears to be a dactyl. In line 24, the first foot is a spondee. Donne is at great care to manipulate these variants carefully, thus augmenting the poem's situation of the speaker complaining to the sun.

WRITING TOPICS. Donne's use of rhyme. The principal metrical foot in the poem, and variations on it. Donne's equation of lovers to the universe. The wittiness of the poem.

WORKS FOR COMPARISON WITH "THE SUN RISING"

Dickinson, *Wild Nights!–Wild Nights!*, 1078
Minty, *Conjoined*, 790
Soto, *Kearney Park*, 1205
Van Duyn, *Earth Tremors Felt in Missouri*, 797

T. S. ELIOT, *Macavity: The Mystery Cat,* *pages 861–62*

Eliot, often considered a hyper-serious poet of either negative or religious themes, published *Old Possum's Book of Practical Cats* in 1939. He was what is called by cat-fanciers a "cat person." There is a 1928 photo of him with a cat named "George" (George V was king at the time), and among some of his other cats were "Wiscus" and "Pettipaws." There were many other cats, no doubt, which he owned or with whom he was friendly or acquainted. His poems about felines achieved popular fame in 1981, with the musical play *Cats*, freely adapted from *Old Possum's Book*. In June, 1997, *Cats* became the longest running play in the history of Broadway, and was not scheduled for closing until the fall of 2000.

The poem illustrates the "nonsense" lyric developed to its highest potential. Eliot admired the nonsense verse of Edward Lear (1812–1888), who is best known for "The Owl and the Pussycat." In writing "Macavity" and the other poems in the *Old Possum* Book, Eliot tried to achieve enjoyment as a major standard of poetic achievement. However, students might also note that "Macavity" is a well-formed poem with an introduction, characteristics of the "hero," accomplishments, refrains, and a climax. There are allusions to large matters of criminal law and international politics, and throughout there is a constant use of overstatement and anti-climax. Thus the nonsense is tightly controlled, showing that poetic craft is essential for all poems, regardless of subject.

Suggestions for Discussing the Study Questions, page 862

(1) Macavity's "crimes" are detailed from lines 21 to 34. The speaker expresses fear and amazement at the crimes, which in a human being would indeed have been heinous. The misdeeds occasion humor, however, because they are part of the overstatement on which the poem is built: To attribute felonious behavior to a cat (a felonious feline) is automatically incongruous and therefore comic.

(2) The line length, according to a conventional scansion, is heptameter or the septenary, with iambic feet as the norm but with occasional lines commencing with anapests (e.g., lines 9, 10, 12, 19, etc).

(3) Once one begins reading and getting into the swing of the lines, however, the dipodic foot takes over, so that each line contains four major stresses accompanied by a number of minor stresses, as in, "He always has an alibi, and one or two to spare." In this line, the dipodic feet put heavy stress on "al," "al," "one," and "spare," even though more formally the line contains seven iambic feet. Because the poem is really on a "nonsense" theme, the transformation of the serious verse form into the bouncier, thumping rhythm adds to the ridiculousness that Eliot is creating.

WRITING TOPICS. The dipodic foot. The development of humor. Macavity as a normal cat. Macavity as a "villain."

WORKS FOR COMPARISON WITH "MACAVITY: THE MYSTERY CAT"

Levine, *A Theory of Prosody, 866*
Tate, *The Blue Booby, 1208*
Tennyson, *The Eagle, 899*
Wright, *A Blessing, 711*

ISABELLA GARDENER, *At a Summer Hotel,* *page 862*

Gardner's short poem is an instance in which rhyme and sound contribute to an ironic portrait of a speaker. The issues in the poem are serious, but the poem demonstrates that the speaker can probably do nothing about them, and that life cannot be held in check when it is bursting in its bounty.

Suggestions for Discussing the Study Questions, page 863

(1) The speaker here is a mother at a "summer hotel" by the sea with her daughter, who is apparently attractive and nubile. The mother is passive; she sits "on the veranda" and worries. The daugh-

ter is active and immersed in nature ("gold in the sun," "bold in the dazzling water"). The speaker wants to relax, but the "beautiful bountiful womanful" daughter causes anxiety in her. The source of the speaker's anxiety is revealed in the closing allusions to Europa, Persephone, and Miranda, for all three fictional women attracted violent sexual attention.

(2) The *b* sound, like the repetitive "ful" and the *r* sounds in "roused by these roses roving," emphasizes the fullness and life of the daughter, and therefore serves as a lively view of the daughter in opposition to the speaker's apprehensiveness.

(3) Internal rhyme, as in "gold–bold" (line 3), "roses–roving" (line 2), and "blond–sand" (line 4), both helps to hold the lines together and produces a slightly comic effect.

(4) The end rhymes also create a certain amount of humor, and enable us to view the speaker in the perspective of being an overly protective mother. "Child–wild" is an exact, rising rhyme that neatly captures some of the daughter's qualities and the mother's anxiety. "Water–daughter" and "veranda–Miranda," however, are falling (trochaic and amphibrachic) rhymes that ring in the comic. Like the first rhyming pair, "water–daughter" captures some of the speaker's anxiety, especially if we see the water as even faintly sexual. "Veranda–Miranda" can only be amusing, as rhymes.

WRITING TOPICS. The effects of rhyme, alliteration, and repetition. The character of the speaker. The presentation of the daughter. The poem's use of allusion.

WORKS FOR COMPARISON WITH "AT A SUMMER HOTEL"

Nye, *Where Children Live, 678*
Oates, *Shopping, 216*
Olsen, *I Stand Here Ironing, 646*
Pastan, *Marks, 1184*

ROBERT HERRICK, *Upon Julia's Voice,* *page 863*

This poem is one of Herrick's poems on the qualities of generalized, conventionalized women. The idea of the poem is not so much to describe specific details about a woman as to demonstrate the poet's sharpness and skill.

Suggestions for Discussing the Study Questions, page 863

(1) The speaker praises Julia's speaking voice, but commends it for its "melodious" qualities. "Silv'ry" and "amber" are euphonious

words as well as rich commodities, therefore reflecting the speaker's high opinion.

(2) The "joke" of the poem is that Julia's voice is beautiful enough to overcome the devil's power of torment, so that damned souls would stop their screams of pain from hell fire to listen to her.

(3) The alliterations are *s* ("so smooth," "so sweet," "so silv'ry"), *n* ("no noise"), *m* ("melting melodious"), and *l* ("melting," "melodious," "lutes"). The *m* sounds complement the praise for the voice, for *m*, being a bilabial nasal continuant, brings the mouth into obvious use.

WRITING TOPICS. The poem as a compliment. The use of alliteration and euphony.

WORKS FOR COMPARISON WITH "UPON JULIA'S VOICE"

Jonson, *Drink to Me, Only, With Thine Eyes, 690*
Joyce, *Araby, 495*
Marvell, *To His Coy Mistress, 1023*
Rückert, *If You Love for the Sake of Beauty, 766*

GERARD MANLEY HOPKINS, *God's Grandeur,* *pages 863–64*

If one did not read the poem word by word, but merely looked at its form, it would seem to be a traditional Italian sonnet, with an extra iambic foot in line 3. An oral reading, however, dramatizes the tension between the formal and the actual rhythms caused by Hopkins's use of "sprung" rhythm. He achieves the vigorous spoken effect through the frequent juxtaposition of single-syllable words together with alliteration. Thus the regular light stresses are replaced by stronger stresses, which "spring" out of the lines.

To stress God's grandeur and power throughout all creation, Hopkins speaks of God as living everywhere in the universe, as ruler and as all-pervasive Holy Ghost who resembles traditional images of angels (with "bright wings"). To show divine omnipresence, he uses metaphors of electricity or flame, the freshness of creation, the dawn, and guardianship.

Suggestions for Discussing the Study Questions, page 864

(1) The first four lines praise God, concluding with a question about human disobedience. The second four lines contain a brief review of the speaker's judgment that human beings are enslaved by commerce. The sestet develops from this octave because it stresses the world's beauty, and suggests the possibility that improvement, like a new dawn, is awaiting those who are open to God's power.

(2) There are many alliterative patterns in the poem, which co-

incide with positions of rhythmical stress and therefore also with important words and ideas. See, for example, line 2, which emphasizes *f* in "flame" and "foil" and *sh* in "shining and "shook," and line 7, with its *sm* pattern in "smudge" and "smell."

(3) For assonance and internal rhyme, see, for example, lines 4 and 5: "men," "then," "reck," and "generations," where the *eh* sound predominates. There are other internal rhymes: "seared," "bleared," "smeared"; and "wears," "shares."

WRITING TOPICS. Hopkins's use of a–alliteration, b–assonance, c–internal rhyme, d–the Italian sonnet form, and e–"sprung" rhythm.

WORKS FOR COMPARISON WITH "GOD'S GRANDEUR"

Arnold, *Dover Beach, 693*
Harjo, *Eagle Poem, 674*
Piercy, *Wellfleet Sabbath, 706*

Langston Hughes, Let America Be America Again, *pages 864–66*

Today the timeliness and the greatness of Hughes's work is becoming widely recognized. His poem *Harlem* (787) is the best known poem, with its powerful phrases *dream deferred* and *raisin in the sun.* Other Hughes poems may be found on pages 822, 1016, and 1166. His play *Mulatto* is on page 1663.

Suggestions for Discussing the Study Questions, page 866

(1, 2) The first sixteen lines contain a statement of an ideal, and thus the quatrains followed by the repetition in lines 5 and 10, with rhyming words in lines 15 and 16, form a unit both topically and rhythmically. The remainder of the poem may be considered a critique of how the ideal has been neglected and corrupted, and hence the units take on irregular lengths, much as in the free form of the ode. Although there are powerful rhymes in the stanzas after line 17, they are not regular, in keeping with the idea that the poet is describing a yet unrealized dream. It is not until line 71 that the poet repeats the line "America never was America to me." Once this theme is reestablished, the remainder is an exhortation to fulfill the dream the poet associates with the founding of the country.

(3) There are many examples of alliteration throughout the poem. Phrases such as *land of love, kings connive, ancient endless chain, grab the gold, sailed those early seas* and *great green*—all invite an incantative recitation and a consequent strong emphasis on the ideas brought out by the phrases. The alliteration hence contributes the poem's effectiveness and assertiveness.

(4) Assonance, rhyme, internal rhyme, and slant rhyme are all employed throughout. One of the prominent rhymes is the use of *ee* in the words *be, free, me, liberty, lea*–a rhyme which appears a number of times. Another prominent set is *again, plain, chain, gain, pain, rain,* and *stain. Again* may be a slant rhyme in this pattern, depending on how one chooses to pronounce it, but it opens the poem (lines 1 and 3) and concludes it (lines 79, 81). Assonance may be seen, for example, in the first stanza on the words *be, dream, be, he,* and *free,* and later (lines 64–66) on the words *me, steel, freedom,* and *leeches.* One might consider this pattern to be also part of the poem's internal rhyme, with the pattern of *ee* rhymes. Slant rhyme is not prominent, but one may see it in the words *dreamed* and *scheme, become* and *home* and *came,* and *pain* and *rain* and *again.* As with the regular rhymes, these features underscore the poem's assertiveness. Because the dream is unfulfilled, perhaps the idea is that a time might come when all rhymes, like making America America again, will be true.

WRITING TOPICS. The varying stanzaic patterns. The use of rhyme. The use of regular meters and free rhythms. The effect of the repetition of the phrase "America never was America to me."

WORKS FOR COMPARISON WITH "LET AMERICA BE AMERICA AGAIN"

Cullen, *Yet Do I Marvel,* 1137
Gaines, *The Sky Is Gray,* 475
Sanchez, *right on: white america,* 1193

PHILIP LEVINE, *A Theory of Prosody,* *pages 866–67*

As with many comic works, this short poem conveys a good deal of truth in its wry development of the speaker's experiences with his cat. The concluding sentence suggests the conclusion of Frost's "A Considerable Speck" (1113)

Suggestions for Discussing the Study Questions, page 867

(1) The situation of letting a cat dictate line lengths and the form of a poem is, on the surface, comic because of the incongruity of letting a cat substitute for a mind. Nellie's theory of prosody is to trim lines by the standard of length alone, regardless of content. The evidence of Nellie's theory may be seen from line 1 to line 2: "When Nellie, my old pussy / cat, . . ." The final lines may be taken with a smile, but the last line, leaving "nothing to chance," is profoundly serious.

(2) Master and cat obviously have a good relationship. Cats usually like to sit on writing paper and generally have a way of

being present on top of current compositions (no longer true if one uses a word processor—unless they can find a nice warm spot on the monitor). Cats also get interested in a moving pen, and chew it as well as swipe at it. Levine makes comic use of these real-life feline habits.

(3) Both Frost and Levine have a good time transferring characteristics of the animal world to the world of writing. Levine stresses the idea of poetic economy; Frost stresses the need for intelligent writing. There is much truth in both poems, and much happiness.

WRITING TOPICS. Nellie as a poetic theorist. The character of the speaker. The poem as comedy.

WORKS FOR COMPARISON WITH "A THEORY OF PROSODY"

Bradstreet, *The Author to Her Book, 818*
Frost, *A Considerable Speck, 1113*
Spender, *I Think Continually of Those Who Were Truly Great, 739*
Wordsworth, *Scorn Not the Sonnet, 1059*

HENRY WADSWORTH LONGFELLOW, *The Sound of the Sea,* *page 867*

This poem represents the transcendentalism characteristic of writers of the nineteenth century. In this respect, one may compare the poem with Arnold's "Dover Beach" (693) and Shelley's "Ode to the West Wind" (877). The ideas also compare well with the thoughts of Hamlet as expressed to Horatio, that there is more to heaven and earth than the philosophy books tell us.

Suggestions for Discussing the Study Questions, pages 867–68

(1) The poem is based on the analogy of sea to soul. The waves of the sea come from some deep and distant source and then rush onward, just as "inspirations, that we deem our own" originate in distant locations that are beyond human comprehension and power. The origin of thought and inspiration, in other words, is divine. This idea demonstrates a combination of philosophy, mysticism, and religiousness–all three. The essential idea here is that there is more to the universe than we can ever know, even the sources of our own ideas and inspirations–an idea that at least represents the start of a religious outlook on the world.

(2) The poem is an Italian or Petrarchan sonnet in form: *abba, abba, cde, cde.*

(3) The basic meter of the poem is iambic pentameter. Substitutions may be seen in line 3 (*wave of the ris–*, a trochee giving the impression of an imperfect foot followed by an anapest; the same

variation occurs in lines 5 and 9), line 13 (*forshadowing and foreseeing* [this requires analysis]), and line 6 (dipodic rhythm). These variations all draw emphasis to the ideas contained within them, and they also demonstrate a good deal of prosodic skill.

(4) There are a number of examples of assonance (*heard, first; sea, we, deem, reason*) and consonance (*rising, rush; sweep, silence; winds, wooded; inaccessible, solitudes, sea-tides, inspirations*). These particular sounds complement the sound of rushing and roaring breakers, and also the sound of wind, thus emphasizing the mysterious origins of both the natural and the intellectual or spiritual worlds.

WRITING TOPICS. The mystery at the heart of human inspiration. The connection between the divine and the human. The nature of the speaker.

WORKS FOR COMPARISON WITH "THE SOUND OF THE SEA"

Francis, *Catch*, 672
Keats, *On First Looking Into Chapman's Homer*, 777
Lux, *The Voice You Hear when You Read Silently*, 763
MacLeish, *Ars Poetica*, 676
Wordsworth, *My Heart Leaps Up*, 1035

OGDEN NASH, *Very Like a Whale*, *pages 868–69*

This poem is an amusing disclaimer against the poetic use of metaphors and similes. It should be read jointly with Byron's "The Destruction of Sennacherib" (1132), upon which it is based. The poem is also instructional, however, for it invites readers to consider the justness and appropriateness of metaphorical language along with the meaning of metaphor.

Suggestions for Discussing the Study Questions, page 869

(1) Nash's point is not so much against the use of metaphor in itself but rather against the use of metaphor to obscure ideas. Nash clearly is basing his poem on the idea that literature should always be perfectly clear. Ray Durem, in "I Know I'm Not Sufficiently Obscure" (758) uses the same idea in a much less detailed way, and also in a more pointedly political way.

(2) Nash's humor is based on the logical fallacy of *reductio ad absurdum*. Virtually any simile or metaphor, if pushed far enough, can seem inappropriate or even silly, and some, like the mice, the snow, and the petticoat, are silly from the start. In lines 1–4, Nash's speaker lays out possible objections to metaphors and similes. Lines 5–22 illustrate the objections, using Byron's poem as the example.

Lines 23–26 describe what the speaker thinks should have been said—without simile or metaphor, had Byron dispensed with them. Lines 27–30 state the need for reality as opposed to metaphor.

(3) Nash uses his rhymes comically, as is seen in combinations like *experience / Assyrians*; *many thing / anythings*; and *interpolate them / purple ate them*, to name just a few of the rhymes. The humor and comedy is made clear by the nonce and clever nature of the rhymes, together with their "falling" rhythms. The original rhymes and the doggerel rhythms make this poem unique and completely memorable.

WRITING TOPICS. The point of Nash's ridicule of metaphors. Nash's rhymes. Nash's rhythms.

WORKS FOR COMPARISON WITH "VERY LIKE A WHALE"

Durem, *I Know I'm Not Sufficiently Obscure*, 758
Francis, *Catch*, 672
Levine, *A Theory of Prosody*, 866
Moore, *How to Become a Writer*, 274

EDGAR ALLAN POE, *Annabel Lee*, *pages 869–70*

The poem is about the death of a young woman and to this degree it fits Poe's idea that the most affecting thing in literature is the death of a young woman. But in reading the poem one should put this concept aside, for "Annabel Lee" may be taken as a sincere lamentation for the loss of his young wife Virginia, who died in 1847.

Suggestions for Discussing the Study Questions, page 870

(1) The speaker indicates that the reason for Annabel Lee's death was that she and the speaker loved "with a love that was more than love," and, moreover, that the "wingèd seraphs of Heaven" were covetous of this love. Also, the angels in Heaven were not as happy as the speaker and Annabel, and therefore they, too, were jealous. Annabel Lee's death was therefore a form of supernatural punishment.

(2) The noteworthy rhythm is created through a blending of anapests which build up a singing speed which is sometimes accented and sometimes halted by iambs.

(3) Stanzas 3, 5, and 6 are longer than the other stanzas because they contain more narrative detail than the others. Stanza 3 describes Annabel Lee's death and her being shut up in the sepulchre. Stanza 5 indicates the speaker's resolve to resist the attempts by both angels and demons to "dissever" his soul from her soul. Stanza 6 concludes the poem by explaining why the speaker spends his time dreaming about her and spending his nights lying alongside her sepulchre.

(4) See page 854 for a brief discussion of Poe's use of internal rhyme in the poem. The various prosodic segmental devices provide the opportunity for the reader to read the poem aloud virtually as an incantation, thus augmenting the speaker's implicit claim that his love for Annabel Lee was so great that it reached the level of a fairy tale. One might note a number of instances of assonance (e.g., *whom / you, "out of the cloud"*), alliteration (e.g., *demons / down, beams / bringing*), and repetitions (e.g., *She was a child and I was a child, loved with a love that was more than love, by the sea / by the side of the sea).*

WRITING TOPICS. Poe's use of rhyme, including internal rhyme. The reason for Annabel Lee's death. The rhythms in the poem.

WORKS FOR COMPARISON WITH "ANNABEL LEE"

Burns, *A Red, Red Rose, 783*
Frost, *The Silken Tent, 1112*
Shakespeare, *Let Me Not to the Marriage of True Minds, 903*

EDGAR ALLAN POE, *The Bells,* *pages 871–73*

"The Bells" evokes the connection between sound and mood. If students come to the poem searching for ideas as such, they will be disappointed. Instead, in "The Bells" the idea is mood, or rather the separate moods evoked by Poe's descriptions. In making this stress upon emotion as a mode of knowledge, this poem, noisy and percussive as it is, is not unlike Emily Dickinson's "There's a Certain Slant of Light" (1077). Dickinson, remember, speaks about the "heft" of cathedral tunes.

Suggestions for Discussing the Study Questions, page 873

(1) The stanzas discuss (a) silver sledge or sleigh bells, (b) golden wedding bells, (c) brass alarm bells, and (d) iron funeral bells. The metals are appropriate because of their colors and textures. Certainly silver and gold suggest happiness and security, while brass and iron are more suitable for the fearsome, somber, and bizarre uses to which Poe puts these bells. The stanzas, particularly the third and fourth, become longer because the situations of alarm and death being described are more far-reaching and complicated than sleighrides and weddings, and perhaps more congenial to his temperament.

(2) In stanza one, the major assonance is the short *i*, and there are a number of repeated *t* and *d* sounds in alliteration. For the wedding bells in stanza two, there is more of a mixture of sounds. Thus one may note assonances in *"eh"* (mellow, wedding), *"oh"* (molten, golden), short *i* (liquid, ditty, listens), and a number of *"oo"* sounds (through,

tune, euphony, voluminously, future). There are more nasals ("*m*" and "*n*") here, and liquids ("*l*") than in the first stanza, so that brittleness gives way to something more like the "mellow" sounds to which Poe refers in line 15. The third section introduces a number of "*r*" sounds to emphasize the noise of terror (as in "scream out their affright"). In the first part of the stanza there is also the plosive "*t*," and the "*k*" sound is introduced in line 53. The fourth stanza, about funeral bells, introduces the fricatives "*s*" and "*sh*," presumably to imitate sounds of sighing and weeping. From line 89 to the end, however, the poem moves from the suggestion of sorrow and shivering into a bizarre, mad dance by a King of the Ghouls. The repetition here is principally on the word "bells," which is a percussive counterpoint to sobbing, moaning, and groaning, which the bells also are doing.

(3) The word *bells*, used sixty-one times in the poem, as a refrain and as the repeated word in lines, is a one-syllable word that begins with the voiced stop b and then moves to *eh*, *l*, and *z*. It suggests a constant hammering and ringing sound. Musical notation (because several lines can be laid out simultaneously) would be better able to capture Poe's desired effect than lines of poetry alone can do.

(4) The pattern of rhymes is complex throughout the four stanzas, but all the stanzas begin and end with "bells" and words that rhyme with it.

Writing topics. The relation of segments to content (any stanza). The progress or change in sounds in the poem.

Works for Comparison with "The Bells"

Eliot, *Macavity: The Mystery Cat, 861*
Masefield, *Cargoes, 749*
Wagoner, *March for a One-Man Band, 991*

Alexander Pope, *from* An Essay on Man, Epistle I, *pages 874–75*

Suggestions for Discussing the Study Questions, page 875

(1) There are a number of topics in the passage, but the principal idea is that human beings (man) cannot understand the reasons for their existence, and that God alone understands these matters. Pope emphasizes the limitations on human perspective about the universe, and points out that humanity is therefore in no position to question or to judge God. Pope's idea is that human beings are as blessed as they can be, for "'Tis but a part we see, and not a whole" (line 59). It is certainly appropriate to consider such matters in poetic form, for Pope believed that a major function of the

poet is to instruct, and also to instruct pleasingly. Accordingly, Pope sought to convey religious and cosmological ideas in the couplet form, which, he thought, his readers would readily understand and remember. A close study reveals that the ideas progress from couplet to couplet. In the first three couplets of the passage, for example, the ideas move from (a) God and man, to (b) the limits of human observation, to (c) a comparison of the vastness of God and the restricted areas open to humanity to discover.

(2) Entire books have been written about Pope's use of the couplet form. Briefly, however, Pope uses mostly one-syllable words, with a blending of two- and three-syllable words. He relies heavily on antithesis ("A hero perish, or a sparrow fall" [line 88], "This hour a slave, the next a deity" [line 68]). Mostly Pope uses end-stopped lines and end-stopped couplets. The thought therefore moves mainly from line to line and couplet to couplet. The pattern of the lines is to have a caesura after the fourth syllable, but Pope varies this pattern considerably, thus creating great interest in the couplets, which might in less skilled hands seem to become repetitive and monotonous.

(3) Pope's rhymes are usually stressed ones. He varies the types of words that rhyme. Commonly, he rhymes verbs with nouns (*comprehend / end, all / fall, confessed / best*, etc.), but there is no hard-and-fast rule, and he finally creates great variation in his rhyming words. His goal in the creation of rhymes is to "clinch" his ideas, so as to assist the memories of his readers.

Writing topics. The relation of segments to content (any stanza). The progress or change in sounds in the poem.

Works for Comparison with the Fragment from "An Essay on Man, Epistle I"

Dickinson, *'Faith' Is a Fine Invention, 1068*
Oliver, *Wild Geese, 967*
Wordsworth, *Ode: Intimations of Immortality, 1049*

Edwin Arlington Robinson, *Miniver Cheevy,* *pages 875–76*

This portrait illustrates the futility of seeking an escape into the romanticized and idealized past. The poem's subject is a failure and a drinker. One might think of him as a perfectionist who, because he cannot achieve perfection, gives up on everything and loses the ability to function. An effective classroom strategy for teaching the poem might be to focus on 1–the portrait of Miniver, 2–the speaker's attitude toward him, and 3–the poetic techniques that Robinson employs to make Miniver all the more ludicrous.

Suggestions for Discussing the Study Questions, page 876

(1) The speaker uses rhyme to emphasize disgust and amusement at Miniver's pathetic silliness. For example, by rhyming ordinary, trite words like "old" and "bold" in the second stanza ("In days of old, / When knights were bold," as a well-known obscene poem begins), the speaker stresses the futility and inaccuracy of Miniver's visions of what life should be. There is also the echo of the legendary "Purple Cow" rhymes ("see one" and "be one") in Robinson's lines 18 and 20:

I've never seen a purple cow.
    I hope I'll never see one.
But I can tell you here and now
    I'd rather see than be one.

(2) The use of "Miniver" at the beginning of each line recalls the word "minimal" (which Miniver's name echoes), and also stresses the idea of littleness and ineffectiveness. The "thought, and thought," phrases of lines 27–28 stress the inconsequentiality of Miniver as a thinker and a person.

(3) Through sound, the falling (trochaic) rhymes in the second and fourth lines of each stanza underscore Miniver's ridiculous situation.

WRITING TOPICS. The use of trochaic rhymes. The use of repetition. The use of irony in the portrait of Miniver.

WORKS FOR COMPARISON WITH "MINIVER CHEEVY"

Anderson, *I'm a Fool, 250*
Kennedy, *Old Men Pitching Horseshoes, 956*
Swift, *A Description of the Morning, 832*

WILLIAM SHAKESPEARE, *That Time of Year Thou May'st in Me Behold,* *page 877*

"That Time of Year" is one of the best known of all the sonnets. Students should memorize it and be able to quote it.

Suggestions for Discussing the Study Questions, page 877

(1) The topics of the quatrains are these: lines 1–4, autumn; lines 5–8, sunset and night; lines 9–12, a dying fire. The common link is diminution or dying. The concluding couplet is tied to the previous twelve lines by the demonstrative pronoun "This," which begins line 13, and which turns the thought to the need for strengthening love.

(2) The spondees create emphasis by slowing the speech and

thereby thrusting the ideas into prominence. Also, the frequency of spondees in this sonnet suggests the heaviness of a slow march or respectful walk appropriate to a funeral procession. The phrases "those boughs" (line 3) and "that well" (line 14) should be added as spondaic substitutions.

(3) Line 2 connects to line 1 because it begins a subordinate adverbial clause, just as line 3 begins an adverbial-prepositional phrase in which the headword "boughs" is modified by the adjective clause "which shake against the cold." The completeness of each line is hence caused by the pause produced between the verbs and the modifying elements. Much the same is true from lines 5 to 6; here, however, the modifying element in line 6 is an adjective clause modifying the noun "day" (or is it "twilight"?).

(4) The caesurae in the lines are placed as follows: Line 2, after syllables 4, 6, and 8. Line 5, after syllables 2 and 7. Line 6, after syllable 5. Line 9, after syllables 2 and 7 (the same as line 5). These pauses cause emphasis or continuity where they appear. In line 2, the effect is one of slowness and heaviness. In lines 5 and 9, which are grammatically and rhythmically identical, the similarity is a means of tying together the two four-line units describing the setting sun and the dying fire. Line 6 is regular, divided medially by the caesura. This regularity throws emphasis on the eternal sameness of the setting sun. In the last two lines, the rising caesurae (in both lines 13 and 14, after the fourth syllables) stress the positive qualities of the love which is the subject of the lines.

WRITING TOPICS. The use of spondees as the main substitute foot. The relationship of caesurae to the ideas in the poem. The repetition of rhythms (e.g., the use of the "in me" patterns, and the adjective clauses).

WORKS FOR COMPARISON WITH "THAT TIME OF YEAR"

Olds, *35/10, 1024*
Porter, *The Jilting of Granny Weatherall, 651*
Whitman, *Facing West from California's Shores, 799*

PERCY BYSSHE SHELLEY, *Ode to the West Wind, pages 877–79*

The "Ode to the West Wind" focuses on the need for poetic inspiration, but here Shelley stresses the practical, political, and ultimately revolutionary results of what the poet, who is in effect a "poète engagé," says. The West Wind symbolizes the force of creativity—that imaginative power that enables the poet to express strong and moving ideas that can ultimately influence people and politicians to change society and create a new social and political order.

Suggestions for Discussing the Study Questions, page 880

(1) The terza rima interlocks and unifies each of the five stanzas through sound; the repeated *b, c,* and *e* rhymes help unify the entire ode. The movement of ideas progresses from a sense of death and despair to one of optimism. Though the speaker may never see the rise of a spring of happiness for humankind, his ideas nevertheless may "quicken a new birth" and, through political means, create happiness after he is gone.

(2) In stanza 1, the wind blows the leaves and seeds; it is both a destroyer and preserver, and the images reflect death and rebirth. In the second and third stanzas, the wind similarly drives clouds and waves. In each instance, the wind represents power, movement, death, and rebirth. In the fourth section, the core of the poem, the speaker presents his problem; he wants to be affected by the wind just as he was in his "boyhood." Life and change have destroyed this ability; maturity and time have *chained and bowed* him. The speaker wants to be lifted as a leaf, wave, or cloud; he wants to become the agent through whom the ideas of change may be transmitted ("Make me thy lyre," line 57).

(3) The ode is in five fourteen-line stanzas of iambic pentameter terza rima concluded by a couplet, as follows:

aba, bcb, cdc, ded, ee
fbf, bgb, ghg, heh, ee
iji, jkj, kck, cec, ee
ele, lml, mnm, non, oo
pqp, qrq, rsr, sts, tt

The three *e* couplets tie stanzas 1–3 together and separate 4 and 5, although the initial repetition of the *e* rhyme in 4 creates a bridge. The stanzaic structure rigorously organizes the poem's ideas: Stanzas 1–3 deal with the West Wind and nature, stanza 4 with the speaker's problem, and stanza 5 with a solution.

(4) There are many memorable phrases in this poem which are underscored by Shelley's use of poetic devices. Some of the best are "autumnal tone" (line 60), "chained / tameless" (lines 55-56), "Angels of rain" (line 18), etc.

WRITING TOPICS. An analysis of the interconnection between form and meaning. The symbolic value of the wind. The character of the speaker. A comparison of "Ode to the West Wind" and Keats's "Ode to a Nightingale" (918).

WORKS FOR COMPARISON WITH "ODE TO THE WEST WIND"

Dryden, *A Song for St. Cecilia's Day*, 1012
Moore, *How to Become a Writer*, 274
Wordsworth, *London, 1802*, 799

ALFRED, LORD TENNYSON, *from* ***Idylls of the King: The Passing of Arthur,*** *pages 880–81*

One of Tennyson's preoccupations was the legendary King Arthur. Tennyson began publishing *Idylls of the King*, consisting of twelve connected poems on Arthurian topics, in 1857, and added more as time went by. The completed version was published only in 1891, the year before his death.

Suggestions for Discussing the Study Questions, page 881

(1) The poem's action produces a mood of depression. Bedivere carries the dying Arthur from a series of ridges to the water, where a barge awaits. Arthur is then taken aboard to the lamentations of three queens. Tennyson develops the mood of depression by including images of cold, darkness, shrill winds, dust, and, primarily the simile of a shattered column. The column may be construed as an allusion to Samson, whose death was brought about when he shattered the columns of the building in which he was imprisoned.

(2) The demonstrative student essay (885–91) analyzes segments in the section from lines 349–360. Further study could produce additional patterns, such as "dark," "scarf," and "stem," "stern" (line 362); "were," "ware" (line 363); "decks," "dense" (line 364); and "dream," "these," "three," "queens" (lines 365–366). These patterns of assonance and alliteration unify these passages and render them particularly suitable for spoken delivery.

(3) The onomatopoeia in lines 349–360 is discussed in the demonstrative essay. The content of lines 369–370 concerns the sounds of lamentation being likened to shrill winds in an empty land. Here Tennyson uses a number of syllable-lengthening consonants, principally "*l*," "*n*," and "*m*," to enable the words to be extended in virtual imitation of wind. Words thus stretched are "lamentation," "wind," "shrills," "land," "one," and "comes." In lines 380–383, Tennyson emphasizes the tears of the tallest queen falling upon Arthur, and also the streaks and spots on him as a result of his mortal battle wounds. Tennyson achieves onomatopoeia here through the use of one-syl-

lable words to emphasize the individual drops (line 380, for example, consists of ten one-syllable words) together with the use of stop sounds which also emphasize the drops (in the words "striped, "dark," "blood," "greaves," "cuisses," "dashed," and "drops"). When he describes Arthur's face he uses words with fewer stop sounds ("face," "white," "colorless," "withered," "moon," "springing"), which when mingled with the monosyllabic words succeed in creating a vivid word picture.

WRITING TOPICS. Tennyson's use of assonance and alliteration in a selected portion of the fragment. The means by which Tennyson creates onomatopoeia.

WORKS FOR COMPARISON WITH "THE PASSING OF ARTHUR"

Anonymous, *Bonny George Campbell, 688*
Anonymous, *Sir Patrick Spens, 668*
Jeffers, *The Purse-Seine, 953*
Whitman, *Dirge for Two Veterans, 1217*

DAVID WAGONER, *March for a One-Man Band,* *page 881*

Wagoner has been extremely productive both as poet and novelist. This poem, "March for a One-Man Band," is a short virtuoso piece, which mixes iambs and anapests together to work up an infectiously rhythmic but also slightly chaotic tetrameter.

Suggestions for Discussing the Study Questions, page 882

(1) The speaker enjoys the one-man band being described: not with awe or respect, but with amused acceptance of a "fun" situation. The noise is so outlandish that "irrational" is a better word than "national" to describe the anthem he plays.

(2) The words italicized in the poem are all echoic; that is, they are onomatopoeic or imitative in origin, having sound-effects as their meaning. The accompanying rhythms are swinging, bouncing, or thumping, designed to imitate and illustrate in words the noisy, desperate motion and sound of one person working all the instruments with hands, feet, knees, and mouth–a frantic, wild spectacle of sight and sound.

(3) At the end of the speaker's description, the *bang* recalls the so-called "button" note which punctuates the second beat of the last bar of a march (hear, for example, the conclusion of Sousa's "The Stars and Stripes Forever"). The one-man band's *bang* (try saying "one-man band's bang" fast) presumably ends the national anthem, creating an amusing sound where none at all ought to be, a sound that is not at all inappropriate if one considers how "The Star-Spangled

Banner" is sometimes excruciatingly performed at many sporting events and public spectacles.

WRITING TOPICS. Onomatopoeia in the poem. Rhythm. Poe's "The Bells" and Wagoner's "March for a One-Man Band."

WORKS FOR COMPARISON WITH "MARCH FOR A ONE-MAN BAND"

Kumin, *Hello, Hello Henry*, 735
Poe, *The Bells*, 871
Tennyson, *The Passing of Arthur*, 880

Writing About Prosody, *pages 882–95*

In teaching the essays on rhythm, segments, or rhyme, you will need to stress accuracy. If students make no errors in their prosodic analyses, then their essays will go forward well. If there are mistakes, however, then the essays will go astray. With normal analytical essays, errors are not quite as crucial, for students may make a good argument even for a misinterpretation. In the study of prosody, however, it is not easy to make a well-reasoned discussion compensate for a mistake.

It is therefore important to stress that students work up a correct and thorough worksheet (see pages 886–88 and 892–93) in the prewriting stages of their essays. You may need to give students classroom time so that their observations may be checked. Have they correctly recorded the sounds? Do they have any doubts or questions about proper rhythms? About rhyme schemes? Especially important is that students have not confused spelling with sound. If, in the poem you have assigned, there are any possible chances for confusion, you may wish to use selected lines as the basis of exercises and queries. Invariably, you will find students who make inaccurate connections of sound and sense. The best time to make corrections and clarify understandings is at those times when students can see where they are likely to be going astray.

When you use the demonstrative essays, it is important to note the comparative modesty of the claims there between content and prosody. Only in the section on onomatopoeia is there a graphic, almost pictorial connection, and here the assertions go no further than can be supported by Tennyson's descriptions.

Also, when you use the demonstrative essays as guides for your students, you might profitably direct them to the strong connection between the central idea and the development. Thus in paragraph 5 of the second demonstrative essay the thematic development is stressed by the following words: "echoes," "major echoing word," "which appears six times," "repeated systematically," "repeats," and "echoes." No matter what central idea students may develop about the rhythm, segments, or rhyme of their assigned poems, the same need for overall thematic unity will prevail.

Special Topics for Writing and Argument about Rhythm and Rhyme in Poetry, *pages 895–96*

(1) The first assignment requires a close analysis of Shakespeare's Sonnet 73 (877). The questions are clear, and if students analyze their worksheets closely, they can produce perceptive and worthwhile essays.

(2) Only one of these poems, Eliot's "Macavity," may be classified as essentially humorous. The others all contain strong elements of seriousness. The point of this question is to emphasize that the lightness of falling rhymes must take place within a context of lightness. One might make the argument that falling rhymes in a serious piece bring out the ideas in a good humor, or bring out the common, everyday nature of the subject material.

(3) Both "The Bells" and "March for a One-Man Band" are bravura pieces, and they therefore furnish a fertile field for a bringing out connections between sound and topic. In both poems, the echoic words transmit real sound to the printed page. Wagoner of course uses more variety than Poe, for while Poe speaks only of bells, Wagoner mentions drums, cornet, harmonica (the "wheeze"?), cymbal, whistle, and perhaps a few other "instruments" thrown in for good measure. Because Poe's poem is so extensive, students may wish to confine their comparisons to only one or two of the stanzas.

(4) The comparison of any two of the five poems should bring out that they are inherently serious. The rhyming words are therefore used in a pattern stressing the basic seriousness of the topic material. Where rhyme occurs, it lends emphasis and builds climax.

(5) This assignment can be interesting. Usually students will commend rhyme as conferring strength through echoing sounds, and unrhymed verse as being more free, and more seemingly natural.

(6) Hardy's rhymes underscore his irony in the poem. The idea in the poem is that the naval guns are making a mockery not only of the dead but of the living, whom they will soon make dead. The fact that trochaic rhymes are often called "dying" rhymes reinforces the irony.

(7) A wise person said that it is more difficult to be funny than

to be serious, and that clarity in humor is much more essential than in ordinary statements (clarity is always essential). Nevertheless, some surprisingly clever poems can result once students get going. Distortion of words is totally acceptable in the interests of humor, such as "I drove to Schenectady / And got into a wrecktady," "I asked for a hot dog / But got a broiled wart hog," or "His jokes were insupportable; His expenses unaffordable." Play of this sort, here, is an object. If some students come up with such rhymes, and some other students groan a bit, that isn't so bad.

(8) This assignment will probably seem difficult for many students until they actually get going on it, particularly the suggestion about how prosody enters into the thoughts of writers. Nevertheless, using the books on the topic should prove illuminating, and the scope of prosodic analysis will make the point that there is more to poetry than just writing down words randomly.

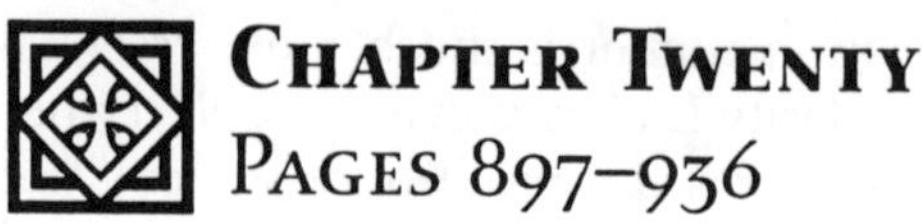

Chapter Twenty
Pages 897–936

Form: The Shape of the Poem

This chapter introduces students to poetic form and structure. It makes no attempt to describe or define every possible traditional form; such an undertaking would require an entire book. Your students may come to poetic form with reluctance or skepticism. They may assume that all closed forms are artificial, and, as such, have been invented by poets in collusion with teachers. While there may be some justification for this claim (poets invent forms, we identify them), it by no means was true before literature was taken up as a disciplinary study in the late nineteenth century. A quick look at several ballads or lyrics written when there were almost no colleges in existence will reveal the natural and organic connection between singing, memory, patterns of repetition, and form. More sophisticated students might condemn all closed forms as too restrictive, or all open forms as too sloppy and disordered. Classroom discussion and emphasis can deal with these positions.

The key distinction in this chapter is between closed and open forms; this central distinction can be reiterated in class. At the same time, you can encourage your students to consider the ways in which the two forms share qualities. Closed-form poets seek the greatest freedom and innovation within rigid structures. Open-form poets undertake an equally difficult task; they must impose order, shape, and meaning in new ways. Encourage your students to appreciate each type of form for its strengths.

The discussion of the building blocks of closed form (897–904) considers one-, two-, three-, and four-line units. The one-line unit (blank verse) is exemplified by a speech from *Hamlet* (a demonstrative essay explicating this passage is in Chapter 27, page 1531). Other poems in the text you might use to illustrate blank verse include Wordsworth's "Tintern Abbey Lines" (1044).

Couplets are illustrated by excerpts from the fragment from Pope's "The Rape of the Lock" (899) and by the epigrams. Other useful poems that exemplify couplets of various lengths include "My Last Duchess" (695), "The Destruction of Sennacherib" (1132), "Very

Like a Whale" (868), "Macavity: The Mystery Cat" (861), "We Real Cool" (858), and "Ars Poetica" (1022).

The three-line unit (triplets, tercets) is exemplified by "The Eagle" (899), "Ode to the West Wind" (877), and the three villanelles in the chapter: Bishop's "One Art" (909), Roethke's "The Waking" (924), and Thomas's "Do Not Go Gentle into That Good Night" (927). Another poem that illustrates the usefulness of the tercet is Dickinson's "To Hear an Oriole Sing" (859). Poems that illustrate the versatility of the quatrain can be found throughout the text; they are far too numerous to mention.

The discussion of types of closed-form poetry deals with some of the major forms that have remained popular for centuries and a few minor forms. Most of the closed forms introduced here are exemplified by one or two poems later in the chapter. Beyond these, examples of most closed forms are scattered throughout the text. Here are some alternate examples for teaching:

- **Italian** or **Petrarchan Sonnets:** Keats, *On First Looking into Chapman's Homer,* 777; Wyatt, *I Find No Peace,* 800; Wordsworth, *London, 1802,* 799; Hopkins, *God's Grandeur,* 863; Yeats, *Leda and the Swan,* 974; Elizabeth Barrett Browning, *How Do I Love Thee,* 1130; Millay, *What Lips My Lips Have Kissed,* page 1178; Hacker, *Sonnet Ending with a Film Subtitle,* 1155.
- **English** or **Shakespearean Sonnets:** All sonnets by Shakespeare; Keats, *Bright Star,* 779; Cullen, *Yet Do I Marvel,* 1137; McKay, *The White City,* 1177. For modifications of the form, see Donne, *Batter My Heart,* 731; Owen, *Anthem for Doomed Youth,* 750.
- **Ballads:** *Sir Patrick Spens,* 668; *Bonny George Campbell,* 688; *Barbara Allan,* 1119; *Lord Randal,* 1121; Keats, *La Belle Dame sans Merci,* 954. See also Carroll's *Jabberwocky,* 730.
- **Common Measure:** Many of Emily Dickinson's poems (Chapter 25).
- **Songs** and **Lyrics:** Berry, *Through the Weeks of Deep Snow,* 1126; Housman, *Loveliest of Trees,* 675; Rossetti, *Echo,* 892; Herrick, *To The Virgins,* 1016; Donne, poems in Chapter 25; Shakespeare, *Fear No More the Heat o' the Sun,* 1197.
- **Odes:** Keats, *Ode on a Grecian Urn,* 1018, *To Autumn,* 1214, *Ode to a Nightingale,* 918; Hughes, *Let America Be America Again,* 864; Wordsworth, *Ode: Intimations of Immortality,* 1049.

William Shakespeare, *Sonnet 116: Let Me Not to the Marriage of True Minds,* page 903

Please see the discussion of this poem in the text, pages 903–904.

Writing topics. Imagery and meaning. Form and meaning.

Works for Comparison with "Let Me Not to the Marriage of True Minds"

Bradstreet, *To My Husband,* 1128
Burns, *A Red, Red Rose,* 783
Wakoski, *Inside Out,* 798

Walt Whitman, *Reconciliation,* page 905

This poem, discussed in the text (905–906), may be compared with Hardy's "The Man He Killed" (673). In addition to contrasting open and closed form poems on the same subject, there is clear contrast in speakers and tones. Whitman's speaker is more sophisticated and clear about his own feelings. The two poems make a good comparison-contrast writing assignment (Chapter 35). The focus of such an essay could be form, tone, speaker, imagery, diction, or meaning. Ralph Vaughan Williams, in his 1936 *Dona Nobis Pacem,* which is based on poems from Whitman's *Drum Taps,* set this poem to music for baritone, chorus, and orchestra, along with "Beat! Beat! Drums!" (1216) and "Dirge for Two Veterans" (1217).

Writing topics. The nature of the speaker. The use of variable line lengths in the poem.

Works for Comparison with "Reconciliation"

Hardy, *The Man He Killed,* 673
Sassoon, *Dreamers,* 1195
Whitman, *Dirge for Two Veterans,* 1217
Zabytko, *Home Soil,* 511

George Herbert, *Easter Wings,* page 907

This splendid and skillful example of shaped verse is well worth class discussion. Teaching can be organized around questions of content and then shape or structure. The ideas are expressed in four movements: humanity's fall, personal salvation, personal fall, and personal flight. The poem takes the form of a petitional prayer, in which the speaker asks the Lord to permit him to sing praises and to feel the joy of the Easter victory over sin. The connection between this desire and the title is that Easter is the celebration of this victory. That the speaker wishes to rise like a lark (line 8) and also like a falcon (lines 19–20) is comparable visually to the Resurrection.

Suggestions for Discussing the Study Questions, page 907

(1) When viewed straight on, the poem's shape resembles two hourglasses (suggesting elapsed personal and cosmic time, the end of time, and also suggesting spiritual thinness and the need for unity with God). When turned sideways, the shape does suggest wings, whether of an angel (visually suggesting grace, Christ, resurrection, salvation), or of a bird. Each line also visually reflects its own meaning through its length (by a diminution or expansion, according to the spiritual stage being described).

(2) The typographical arrangements follow the sense closely, with both stanzas narrowing to a central point, as with lines 5 and 15, and then, as the emotion surges, expanding to the approximate beginning widths.

(3) The first five lines show, both graphically and assertively, how humankind has been spiritually diminished as a result of the choice of the first disobedience (the "fall," line 10). The speaker reiterates the same conclusion about himself in lines 11–15, and the lengths of these lines match those of 1–5.

WRITING TOPICS. The visual connection between form and content. The reasons for the shortening and lengthening lines. The importance of the larks and the falcon.

WORKS FOR COMPARISON WITH "EASTER WINGS"

Collins, *Days, 1135*
MacNeice, *Snow, 676*
Wordsworth, *It Is a Beauteous Evening, 1058*

ELIZABETH BISHOP, *One Art,* *page 909*

"One Art" represents an antidote to the idea that "Winning isn't just the main thing; it's the only thing," which many of our students might hold as a guide to life. In team sports, there is only one championship winner, and all the others are "also rans." Does this fact make them lesser as human beings? Should it be the cause of self-reproach and depression? These are good personal questions for students to consider and discuss.

Suggestions for Discussing the Study Questions, page 909

(1) The villanelle is a form borrowed by English poets from the French, who originally acquired it from the Italian. Traditionally it contains five tercets rhyming *aba,* and it concludes with a quatrain rhyming *abaa,* as is shown by Bishop, Roethke, and Thomas in the

villanelles in this chapter. The first line of the first tercet is repeated as the last line of the second and fourth tercets, and the last line of the first tercet is repeated as the last line of the third and fifth tercets (in these poems, some of these lines are varied). Both these lines, in addition, conclude the poem as the eighteenth and nineteenth lines. Although the form has been used as the vehicle for lighter subject matter, the three poets here illustrate its potential for the most serious of topics. All three villanelles illustrate the use of both serious and personal topic matter, with the repeated lines developing an increasing weight of meaning as the poems evolve.

Because of the repeated rhyming words, the villanelle form requires only two rhymes (with whatever variations the poets choose to introduce) is used thirteen times and the other six, and each of these second rhymes is the second line of each of the stanzas. The opening line in each poem is repeated three times, and the third line is repeated (or varied) three times. The three poems included in this chapter poems are about the idea of loss and its repetitive nature. With Bishop, loss is an inseparable part of life; the lines themselves emphasize the continuity of loss. With Roethke, life is not permanent; it is always receding. With Thomas, loss encroaches on life, but the person affected should "rage, rage against the dying of the light."

(2, 3) The basic idea of the poem is brought out in lines 2 and 3. Things are "filled with the intent / to be lost," and therefore, their "loss is no disaster." The things exemplifying this idea are: door keys, the hour badly spent, places, names, travel destinations, her mother's watch, three loved houses, two cities of residence, two riverfront properties, a nation (continent; the poet left the United States and lived in South America for many years), and the listener (the "you" of line 16). The idea is that one learns to live with loss.

Writing topics. The unusual nature of the poem's topic. What things do people lose without experiencing "disaster"? The form of the villanelle, and Bishop's use of it in this poem.

Works for Comparison with "One Art"

Eliot, *The Love Song of J. Alfred Prufrock*, 1147
Hacker, *Sonnet Ending with a Film Subtitle*, 1155
Kincaid, *What I Have Been Doing Lately*, 148
Oliver, *Ghosts*, 1182
Sexton, *To a Friend Whose Work Has Come to Triumph*, 989

BILLY COLLINS, *Sonnet*, *page 910*

This is a quite engaging poem which students should take to readily. The major question to raise is whether the speaker is ridiculing the sonnet tradition specifically or literature generally, or whether he is asking readers to share his joke about the sonnet tradition, or whether he is serious about advocating a more open-form type of personal lyric that is exemplified by the sonnet.

Suggestions for Discussing the Study Questions, page 910

(1) The first line takes up the humorous vein of the poem, with the subtraction of one from fourteen leaving "thirteen now." After this, the reference to "iambic bongos" (line 6) refers comically to traditional iambic pentameter lines in sonnets, and the reference to Petrarch and Laura (lines 12–14) describes the reality behind the idealistic feelings described in the earliest sonnets. The poem is closely tied to the sonnet tradition, but it takes the tradition lightly.

(2) Lines 5–7 assert the ease of composition if meter and rhyme could be avoided. Underlying the lines is the notion that open form verse is superior to the closed form because it avoid artificiality. If one needs to know what an open-form sonnet would be like, the poem "Sonnet" is an example. The reference to "every station of the cross" refers humorously to needless formality and regularity in poetry.

(3) The "ship" is the love sonnet, of which many were composed during the Renaissance and later.

(4) The poem concludes with the reference to Petrarch and Laura because Petrarch was the originator of the sonnet form, and because many Petrarchan sonnets were composed to give testimony to Petrarch's ideal love for her. The idea here is that Laura, like Petrarch, was a real person who did not live every moment of her life within a literary tradition. Her clothing was down to earth, and she went to bed to rest. She was, in other words, real.

WRITING TOPICS. The nature of the speaker. Is the speaker attacking the sonnet form? The meaning of the references "rows of beans" and "the turn / into the final six [lines] where all will be resolved."

WORKS FOR COMPARISON WITH "SONNET"

Burney, *Can. Lit. 1126*
Levine, *Theory of Prosody, 866*
Nash, *Very Like a Whale, 868*
Strand, *Eating Poetry, 740*

E. E. CUMMINGS, *Buffalo Bill's Defunct*, *page 910*

This poem exemplifies the importance of how the printed form affects comprehension of a subject. It has a conversational ring, and an ambiguous, mocking tone, considering that the famous Buffalo Bill had actually transformed himself from an individual to a business or a myth. cummings's form is worth extended discussion.

Suggestions for Discussing the Study Questions, page 911

(1) Lines made up of single words or names (1, 5, 7, 11) depend on typography and space to emphasize the images/ideas. *Buffalo Bill's* and *Mister Death*, as the opening and closing lines/names, are balanced and opposed against one another.

(2) The run-on words create an initial difficulty in reading on the page, and they also emphasize the activity of Bill and the sounds of the speaking voice. You might remind students that spaces between words are one of the major conventions of writing.

(3) *Defunct* is a Latin word originally meaning "non-functional"; that is, dead. It is to be found in the Latin Mass for the Dead, and there it is quite serious ("*Libera animas defunctorum*"). In English, however, it is a comic, overblown word. "Dead" is the straightforward English word, while *deceased* has a formal and somewhat obnoxious ring to it.

(4) This poem can lead to a spirited class discussion. It is certainly a portrait, but your students will have to decide if it is admiring, mocking, or something in between.

WRITING TOPICS. The spatial relationships on the page. The relationship of these to cummings's ideas in the poem. The tone. The image of death.

WORKS FOR COMPARISON WITH "BUFFALO BILL'S DEFUNCT"

Dickinson, *The Bustle in a House*, 978
Nemerov, *Life Cycle of Common Man*, 1078

JOHN DRYDEN, *To The Memory of Mr. Oldham*, *page 911*

This short poem commemorates the death in 1684 of the young poet John Oldham, whose major contribution to literature was a satire against the Jesuits (in 1679, a time of great anti-Catholic feeling in England). In 1684, Dryden had not yet switched his religious allegiance to Catholicism, and therefore he was still supportive of Anglicanism. Dryden's most memorable line is the last one, which, being an alexandrine (six iambic feet) rather than a pentameter, effectively summarizes the poet's view of the finality of death.

As Dryden presents the consolations of early death here, they are pagan and classical, not Christian and redemptive. The speaker asserts that Oldham might have improved by writing smoother lines (*numbers*) had he lived longer, but that the "rugged" verse he actually wrote was all right for satire (condescending?). *Marcellus* (line 23) implies that Oldham would have succeeded as a brilliant poet; the *laurels* suggest that he had already achieved greatness. Rhymes are useful in clinching ideas and linking concepts; you might ask your class about pairs like *thine/mine, shine/line,* and *prime/time/rhyme* (the triplet). See if your students think the repetition of the *young/tongue* rhyme (lines 13–14, 22–23) helps or hurts the poem.

One might compare this poem with other poems on death, such as Gray's "Elegy," Frost's "Out, out–," and cummings's "buffalo bill's defunct." Most such poems stress the lost potential of the dead person, and conclude on a note of reconciliation, even if that reconciliation is to raise questions about the fairness of life.

Suggestions for Discussing the Study Questions, page 912

(1) The poem is in the closed form of heroic couplets (iambic pentameter: *aa, bb,* etc., with a triple rhyme in lines 19–21). The couplet form is a self-enclosed unit of development, giving the poet the opportunity to shift ideas quickly when needed (as in line 22, the beginning of the last unit of the poem), and also bestowing upon the poem a dignified and stately tempo appropriate to its elegiac tone. Dryden uses an *alexandrine* (line 21) to slow the poem still further before its final "hail and farewell." The couplet form, also used by Oldham himself, was particularly important in the late seventeenth century because the developing admiration for science created a pressure for poets to develop their thoughts in a pithy, axiomatic form analogous to the conclusions and generalizations of science.

(2) In the opening ten lines, the speaker describes his affinity with Oldham, noting that their souls were *near allied* and that they both wrote verse satire. The allusion to *Nisus* (line 9) puts the friendship in a classical and poetic context.

(3) The classical *ethos* also dominates lines 11–25, where the speaker attempts to explain that dying young may not be all bad. The idea is that one's full power comes early, and that age merely "mellows" the achievement of an older person. Therefore, Oldham did reach his full power, and time would not have granted him additional strength for further contributions.

WRITING TOPICS. Form, rhyme, diction, or allusion in connection with character or meaning.

WORKS FOR COMPARISON WITH
"TO THE MEMORY OF MR. OLDHAM"

cummings, *Buffalo Bill's Defunct, 910*
Frost, *Out, Out–, 1109*
Gray, *Elegy Written in a Country Churchyard, 698*
Gray, *Sonnet on the Death of Richard West, 733*
Plath, *Last Words, 1186*

ROBERT FROST, *Desert Places,* *page 912*

Frost employs repetition, alliteration, and rhyme in this lyric to create a network of related images and sounds that reinforce meaning. Reading the poem aloud in class may help your students pick up the repetitions of *snow*, the alliteration on *f* (*falling, fast, field, few*) and the web of sounds/words linked to *loneliness.*

Suggestions for Discussing the Study Questions, 912

(1) The poem is a four-stanza lyric (iambic pentameter, *aaba, ccdc, eefe, ffgf*).

(2) The setting and situation are that snow is falling on a field and covering everything in a monochromatic white. The snow affects the landscape, the animals, the field, and, through metaphor, the universe and also the speaker himself.

(3) Even though at the time of the poem astronomers were learning that the universe was incalculably more vast than anyone had ever supposed, the speaker asserts that the mind-boggling distances of the universe, and the virtually infinite emptiness, are less important and frightening than the "desert places" within his own spirit.

(4) The falling rhymes in the last stanza—*spaces/race is/places*—do not lighten the poem's tone; they add a twist of grim irony.

(5) In stanzas 1 and 2, the snow covers and isolates, turning the earth into a *desert place.* The speaker is included in this loneliness *unawares* because he is too "absent-spirited to count." In the third stanza, the speaker begins to meditate on this desert of loneliness, and implies that there is nothing within or without (*nothing to express*) to mitigate the desolation. The snow, landscape, speaker, and nature are all *benighted.*

WRITING TOPICS. An analysis of form, repetition, rhyme, or sound in connection with tone, speaker, or meaning.

WORKS FOR COMPARISON WITH "DESERT PLACES"

Frost, *Acquainted with the Night, 1111*
Frost, *Fire and Ice, 1110*
Larkin, *Next, Please, 1021*
Shakespeare, *When in Disgrace with Fortune and Men's Eyes, 1198*

ALLEN GINSBERG, *A Supermarket in California*, *page 913*

This tribute to Walt Whitman imitates several features of Whitman's style, including his poetic cadences, enumerative lists, and long sentences.

Suggestions for Discussing the Study Questions, page 913

(1) The speaker is alone at night looking for *images.* The *neon fruit super market* is the contemporary America (of 1955) of conspicuous consumption and wealth; the Whitmanesque lists reflect this abundance.

(2) Lorca and Whitman are the speaker's spiritual progenitors. The speaker, like the Whitman presented in the poem, is an outcast on a journey without a destination. For all these complementary figures, the key terms are *childless, lonely, solitary,* and *silent.* Whitman's journey to death (*Charon, Lethe*) is as silent and lonely as the speaker's journey through the night.

(3) The enumeration of various elements is consciously mentioned by the speaker in lines 5–6. The detail is a tribute to the concreteness of Whitman's poetic style, and might also be considered particularly American because of the sense of abundance.

(4) Even though the individual lines are long, the poem should not be considered prose because it is not expansive. In addition, the rhythms produce more strong accents than in prose, and there are a number of repetitive "I walked," "I went," and "I heard" structures–more characteristic of a poetic than a prose style.

WRITING TOPICS. The impact of setting, form, diction, or imagery. The link between the speaker and Whitman. The ideas about modern America and its values.

WORKS FOR COMPARISON WITH "A SUPERMARKET IN CALIFORNIA"

Jeffers, *The Answer, 1167*
Kennedy, *Old Men Pitching Horseshoes, 956*
McHugh, *Lines, 1177*

NIKKI GIOVANNI, *Nikki-Rosa*, *page 914*

Giovanni is a poet whose reputation has coincided with the development of African-American consciousness and pride. Often her material is political, although a strain of the personal may also be found in her work, as in this poem, which is selected from the 1968 volume entitled *Black Feeling, Black Talk.*

Suggestions for Discussing the Study Questions, page 915

(1) Short lines and cadences alternate with longer ones here to punctuate ideas; conjunctions at the opening of lines speed up the tempo.

(2) The poem is full of positive and loving images of childhood, even when they are linked with hard times. Some of these images are the big tubs, the meetings, and the togetherness of the family. The speaker shows an attitude of self-awareness and assurance about herself, and a sense of identification with African Americans. Her expectation is that she will be successful enough so that someday someone will write about her.

(3) The assumption attributed to whites by the speaker is that poverty, fighting, and drunkenness must automatically make a child unhappy. She denies this assumption, asserting instead that she was quite happy because, whatever her sorrows, she always felt a sense of Black identity. The speaker's central assertion is in the last four lines; he or she claims that *no white person* will ever understand that *Black love is Black wealth.*

WRITING TOPICS. The use of detail. The variable lines and the free form. The contrast between the speaker's good memories of childhood and the assumptions that the speaker claims they (biographers, line 6) will make about the childhood.

WORKS FOR COMPARISON WITH "NIKKI-ROSA"

Evans, *I Am a Black Woman, 821*
Stanton, *Childhood, 710*
Wheatley, *On Being Brought from Africa, 1216*

ROBERT HASS, *Museum,* *page 915*

Students will at first wonder why an apparent paragraph is appearing in a section on poetry, but prose poems are quite plentiful today in poetry collections. Classroom discussion should demonstrate that the major difference between "Museum" and lined-out poetry is the appearance on the page.

Suggestions for Discussing the Study Questions, page 915

(1) The appearance of this prose poem does not immediately suggest poetry. What seems poetic about the poem is the concentration on detail, speech rhythms, and segmental devices such as assonance (s*u*ffering the n*u*mbest; t*a*lent or cap*a*city, etc.) and alliteration (*K*äthe *K*ollwitz *c*arved; *g*reen has be*g*un). What seems "unpoetic" is that for most of the poem the subject does not seem to be anything more than reportorial.

(2) The poem is not set up in lines because Hass is emphasizing the closeness of speech to poetry. The poem is not to be considered prose, which requires argument and logic. Instead the poet presents the scene as it is, emphasizing the description of the activity. Certainly the poem would yield easily to a line arrangement based on content and rhythms. Here is a brief example:

> Her hair is tousled, her eyes are puffy.
> they look like they were thrown down
> into sleep
> and then yanked out of it
> like divers coming up for air.

Such a line arrangement would change the emphasis and therefore change how the poem is perceived by readers (but perhaps not for listeners).

(3, 4) The contrast is that Hass's young couple are at ease, at peace, and secure in their assumption that no harm will be done to them. The art of Käthe Kollwitz concerns people who can make no such assumptions, for her best-known artistic works depict people in the grips of poverty and war. The poem's final statement, in the light of this contrast, seems right for the situation. Note that the final word is *possible*, not *inevitable* or *certain*.

WRITING TOPICS. The nature of a prose poem as shown in "Museum." The optimistic conclusion. The poet's observations of the couple.

WORKS FOR COMPARISON WITH "MUSEUM"

Pound, *In a Station of the Metro, 766*
Whitman, *Full of Life Now, 1216*
Wordsworth, *It Is a Beauteous Evening, Calm and Free, 1058*

GEORGE HERBERT, *Virtue,* *page 916*

This wonderful lyric explores the differences between transient worldly things and the immortal soul. The poem is discussed at some length in the demonstrative essay in this chapter (933–35).

WRITING TOPICS. Form and meaning. Rhyme and meaning. Meter and meaning. The imagery (especially the *day, rose,* and *spring*).

WORKS FOR COMPARISON WITH "VIRTUE"

Arnold, *Dover Beach, 693*
Crashaw, *On Our Crucified Lord, 758*
Harjo, *Eagle Poem, 674*

William Heyen, *Mantle*, *page 917*

Heyen's fresh and original shaped poem might be of special interest to students who realize that the stanzas are intended to take the shape of a curve ball. It is not certain that these students will be vigorous exponents of poetry after they make this realization, but it is certain that they will be talking about this poem.

Suggestions for Discussing the Study Questions, page 917

(1) This poem resembles a curve ball. The last stanza represents the ball going over the plate. The mark of the great major league hitter, of course, is the ability to hit curve balls. Mickey Mantle (1931–1995), the subject of the poem, hit curve balls, and he also hit fast balls, sliders, and changes. He did confess, however, that he had trouble with a high inside pitch. He therefore struck out many times.

(2) In the poem Mantle symbolizes the loss of youth and the need to carry on after the shouting stops. Housman's poem "To an Athlete Dying Young" (not in the anthology) is comparable, but Housman's athlete's life is over, and he therefore does not need to face the circumstance in which "the name" dies "before the man." After Mantle retired from baseball in 1969, he made personal appearances, endorsed bread and hair cream, autographed baseballs, operated a restaurant, and attempted in other ways to capitalize on his fame.

(3) George Herman Ruth ("Babe" Ruth, the "Sultan of Swat"), Lou Gehrig (the "Iron Man"), and Joe DiMaggio (the "Yankee Clipper") were all New York Yankees and were awesome power hitters. All set records. Ruth's record of 60 home runs in one season was broken in 1961 by another Yankee, Roger Maris. This record was in turn broken in 1998 by Mark McGwire (70 homers) and Sammy Sosa (66 homers). Gehrig's record of playing in consecutive games was exceeded only by Cal Ripkin, Jr., of the Baltimore Orioles. No one else has even come close to Gehrig's record. DiMaggio's record of hitting safely in 56 straight games in 1941 has never been seriously threatened. Both Ruth and Gehrig died young (Mantle died at the age of 63 in August, 1995). DiMaggio spent his later career throwing out balls at season openings, and also in advertising on television for a bank and a coffee-maker. They are all like Mantle because of their ability and successful baseball careers. DiMaggio was closest to Mantle, however, in living in the shadow of former greatness.

Writing topics. The relationship between the poem's shape and its subject. The major idea in the poem.

Works for Comparison with "Mantle"

Frost, *Nothing Gold Can Stay*, 1111
Frost, *The Oven Bird*, 1110
Millay, *What Lips My Lips Have Kissed*, 1178

John Hollander, *Swan and Shadow*, page 918

Like "Mantle" immediately preceding it, this poem makes an immediate impact on the page. It is interesting to have students make connections between words in the neck and on the swan's back (e.g., *What A pale signal will appear*, etc.).

Suggestions for Discussing the Study Questions, pages 918–19

(1–4) This poem works as shaped verse, but not quite as well as Herbert's "Easter Wings" (907); there is no multiple image here, and every line length does not reinforce meaning. The poem is about perception, memory, and time; the swan is only a convenient example. The image awakens recognition in the beholder, creates illumination in the mind, and then fades into memory. The relation of swan to shadow is parallel to present and past, image and reflection, perception and memory. Typography and shape produce some interesting effects. The *what when where* (lines 10–12) are all answered in the same lines of the body. Line 18 divides swan from shadow, present from past, perception from memory. It is the "perfect sad instant now." A single rhyme (*light/sight*) frames and emphasizes the transition. At the close, Hollander introduces a visual-verbal pun. The "swan / sang" is an allusion to the *swan song*, the myth that a swan sings once in its life immediately before dying. The single word *sang* visually embodies that dying and fading away, a last glimmer of memory.

Writing topics. The relationship of shape to meaning. The limits of spatial poetry.

Works for Comparison with "Swan and Shadow"

Herbert, *Easter Wings*, 907
Heyen, *Mantle*, 917
Swenson, *Women*, 926

John Keats, *Ode to a Nightingale*, pages 919–21

This poem is one of Keats's most important, written in his last, "living year" of great poetic creativity. It is by no means easy, and may require some explanation of Keats's idea of "negative capability." That is, the person of great creative power, being a kind of receiver of divine information much like the ancient Biblical prophets, is satisfied with recording the results of creative impulses without seeking explanations and without erasing what comes from the "penetralium (penetralia) of mystery" that constitutes the source of inspiration. The poem develops through a comparison of the song of the invisible nightingale with the everyday, here-and-now life of the speaker, and it may be construed as a statement of faith that there is a force in the universe that can reach us through imagination. Needless to say, these ideas need discussion and exemplification.

Suggestions for Discussing the Study Questions, page 921

(1) The stanza form Keats employs throughout is a truncated Italian sonnet (iambic pentameter, *abab cde 3cde*).

(2) The first stanza establishes the speaker's mental and emotional state; he is unhappy and pained. Key metaphors relate this condition to poison (hemlock) and narcotics (*opium*), but it is the nightingale's song that has produced the lethargy.

(3) The speaker (in stanza 2) thinks of drinking wine (vintage, warm south, Hippocrene, inspiration, spirit) so that he can join the nightingale and vanish "into the forest dim." His wish is somehow to escape the sickness, age, loss of power, and death that constitute living in the world.

(4) In stanzas 4 and 5 the speaker's tone changes. He claims that he will join the nightingale through the power of poetic inspiration/imagination ("the viewless wings of Poesy"). In his imagination, he transfers himself to the nightingale's green, fragrant, murmurous, and dark world. The sensual images here are visual, olfactory, and auditory.

(5) In the seventh stanza, the heart of the ode, the speaker establishes the transcendent, symbolic meaning of the nightingale's song, which has been heard throughout human history by emperors, clowns, and even spirits ("in faery lands"). The bird's song, in other words, symbolizes something more permanent than the short lifespan of individual human beings. After this climax, the speaker describes the loss of his visionary insights, claiming that his "fancy," or imagination, may have cheated him. Characteristically, and perhaps paradoxically, it is this sort of questioning and chiding ("deceiving elf") that is the essential quality of everyday, ordinary (boring) existence, and the speaker concludes on the question of his uncertainty about the state of his waking consciousness. His assertions may thus reflect more hope than certainty.

WRITING TOPICS. The organization of the poem's ideas or argument through form. The impact of rhyme or diction. The ideas about the world, poetry, or imagination.

WORKS FOR COMPARISON WITH "ODE TO A NIGHTINGALE"

Hopkins, *God's Grandeur, 918*
Oliver, *Wild Geese, 957*
Wordsworth, *Lines Written in Early Spring, 1048*

CLAUDE MCKAY, *In Bondage,* *pages 921–22*

In its first twelve lines, this poem is builds a quiet and courageous vision of what life could be like and should become. The conclusion, however, creates a strong contrast and therefore makes a powerful impact.

Suggestions for Discussing the Study Questions, page 922

(1) "In Bondage" is a Shakespearean sonnet (iambic pentameter, *abab, cdcd, efef, gg*). McKay uses the three quatrains and the couplet to organize his ideas. In teaching, it is important to get your students to see the radical shift (or disjunction) between the hypothetical (lines 1–12) and the actual (lines 13–14), indicated by *would* and *but.*

(2) In lines 1–8, the word *would* signifies the hypothetical nature of a world of freedom, leisure, fairness, and time.

(3) The third quatrain (lines 9–12) draws back from this world and explains its importance: Life is more important and enduring than petty and short human conflict.

(4) All this is sharply undercut by the couplet, which jerks us back to the reality of African-Americans in the United States during McKay's life. Here, the rhyming words—*grave/slave*—pound home the image of what *is* instead of what should be.

WRITING TOPICS. The relation of form to meaning. The ideas explored about life, reality, humanity. The effects of rhyme, especially in the couplet.

WORKS FOR COMPARISON WITH "IN BONDAGE"

Coleman, *Unfinished Masterpieces, 433*
Harper, *She's Free!, 1159*
Hughes, *Negro, 1166*
McKay, *The White City, 1177*

JOHN MILTON, *When I Consider How My Light is Spent*, *page 922*

This sonnet is one of Milton's most famous, having been for many years, in many schools, a requirement for memorization. The concluding line, "They also serve who only stand and wait," is quoted as often, if not more often, than any other Milton line. This is not to suggest, however, that the line is well understood.

Suggestions for Discussing the Study Questions, page 923

(1, 2) In this Italian sonnet (iambic pentameter: *abba, abba, cde, cde*), Milton employs the octave-sestet structure to organize the poem's movement and meaning.

(3) In the octave, the speaker complains about his failures and frustrations, only one of which is blindness. More significant is the crisis of faith in which the speaker expresses uncertainty about God's expectations, and assumes that he will be rejected. The speaker *almost* asks if God exacts "day-labor, light denied" (*light* here means sight, faith, inspiration), and he admits that it is a foolish question. The problem is resolved in the sestet, where the speaker's (personified) Patience prevents him from asking the question by explaining God's expectations. Patience makes it clear that God is self-sufficient, not needing either "man's work or his gifts." The *best* service to God is to "bear His mild yoke," and that can be done by those "who only stand and wait" (*wait* suggests a series of actions connected with service, including *wait on, wait for, attend,* and *expect*).

(4) In a limited sense, the *one talent* refers to the speaker's skill at poetry and political writing (Milton was a brilliant propagandist for the Puritans during much of the Interregnum). As an allusion to the parable in *Matthew*, however, *talent* refers additionally to the active and energetic preparation for the Lord's return.

WRITING TOPICS. The connection between form and meaning. The character of the speaker or of Patience. The image of God.

WORKS FOR COMPARISON WITH
"WHEN I CONSIDER HOW MY LIGHT IS SPENT"

Donne, *Batter My Heart*, 731
Herbert, *Love (III)*, 1162
Rossetti, *A Christmas Carol*, 708
Joy Williams, *Taking Care*, 95

DUDLEY RANDALL, *Ballad of Birmingham*, *pages 923–24*

In 1965, Randall founded the Broadside Press, an important and valuable publisher of modern Black poetry. One of the first poems he published as a broadside (a single sheet, often political in topic matter) was this ballad. The poem demonstrates that the ballad survives as an effective and moving poetic form.

Suggestions for Discussing the Study Questions, page 924

(1) The poem is traditional in form and subject matter. The rhyme scheme (*xaxa, xbxb,* etc.) and meter (iambic tetrameter and trimeter) reflect medieval practice, as do the use of quotation and the sensational and disturbing events.

(2) The quoted speaker in stanzas 1 and 3 is the child; the mother is quoted in stanzas 2, 4, and 8. This dialogue slows the ballad down and delays the climax.

(3) The story of the bombing is told through dialogue and third-person narration. The speaker is dispassionate; emotion is conveyed through description and dialogue. The daughter wants to join a freedom march; the mother, considering this too dangerous, instead sends the daughter to church. The irony here is complex. The mother is ironically wrong about safety. American society is also presented in an ironic light; in the world of the ballad, it is safer to face "clubs and hoses, guns and jails" than to go to church. The little girl's shoe (line 30), like the hats of Sir Patrick Spens's crew (605), is a more gruesome and ironic symbol of death than the actual body would be.

(4) All three poems share a narrative structure with speeches added to increase dramatic tension. They also share the common subject matter of death, with the causality being either directly or indirectly political.

WRITING TOPICS. The relation of form to impact, the characters, tone, and ideas about society. The character of the mother, daughter, and/or speaker.

WORKS FOR COMPARISON WITH "BALLAD OF BIRMINGHAM"

Anonymous, *Barbara Allen, 1119*
Anonymous, *Bonny George Campbell, 688*
Anonymous, *Sir Patrick Spens, 668*

THEODORE ROETHKE, *The Waking,* *pages 924–25*

The villanelle form used here, as with the villanelles in this chapter by Bishop and Thomas, is immensely demanding in English poetry, and it creates a complex and incantational concentration of rhyme and verbal repetition. The form is hence appropriate to the topic material about the evanescence of life.

Suggestions for Discussing the Study Questions, page 924

(1) See the discussion of the villanelle form in this manual under Bishop's "One Art."

(2) The poem deals with the closeness of death (sleep), and the truth that life (wakefulness) leads us inevitably toward death; therefore, wisdom suggests that we take that "waking slow," savoring life while we have it.

(3) The speaker is probably saying that there are no set rules to life. One learns about living by living, and not by adhering to any preestablished set forms. Thus he learns "by going where I have to go." That all things are subject to "what falls away" (line 17) suggests that time is never grasped, but that each moment is receding into the past. Nothing is clear; no one "can tell us how" "Light takes the Tree," and so we are wandering about in a state of perpetual ignorance. The solution is to live as best as one can. The poem is thus like other poems that have a basis in the *carpe diem* or "seize the day" tradition. This poem, however, has not even a remote basis in the seduction aspects of *carpe diem.*

WRITING TOPICS. The relation of form to impact, the characters, tone, and ideas about society. The character of the mother, daughter, and/or speaker.

WORKS FOR COMPARISON WITH "THE WAKING"

Frost, *The Road Not Taken, 1109*
Lochhead, *The Choosing, 1172*
Whitman, *Facing West from California's Shores, 799*

PERCY BYSSHE SHELLEY, *Ozymandias,* *page 925*

When Shelley wrote "Ozymandias," the science of Egyptology was in its infant stage. Scholars could not yet read Ancient Egyptian, although Jean François Champollion (1790–1832) was making breakthroughs and published a guide in 1821. Shelley's choice of topic, in short, was timely, and was based on recent archaeological studies of the Rameseum, the palace and tomb of the ancient Pharaoh Rameses II. The sonnet is one of the many poems dealing with change and mutability. Shelley implies that the *lone and level sands* will in time cover everything—artifacts like the colossal statue, and also the memory of the power of persons like Ozymandias (Rameses). Ironically, however, the ancient artist's skill still endures.

Suggestions for Discussing the Study Questions, page 925

(1) This is a modified Italian sonnet (iambic pentameter: *abab,*

acdc, ede, fef). The modified rhyme scheme allows each unit to be interconnected with the next.

(2) The octave-sestet structure organizes the poem's images and ideas. The statue, or its remains, are described in the octave, the inscription in the first triplet of the sestet, and the surrounding desolation in the second triplet of the sestet.

(3) The image of the face and the inscription convey Ozymandias' arrogance, pride, and vanity. There are three remaining parts of the statue: the head, the legs, and the pedestal containing the inscription. The effect of distributing the parts throughout the poem is to emphasize the fragility and impermanence of human works. Thus, the sonnet illustrates the vanity of human tyrants and the power of time and change. The artist, who recognized this vanity, mocked both the king's vain passions and the pompous heart that "fed" the king's yearning to seem grandiose.

WRITING TOPICS. The relation of form to meaning. The ideas explored about tyranny, time, and art.

WORKS FOR COMPARISON WITH "OZYMANDIAS"

cummings, *next to of course god america i, 1012*
Stevens, *Disillusionment of Ten O'Clock, 739*
Wordsworth, *On the Extinction of the Venetian Republic, 1058*

MAY SWENSON, *Women*, *page 926*

One of Swenson's objectives is to create a position for poetry in space as well as time (poetry, like music, being understandable only when moving through time or else being read in the order of lines on a page). The result is exemplified in this poem, which suggests some of the qualities of movement and character to be attributed to her topic, women.

Suggestions for Discussing the Study Questions, page 926

(1) The form of this poem suggests but does not specifically depict a swaying, dancing (female) figure. The poem can be read at least two ways: down the left column and then the right, or in ten-line two-column units divided at lines 10 and 20; the second method may provide a more coherent reading.

(2) The undulating typography suggests curves, movement, and pliancy—all consistent with the textual images of women "moving to the motions of men" as "rocking horses rockingly ridden." If the poem were in straight lines it certainly would be less noticeable visually.

(3) The devices of repetition and alliteration move in sympathy to the poet's ideas. For example, "ridden / rockingly / ridden until / the restored ..." provides a rhythmic undertow to the poet's sexual references.

(4) The poem asserts that women may be envisioned as "pedestals moving to the motions of men, " as "painted rocking horses," and as "immobile," always "waiting willing to be set in motion"; they are the "gladdest things in the toyroom." These images are sexual and ironic; women are ironically presented as passive objects (toys) to be used and then abandoned by men ("the restored / egos dismount and the legs stride away"). The speaker's irony suggests that the social/sexual formulation is wrong. The poem also implies that those men who accept this view of women are really perpetuating their own childhood. Indeed, the social structure depending on this view is itself immature, for by stereotyping women it denies the rights of freedom and individuality to all.

Writing topics. The various ways to read the poem. The suggestiveness of the poem's shape. The irony of the view of women. A defense of an opposing view.

Works for Comparison with Swenson's "Women"

Bogan, *Women, 1127*
Herbert, *Easter Wings, 907*
Parker, *Penelope, 980*

Dylan Thomas, *Do Not Go Gentle into That Good Night,* *page 927*

In the 1980s, John Cale set "Do Not Go Gentle" and other poems by Thomas to music as part of his *Falklands Suite* (found on *Words for the Dying*, Opal/Warner Bros. 9 26024-2).

Suggestions for Discussing the Study Questions, page 927

(1) See the discussion in this manual at question 1 for Bishop's "One Art."

(2) The poem reflects the speaker's dismay at his father's emotional and physical decay (Thomas's father had been a strong and authoritarian teacher; in his eighties, however, he became blind and ill). The speaker addresses the poem to his father (line 16) as an incentive to maintain his courage in the face of blindness.

(3) The speaker wants his father to emulate "wise men" (lines 4–6), "Good men" (lines 7–9), "Wild men" (lines 10–12), and "Grave men" (13–15), all of whom have raged against death, and have not gone "gentle into that good night."

(4) The poem is enlivened by puns on *good night* (dying and "farewell") and *grave* (serious and dead–a pun made famous by Mercutio in Shakespeare's *Romeo and Juliet*). Connotative words and phrases are "close of day" (i.e., dying), "bright" (a result of the activity of vigorous life), and "gentle" (well-bred, and also passive).

WRITING TOPICS. Use of the villanelle form. The function and meaning of the repeated lines.

WORKS FOR COMPARISON WITH "DO NOT GO GENTLE"

Frost, *Out, Out–*, 1109
Olds, *35/10*, 1024
Porter, *The Jilting of Granny Weatherall*, 651
Shakespeare, *That Time of Year*, 877

JEAN TOOMER, *Reapers*, *pages 927–28*

This poem ostensibly is about a harvest involving scythes and a horse-drawn mower that cuts into a field rat. On the symbolic level, it stands for the ways in which individuals are harmed and killed as business and industry carry on without regard to the consequences. The poem's implication is that the subject matter is the subjugation of blacks.

Suggestions for Discussing the Study Questions, page 928

(1) "Reapers" is in iambic pentameter rhymed couplets that are enjambed rather than end-stopped (as, mainly, with Dryden). The enjambment, especially in lines 1–2 and 7–8, moderates the effect of the couplets and keeps the poem moving quickly.

(2) The auditory images of the poem contrast the silence of reaping to the *sound of steel on stones* and the *squealing* of the field rat. The visual images form a linked chain that related to death: *black reapers, scythes . . . silently swinging, black horses,* the bleeding field rat, and the *blood-stained blade.* Like the squeal, the blood (lines 6–8) shocks by contrasting vivid red with the dominant black of the poem.

(3) Alliteration of the *s* sound links together the various images. One might particularly notice the similarity of the *s* to the actual hissing of a scythe cutting through "weeds and shade." In addition, the *b* sound in the concluding lines links the inanimate mechanism of the blade to the belly of the dying animal.

WRITING TOPICS. The impact of the rhymed couplets on meaning. The reapers as metaphorical images of life or of death. The play of colors (especially black and red) in the poem.

WORKS FOR COMPARISON WITH TOOMER'S "REAPERS"

Hughes, *Mulatto, 1663*
Lessing, *The Old Chief Mshlanga, 628*
Villanueva, *Day-Long Day, 1210*

CHARLES H. WEBB, *The Shape of History, page 928*

The shape of this poem is arresting, and the content with which the poet fills the shape creates a short version of civilization. Students may wish to discuss the various meanings of the shapes that they believe the poem takes.

Suggestions for Discussing the Study Questions, page 929

(1) The poet gives history the shape of a cone, or a whirlwind, or a top, or perhaps a tornado (can students think of any others?) beginning at a narrow point and gradually widening outward as human populations expand and civilizations grow. Granting the plethora of news at the present time, and the non-existence of it at the beginning of civilization, the image is a good one.

(2) The first line has thirteen words; the last two lines have three, certainly a contrast between our current state of news and the news at the beginning. The "top stories" of the first two lines were headlines in 1995, the year the poem first appeared (Somalia, Yugoslavia, qualifications for military service). Since then, other important stories have appeared. Who knows how long the first references in Webb's poem will remain important?

(3) To pursue Yeats's image, civilization will lose control and humanity will be harder to define and govern. If things don't "fall apart" soon, they eventually will.

(4) "Nothing at / all" could refer to the singularity with which the universe began, when the entire universe was confined within an infinitely small point, or it could refer to the very beginnings of civilization, wherever it began, at some remote and agelessly prehistoric time. It is difficult to define "nothing" in these terms, since we know very little about whether or not there was "something" at the same time, or when "something" came into being.

WRITING TOPICS. The shape of the poem as an expression of idea. How accurately does the shape conform to history?

WORKS FOR COMPARISON WITH "THE SHAPE OF HISTORY"

Dryden, *A Song for St. Cecilia's Day, 1012*
Nemerov, *Life Cycle of Common Man, 1179*
Whitman, *Full of Life Now, 1216*
Yeats, *Leda and the Swan, 974*

PHYLLIS WEBB, *Poetics Against the Angel of Death,* *page 929*

The poem is built on a sense of what values should be in light of the inexorability of death. The reference to Wordsworth's "The Prelude," a vast autobiographical poem (1040) comes as a surprise. Also a surprise is the speaker's thought after this reference. Understanding why Wordsworth wrote as he did, she also realizes that she herself must find her own voice to give expression to her own ideas about what is importance under the shadows of the wings of the Angel of Death.

Suggestions for Discussing the Study Questions, page 929

(1) The "Angel of Death" could be a literary reference to Byron, or it could refer to the original Passover of the Hebrew people in the land of Egypt (Exodus 12), or it could be a figure representing the inevitability of death and the end of life. Whatever the precise meaning, the speaker uses the angel to initiate a pattern of thought about how she should live her life and about her ultimate values.

(2, 3) The speaker expresses a certain mockery of "the Great Iambic Pentameter." She discovers that this kind of expansive, philosophical verse is not for her, but instead she prefers the tightly compact form of haiku, or if she wants expansiveness she prefers to let the lines themselves govern their length. There is little question that this attitude is totally defensible, especially now when form follows sense, regardless of how short or long verse should be. The form of "Poetics Against the Angel of Death," particularly the last lines, illustrate the shortness of haiku and the extensive length of knotted bamboo.

WRITING TOPICS. What is the poem's topic, death or poetry? The character of the speaker. The form of the poem as an embodiment of the thoughts expressed about poetry

WORKS FOR COMPARISON WITH
"POETICS AGAINST THE ANGEL OF DEATH"

Hacker, *Sonnet Ending with a Film Subtitle, 1155*
Hass, *Museum, 915*
Moore, *How to Become a Writer, 274*
Tremblay, *The Thimble, 455*
C. K. Williams, *Dimensions, 834*

WILLIAM CARLOS WILLIAMS, *The Dance,* *page 930*

Williams captures in verse the movement and energy rendered visually in Brueghel's painting. The key question for class discussion is how Williams recreates the essence of the painting in the poem. Since the painting is reproduced above the poem in the text, students may study both poem and image simultaneously.

Suggestions for Discussing the Study Questions, page 931

(1) The repetition of the first line at the close creates a circular movement; the poem could start all over again. The identical lines also create a frame, like the edges of an artist's canvas.

(2) The repetition of sounds, syllables, and words drives the poem rapidly forward, and forms internal connections (notice, for example, the web created by "round ... round ... around ... round ... impound ... sound"). Williams employs onomatopoeia to suggest/duplicate the sounds of the instruments (*squeal, blare, tweedle*). While end-rhyme is lacking, internal rhyme (*around/impound* or *prance/dance*) pulls different parts of the poem together and speeds up the movement. The participles (*tipping, kicking, rolling, swinging, rollicking*) suggest the confusion and energy of ongoing activity.

(3) The poem capitalizes only the first words of two sentences, and the other capitals are placed at the beginnings of proper nouns. The absence of capitals elsewhere, particularly at the line beginnings, produces a steady pace, a visual enjambment, much in keeping with the constant round of activity in the painting.

(4) Williams avoids regular meter. Instead he juxtaposes accented and unaccented syllables to develop the dancing cadences of anapests and dactyls. The unstressed or split words that end lines (*and, the, thick-, those, such*) push the reader on from line to line.

(5) A close look at the painting shows that Williams captures the boisterousness of Brueghel's figures. The open form is appropriate to convey the random, hustle-and-bustle movement in the painting.

WRITING TOPICS. The absence of capitals. The use of verbals. The use of alliteration. The repetition of the first line at the end.

WORKS FOR COMPARISON WITH "THE DANCE"

Wagoner, *March for a One-Man Band, 881*
Williams, *Landscape with the Fall of Icarus, 990*
Wojahn, *"It's Only Rock and Roll, But I Like It", 768*

Writing About Form in Poetry, *pages 931–35*

Although the demonstrative essay (933–35) deals with a closed-form poem, the discussion on writing about form provides approaches that work effectively for closed or open poems. In an essay on form, it is important to consider the relationship between form and content (speaker, idea, tone, meaning) rather than form or idea themselves. The questions for discovering ideas on pages 931–32 will help shape basic ideas from which to organize and develop essays on the topic.

Special Topics for Writing and Argument about Poetic Form, *pages 935–36*

(1) The first topic introduces a comparison-contrast of poems by Shelley and Keats. Students may wander away from the topic of form and produce instead a comparison of ideas. It is therefore important to stress the relationship of form and content.

(2) The four poems offer differing treatments of the topic of death. As with many essays on more than two works, the problem here is keeping within reasonable limits. Ask students to study Chapter 35, on Extended Comparison-Contrast (1854) for using groups of poems as the basis of the comparison.

(3) This question has a number of subtopics, all of which together might produce a term-length essay. You might wish to narrow things a bit, depending on how much you want your students to produce. Of great interest is the relationship of visual art, as represented by Brueghel, and poetic art.

(4) For this subject, please consult the first discussion suggestion under Bishop's "One Art" in this manual.

(5) To write a visual poem may at first seem difficult. You might suggest that students first create the shape they wish the poem to take, and then start working out lines to fill that shape. Once they get the "hang" of pouring words into shapes, they will discover that the technique is not considerably more difficult than writing a poem, say, in a given number of iambics. The real challenge of this assignment is to relate the line lengths not only to the shape, but also to the topic itself (see Herbert's "Easter Wings" for a successful example).

(6) The writing of haiku has been a favorite assignment for many years in schools throughout the country. The virtue of haiku is that they are short, and that students discover the need for short, specific, and concrete words rather than long and abstract ones. It is interesting to shorten the lines, for this exercise also enables writers to achieve even greater clarity, and often more pointed imagery.

(7) You might add other topics for student reference, as you wish. What is important here is that library reference systems list holdings not only under authorial names, but also under topics such as "ballads, England," and so on.

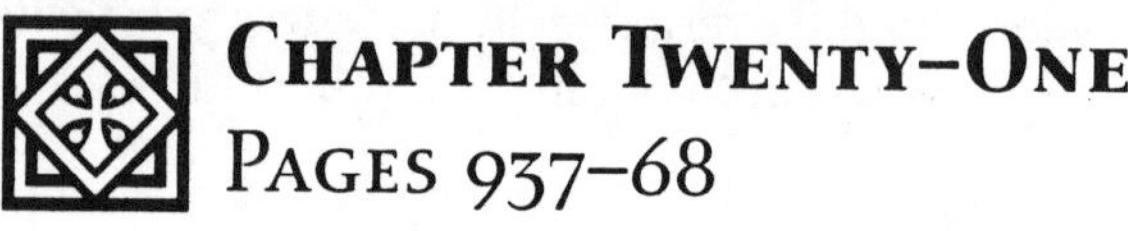

Chapter Twenty-One
Pages 937–68

Symbolism and Allusion: Windows to a Wide Expanse of Meaning

If you have already taught symbolism in fiction (Chapter 9), you may wish to use this introductory section simply as a review. If you omitted Chapter 9, however, there will be much here that is new. Particularly important is that poetry, being more compact than fiction, does not go into as much detail with symbols as one is likely to find in fiction. Students should thus be sensitive to the rapidity with which symbolism is often rendered in poems, through words, actions, settings, characters, and situations (941).

Allusion (942–43) is sometimes difficult for students because they may not have built up the background needed for recognition. Even with good explanatory notes, they need guidance, so that they may understand the context and therefore the meaning of allusions.

On pages 943–44 we address one of the perennial problems of students: how to recognize symbols and allusions. Often we ourselves may take these things for granted, but students are less sure of their ground. A frank discussion about how students may try independently to determine the presence of symbols and allusions will hence be much appreciated.

Virginia Scott, *Snow*, *page 939*

The matters raised in the questions about this poem are considered on pages 940 and 943. Writing topics may deal with any of the questions.

E. E. Cummings, *in just-*, *page 945*

This poem is one of the more joyful that Cummings wrote, although students may be perplexed at first about the appearances of the balloonman. Sometimes they may need some prodding to see that the poem is about development and sexual growth, for the subject may superficially seem like a nostalgic memory of childhood. Here the change of the balloonman is important, for he alters from a colorful salesman to a symbolic, Pan-like figure representing spring and ritual fertility.

Suggestions for Discussing the Study Questions, page 946

(1) As symbols, *mud-luscious, marbles, puddle wonderful,* and *hopscotch* all signify the excitement and joy of childhood. Spring symbolizes growth, and also incipient sexuality. The whistle, at first not more than a realistic sales-call of the balloonman, by the end of the poem symbolizes the urges and needs of sexuality.

(2) At first the balloonman suggests the joy and color of childhood discovery. Once Cummings introduces the goat feet, however, the connection with Pan and symbolic sexuality is plain.

(3) Beyond the "wee," or "we," who may be an unidentified first-person plural group, the four characters are Betty, Isbel (or Isabel), Eddie, and Bill. cummings runs their names together to stress their common identity as children, and, additionally, to symbolize their growth as sexual beings.

(4) The spacing and alignment definitely influence one's perception of the poem. Students may wish to experiment in spoken delivery. Interestingly, many students prefer the poem on the page, as a visual, seen artifact alone, rather than a poem to be read aloud or heard.

WRITING TOPICS. The use of symbols. The relationship of spring to sexuality. The effects of spacing, alignment, and lack of capitalization.

WORKS FOR COMPARISON WITH "IN JUST-"

Collins, *Schoolsville*, 599
Joyce, *Araby*, 430
Soto, *Oranges*, 992

John **DONNE,** ***The Canonization,*** *pages 946–47*

This lyric is a defense of love and passion in which both are linked with mysteries of myth and religion. At first the idea that love transforms and exalts lovers and is therefore a religious experience may seem far-fetched. But it is to Donne's credit that he makes this idea work. Indeed, "The Canonization" is one of Donne's best known poems, on which his reputation for wittiness and courageous rhetoric rests.

Suggestions for Discussing the Study Questions, pages 947-48

(1) The poem develops out of a dramatic situation. The speaker has been listening to someone (a parent? a guardian? a friend?) who tries to dissuade him from his affair with his sweetheart. Finally the speaker loses his patience and exclaims "For Godsake hold your tongue and let me love." He then goes on to point out that his love is not a minor thing but is rather a holy involvement.

(2) Donne introduces symbols (*eagle* and *dove*), allusion (the *phoenix*) and sexual puns (*die* = to achieve orgasm) to emphasize the mysterious, overwhelming power of love.

(3) The reference to the phoenix and the phrase *die and rise* point toward both resurrection and the reawakening of sexual desire after orgasm. *Canonization* refers to the making of religious saints. In the poem Donne asserts that love transforms lovers into saints of love who will become exemplars and also intercessors for future lovers. There are no outside accreditation for this sort of sainthood of love; instead, the two lovers, through the intensity of their love, qualify for their exalted role.

(4) In the fourth stanza, the speaker claims that his and his lady's love will be chronicled in verse (this very poem) and the lovers will thus be canonized and immortalized–they will become saints of love. Future lovers (quoted in lines 37–45) will pray to these saints for a *pattern* of love. The poem thus explores both the power of love and the immortality of verse.

WRITING TOPICS. Donne's use of symbols. The idea of lovers becoming saints. Is the poem sacrilegious? The poem's speaker.

WORKS FOR COMPARISON WITH "THE CANONIZATION"

Elizabeth Barrett Browning, *If Thou Must Love Me*, 755
Frost, *The Silken Tent*, 1112
Marvell, *To His Coy Mistress*, 1023
Shakespeare, *Let Me Not to the Marriage of True Minds*, 903

ISABELLA GARDNER, *Collage of Echoes*, *page 948*

In her lifetime, Gardner acted, edited *Poetry* magazine, taught, published four volumes of poems, and gave frequent poetry readings. This poem, "Collage of Echoes," is from her final volume, which appeared two years before her death.

Suggestions for Discussing the Study Questions, page 948

(1) Granted the allusiveness, the poet clearly assumes that read-

ers have the knowledge to recognize the total context upon which she is drawing.

(2) Gardner's many echoes truly make the lines resonate, for the poem would have little meaning without the lexical strength of the allusions.

(3) The phrases all suggest weariness, a feeling of having fulfilled obligations and borne many cares. Because the originals are easily recognized, they might be considered comic in this new context. The "collage" of quotations is therefore a different and totally new application of something well known (a collage is usually thought of as an assemblage of cuttings and pastings, often by children in the early grades). "Witty" is perhaps a better description of the allusions than "comic."

WRITING TOPICS. The integration of the echoes. The meaning and application of the allusions.

WORKS FOR COMPARISON WITH "COLLAGE OF ECHOES"

Keller, *Tea Party*, 1266
Millay, *What Lips My Lips Have Kissed*, 1178
Porter, *The Jilting of Granny Weatherall*, 651

JORIE GRAHAM, *The Geese*, *pages 948–49*

This poem offers the reader a challenge in understanding and interpretation. The symbolism of the geese and the spiders and how they apply to human life is not easily grasped. Students will need a good deal of close reading and reflection to arrive at satisfactory interpretations of Graham's lines.

Suggestions for Discussing the Study Questions, page 949

(1) The tense is dominantly present, with a sprinkling of conditional tenses to raise questions about the possibilities of certain courses of action. The effect of the tense is that things are happening now, at the present time, no matter when the reader reads the poem. The poet thus gains immediacy for her ideas.

(2) The speaker hangs out the wash and looks up to see geese flying, either north for the summer or south for the winter. She does not say. After a time of contemplating the geese, she goes indoors and continues her meditation on the meaning of the geese, the spiders, and the ways in which these creatures symbolize the problematic nature of existence.

(3) The symbolism is broad and does not yield to a simple formulation. Essentially, the geese and the spiders create lines of cross-

ing and texturing. The creatures move in natural and preordained paths, from which they do not deviate. As these observations apply to humanity, they symbolize human possibilities for breaking the lines and entering another plane of existence (which takes the form of a question: Where would human beings be if there were nothing more for animated creation than the rigid lines of the geese and the spiders?). We are therefore in a pattern of the "everyday" but this existence may be nothing more than a "delay" in our reaching some greater, undefined goal.

(4) Graham alludes to Yeats by putting the connectedness and dissolution of "The Second Coming" into a pattern of ambiguity. We live in the "everyday" as a defense against things falling apart, even though the everyday world is perhaps "false" (line 30). We therefore try to live connected lives because we, like the geese and spiders, know nothing superior.

WRITING TOPICS. The meaning of the crossing patterns and webs of the geese and the spiders. The complexity of human existence contrasted with that of the creatures. The character of the speaker. Why does a description of hanging out the washing begin the poem?

WORKS FOR COMPARISON WITH "THE GEESE"

Keats, *Ode to a Nightingale, 918*
Levertov, *A Time Past, 762*
Oliver, *Wild Geese, 957*
Yeats, *The Wild Swans at Coole, 1219*

THOMAS HARDY, *In Time of 'The Breaking of Nations,'* *page 950*

With this poem, students may wish to discuss whether the topic is politics or people. Another interesting subject is whether such a poem could be written today, with the threat that nuclear warfare could penetrate even the remotest corners of earth to destroy maids and their wights.

Suggestions for Discussing the Study Questions, page 950

(1) The man and woman are easily recognized as a universal symbol of love. The man and the horse are also a universal symbol. The smoke coming from the grass, however, is contextual; the poet must arrange the stanza to make the smoke symbolic. As images, these symbols refer to sight, sound (whispering) and smell (smoke).

(2) Hardy emphasizes the symbolism of the phrase "breaking of nations" by speaking of dynasties and war's annals in lines 7–8 and

11–12. The Biblical allusion adds the sense that wars and political changes have been going on for millennia, but that human life has been predominating and will prevail, because strength is in human affection, not anger.

(3) Stanza one is descriptive, whereas in stanzas two and three only the first halves are descriptive. In developing his assertions, Hardy refers to these halves as "this" (line 7) and "their story" (line 12).

(4) Hardy's speaker makes his evaluation by citing the quietness and permanence of his pictures of life among the people, the folk. He dismisses the great business of war and dynastic change by relegating it to the second parts of the stanzas, and by negating it in favor of common life.

Writing topics. The visual symbols. The importance of the Biblical allusion and the quotation marks in the title.

Works for Comparison with "In Time of 'The Breaking of Nations'"

Emanuel, *Like God*, 1151
Haines, *Little Cosmic Dust Poem*, 1156
Wilbur, *Year's End*, 958
C. K. Williams, *Dimensions*, 834

George Herbert, *The Collar*, *pages 950–51*

Herbert's poems, which dramatize his religious conflicts before he became a priest, were not published during his lifetime. "The Collar" describes one of these conflicts. Herbert's speaker cites the following reasons for pursuing his own secular goals: freedom, impatience, earthly reward, capacity and opportunity to do other things, independence, and possible adventure. The sole reason in favor of the clergy role is God's call (line 35), and this is overwhelmingly persuasive.

Suggestions for Discussing the Study Questions, page 951

(1) At the beginning the speaker describes a moment when in frustration he beat a table and began the train of inward debate contained in the rest of the poem. The speaker is thinking about accepting a calling to divine service, and for most of the lines he cites reasons for which he should resist it.

(2) The title of the poem is a multiple symbol, because it involves an elaborate pun. It represents the speaker's anger (choler) against what he considers the yoke (collar) of service for which God (the caller) is calling him, and also the power of service because the clerical collar is round and therefore enveloping and enclosing. Because

of the way the poem concludes, the calling by God and the collar as an enclosure are dominant.

(3) The symbols of the poem may be classed as follows: A– Positive religious symbols are thorn, blood, wine, and the parent-child relationship. B– Positive secular symbols of independent self-fulfillment are bays, flowers, and garlands. C– Negative religious symbols (prompting the speaker's anger or "choler") are cage, the death's head, and the rope of sands (symbolizing the many complex, endless, and never-to-be-finished duties of the clergy).

WRITING TOPICS. The use of "collar" as a symbol and as a pun. The conflicting symbols. Herbert's use of allusion.

WORKS FOR COMPARISON WITH "THE COLLAR"

Donne, *Batter My Heart*, 731
Herbert, *The Pulley*, 716
Joy Williams, *Taking Care*, 95

JOSEPHINE JACOBSEN, *Tears*, *pages 951–53*

"Tears" is a unique reflection on a very unusual subject for poetry. Crying, the poet states, is a purely human condition. To feel pain and to respond with tears, and to sympathize with the plight of others and to cry for them, are human characteristics. Without the capacity for tears, the poet states, we lose our humanity.

Suggestions for Discussing the Study Questions, page 953

(1) As a symbol, tears signify the immense suffering, agony, and cruelty that the human race has experienced since its beginnings. The memory of past tears has vanished, however, just as the tears themselves have vanished without trace. Symbolically, the tears thus suggest that each generation of humanity must go through the same experiences, even though one would hope that generations would benefit from the sufferings and persecutions of the past.

(2, 4) The poem applies the symbol to past civilizations (Ur [ancient Sumerian], Persepolis [ancient Persian], to other cultures ("in some countries, openly, in others, not" [line 21], to the future, and to literature (Shakespeare, Thomson). All these allusions are introduced to demonstrate that grief, together with the human causes of grief, is perpetuated throughout all times and all societies.

(3) It would appear, from the poem, that tears are a response to suffering in its various forms, both past, present, and to come. Animals, however, have no recorded history, and live primarily in the moment. The poem's final two lines refer to the fact that many

human beings, in their desire for power and control, forsake their capacity to understand and sympathize with suffering, and hence their eyes become figuratively dry as they pursue their goals. In essence, they give up their humanity as they give up their ability to sympathize with others and to shed tears for them. Symbolically, then, there is no humanity without tears. If one seeks to define the essence of human beings, it is the capacity to cry.

WRITING TOPICS. The symbolic value of tears. The meaning of the final two lines. The character of the speaker. The poem's use of allusion.

WORKS FOR COMPARISON WITH "TEARS"

Quasímodo, *Auschwitz, 829*
Serotte, *My Mother's Face, 1196*
Stern, *Burying an Animal on the Way to New York, 1206*

ROBINSON JEFFERS, *The Purse-Seine,* *pages 953–54*

One of Jeffers's major themes is the capacity of human beings to self-destruct. Out of the destruction, however, may come a restoration of the pristine beauty of the natural world. "The Purse-Seine" deals with this theme, although in the poem Jeffers is not concerned with the potentially positive aftermath.

Suggestions for Discussing the Study Questions, page 954

(1) A purse-seine contains floats at the top and a draw-cable at the bottom. When drawn, the net does not permit any fish to escape. In the second stanza the speaker responds to the seining by claiming that it is terrible because of the certainty of capture, but he also stresses details about the beauty of the fish as they struggle to free themselves.

(2) In stanza three, the speaker shows the symbolic nature of the purse-seine by equating it to the inability of industrialized humanity to survive independently. He points out that the draw cable may take the form of dictatorship, revolution, repression, anarchy, or mass disasters, from which there is no escape. The sardines hence symbolize the present world population, and the seine symbolizes destructive political forces.

(3) Both Jeffers and Yeats agree that a sinister force will soon become powerful. To Yeats, however, things happen in 2,000-year cycles, with the possibility of a better cycle replacing the evil one now approaching. Jeffers is less systematic than Yeats, for Jeffers makes plain that repressive political processes are destroying world civilization.

(4) The concluding assertion (line 31) about death as the end of life is both a recognition and an acceptance. Because the fish are described as "caught" (line 9), the poem does not offer the possibility of escape for human beings. The speaker is clearly concerned, if not fearful, about the loss of beauty represented by the city and its lights (line 17).

(5) The sighing watch of the sea lions in line 12 may be seen as a symbolic lament for the loss of the freedom and natural beauty represented by the fish. The "you" of the concluding lines is the reader being drawn in to the scene of the poem as a virtual witness, who would need to be insensitive not to sigh at the prospects of destructiveness symbolized in the poem.

Writing topics. The symbolism of the purse-seine. The symbolism of the lighted city and the fish. The cataclysmic views of Jeffers and Yeats compared and contrasted.

Works for Comparison with "The Purse-Seine"

Bishop, *The Fish, 751*
Kumin, *Woodchucks, 1168*
Tate, *The Blue Booby, 1208*
Wright, *A Blessing, 711*

John Keats, *La Belle Dame Sans Merci*, *pages 954–56*

Because of Keats's letters, we know the precise time when he wrote the first version of this poem (April 21, 1819) and also the circumstances (soon after he had taken care of the personal effects of his dead brother, Tom). Critical biographers have tried to demonstrate the influence of this situation on the poem, together with Keats's own uncertainty about his love for Fanny Brawne. Despite the wealth of information about the circumstances of composition, and also despite attempts to relate the poem to a linkage of death and life in the poet's psyche, "La Belle Dame Sans Merci" has an independent existence that defies categorization. All poems of course require great perception and care. With this poem, special care is needed.

Suggestions for Discussing the Study Questions, page 956

(1) The first three stanzas contain the first speaker's questions. The remaining eight stanzas contain the knight's narrative about his encounter with the lady, the "Belle Dame." The knight's narrative is structured according to the meeting, the first loving, and the magical journey (stanzas 4–7). In stanzas 8–11, the knight goes with the lady to her grotto; they make love and the knight falls asleep

and dreams the ghostly dream, only to awake on the hill's side. The last stanza (12) is the knight's answer to the speaker's question in the first stanza. The source of the knight's information about his thralldom is only his own dream, his own imagination.

(2) That the knight's narrative is a dream requires that it be read as a symbol. The meaning, however, is not certain. Is it disillusionment with love? A sense of doom about life itself? A disparagement of the regrettable power of the human imagination to misconstrue and negate positive experiences? Sorrow about the hauntingly brief nature of happiness? Your students might wish to discuss any or all of these possibilities.

(3) Relish, honey, and manna are all magical, unreal symbols. Manna, particularly, is the food provided by God to the ancient Israelites after they fled from Egypt (Exodus 16). Keats probably intends by it no more than a magical nourishment. The pale kings and warriors symbolize powers of doubt and negation.

(4) The multiple setting of withered sedge, the meadows, the herbs, and the grotto all symbolically complement the knight's dazed state of mind.

Writing topics. The narrative structure of the poem. The puzzle of the meaning of the poem's major symbols. The nature of the fairy lady, apart from the knight's perception.

Works for Comparison with "La Belle Dame Sans Merci"

Atwood, *Siren Song, 977*
Dickinson, *I Cannot Live with You, 1069*
Drayton, *Since There's No Help, 1146*
Minty, *Conjoined, 790*
Wyatt, *I Find No Peace, 800*

X. J. Kennedy, *Old Men Pitching Horseshoes,* *pages 956–57*

Although this poem invites a symbolic reading, it makes no overt claims about being symbolic or profoundly meaningful. The title is totally descriptive: Four men are playing a game of horseshoes. One man throws a horseshoe and misses, but his second one is a ringer. While his side cheers, his opponents mutter. After this, the four men change sides, and continue the game. Yet the poem suggests that such actions are as old as the ages, as old as human civilization itself. The poem therefore is an example of how a work may be contextually symbolic.

Suggestions for Discussing the Study Questions, page 957

(1, 2) The symbolic nature of the game is brought out not so much by the description of the action, but by the permanence suggested by the diction. *Dirt-burnished iron,* for example, is an observation about a horseshoe that invests it with a long-term connection with the earth. Words like *congregate, appraising, inhabits, extended, outpost, withered, worn path of earth, sheaves of air, warm distortions,* and *force* all together support the idea that the single game of horseshoes is like all previous games, like all games to follow, and like all games of all sorts. As long as there are people, in short, there will be old men pitching horseshoes, an activity in which they engage after their years of work and service are past, and they retreat into the recreational years of retirement.

(3) Eliot's poem concludes with the image of "ancient women gathering fuel in vacant lots." The image is one of effortful work, gleaning energy and continuing life under unpromising conditions. Kennedy's characters are old men, and his location is a recreational area set aside for play. Kennedy's poem therefore suggests a world of greater stability and security than Eliot's. Or do the roles assigned to men and women in both poems suggest that women must always work, even in age, while men ultimately reach a state in which they may afford to spend their time in relaxing games?

WRITING TOPICS. The poem's symbolism. The use of descriptive and abstract diction.

WORKS FOR COMPARISON WITH
"OLD MEN PITCHING HORSESHOES"

Eliot, *Preludes,* 759
Hardy, *In Time of 'The Breaking of Nations,'* 950
Porter, *The Jilting of Granny Weatherall,* 651

MARY OLIVER, *Wild Geese,* *page 957*

In terms of its opening and development, this poem may be compared with Donne's "The Canonization." Both are arguments that serve as the final words in a discussion. If the previous speaker had anything to say, the poems themselves overcome whatever arguments he or she might have advanced.

Suggestions for Discussing the Study Questions, page 957

(1) The first five lines stem out of a previous dramatic situation. Someone has apparently said that it is necessary to lead a good life and to perform expiation for one's sins. The speaker responds

with the opening of the poem, indicating that conduct need not be humble and penitent, for all that is needed is to permit love to become the dominant impulse of life. In lines 6–12 the speaker puts human life in the larger context of world, sun, rain, and homeward migrations of geese, to signal the constant changing of seasons; compared to these, our lives are temporary. Lines 13–17 form a climax: Small as we are, we have a part in nature and the universe, in "the family of things." These ideas formulate a code of conduct and philosophy that stem naturally from the more formal position to one of relaxed acceptance and reconciliation with nature.

(2) These references symbolize the continuity of the creation and the consequent roles that all living things have within this pattern. They are hopeful because the symbols offer a natural pattern of behavior that excludes the need for "goodness" and expiation.

(3) The wild geese symbolize recurring and cyclical regeneration, and they are vital because they form visible patterns of flight in the sky. All the suggested words are fitting as formulations of the poem's ideas. Students in discussion will doubtless contribute other suitable words.

WRITING TOPICS. The poem as an argument with an unidentified listener. Symbols of optimism in the poem.

WORKS FOR COMPARISON WITH "WILD GEESE"

Berry, *Through the Weeks of Deep Snow, 1126*
Graham, *The Geese, 948*
Jeffers, *The Answer, 1167*
Tate, *The Blue Booby, 1208*

WALT WHITMAN, *A Noiseless Patient Spider,* *page 958*

In this brief poem Whitman captures the human yearning to be connected, a part of the whole, which otherwise is "detached, in measureless oceans of space." The second stanza is particularly powerful in rendering the speaker's desire to overcome his sense of alienation in the immense universe.

Suggestions for Discussing the Study Questions, page 958

(1) In the second stanza the speaker shifts from the narrative of the first by turning to his own soul, and asking why his soul has not made something substantial, but instead never seems to catch hold, as the spider does in the "noiseless patient" pattern of weaving and making a place.

(2) The speaker uses the spider and its web to symbolize the

need of the human spirit to find a secure place in the universe. Granted the nature of human life, however—at least the speaker's life—nothing ever seems to be finished. Thus the speaker's soul is always surrounded, but is detached, always venturing and seeking, but never with an anchor.

(3) The second stanza is not a complete sentence because the quest of the speaker is incomplete. Thus he views life as a process of searching and hope, but never seems to find the bridge to completion, the anchor that will keep him in place, or the gossamer thread that will tie him to someone or something.

WRITING TOPICS. The shift of subject matter in stanza 2. The spider as a symbol of the speaker's soul.

WORKS FOR COMPARISON WITH "A NOISELESS PATIENT SPIDER"

Oliver, *Wild Geese, 957*
Graham, *The Geese, 948*
Whitman, *Facing West from California's Shores, 799*

RICHARD WILBUR, *Year's End,* *pages 958–59*

This poem contains many negative symbols. Students will wish to consider whether "Year's End" should refer to the end of all endeavor, however, or whether the "New-year bells" which "are wrangling with the snow" may contain a contrary note of hope and optimism.

Suggestions for Discussing the Study Questions, page 959

(1) Stanzas 1–3 introduce natural symbols of impermanence. Winter snow, lake ice, dead ferns, and great mammoths—all symbolize the end of life and power. In stanza 4 Wilbur refers to Pompeii, the long-buried Roman city, and the dog curled up and covered in lava while his masters still felt incomplete and were still planning to "do the thing they had not done." Death, in other words, inexorably interrupts natural and human plans, and has always done so.

(2) The alliterative and consonance groups are so prominent (e.g., *st*ill . . . *st*irring, *pe*o*pl*e incom*pl*e*t*e, etc.) that they clearly refer to the poetic units of Old English. Because the poem contains many references to the ages-old passing of life into death, it is appropriate to have a poetic form that is connected to the earliest period of English poetry.

(3) The details symbolize the idea that life contains within itself the principle of death. Thus the glorious life we have now (as large and lovely as tapestries) is in the process of fraying. The constant problem of humanity is that we do not do the needed things now,

but think of them only as an afterthought, just as the Pompeiians did not think of "the shapely things they had not done" until they were being buried under hot ashes from Vesuvius. Even the sounds of the radio seem muffled when they are buried in other rooms and other places. But the process of life goes on, and hence our optimism over the New Year enables us, in perspective, to go on too, despite the fact that snow is always present and ready to freeze us before we can reach our hoped-for levels of achievement.

(4) The symbol here is "sudden ends of time," which "must give us pause." In one sense there is no solution: As we think of the future, the present overcomes us. For this reason the poem may be taken negatively. In another sense, however, the "New-year bells" give some chance for hope. The now and the future are not yet past, and as long as they exist there is the possibility of achievement. Thus the poem may also be taken as an expression of hope even if, admittedly, most of the poem's details emphasize impermanence and death.

WRITING TOPICS. Symbols of impermanence and death. The purpose of the mammoth and the Pompeiian dog as symbols. The significance of the concluding stanza.

WORKS FOR COMPARISON WITH "YEAR'S END"

Berry, *Through the Weeks of Deep Snow, 1126*
Frost, *Birches, 1107*
Lee, *A Final Thing, 1170*
Mueller, *Hope, 661*
Page, *Photos of a Salt Mine, 764*

WILLIAM BUTLER YEATS, *Sailing to Byzantium, page 960*

"Sailing to Byzantium" is one of Yeats's reputation poems. It presents a vivid contrast between life and death, and also between human impermanence and artistic permanence. Unless there are students of late Roman and medieval history in your class, it may be necessary briefly to describe some of the achievements of Byzantium from post Roman times to the invasions of the Ottoman Turks in 1453.

Suggestions for Discussing the Study Questions, page 961

(1) From the vantage point of age, the speaker reflects upon life (stanza 1), stressing love, music, and "fish, flesh, or fowl," which "commend all summer long." In youth we are caught up in "sensual music" (line 7) and ignore the more permanent things of the intellect. There is little need for old people in such an environment.

(2) In stanza 2 the speaker compares the aged man—referring specifically to himself—to a scarecrow. He has the appearance of life but is in fact "paltry" (line 9). The only contribution the aged person can make is to enable his soul to sing songs of intellectual and spiritual achievement. The speaker then evokes the memory of Byzantium, the medieval culture that to Yeats was the primary symbol of civilized achievement, in order to learn from its history and philosophy ("sages") how to become part of "the artifice of eternity" (line 24) and thereby to make the songs that will be his contribution.

(3, 4) Dreaming in stanza 4 of this post-physical state, the speaker sees himself as an intricate and beautiful work of art embodying creative wisdom. Thus in this poem Yeats stresses the importance of art (which is as intellectual as science or philosophy), which is the only means by which time-bound human beings can gain the eternity which many religions have promised. Youth, in short, is impermanent, and art is eternal, for it alone has an existence that transcends life.

WRITING TOPICS. Symbols of life and death. Amid death, what alone constitutes life? The position of the speaker. Why does the poet choose "Byzantium" as his symbol of life and art?

WORKS FOR COMPARISON WITH "SAILING TO BYZANTIUM"

Coleridge, *Kubla Khan*, 756
Keats, *Ode to a Grecian Urn*, 1018
Shelley, *Ode to the West Wind*, 877
Wilbur, *Year's End*, 958

WILLIAM BUTLER YEATS, *The Second Coming*, *pages 961–62*

The issues in the questions are treated in the notes, and also in the demonstrative essay (965–66). In 1991, Joni Mitchell wrote a musical adaptation of this poem, entitled "Slouching Toward Bethlehem" (on *Night Ride Home*, Geffen GEFD-24302).

WRITING TOPICS. The structure of the poem. A major symbol in detail (e.g., the gyre, the rough beast). Yeats's theory of cyclic changes in history.

WORKS FOR COMPARISON WITH "THE SECOND COMING"

Frost, *'Out, Out—'*, 1109
Jeffers, *The Answer*, 1167
Jeffers, *The Purse-Seine*, 953
Nash, *Exit, Pursued by a Bear*, 791
Webb, *Poetics Against the Angel of Death*, 929

Writing About Symbolism and Allusion in Poetry, *pages 962–67*

In teaching this section, you will probably need to stress the strategies for organizing ideas (963–65). Questions that your students raise about these patterns may be sufficient for your discussion. However, you might additionally need to go over the material in detail. It is best, always, to combine a discussion of essay forms with the reading and interpretation of a specific poem that is relevant to the forms. If you assign approach 2, for example, you might use Isabella Gardner's "Collage of Echoes" to illustrate how a poem may be shaped by allusion. Or you might find that Oliver's "Wild Geese" is effective in illustrating approach 1, the meaning of symbols. In your use of the demonstrative essay (965–66), it would be best also to teach "The Second Coming" as a base from which to show students how they, too, may apply an interpretation of symbols and allusions to the task of writing.

Special Topics for Writing and Argument about Symbolism and Allusion, *pages 967–68*

(1) The symbols of capture are love and sex (Keats), dedication and guilt (Herbert), and the net and the consequences of civilization (Jeffers). In context, all these symbols are totally appropriate.

(2) All these poets are highly allusive in their respective poems. Graham uses simple natural references to convey complex ideas; both cummings and Yeats refer to material from the classics, but Yeats adds Christian apocalyptic allusions and combines them with his own specific system.

(3) For the first three stanzas Donne's symbolism is secular. In stanzas 4 and 5 his religious symbols are drawn first from death and burial and from the canonization of saints. His idea that the speaker and his lady are saints of love is quite bold if one is strictly religious. Students may be able to provide opinions on this subject. Herbert's poem begins in the home, but then shifts to more liturgical symbols (blood, wine) and psychological symbols (dispute, petty thoughts, death's head, the following of the religious profession).

(4) The symbolism of these three poems is domestic and natural. Although this aspect is common, each poet moves the topics in differing directions: childhood and the celebration of life, the permanence of folkways, and the yearning to connect oneself with the universe and infinity.

(5) Topic 5 should produce some interesting poems featuring major symbols. Students, always, may select their own subject, but be sure that they consult you before doing so. The self-analysis is of course an important aspect of this assignment, as with all other such assignments made in the writing topics.

(6) As with topic 5, topic 6, involving the use of allusions, is designed to get students thinking about people, activities, governments, and publications in the world around them, and, through allusion, determining how these things have both direct and indirect influences on their own lives. You might indicate that students might make allusions through names, quotations, and situations.

(7) Although topic 7 suggests that Yeats or Jeffers should be the subject, you may wish to use cummings, or Donne, or Hardy, or another poet that would provide a challenging assignment. Because students will be using secondary sources, they should be sure to provide adequate documentation for whatever reports they submit.

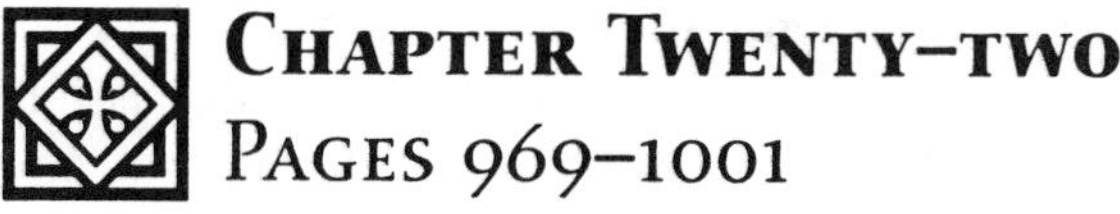

Chapter Twenty-two
Pages 969–1001

Myth: Systems of Symbolic Allusion in Poetry

This chapter has the double aim of giving students a quick introduction to mythology and a longer consideration of the ways in which poets employ myths as symbolic allusions that add layers of meaning and resonance to their poems. The introductory discussion of mythology (881-84) seeks to establish the importance of myth to humanity and to emphasize the symbolic nature of myth. "Mythology and Literature" (969-72) takes up the essential differences between the two, and the ways they can intersect. The Ansel Adams photograph (971), may serve as a touchstone for a discussion of the relationship of mythology and perception.

Problems may arise when you deal with myth and poetry. Some students might question the relationship of myth to revealed religion. It is important to respect this question, and carefully to establish the boundary lines between the two. Additionally, it is often difficult for students immediately to recognize the mythic aspects of a poem. This process often idealistically assumes a high level of familiarity with a variety of mythic systems, including Buddhist, Hindu, American Indian, Norse, and Chinese myth. We have tried to avoid this problem by limiting the mythic systems evoked in the poetry here to the system familiar and accessible to most students–Greco-Roman myth. In addition, the section entitled "Mythological References Are Common in Poetry" (973-74) should guide students to undertake the research necessary for their understanding of a particular mythic system.

Besides the poems in this chapter, the text contains many others that lend themselves to an exploration of the impact of myth in poetry. These include Gardner's "At a Summer Hotel" (862, Greco-Roman myth), Keats's "La Belle Dame sans Merci" (954, folk mythology), Yeats's "The Second Coming" (961, Christian tradition and private mythology), cummings's "In Just" (945), Plath's "Last Words" (1186, Egyptian and Babylonian myth), and Silko's "Where Mountain Lion Lay Down with Deer" (1200, Navajo Indian myth).

WILLIAM BUTLER YEATS, *Leda and the Swan,* *page 974*

The poem is explicated in the text (974–75). In class discussion, you might begin with myth and meaning, but meter, rhyme, and form are also worth class time. Yeats employs iambic pentameter with substitute feet to stress important words and ideas (e.g., the spondee *on great wings* in line 1 that produces three heavy beats in a row). The Italian sonnet form organizes the poem's argument and ideas; rhymes present some elegant and suggestive connections (e.g., *thighs/lies, up/drop*).

WRITING TOPICS. The form of the poem. Yeats's use of ancient mythology. The brief view of history in the poem.

WORKS FOR COMPARISON WITH "LEDA AND THE SWAN"

Byron, *The Destruction of Sennacherib, 1132*
Herbert, *The Pulley, 716*
Rossetti, *A Christmas Carol, 708*

■ Eight Poems Related to the Myth of Odysseus, *pages 976–84*

MARGARET ATWOOD, *Siren Song,* *page 977*

The adventure with the sirens is an important episode in Homer's *Odyssey*. Always a lover of danger, music, and temptation, Odysseus fills the ears of his crew with wax to prevent their hearing, while he himself is lashed to the mast so that he will not throw himself overboard and kill himself when cast under the spell of the sirens. Students are interested in discussing the views presented in the poem about male-female relationships. Atwood may be suggesting that males will always succumb (because of sexual attraction, their egos, their interest and love?). She may also be implying that some women may find the pattern of interaction boring, inevitable, predictable, and repetitious.

A famous musical version of the sirens is the 1898 nocturne for orchestra and women's voices, *Sirènes,* by Claude Debussy. David Bedford composed a musical impression of the sirens in 1976 ("The Odyssey," Caroline-Blue Plate CDOVD444 • 7243 8 39574 22).

Suggestions for Discussing the Study Questions, page 977

(1) In the mythology as told by Homer, the sirens were a trio of bird-women mythology who enchanted sailors in passing ships with their beauty and songs. The sirens' singing was so alluring that the captivated sailors inevitably forgot their native land, lost their

will to go on, and landed (or wrecked themselves) on the island where they starved to death. The shores around the sirens were therefore covered with bleached bones.

(2) Atwood focuses on the sexual allure of the sirens—their seductive power which undermines masculine resistance. Atwood's speaker is a contemporary siren who is tired of being with her two sisters. Her colloquial language brings her into the present, as does her claim that she is trapped in a bird suit (line 12).

(3) In lines 1–9 the speaker defines her song; it is irresistible and unknown (to what extent is it this very poem?). This is the hook that the siren speaker uses to get *you* (the reader, men) interested. In lines 10–18 the siren offers what appears to be an offer that cannot be refused: She will reveal the secret/song if *you* will help her escape. The listener is drawn in deeper. Finally, the speaker appeals to the listener's (male) ego: "I will tell the secret to you, / ... only to you" and "Help me! / Only you, only you can, / you are unique" (lines 19–24). But of course *you* are not unique because the song (poem, seduction) *works every time.*

WRITING TOPICS. The speaker or the listener, language, tone, or form. The irony and humor of the poem.

WORKS FOR COMPARISON WITH "SIREN SONG"

Chekhov, *The Bear, 1625*
Keats, *La Belle Dame Sans Merci, 954*
Wyatt, *I Find No Peace, 800*

OLGA BROUMAS, *Circe,* *page 978*

The myth of Circe is told not only by Homer, but also by Hesiod (*Works and Days*) and by Ovid (*Metamorphoses*). Like Parker in Penelope, Broumas looks at the myth not through the male eye, but through the female. Bedford's "The Odyssey" also includes a musical representation of Circe based on a modulation of the Sirens' song into a minor key.

Suggestions for Discussing the Study Questions, pages 978–79

(1) Circe is a sorceress in Greco-Roman mythology who has the power to turn men into pigs. Her most famous encounter is with Odysseus and his crew (*Odyssey,* Book 10). She transforms half of Odysseus's men, but Hermes fortifies Odysseus against her spells, and Odysseus forces her to restore the men. Circe then honors Odysseus and gives him her love. He spends a year with her on her island. Like the sirens, Circe symbolizes female sexual power.

(2) The title identifies the speaker as Circe. Her sexual power here, as in the myth, can turn "men into swine" (line 25).

(3) While Homer presents the Circe myth from a male point of view, Broumas here presents it from Circe's point of view. The speaker and poem thus symbolize the resentful attitude of women who are often used or even victimized in the relationships between the sexes. Circe's mythical power consisted of her herbal potions. Here her power seems to be venomous and spiderlike.

(4) The *charm* and the *fire* (lines 1–5) represent both Circe's power and her desire to use the power. *The Anticipation* (lines 6–15) sets up the social and sexual context in which Circe's power can work. *They* are men, society, and the followers and enforcers of social custom; they court (weave, entrap, tie up) the speaker (Circe, women) and, in doing so, create the situation (the spell) that will undo them. The *courting hands* (limitations, customs, boundaries, demands) of the men are balanced against Circe's *spiderlike* waiting and knowledge that she has the power to change them. *The Bite* (lines 16–26) presents anew the transformation myth. The speaker is confident, powerful, self-satisfied, joyful, and *divine*.

(5) After line 21 the scene shifts to modern settings, and Circe is an individual woman who is watched by nearby construction workers and by men hanging out at local bars and stores. The men's responses to her reduce their humanity; indeed, women may testify that the whistling and grunting they hear are truly "wild" sounds that one might expect of "swine" (lines 26, 25). The repetition of *corner* (lines 22–23) stresses the point of turning or transformation that both the speaker and the men experience. Classroom responses to this poem should be vigorous.

WRITING TOPICS. Male-female relations as portrayed in "Circe." The ambiguity of location in the poem. The spell-like powers of Circe.

WORKS FOR COMPARISON WITH "CIRCE"

Anonymous, *Barbara Allan, 1119*
Anonymous, *Lord Randal, 1121*
Jonson, *Drink to Me, Only, with Thine Eyes, 690*
Lawrence, *The Horse Dealer's Daughter, 500*

LOUISE GLÜCK, *Penelope's Song*, *page 979*

Ostensibly the poem could actually have been "sung" by Penelope as she waited for her returning hero, Odysseus. If so, it reveals feelings that are ordinarily associated with Penelope. If one treats the poem as strictly modern, the irony and ambiguity are evident, and the poem may be read as a feminist critique of traditional female-male roles.

Suggestions for Discussing the Study Questions, page 979

(1) The speaker is a woman addressing her "little soul"—that is, herself—and sending the soul to look for a returning man, presumably her husband, Odysseus. The speaker (lines 7–10) states that she has "not been completely / perfect either," as though she, as well as her husband, has strayed during the time the husband has been away. There is nothing in Homer to indicate any complexity in her life or in her attitude toward Odysseus.

(2) If the speaker is actually Penelope she introduces a number of domestic details, common and ordinary like grilled chicken, that could apply to ancient times as well as to our own. The exception is the reference to Maria Callas, the mention of whom creates a body of reference relevant to modern times as well as ancient. One might mention that one of Callas' best-known roles was Tosca, in Puccini's *Tosca,* who in the second act kills the police chief Scarpia with a dagger. In this poem, however, the speaker tells herself to resist her anger, to make sure that shaking the spruce tree will not drop needles on her husband's "beautiful face." The idea is that Penelope must put away her personal feelings and any grudges she might harbor against her husband, and prepare to continue in her subordinate role.

(3, 4) If the poem is about a woman waiting for her husband to return from a football afternoon, the poem takes on a comic and ironic cast. The chicken is actually to be grilled on an outdoor grill, and the details refer not to an ancient Ithacan palace but to a modern home. The situation, however, is esssentially the same, and Glück is using the poem's details to illustrate the historical continuity of a woman's secondary status.

WRITING TOPICS. The circumstances of the speaker. The story's irony. The ambiguity of Glück's use of the ancient myth.

WORKS FOR COMPARISON WITH "PENELOPE'S SONG"

Atwood, *Siren Song,* 977
Anonymous, *Lord Randal,* 1121
Gilman, *The Yellow Wallpaper,* 617
Raleigh, *The Nymph's Reply to the Shepherd,* 707

W. S. MERWIN, *Odysseus,* *page 980*

This poem draws on the mythic associations of Odysseus as a wanderer and adventurer to suggest that such a life can become redundant and meaningless. A good approach to teaching the poem is to ask students to comment on the words *same* in lines 1–2 and *identical* in line 5. When they determine the idea that Odysseus's life has become repetitive and boring, they will have a good perception of the poem's tone and central idea.

Suggestions for Discussing the Study Questions, page 980

(1) The aspects of the myth concern the life of Odysseus after his return from his wanderings. He must go in quest over and over again, to the point where his life becomes confused, purposeless, and monotonous. The speaker (outside the poem, detached) suggests that it is "As though he had got nowhere but older" (line 3). Beginning at line 5, the speaker reviews Odysseus's adventures, blending them through the use of unspecified allusions and Odysseus's own confusion into a repeated pattern of betrayal and abandonment.

(2) The originality and surprise of the poem is that Odysseus is lost as the traditional symbol of going out on the quest, and instead becomes a symbol of desertion and infidelity. He abandons the women he lives with and encounters, including Penelope, Circe, and Calypso. The last six lines suggest that Odysseus can no longer distinguish these women from one another or keep Penelope fixed in his mind. Odysseus's life becomes almost meaningless; "it was the same whether he stayed / Or went" (lines 11–12).

(3, 4) The poems by Merwin and Parker in the *Poems for Study* section form a combination based on the same mythic material; they demonstrate the ways that poets can evoke the same myth for differing purposes. Merwin focuses on the boredom and infidelity of Odysseus. Parker, who makes Penelope the central figure in her view of the myth, ignores the career of Odysseus while focusing on the woman left behind (980). The result is that Parker throws the King's adventures into the class of dereliction of responsibility. Progressively, therefore, Odysseus's restlessness and adventurousness moves from the positive in the original myth to the totally negative with Merwin and Parker.

WRITING TOPICS. A comparison of the poems by Merwin, and Parker. Merwin's view of the adventurer. Varying concepts of heroism and lengthy life.

OTHER WORKS FOR COMPARISON WITH "ODYSSEUS"

Field, *Icarus*, 987
Heyen, *Mantle*, 917
Pastan, *The Suitor*, 981

DOROTHY PARKER, *Penelope*, *page 980*

(1, 2) This short lyric, the subject of the chapter's demonstrative essay (998–99), also gains resonance from its evocation of myths in the *Iliad* and the *Odyssey*. Here however, the focus is on Penelope, Odysseus's wife. The ironic conclusion is a testimony to the fact that the heroic quest depends on the sacrifices of loved ones and dependents, and that therefore this quest may very well be characterized as juvenile as well as heroic.

WRITING TOPICS. The use of myth in the poem. The view of war and wandering from Penelope's side. The irony of the poem.

WORKS FOR COMPARISON WITH "PENELOPE"

Glück, *Penelope's Song*, 979
Piercy, *A Work of Artifice*, 792
Steinbeck, *The Chrysanthemums*, 447
Whur, *The First-Rate Wife*, 809

LINDA PASTAN, *The Suitor*, *981*

"The Suitor" is a mythologically based poem which takes the viewpoint of another "side" in the story, in this case, that of a "younger son of a younger son"; in other words, a man of little or no power, who is no more than a bystander in the hostile situation involving others.

Suggestions for Discussing the Study Questions, page 981

(1) A young man, insignificant among the adult suitors ("boisterous men") who stay in the Ithacan court and consume the court's resources, is a fitting subject because he is innocent of any offense. In keeping with the idea of how the world works, it is often just such innocent and inoffensive persons who are destroyed when violence takes place around them.

(2) The suitor views Penelope at a distance and admires her. He has to gain only the possibility that "it could be him she'll choose" (line 18).

(3) The young suitor will be killed with the rest when Odysseus and Telemachus exact their reprisal against the suitors. The idea of "wasted blood" does not apply just to the suitors, but to all who embark on foolish political and military ventures.

WRITING TOPICS. The use of myth in the poem. The view of war and wandering from Penelope's side of things. The irony of the poem.

WORKS FOR COMPARISON WITH "THE SUITOR"

Hardy, *The Man He Killed,* 673
Parker, *Penelope,* 980
Ulisse, *Odyssey: 20 Years Later,* 984

ALFRED, LORD TENNYSON, *Ulysses,* *pages 982–83*

Tennyson's "Ulysses" (Latin) and Merwin's "Odysseus" (Greek) allude to the same hero of Homer's Odyssey. In myth, Odysseus is characterized as shrewd, intelligent, crafty, and eloquent. It was he who brought about the end of the war by developing the strategy of the Trojan Horse. It is worth remarking that the concluding lines are among the most famous and often quoted in English literature.

Suggestions for Discussing the Study Questions, page 983

(1) Tennyson's dramatic monologue (in blank verse) is spoken by Ulysses many years after his return. In the poem, Ulysses represents a commitment to the active life and the continual search for new experiences. The poem draws on the mythic figure's intelligence and symbolic value as an adventurer and wanderer.

(2, 3) Students may debate what Ulysses wants: adventure, knowledge, death, or escape. The speaker, Ulysses, establishes his attitude toward life in Ithaca (lines 1–5) with phrases like *little profit, idle, still hearth,* and *barren crags* that are images of waste and boredom. He has nothing in common with the people he rules; they do not know him. At line 6, he considers his attitudes toward life; he wants to live it to the fullest, for one life is almost not enough. He notes that it is dull to "pause . . . make an end . . . rust . . . not to shine" (lines 22–23). His past adventures (lines 7–17) have become part of his present (line 18) and this pushes him onward to "that untraveled world whose margin fades / Forever and forever." He contrasts his need to move (explore, discover) with his son's complacency (lines 33–43). Telemachus will be a good and happy king, but Ulysses has other work. His quest is for knowledge (line 31), and his journey westward will be a new experience. He admits that he and his men are old and weak, yet he affirms that they are "strong in will" The poem thus absorbs the features of the myth of Ulysses as adventurer, and expands on them, turning the mythic figure into a symbolic affirmation of the life that never yields to habit or decay.

WRITING TOPICS. The problem of settling down after an exciting period of life (e.g., war, expeditions, athletics). The character of the speaker of "Ulysses."

WORKS FOR COMPARISON WITH TENNYSON'S "ULYSSES"

Auden, *The Unknown Citizen*, 1125
Frost, *The Road Not Taken*, 1109
Hemingway, *Soldier's Home*, 348
St. Luke, *The Parable of the Prodigal Son*, 445

PETER ULISSE, *Odyssey: 20 Years Later*, *page 984*

The title suggests that the poem will be about Odysseus, but a closer look discloses that it is a more general poem and that the direction of choice for the speaker is not further exploration but is rather a return to home as a place of strength and satisfaction.

Suggestions for Discussing the Study Questions, page 984

(1) The speaker is a follower of Odysseus, who as the poem progresses assumes the traditional role of the wanderer (see line 7, "Wandering Jew, Prodigal Son, opener / of doors in empty streets"). The speaker, in short, is an unnamed character who has gone along on innumerable quests. He is unlike the speaker of Tennyson's poem because he is interested in going home, not in pursuing continuous goals of travel.

(2, 3) In the first fourteen lines the speaker describes his various quests, but in the remainder of the poem he realizes that he is like a fish swimming against the current to reach home, like a turtle returning to the Galapagos to lay eggs, and like a bird returning to its nesting grounds after migration. These feminine images of settling down indicate the strong pull of making a home, even if it is no more than a temporary one. The major educational experience is that "coming home" is the most powerful attraction that life presents.

WRITING TOPICS. The value of the quest according to the speaker. Why does the speaker use feminine images of nesting and procreation to define his wish to return home?

WORKS FOR COMPARISON WITH "ODYSSEY: 20 YEARS LATER"

Kennedy, *Old Men Pitching Horseshoes*, 956
Whitman, *Facing West from California's Shores*, 798
St. Luke, *The Parable of the Prodigal Son*, 445

■ Seven Poems Related to the Myth of Icarus, *pages 984–91*

The story of Daedalus and Icarus is told most fully by Ovid in the *Metamorphoses* and the *Heroides*. The reproduction of the Brueghel painting (*see insert*) provides a graphic interpretation of the story, and also are the base of the poems by Auden and Williams.

In general, the mythic figure of Icarus symbolizes pride, ambition, arrogance, striving, and daring as well as recklessness, foolishness, and suffering. The myth presents the outline of a tragedy in microcosm; the striving toward the sun is heroic, while the fall into the sea is tragic (or at least pathetic—there is no explicit self-knowledge attained). The various poets use the figure of Icarus to embody a series of different qualities and ideas. As with the poems based on Odysseus and Penelope, these illustrate the way the same mythic figure can be employed to very different ends by writers.

Brian W. Aldiss, *Flight 063*, *pages 985–86*

Interestingly, many of the poems about Icarus deal with his failure, just as this one does. However, "Flight 063" considers the value of searching and reaching for goals. Aldiss is asking us to consider what things might be like today if the first test pilots had never tried flight, or if early explorers had never ventured into the new world.

Suggestions for Discussing the Study Questions, page 986

(1) The speaker views Icarus as a brave soul, trying his utmost to go just as high and far as he can, unlike the passengers on flight 063, who eat their dinner and are oblivious to the cold of the Arctic and to the damage that the sun's rays at high altitude can cause. The speaker speculates on the imagination and daring of trying something for the first time ("Before the fall the flight was," line 14), just like Icarus and also like Adam before the fall from grace (lines 15–17).

(3) The word "think" is emphasized as a means of stressing the magnificence of daring and creativity. The limitation of the melting point of wax is "silly" when compared with the greatness of achieving a great goal for the first time. The risk of failure and the danger to life are worth the final achievement.

Writing topics. The nature of the speaker. Why are goals like the first flight and the first innocent love worth the risks one must take to gain them?

Works for Comparison with "Flight 063"

Tennyson, *Ulysses, 982*
Sexton, *To a Friend Whose Work Has Come to Triumph, 989*
Lee, *A Final Thing, 1170*

W. H. Auden, *Musée des Beaux Arts,* *pages 986–87*

This poem focuses on Brueghel's painting of the Icarus myth (*see insert*) in a Museum of Fine Arts. The painting ignores the heroic aspirations of the mythic figure, dealing only with the fall. Auden, in turn, uses Brueghel's placement of the figure (the legs) to underscore his point that people like the plowman and like those on the ship (and also like the sun above and the natural world generally) go about their business, indifferent to the falling and dying young man.

Suggestions for Discussing the Study Questions, page 987

(1, 2) In this poem Auden moves from general to specific. He uses Icarus to explore ideas about the world's reaction to the misfortunes of others. In lines 1–13, the speaker asserts that the *Old Masters* (painters) were right about suffering; the victims always go through their agony alone while others remain indifferent and life goes on. He cites two unnamed paintings (one of the nativity and the other possibly of the crucifixion) as examples. Each presents a momentous event and a victim surrounded by indifference—the children, the dogs, the torturer's horse. The last eight lines focus on the example of Brueghel's "Icarus" (you may need to point out the legs entering the water at the right just below the ship).

Auden illustrates his idea by making the mythic figure seem insignificant. The effect only works, however, if the reader brings the whole symbolic impact of Icarus to the poem. We must assume his heroic and tragic stature so that we can see how it is ignored by the figures in the painting and by the figures cited by the speaker.

(3) In "Out, Out–" the bystanders go about their business after the little boy dies. Both poets stress that such disasters are, in the larger schemes of things, of little concern. The words describing both poems are correct. Note that it is *not* the poets who are not concerned, but rather the *people* whom the poets describe.

Writing topics. The ideas of suffering in Auden and Brueghel, and also in Frost's 'Out, Out–' (1109) The poem as an accusation about human indifference to others.

Works for Comparison with "Musée des Beaux Arts"

Frost, *'Out, Out–', 1109*
Nemerov, *Life cycle of Common Man, 1179*
Welty, *A Worn Path, 150*
William Carlos Williams, *Landscape with the Fall of Icarus, 990*

EDWARD FIELD, *Icarus*, *pages 987–88*

"Icarus" is like a number of the earlier Odysseus poems which deal with the hero who goes on living long after the moment of glory, and who is puzzled, bored, and unhappy with the drabness of the uneventful life.

Suggestions for Discussing the Study Questions, page 988

(1) Field directs attention to the mythic figure of Icarus. Even here, however, there is a displacement; the heroic and tragic values in the myth make ironic the central figure's descent into the dull and boring world of suburban commuters. The poem explores the idea that the mythic, heroic, and tragic can be reduced in our modern world to the ordinary, common, and pathetic.

(2) In the first stanza, the speaker reviews the disaster, reduces it to the *usual drowning*, and rewrites the end of the myth; Icarus has *swum away* and come to the city, *where he rented a house and tended a garden* (line 9). The remaining stanzas explore Icarus's feelings and his place in this unexciting existence. The mythic figure in the suburban world of *neat front yards* and *commuter trains* embodies alienation and despair.

(3) Field uses accurate but ordinary language to underscore this transformation (e.g., *usual drowning, gang war, nice Mr. Hicks, neat front yards*), and shifts from the past tense narrative to the present tense in line 21–end to indicate the ordinary existence of Icarus in modern society.

WRITING TOPICS. The way the mythic figure is undercut in the poem. The problem of Icarus in the modern suburban world: Why does Icarus, as an alienated figure who *wishes he had drowned*, seem to illustrate that the modern world can accommodate neither heroic aspiration nor tragic fall?

WORKS FOR COMPARISON WITH FIELD'S "ICARUS"

Auden, *The Unknown Citizen, 1125*
Spender, *Icarus, 990*
Tennyson, *Ulysses, 982*

MURIEL RUKEYSER, *Waiting for Icarus*, *pages 988–89*

Rukeyser's poem treats the ancient subject not from the hero's point of view, but rather the point of view of his girlfriend, who speaks not as an ancient heroine but as a modern young woman without a sense of identity or purpose. The poem thus does not describe heroic achievement but rather dramatizes romantic disappointment.

Suggestions for Discussing the Study Questions, page 989

(1) The speaker is Icarus's girlfriend who has been waiting all day, "or perhaps longer," for Icarus to return after flying away. She is on a beach in Crete, the location of the kingdom of Minos, and does not know what has happened to Icarus. Her complaints fully indicate her situation and her frustration.

(2) She complains about having been apparently abandoned. The similarity of her topics to the topics that might be made by a modern person bring the heroic world of Daedalus and Icarus to a common level and also to a level of commonness.

(3) The anaphora—that is, the methodical repetition of certain words and phrases (*He said, I remember, would have*)—succeeds in making the poem comic because it has a cumulative effect of bursting the heroic bubble of ancient myth.

WRITING TOPICS. The use of anaphora. The problem of deflating the heroic image of Icarus. The nature of the speaker.

WORKS FOR COMPARISON WITH "WAITING FOR ICARUS"

Rukeyser, *Looking at Each Other, 794*
William Carlos Williams, *Landscape with the Fall of Icarus, 990*
Spender, *Icarus, 990*

ANNE SEXTON, *To a Friend Whose Work Has Come to Triumph,* page 989

If one considers the poem as being addressed to a person "whose work has come to triumph," Icarus's failure could be taken as a contrast and also as an incentive. Sexton, like Aldiss, puts the achievement into focus, and measures success as having completed one's goals. There is irony in Sexton's poem inasmuch as the whole story of Icarus could not be held up as a successful model.

Suggestions for Discussing the Study Questions, page 989

(1) Sexton's sonnet (*abab cdcd efgf hh,* with many slant rhymes) focuses on the heroic triumph of Icarus's flight. Icarus *acclaiming the sun* is contrasted with his *sensible daddy* (Daedalus) and with other things on earth (*trees*) and air (*starlings*).

(2) The fall of Icarus, mentioned in line 12, is dismissed; it is secondary to the image and the fact of the flight.

(3) The tone—familiar, admiring, a bit condescending—undercuts the heroic presentation; it is established through diction and understatement. Note especially *sticky* (line 1), *little tug* (line 2), *quite well* (line 7), and *sensible daddy* (line 14).

WRITING TOPICS. The figure of Icarus. Icarus contrasted to Daedalus. Diction and tone. Sexton's use of mythic material.

WORKS FOR COMPARISON WITH "TO A FRIEND WHOSE WORK HAS COME TO TRIUMPH"

Aldiss, *Flight 063, p. 985*
Spender, *Icarus, 990*
Tennyson, *Ulysses, 982*

STEPHEN SPENDER, *Icarus,* *page 990*

Spender was a close friend of Auden's, and his reputation as a poet reflects the tendency to compare the men's work. This poem, published in *Poems* (1933), evokes both the daring flight and the tragic fall. It is often read as a description of the flight and crash of a World War I aviator; you can try this suggestion with your students and see if it changes their perception of the poem.

Suggestions for Discussing the Study Questions, page 990

(1) The first ten lines focus on the flight and pride of Icarus, his *War on the sun* (line 10). The last two focus on the fall; the figure is shattered into *Hands, wings*–an image that stresses the destruction of Icarus and the finality of his fall. Spender uses the whole myth (flight and fall) with most of its symbolic overtones intact; the focus remains on Icarus. The Icarus figure in the poem is proud of his achievement in flight. He therefore possesses an aristocracy of accomplishment, and is *indifferent* to those beneath him (hawk, men, eagles).

(2) The "almost" winning of the war on the sun, together with the final two lines, indicates that Icarus, like everyone else, was human and therefore subject to human limitations even if his imagination was great. The modern lesson is perhaps also an ancient lesson: The higher the flight, the greater the fall.

(3) The shifting in verbs from the first to the second stanza mark a shift in the treatment of topic. In the second stanza the verbs present the narrative of Icarus. In the first stanza, however, the future and present tenses emphasize the continuous importance of Icarus as a symbol of striving high and achieving greatly.

WRITING TOPICS. The figure of Icarus. Icarus contrasted to Daedalus. Diction and tone. Sexton's use of mythic material.

WORKS FOR COMPARISON WITH SPENDER'S "ICARUS"

Aldiss, *Flight 063, 985*
Sexton, *To a Friend Whose Work Has Come to Triumph, 989*
Tennyson, *Ulysses, 982*

WILLIAM CARLOS WILLIAMS, *Landscape with the Fall of Icarus,* pages 990–91

Like Auden, Williams filters Icarus through the pictorial medium of Brueghel's painting (*see insert*). Williams, however, does not explore a separate issue such as human suffering; rather, he recreates the painting in verbal images. As in "Musée," the mythical Icarus is essential to the poem but secondary to the poem's subject.

Suggestions for Discussing the Study Questions, page 991

(1) The center of the poem, like the painting, focuses on the landscape rather than the fall.

(2) A possible answer to this question is that the painting speaks for itself, as a work of art, and the poet uses the terse diction and minimal line structure to emphasize the minimal effect of Icarus in the larger world.

(3) References to Icarus's fall frame the poem, even though most of the poem turns away from the event and the figure—relegating Icarus to the opening (line 2) and the close (lines 14–20), just as Brueghel displaces Icarus from the center to the lower right-hand corner. The speaker "pans" the painting from left to right, noting the *farmer,* the regeneration of nature, the *edge of the sea* and the sun. In lines 16–21, Williams focuses on the *splash quite unnoticed* of *Icarus drowning,* and therefore marks the global insignificance of Icarus.

(4) To help students with this topic, have them consult Chapter 35 (1854). All the poems use the Icarus story to bring out varying degrees of criticism, but Aldiss and Spender also include elements of praise of the efforts of Icarus. Field stresses the antiheroism of Icarus, and Williams and Auden bring out the insignificance of the hero, and the event, in human history. Though all the poems commonly treat Icarus, each poem is unique, with Auden, for example, treating indifference to human suffering and Williams treating the ancient subject as little more than a dot in the ocean.

WRITING TOPICS. The use of the tercets in the poem's development. The contrast between Icarus's death and the season of spring. The poem's diction.

WORKS FOR COMPARISON WITH "LANDSCAPE WITH THE FALL OF ICARUS"

Aldiss, *Flight 063,* 985
Auden, *Musée des Beaux Arts,* 986
Field, *Icarus,* 987
Spender, *Icarus,* 990

■ Three Poems Related to the Myth of the Phoenix, *pages 991–94*

AMY CLAMPITT, *Berceuse*, *page 992*

A *berceuse* is a cradle song which usually uses gentle rocking rhythms and is sung quietly, with no loud climaxes. The references to sleep in Clampitt's poem are thus appropriate to a berceuse. Here the references are ironic for the sleep she writes about is in effect a closing off of the grim realities of modern political and military conditions.

Suggestions for Discussing the Study Questions, page 992

(1–3) The poem is pessimistic to the degree that the life that is to rise like the Phoenix will not be a revival of the piano music of Chopin played by a master like Gieseking, but rather will be like a return of a horror like Auschwitz and the continuation of intellectual and moral decay. If the future is like the past, moral turpitude will coexist with the "purest art," and doomsday will come. The "thousand replicas in upright silos" (nuclear missiles in missile silos) will claim power, as they have in the past. The alternative is to sleep in a state of "scathed felicity" (a turning away from reality to create a happy world that does not exist). Although the Phoenix usually signifies rebirth, here it symbolizes a cycle of continued evil—a redeath—as in the past.

WRITING TOPICS. The poem's use of negative imagery. Why is the sunrise "incorrigible"? What contradictions of human life does the poem explore? What is the significance of the title?

WORKS FOR COMPARISON WITH "BERCEUSE"

Layton, *Rhine Boat Trip, 1169*
Nash, *Exit, Pursued by a Bear, 791*
Quasímodo, *Auschwitz, 829*
Sassoon, *Dreamers, 1195*
Yeats, *The Second Coming, 961*

DENISE LEVERTOV, *Hunting the Phoenix*, *pages 992–93*

This brief and interesting poem makes great use of the Phoenix myth, but uses it not as a passive hope but as an active incentive. In this respect "Hunting the Phoenix" is both realistic and salutary.

Suggestions for Discussing the Study Questions, page 993

(1–3) The poem is based on the idea that things do not regenerate by themselves, as the Phoenix myth might suggest. Rather, the Phoenix must be hunted, must be found, and must be re-created. A person must symbolically dig into the "ashy nest itself," which is presumably the remains of past ideas, past experiences, past tries at expression, past relationships—for everything in the present was once a part of the past. Only then will the ashes of the past be reconstituted and assume a new shape, just as the Phoenix rose from the dust of its own ashes. It is up to us, the poet states, to make the world anew, to put living things together that will have new blood. Magic does not exist, but hard work, study, and sweat do exist, and these will enable us to create the future. If one does not seek out the nest of the past, there will be nothing to build on–no eggs, no nurture, no guidance, no future.

WRITING TOPICS. The use made of the Phoenix myth in "Hunting the Phoenix." Why is regeneration not automatic? Why must it be sought after, and worked for?

WORKS FOR COMPARISON WITH "HUNTING THE PHOENIX"

Frost, *Choose Something Like a Star, 1114*
Emanuel, *Like God, 1151*
Abbie Huston Evans, *The Iceberg Seven-eighths Under, 786*
Wilbur, *Year's End, 958*

MAY SARTON, *The Phoenix Again,* *pages 993–94*

Often poems emphasize the negative aspect of life. "The Phoenix Again," however, is positive: Life will prevail against difficult odds and in spite of grievous circumstances.

Suggestions for Discussing the Study Questions, page 994

(1) The Phoenix in this poem is the Phoenix of ancient and modern myth. It signifies a renewal, even if to gain rebirth it must struggle against "death and self-doubt."

(2) The speaker is aware of all the negative elements against which renewal must contend, but she nevertheless believes that song will come again and that the Phoenix will fly above seas of grief. The personal situations are not specified, except that they have had much to do with grief, self-doubt, and death—all experiences that make one doubt that the future will have meaning.

(3) Sarton uses the Phoenix as a symbol of getting on with existence despite grief and disappointment; Donne uses the Phoenix to symbolize the renewal that his speaker experiences in his love;

Clampitt uses the Phoenix as a negative symbol of renewing death and terror as well as the "purest art."

WRITING TOPICS. Positive and negative images in the poem. Why can no Phoenix be told that death "is the end of song"? What is the strength of the Phoenix to the speaker?

WORKS FOR COMPARISON WITH "THE PHOENIX AGAIN"

Clampitt, *Berceuse, 992*
Levertov, *Hunting the Phoenix, 992*
Donne, *The Canonization, 946*

Two Poems Related to the Myth of Oedipus, *pages 994–96*

MURIEL RUKEYSER, *Myth, page 995*

For background on this poem, see *Oedipus The King* together with the introduction (1305).

Suggestions for Discussing the Study Questions, page 995

(1–4) Briefly, Oedipus's solving of the Sphinx's riddle—he answered "man"—freed Thebes from the terror of the Sphinx. In return, he was rewarded with the throne and the recently widowed queen, Jocasta. Class discussion can focus on the form of the poem and on Rukeyser's ambiguous and witty use of the word *myth*.

Rukeyser, like Atwood and Broumas, employs mythic material to comment on a contemporary (and perhaps universal) aspect of the relationship/difference between men and women. At one level, the word *myth* refers to the story of Oedipus and the Sphinx. At another, however, it refers to Oedipus's assertion that "When you say Man . . . you include women / too. Everyone knows that" (lines 10–11). The Sphinx's reply exposes the linguistic and sociological problem with the myth; it suggests that exclusion rather than inclusion has been the order of language and society for eons.

WRITING TOPICS. Rukeyser's modern application of the ancient myth. Humor in the poem. The characterizations of Oedipus, or the Sphinx.

WORKS FOR COMPARISON WITH RUKEYSER'S "MYTH"

Bogan, *Women, 1127*
Piercy, *The Secretary Chant, 1185*
Sophocles, *Oedipus the King, 1305*

John Updike, *On the Way to Delphi,* *pages 995–96*

Suggestions for Discussing the Study Questions, page 996

(1, 2) The speaker is on a tour that travels to the ancient sites made famous in the myth of Oedipus and also in the myths of the Gods (Parnassus) and art (Helicon). When traveling to these sites, the speaker meditates on their significance in ancient times and the changes that have occurred up to the present day. The myths of ancient times were romantic, and they told of ancient power struggles, heroism, and sacrifice. The reality now, however, and probably the reality of the past, is that the locations where the mythical actions took place were no different from the "muddy field" which the speaker observes from his tour bus.

(3) The second stanza is a complex one, bringing out the notion that the ancient myths were created about "dim chieftains." That is, the people of myth were no different from people of today, but, nevertheless, they "grew huge." Now all this is forgotten. The sites are "overrun by roads and fame" and polluted by "cement and smoke," so that the low houses of the present inhabitants is not visibly different from the rubble of a landslide (scree). In short, life in modern times has not progressed from that in ancient times, but has gotten uglier and grubbier.

Writing topics. The geography of the present and the myth of the past. The significance of Helicon and Parnassus in the poem. Why does the "lean geology" want to forget "the myths it bred"?

Works for Comparison with "On the Way to Delphi"

Levertov, *A Time Past,* 762
Lochhead, *The Choosing,* 1172
Masefield, *Cargoes,* 748
Sophocles, *Oedipus the King,* 1305
Webb, *The Shape of History,* 928

Writing About Myth in Poetry, *pages 996–1000*

Writing about myth requires that it be connected with some other aspect of poetry, such as speaker, tone, or meaning. Your students will be tempted to write a merely descriptive essay, noting and explaining in series the mythic allusions in a poem. When you assign an essay about myth in poetry, warn students to avoid such an exercise in description. The demonstrative essay on Parker's "Penelope" (998–99) illustrates how the material of mythology may be connected with character and meaning.

Special Topics for Writing and Argument about Myth in Poetry, *pages 1000–1001*

(1) The eight poems illustrate a wide divergence of treatment. Students will thus find more material for differences than similarities. The task will be to relate these differences to similar topics (e.g., the wandering figure of excitement, the woman left behind, the yearning for adventure, the dismay at a life without danger, etc.). Use Chapter 35 (1979) for help with the extended comparison-contrast.

(2) The topic of Icarus is somewhat different, because it brings out the plight of those experiencing misfortune and the responses of those who are not directly involved. For this subject, it is also essential to refer to the reproduction of Brueghel's painting (*see insert*).

(3) Rukeyser's "Myth" brings up the topic of feminism and inclusive language, a topic that goes far beyond the subject of Oedipus's misfortunes. Students undertaking to write on this question should make a special point to keep referring to "Myth" as they make their various points.

(4) These three poems make an excellent unit of comparison. They all share in the idea about life's being cyclic, but the direction of change makes for the points of interest. Clampitt suggests that life is a strong force that will overcome the dead past. Levertov draws attention to the need for organized effort to create the future. Sarton shares much with Clampitt, and, further, suggests that renewal will begin on "one cold starry night"; that is, when change and improvement are least expected.

(5) The fifth direction suggests a freedom of selection of topic, which you might wish to limit, or about which you may want to confer. The suggested books will furnish many materials for selection, and selectivity will therefore need to be the key. There are many examples of poems in this chapter, such as Field's "Icarus" and Aldiss's "Flight 063," which should give students guidance for transforming old materials within a contemporary context. As with most of the creative-writing assignments, it is important for students to turn critics of their own works, and try to recall and analyze how and why their treatments have taken the form they have created.

Chapter Twenty-three
Pages 1002–1031

Meaning: Idea and Theme In Poetry

This chapter takes up in detail a topic that runs throughout all the poetry chapters—the theme or meaning of a poem (see also Chapter 10, on ideas in fiction). In the introductory material, we attempt to describe the terms *theme, idea, motif*, and *meaning*. These are elusive, but *idea* refers to a thought or concept in the abstract; *theme* and *motif* are nearly identical terms referring to the operation of an idea in a work; and *meaning* is the product of idea, theme, and motif taken as a totality in relationship to the work. Once you make these initial distinctions, you can allow the concepts to flow back together, for they invariably do whenever people speak about literature.

Students sometimes present a simplification of the view in MacLeish's "Ars Poetica" (1022) that poetry should simply "be," and therefore they raise the question of whether poems must have themes at all. *Mutatis mutandis*, students sometimes believe that there is a "message" in every poem, and spend their time seeking one out, even inventing messages if they find that nothing comes immediately to mind.

The best teaching strategy is therefore to steer a middle course between too much and too little emphasis on theme. The key idea to communicate in teaching is that every element of a poem *can* contribute to its theme and meaning. In any given poem, however, not all the elements will be equally important or effective. One of your goals in teaching poetry (and this chapter) might be to develop your students' ability to focus quickly on the poetic elements that are most prominent in creating meaning.

Judith Viorst, *True Love*, *pages 1008–1009*

The ideas about love in this comic and honest poem are valuable for people at any age.

Suggestions for Discussing the Study Questions, page 1009

(1) Although the poem is an amusing review of married life, its

concluding statement is serious: "We still feel something / We can call / True love." There are no romantic pretensions about this "True love," but in light of the previous material in the poem, the poem asserts that love can last–must last–through many trials.

(2) Most of the poem is devoted to anti-romantic details about daily aspects of married life, such as contrasting views about watching football, wishing death on the husband in preference to his having an affair, "acid indigestion," and so on. They are important in the wife-husband relationship because they are an inevitable and necessary aspect of real life as it is actually lived, not as it is dreamed.

(3) There are many comic situations and statements in the poem, such as lines 9, 17–18, 20–21, and so on. Because of the reality of such situations in life, and because marriage is the part of life the poet is discussing, these situations draw assent about the day-by-day difficulties that life brings. Because the poem's comic view of life makes no claim that elements of daily living are disasters or causes for divisiveness in marriage, they undergird the idea that "true love" must be positive enough to persist even under negative circumstances.

(4) These lines resemble the kinds of things people save up for inclusion during a family argument. They are minor climaxes of the development of the poem, and focus the poem's negative but nevertheless comic details. The other lines of the poem either lead up to these passages or represent conclusions drawn from them.

WRITING TOPICS. Is the idea of "true love" in the poem romantic or anti-romantic? Can "true love" sustain the "hate" situations like those described in lines 21 and 24?

WORKS FOR COMPARISON WITH "TRUE LOVE"

Atwood, *Variation on the Word Sleep*, 1124
Donne, *The Canonization*, 946
Kauffmann, *The More the Merrier*, 1255
Joy Williams, *Taking Care*, 95

AMY CLAMPITT, *Beach Glass*, *pages 1010–11*

"Beach Glass" is a poem about the impermanence of human life as contrasted with the eternity of the world and the universe. The beach glass thrown up on shore by the ocean is insignificant, but it is also beautiful and worthy of being collected for its one-time utility, the castoff products of our throwaway culture.

Suggestions for Discussing the Study Questions, page 1011

(1) The reef-bell is a signal that danger lies ahead for approaching vessels. The fact that it is associated with the mythical figure Cassandra makes it further associated with premonitions of bad things to come. The idea is that even during calm, easy times there exists the possibility of danger.

(2, 3) The former living forms, now jetsam, are shells of mussels and periwinkles which have long been dead. The speaker chooses to collect beach glass for its colors. The various pieces of glass thrown up by the shore are remnants of life: beer and wine bottles and bottles that formerly contained anti-diarrhea medicine. Despite the unlikely origins, the glass is beautifully colored, suggesting that human life is capable of grace and beauty even if it is not always so. Going on, the speaker states that the Glass resembles fine glass from Venice and Chartres. The idea is that human existence and creativity, however beautiful they might be, or however utilitarian and impermanent, are temporary when considered in the perspective of the ebbing and flowing ocean, which "goes on forever."

WRITING TOPICS. The purpose of the imagery of jetsam. The contrast between beach glass and more artistic glass. The view of humanity in the poem.

WORKS FOR COMPARISON WITH "BEACH GLASS"

Dryden, *A Song for St. Cecilia's Day*, 1012
Updike, *Perfection Wasted*, 1218
Wordsworth, *On the Extinction of the Venetian Republic*, 1058

E. E. CUMMINGS, ***next to of course god america i***, *page 1012*

This poem is a minor masterpiece of poetic satire, in which the main speaker talks himself into stupidity. cummings suggests that numbskulls who voice such platitudes give patriotism a bad name.

Suggestions for Discussing the Study Questions, page 1012

(1) The poem is a sonnet, with the form being *abab, cdcd, efgfeg*. The rhyming words are colloquial, in keeping with the nature of the speaker and his purpose as a July 4 type of orator. By eliminating capitalization and punctuation cummings renders the common speech quality of the speaker's oratory.

(2) The speaker is an impassioned yet ignorant traditionalist who sees death in war as heroic and admirable (compare Owen's "Dulce et Decorum Est" [810], and Crane's "Do Not Weep, Maiden"

[1137]). His monologue is full of half-witted, half-digested, and fragmented phrases from patriotic songs.

(3) The poem satirizes the clichés and banalities of super-patriotism. The alliteration and repetition (especially in lines 7–8) underscore the speaker's fatuousness. Line 14, spoken by a detached observer, puts the preceding diatribe into perspective and also indicates that this particular "voice of liberty," now mute, is really a voice that tries to suppress, not liberate, the human spirit.

WRITING TOPICS. The serious idea of patriotism underlying the poem. cummings's use of colloquialisms and slang to characterize the speaker.

WORKS FOR COMPARISON WITH "NEXT TO OF COURSE GOD AMERICA I"

Owen, *Dulce et Decorum Est, 810*
Crane, *Do Not Weep, Maiden, for War Is Kind, 1137*
Spender, *I Think continually of Those Who Were Truly Great, 739*

JOHN DRYDEN, *A Song for St. Cecilia's Day,* *pages 1012–14*

The issues raised in the study questions are considered on page 1003.

WRITING TOPICS. The significance of Dryden's idea that a creator God shaped the universe as a work of art, according to musical principles of order. The qualities attributed to musical instruments. The occasion of the poem as a celebration of St. Cecilia (Nov. 22).

WORKS FOR COMPARISON WITH "A SONG FOR ST. CECILIA'S DAY"

Blake, *The Tyger, 754*
Hopkins, *God's Grandeur, 863*
Wordsworth, *My Heart Leaps Up, 1035*

DONALD HALL, *Whip-poor-will,* *page 1015*

"Whip-poor-will" is firmly established in the countryside of farms and work. In this respect it is like many of the poems of Frost (see Chapter 25) and Kumin (735, 1168).

Suggestions for Discussing the Study Questionspage 1015

(1, 2) The whippoorwill is an evening bird with a distinctive song that resembles the words "whip-poor-will." The song is vital in affecting the speaker's imagination when he is asleep. Rather than "whip-poor-will," the sound seems more like "Wes-ley-Wells," the name of the poet's grandfather, who inhabited and worked the property for fifty years. The connection between speaker and Wells is the property, the bird, the bed, the experience on the property, and the active life of keeping things going and keeping life together. The poem establishes all these links, thus showing how life and work continue from one generation of people to the next.

(3) The attention to the bird is an important means by which Hall establishes the reality of the situation. Logically, if such details are true and real, then the poet's conclusions will seem sound and incontrovertible.

(4) The two poems both link the speaker with the sounds of birds, and both use the sounds to draw conclusions about the nature of life. In "Whip-poor-will," Hall's conclusion is that the bird and his grandfather symbolize the continuity of life and work (especially lines 20–26), while Keats's idea is that the bird's song symbolizes the mystery of the universe and the eternal nature of artistic beauty.

WRITING TOPICS. The bird as a symbol. The idea of continuity. The meaning of the concluding seven lines.

WORKS FOR COMPARISON WITH "WHIP-POOR-WILL"

Oliver, *Ghosts, 1182*
Smith, *Bluejays, 1200*
Tate, *The Blue Booby, 1208*

ROBERT HERRICK, *To the Virgins, to Make Much of Time,* *page 1016*

Herrick's lyric, is an example of the moral and less personal *carpe diem* poems. The title indicates that it is addressed to a group rather than an individual.

Suggestions for Discussing the Study Questions, page 1016

(1) The title suggests that the listeners, who are "virgins," lose their virginity. The poem, however, suggests a moral avenue of sexuality ("go marry"). The speaker is not directly involved as a seducing participant, and is simply offering advice about how to live.

(2) Time, life, love, youth—all pass. They are given to us for use, and if we do not use them while we can, we will "forever tarry" (i.e., lose out totally on an aspect of life that was made for happiness and fulfillment).

(3) In stanza 1, the *rosebuds* symbolize life—here today and gone tomorrow. The *sun* (stanza 2) serves a parallel function; one day becomes a lifetime. The *carpe diem* theme is stated explicitly in stanzas 3 and 4.

(4) The pattern of rhyme in the stanzas alternates between rising rhymes in the first and third lines and trochaic rhymes in the second and fourth. The effect is both colloquial and natural; this is the way it is, in everyday, common speech. The tone of the poem is public, advisory, paternal, and hortatory; the speaker is concerned and moralistic.

(5) The speaker's advice that the virgins should *marry* emphasizes the distinctions between this poem and the two previous ones.

WRITING TOPICS. Analyze speaker, tone, or theme. Compare this poem with Marvell's "To His Coy Mistress." The imagery. The rhyme.

POEMS IN THE *Carpe Diem* TRADITION FOR COMPARISON

Jonson, *To Celia, 1017*
Larkin, *Next, Please, 1021*
Marvell, *To His Coy Mistress, 1023*

LANGSTON HUGHES, *The Negro Speaks of Rivers,* *pages 1016–17*

"The Negro Speaks of Rivers" promises to bring out much discussion and many deeply held opinions and feelings. An attempt to analyze the ideas implicit in the word "deep" will be particularly important in discussion about this poem.

Suggestions for Discussing the Study Questions, page 1017

(1) The meaning of the sentence, which is used as lines 3 and 10 of the poem, is that the cumulative experience of "The Negro" has created a depth of knowledge and feeling that is virtually as old as the human race. The idea is that there is both a personal and collective memory, involving bitterness and anger, that has developed as a result of slavery and oppression. As it were, history and the individual are one.

(2) The Euphrates refers to ancient Mesopotamian civilization; the Congo refers to nineteenth-century European colonization of Africa; the Nile refers to the ancient Egyptian dynasties which created the pyramids (which the speaker states were built by the Negro); the Mississippi refers to slavery in the United States. These rivers, in the speaker's judgment, symbolize the idea that human beings are unequal, specifically that people of the civilizations along the rivers, from ancient times to our own, are superior to the Blacks whom they enslaved. It was such an idea of racial superiority that has been used to justify the oppression of Black people.

(3) Lines 8–10 echo lines 1–3 summarize and recapitulate the speaker's attack on the idea of inequality that permitted the various

civilizations to flourish at the expense of the slaves who sustained them.

WRITING TOPICS. The nature of the speaker. What ideas are being criticized in the poem? What ideas are implied in the sentence "My soul has grown deep like the rivers"?

WORKS FOR COMPARISON WITH "THE NEGRO SPEAKS OF RIVERS"

Brooks, *Primer for Blacks, 1128*
Lorde. *Every Traveler Has One Vermont Poem, 1173*
Toomer, *Reapers, 927*
Villanueva, *Day-Long Day, 1210*
Whitecloud, *Blue Winds Dancing, 156*

BEN JONSON, *To Celia,* *page 1017*

In teaching this *carpe diem* poem you can show your students that meaning is a function of ideas, speaker, tone, and diction. The cynicism of Jonson's speaker (a negative person, from one of his plays) is clear. In support of his quest for seduction, he argues that reputation is unimportant, and that Celia's husband can easily be deceived. His theme is that immediate action will satisfy desire; in short, that the ends justify the means. The total meaning combines these ideas with our emotional and intellectual rejection of the speaker's cynical position.

Suggestions for Discussing the Study Questions, page 1018

(1) The speaker is presented as eager, cynical, and greedy, ready to prey upon those who are gullible and weak. In this respect he is a satiric figure who, in himself, illustrates the qualities being satirized. He wants to possess a woman who is not willing or available. He sees time as an enemy, love as a commodity, and Celia as an attractive object to be used.

(2) In lines 3–5, time is personified as an enemy who severs lives.

(3) The first eight lines contain the traditional *carpe diem* argument. The speaker asserts that he and Celia should act before *perpetual night* (death) overtakes them.

(4) The speaker shifts his ground at line 9; he is no longer concerned with time, but rather with reputation and the ease with which he and Celia may get away with their *theft.*

(5) The central idea emphasizes the speaker's cynical amorality; he asserts that an act is a crime only if one is caught at it (lines 15–18). The diction also emphasizes the speaker's demeaning and cynical tone; phrases like *sports of love* and *sweet theft* trivialize love (sex) and

demean Celia. The argument is thus undercut by the cynical tone and amoral attitude.

WRITING TOPICS. The character of the speaker. The situation of the poem and the structure of the speaker's argument. The meaning of "carpe diem" as presented in the poem. The flaws in the speaker's argument.

POEMS IN THE *Carpe Diem* TRADITION FOR COMPARISON

Herrick, *To the Virgins, to Make Much of Time, 1016*
Larkin, *Next, Please, 1021*
Marvell, *To His Coy Mistress, 1023*

DONALD JUSTICE, *On the Death of Friends in Childhood,* *page 1018*

This short poem recalls Dryden's "To the Memory of Mr. Oldham" (911) in its brevity and poignancy, and also in its conclusion; Justice's friends are in the "shadows," while Oldham is encompassed by "fate and gloomy night." "On the Death of Friends" is extremely sad even though it mentions no specific friends. The concern of the poem is more about the living, and the dimming of our intellectual lights, than about the dead themselves.

Suggestions for Discussing the Study Questions, page 1018

(1) While the subject of the poem may be friends who died in childhood, the theme concerns the difficulty or even impossibility of recovering the past through memory.

(2) Time stops for the dead children; they will not grow beards or become bald in heaven or hell. For the speaker and reader, however, time produces change; we no longer remember the names of the games we played.

(3) The first two lines present images of heaven and hell, and the speaker rejects these locations as being real. "If anywhere," then, memories of the dead might be revived in real locations where we knew them and played with them, even though we have forgotten the exact circumstances of our experiences. The tone suggested by "bearded" and "sunning themselves" is mildly comic and somewhat regretful (can we believe that dead souls in hell sun themselves by the fires there?). The rhetorical strategy of the poem is the exploration of the "decaying sense" of our memory of the past: We lose everything–our memory of others, our youthful beliefs, and our memories even of our own past. The concluding personification of memory as a guide to help us search for images of the lost friends in the "shadows" (a pun on the darkness of twilight and also the

shades or ghosts of the dead) is a fitting climax for this sad and wistful poem.

WRITING TOPICS. The tone of the poem. The topic: death of friends or the death of memory? Also, questions 2 and 3.

WORKS FOR COMPARISON WITH
"ON THE DEATH OF FRIENDS IN CHILDHOOD"

Dickinson, *I Never Lost as Much but Twice,* 1073
Field, *Icarus,* 987
Heyen, *Mantle,* 917

JOHN KEATS, *Ode on a Grecian Urn,* *pages 1018–20*

A major idea of Keats is explored extensively in "Ode on a Grecian Urn." This is the contrast between the inability of human beings to comprehend the mysteries of art and the universe. Even the song of a bird in a tree represents more than human beings, with their "dull brain(s)," can encompass ("Ode to a Nightingale," page 918). We know, or think we know, what we see and hear, but we have no understanding, words, or ability to describe the ultimate realities which underlie our earthly experiences. We create and see fine things and attribute beauty to them, and these give us our only hints at the immense and vast but still unseen universe of truth that remains beyond our small abilities to understand. It is in this sense that beauty is truth and truth is beauty.

Students might want to compare the poem with the photo of the Grecian vase (1019). Keats could have seen many such vases in the British Museum. Most probably he was imagining a composite vase, for there is not enough space on ancient vases for all the details he describes.

Suggestions for Discussing the Study Questions, page 1020

(1) The ode suggests a dramatic situation; the speaker is contemplating the urn and the reader overhears the resulting meditation.

(2) The paradoxical nature of the urn is established immediately through phrases like *unravished bride* and *foster child of silence and slow time;* the urn exists in real time but is little touched by it. Paradox continues in the description of the figures on the urn (gods or men, eternal or mortal) and in the contrast between the energy (passion) figured on the urn and the calm silence of the urn itself. The urn is a *sylvan historian* that can sing a better song than the poet (*our rhyme*) because it has already transcended time. The images are eternal; the poet's words are temporal.

(3) *Unheard* melodies and "ditties of no tone" are heard in the mind (imagination) rather than through the *sensual ear.* In other words, the idea (Platonic ideal) of the song (poetry, art, beauty) is more permanent than the actual song itself.

(4) Three sets of images are developed in stanzas 1–3 to show this concept of the ideal: nature (leaf-fringed border, tree that will never lose its leaves), love (pursuit, lovers who will never kiss), and music (pipes and timbrels, the youth who will never leave his song). All these images are frozen in time on the urn, unchanging and eternal. These are contrasted (in stanza 3) to *human passion* that leaves only sickness and sorrow.

To this point, Keats has developed paradoxes that oppose real and ideal; these reach a climax in stanza 5. The urn is a silent form and a Cold Pastoral (both contradictory). It is also a "friend to man" because it tells us that "Beauty is truth, truth beauty" (line 49). Keats sustains the *oxymora* of the urn and the poem throughout. Both poem and urn ask us to balance in our minds the real (time, change) and the ideal (permanence, eternity) simultaneously. Ultimately, of course, human beings cannot understand, and thus both urn and poem, like eternity, "tease us out of thought."

WRITING TOPICS. The distinction between heard and unheard melodies. The importance of art and the inadequacy of human beings to understand both human and universal creation. The nature of Keats's speaker.

WORKS FOR COMPARISON WITH "ODE ON A GRECIAN URN"

Dickinson, *This World Is Not Conclusion, 1078*
Shakespeare, *Not Marble, Nor the Gilded Monuments, 679*
Shelley, *Ode to the West Wind, 877*

PHILIP LARKIN, *Next, Please, page 1021*

(1–4) This poem, discussed in the demonstrative essay (1028–29), can be taught in conjunction with the other *carpe diem* poems in this chapter. Any of the questions can be adapted as topics for writing.

WRITING TOPICS. The meaning of the metaphor of the "armada of promises." The nature of the speaker. The mood of the poem's conclusion.

WORKS FOR COMPARISON WITH "NEXT, PLEASE"

Dickinson, *Because I Could Not Stop for Death, 671*
Frost, *The Road Not Taken, 1109*
Gray, *Elegy Written in a Country Churchyard, 698*

ARCHIBALD MACLEISH, *Ars Poetica,* page 1022

The poem explores the question of meaning versus being. In a real sense, "Ars Poetica" asserts that poems and poets can have it both ways–that a poem can mean and be at the same time.

Suggestions for Discussing the Study Questions, page 1022

(1, 2) The first section tells us that a poem should be mute, dumb, silent, and wordless—an apparent paradox, for poems are made of words. But MacLeish explains through similes that the meaning of poems is communicated not mentally but through the feelings, much as people experience fruit, metalwork, statuary, and the flight of birds.

(3) The second section of the poem explains how paradoxes about poetry, such as being motionless and yet climbing at the same time, may be resolved. The moon appears to be stationary, yet over an entire night it moves, rising in the east, crossing the sky, and setting in the west. "Motionless," like "wordless," has more to do with the way we perceive things than it does with actuality. Just as the moonlight releases shadows of trees "twig by twig," so a poem should penetrate the mind "memory by memory," in this way timelessly altering the consciousness of the reader. The lines opening the section also close it. This repetition, as it were, emphasizes the constancy and generality of the poetic experience.

(4) The third section treats the poem as an aspect of life itself. Poetry has nothing to do with "truth" (line 18), for it is not scientific; instead, it is the same as experience, in this way taking on reality without any need for analysis or proof. Whether for grief or love, poetry creates images that touch the human spirit, such as the sadness of "an empty doorway and a maple leaf" or the commonness of the "leaning grasses" or the rareness of "two lights above the sea."

(5) "Ars Poetica" asserts that poems should create a "palpable" set of perceptions that parallel all of life's experiences. The methods of poetry are imagery, metaphor, and symbolism. MacLeish also makes clear that the experience of poetry is more important than either the words that create it or the intellectual judgments of readers. In that sense, a poem is "mute" and "wordless," and in that sense the poem takes on life, the being and existence of great art. The concluding line is a famous climax of all these ideas.

WRITING TOPICS. The poem's paradoxes about poetry. The relationship of art to experience. How poetry is unlike other intellectual forms of expression.

Works for Comparison with "Ars Poetica"

Keats, *On First Looking into Chapman's Homer*, 777
Lux, *The Voice You Hear When You Read Silently*, 763
Moore, *How to Become a Writer*, 274
Wordsworth, *Scorn Not the Sonnet*, 1059

Andrew Marvell, *To His Coy Mistress*, *pages 1023–24*

This is the most famous *carpe diem* poem. Your students may already know it, but it will always yield new surprises in class discussion. In teaching, you might focus on the connotation of *coy*, and then consider the logic of the poem, the hyperbole of the first section, and the shifting imagery throughout. The poem is in iambic tetrameter rhymed couplets, and it contains some effective rhyming pairs (e.g., *dust/lust*). The title identifies the characters; the speaker, a would-be lover, addresses his coy (reluctant, playing hard-to-get) lady. *Coy* is a loaded word here; it certainly does not suggest virtue.

Suggestions for Discussing the Study Questions, page 1024

(1) In lines 1–20, the speaker sets up a hypothetical situation (*Had we*) in which there would be large amounts of space and time in which to engage slowly in preliminaries to making love. The argument will be, of course, that the world does not furnish these amounts.

(2) Geographical references to the *Ganges* and *Humber* Rivers place the lovers on opposite sides of the earth (use a map or get your students to imagine one). The allusions to Noah's flood and the conversion of the Jews evoke a huge span of time (from Genesis to the Last Judgment). The amatory arithmetic associated with the speaker's admiration of each part of his mistress is extravagantly exaggerated—an ideal example of hyperbole or overstatement.

(3) The hypothetical *world enough and time* are negated in lines 21–32; the word *But* identifies and begins the refutation. Time is personified as an ever-pursuing enemy (line 22). The lines are full of images of death and the grave, all suggesting sterility, dryness, dust, and isolation (*quaint virtue* in line 29 is a sexual *double entendre*).

(4) The third stage of the argument (lines 33–46) offers the speaker's logical conclusion: *Now therefore* we should act with urgency and immediacy to "tear our pleasures with rough strife / Thorough the iron gates of life." The imagery suggests moist heat (*dew, fires*) and violence, all pointing toward urgency. The image of *amorous birds of prey* is both playful and daring. By looking at diction and tone in class, students can see the differences between this poem and Jonson's "To Celia" (925). The speaker here is much more playful and

witty, without any of the demeaning cynicism of Jonson's speaker. The effect of Marvell's poem, however, is one of philosophical sobriety, far removed from immediate action.

WRITING TOPICS. The logical development of the poem. The tone: cynical or serious? The character of the speaker. The meaning. The use of exaggeration. The meaning of "carpe diem" shown in the poem.

POEMS IN THE *Carpe Diem* TRADITION FOR COMPARISON

Herrick, *To the Virgins, to Make Much of Time, 1016*
Jonson, *To Celia, 1017*
Larkin, *Next, Please, 1021*

SHARON OLDS, 35/10, *page 1024*

Olds uses a domestic context to explore the idea that life is cyclical and that children replace adults. The first sixteen lines make these points metaphorically through imagery and language; the last two lines state them directly. The total meaning grows out of the situation and setting, action, language, and the emotions the poem evokes.

Suggestions for Discussing the Study Questions, pages 1024–25

(1) The speaker is a thirty-five-year-old mother who is brushing her ten-year-old daughter's hair at bedtime.

(2) The idea of youth's displacing and replacing age is conveyed in three sets of images related to hair (*dark, gray*), skin (*fine, dry*), and sexuality (the image of ovaries as an empty or bursting purse).

(3) As with Pastan's "Ethics" (1025), emotional engagement with the poem may depend on the reader's ability to experience (or imagine) age.

WRITING TOPICS. The comparison of youth and age. The meaning of replacement.

WORKS FOR COMPARISON WITH "35/10"

Dixon, *All Gone, 595*
Justice, *On the Death of Friends in Childhood, 1018*
Oates, *Shopping, 216*
Olsen, *I Stand Here Ironing, 646*
Wagner, *Boxes, 1211*

LINDA PASTAN, Ethics, *page 1025*

This poem concerns an imponderable question, and it does not give a hard-and-fast answer. Perhaps the concern itself is as far as people can go, for their actions may not have influence beyond the specific things they do.

Suggestions for Discussing the Study Questions, pages 1025–26

(1) The speaker is a thoughtful person who has benefited from the ethical question raised in her ethics class "so many years ago." However, she is not nearer an exact answer than she was when young, except that her adult thought is that all things are valuable, but that their existence does not depend upon the power of individuals.

(2) In the poem there are two distinct situations (school, museum), and a shift of time and place at line 17. The speaker's response to the ethical question changes, and the poem thus explores the shallowness of youth and the mature consciousness about the impermanence of both art and life.

(3) In lines 1–16, the speaker recalls the ethics classes of her youth and the recurring question about the burning museum. The problem was irrelevant to the young people; they were caring little and chose one answer or the other "half-heartedly." Even when the speaker attempted to personalize the issue by imagining that the old woman was her grandmother (lines 9–16), the matter was of little consequence.

(4) One may claim that the subject of the poem is that growth does not produce absolute knowledge. The theme is that ethical judgments are eternally difficult, for art, life, time and values are almost the same, and all are beyond saving by children (line 25).

WRITING TOPICS. The meaning as conveyed though speaker, setting and situation, imagery, or diction.

WORKS FOR COMPARISON WITH "ETHICS"

Dickinson, *The Heart Is the Capital of the Mind, 1069*
Frost, *Birches, 1107*
Jeffers, *The Answer, 1167*
Wordsworth, *from The Prelude, 1040*

Writing About Theme and Meaning in Poetry, *pages 1026–30*

Prewriting and organization here are important because theme and meaning can be approached from so many different directions. It is necessary to tell students that in a single essay they cannot consider every element that contributes to meaning—indeed, they should not try—and therefore it is necessary that they consider only the most striking and significant elements. The demonstrative essay on Larkin's "Next, Please" (1028–29) illustrates the way meaning can be explored through metaphor. Your students should be encouraged to read this essay and the commentary before they plan their own essays.

Special Topics for Writing and Argument about Meaning in Poetry, *pages 1030–31*

(1) See pages 1006-1007 for a few ideas for this essay. An extended comparison-contrast essay might be augmented with library sources, and if it reaches this scope might serve as the final essay in your course. Please ask your students to consult Chapter 35, on Comparison-Contrast (1997), for guidance in writing. If research materials are to be used, please assign Chapter 33, on Research.

(2) The subject matter of the four poems is divergent, but they all share the topics of aging and death. Justice explains the loss not only of childhood friends but also of adult memory. Marvell bases his arguments on the inevitable encroachment of age and the grave. Olds wonders about the "replacement" of age by youth. Pastan is concerned with the ethical question of choice in both youth and age. A comparison-contrast of the four works should emphasize the common thread of growth, aging, continuity, replacement, and change, together with the diverging ways in which the poets treat the topic.

(3) The three poems treat love, patriotism, and scientific truth—all seriously vital personal, political, and educational topics. By introducing elements of farce into the poems, the poets make even stronger points than they might do if they treated the topics in deadly earnest seriousness, and they succeed in amusing as they do so. It is difficult to imagine totally serious poems being as effective as these are.

(4) The creative-writing topic might at first seem to require a discursive poem, which might become an essay in brief. But if students are reminded that literature communicates ideas through metaphors and symbols, together with word choices, etc., they will see that a narrative or descriptive framework for their poems will be satisfactory as long as the events and details are carefully included. Their brief essays explaining their practices and procedures as poets will also enable them to show how they have applied the principles of Chapter 23.

(5) This assignment does not involve poetry as such, but rather is designed to introduce students to the depth with which ideas may be defined and illustrated. Students—college students particularly—need to know that the expression of an idea is not to be encapsulated in just a sentence or two, but rather requires extensive exemplification and analysis.

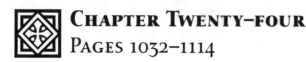

Chapter Twenty-four
Pages 1032–1114

Three Poetic Careers: William Wordsworth, Emily Dickinson, and Robert Frost

William Wordsworth, *pages 1032–59*

My Heart Leaps Up, *pages 1035–36*

1 • *What is the comparison made by the speaker in this poem?*

2 • *Describe the structure of this poem.*

(1) The comparison is that the "Child is father of the Man" and that therefore the speaker wishes to retain in adulthood the same spontaneity and "natural piety" he knew as a child.

(2) The first six lines develop from the specific experience of seeing and delighting in natural scenes, such as a rainbow. The final three are abstract, a dedication to a continuous linking of his present and future with his past.

From **The Prelude Book I,** *Lines 301–474, pages 1040–44*

The topic of this vast autobiographical poem, only a fragment of which is included in the text, is to account for how Wordsworth's "poetic mind" grew. In this respect the poem is a spiritual and artistic autobiography, not a detailed day-by-day and year-by-year one.

1 • *What is meant by the passage "Fair seed-time had by soul, and I grew up / Fostered alike by beauty and by fear" (lines 301-02)?*

2 • *What is the pattern of development in this passage?*

3 • *What points does the speaker make by the episodes of the traps, the taking of raven's eggs, the boat, and the skating?*

(1) The idea in the lines is that the speaker's upbringing was both positive (through beauty) and negative (through fear). That is, his growing imagination was affected by the many sights of beauty that he beheld while walking and playing in fields and woods, and also that checks were made on his behavior by nature itself. His concept is

that natural forces were always affecting him and leading him onward, sometimes by instilling joy and other times by creating fear. The notion of positive and negative reinforcement is not unusual when applied to child-rearing. What is unusual, however, is the power and importance that Wordsworth attributes to his childhood experiences with nature.

(2) The pattern is that there are lengthy narratives, such as his stealing the traps of others, as a boy of about ten, and taking raven's eggs from the nest (lines 306–25), followed by passages of reflection on the meaning of how these episodes caused him to develop that "calm existence that is mine when I / Am worthy of myself."

(3) The commentaries on these actions begin in lines 340, 401, and 464, and they all follow the blank verse narratives. They are reflections on the constructive interaction of a vast natural spirit (i.e., "Wisdom and Spirit of the universe!" line 401, perhaps the most famous of these reflections) with the boy's developing mind. Wordsworth's argument is that the heightened awareness that characterizes the poet were lovingly nurtured by forces that reached him primarily through feeling and intuition (and only secondarily through reason and logic).

Lines Composed a Few Miles Above Tintern Abbey, *pages 1044–48*

A critic once said that writers of the Romantic movement wrote poetry, not poems. "Tintern Abbey" fits this description. Note that Wordsworth himself describes the work as "Lines," implying that he did not have specific limitations of form in mind when he composed it. "Tintern Abbey" also illustrates an idea of the Romantics that the source of poetry was mysterious and also holy. Thus Wordsworth states that the poem came to him as he was completing a walking tour in 1798. He says that when he wrote it down, he changed nothing, thus observing the sacredness of his own inspiration.

1 • *What is the opening scene, and what meaning does the poet ascribe to it?*

2 • *To the speaker, what is the relationship of remembered scenes and the growth of moral behavior?*

3 • *What effect does the speaker believe the present will have on his future?*

4 • *In lines 93–111, how successfully does the speaker make concrete his ideas about moral forces?*

5 • *What is the power that the speaker attributes to nature? What is the "cheerful faith" of lines 133–34?*

(1) The speaker visualizes the scene as taking place in the present moment. He is lying beneath a sycamore on the banks of the Wye River, surrounded by steep cliffs and an agricultural landscape. The scene is specific because the speaker describes it as he sees it and locates it clearly at a particular place near Tintern Abbey. In the past five years he has often been in towns and cities, and there, in his lonely rooms, the memory of these scenes has given him great strength.

(2) The speaker believes that experiences of natural beauty, and the pleasure they give both as they occur and as they are remembered, directly cause human beings to be moral, kind, and loving. He clearly finds in nature a transcendent experience, a "motion and a spirit," that unites all created things with the unseen and mysterious life force of the universe.

(3) The speaker believes that this experience will be "life and food for future years" (lines 64–65).

(4) The speaker's argument is subtle. He believes that a spirit both in and beyond nature speaks to human beings at special or heightened moments. It is a two-way street: The individual must be willing both to see and listen, knowing that eye and ear also help create the experience which allows the speaker to find this "presence" in the world. The setting is therefore fully integrated into the speaker's philosophy. Without the two-way relationship (the speaker bringing his thoughts, experiences, and responsiveness to the scene; Nature providing the beauty from which many of his intellectual and emotional responses spring) the philosophy would not have its coherence and emotional power.

(5) Nature, the speaker believes, has the power to create scenes of beauty which, in their overwhelming power and effect upon the mind and senses, bring the receptive viewer to a state in which "we are laid asleep / In body, and become a living soul," (lines 45–46) and penetrate to the essence of reality and life itself. The "cheerful faith" (line 133), shared by the speaker and his "friend," is that nature will never fail to give this joy if people continue to love her; that with the strength given by this happiness they can withstand life's disappointments or human betrayals, and that everything around them is "full of blessings" (line 134).

Daffodils (I Wandered Lonely as a Cloud)*, page 1048*

This poem demonstrates a characteristic aspect of Wordsworth's thought. He is not a poet who provides botanical details about flowers and trees (though in an early draft of one poem he measures the dimensions of a puddle: "I've measured it from side to side. / 'Tis three feet long and two feet wide." Instead, what Wordsworth wants from Nature is evidence of divine or universal power. To him, the invisible strength of the universe, together with the consequent shaping of human character, come mystically through the interactions of human beings and natural phenomena. To Wordsworth, this same mystic power constitutes the subject of poetry and causes the development of the poetic mind.

1 • *Describe the occasion of the poem. Why does the speaker specify that he was alone?*

2 • *What is the significance of the verbs and verbals describing the flowers? What idea about nature is suggested by these words?*

3 • *How has the scene affected the speaker? What conclusions about human beings and nature are we invited to draw?*

(1) The occasion is that the speaker is alone, and observes a vast array of springtime daffodils blooming beside a lake. The solitude is important because it permits the direct connection, without interference, of the speaker and the scene.

(2) The participles *fluttering, dancing,* and *tossing,* together with the verbs *stretched, out-did,* and *had brought*—all suggest the living vitality of the flowers. The idea about Nature is that the vegetative world, like the Natural world generally, is not dead, but living, and is a direct manifestation of the universal power of life.

(3) The key to the poem is the fourth stanza, in which the speaker describes the effect that the scene has upon him. He keeps the memory, and in later times, when he is alone "In vacant or in pensive mood," the scene floods his consciousness, and the pleasure fills his heart. This process is not only happy, but it is also a creative, constructive, re-creative experience which renews and strengthens the speaker.

Lines Written in Early Spring, *pages 1048–49*

This brief poem generally outlines a process of thought that underlay the Romantic theories of government. Because the world permits all creatures the possibility of joy, the function of society should be, politically, to enable this possibility to be realized.

1 • *What is the situation of the poem? What sounds does the speaker hear?*

2 • *What experience is described in stanza 2? What faith does the speaker proclaim?*

3 • *How does his faith prompt him to meditate on the human mistreatment of human beings?*

(1) The speaker tells us that on a spring day he was sitting in a grove in the woods, listening to "a thousand blended notes" of nearby singing birds. It is the pleasantness of the scene that evokes "sad thoughts" in the speaker.

(2) The idea of stanza 2 is that a direct link existed between the "fair works" of nature (i.e., the birds and their song, and the sights) and his own "human soul." In other words, his thoughts were being governed not by himself and his own mind, but rather were being created and stimulated by the power coming to him from nature through the linkage. He declares his faith that animated nature (flowers, birds, twigs) actually delights in being part of creation. All living creatures, in short, are entitled by nature to enjoy being alive, and no agency has the right to curtail this joy.

(3) On the grounds that living and participating in the joy of creation is an entitlement, the speaker's faith prompts him, in his "sad thoughts," to lament the misdirection of governments. Instead of securing power through the exploitation of others, it should be the task of government to free human beings to enjoy the blessings of liberty and fulfill their own destinies.

Ode: Intimations of Immortality from Recollections of Early Childhood, *pages 1049–54*

This poem repays close attention. Its basic ideas address the inevitable changes that occur as we become older and older. Do we lose divinely inspired spontaneity as we become jaded, cynical adults, or do we become mature as we leave behind our childishness? There is no answer to this question, but it is certainly one that Wordsworth attempts to answer and therefore the poem is one of the valuable poems in the language.

1 • *Why does the speaker open the poem speaking of loss? What did he lose? How does he perceive that things have changed? How do the questions ending stanza 4 summarize these changes?*

2 • *What does the speaker assert about the soul (stanzas 5 and 6)? What happens to the soul as a person grows older?*

3 • *What is the answer to the question of what happens during the development of maturity and the loss of our "visionary gleam"? What replaces the "gleam"?*

(1) In stanzas 1–4, the speaker realizes that the glory that transfigured everything he saw in his youth has faded away. The contrast here is between the visionary past ("There was a time") and the mundane present ("It is not now as it hath been of yore"). Stanza 2 reveals that not nature but the speaker's *perception* of nature has changed. The nature imagery here defines the speaker's loss. The poem's central questions stem out of this loss: "Whither is fled the visionary gleam? / Where is it now, the glory and the dream?: (lines 57–58).

(2) The soul—a concept of existence that Wordsworth accepts—has come "from afar" to rise with us (to coexist with us). This Platonic theory explains why living dulls us, for the soul preexists with God, who is our home, and comes to us at our birth "trailing clouds of glory," but then becomes obscured as we get on with our lives, eventually fading into the light of common day. By accepting the everyday pleasures that earth has, we grow dull and lose the joy and enthusiasm (i.e. "god [being] within") of our spontaneous and exuberant years.

(3) The problem of maturity can be addressed if we use the memory of our earlier visionary power to compensate for our loss. Our power is now gone but is replaced by memory and a calmer and more philosophical sympathy for human suffering. Ultimately, the ode is about the inevitability of growth and change, and about the inheritance that the child leaves the adult.

Expostulation and Reply, *pages 1054–55*

"Expostulation and Reply" is one of two companion poems on the contrast between seeking and receiving. It fits into Wordsworth's reliance on intuition as a guide to truth. We of course learn from books and from our history, but we also learn just by looking around and developing understanding of the ways of the universe.

1 • *What is the situation of the poem? Who is speaking to whom? Why does the first speaker remonstrate with William?*

2 • *What is William's answer? What contradiction does he explore, and what response to the contradiction does he propose?*

(1) The situation is a dramatic one, unusual for Wordsworth. A good friend named Matthew has come upon William, who is the speaker, and tells him that he is wasting his time doing nothing more than sitting on an "old grey stone." Matthew says that he should be up and doing, studying, and learning, and not just sitting and behaving as though he had no purpose in life.

(2) The speaker, William, responds by defending his purpose in sitting on the rock. His idea is that there is a distinction between seeking and receiving. He denies that we must always be seeking after truth, for he believes that one can receive by feeding the mind "In a wise passiveness." By allowing our eyes, ears, and bodies to feel, where'er they be / Against or with our will," we can perceive the wisdom of creation through a mystical power of assimilation. In short, though books have great value, so also does meditation.

The Tables Turned, *pages 1055–56*

"The Tables Turned," like "Expostulation and Reply," shows Wordsworth in a light mood, but his ideas nevertheless are similar to those he brings out in the Tintern Abbey lines and the "Intimations of Immortality" ode, and also in his extensive autobiographical poem *The Prelude.*

1 • *What is the situation in this poem? In what way is "The Tables Turned" a companion poem to "Expostulation and Reply"?*

2 • *What is the argument of the poem? Of what importance are the final lines: "Come forth, and bring with you a heart / That watches and receives"?*

(1) Here the "tables" are genuinely turned, for it is the speaker who remonstrates with his friend. Matthew, however, does not get an opportunity to reply, as William does in the other poem. The speaker finds his friend reading, and urges him to put the books away and go outside to hear the woodland linnet and the throstle, and to let Nature be his teacher.

(2) The last four stanzas bring out Wordsworth's argument, also developed in "Expostulation and Reply," that Nature is the best teacher of all, who teaches spontaneously without murdering ideas by dissecting them (i.e., analyzing problems, using reason to examine things to the point where the reason for undertaking the search is forgotten). The point is that with the heart that "watches and receives" a person can achieve the wisdom of experience and of the universe, not the wisdom of history, science, and systematic philosophy.

Stepping Westward, *page 1056*

This poem, written in June, 1805, was inspired by an incident which Wordsworth describes in the note. It occurred when he was on a walking tour in Scotland in 1803, and it is of interest because the greeting, to Wordsworth, bespoke kindness. One might remember that he speaks of "greetings where no kindness is" in the "Tintern Abbey" lines (line 131), and the "stepping westward" greeting must have impressed him as one made totally with kindness. It is his perception of kindness and its human and natural associations that undergird the poem.

1 • *What prompts the poem? Where does the speaker hear the phrase? What is significant about the phrase "stepping westward"?*

2 • *What does the greeting do to the speaker's perceptions? Why does he mention that the woman's voice was "enwrought" with "human sweetness"?*

(1) After sunset, the walkers are greeted when going toward a specific hut in a specific location, and specific people give him a warm greeting that was apparently idiomatic in the area. "Westward" is often considered a direction of death, but in this instance Wordsworth takes it to imply a "heavenly destiny," a kindly greeting indicating good will and a human bond.

(2) The greeting transforms the speaker. The ground had been dewy, dark, and cold, and evening gloom was coming on, but the greeting enables him to sense that he has been given the spiritual right to travel "through that region bright." Clearly the location does not change, but his feelings change. In light of the ideas about existence he propounds in other poems, it is clear that he perceives the greetings as a sign that nature has created "human sweetness" in others, and thus his belief in a bond of humanity knitted together by nature is affirmed.

The Solitary Reaper, *pages 1056–57*

"The Solitary Reaper," written in 1805, is one of the perfect poems in the language. It embodies the delight that Wordsworth felt in poetry and song, and it conveys his sense of joy in experience and in the deep value of the power of memory to shape character.

1 • *What is the scene described in the poem?*

2 • *Why does the poet shift from present to past tense at line 25? What is gained by this shift?*

3 • *What speculation does the speaker make about the meaning of the woman's song?*

(1) The initial situation described in the poem is simple and compelling. The speaker, walking in the Scottish Highlands, comes

upon a young woman who is cutting and binding grain, and who is singing as she works. He listens and admires the beautiful song, and speculates about the meaning when he realizes that he cannot understand her language. Then he leaves, but remembers the song long afterwards.

(2) The first twenty-four lines are in the present tense, a presentation that emphasizes the vividness of the woman's song and the strength of his memories.

(3) Because the speaker cannot understand the words of the reaper's song, he speculates upon the meaning. In doing so, his thoughts take the experience far beyond the specific time and place, making of it a universal moment, one which remains in memory long afterwards. The solitary singer is emblematic of the mystery of the sources of art; her song is the symbol of the wide ranges of human experience and deep feelings.

Composed upon Westminster Bridge, *page 1057–58*

The poem's date, September 3, 1802, may be misleading, for it likely that Wordsworth first developed his ideas for the sonnet when on his way, in July, 1802, to France to see Annette Vallon and to speak with her about a permanent settlement (1034). The poem is interesting because it demonstrates Wordsworth's characteristic habit of composition–accepting experiences as they came, and then writing his poems as his thoughts about the experiences developed.

1 • *What is the situation of the poem? Where is the speaker? What is he describing?*

2 • *How is the poem organized?*

3 • *What conclusions does the poem make about the London morning scene.*

(1) The situation is described in the title, which indicates that the poem was composed when the poet was riding on Westminster Bridge on the given date. From the bridge many of the London landmarks are visible ("ships, towers, domes, theatres, and temples"), and as the speaker looks at them he is impressed with their beauty and with the evidence they provide of divine power. With Wordsworth, it is possible to believe that he conceived the poem on the occasion he specifies, even though he might not have written down the actual poem itself until later.

(2) The poem is an Italian sonnet. The octave contains the observations of the London scene. The sestet contains Wordsworth's

thoughts about the scene's beauty and importance. The concluding words make the poem seem almost like a prayer.

(3) Usually Wordsworth is remembered for his visions of nature and for the power he discovered in natural objects and scenes. In this poem, however, he uses the experience of seeing the city early in the morning to as evidence for the "mighty heart" of the people. The sonnet demonstrates that Wordsworth was a poet who was interested in life and lives, and that what he found in life was evidence for the divine power and wisdom of the universe.

I Grieved for Buonaparté, with a Vain, *page 1058*

This sonnet, written in 1802, is sometimes titled "1801." It is one of Wordsworth's political poems, which are based in the need for freedom of thought. Any truncation of freedom is theoretically and actually wrong because it violates Wordsworth's idea that the goal of politics should be to allow the human spirit to flourish. Anyone who suppresses humanity, for whatever reason, such as Napoleon, is wrong.

1 • *How does the speaker criticize Napoleon?*

2 • *What is the basis for the criticism? What is Wordsworth's judgment of how real political power is developed?* .

(1) The first four lines contain the speaker's criticism of Napoleon's lack of compassion, constructive thought, and knowledge. The man was ignorant and unfeeling, a failure as a leader [just as he was, for a time, a success as a general]. The idea is that the general could not be tender because he had no life's experience with tenderness.

(2) The basis for Wordsworth's criticism (and grief) is that Napoleon's life was composed of a succession of wrong experiences. Napoleon could never be tender or merciful because he was brought up without these qualities, and, if such qualities are to be found in the adult they must be instilled in the child. ("The child is the father of the man.") The principle is that if an educational goal is to be reached, it must either be taught or else be allowed to be reached. Wordsworth claims that a successful leader must be brought up to have "thoughts motherly, and meek as womanhood," and to use and love books, leisure, and perfect freedom. A man raised only in battles, without the arts of peace, could not help being a tyrant and a menace to humanity. The first two lines of the sonnet, which may seem strange at first, thus represent sorrow for Napoleon's ill education.

It Is a Beauteous Evening, Calm and Free, *page 1058*

This sonnet was written in August, 1802, at the seaside near Calais, when Wordsworth was visiting in France. The "Dear Child" of line 9 is commonly thought to be his daughter Caroline.

1 • *Describe the organization and rhyme scheme of the sonnet.*

2 • *Should this poem be considered religious or philosophical? Why?*

(1)The octave of the sonnet contains a variation of the usual rhyme scheme: *abba, acca.* In this section the speaker makes an observation about the beauteous evening being calm, free, and quiet. Despite the quiet, however, the speaker draws attention to the nearby surf, which he compares to a sound "like thunder" and which indicates the presence of the "mighty Being." In the sestet, in the pattern *defdfe,* the speaker addresses a child, "dear Girl!" near him, and observes that the holiness of the natural scene is a part of her.

(2) The poem is religious without being sectarian. Wordsworth uses a number of common religious words: *holy, Nun, adoration, heaven, mighty Being, divine, Abraham's bosom, worshipp'st, Temple's inner shrine,* and *God.* The ideas contained here, particularly in the sestet, are like those in the "Intimations of Immortality" ode. In observing the child, who appears "untouched by solemn thought," the child nevertheless gives evidence of her Godly home, from which she came, for the poet concludes that God is with her (and us) "when we know it not."

On the Extinction of the Venetian Republic, *pages 1058–59*

Wordsworth probably wrote this sonnet in 1802 as a belated lament for Napoleon's having declared the dissolution of the republic of Venice several years before. The basis of his grief is that a free society has been deprived of its freedom, and without freedom, people are inhibited from establishing their own connections with the power of nature and the wisdom and spirit of the universe.

1 • *Why does the speaker value in Venice?*

2 • *Why does the speaker grieve over the abolition of Venice as a political entity?*

(1) The speaker values the greatness of Venice, for at one time the Venetian republic controlled the "gorgeous east" and also served as a bulwark of freedom in Europe. She formed one of the first free governments ("the eldest child of Liberty"). Her only alliance was to the sea, and each year the Venetians celebrated the city's marriage to the sea by throwing a ceremonial ring into the water.

(2) The speaker grieves over the extinction because a strong element of life has passed way. Even if the Venetian power had been waning and was no longer any more than a "Shade / Of that which once was great," it had represented the strength and power that comes, in the speaker's estimation, from freedom. Implied in the poem is the idea that when such enlightened power is lost it is possible that repression will fill the void. One thinks of Wordsworth's sonnet "I grieved for Buonaparté," for in 1802 the specter of warfare and suppression was represented by Napoleon.

Scorn Not the Sonnet, *page 1059*

"Scorn Not the Sonnet" was apparently written between 1820 and 1827, and was published in 1827. Wordsworth is often regarded as a poet of the lengthy blank verse poems, as represented particularly by *The Prelude* (see Phyllis Webb's "Poetics Against the Angel of Death," [929]). However, he wrote many stanzaic poems, some of which are represented here, and as many as 500 sonnets. This sonnet is his celebration of the form that he much admired. Of special note in the poem are the succinct appraisals that Wordsworth makes of seven poets, from Petrarch to Milton, who used the sonnet form.

1 • What is the dramatic situation in the poem? Whom is the speaker addressing?

2 • What evidence does the speaker present to illustrate the value and power of the sonnet?

(1) The poem stems from a dramatic situation in which the speaker addresses a literary critic who has expressed scorn of the sonnet form on unspecified grounds. We may surmise, however, that the critic's charge is that the sonnet form was considered a minor one because a sonnet-writing poet could not bring out extensive great thoughts within the confines of just fourteen lines.

(2) The speaker rises to defend the sonnet and cites seven great writers who used the form, including the English writers Shakespeare, Spenser, and Milton, in whose hands the sonnet "became a trumpet." His ideas, we may surmise, are that the sonnet form requires great compression and therefore great selectivity. The form also requires strong concentration and focus—a type of poetic discipline that poets using longer forms might neglect.

To Toussaint L'Ouverture, *page 1059*

Wordsworth wrote this sonnet in late 1802 as an attempt to find meaning in the face of one of Napoleon's great outrages. Toussaint L'Ouverture was a former slave who had led a rebellion in Haiti. Napoleon suppressed the uprising and had Toussaint taken to Paris, where he was imprisoned and where he died in 1803.

1 • *Why is the present tense the dominant tense of this poem?*

2 • *Why does the speaker not express despair for the imprisoned leader? What grounds does the poet assert for future freedom?*

(1) The poem is written in the present tense because Wordsworth was speaking about a present situation. Toussaint was suffering in a Paris prison, from which he could not escape. The poet therefore necessarily uses the present, for he is seeking to find meaning in the fact of the imprisonment and the suppression of the Haitian rebellion.

(2) Toussaint's legacy is explained in the poem's sestet. The major Wordsworthian word is *Powers*, which will continue to influence those who come in the future and who will therefore take up the cause of freedom again. Although the speaker admits that Toussaint will never be given freedom, he finds grounds for hope. He cites eight "allies" (e.g., "air, earth, and skies," etc.) that will eventually cause people to seek freedom, including the last and most memorable ally, "man's unconquerable mind."

■ EMILY DICKINSON, *pages 1060–1100*

After Great Pain, a Formal Feeling Comes (*J341, F372*), *page 1068*

1 • *What is meant by* formal *in line 1?*

2 • *What do the images of the poem have in common?*

3 • *What is the connection of the poem's subject with the* He *of line 3?*

(1) Ordinarily *formal* refers to appropriate and ritualized manners. That is partly its meaning here, but also the word suggests the images that follow. The feelings after great pain, in other words, are molded into rigid patterns beyond the conscious control of the individual—almost into a set of analogous physical shapes.

(2) The images have a common thread of stiffness, numbness, heaviness, and rigidity, as though the feelings with which they are compared are being held in suspended animation and emotional isolation. Thus *Tombs* (line 2) force people into appropriate ceremoniousness, literally forbidding anything but solemnity. The *Wooden* way

(line 7) suggests a lack of spring and spontaneity, a total heaviness of foot and of spirit. The *Quartz contentment* is hard and shiny, crystallizing and encapsulating the individual in passivity and incapacitating him or her to have further emotional interchanges. The *Freezing* image of lines 12 and 13 (is the total number of lines in the poem—thirteen—significant?) connects the ending of the poem with *Tombs* at the beginning: The response to great pain is a kind of death, even though the individual goes on living, because the emotional connections he or she once had are now gone, and thus a link with life has been frozen or killed. For comparison, see "My Life Closed Twice" (1074).

(3) The *He that bore* of line 3 is a reference to Christ's carrying the cross (see John 19:17). The connection with the poem is made at the end of the second line with *Tombs*, presumably an association with the tomb in which Jesus was laid (see Matthew 27:60 and elsewhere) and therefore also prompting the third-line outcry about the passion.

The reference underlies the intensity of the *great pain* of line 1, for it makes the passion seem both comparable and immediate. Even though line 4 does not cohere grammatically with line 3, it nevertheless preserves the topical and thematic connection because it is a virtual reenactment of the disorientation about time that a person in great grief might experience. Though the line is fragmentary, therefore, it is especially dramatic.

The Bustle in a House *(J1078, F1108), pages 1068–69*

1 • *How does the first line of the poem promise a certain kind of setting? How does the second stanza indicate that the setting is metaphorical?*

2 • *A student once suggested that line 6 of this poem, "And putting love away," is cold and unfeeling. What argument might be made to support this assertion? How do the remaining two lines suggest that the student may have been wrong?*

3 • *In what way does this poem depart from the ballad measure Dickinson often uses?*

(1) The opening line suggests a household where a family member has died the day before. The "Bustle" refers to the hushed solemn preparations that need to be made before the funeral—cleaning, preparing invitations, writing notices to friends, and so on. In the second stanza the "Sweeping of the Heart" (line 5) indicates an entirely different setting—the interior one of adjusting to life in view of the reality and permanence of death. The appearance of the word *Heart* indicates the beginning of the metaphor.

(2) The thought of "putting Love away," if taken out of context, might seem cold and unfeeling if it is taken to mean that the living can forget the dead. In the poem however, the metaphor of housework applies. Hence the love being put away is like storing something in a closet, or on a shelf until a change of season makes it necessary again. This analogy, together with the concluding reference to the reuniting of the dead in Eternity, lends a strong note of poignancy and yearning to the poem. The second stanza hence expresses deep feeling, though it also expresses resignation and acceptance.

(3) In this poem Dickinson modifies the first lines of the two stanzas. Each line (1 and 5) has six syllables, and therefore three rather than four iambic feet. The effect is that the syllables *Bus, House,* and *Sweep, Heart,* are stressed rhythmically. Both the lines, in fact, are almost metrical twins. For this reason, the rhythmical echo that line 5 makes of line 1 creates an element of surprise once the word *Heart* is found in the same position as *House.* This type of control enables Dickinson to achieve a powerful effect within a very brief compass.

"Faith" Is a Fine Invention *(J185, F202), page 1069*

1 • *Why is "Faith" included within quotation marks? What do the quotation marks add to the meaning that the absence of quotation marks would indicate?*

2 • *What does* microscopes *suggest or symbolize in line 3? What "Emergency" might make microscopes better than faith?*

3 • *Explain the idea of the second line reference to "Gentlemen can* see–."

(1) The quotation marks suggest that Dickinson is referring to a generally or popularly understood definition of the word. Here, it seems clear from the "can see" in the second line, Dickinson is alluding to the famous definition of faith in Hebrews 11:1, "Now faith is the substance of things hoped for, the evidence of things not seen." The entire eleventh chapter of Hebrews, in fact, is testimony to the power of faith. Without the quotation marks the usage might not necessarily be construed as an allusion.

(2,3) *Microscopes* suggests here the analysis and questioning of events of life. The microscope is an instrument that gets beyond the obvious, and therefore it symbolizes a questioning attitude, not the accepting one suggested by faith alone. Thus the microscope marks a rejection of quiescence, and an acceptance of inquiry. The "Emergency" could be a significant event, such as a departure or death, that creates an individual crisis. The phrase is paradoxical. It suggests that "Gentlemen can *see*," or understand, the usual religious explanations for misfortune, but that they are in fact insensible as human beings to the real sufferings of others. In addition, *Gentlemen* suggests exclusion, likely based on hierarchy. The gentlemen form the group who interpret faith and provide comforting platitudes for those experiencing pain, but their answers do not deal with the pain itself.

The Heart is the Capital of the Mind *(J1354, F1381), page 1069*

1 • *What is the metaphor on which the poem is based? What is the effect of this metaphor?*

2 • *The second stanza seems difficult grammatically. How can the language be read?*

3 • *How may this poem be compared with "One Need Not Be a Chamber" (1075)?*

(1) The metaphor is that the individual is like a country, a continent, with the mind as a single political unit coincidental with this country. The capital is the heart; that is, the emotions are the primary source of strength and control, and the recipient of the individual's mental and physical resources. The population is one. The argument might seem solipsistic, but the poem is more about knowing oneself than about making the world over in one's self-image. The effect is surely, however, to indicate Dickinson's stress on individual consciousness and identity.

(2) The stanza is ambiguous primarily because of the punctuation and also because of the elliptical constructions. There are two possible ways to read the lines, with each being acceptable because both stress the need for learning about oneself:

[a] The population [of this Continent] is One — numerous enough. Seek this ecstatic Nation: It is Yourself.

[b] The population [of this Continent] is One. This ecstatic Nation [is] Numerous enough. Seek [it]; it is Yourself.

(3) The poems are comparable because both metaphorically equate an individual with houses and nations. There the similarity stops, for "The Heart" is optimistic while "One Need" is pessimistic. "One Need" asserts the potential horror of the mind, and it compares this horror to a haunting ghost that frightens the individual

in both familiar and lonely settings. By contrast, "The Heart" is more expansive just as it is more in accord with the need for adjustment and self-knowledge. Ironically, "The Heart" by its comprehensiveness includes the view of "One Need," because one of the things a person might face in seeking self-knowledge is the potential for horror described in "One Need."

I Cannot Live with You *(J640, F706), pages 1069–70*

1 • *What is the dramatic situation imagined in the poem? Who is the "you" being addressed?*

2 • *What reasons does the speaker cite in support of the opening denial? How is the poem structured to embody these responses?*

3 • *How do the thought and the sentences cohere from lines 5–10? What purpose is served by the difficulty of these lines?*

(1) The speaker responds to a question of the "you" listener that the two should live together, presumably in marriage. The speaker answers negatively, and then explains her refusal. Her reasons, together with the concluding summary, form the poem, which is more a personal, written letter than an intimate, spoken speech. Once the poem is completed, there is no opportunity for response, and the concluding word, "Despair," indicates the finality of the statement and the speaker's deep grief.

(2) Lines 1–12 form a negative denying the possibility of living together, citing a religious barrier (the Key kept by the Sexton, line 5). Lines 13–20 further deny living together because of the impossibility of the two dying together; neither could predecease the other. A third section is lines 21–44, in which the denial extends to the impossibility of the two being resurrected together: A– the speaker could not admire Jesus more than the "you" in Heaven because she admires "you" for shining nearer. B– She would be ill judged for crowding out her vision of Paradise by filling her sight with "you." C– She could never bear to be anywhere in Heaven without the "you," because being apart, even in Heaven, would be "Hell" to her. The conclusion, lines 45–50, summarizes the vastness between the two, who have only prayer for consolation and despair as a permanent condition.

(3) The passage is difficult, even after repeated readings. If one includes the fourth line, however, a continuous grammatical connection may be formed:

Behind the Shelf [which] the Sexton keeps the key to,
Putting up [on the shelf] our Life - His Porcelain - Like

a Housewife's discarded cup [that is] quaint or broke[n].

The fragmentary, difficult lines complement the elliptical thought of a person trying to speak while in extreme emotional pain. Hence the style here is appropriate for the subject and for the grief of the speaker. Beyond the religious barrier mentioned in lines 5–10, the speaker suggests that the "you" may have gone on to a new relationship (the "newer Sevres" china that "pleases") to replace the cracked and now dead one.

I Died for Beauty—but Was Scarce *(J449, F448), pages 1070–71*

1 • *Who is the speaker and what has happened to her? What has happened to the man in the "adjoining Room"? What dramatic situation is described in the poem?*

2 • *Why does the man who died for Truth ask the speaker why she "failed" (line 5)?*

3 • *Explain the final stanza. What idea do you think it represents on the part of the speaker? The poet?*

(1) The speaker of this poem, like the speakers of "I Heard a Fly Buzz" (1071) and "Because I Could Not Stop for Death" (671), is speaking after the fact of death. She states that she has died "for Beauty" and has been "adjusted in the tomb." The man in the adjoining grave claims a kinship with the speaker because, as he says, he died "for Truth." The identification of beauty and truth ("Themself are One") makes a bond between the two, and so they meet "a Night" and talk to each other "between the Rooms." They speak for an indefinite period of time until the Moss reaches their lips and covers up their names.

(2) "Failed" is a synonym for dying, but it also implies that the speaker's goals may not have been fully visualized or realized. The use of this word hence suggests that the concepts of beauty (and truth) may not be fully understood or understandable.

(3) The final stanza represents the view that death and time make human concerns meaningless. If there is a reality of universals existing in an eternal world of ideas, human beings cannot know about them because of the finiteness of life and the overwhelming power of the grave. For this reason this poem may be contrasted with poems such as "This World Is Not Conclusion" (1078), in which Dickinson expresses a more optimistic understanding of an afterlife. "I Died for Beauty" is an expression of sorrowful, extreme pessimism.

The connection between beauty and truth is made in the conclusion of Keats's "Ode on a Grecian Urn" (1018). In terms of the finality of death as a cessation of human dreams and potential, "I Died for Beauty" may be compared with Gray's "Sonnet on the Death of Richard West" (733) and Ransom's "Bells for John Whiteside's Daughter" (1189).

I Felt a Funeral in My Brain (J280, F340), page 1071

(See David Porter's discussion of this very personal, difficult, and perplexing poem, page 1084.)

1 • *Describe the narrative in this poem. What is meant by a funeral in the speaker's brain?*

2 • *To what degree is the poem confessional? What is the psychological or spiritual state that the speaker is describing? What does it mean to state that Being is "but an Ear," and that the speaker and Silence make up "some strange Race / Wrecked, solitary, here –"?*

3 • *Explain the circumstances and meaning of the last stanza. If the speaker is describing a dream, what does the dream mean?*

(1) The past tense narrative is used to describe a series of events that might or might not coincide with a disturbed or psychotic episode. The speaker felt or imagined that a funeral was taking place within her brain. The major elements of a funeral are included in this vision: the mourners, the funeral service (beating "like a Drum"), the removal of the coffin, the heavy tread of the pallbearers, and the tolling bell A funeral of course is something final–the end of life, the formal leave-taking by the living for the dead. The speaker is stating that, internally, she has gone through such a ritual and that the experience has left her devastated.

(2) The poem is confessional, but was almost certainly never intended for circulation to a wide audience. The occasion of the speaker's narrative is her response to an extreme disturbance, a response to something disastrous and traumatic. Therefore we must conclude that some part of life has vanished, that some relationship is over about which we know nothing, or that some endeavor has come to naught. The speaker implies that the experience has left her "Wrecked, solitary" along with Silence. The occasion was so vast for her that the tolling Bell she envisions seems to be coming from "all the Heavens," and the speaker is so fixed on the circumstances that her entire existence has been taken up with the sound. This preoccupation has left her emotionally drained, so much so that she

has been virtually changed into another species, a "strange Race." What she describes is psychological and spiritual enervation and "breakdown," to quote David Porter.

(3) The poem is in the form not so much of a dream but rather of a nightmare. Even a bad dream could not include the details Dickinson puts into this poem. The conclusion of the vision in the last stanza is difficult to follow, for the speaker imagines that she has been walking on the floor of reason, but then a plank breaks; she plunges downward and has "Finished knowing – then –". It would appear that the speaker's hurt is so great that she has no interest in any further kinds of experience from which she could learn. One is reminded of the conclusion of "The Soul Selects Her Own Society," in which Dickinson describes the closing of the "Valves" of attention "Like Stone" (1076). Some experiences are so traumatic, in other words, that they make life difficult if not impossible.

I Heard a Fly Buzz—When I Died (J465, F591), *pages 1071–72*

1 • *What is the imaginary situation being narrated in the poem?*

2 • *How does the buzzing fly affect the poem's tone?*

3 • *What is the meaning of the last two lines? What is their effect?*

(1) The situation is a deathbed scene. In the nineteenth century people who were gravely ill did not die in hospitals, but rather at home, often directly in front of family and friends who were maintaining a bedside vigil. The witnesses would be tearful (line 5) and would prepare themselves for the moment of death (line 7). The dying person would give personal effects and properties to the persons present, who were also witnesses of the gifts and final wishes and even wills (lines 9–11). The giving of testimony and acknowledgment of the presence of God ("the King," lines 7, 8) would also take place. Amid the scene, the speaker notes the appearance of a buzzing fly, which is her last connection with the living world. The personalized imagining of death or deathbed scenes is not unusual even today, and it was even less unusual at Dickinson's time, when death was more common among the young than it is now. Swift, for example, wrote "Verses on the Death of Dr. Swift, D.S.P.C.D.," a poem about how people would respond to his own death. Death is also a frequent topic of Donne's poetry, and Gray's "Elegy Written in a Country Churchyard" contains an "Epitaph" demonstrating the poet's concern with Death (698). Mark Twain satirized such preoccupations in *Huckleberry Finn*, with the dead Emmeline Grangerford's poem about the death of "Stephen Dowling Botts Dec'd" (Chapter 17).

(2) The fly is an intrusion upon what should be a serious occasion; it is "uncertain, stumbling," and therefore it is mildly comic. With respect to the tone, the fly saves the imaginary situation from becoming sentimentalized because it represents reality and everyday life. As it were, the fly enables Dickinson to focus on the seriousness of the last lines, and to deepen their humanness because they describe real life more adequately than tearful farewells by vigil-keepers would do.

(3) The last two lines constitute a powerful ending. They are connected to the sound and light represented by the fly because the fly interposes itself between the light and the speaker. Thus the phrase "the Windows failed" is logical in the narrative because the speaker has been conscious of the fly outlined against the light. The use of *Windows* is a metonym—the substitution of one thing (*Windows*) for another with which it is closely associated (light), and here it emphasizes the idea that death is a termination of the world externally as well as internally. In the last line, *see to see* is a way of describing death as a loss of capacity. The first *see* is thus the power to perceive, and the second *see* is the visual function of this power.

I Like to See It Lap the Miles (*J585, F383*), *page 1072*

1 • *How does Dickinson succeed in describing a sense of motion about the train, even though there is only one complete sentence in the poem?*

2 • *What is the dominant metaphor in the poem? How does Dickinson keep the metaphor from seeming ordinary?*

3 • *How does Dickinson preserve a comic, playful tone throughout the poem?*

(1) She begins the poem with the construction "I like to see it . . ." and then she includes ten one-syllable infinitives in this complementary position, of which *it* is the recurrent subject. Thus the speaker likes to see it *lap, lick, stop, step, peer, pare, crawl, chase, neigh,* and *stop,* with the present participle *complaining* in line 11. All the infinitive complements and the participle stress the movement of the train.

(2) The major metaphor is common: The train is like an iron horse. (Dickinson may be speaking of the Amherst-Belchertown railroad, which had opened in 1853.) She keeps the metaphor fresh, first, by not mentioning ever that she is describing a train, second, by stressing the train's movement, and, third, by withholding the verb most appropriate to a horse, *neigh,* until line 15. The metaphor thus is not completely fixed in the reader's mind until the poem is almost

ended, and therefore the poet has given the topic the descriptive freshness of the first fourteen lines. The metaphor, in fact, is rather surprising when it becomes apparent, and it is certainly fun.

(3) She uses a number of overstatements which by being overblown create amusement. There are *prodigious* (line 4), *supercilious* (line 6), *Boanerges* (line 14), and *omnipotent* (line 16). In addition, the complaining in a horrid, hooting stanza (lines 11, 12), the chasing (line 12), and the neighing (line 14) are also comic. Another playful idea is that after all the hooting, the creature-train becomes *docile* once it stops (line 15). The metaphor *stable* for a railway roundhouse is also comic. These are only the major ways in which Dickinson exhibits good humor and geniality in the poem.

I'm Nobody! Who Are You? *(J288, F260), pages 1072–73*

1 • What does the designation "Nobody" mean in the poem? What advantages are educed for being nobody?

2 • What is meant by the poem's distinction between "Nobody" and "Somebody"?

3 • What attitude toward the public does the speaker express? How consistent is this attitude with the claim the speaker makes to be "Nobody"?

(1) "Nobody" likely refers to a status of privacy or anonymity. The speaker expressly denies any kind of public admission of her need for privacy. The cleverness of the first stanza results from the fact that the listener, who is also "Nobody," should not tell anybody about this detail. The existence of anyone admitting to be "Nobody," in other words, would probably then become "Somebody." This detail would then focus such attention on the new Somebodies that they would lose their preferred seclusion.

(2) The play on the words *nobody* and *somebody* is probably as old as the language. The common interchange is the following:

> "Who did this?"
> "Nobody."
> "It must have been Somebody."

Somebody, in other words, is always responsible, and is therefore the public one. Ironically, both Nobody and Somebody are always doing something, and thus both are equally responsible for what happens.

(3) The attitude of the speaker toward the public is contained

in the phrase "admiring Bog" in the last line. It is difficult to define exactly the reasons for the negative attitude, but clearly the speaker considers being a Somebody in the public spotlight as being like a frog, croaking out unpleasant noises for the bog to hear. Certainly the speaker's attitude is negative and censorious.

I Never Felt at Home—Below *(J413, F437), page 1073*

1 • *What ideas does the speaker explore in this poem? What restraint does the speaker recognize upon her rebellious attitudes?*

2 • *What is suggested by the use of quotation marks around the final words, "Judgment Day"?*

3 • *Describe the relationship between the form and rhyme, on the one hand, and the content, on the other.*

(1) The poem begins with the speaker's description of her sense of alienation, both "Below" and in the "Handsome Skies." This is a broad, sweeping claim, and when she applies it to "Paradise" she makes the analogy that an afterlife will be no more congenial to her than this life has been. She continues in this vein for the next eleven lines, citing comic instances to assert that the afterlife will be a bore. One will always have to wear Sunday best; there never will be any chance to play; Wednesday afternoon will be lonesome; and, above all, God will be like a telescope that provides a continual supervision of Edenic residents who want to be wayward. The restraint is of course explained as the "Judgment Day" in the final line.

(2) The last line represents the major heavenly restraint upon the speaker's rebellious feelings; it is the "Judgment Day." Interestingly, the inclusion of "Judgment Day" within quotation marks suggests that the speaker is introducing an idea that she has not felt at home with, but about which she has been told. Even at the end, in other words, the speaker is still rebellious.

(3) The first stanza is a normal hymnal stanza, with a regular *4a, 3b, 4a, 3b* pattern and with rhymes on lines 1–3 and 2–4. This regularity seems consistent with the speaker's positive expression of her sense of never feeling at home. As the poem develops, the rhythm becomes more varied and the poet uses inexact rhymes, such as "time" with "lonesome," and "Nap" with "Telescope." One might claim that this employment of irregularity is appropriate to the topic of the speaker's general malaise with a rigid concept of an eternally regularized paradise. Interestingly, with line 11 the rhyming word "say" is introduced, and this rhymes with "away" and the

final word "Day." This return to regularity is consistent with the idea of "Judgment Day" closing the poem. There is a judgment, and it does keep her thoughts—and rhymes—in line.

I Never Lost as Much But Twice *(J49, F39), page 1073*

1 • *Is it necessary to know the specific occasions to which the speaker is referring in this poem?*

2 • *What situation does the speaker propose for herself as a petitioner before God?*

3 • *What is the religious basis of the image of the beggar at the door?*

4 • *What is the effect in this poem of Dickinson's use of internal rhyme?*

(1) We cannot tell from the poem whose loss the speaker is mourning. Regardless of the specific causes of grief, the poem itself stands alone as an expression of the speaker's need for consolation because this need is the poem's major substance.

(2) The speaker envisages an idea of wealth and loss. Twice she has been a beggar asking God for help. She received help twice, but now a new loss has occurred and she is again poor. The imagery intimating that God is a "Burglar" complicates the speaker's attitudes, however, for this word calls into question the assumption that God is always and eternally good.

3. The beggar as a person whom God raises from the dust is contained in I Samuel 2:8. Bartimaeus, a blind beggar, sat at the side of the road in Mark 10:48, and Jesus, on the way to Jerusalem, restored his sight. The "door" of God may refer to John 10:9, "I am the door." Lazarus the beggar of course was given the heavenly reward of sitting in Abraham's bosom (Luke 16:23). The image of human beings as beggars-petitioners, and of God as the giver of alms, is therefore well established scripturally.

4. The *-ore* sound occurs five times in *Before, door, store, poor,* and *more,* even though it is a concluding rhyme only in lines 6 and 8. Because the poem is so short, the sound itself becomes a prominent internal rhyme, stressing the idea of the emotional impoverishment of the speaker and therefore of her need for divine restoration.

I Taste a Liquor Never Brewed *(J214, F207), pages 1073–74*

1 • *What is the topic of this poem? Why is a prose restatement of the ideas inferior to the poem itself?*

2 • *In minimizing Dickinson's verse, Thomas Bailey Aldrich in 1903*

offered a rewritten first stanza by, as he said, "tossing a rhyme into it," as follows:

I taste a liquor never brewed
In vats upon the Rhine;
No tankard ever held a draught
Of alcohol like mine.

What is the principle on which Aldrich made his revision, and in what way is it relevant to an evaluation of Dickinson's stanza?

3 • *For the last line, Emily Dickinson herself composed an alternative, which she wrote in the manuscript of this poem:*

Leaning against the–Sun–

Because she did not publish the poem, we do not know her final intention. However, what improvement, if any, does the alternative line offer the poem?

(1) The topic is the speaker's statement about the ecstasy and exhilaration she feels with life, both now and in the future. Dickinson bases the poem on the analogy of being "drunk with the wine of life." She uses the phrase "liquor never brewed" to explain the expansive mood. She may also be creating a riddle, for she may be using the persona of blades of grass—certainly a riddle of which readers should be aware. Under this reading, the liquor never brewed may be no more than rain and dew. Any prose restatement is dull by comparison with the poem because the paraphrase kills the imaginativeness and daring of Dickinson's word choices.

(2) Aldrich's principle is that the ballad stanza should be regular, with four stresses in lines 1 and 3, and rhyming words ending lines 2 and 4. Aldrich obviously concluded that Dickinson had violated this principle because she made line 3 have seven rather that eight syllables, and used *Alcohol* in line 4 as a very slant rhyme with *Pearl* in line 2. Modern readers are likely to find such insistence on mechanical regularity totally irrelevant to the joyful state of mind Dickinson presents in the poem. Today we read Dickinson, but who now reads Aldrich?

(3) The image in the alternative suggests that its speaker would be leaning drunkenly against the sun as though it were a lamppost. The image is clever, joyful, ridiculous, far-fetched, and daring, and for this reason it would be a definite improvement over the image in the text, which suggests simply that the speaker (the "tippler") has come from "Manzanilla" (i.e. drinking wine). Moreover, the last word of the alternative—*sun*—creates a perfect rhyme on which to end the poem.

Although perfect rhymes were not one of Dickinson's objectives, here the word that makes the good rhyme is an improvement.

Much Madness Is Divinest Sense *(J435, F620), page 1074*

1 • *How may the first three lines be resolved grammatically? How does this resolution assist comprehension of these lines?*

2 • *How does the speaker suggest that the opening paradox is applicable to politics?*

3 • *Why does the speaker refer to "you" in line 6 and "you're" in line 7?*

(1) In the first three lines, Dickinson's use of the dash creates an immediate difficulty of understanding. This problem may be resolved, however, if the lines are understood thus:

> To a discerning eye, much madness is divinest sense
> [and] much sense [is] the starkest madness.

This resolution enables the lines to be seen as a description of a topsy-turvy world, in which things are seldom what they seem. The rhetorical arrangement of lines 1 and 3, a chiasmus or antimetabole on *madness-sense,* and *sense-madness,* also suggests that the lines are to be read as a unit, with *To a discerning Eye* as the modifying phrase grammatically.

(2) The use of the words *Majority ... prevail* in lines 4 and 5 indicates that the speaker is criticizing the political decision making process of democracy. The idea is a play on the idea of the proverb "vox populi, vox dei" ("the voice of the people is the voice of God"). If the people embody collective madness in their voting patterns, therefore, that madness is the "divinest sense" that will prevail. By the same token, the sensible person who dissents on reasonable grounds will be branded the mad one. Also, the concluding image of being "handled with a Chain" suggests the political associations of the poem.

(3) When speaking of personal, inner feelings, Dickinson does not have her speakers include references to the second person. In this poem, however, the use of the second person may be suggested by the "majority" of line 4 and the political associations considered in question 2. The *you* is introduced as a means of extending the context and general application of the poem as statement. In other words, the "discerning" reader is being drawn into this poem to verify the ideas there, whereas in Dickinson's purely personal poetry the speaker is the sole voice verifying personal experiences that the reader has not necessarily shared.

My Life Closed Twice Before Its Close *(J1732, F1773), page 1074*

1 • *In what way does the structure of this poem not conform to the strict confines of the two-stanza ballad measure?*

2 • *In lines 2–6, the speaker raises questions about the nature of a possible "third event" that might occur to her. Does the speaker therefore anticipate that this third event will be disastrous?*

3 • *How are the last two lines connected to the topic matter of the poem?*

(1) The sentences do not fall regularly within the pattern of the stanzas. Line 1 is a complete sentence that features the use of *close* in both a figurative and literal sense of dying. Lines 2–6 form an extensive sentence that continues for five lines; these lines do not strictly fall within the line and stanza patterns. The last two lines, like the first, form a separate statement. Thus the two stanzas, though the rhythms and rhymes are fairly regular, are stretched by the content of the poem.

(2) Because the first two events were figurative endings of the speaker's life, the implication of lines 2–6 is that "Immortality" might have a third event equally bad in store. But the language is ambiguous, for the description "So huge, so hopeless to conceive" may equally describe a favorable as well as unfavorable event. The question of what Immortality might "unveil" is therefore still open, even though the previous experiences have been bad. In the light of the last two lines, the "third event" is clearly about the nature of heaven and hell in an afterlife. Dickinson considers similar subject material in "I Never Lost As Much But Twice" (982).

(3) These lines are perhaps the best known of any that Dickinson wrote. Though they are often excerpted they belong within the poem, and are essential to the poem's ideas. In effect they constitute a denial of the speculation about the magnitude of anything that immortality might offer to the speaker. We commonly regard going either to heaven or hell as the two big events that death has in store for human beings. But, says the speaker, because her life has already been "closed" twice before her actual death, she has already experienced both heaven and hell. The poem therefore ends on a skeptical as well as a memorable note: Nothing that Immortality can provide—not heaven, and not hell—could be either better or worse than what she has known in life because of the partings she has experienced.

My Triumph Lasted Till the Drums *(J1227, F1212), pages 1074–75*

1 • *Who is the speaker of this poem? What dramatic situation has prompted the speaker to begin the poem?*

2 • *In what way are lines 9–16 a contrast to the first eight lines, and in what way are they a reflection upon them?*

3 • *What kind of image of the dead in warfare is developed here? Does Dickinson stress the horror or the anguish of war?*

1. There is no clear identification, but from the situation the speaker is a member of a victorious army, perhaps even a commanding officer. The victory has been celebrated by drum rolls, and the speaker is elated. After the noise, however, the speaker inspects the dead, and upon seeing their "finished Faces" (line 5), he, or she, loses all elation, and in fact feels so "chastened" (line 4) that the speaker wishes to become one of the dead.

2. The last eight lines, the second half of the poem, are a reflection upon warfare and upon what people might learn from it if only they could be sensible and caring. The speaker of this second half is the same as in the first, except that here the topic is contrasted because it is abstracted from the specific situation of the first half. In this second part the question of how we know the future is treated, specifically how we could use the memory of past warfare to predict that future warfare would produce the same regret and guilt in the victors as described in the first part. The concluding reference to the bayonets (a metonym for those who have killed) becoming contrite only after the act of killing is an effective coda to this thoughtful and sensitive meditation.

3. The image of the dead is not immediate or visual. We read only that the dead have "finished Faces" and that they have "turned" their "Conclusion" on the speaker (lines 5, 6). There is hence nothing graphic, but rather Dickinson directs the topic inward to the responses of the speaker. The subject is therefore more the anguish of war than physical horror and agony.

One Need Not Be a Chamber – To Be Haunted *(J670, F407), page 1075*

1 • *How is the metaphor comparing a house to the mind developed in the poem to demonstrate the frightening nature of identity?*

2 • *To what degree is "One Need Not" a successful poem?*

(1) In stanza 1 the poem asserts that our brains have their own corridors, or hallways, where we may meet horrid fantasies. At the end the image is a single room where a "superior spectre / Or More"

is waiting within the room of the mind, more deadly than a real-life assassin. In between, the mind is compared to a "cooler Host" (line 8), ready to give a terrorizing party for the individual. In line 12 the metaphor of the house is briefly abandoned for a "lonesome Place," which could be anywhere, most likely outdoors. Here, the image is that the mind—"one's self"—is like a lurking bandit. Even here, however, the room image is the Abbey (lines 9, 10), where the stones themselves might chase the terror-stricken victim. The poem suggests that such fright is less harmful than the horrors within the mind. These many separate representations of the mind as a haunted house, five in all within the five stanzas, create consistency and unity.

(2) "One Need Not" deals abstractly but successfully with a difficult topic. With its many comparisons, it does not reflect a single experience—difficult as it is anyway to determine the exact incidents which may have given rise to Dickinson's other very personal poems. The success of the poem depends on the reader's willingness to concede, at least for poetic purposes, that the mind's inner recesses are like a vast mansion that may be haunted by invasive and frightening ghosts. For comparison, see "The Heart is the Capital of the Mind" (1069), and also Frost's "Desert Places" (912).

Safe in Their Alabaster Chambers *(J216, F124), pages 1075–76*

1 • *Who are the "members of the Resurrection?" Why are they* meek? *In what way are they safe?*

2 • *Contrast the subject matter of the second stanza with that of the first.*

3 • *Consider the words* Crescent, Arcs, Firmaments, Diadems, *and* Doges. *How do the associations of these words broaden the meaning of the poem?*

4 • *In the last line, why is everything* soundless? *What idea does Dickinson suggest with this word?*

(1) The "members of the Resurrection" are the dead, so named here because often on tombstones inscriptions read that the dead person lies below awaiting and anticipating a joyful resurrection. The word *meek* refers to Matthew 5:5, "Blessed are the meek, for they shall inherit the earth." The dead in the grave are safe from any more worldly pain.

(2) Stanza 2 refers to the passage of time, to the eternal movement of heavenly bodies, and to the constant change in governments and therefore in human society. This stanza suggests how long the dead must wait for their eventual resurrection.

(3) *Crescent*, in addition to its probable reference to the earth's curved surface, suggest the location in the middle east—the fertile crescent—where the mythical garden of Eden was located. *Arcs* suggests the Ark of the Covenant—the pact God made with the ancient Hebrews (Exodus 25:16–21; Numbers 10:33 and elsewhere). *Firmament* is also a Biblical word, signifying the heavens, in the shape of an arch. The word is also prominent in Joseph Addison's hymn "The Spacious Firmament on High," for which Haydn set his well-known music. *Diadems* is Biblical (see Isaiah 62:3) and is also an important and repeated word in the common hymn by Edward Perronet (1726–1792), "All Hail the Power of Jesus' Name," with music by Oliver Holden (1765–1844). *Doges*, or *dukes*, suggests the Venetian Republic, which had lost its eminence early in the nineteenth century. All these words suggest the broad historical and religious milieu of Dickinson's ideas.

4. *Soundless* suggests the insignificance of human activities in the context of eternity. Worldly power and the worlds which contain it shall pass, and they will be unimportant compared with God's resurrective power.

Some Keep the Sabbath Going to Church *(J324, F236), page 1076*

1 • *What concept of worship is presented in this poem?*

2 • *Consider the lines in which the speaker refers to "I" (lines 2, 6, 12). What is the tone of these lines?*

3 • *In what way does God, the "noted Clergyman," preach in the orchard of worship in which the speaker observes the Sabbath?*

(1) The poem contrasts a formal church service with the spontaneous experience of being with Nature in the home orchard. The idea is that in the natural world a person is closer to God than in a worship service where the service itself, because it is the focus of attention, interferes with his or her relationship to God.

(2) The tone is one of cleverness and challenge—playful pride and mockery. In line 2 the speaker admits to keeping the Sabbath by staying away from church. (Remember that Exodus 20:8–11 commands the keeping of the Sabbath; also remember that this commandment was usually heeded in the nineteenth century.) In line 6 the speaker endows herself with wings, and in the last line she indicates a belief that her way of keeping the Sabbath makes her life a constant process of going to Heaven. Certainly these statements were intended to shock the more conventional readers of 1864, the date of first publication. This poem was one of the few poems of Dickinson published during her lifetime.

(3) The exact means are not disclosed, unless one assumes that Dickinson is alluding to statements like that in Psalms 24:1, "The earth is the Lord's, and the fullness thereof, the world and those that dwell therein." If the allusion is admitted, then all the elements of nature—the bobolink, the orchard, the singing sexton (presumably a bird)—become the means through which "God preaches." By the natural, pantheistic idea of the poem, any title attributed to God is an understatement. Therefore the appellation "noble Clergyman" is designed as a rhetorical reminder of the intensity of God's power. There is also a strong note of defiance and unconventionality in the choice of phrase.

The Soul Selects Her Own Society *(J303, F409), page 1076*

1 • *What condition of the soul does Dickinson describe in this poem?*

2 • *What metaphor does Dickinson use for the soul? What meaning does the metaphor lend to the concept of soul?*

3 • *How does Dickinson use the lengths of the second and fourth lines of the stanzas to complement the shutting down of communication she describes in the poem?*

(1) The soul as imagined in this poem is independent of the will of a person because it ("she" in the poem) dictates the friendships and associations that the person might have. Thus the soul, after determining the associates, closes the door to others (line 2) and remains unmoved even by those with great power and prestige (stanza 2). So firm is the soul that it literally closes the person off from others, as though a stone (gravestone?) has been put into place between the person and the world.

(2) The metaphor is that the soul is a queen or even a goddess, living within a holy of holies which may be closed to prevent future communication with subjects ("her divine Majority," line 3), with busy people of the world pausing in chariots to seek admittance (lines 5 and 6), and even with "an Emperor" (line 7). The soul thus has great worth and value, being empowered to make one selection from everyone within the sphere of acquaintance (lines 9, 10). At the end, the metaphor of "valves of her attention" suggests that the soul is like a great organ playing all pipes from high to low. Once these valves are closed, however, the instrument becomes as silent as stone.

(3) In stanzas one and two these lines contain, respectively, four and then three words. In the last stanza, however, the lines are reduced to two words each, being, metrically, a spondee ("Choose

One," line 10) and a single iamb ("Like Stone," line 12). Rhythmically, this reduction creates emphasis upon the abruptness of the action and the simile with which the poem closes.

Success is Counted Sweetest *(J67, F112), page 1077*

1 • *Describe the main idea of this poem.*

2 • *What example is developed in lines 5–12? How does this example develop the idea of the first stanza?*

3 • *Describe Dickinson's use of metrical form in this poem. How does the form operate in the first stanza? In the second and third?*

4 • *Consider the nature of Dickinson's diction in this poem. Would you classify it as specific, general, concrete, abstract?*

(1) The main idea, stated in lines 1–2, is that those who do not achieve success would best be able to appreciate it, likely because people are always dissatisfied with what they have and always seem to want more. The topic is broadened not only to include success, but also victory and triumph.

(2) The example is drawn from the victor and vanquished on a battlefield. The image is that the person who has lost and is dying can define victory far more accurately than those who have taken "the Flag today." By extending the subject to the extremes of losing and dying, Dickinson emphasizes the regret, loss, envy, and disappointment that makes the loser benefit from the loss by gaining vision and understanding even in defeat. For comparison, see "My Triumph Lasted Till the Drums" (983).

(3) The pattern is a modified ballad measure, which should be *4x, 3b, 4x, 3b,* in quatrains. Only in line 5, however, does Dickinson provide a four-stress line. In all the other lines normally requiring four stresses she substitutes three. The measure operates normally in stanza one, where line 2 modifies the verb of line 1, and line 4 is the predicate of the subject in line 3. The last eight lines form a single sentence. Thus the measure of stanzas 2 and 3 is almost incidental to the formal pattern. It is as though Dickinson, to stress the idea of the defeated warrior, stretches the grammar along with the anguish.

(4) The diction is a combination of general and abstract, though the poem itself is concrete because of the situations. Thus *success* is abstract, and *those who ne'er succeed* is general. *Nectar* is specific, but here it is used as a symbol of the sweet drink of the gods, to be shared by mortals who achieve triumphs. The phrase *sorest need* is applicable to anyone who is trying to find success, and therefore it

is abstract. The flag is of course specific, and here it is a metonym for those who have won and accepted the flag of the vanquished as a token to their victory. In short, Dickinson's language is broadly meaningful; the success of the poem is created by the truth and the inclusiveness—the accuracy—of her observations.

Tell All the Truth but Tell It Slant *(J1129, F1263), page 1077*

1 • *What is this poem saying about truth? Why should truth be told "slant"?*

2 • *Describe the poem's concluding image. How true do you think the "slant" truth is?*

(1) Truth is truth, and it must be told. However, Dickinson is here playing with an idea that too much of a good thing can be harmful. Sometimes, in other words, it is better to "slant" the truth, and make the revelation come out slowly. People are often not receptive to the entire truth, for truth may force them into changes that they would not like to make, regardless of truth.

(2) The image of explaining the phenomenon of lightning to children makes clear that the truth may dazzle so much that the viewers of truth may go blind. It is not that people do not desire truth, but rather that they should grow accustomed to the light gradually. Therefore, being successful at persuading and informing people lies "in Circuit." That is, one should present the details gradually and in round-about ways, always aiming for complete revelation. Pope, in *An Essay on Criticism*, deals with the issue similarly, for while pointing out the need for "truth and candor" to shine, he states that "blunt truths" often do more harm than well considered "falsehoods." This is an interesting issue that students will want to discuss.

There's a Certain Slant of Light *(J258, F320), pages 1077–78*

1 • *How does the poem relate the "certain slant" of light to human mood and character?*

2 • *Describe the tone of the first stanza.*

3 • *Explain the line "Where the Meanings are" (line 8).*

4 • *What is the relationship of the last stanza's metaphors and simile to the principal idea of the poem?*

(1) The premise of the poem is that mood and character are not fixed but rather are continuously shaped by changing conditions. In this poem, the condition is a "certain slant of light" that is

disturbing, unsettling, and depressing. The hurt is not temporary, like the slant of light, but is a permanent "internal difference" that remains as a part of life's conditions, literally an "imperial affliction" from the universe.

(2) The tone is built up out of the swift movement from the reference to the slant of light to the weight, or "Heft," of "Cathedral Tunes." The shift from one sense—sight—to two others—the perception of weight and also the sound of music—creates surprise and also humor. Cathedral music is usually considered as dignified, but the choice of the word "Tunes" minimizes the sound, creating an anti-climax from the idea of "Heft." In addition, the reference to "Cathedral" is irreverent. These combinations create the complex tone that is both serious and comic.

(3) The meanings of life, as suggested in line 7, are all internalized, whether through the conscious process characteristic of much of our learning, or through the unconscious process suggested in this poem. The poem indicates that such meaning may not be perceived consciously; the effect of the certain slant of light is nevertheless real.

(4) In lines 13 and 14 there are two personifications: landscapes listen and shadows momentarily stop breathing. In lines 15 and 16 the simile is to the appearance of a dying person (the "Distance / On the look of Death"). These figures, joining landscape and death to the slant of light, are a climax to the main idea, suggesting both the universality and finality of the mood and feelings created on "Winter Afternoons."

This World Is Not Conclusion *(J501, F373), page 1078*

1 • What does the speaker mean by "This World is not Conclusion"?

2 • What does the speaker mean by "through a Riddle" in line 7?

3 • Explain the conclusion about the Tooth nibbling at the soul.

(1) The statement "This World Is not Conclusion" seems to be an outright claim of belief in life after death. There is no claim for a resurrection of the body, as would be consistent with certain orthodox Christian views of Heaven, but the speaker does note that the world after death is "invisible, as Music– / But positive, as Sound." These statements are made without qualification or ambiguity, unlike the ideas about Paradise in "I never Felt at Home–Below" (1073).

(2) The phrase "through a Riddle, at the last" is stated in the context of Philosophy that does not know, Sagacity that must go,

and scholars who are puzzled as they try to make guesses. Consistent with these situations of uncertainty, the riddle likely refers to some of the paradoxes that are expressed in the New Testament, such as the last being first (Mark 10:31 and elsewhere) and the need for losing one's life in order to find it (Matthew 16:25 and elsewhere). Dickinson does not explain the phrase any further, however, and readers must therefore make inferences about her meaning.

(3) The final two lines state that narcotics or painkillers cannot "still the Tooth / That nibbles at the soul." These lines are best understood in the context of the previous six lines. The narcotics seem to be A– the tenuous grasp at truth by Faith, B– the gesturing of preachers from their pulpits, and C– the strong Hallelujahs sung by congregations. These, the speaker implies, deter understanding of eternal life. The yearning for an afterlife, however, is never quite stilled in the individual, for it is constant and unremitting, like a toothache. In short, when all the claims of philosophy and theology fall short in persuading the individual that the world is not conclusion, the still small voice within is silently asserting this truth.

Wild Nights–Wild Nights *(Poem 249), page 1078*

1 • *How literally should the title, "Wild Nights," be taken?*

2 • *What is the reading and interpretation of "done" in lines 7 and 8?*

3 • *What is the metaphor of stanzas 2 and 3?*

4 • *In stanza 2 there are no complete sentences, and in stanza 3 the last two lines comprise a sentence in the subjunctive mode. Relate this relative incompleteness to the theme of the poem.*

(1) The title cannot be interpreted literally because it is general. However, *nights* in this context clearly signifies a time of love. Therefore the speaker is suggesting emotional, and also physical, abandon and release.

(2) The reading should probably be that once a person knows the satisfaction of unity with a loved one, there is no further need for the controls (the "chart" and "compass") that keep a person seeking for love and tentatively establishing and then relinquishing unsatisfactory relationships. Hence, chart and compass may be "done" away with.

(4) The metaphor is that of a ship going to port (line 6) and reaching a state of paradise (line 9). The metaphor is coextensive with lines 5–12, comparing the emotional identity (the "Heart" syn-

ecdoche in line 6) of an individual to a ship sailing to a safe and secure port. In this poem, the port is the *thee* of lines 2 and 12.

(5) The poem is about the speaker's yearning for the "thee" listener. Because the relationship does not exist, the poignancy of the unfulfilled desire is underscored by the absence of declarative sentences.

Edited Selections from Criticism of Dickinson's Poems, *pages 1079–1100*

Like the selections from Poe criticism (567), the selections from criticism of Emily Dickinson are intended collectively as a brief "casebook," with an emphasis on the poems included in the anthology. (There are also discussions of other Dickinson poems.) Writing topics may be drawn from the list on page 1067, to which you may add your own topics and changes. The selections will readily serve students as the basis for short research essays. The marginal page numbers provide the opportunity to use original pagination, and therefore the selections can give students experience with documenting research essays. For a detailed discussion of research, see Chapter 33 (1925).

■ Robert Frost, *pages 1100–1114*

A Line-Storm Song (1913), *page 1106*

1 • *Describe the relationship between the form of the poem and its subject matter.*

2 • *Describe Frost's use of natural references, amid which the speaker asks his loved one to join him in love.*

(1) This love song uses conventional rhyme and a varying pattern of rhythm, building what is essentially a hymnal stanza into eight-line units, and repeating its refrain at the ends of the first and last stanzas ("And be my love in the rain").

(2) For a love poem, the references are unique. There is no mention of moonlight and roses, but rather the flowers are "wet," clouds are "tattered and swift," waters are "aflutter," feet are "dry-shod," and the east wind is "whelming." Like a typical ballad, this poem tells the story of love that has persisted in all ages and times of human history. To the speaker, love is as old as the "ancient lands where" the sea has ebbed and flowed again and again ever since the early days of the world. The experience of love is like the sea's recovering the land,

a constantly repeating event that takes place "in the rain." Through this and other images of nature and natural forces (a storm-tossed world of silent birds and a wood-world filled with "torn despair"), the speaker allies the reemergence of love to the natural history of the world itself. The bold sweetness of the poem's sentiments is underlined by the power of the language describing the natural world in which love must emerge from storm and shower.

Mending Wall *(1914), pages 1106–1107*

1 • What is the setting and situation? Who are the characters?

2 • What is the neighbor's attitude toward walls? How did he get this attitude? What is he like?

3 • What is the speaker's attitude toward walls? How does Frost show that the speaker is ambivalent? How is the speaker different from the neighbor?

(1) The poem (in blank verse) isn't really about walls. Instead, it employs a specific action and situation to explore the differences between two types of personalities. The two characters—speaker and neighbor—are repairing the wall between their farms.

(2) The neighbor believes that "Good fences make good neighbors" (lines 27, 45); his views are conservative and traditional, inherited from his father (line 43). He is neither introspective nor philosophical; he does not question inherited wisdom.

(3) The speaker is much more philosophical, ironic, introspective, skeptical, and amused. He knows that walls can be silly or worse—"Something there is that doesn't love a wall"—but he is ambivalent about them; he calls the neighbor to start work (line 12) and helps rebuild the wall. The speaker's tone and attitude combine questioning with ironic humor and whimsy. These are reflected in the speaker's assertions that *a spell* must be used to make some stones balance, that wall-building is "just another kind of outdoor game," that his apple trees will never invade his neighbor's pines, and that the *Elves* knock walls down. The speaker is thus uneasy and unsure about walls; he makes quiet fun of his neighbor's attitude, but he recognizes the need for some walls and he helps rebuild this one year after year.

One might note that the line "Good fences make good neighbors," is often misquoted by people who attribute the idea to Frost, without realizing that it is really the benighted fence-mender who says it. Unfortunately, many writers are subject to similar misquoting—a hazard, probably, of having the ability to present an opposing view dramatically.

Birches *(1915), pages 1107–1109*

1 • *What two ways of bending birches does the speaker describe? Which way damages the trees? What does each way symbolize?*

2 • *What kind of escape from earthly care does the speaker want? Why is the word* toward *(line 56) in italic?*

(1) Bowed birches remind the speaker of two ways that trees can be bent: ice storms and swinging boys. The ice-storms (lines 5–20) damage the trees permanently; the birches "never right themselves." Such bending is harmful, destructive, symbolic of death. A child swinging on the birches (lines 21–40) does not do such damage; instead, such swinging, according to the speaker, takes "the stiffness out of them" (line 30).

(2) The speaker was once a "swinger of birches," and he dreams of returning to this pastime as a regenerative process, to escape from the earth (drudgery) for a while and then to "begin over" (line 50). Birch swinging symbolizes a temporary escape that will not break or damage the speaker permanently; he seeks escape and then return. The italic *toward* indicates the denial of permanent removal.

The Road Not Taken *(1915), page 1109*

This poem is one of those set to music by Randall Thompson in his 1941 *Frostiana* for chorus and piano. Along with "Stopping by Woods on a Snowy Evening" (673), it is one of the best known of Frost's poems.

1 • *What do the two roads symbolize? What is the speaker's attitude toward them? What must he decide?*

2 • *How are the roads different? Which does the speaker choose? Why?*

3 • *What does the speaker know about the unchosen road? What will be the effect of his choice?*

(1) This poem explores the idea that every choice we make determines what we are and what we will be. The two roads symbolize choices of direction—career, personal involvements, activities, development of character. Stanza 1 sets up the circumstances of the choice; the roads *diverged* and the speaker was *sorry* he could not choose both.

(2) Stanza 2 suggests that the two roads (choices) were almost equal, but there is a difference. The speaker picked the one that *wanted wear* and was *less traveled* (less conformist, traditional, normal, and popular).

(3) Stanza 3 takes up the inevitable closure produced by choice; the speaker saved the unchosen road "for another day," but he knew that he would never "come back" (face the same choice again) because "way leads on to way" (each choice leads on to subsequent choices predicated upon the first). All this is in the past; there is no present in the poem. In the last stanza, the speaker considers the impact of such choices on the future; although one choice may seem insignificant, it will have made "all the difference."

'Out, Out—' *(1916), page 1109–1110*

1 • *To what does the title allude? How does the allusion help shape meaning?*

2 • *What is the setting and situation? What types of imagery are employed here? What is the boy doing? What happens?*

3 • *Trace the poem's movement from accident to injury to death. How does the speaker make each seem accidental, surprising, and relatively insignificant?*

(1) The title is an allusion to Shakespeare's *Macbeth;* it is quoted from Macbeth's speech about the emptiness of life:

> Out, out, brief candle!
> Life's but a walking shadow, a poor player
> That struts and frets his hour upon the stage
> And then is heard no more. It is a tale
> Told by an idiot, full of sound and fury,
> Signifying nothing. (V.5.23–28)

The title thus suggests that the poem will explore the uncertainty and emptiness of life. Even without the allusion, this sense of unpredictability and uncertainty comes across.

(2) The setting and situation are set up in lines 1–8 with images of sound (onomatopoetic *snarled and rattled*), smell (*sweet-scented stuff*), and sight (dust, sticks, mountains). Our sense of the instant is expanded in lines 9–14; we learn that the day has been uneventful, work is over, and it's supper time. The boy's hand is severed by accident in one moment of inattention.

(3) The poem is structured by stages toward death; each one is unanticipated. The *rueful laugh* and the *spoiled* life are followed by fading pulse (*No one believed*) and then death. No one understands what is happening; the death, like the cut, is a product of chance. Those (we don't know who *they* are) who *turned to their affairs* underscore the insignificance and randomness of chance events.

The Oven Bird *(1916), page 1110*

1 • *What is the oven bird? What is the significance of the time of the bird's appearance? Why does the bird stop singing?*

2 • *What is the meaning of the final lines? How may they be interpreted as symbols?*

(1) The oven bird is apparently native to New England. Not all students have heard it, but they do know bird songs in general. The speaker introduces the bird as a creature of mid-summer and autumn ("the other fall we name the fall"). The call of the bird therefore signifies the changing of the season, from summer growth and fall harvest to the diminution of activity and the stasis of winter. After most birds have made their calls and created their nesting broods, they stop singing, but this one is different, and apparently continues singing (line 12).

(2) The concluding final lines are typical of Frost's carefully controlled symbolism. The "diminished thing" refers specifically to the loss of the harvest available to birds, but it also, symbolically, refers to reductions in the quality of human life—through age, changes in customs, reductions in the allocation of resources, and so on. The final lines are among Frost's most memorable.

Fire and Ice *(1920), page 1110*

1 • *What two types of cosmic destruction does the poem describe?*

2 • *With what emotions are fire and ice associated?*

(1) The title and lines 1–2 refer to two modes of ending the world; fire (war, apocalypse, being swallowed up by a gigantic explosion of the sun into a supernova) and ice (ice age, cooling, dying of the sun and the consequent extinction of all life).

(2) By extension, the poem investigates the destructive power of human passion (desire and hate) through the symbolism of cosmic destruction by fire or ice. Fire is linked with desire; ice with hatred. The speaker knows both, and knows that both are strong enough to end the world.

Misgiving *(1923), page 1111*

1 • *What do the leaves promise in spring? How are they changed by the fall?*

2 • *What do the leaves symbolize? The spring and fall? The wind?*

3 • *In what ways does the speaker hope to be different from the leaves?*

(1) In spring (youth), the leaves promise to travel with the wind. In fall (age), however, the leaves become *oppressed* by sleep (fear, reluctance) and they ask the wind to *stay with them.* Early promises of flight give way to a *vaguer and vaguer stir* or a *reluctant whir* that does not change or move the leaves.

(2) The poem investigates the human fear of the unknown (adventure, death) through the metaphor of leaves driven by the wind (the power of life, hope, aspiration). Stanzas 1–3 develop the metaphor and the leaves as a symbol for aging humanity.

(3) In the last stanza, which is a plaintive expression of hope, the speaker expresses the wish to be different and to have the courage to move *beyond the bounds of life* in question of knowledge when he is *free.*

Nothing Gold Can Stay *(1923), page 1111*

1 • What do the leaf, human history, and a single day have in common? In what sense do all begin in gold?

2 • What does "gold" symbolize? What happens to everything that is gold?

(1) The poem explores the idea that happiness, perfection, bliss (all symbolized by gold) cannot and will not endure. The apparent paradox of line 1 is based on the fact that buds appear to be gold rather than green.

(2) The speaker looks at the falling away from gold in nature, human history, and time. The leaf, humanity, and the day all begin in gold (bud, Eden, dawn) and decay quickly; perfection in any form lasts only for *an hour.*

Acquainted with the Night *(1928), pages 1111–12*

1 • What is the speaker like? What does he know? What has he done?

2 • What are the central symbols in the poem? How do they create meaning?

3 • What aspects of human existence does the poem reveal?

(1, 2) The speaker's acquaintance *with the night* suggests that he has experienced life's bitterness; *acquaintance* also implies cold knowledge rather than warm familiarity. Subsequent images (*rain, furthest city light, saddest city lane*) reinforce the initial symbol of night as sadness, misery, isolation. The watchman that the speaker passes suggests a denial of human contact and perhaps suspicion and guilt; the silence and *interrupted cry* (stanza 3) hint at isolation and violence.

The *luminary clock* (a lighted clock on a post or perhaps the moon) is detached and non-judgmental; it indicates that time is *neither wrong nor right.* The repetition of *I have* seven times, the repeated end rhyme, and the interlocking terza rima all pull the poem together. The rhymes (e.g., *beat/feet/street*) clinch ideas. The high number of end-stopped lines combined with the repetition suggests compression and sparseness.

(3) The poem, in iambic pentameter terza rima (*aba, bcb, cdc, dad, aa*), investigates the human dilemma of loneliness and isolation. Night is the central symbol for sadness, loneliness, and all the negative aspects of life.

Design *(1936), page 1112*

1 • *What three white objects are described in lines 1–8? What do they symbolize? What* design *do they suggest?*

2 • *What question does the speaker consider in lines 9–12? What answer does the closing couplet suggest? What does the answer imply about the cosmos?*

(1) The speaker uses the coincidence of three white things coming together in nature to imply that the universe is controlled by evil designs or by no intelligent plan at all. Frost uses a modified sonnet form (*abba, abba, acaa, cc*) to organize these ideas and to create a tight network of rhyme sounds that clinch ideas throughout. In lines 1–8, the speaker observes the deadly convergence of white flower, spider, and moth; all three ironically (because white) symbolize *death and blight* and evil (*witches' broth*).

(2) The third quatrain asks what brought these three things together; the idea of design is emphasized in the unnatural whiteness of a normal blue flower. The couplet answers the question: either malevolent intelligence (*design of darkness to appall*) or pure chaotic chance (*if design govern*).

The Silken Tent *(1936), page 1112*

1 • *Why is the first sentence of the poem a complete sentence, while all the other parts of the poem are modifying or subordinate elements to the first sentence?*

2 • *For what reasons does the speaker praise the loosely maintained power of the subject over "one" (line 12) while not praising her beauty.*

(1) In this poem, grammatically, the main clause is contained in the first sentence. One may observe that the image of the silken

tent, in which the tent is "loosely bound" by many cords, maintains its integrity without ever depending on one alone. The speaker's "slightest bondage," therefore (line 14) is complemented by the looseness of the grammatical ties. The achievement is pictorial and also quite remarkable.

(2) The beauty of the subject is not one of physicality. Nowhere does the speaker talk about his desire and about the extent of what he would do for his lady love. Rather the poem is about the character of the subject, who with great graciousness, no grand plan, and "countless silken ties of love and thought" (line 10) has established a connection with the speaker that points "heavenward" (line 6).

The Strong Are Saying Nothing *(1937), page 1113*

1 • *What situation is described in the first fourteen lines? What is the virtue of the references to the spring plowing and planting?*

2 • *A reader has asserted that the final two lines are abrupt and that they change the context of the poem so significantly that they are obscure. How justifiable is this criticism?*

(1) The poem is a well visualized picture of the activities of an agricultural spring. The "rumpling" of the soil is of course spring plowing; the hoe is used for certain "selected" seeds that are planted in the hopes of a summer harvest of table vegetables. The second stanza is particularly noteworthy in its presentation of an almost painterly vision of people in the fields working at their springtime tasks.

We should notice that the details of planting all refer to the earliest work that is done in the earliest spring, in the hopes that there will be no killing frosts to destroy the work. It may be too cold, for example, for the bees to arrive to carry on their springtime and summer tasks of pollinating blossoms for the summer fruiting of blooming vegetables and fruits. In short, all the tasks that Frost describes involve hope and anticipation; the world still looks barren, with "no cry of what is hoped to be."

(2) Therefore there is a connection between the first fourteen lines and the concluding two, even though the shift from agriculture to "little or much beyond the grave" may at first seem abrupt. The connection is that the seeds of faith must be sown even when there is no absolute certainty that they will ever reach harvest. The implication for assuming the existence of an afterlife is that it does not just happen. It must be cultivated during the life we have, just as the earliest spring preparation is needed if a good fall harvest is to be

obtained. Although the final two lines still may seem abrupt, they are nevertheless connected in this symbolic way.

Frost's final sentence preserves the symbolism of the early preparation of the earth. Just as springtime and summer growth, along with fall harvest, may occur, it is too early to judge what will happen until the conditions for harvest are actually seen. Thus, "the strong" will say nothing positive until they see more and learn more. This conclusion is negative in comparison with the final stanza in Frost's "Misgiving" (1111).

A Considerable Speck (Microscopic) *(1942), pages 1113–14*

1 • *What is the setting and situation? What does the speaker find on his paper? How does he deal with it? Why?*

2 • *To what extent do rhyme, meter, and diction contribute to tone and theme?*

3 • *How is "on any sheet the least display of mind" used with a double meaning?*

(1) The speaker finds a microscopic insect on his blank paper and after watching it for a time recognizes it as "an intelligence" (line 15). He therefore respects the mite, and does not swat it, as he otherwise might do.

(2) Frost's tone in "A Considerable Speck" is playful, ironic, and wry. He uses the crawling and insignificant insect as the cause for asserting that there is a general dearth of intelligence in the world. Tone is also established by the iambic meter, the rhymes (e.g., "ink-think," "feet-complete"), and the colloquial diction.

(3) The speaker spares the mite partly because it is innocent and partly because he is glad to find "On any sheet the least display of mind." The implication is that many written and printed things are mindless. When there are signs of mental excellence, however, such signs are worthy of study and preservation. This conclusion makes "A Considerable Speck" amusing and memorable.

Choose Something Like a Star *(1946), page 1114*

This poem is one of those set to music by Randall Thompson in his 1941 *Frostiana* for chorus and piano.

1 • *What is symbolized by "Something Like a Star"?*

2 • *Why does Frost include references to Fahrenheit and Centigrade?*

3 • *What can the star do to prevent us from being swayed by "the mob," which may be "swayed /To carry praise or blame too far"?*

(1) The star represents ideals and aspirations, something that is like Shakespeare's "ever fixèd mark" in the sonnet "Let Me Not to the Marriage of True Minds" (903) and also, of course, "Keats' Eremite, which Frost specifically mentions in line 18 (779). The idea is that we as human beings are adrift unless we have something fixed and unchanging for guidance.

(2) Frost knew a great deal about science, and spoke with many of the leading scientists of his day. For example, he spoke with Edwin Hubble, whose name and achievement have been enshrined in the orbiting Hubble space telescope, about the expanding universe and the probable way in which the solar system and the universe would end. His response to his conversations with Hubble was to write the poem "Fire and Ice" (1110). So his references to systems of measuring heat here refer to his characteristic desire to create poems based in specific things. Perhaps comically, when we say "I burn," then, we should not be overly emotional and inexact, but should rather be specific about what we are doing. Hence, Frost points out that our ideals should never permit us to go too far into irrationality, but should always keep us balanced through an observation of fact and theory.

(3) These phrases refer to the dangers of going overboard politically in favor of slogans for or against candidates. Accepting everything one party says may push us in the direction of dictatorial power, and promoting hate against another party may cause damage. It is our ideals—"Something Like a Star"—that give us something to stay our minds on, even if some might claim that such middle positions might be unexciting and even "staid."

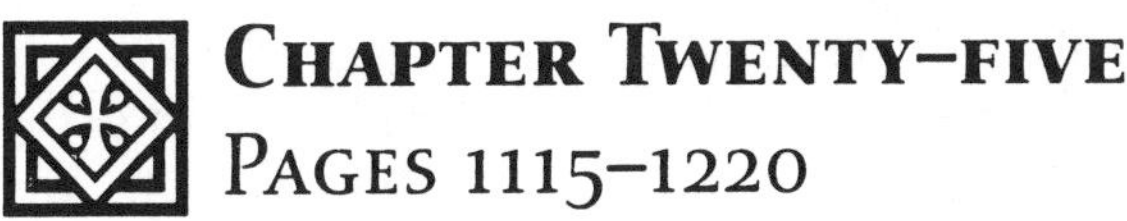

Chapter Twenty-five
Pages 1115–1220

Poems for Additional Study

A. R. Ammons, *80-Proof*, *pages 1118-19*

This poem combines humor and seriousness. The poet is writing in a comic mode. Ammons's speaker determines the composition of his body based on a weight of 175 pounds, and concludes that he himself is only a fifth of that—35 pounds. All the rest consists of matter such as "steaks & chops & / chicken fat." Inasmuch as poets often employ poetry to determine their own identities and their place in the universe, the speaker's self-analysis creates laughter and surprise. The stress on the word "fifth" (lines 1, 19) refers not only to the fraction of the speaker's body that is himself, but also to a bottle of whiskey. The concluding ambiguity on "100 % spiritual" therefore refers both to the mind or soul and also to spirituous liquor.

Maya Angelou, *My Arkansas*, *page 1119*

Angelou explores her own reactions ("My Arkansas" rather than simply "Arkansas") to a state deeply scarred by racial strife. Arkansas' history of violence against African Americans disturbs the speaker's perceptions of the land and nature. The "old crimes" that "pend from poplar trees" describe lynchings. The "sullen earth" (see Shakespeare's "When in Disgrace," page 1198) is "red" with clay and blood. In stanza 2, the speaker observes that the history of racism has eroded even the light shining on the land, and, if light may be construed as a symbol of tolerance and intelligence, the land is yet to be illumined. In stanza 3, she states that racial hatred and attitudes ("ante-bellum lace") of the past are still very much alive. Indeed, the past is still the present, and the present is "yet to come."

Anonymous, *Barbara Allan*, *pages 1119*
Anonymous, *Lord Randal*, *pages 1121–22*
Anonymous, *The Three Ravens*, *pages 1122–23*
Anonymous, *Waly, Waly*, *pages 1123–24*

These late renaissance and neo-classical narrative popular ballads tell of both horrible and touching events. Barbara Allan, by slighting a young swain, has caused his death, and his death is causing hers. Lord Randal is poisoned by his true love. The sweetheart of the dead warrior in "The Three Ravens" quickly joins him in death. The young woman bemoans the disappearance of her lover and the loss of her innocence and virtue. All the narratives present only the high points and concluding scenes. Commonly, there is much dialogue to make the poems dramatic. In "Lord Randal" the mother asks questions and the son answers. In "Barbara Allan" the sick swain and Barbara Allan engage in dialogue, and the last stanza is Barbara's farewell to life. In "The Three Ravens," the three birds observe and describe the sad drama unfolding below them. In "Waly, Waly" the speaker tries to will death upon herself because of her shame and heartbreak.

An important technique of the ballad, in light of the fact that there are many stanzas and that interest must be preserved, is the dramatic delay in the disclosure of what has happened. Thus, the guilt must build in Barbara Allan before she, like her slighted lover, succumbs to death. The last will and testament of Lord Randal, the mention of which is delayed until the final stanza, indicates that his death has been caused by his sweetheart. The drama of the "lemman" and the knight unfolds as one of the birds describes the place of death as a potential spot where they may obtain food, and where they will be opposed by the hawk, the hounds, and the sweetheart as long as she lives.

The ballads commonly have a refrain, which may be like the *With a down, derry, derry, derry, down, down* of "The Three Ravens" or the varying repetitions in "Barbara Allan." These refrains may be integrated with the action of the narrative, or they may serve as brief interludes separating the stanzas of narrative and dialogue. Interestingly, the traditional music of "Waly, Waly" has been used in modern folk songs and also, perhaps surprisingly, has been adapted for church anthems.

ANONYMOUS (NAVAJO), *Healing Prayer from the Beautyway Chant,* pages 1120–21

This poem is, as the title indicates, a chant, designed to be sung and danced by Navajo healers to assist a sick person in the pathway to recovery. Notice the imagery of enveloping or surrounding (East, South, West, North), and notice how all the images are positive. The word "beauty" has many connotations as it figures in this chant. Beauty is not confined to physical beauty, but also implies health, happiness, healing, reconciliation, peacefulness, optimism, and love of the "highest heavens and the lowest lands."

Anonymous, *Waly, Waly*

See the discussion, above, of the anonymous ballads.

Margaret Atwood, *Variation on the Word "Sleep,"* page 1124

This is a love poem of intense longing. Using the phrase "I would like to" over and over, like an incantation, the speaker conveys deep emotion, creating thereby a continuous motif of desire. Wanting to enter into the loved one's sleep—one of the most personal and intimate of experiences—shows the intensity of the speaker's wish. There is tenderness in the way going to sleep is presented—like entering a waterworld of beauty in motion—emphasized by the speaker's desire to protect the loved one against whatever might be fearful in the dream. Finally, the speaker's wish to be as necessary and as natural to the loved one as the very air he/she breathes tells us that the speaker wants to be essential to life of the loved one. A major achievement of the poem is that it conveys so passionate a desire with such simplicity and calm.

W. H. Auden, *The Unknown Citizen,* page 1125

Auden employs an ironic tone and sociological jargon to satirize the loss of identity and individuality in modern society. The epitaph and the poem are spoken by a representative of the state, who identifies the citizen by number rather than name. The speaker knows the citizen's statistics thoroughly, and he praises the citizen's tendency to conform in all matters. The citizen's work habits, social behavior, consumption, and ideology were all known and normal. He had the right appliances ("everything necessary to the Modern Man"), opinions, and number of children. In most respects, the citizen is certainly not "unknown" in the sense of "unknown soldier." But the state cares nothing about the inner man ("Was he free?" "Was he happy?"). In this sense, the citizen is *unknown.* While the speaker's tone is smug and admiring, the tone of the poem is ironic and contemptuous. The poet deplores modern dehumanization and conformity. Auden also uses the rhyme to create the tone and clinch ideas; note that even the epitaph rhymes (*78/State*). For comparison, see Howard Nemerov's "Life Cycle of Common Man" (1179).

Imamu Amiri Baraka (LeRoi Jones), *Ka 'Ba,* pages 1125–26

The poem contrasts the beauty of black lives and the glory of the African-American heritage with the enslavement and degradation encountered by blacks in the society of the United States. African Americans defy the chains and limitations of their world ("dirty courtyards," "physics," "grey chains in a place full of winters") through "the stream of their will." Although they suffer, kill, and fail, their world is vital and lovely. Their heritage is freedom, sunlight, and Africa. At the close, the speaker wonders what "magic spells" or "sacred words" will restore African Americans to themselves and their "ancient image." Compare this poem to Gwendolyn Brooks's "Primer for Blacks" (1128), which also deals with the problem of black self-images.

Wendell Berry, *Through the Weeks of Deep Snow,* *page 1126*

The main metaphor of this brief, direct, and optimistic poem is that snow, with its seasonal cold and its muffling of life ("root and leaf"), alienates the "we" of the poem (line 3). Therefore, the season of snow creates "only air and weather / for our difficult home" (lines 5, 6). The advent of early spring in March marks a real renewal of life and light, and the "we" can once again be metaphorically linked to the earth. The connection of human life to natural life is thus a major idea in the poem.

Earle Birney, *Can. Lit.,* *pages 1126–27*

The speaker blames Canadian history and habits for the dearth of great Canadian literature. The first stanza establishes a metaphor based on birds that fly away. The vast spaces of Canada and the ongoing *civil war* between the French and the English subverted the impulse to develop great national poets such as Dickinson or Whitman (both of whom are named in the poem). Energy has gone into conflict and control instead of literature.

Louise Bogan, *Women,* *page 1127*

"Women" explores the idea that women, placed in a largely dependent position, have assumed a character that is self-limiting and self-demeaning. In a world where they have no responsibility, and where men make decisions, women withdraw into the "tight hot cell" of themselves (like an oven) and do not experience life fully. They are passive ("wait") and lack flexibility or moderation ("stiffen," "Too tense, or too lax"). The concluding stanza is reminiscent of the "Alice Ben-Bolt" type of woman ("She shook with delight when you gave her a smile, / But trembled with fear at your frown."), but the speaker implies in the last two lines—but only implies, for this is not a revolutionary poem—that women would be better off if they would let this sort of life "go by"; i.e., stop giving in to the circumstances of exclusive domesticity and self-effacement that are suppressing them.

Arna Bontemps, *A Black Man Talks of Reaping,* *page 1128*

This lyric is a truncated sonnet (*abab, cdcd, efef*). The quatrains organize the speaker's thoughts and feelings. The poem expresses the sorrow and bitterness of black existence. The central metaphors are sowing (i.e., labor of any sort, but usually "stoop labor") and reaping (wealth, happiness, reward, advancement). The speaker observes the vast extent of his own sowing (lines 1–6), the meagerness of his harvest (7–8), and the fact that his "brother's sons" (i.e., white brother's sons) benefit from his labor (9–10) while his own children (people, blacks) collect the leavings in fields "they have not sown, and feed on bitter fruit." The poem thus implies that African Americans labor in vain, since they are excluded from reward or advancement of any kind. This point is underscored by the absence of the last two lines, indicating graphically the lack of reward about which the poem speaks.

Anne Bradstreet, *To My Dear and Loving Husband,* *page 1128*

The poem is unusual because it is about the fulfillment the speaker finds in married love, for usually love poems are about the love, yearning, and dedication of unmarried lovers who speak more about their own feelings than about their objective assessments of their loved ones. The poem is also unusual because the speaker is a woman praising her husband. She speaks of the closeness, passion, and value of their love, which seems so strong that she intimates that her concept of immortality is to continue loving her husband "when we live no more" (line 12). For comparison, see Elizabeth Barrett Browning's "Sonnet 43: How Do I Love Thee" (1130), the conclusion of which is similar to that of Bradstreet's poem.

Gwendolyn Brooks, *Primer for Blacks,* *pages 1128–30*

Brooks is a black whose first audiences were mostly white. In 1967 she began directing her work toward black readers. This poem reflects that shift; it attacks African Americans for self-denigration and low self-esteem ("self-shriveled"), and asserts that blackness is power and glory. The speaker castigates the "slack in Black" who believe that "It's great to be White." The speaker argues that African Americans have geographic power, and she concludes that all blacks must learn to find value and strength in their blackness.

Elizabeth Barrett Browning, *How Do I Love Thee,* *page 1130*

This is the most famous of Elizabeth Browning's *Sonnets from the Portuguese*. Her speaker describes the abundance of her love with reference to infinite spaces and abstract ideas ("the ends of Being"). In the second quatrain, the love is measured against daily necessities ("quiet need") and ideals of freedom and purity. In lines 9–12, the speaker asserts that her entire life expresses her love; she loves with a child's faith and with all her "breath." Lines 13–14 suggest that the love will continue after death. Note that the speaker describes her own attitudes and dedication, and says nothing at all about specific qualities of the husband. Compare this poem with Bradstreet's "To My Dear and Loving Husband" (1128).

Robert Browning, *Soliloquy of the Spanish Cloister,* *pages 1130–32*

This poem is a masterpiece in the mode of the dramatic monologue. As the speaker, a cloistered priest or monk, talks himself alive, he also reveals that he is a fish out of water, a man filled with anger and contradictions. The poem is simultaneously comic and frightening; the speaker is a monster of envy, but he does not know it. He is in the same order with "Brother Lawrence," but he believes that Lawrence's apparent indifference to lovely women is a cover for lechery. In fact, however, the speaker is projecting his own desires onto Lawrence, for it is he, the speaker, who speaks longingly of "Dolores" and "Sanchicha" as they wash their hair in the tank outside the "Convent bank." To gain revenge on Lawrence, he states that he intends to hide his pornographic novel, open to a particularly juicy part, amid Lawrence's harvest, to get him damned by seeing the profane text (whose book is it, and who will be damned by looking at it?). The speaker has other schemes, all of which contrast sharply with his ordained role of monk. Of course, Lawrence is a virtual saint, while the speaker shows himself to be in a state of anger, envy, hatred, suppressed lust, and hypocrisy. A similar poem by Browning is "The Bishop Orders His Tomb at St. Praxed's Church."

George Gordon, Lord Byron, *The Destruction of Sennacherib,* *pages 1132–33*

This poem is the best known of the poems in Byron's *Hebrew Melodies* (1815), the last major work he published before he left England, to remain in virtual exile until his death. The poem demonstrates Byron's virtuosic metrical skill, being almost entirely in anapests, with occasional amphibrachs and iambs as substitute feet. Byron's opening simile, comparing a wolf attacking a sheepfold to the Assyrian army attacking the Hebrews, is striking, filled as it is with the implication of the innocent and helpless sheep and the vicious attacker. The power of human warriors, however, is nothing before Divine power, for it is the "Angel of Death" which lays the Assyrian host low. In the final stanza, Byron mentions the "widows of Ashur" who lament their dead. But by returning quickly to the supposed falsity of the Assyrian religion ("the temple of Baal"), Byron avoids concentrating on the fact that the Assyrians were people too, with homes, wives, and responsibilities, and that their deaths might be cause for pity and sorrow. Instead, he concludes on the note that God will protect the Chosen People against war and injustice. Ogden Nash, in "Very Like a Whale" (868), parodies Byron's metaphor of the wolf on the fold.

Thomas Campion, *Cherry Ripe*, *page 1133*

Campion himself set many of his poems to music, this among them. Those listening to a musical rendition, however, would need to pay close attention upon first hearing, for the text is complex. The basic metaphor of the poem is the garden, which stands for the lady's beauty—a conventional comparison. The roses are her cheeks, the lilies her skin, along with other metaphors to suggest her beauty and desirability. The cry "cherry ripe" was apparently commonly used during the Renaissance by fruit sellers to advertise their wares. In the poem, it suggests that no one may have the fruit (i.e.. kiss the lady's lips) unless she herself declares her willingness, perhaps when she is mature, perhaps when in love. At first, the poem therefore seems to suggest that the lady's beauty might be for sale. But by the last stanza we have seen that her beauty brings the need for wise decisions about where she will give her love. The poem is thus a morality lesson, one which shows surprising respect for a woman's freedom of choice and destiny.

Lucille Clifton, *this morning*, *page 1134*

Prosodically, this poem is an exercise in rhythm and emphasis. The topic is self-recognition and pride in oneself. Whereas at an earlier time a black might be ashamed of the African background, now this heritage is one of which the speaker is proud ("i met myself / coming in / a bright / jungle girl"). The speaker goes on to compare herself metaphorically with a "black bell" that rings out her vitality for all to hear and see. "Bell" may also be a pun on "belle," for the speaker's sense of identity encompasses and comprises all images of beauty and joy.

Lucille Clifton, *the poet*, *page 1134*

In this brief poem of six lines the speaker cites a number of reasons for which she creates poetry. She would like to be restrained, but poetry is in her bones, in her very being, and her need for expression is spinning and churning at the center of her existence. Though she has fears of seeming foolish, her poetry is like a dance that she must perform. Indeed, she cannot separate her art from her life, despite the obstacles she might encounter.

LEONARD COHEN, *'The killers that run . . .',* *pages 1134–35*

The poem is deeply ironic, even cynical, and somewhat comic for this reason. There are killers in the world, all of them wanting to kill everyone else, but the speaker states that he wants to keep the killers he has rather than accept killers "that run / the other countries." The reluctance to accept foreign killers leads him to become "a patriot" to prevent killers from invading us. Thus, engaging in demonstrations with burning flags is not acceptable because it "excites / the killers on either side /to unfortunate excess / which goes on gaily / quite unchecked / until everyone is dead." The speaker is not expressing a systematic political philosophy, but certainly is speaking about a practical one.

BILLY COLLINS, *Days,* *pages 1135–36*

"Days" is a reminder of just how much of "a gift, no doubt" each day is that we are priviliged to live. The major simile in the poem, beginning with line 14, is that of the high stack of dishes that "entertainers used to build on stage." The simile is symbolically perfect, for it emphasizes both the tenuousness and fragility of life. There is no guarantee of another day, and we hold our breath as we put each day's cup on "yesterday's saucer." When we hear not "the slightest clink" we go on with the day, but we are always atop a "tall ladder."

FRANCES CORNFORD, *From a Letter to America on a Visit to Sussex,* *page 1136*

The situation of the poem is that the speaker has been in the countryside of Sussex in England during the Second World War, which was at its height in 1942 for England. The United States had just recently entered the war, and a victorious outcome in those days was by no means certain. The speaker describes a situation of maneuvers being carried out in this countryside. She sees a gunner hiding "in the gorse" (i.e., high grass), and also sees a tank. However, in the last seven lines she puts the situation in perspective. She draws attention to the fact that the relatively harmless maneuvers have dire consequences. She points out that the ancient Greek furies may come out of the air instead of "our Squadron's wings," and the soldier she has seen in the gorse may "lie beside his gun / His mud-brown tunic gently staining red." The final perspective is that the earth and nature are relatively unconcerned about human conflicts, for, no matter what soldiers do in warfare, "larks get on with their old job of singing."

STEPHEN CRANE, *Do Not Weep, Maiden, for War Is Kind,* *page 1137*

The poem is a strong and ironic anti-war statement. Stanzas 1, 3, and 5 focus on the losses and deaths produced through war: A maiden loses her lover (lines 1–5), a baby loses her father (lines 12–16), and a mother loses her son (lines 23–26). There is nothing "kind" about the losses or about war. Stanzas 2 and 4 mock the symbols of passion that encourage war: booming drums, unexplained glory, the blazing flag of the regiment, the eagle on the flag. Both stanzas close with the same image of war's reality: "A field where a thousand corpses lie." The realities of carnage and loss are thus contrasted with the illusions of ideals. Compare this poem with Cornford's "From a Letter to America" (1136), Owen's "Dulce et Decorum Est" (810) and cummings's "next to of course god america i" (1012).

COUNTÉE CULLEN, *Yet Do I Marvel,* *pages 1137–38*

Cullen, a poet of the Harlem Renaissance, was a pioneer in dealing with topics concerning the conditions and aspirations of African Americans. In this poem, which is in the Shakespearean sonnet form, Cullen's speaker uses each of the quatrains to take up a different aspect of the mysteries of God's ways. In the first, the speaker questions the necessity of death. "Good" and "kind" are ironic, and "well-meaning" suggests less than ideal results. The allusions to the myths of Tantalus and Sisyphus (lines 5–8) emphasize the futility of existence; these men are fated never to complete their assigned tasks. The third quatrain explores humanity's inability to understand any of God's purposes. The couplet offers the most mysterious and paradoxical problem—a black poet asked to "sing" (write poetry) out of the bleak wretchedness of black existence; this is the mystery of God's demands that the speaker finds most remarkable.

E. E. CUMMINGS, *if there are any heavens,* *page 1138*

This is a successful poem about a topic—love for one's mother—that is frequently sentimental. Without claiming that he/she loves dear old Mom, the speaker conveys a deeper affection. The setting is a heaven that the speaker's mother will have "all by herself." (Although the poem does not explain why the mother might be deserving of her own heaven, we might assume that it is a reward for hardships, perhaps caused by the speaker, tolerated in life.) This heaven will not be strewn with pansies or fragile lilies of the valley, but rather will be filled with "blackred roses" (line 4). The scene visualized is one in which the mother will almost be holding court, as if she were a queen, with the speaker's father standing by, "swaying over her / silent." The final three lines capture a sudden scene of respect and adoration, and the poem ends strongly. Because cummings is often ironic, some critics have claimed irony here, but this poem seems straightforward, without ironic complications. It is a masterly personal tribute. Compare this poem with Serotte's "My Mother's Face" (1196).

JAMES DICKEY, *Kudzu*, *pages 1138–40*

Kudzu is a plant used for animal food and forage in its native countries of China and Japan. It was imported into this country for experimental purposes, and, naturally, got out of hand, just as creatures like the Starling and the Gypsy Moth did. In the United States kudzu is invasive, covering native shrubs, bushes, and trees, and starving out its host plants. In much of "Kudzu," Dickey describes the habits of this plant, telling the story that in Georgia, "the legend says / That you must close your windows / At night to keep it out of the house" (lines 9–11). Dickey's speaker notes that kudzu covers telephone poles, houses, cows, and pigs, and that its confines offer a perfect hiding place for poisonous snakes. Dickey observes how an organized group of men uses sticks to destroy the hiding snakes. As a final insult of the plant, the speaker notes, kudzu becomes ugly and black when it freezes. The kudzu may be taken as a symbol for the invasiveness of foreign plants upon native American *flora,* but it may also be read as a symbol of similarly invasive foreign—specifically Japanese—industrial products. The conclusion is a general one: There are terrors within and without, and kudzu is one of the most prominent of external terrors. The poem is characteristic of Dickey's poetic craft, for it exhibits a good deal of description, with an accent on the violent, dangerous, and threatening.

JAMES DICKEY, *The Lifeguard*, *pages 1140–41*

In this poem about death, guilt, and resurrection, the speaker-lifeguard becomes a Christ figure in his own dream vision. Stanza 1 establishes setting and situation. The children (probably at summer camp) are asleep at night; the lifeguard is alone, lying in a boat tied up in a boathouse. In stanza 2, he walks on the water in quest of the miracle of resurrection. Stanzas 3–6 flash back to an earlier failure at salvation (saving a drowning child that afternoon). Although the children had faith, the speaker failed to save the "one who had sunk from my sight" despite many attempts to see and recover the dead child. Stanza 4 is full of images of cold, water, dark, and death, while stanza 5 conveys the speaker's "defeat" and the children's disappointment. In stanza 6, the speaker hides in the boathouse awaiting night and the moon reflected on the water. Stanzas 7–10 embody the present dream (or reality) of resurrection; the lifeguard walks to the center of the lake to be the "savior of one who has already died in my care." He calls out; the child answers and rises from the depths. The child of "water" can represent either rebirth (and baptism) or illusion (and death).

James Dickey, *The Performance*, *pages 1142–43*

This poem is a product of the Pacific theater of World War II between the United States and Japan from 1941 to 1945. Early in the war the Japanese invaded and occupied the Philippine Islands, and many Americans were captured and were subject to atrocities. Dickey's speaker tells the story about one of the captive pilots, Donald Armstrong. In relaxed moments before his capture, the speaker says, Armstrong had performed physical feats like standing on his head. When captured by the Japanese he continued to do this exercise, even though he was about to be beheaded. Ironically, the speaker points out that the executioner would just as soon have cut off Armstrong's feet as his head, except that Armstrong, after having dug his own grave, knelt before it with dignity to receive the blow.

"The Performance" hence demonstrates, on the one hand, the sort of violence that characterizes Dickey's well-received novel *Deliverance* (1970), and on the other, the courageousness of a human being, insisting on his individuality and rights even against the greatest odds. Readers may note that the name "Armstrong" is the name of the radio hero "Jack Armstrong" of the 1930s and 1940s. To the highest degree, this name embodied the idea of the "All-America Boy," who excelled in all athletic competition and carried this excellence into all avenues of life.

John Donne, *The Good Morrow*, *page 1143*

The speaker (a lover) praises his beloved and their passion by comparing them favorably to all his previous romances; he sees their previous lives as a sleep or infancy. The *good morrow* refers to the awakening of their love and the actual events—two lovers awakening in bed. The second stanza takes up the power of love—it controls emotion and perception—and begins an extended conceit on the image of *worlds*. The speaker creates a clear distinction between the public world (*sea-discoverers, new worlds, maps*), and the private world of the lovers that becomes an *everywhere.* The one world of the lovers becomes two (line 14) and then the two *hemispheres* of eyeballs reflecting faces (lines 15–16), finally resolving back into a single world *Without sharp North, without declining West* (line 18). The tone is exaggerated and affirmative; love and passion are presented as valuable and powerful.

John Donne, *Holy Sonnet 6: This Is My Play's Last Scene,* *page 1144*

This Petrarchan sonnet (*abba abba cdcd ee*) is a meditation on death and salvation. The first two quatrains focus on the moment of death, which is evoked by seven metaphors that imply an ending. The body will become earth, but the soul will see God's face. The last six lines focus on salvation and the purgation of sin. The form of the sonnet organizes the meditation and the ideas; the rhymes (e.g., *evil/devil*) emphasize the meaning.

John Donne, *Holy Sonnet 7: At The Round Earth's Imagined Corners,* *page 1144*

Like most of Donne's Holy Sonnets, this one begins as a meditation on a specific moment—the apocalypse and Judgment Day. Lines 1–8 (*abba abba*) create a vivid and immediate image of bodies rising from their graves for judgment; lines 5–8 contain a catalogues of those who will rise from the dead or more directly to judgment from life. In lines 9–14, the sestet, (*cdcd ee*), the speaker reflects on his own spiritual corruption; he prays for more time to repent his sins and to seek God's grace.

John Donne, *Holy Sonnet 10: Death Be Not Proud,* *page 1145*

This is Donne's best-known sonnet. A meditation on death and salvation, its apparent paradoxes are all resolved by the idea of death as the beginning of eternal life. In this respect, it might be compared with Shakespeare's Sonnet 146, "Poor Soul" (1198).

The rhyme scheme here organizes the poem into three quatrains and a couplet. The first two quatrains are linked by repeated rhymes (iambic pentameter: *abba, abba, cddc, ee*). In the first quatrain, the speaker characterizes death as needlessly proud, for death really does not have the power to "overthrow" or "kill" anyone. The second quatrain presents two interesting put-downs of death. The speaker claims that death is only another version of "rest and sleep," which are both sources of pleasure. Then, he argues that the "best men" go to death "soonest," implying that death creates a state that people should not fear but envy. The speaker continues to belittle death in the third quatrain, observing that it is controlled by ("slave to") "fate, chance, kings, and desperate men" and resides with "poison, war, and sickness." The paradox in the couplet resolves in the realization that death is the way to eternal life. Donne's sonnet thus explores the idea that death is powerless and insignificant compared to salvation and Divine Grace.

Donne's rhymes are mostly exact and rising, thus helping to make the poem both powerful and memorable. Interesting (and often antithetical) rhyming pairs include "thee-me-be-delivery," "dwell-well," and "eternally-die." The last rhyme, occurring in the couplet, sums up the basic opposition that runs through the poem as a theme. One might recall that the rhyme might still have been exact in Donne's time, for the "Great Vowel Shift" had not fully effected the diphthong sound of / *ay* / that we pronounce today.

JOHN DONNE, *A Hymn to God the Father,* *page 1145*

This poem, a prayer spoken to God, is a confession of sins in which the speaker catalogues his own corruption and seeks divine grace. An important pun is the traditional one on sun-son (*Thy sun* = Son). The speaker's sins are listed in lines 1–14; the request for grace is voiced in lines 15–18. The central pun is on *done* (Donne). In stanzas 1–2, God's work is not *done* and God has not redeemed Donne because the speaker has *more* (sins). Some scholars suggest that *more* is also a pun on the name of Donne's wife (Anne More).

JOHN DONNE, *Song: Go and Catch a Falling Star,* *page 1146*

The theme here is that no woman can be *fair* (beautiful) and *true* (loyal, honest) at the same time. The speaker lists a series of impossible tasks in stanza 1 to establish an aura of cynicism and difficulty. Some of these (envy, the lack of advancement for honest minds) evoke social ills. The second stanza introduces the impossibility of the woman who is both true and fair. The third reinforces this cynical view by claiming that such a woman would become *false* before the speaker could meet her. The lyric is composed of three stanzas, each of which combines a quatrain, couplet, and triplet into a single sentence (iambic, *4a 4b 4a 4b 4c 4c 1d 4d*); the pattern of stanza 1 is repeated in 2 and 3. Rhyme (e.g., *singing/stinging*) and the short seventh and eighth lines of each stanza are especially effective.

MICHAEL DRAYTON, *Since There's No Help,* *pages 1146–47*

This English or Shakespearean sonnet, spoken by a male lover to his mistress, captures the moment in which their relationship is about to fall apart. While the poem may be somewhat difficult for students, it deals with easily understandable feelings. In the first quatrain, the relationship seems doomed and the speaker seems resigned (and even "glad") about it. The second quatrain continues in the same vein. Here, however, a claim might be made that the speaker is protesting too much. His hyperbole is shown in words like "forever," "all our vows," and "not one jot." We get a clearer view of the speaker's feelings in lines 9–14, where he claims that his mistress could save the relationship. He is willing, and needs her words to save their love, which like a dying person ("bed of death") will expire without her saving intervention. The tone of the sonnet thus shifts from the apparently cavalier "you get no more of me" of line 2, to the hopeful "From death to life thou mightst him yet recover" of line 14.

Paul Laurence Dunbar, *Sympathy*, *page 1147*

This lyric voices the emotions and desires of African Americans in general and of a black poet in particular. The caged bird symbolizes blacks and the black poet. The bird's imprisonment metaphorically captures the essence of black status. Stanza 1 contrasts the bird's cage (imposed limitations) with natural freedom and beauty. Stanza 2 expresses the bird's driving desire to be free. Stanza 3 identifies the bird's song (a traditional symbol of poetry) as a plea for freedom. Compare Cullen's "Yet Do I Marvel" (1137).

T. S. Eliot, *The Love Song of J. Alfred Prufrock*, *pages 1147–51*

This poem is difficult but rewarding. It offers a splendid opportunity to examine speaker, setting and situation, imagery, metaphor, allusion, and theme. The dramatic monologue is spoken by Prufrock (the name is both a pun [on "prudish"] and a parody [of elegant names]), a man who feels trapped in the hell of his own inadequacies (hence the epigraph from Dante's *Inferno*).

The dramatic situation is that Prufrock, a cultured man going to an afternoon tea, is consumed with an "overwhelming question" of whether or not to make a proposition to one of the cultured women taking "toast and tea" (hence the ironic title "Love Song"). His reluctance, indecision, and fear of rejection dominate lines 1–83. The "you and I" in line 1 have been variously identified as Prufrock and a friend, Prufrock and the reader, or Prufrock and himself (perhaps even Prufrock's ego and superego or desires and self-consciousness). The metaphor of evening as an etherized patient (lines 2–3) suggests Prufrock's difficulty in dealing with his feelings. This is contrasted throughout the poem with the sexual life of the lower classes ("cheap hotels"), almost always linked with water images ("oyster shells") that suggest sexual activity.

The impending visit and the "overwhelming question," combined with Prufrock's ongoing impulse to revise, rethink, and retreat, recur as the central *motif* of the first section of the poem in lines 10–14, 25–31, 46–49, and 79–83. Failure, reticence, and withdrawal, the crisis of the poem, occurs in lines 84–86: Prufrock has been "afraid." He rationalizes and justifies his failure in lines 87–111, assuming that his approach would have been out of place, badly done, misunderstood, and rejected. He imagines that the woman to whom he spoke would have told him that "That is not what I meant at all."

In the last twenty lines, Prufrock offers an accurate assessment of his own present and future. The *Hamlet* metaphor (lines 111–119) identifies him as an insignificant and foolish character, far removed from the vital centers of life. He realizes that life and time have passed him by. The mermaids (sea imagery, sexuality) represent a fulfillment that Prufrock will never have ("I do not think that they will sing to me"—one of the most sorrowful lines in modern poetry). He can experience such vision in his dreams (lines 125–130), but *human voices* (reality, society, responsibility) remind him of his failures and inadequacies.

James Emanuel, *The Negro*, *page 1151*

This poem is even more cryptic than the dramatically presented "We Real Cool" of Gwendolyn Brooks, with which it may be compared (858). In classroom discussion, students can bring out the poem's ideas but may need leading questions to do so.

In lines 1–4, the attribute of the black is "invisibility." In other words, the black is not visible because he has never had a chance to develop knowledge, character, and identity. Lines 5 and 6 bring out the traditional servile role in which blacks have been cast. Lines 7 and 8 refer to the wasteful and destructive ways of life pursued by many blacks because they were denied more fulfilling opportunities. A problem may arise with the phrases "The-ness" in line 9 and "A-ness" in line 11. You might point out that "the" is a definite article and "a" is the indefinite. Therefore, a likely explanation is that "The-ness" represents the traditionally circumscribed and subservient role of black people, while "A-ness" represents the freedom and the opportunity to grow as an individual without the restrictions of race Another good poem for comparison is Hughes's "The Negro Speaks of Rivers" (1016).

Lynn Emanuel, *Like God*, *pages 1151–52*

This is a poem requiring a vivid imagination to read and a certain ability of abstraction and dissociation. The idea is that the "you" (second-person point of view; who is the "you"?) are engaged in the task of reading, and are so taken up with the story that you literally become a part of it, albeit not necessarily the part you would have chosen if everything had been "affable and sleek" (line 38). The scenes described in the poem thus become your world, a world of "fellow travelers" involving a "logjam of / images of hats and umbrellas and / Vuitton luggage" (lines 23–25). The idea is that we must take life as we find it, not as we would like it to be, and therefore we must adjust to what we find. The poem is restored to something like reality at the very end, when the speaker talks about "you, who have been hovering / above this page, holding the book in / your hands, like God, reading" (lines 52–54) to remind us of the separation of imagination and life. But, metaphorically, Emanuel raises the issue of how much imagination it takes us to perceive and create our life's experiences. Works for comparison are Stanton's "Childhood" (710), Kincaid's "What I Have Been Doing Lately" (148), and Lux's "The Voice You Hear when You Read Silently" (763).

JOHN ENGELS, *Naming the Animals,* *page 1153*

The title, which is ironic, alludes to Adam's "naming the animals" in Eden (in Genesis). The dead deer and the captured one (lines 1–10) represent the speaker's desire for control, as though in a perverted way he can count only those things over which he has "dominion" (the word is Biblical). In a real sense, the poem represents an attack upon our civilization, as represented by the speaker, which has sought to control Nature, and to use the things of the earth exclusively for human benefit. Once we subdue and kill things, so that they do "not watch back" (line 17) we have controlled them and have therefore "named" them. The three does (line 11) do not count because they are still alive and wild, still a part of Nature, and not a part of human history until they are captured or killed.

Carolyn Forché, *Because One Is Always Forgotten,* *page 1153*

This poem is a product of two years that Forché spent in El Salvador in the late 1970s. The atrocity described calmly in lines 7–10 refers to a custom of hanging trash on the boughs of fruit trees that were not producing. The Salvadoran army mocked this custom by murdering rebellious peasants, peeling their facial skin, and hanging it on trees. The speaker of the poem contrasts this barbarism with the need for strength like that possessed by Viera and others. Thus, the concluding paradox that "the heart is the toughest part of the body" (line 12) is that great skill is needed to commit the horror being committed by the "boy soldier." If this skill and care were turned to a good end, the poem implies, there would be no need for the toughness and callousness that must be developed to stand up to the brutalities of warfare and the suppression of innocent populations.

Dan Georgakas, *Hiroshima Crewman,* *page 1154*

The first atomic bomb was dropped over Hiroshima, Japan, in August of 1945. The American plane that carried the bomb bore the name "Enola Gay," after the mother of one of the crewmen, and the men did not understand until later the true dimensions of the destruction that they had unleashed. In "Hiroshima Crewman," Georgakas centers on one crew member who in dealing with his feelings entered holy orders and took vows of silence. The concluding lines focus on atrocities committed by the Germans (Auschwitz, Dachau), but the speaker implies that no one side was guilty of all the atrocities, for "war produces many brands" of horror. It is war itself, in other words, that is guilty.

Chief Dan George, *The Beauty of the Trees,* *page 1154*

This poem seems to be a prayer of thanksgiving. It is significant that it contains four stanzas, the traditional North / East / South / West symbolism of the four directions and the four winds that is so significant symbolically for Native Americans. From each direction the speaker cites things of beauty and power that are a part of his consciousness. He states that the entire world, from the fragrance of the grass to the thunder of the sky to the faintness of the stars, speaks directly to him. The conclusion is simple and plain: The speaker's "heart soars" and he is attuned to the universe and at peace with the world around him.

Nikki Giovanni, *Woman,* *pages 1154–55*

The speaker asserts that men have not supported the aspirations (needs, dreams, desires) of women—an argument couched in five metaphors ("blade," "robin," "web," "book," and "bulb"). Each metaphor suggests growth, creation, and order. In each, "he" refused to cooperate in the process of fulfillment. The final stanza suggests that women must seek such fulfillment, definition, and value within themselves, without recourse to the support of men.

Marilyn Hacker, *Sonnet Ending with a Film Subtitle,* *page 1155*

This is a traditional Shakespearean sonnet, with only a slight variation in the last two lines (*abab, cdcd, efef, ef*). Though the form is traditional, however, the content is not. It is a personal expression by a rebellious speaker who is furious against a "bastard" who was apparently a departed husband or lover, who may perhaps have given her a "Venereal Disease" (line 3). The rebellion takes the possible directions of recommending that women "break our fetters / And raise our daughters to be Lesbians," or that the speaker could fortify her "rhetoric with guns" (line 10). Despite the rage smoldering in the poem, however, one might note the humor of the concluding line. The line might be construed as an admission of helplessness, or else as a modification of the French saying, "Je ris pour ne pas pleurer" (*I laugh in order not to cry*).

JOHN HAINES, *Little Cosmic Dust Poem*, *page 1156*

This poem contrasts the immensity of the universe with the miracle of life and love. Astronomers have concluded that our solar system, including the earth, was created out of the "debris of dying stars." In its death throes, an exploding star underwent catastrophic expansion, and created the many elements, such as oxygen, carbon, silicon, iron, silver, and gold, that have made life on earth possible. Astronomers have further speculated that the solar system will one day (in perhaps five billion years) be enveloped by the sun as it expands and dies, thus returning everything on earth to the status of "cosmic dust." In the light of these cosmic mind-boggling details, of this "silence and waste to come," life of any sort is miraculous, and love is one of the greatest and most precious of miracles.

DONALD HALL, *Scenic View*, *pages 1156–57*

This poem demonstrates how poetic imagination and playfulness may combine with ironic seriousness. On the surface, "Scenic View" is based on the comic hypothesis that cameras taking pictures of a mountainous landscape drain the mountain scene of color. Eventually there will be so many photographs—so popular is the scene among amateur photographers—that all the color from the green and white mountains will have been transferred, bit by bit, into photograph albums, and the mountains will be "unseeable." The "intractable granite" peaks will still be there, however, but because of their invisibility, passing airplanes may crash into them. The serious undercurrent of the poem, implied but not mentioned by the poet, is that increasing pollution, smog, acid rain, and haze may be the influence causing the fading-out of the scene. Thus the point may eventually be reached when the air will indeed make the mountains "unseeable," but the cause may be horribly real, not fanciful.

Daniel Halpern, *Snapshot of Hué,* *page 1157*

Hué, a major Vietnamese city, was the scene of particular heavy attack and counterattack, bombing and shelling, and bitter street-fighting during the Tet Offensive of the War in Vietnam. The poem supposes that the speaker visits the city after the war is over and after the wreckage has been cleared away. The bridges are restored, and there is much traffic on the streets, and the sun is "posted above"; in short, things are back to normal. The implication of the poem is that if things can now be normal, why should they ever have been otherwise? What was the purpose of the war, the "telling piles on corners" (line 5), the "debris that contained a little of everything" (line 6) and the "impenetrable" sky, presumably blackened by smoke by burning buildings (line 8)?

Daniel Halpern, *Summer in the Middle Class,* *pages 1157–58*

Beneath what seems a cheerful description of America in a holiday mood there emerges a picture of lives undifferentiated by individuality, moving inexorably from banality to extinction. The tone is complex: There is humor in the picture of overweight fathers playing ball with their sons and of cooks preparing food and setting the tables for the mosquitoes to have their "evening meal" by biting the people. But the picture of a world "in unison" as being quintessentially American is chilling, and the final "total darkness" once the TV goes off constitutes a seriously negative judgment on American life.

H. S. (Sam) Hamod, *Leaves,* *pages 1158–59*

In this poem the speaker tells of his Arabic father, who constantly sent grape leaves to him and his wife when he was alive, and whose leaves are still to be found in their home freezer, as though the father were still alive. This concrete evidence of the tradition of the old country causes the speaker to think of his heritage, and to trace his own development as a poet to the poetic impulses of his father. Although he did not understand his father's songs because they were in Arabic, the songs were poetry nevertheless. The idea of "Leaves" is that the human spirit is influenced not only consciously, but subliminally. The memory and creativity of the speaker's father will continue to exist, like the symbol of the grape leaves, within the speaker's mind, and they will influence his ideas and words as long as he lives. It is in this way that a national tradition is passed down from generation to generation.

Frances E. W. Harper, *She's Free,* *pages 1159–60*

The poem, with four-stress lines mainly in anapests with commencing iambs, and with rhyming couplets (*aa, bb, cc, dd; ee, dd, cc*), is a modified sonnet, with the octave describing the flight of a black slave woman going north to flee slavery in the South. She braves great danger to leave "the hand of oppression," even though her only "crime is the hue of her face." The concluding sestet describes her success at evading bloodhounds, hunter, and posse; her life of difficulty is not over, for she will still "brave" the troubles of "poverty, danger, and death." But the glory of her flight is that she "is no longer a slave."

Michael S. Harper, *Called,* *page 1160*

The poem, describing the burial of a dog which had formerly been chained but which has broken loose and been killed, offers a series of images that contrast life and death, heat and coolness, light and dark, movement and stillness. The grave, black dirt, the animal's body, and the image of "the bed" and "earth and rock / which will hold her," the sunset, and the past tense of "called" all embody half of this contrast. The opposition is established in the "heat" (apparently the heat of oestrus, which caused the dog to break free) the "brother," the three questions that end the poem, and the present tense of "calls." The act of burial brings the speaker and his companion into direct contact with these two opposite aspects of a natural cycle.

Robert Hass, *Spring Rain,* *page 1161*

This poem is a description of what happens to spring rain that begins as "a Pacific squall" and then "moves its own way" over land. The rain falls on the mountains (The Sierras) and there it nourishes larkspur and penstemon which sprout much later and are then available to nourish gray jays. The jays, in their turn, excrete the seeds which then form new plants to create a new cycle the next time spring rains come. The idea is that the processes of nature are cyclical and interrelated, but if human beings try intervening in the process it becomes complicated (lines 15–18) and difficult. "Spring Rain" is therefore built on the contrast between the inevitable certainties of nature and the awkward intervention of human beings. A question might concern the degree to which citified, industrialized humanity belongs in the cycles of nature.

Robert Hayden, *Those Winter Sundays,* *1161*

In this well-loved poem Hayden's speaker tells of his father's love, expressed through mundane acts, and of his childhood inability to understand or appreciate that love. The speaker focuses on his father's habitual Sunday morning efforts to warm the house for the family, for which "No one ever thanked him" (line 5). The poor and hard life is vividly expressed in images like "blueblack cold" and "cracked hands." Life was bitter for both father and son; the father always "got up early," but the son was reticent because he feared the "chronic angers of that house." The adult speaker understands, in retrospect, that driving "out the cold" and polishing "my good shoes" were acts of love. He calls them "love's austere and lonely offices." But the child never realized this; he spoke "indifferently" to his father, and now, even though he understands his past, he thinks about his childhood with regret.

In this age of automatic thermostats and easy heating, students might benefit from learning that during the days when houses were heated by coal-burning furnaces, coal fires had to be "banked" each night, so that they would not burn out and leave the house freezing. In the mornings, however, the house was cold, and someone would need to go downstairs to the furnace, shake out the ashes, and put on fresh coal to get a roaring fire going to warm up the house. In "Those Winter Sundays," this task is the regular responsibility of the speaker's father.

Seamus Heaney, *The Otter*, *page 1162*

This poem is spoken or written to a listener who does not respond but only hears (or reads). The listener is clearly a sweetheart, and the speaker addresses her ambiguously as though she is an otter, which is one of the happiest and most charming little creatures to swim the ocean. The comparison draws attention to the sweetheart's athleticism in water, for much of the imagery concerns swimming and other water movements. Under these circumstances, the lines "When I hold you now / We are closed and deep / As the atmosphere on water" apparently refer to ardent lovemaking. Through the comparison, therefore, the poet links human and animal desires and intensifies the speaker's love for the listener.

George Herbert, *Love (III)*, *pages 1162–63*

This three-stanza lyric is a combined meditation and brief drama about the relationship between God (Love) and the soul ("me," the speaker), expressed in an extended metaphor in which Love is an Innkeeper and the speaker is a Guest at the Inn. The primary speaker is the "I" of the poem, the soul of the speaker, who tells the story of the encounter with God and who quotes his dialogue with

God. The speaker believes that he is an unworthy guest because he is guilty of "dust and sin" (i.e., being mortal and therefore sinful). Despite the soul's self-deprecation, however, Love welcomes the soul as a guest "worthy to be here," and gives two explanations of why the soul is worthy: In the second stanza, Love smiles while asking the rhetorical question, "Who made the eyes but I?" In other words, the soul was created and formed entirely by God. In stanza 3, Love points out that He "bore the blame" for the soul's imperfections. Thus Love alludes to the divine roles of creator and redeemer. Love's "meat," the body and blood of Christ, is the sacrament of communion—the conduit of divine Grace.

WILLIAM HEYEN, *The Hair: Jacob Korman's Story,* *page 1163*

Heyen's poem responds to images deep in the memory of twentieth century life—the roundups of Jews to be taken to the death camps and the huge mounds of hair taken from Jews, especially Jewish women, to be used in Germany for household items such as pillows and rugs. Conventional wisdom for many years had it that the Jews went passively to their death, but Heyen corrects that misapprehension by describing a scene of wild though unsuccessful resistance. The image in line 4, of a wheel turning, recalls the image of the Goddess Fortune who, with her wheel, spun out the fate of individuals with total indifference to whether people lived or died. The concluding image of the field of hair demonstrates the ferocity with which the women who died tried to defend themselves against the inhuman actions of the German SS guards.

A. D. HOPE, *Advice to Young Ladies,* *pages 1163–64*

This is an excellent poem. It is an ardent defense of female rights, beginning with a narrative about the ways in which the ancient Romans treated women, and making judgments on later treatment. The first story concerns Postumia, a vestal virgin, who was tried on charges of impurity in A.U.C. 334 but was acquitted. The speaker states that she was really indicted because she tried to behave like a human being and therefore incurred the resentment of the Roman male power elite. The circumstances of Postumia are related to the decline of Rome which, according to the historian Tacitus, became "rotten through and through." Hope includes additional references to women who later were literally torn to pieces (Hypatia, line 43) or burned (Joan of Arc, line 44) for presuming to usurp traditionally male domains. The final stanza is bitterly ironic, for the speaker implies that civilizations have destroyed themselves for failing to trust "the servile womb to breed free men." Students will be anxious to discuss this poem in great detail whether or not they are willing to accept the feminist critical approach (*see page 1832*).

GERARD MANLEY HOPKINS, *Pied Beauty,* *page 1165*

This lyric praises God by enumerating an assortment of "pied" (dappled, varied, dazzling, freckled) aspects of creation. The "skies," "cow," "trout," "chestnut-falls," "finches' wings," and "Landscapes" are all streaked, spotted, or multicolored. The tools ("gear," "tackle," "trim") of trades are "pied" in their overwhelming variety. In lines 7–9, the speaker moves to images of variety in movement, behavior, and taste. Lines 10–11 gather all the images to their focus. God "fathers-forth" all the infinite variety of creation. All this variety justifies praise of God, and the speaker encourages readers to praise God also.

GERARD MANLEY HOPKINS, *The Windhover,* *page 1165*

This song of praise to Christ gains much of its impact from Hopkins's "sprung" rhythms and vibrant alliteration. The rhymes are also powerful; the scheme is that of an Italian sonnet (*abba abba cdcdcd*). Lines 1–8, the octave, describe the glorious energy and valor of the falcon (Windhover) that the speaker "caught" sight of "this morning." This glory is conveyed in the image of the noble ("dauphin") bird "riding" the wind. The first triplet (lines 9–11) produces the transition from falcon to Christ. The bird combines beauty, valor, pride, strength, and action, but the "fire" of Christ ("thee, O my chevalier") is a trillion (in British English "billion" means "trillion") times more lovely and dangerous. Christ's glory (lines 12–14) transfigures the earth and makes "embers" "gash gold-vermilion."

JULIA WARD HOWE, *Battle Hymn of the Republic,* *page 1166*

Howe was a well-known nineteenth-century activist in causes for women's liberation and the emancipation of the slaves. The "Battle Hymn of the Republic" became immediately popular among Union soldiers during the Civil War, and has remained her most popular poem and one of America's major patriotic songs (sung to the music of "John Brown's Body"). The poem is noteworthy because it unites Christian faith with the cause of freedom. It is based on the idea that religion should bring about social action ("let us die to make men free," line 27), and therefore it shares with the well-known hymn "Onward, Christian Soldiers" (by Sabine Baring-Gould and Sir Arthur Sullivan) the idea that religious faith recruits its believers into a battle on the side of righteousness and reform.

Langston Hughes, *Negro*, *pages 1166–67*

Hughes looks at the plight of African Americans through a series of images that encompass wide expanses of time and space. The identical first and sixth stanzas frame and unify the poem, defining the speaker as a symbol for all African Americans and linking him with "night" and Africa. The repetition of *I*, *I am*, or *I've* as the first words of ten of the lines maintains this clear focus on speaker and symbol. The speaker identifies himself as a "slave," "worker," "singer," and "victim." In each case the subsequent lines create a historical or geographical context suggesting that the suffering of bondage and enforced labor has continued throughout time (Caesar to Washington, the pyramids to the Woolworth Building) and all over the world (Africa to Georgia, the Congo to the Mississippi).

Robinson Jeffers, *The Answer*, *page 1167*

This poem, like "The Purse-Seine" (953), reflects Jeffers's conviction that humanity is much less than admirable. The question, unstated here, is how to preserve life on earth, inasmuch as human beings have now developed the power, if misused, to destroy it. The speaker offers a series of answers, each of which catalogues aspects of suffering. He suggests that we not be "deluded" by false dreams of "universal justice or happiness" and that we look to history for a pattern of survival. He also suggests that we avoid violence, keep our integrity, and "not wish for evil." Integrity and wholeness represent the best solution. This unified perceptiveness requires seeing human life in the context of the "wholeness of life and things" and "the divine beauty of the universe" (line 9). Only if we "love" the whole cosmos, and not just "man / Apart from" it, can we avoid despair and the continued deterioration of the environment. The idea is that all future decisions must be made not only in the light of economic, social, and political expediency, but also in the light of environmental consequences.

Etheridge Knight, *Haiku*, *pages 1167–68*

These haiku from Knight's first book, *Poems from Prison*, reflect the poet's experiences when he spent six years in prison for robbery (1960–1966). The sequence begins by presenting three images of prison life, and then deals with African-American existence, nature, and poetry. Images are central here; they define the world and evoke overtones. Convicts being "like lizards," for example, suggests both cautious movement and wary intelligence. Poems 4 and 9 focus on the discipline and the power of art. The "blues song" and "jazz" are both ways for Knight to talk about his own poetry. Indeed, the concluding haiku focus on his poetic skill; he identifies his craft as "jazz" and claims that there is nothing "square" about it.

MAXINE KUMIN, *Woodchucks,* *pages 1168–69*

The speaker comes to painful realizations about herself (and human beings) as she tries to destroy the woodchucks that are gobbling up her garden. Her "case" against the critters is "airtight," like the gas chambers alluded to in the last two lines, and she plans to use a "knockout bomb." The gas fails (stanza 2), and the woodchucks continue to feast. The speaker's "Darwinian pieties" lead her to a more effective means of destruction. The poem expresses the beginnings of pity and regret in the image of the "littlest woodchuck's face" and the body in the "everbearing roses." At the same time, the speaker experiences the rise of the "murderer" and the "hawk-eye killer" lurking inside her. Killing the last woodchuck becomes a contest of extermination, and the last two lines suggest a link between the speaker and Nazi Germany. The poem finally suggests that all killing is dehumanizing and destructive for both killer and victim. The speaker is horrified and fascinated at the same time. She moves from a state of innocence to experience, and thus learns unpleasant things about herself. Kumin, a Pulitzer-Prize winning poet, combines a closed form (*abcacb; defdfe; ghigih; jkljlk; mnomon*) with slant rhymes and some run-on lines, to create a narrative in which rhyme works almost subconsciously to reinforce meaning.

IRVING LAYTON, *Rhine Boat Trip,* *pages 1169–70*

Layton, a major Canadian poet, draws together two strands of imagery related to German history and myth to suggest that modern atrocities of death have blotted out all that went before. Each image of the mythic past ("castles," "grapes," "Lorelei," sweet singing) is canceled and displaced by an image of carnage and death (*ghosts, blinded eyes, crimson beards of murdered rabbis, wailing of cattle-cars*).

LI-YOUNG LEE, *A Final Thing,* *pages 1170–71*

"A Final Thing" is a meditation on love and how even though we are isolated we are also connected. The poem is a meditation growing out of an occasion common to most people. The speaker is lying in bed and hears voices outside his room, interpreting what is being said—a story perhaps, an expression of feeling, a request to consider an idea. As he speculates on what he vaguely hears he believes that the voices form a connection with him. He dwells on how he, his wife, and their child cling "in expectancy" to each other, and, presumably, he senses that this bond is what life is about. He delights in the fact of his love, of having someone to love, and of being loved himself. The poem, beginning in tercets but growing to four- and then five-line stanzas, asserts that the speaker's thoughts have been based on the simplest and most basic facts about life, but these simple details are symbolic of life itself to him. The speaker concludes by stating that someday he will close his eyes "to recall" his feelings on this morning. The memory will clearly be the "final thing" of his life.

ALAN P. LIGHTMAN, *In Computers,* *page 1171*

This poem is a product of our computer age, in which more and more miraculous functions and achievements are being claimed for computers. At the same time, increased industrialization is increasing pollution and is therefore making it less likely that the earth can continue to support life. At some point, scientists have speculated, waves of human emigrants might be forced to leave the dying earth to take up residence on the moon, or on Mars, where they will have to live in artificially created and controlled environments. At that point, all they will have from earth will be recorded on computers—things such as sunsets, the movements of gazelle, the winds, and snowfalls. The final two lines are a grimly ironic response to this prospect.

LIZ LOCHHEAD, *The Choosing,* *pages 1172–73*

Students will likely cite apparent sociological differences between the speaker and Mary in explanation of the separate lives the two have led. This analysis will certainly work. Mary's father can be seen as a major factor in the direction her life took, for "He didn't believe in high school education, / especially for girls, / or in forking out for uniforms" (lines 28–30). We may infer that Mary was not given the opportunity to go on, despite her obvious brilliance in studies. With this analysis, it is important to stress that the poem does not claim superiority for either choice followed by the two major characters. The speaker comes from the library with her "arms full of books" (line 44), while Mary has a "husband who is tall, / curly haired, has eyes / for no one else but Mary" (lines 35–37). The two girls who "were first equal" in school have traveled in different directions.

An additional dimension may be introduced, however, if you raise the issue of how choices are made in a person's life. Are the choices inherent from birth? Do people actually make choices, or are choices made for them as a result of their inherent abilities? Would the speaker have made the same choice as Mary, granted an equal background (we assume the speaker's family provided the speaker with support and encouragement, but we are not told that)? A larger issue is of course that of free will as opposed to determinism. And, if determinism is the major factor in people's lives, could people not be determined to exercise their free will when important occasions arise? Thus the poem concludes when the speaker wonders "when the choices got made / we don't remember making" (lines 46, 47). Students should enjoy discussing this poem.

AUDRE LORDE, *Every Traveler Has One Vermont Poem,* *page 1173*

"Every Traveler Has One Vermont Poem" builds to the shock of the next-to-last line, when into the natural beauty of the countryside there intrudes the reality of human ugliness in the form of racism. The pastoral then becomes social commentary, and one is led to wonder about these "tanned boys" and the unreflective and self-centered world in which they live. The title is at first amusing because of its assertion that a "Vermont poem" (probably a poem on the beauties of the state, as this one starts out to be), is almost obligatory for a traveling poet. But the title becomes bitterly ironic, almost tragic, when one realizes the content of such a poem for a poet of color, because even the beauty of the landscape cannot compensate for the violation the poem describes.

RICHARD LOVELACE, *To Lucasta, Going to the Wars,* *page 1173*

This lyric asserts that love cannot exist without honor. Although the tone is light and witty, the poem is serious. The speaker is leaving Lucasta because his honor demands that he go to war to serve King and Country. Lucasta is "chaste" and "quiet." War is personified as a "new mistress" with great vitality, and the speaker comically calls his departure, therefore, a type of "inconstancy." Finally, the speaker asserts that his love for Lucasta is based on a greater love for honor, a driving force in his life.

AMY LOWELL, *Patterns,* *pages 1174–76*

Lowell's anti-war poem protests the rigid "patterns" of thinking and behavior that constrict life and lead to war. The speaker, an aristocratic woman walking in her garden and mourning the death of her fiancé in battle, grounds her protest in images that evoke four distinct patterns: formal gardens, stiff clothing, social and sexual decorum, and warfare. Stanzas 1 and 2 combine the patterns of garden and clothing; the speaker's "whalebone and brocade" (clothing of the eighteenth century) make her "a rare pattern" like the formal garden. Her "passion" fights against both patterns. Stanzas 3–4 add the pattern of social and sexual restraint. Again the speaker notes that her "stiffened gown" conflicts with the "softness of a woman." The stanzas present an erotic dream (and an escape from patterns) in which the speaker discards her rigid dress, bathes in a fountain, and is discovered and embraced by her lover, but the dream conflicts with the reality of patterns. Stanzas 5–6 introduce two further aspects of pattern—war and the proper behavior for grief. The letters on the paper informing her of her lover's death "squirmed like snakes," but the speaker stiffly "stood upright" and returned "no answer"; i.e., her desire to mourn is held in check by patterns of social restraint. In stanza 7, the speaker has a vision of what might have been—an escape from patterns through love with her dead fiancé. This is canceled in stanza 8, which reveals the speaker's future. She is condemned to rigid and unchanging patterns of dress, behavior, chastity, and loneliness. In the last lines the speaker breaks decorum—the pattern of appropriate language—and rages against all these patterns. For a detailed discussion of this poem see page 1985.

GWENDOLYN MCEWEN, *Dark Pines under Water,* *page 1176*

This poem is suggestive and symbolic, for the narrative framework is personal and uncertain. The main symbol is "dark pines under water," which is literally based on the vision of sunken logs in a lake bottom. What seems clear is that the poet is speaking about ideas and feelings in the depths and recesses of the mind. The poet does not make any specifics clear, but what is clear is that we should express thoughts, feelings, and apprehensiveness that ordinarily we hide. The symbolism thus involves a surfacing of things, for there is "something down there" to be told. In ordinary, day-to-day terms, things should be brought out into the open and talked about.

The speaker is addressing a "you" and the *you-your* pronoun is used eleven times in the poem. In effect one might say that the poem's point of view is the second person—the listener—whom the speaker may be counseling. The speaker is attempting to bring the listener in to the symbolism of the dark pines under water so that the speaker can bring out whatever is submerged in his or her mind.

HEATHER MCHUGH, *Lines,* *page 1177*

The poem addresses the disparity between what we want in life and the things for which we will settle. Through a series of images—one very appealing, that of the subway as a wind instrument with many stops—the poet brings us to the sense that everything comes to an end. Even the man who is deeply in love has just heard the word "goodbye." But by contrast, an old man, rejoices "just to be alive." Thus at different points in our lives we are all happy with different things, and truth is always contingent upon individuals and circumstances. This poem may be compared with "Like God" by Lynn Emanuel (1151).

CLAUDE MCKAY, *The White City,* *page 1177*

This sonnet introduces elements of the Petrarchan sonnet in its paradoxes, irony, and capitalized personification. McKay uses this tradition to express his simultaneous acknowledgment of the material grandeur and appeal of white society, and of the rage and resentment it can elicit from an African-American who both is and is not a part of it. The speaker is obviously highly educated in the traditions of White European culture. But he does not belong, and uses one of that culture's most complex literary achievements to declare both his mastery and his rejection of the white world and the city which is its symbol.

W. S. MERWIN, *Listen,* *pages 1177–78*

This is a surprising poem and virtual prayer of gratefulness: Despite all the things in the world that are bad, the "We" of the poem are saying "thank you." The speaker cites seventeen negative aspects of the modern world (mugging, funerals , death, shame, stench, dead animals, lost feelings, denuded forests, etc.), but also stresses the need for "thank you." The rhetorical device here is that of *anaphora*, or repetition (Chapter 17), and the phrase "thank you" is repeated fourteen times. The point is that there is so much to be depressed about that the idea of gratitude needs to be stressed and overstressed. The silent agenda is that without gratitude for what we have left after all the negatives, we would have nothing. Student responses to this poem should be most interesting.

EDNA ST. VINCENT MILLAY, *What Lips My Lips Have Kissed,* *pages 1178–79*

This poem is a sonnet, using the traditional subject matter of love. But there are several surprises: The speaker is female; the love is remembered, not actual, and thus the tone is nostalgic; finally, the female speaker is apparently reflecting upon a past series of lovers—so many that she has forgotten them as individuals. Such a confession has traditionally been unusual for a woman, since it opens her to charges of promiscuity. The speaker keeps that judgment in abeyance, however, by turning the subject, in the sestet, fully to her present state. Now, she asserts, she is old and alone, and her summer has gone.

N. Scott Momaday, *The Bear,* *page 1179*

The speaker uses an aged and venerable bear to symbolize the power, mystery, and durability of nature. The bear has suffered from being held at one time in a trap, and he experiences pain and has had one of his legs withered. Despite the hardships he has endured, however, he has outworn "valor, all but the fact of courage" (lines 7–8). The idea is that Nature (with a capital *N*) has been assaulted by human beings, but that it will continue in some form and elude all human efforts to bring it down. Ultimately, Nature contains power about which human beings know nothing, and, presumably, this power will persist because it is part of a "whole" (line 17) that transcends human civilization.

Howard Nemerov, *Life Cycle of Common Man,* *pages 1179–80*

"Life Cycle of Common Man" is unusual because it relentlessly considers what human life has become in our age of consumerism. To verify Nemerov's statistics, his common man must have consumed a fifth of gin in an average of about six days, and daily must have smoked cigarettes at an alarming rate of combustion. On a sobering note is the vast number of "beasts" (beef cattle, chickens, hogs, lambs, fish, crustaceans) who had to die "to provide" the common man "with meat, belt and shoes." The irony at the poem's end is particularly powerful, for the common man is there considered as a comic-strip figure, speaking not in the real world of communication but rather in speech balloons. While human beings profess nobility and dignity, the commercial and advertising emphasis on making the common man a consuming unit rather than a complete human being has vitiated this claim. "Life Cycle" may be compared with Auden's "The Unknown Citizen" (1125).

Jim Northrup, *wahbegan,* *pages 1180–81*

Although the title is an Ojibway name, its sound is close enough to the English word "woebegone" to convey the feeling of the poem. From the first word of the poem—"Didja," used twice—it is clear that the speaker wants to address the reader intimately and directly. His description of his brother who "died in the war but didn't fall down for fifteen tortured years" reminds us of the terrible scars left on America by the war in Vietnam and, by extension, by all wars. We are left to reflect on the real price of war, and to wonder how we determine whether our course in turning so often to warfare has been justified by the cost in mental anguish and suffering.

FRANK O'HARA, *Poem,* *page 1181*

"Poem" is built on a bizarre reversal of expectations and their tragic and ironic outcome. There seem to be two time schemes in simultaneous operation: The speaker's receipt of the eager and apparently happy note, prompting him to pack quickly and head "straight for the door," is played against the mystery of the statement "It was autumn / by the time I got around the corner" (lines 5–6) and the concluding statement that the invitation had been issued "several months ago" (line 16). The speaker's understated words "I did appreciate it" (i.e., the death), and his effort to pretend that the death is part of a host's careful preparation for a guest, all suggest a considerable depth of emotion beneath this deliberately commonplace description of a nightmarish, macabre experience.

MARY OLIVER, *Ghosts,* *pages 1182–83*

"Ghosts" is a meditation and lamentation for the loss of the vast herds of buffalo that once roamed the midwestern plains of the United States, and also for the destruction of the Plains Indian civilization which depended on the animals for virtually every aspect of their lives. The speaker describes the insensitivity and callousness of the passengers shooting the animals from train windows, leaving piles of bodies to stink in the prairie air. With remarkable sensitivity and beauty she asks readers to "*notice*" the loss and the evidence of the life that had once existed where the bison had lived (stanza 6). The poem develops three major symbols: (1) the buffalo who gave life to the Indians, (2) the unbelievably cruel shootings, and (3) the attempts by the Sioux to revive the past through their ghost dancing (a major reason for which they were killed at Wounded Knee in 1890). The symbolic commentary on the wanton destruction is the stink of the dead buffalo (lines 37–41). At the end the speaker dreams of having room made for her in the beauty of the long-vanished life. Compare this poem with Momaday's "The Bear" (1179).

SIMON ORTIZ, *A Story of How a Wall Stands,* *pages 1183–84*

"A Story of How a Wall Stands" is a graphic illustration of how metaphor operates. The story is that of how a wall at Aacqu (Acoma in New Mexico) is put together, with much that shows but much more that does not show. It is the foundation, the patience, and the workmanship that make the wall last. Metaphorically, the same method nurtures the young, gives them a place in their society, and creates the strength which makes them endure "a long, long time."

DOROTHY PARKER, *Résumé*, *page 1184*

This ironic and funny poem is based on the startling idea that one "might as well live" simply because all the ways of committing suicide are either uncomfortable or unreliable. Each statement is understated in some way: For example, razors don't just "pain you" and rivers are far deeper and wetter than "damp." The speaker's tone of sophisticated ennui suggests that one lives because doing otherwise is just too much trouble. The title "Résumé" (suggesting both a summary and also the vita that one presents as part of a job application) is an understated, whimsical, offhand defense of life, with the implication that there are many strong reasons for living—including enjoying the laughter from a poem like this one.

LINDA PASTAN, *Marks*, *pages 1184–85*

Students take delight in the metaphor of this poem. Some may want to take the conclusion seriously, and it is therefore important to stress that this part can be read in context as a joke or quip. Even so, however, the poem contains an underlying note of annoyance. The extended metaphor is that of school and grades. Housework is like taking a course: The speaker receives a varying report card, including an ***A*** for cooking and an *Incomplete* for ironing. The son and daughter give grades based on a superior-average and a pass/fail system. The conclusion, "Wait 'til they learn," is an implied threat, but granted the poem's tone of affectionate banter, the threat is to be seen as a joke. The poem thus explores the speaker's sense that she, like most people, is constantly being rated, and that even those who love her find her not fully adequate. The playful metaphor, which puts this situation in an original light, is accurate, vivid, and refreshing.

MARGE PIERCY, *The Secretary Chant*, *page 1185*

The subject of this poem is the dehumanization of women secretaries, since this is ***The*** *Secretary Chant*, not ***a*** *secretary's chant*. The first-person speaker describes how her character is submerged by the functions and sounds of her work, for in the business world she is little better than the machines she uses. The parts of her body described and many of the activities in which she engages are quintessentially female (such as hips, breasts, navel, delivery of a baby), but here they perform mechanical rather than human functions.

Marge Piercy, *Will We Work Together?*, *pages 1185–86*

This poem is a powerful dramatic monologue, spoken by a woman speaker (let us assume a woman) to her lover. It is an expression of intense love, as its metaphors demonstrate. The speaker is like a lantern, for she lights up "the corners" when the two are together. She also becomes a source of warmth, "bright / as a fireplace roaring / with love." A movingly observed part of the speaker's words are the lines "My body wears / sore before I can express / on yours the smallest part / of what moves me. Words / shred and splinter." Granted the intensity of the speaker's monologue, the conclusion is not an anti-climax, but rather a continuation of her desire to find and create meaning and usefulness "from this fierce sturdy / rampant love." An interesting issue for classroom discussion is the reason for which the poem's title is phrased as a question.

Sylvia Plath, *Last Words*, *pages 1186–87*

The poem juxtaposes images from ancient Egyptian practices of mummification and from daily life in the modern kitchen. The speaker sees herself losing life slowly, to the point where a mirror held against her lips (like that used in Shakespeare's *King Lear* to see if Cordelia still breathes) will soon show nothing. Yet oddly enough, the speaker demonstrates a macabre rejoicing in the household things which are part of her burial, because they are lustrous and "warmed by much handling" (line 18), and might be a comfort in the grave. Indeed, line 23 describes an almost ecstatic joy at the virtual loss of personality ("I shall hardly know myself") in the dark sarcophagus. It is as though, finding motherhood and housekeeping to be destructive, this speaker determines to love the things killing her rather than escape them.

Sylvia Plath, *Mirror*, *page 1187*

The personified mirror speaks of its life, in which it reflects and has come to love the wall opposite itself. Yet it also reflects the woman who sees herself aging daily, changing from a young girl into an old woman resembling a "terrible fish" (lines 17, 18). The fish is clearly a symbol of a horrible and inevitable transformation from loveliness to ugliness. The "truthful" mirror (line 4) reminds its owner that her days are running out, and that when her beauty is gone she will be considered less than human.

Katha Pollitt, *Archaeology*, *pages 1187–88*

Using the activities of an archaeologist as a metaphor, the author raises questions about the choices we make in life. The speaker suggests that any choice might turn out to be a disappointment, like the "ancient grocery lists" an archaeologist uncovers rather than some wonderful, history-changing document. In light of such possibilities, one may regret the time and effort spent on foolish dreams. But then comes the speaker's advice: "Pack up your fragments," and continue the effort; try to make something meaningful and beautiful out of the work that has been done. The poem is a call to dreams and to commitment to them. While admitting the doubts that may come, Pollitt asserts that human inventiveness can create meaning out of disorder as it summons up the life of the past.

Ezra Pound, *The River-Merchant's Wife: A Letter,* *pages 1188–89*

The poem tenderly reflects a happy marriage, albeit one very different from modern assumptions about marriages of choice. The speaker is the young wife, who is subservient by our standards (see her reference to her husband as "My Lord you" [line 7]). Clearly, however, their love is deep and fulfilling. The details of Chinese village life in the eighth century (the children's occupations, the monkeys overhead, and the young wife's description of her decorous bashfulness) are vivid and compelling. The speaker's unexpected declaration of transcendent love (lines 12–13), her sorrow at their separation (line 18), and her eagerness to rejoin her young husband (lines 26–29) are poignantly rendered, and in this way the poem re-creates an alien time and place.

John Crowe Ransom, *Bells for John Whiteside's Daughter,* *page 1189*

This poem avoids sentimentality, despite its painful subject matter, by describing the child's death as a "brown study" (line 3), as though she could awaken and return to her usual busy life. Similarly, those who knew her are astonished and vexed, but not overwhelmed in tears (line 19). The contrast between the child alive and dead, now "lying so primly propped" (line 20) is sharply drawn, since her life is described in images of sound and joy, color, and motion. The speaker's tribute, that the geese themselves cried "in goose, Alas" (line 12), expresses the poem's mixture of fond memory and deep sorrow. For comparison, see Wagner's "The Boxes" (1211).

John Raven, *Assailant,* *page 1190*

The dramatic scene visualized here is that the speaker is telling his story to a group of policemen. The first eight lines lead the officers to believe that the speaker is describing an assailant and that the crime was an assault. It is not until the last line, the ninth, the poem reveals that the assailant was a rat. Implied in this surprise is that the life circumstances of the black speaker is one of poverty in which municipal services are lacking. The result is that people are living in squalor, prey not just to rats but to disease, lack of education, and to all the consequent personal and social ills of contemporary society.

Adrienne Rich, *Diving into the Wreck,* *page 1190–92*

The poem describes the search of modern women through the symbolic history and myths of patriarchal culture (the "wreck," also short for "record") to recover their own identity. That reality is buried beneath the accretions of story (the "book of myths" [line 92]) written by others whose point of view excludes female experience. To achieve freedom and knowledge, the poem implies, women must take direct possession of their own experience (i.e., dive into the wreck), not as that experience is mediated through males, but through themselves. The symbolic equipment needed by women diving into the wreck of history includes a knife to cut away appearance from reality (line 3); a camera, to record that reality (line 2); and diving equipment, to keep them alive during the dangerous search and discovery (line 5). The idea that history is a wreck and a shambles is the poem's governing symbol, and the descent of women into the wreck symbolically suggests the need for women to salvage whatever in the past is valuable, despite the wreckage.

Theodore Roethke, *The Light Comes Brighter,* *page 1192*

This is a brief and optimistic poem. The brightening of light is a sure signal of spring in the northern latitudes, and all of nature responds to it. The poem's governing metaphor is light, which is certainly the realistic and perceivable light of the sun (line 5) but is also an intellectual light. Thus the final stanza tells us that the "leafy mind, that long was tightly furled, / Will turn its private substance into green, / And young shoots spread upon our inner world" (lines 18–20). Metaphorically, ideas spring forth when sufficient intellectual light shines on the mind. It is such thought that underlies the ancient concept that Apollo, the sun god, is also the god of intellect, art, music, and poetry. It is also the same idea that underlies the biblical passage from Isaiah: "The people that walked in darkness have seen a great light: they that dwell in the land of the shadow of death, upon them hath the light shined" (Isaiah 9:2).

One might draw attention to the poem's ninth line, which describes the alteration in trees in springtime: "Once more the trees assume familiar shapes." This line may be compared with "Or cheerful fields resume their green attire" in Gray's "Sonnet on the Death of Richard West" (733). The image here is quite apt as a description of trees leafing out in early spring.

Luis Omar Salinas, *In a Farmhouse*, *page 1193*

The speaker of "In a Farmhouse" is an eight-year old migrant worker child, forced to work in the fields with the other family members so that they can live through the year. The ironic last stanza points out the disparity between the Christian promise of happiness in a life to come and the reality of the child's earthly life. The irony is signaled by words that are oddly incompatible with the expected vocabulary of the speaker: "profoundly, / animated by the day's work / in the cottonfields" (lines 5–8). The poem thus questions the moral basis of our national economic well-being, and about our society's professed concern for children.

Sonia Sanchez, *right on; white america*, *pages 1193–94*

A striking thing about this poem initially is its disjointed presentation on the printed page, a graphic reminder that the world is disordered. The speaker refers to two major moments in American history: Custer's last stand, and the daily shootouts which popular history tells us were real parts of our past. Although native Americans lost most of their land and their culture, they literally blew "custer's mind / with a different / image of amer-ica" (lines 8–10), a point made with savage humor. The prophetic assertion is that the past persecution of minorities has not stopped, but is an ongoing condition in white America.

Carl Sandburg, *Chicago*, *pages 1194–95*

The speaker's recitation of the attributes of this raucous city, repeated with pride in the concluding section, gives the poem a far tighter organization than at first appears. The images are pictorial—a series of action vignettes out of which the young, strong, vitally male city emerges with brashness. The speaker's descriptions of the city in its vital processes of "Building, breaking, rebuilding," parallel the attributes for which poets have praised the earth: fecundity and the capacity to live and grow.

Siegfried Sassoon, *Dreamers*, *page 1195*

That the poem is a sonnet reminds us of the customary content of that form. Here, the speaker contrasts the ugliness, pain, and suffering of the soldier and the ordinary pleasures of civilized life. Even the daily grind of "going to the office in the train" (line 14) is part of the "hopeless longing" (line 12) of these "citizens of death's gray land" (line 1). The trench warfare of the first World War may be far different from future wars, but the suffering and waste of war will never change.

GJERTRUD SCHNACKENBERG, *The Paperweight,* *pages 1195–96*

The proportion on which this five-quatrain poem is based is that there is a vast force beyond us that looks down at us just as we look down at the world within the paperweight. The narrative of the poem is that the speaker holds a swirling-snow globular paperweight in her hand, and questions the nature of the artistic man-and-wife visible in the scene. Then, in stanza four, the "winter night" "bends to see / Our isolated little world of light." The idea is that there is much in the universe beyond what we see, for our world contains "drifts and swirls too deep to understand" (line 18). A problematic statement is made by the speaker in line 20: "With so much winter in my head and hand." Discussion should produce thoughts about the meaning of this line. The poem reminds one of the questions Keats raises in the "Ode on a Grecian Urn" (1018), and the speculations about reality and apparent reality are reminiscent of Stanton's "Childhood" (710) and Lynn Emanuel's "Like God" (1151).

ALAN SEEGER, *I Have a Rendezvous with Death,* *pages 1196*

The poem turns on the paradox of A–springtime as a time of death, not life, and B–the acceptance of this fact as a "rendezvous," i.e., a love meeting to which he is "pledged" (line 23). It is the ironic situation, in which soldiers are nothing but helpless pawns, that creates the argument of the poem. Implicitly, Seeger ironically deplores the institution of warfare in light of the earth's fecundity and the attractions of human love.

BRENDA SEROTTE, *My Mother's Face,* *page 1196*

This poem begins with an ordinary situation that takes place millions of times daily throughout the world: The speaker looks in a mirror while getting ready for work. But she observes there not herself but rather her mother. The poem leads the reader into a magical transformation of appearance and reality. Not only is the facial appearance real, but so is the entire image, including the mother's movements reflected in the mirror ("like I do," line 10). The speaker's observations are deeply moving, and the poem's muted but powerful conclusion cannot be forgotten. For comparison, see cummings's "if there are any heavens" (1138), Hamod's "Leaves" (1158), Hayden's "Those Winter Sundays" (1161), and Roethke's "My Papa's Waltz" (831).

William Shakespeare, *Fear No More the Heat o' the Sun,* *pages 1197–98*

This song from Act IV of *Cymbeline* blends two themes: The first is that death is the great leveler, the end to which all persons, however powerful or powerless, must come. The second is that death is a restful and safe haven, where one is free from injustice, discomfort (like the sun's heat), slander, and censure. The final stanza is a blessing, a magic spell over the grave, to keep it safe from predators or spirits, so that the lost one may rest in peace.

William Shakespeare, *Sonnet 29: When in Disgrace,* *page 1198*

This is one of the better-known sonnets, and it is noteworthy because it departs from the usual Shakespearean sonnet structure: Lines 9–14 form a unit, a sestet. In lines 1–8 the speaker cites circumstances in which his self-doubts overwhelm him. In lines 9–12 the speaker notes that the remembrance of the *thee* who is the listener of the poem, a memory occurring almost at random, lifts his spirits. The analogy of these lines is that of the soul departing from earth and singing as it passes into heaven. The simile also indicates that the speaker's joy is like the return of the lark's song at day's beginning.

William Shakespeare, *Sonnet 146: Poor Soul,* *page 1198*

This sonnet attempts to put into perspective the things that are important and valuable in life. The speaker laments the over-attention that he or she has paid to physical needs, the metaphorical "outward walls" (line 4) of the "fading mansion" (line 6) of the body, which, we are reminded, is made up of nothing more than "sinful earth" (line 1). Concluding that the metaphorical "lease" on life is short (line 5), and that flesh will decay, the speaker exhorts his or her soul to focus on things divine, to cultivate the spiritual rather than the physical, so that eternal life will overcome death.

If you have time, you might indicate that this poem brings up the interesting question of conjectural emendation in the text of Shakespeare's work. In the 1609 edition of the sonnets, the second line begins "My sinful earth," thus repeating the last three words of the first line ("My sinful earth these rebel powers that thee array." Editors have made a number of suggestions about what should be there to replace the obvious compositorial error. "Thrall to" is only one of the conjectures, but no one can ever know for certain what Shakespeare actually wrote.

Karl Shapiro, *Auto Wreck,* *page 1199*

This poem could not have been written except in our age of cars. As witness to a terrible automobile accident, the speaker confronts the horror of accidental mutilation and death, pointing out that, while many deaths are explicable or at least understandable, the carnage of collision is especially terrible because it is also especially illogical. The vivid description, and the uses of color, sound, light, and darkness, all contribute to the poem's impact. The survivors, in a state of shock (line 14), confront unanswerable questions which in their mystery can only be dealt with by "the occult mind" (line 36), for accidental death makes logic and reason irrelevant.

Leslie Marmon Silko, *Where Mountain Lion Lay Down with Deer,* *page 1200*

The poem is cast visually in the form of a physical journey up a mountain to a high point, which is paralleled by a journey through time, back almost into a racial memory to the beginning of creation. In a sense the speaker (if he or she is meant to be a literal person) is telling a Creation myth and at the same time lamenting the changes that have occurred in recent history. The tragedy is that the Navajo people, tribes, cultures, and past ways of life, are now forgotten, along with the "old songs" that told the stories (line 17). By implication, no one now cares, except those who are affected by the poem.

Dave Smith, *Bluejays,* *pages 1200–1201*

The situation is the interplay between a girl and a flock of bluejays. These birds are noisy and raucous, responding only with more noise to the girl's efforts to get them to come to her. But they do not fly away, and thus the speaker compares them to boys, afraid of beauty but fascinated by it. In that sense the poem is a paradigm of a pre-adult sexuality, in which the female attracts males, and they hover about her, unable to leave but also unable to approach her except in groups, and even then at a distance.

Stevie Smith, *Not Waving But Drowning,* *page 1201*

The justly famous poem uses the image of a drowning man waving frantically to those ashore, who mistake his gestures for greetings. The symbolic parallel is the frequency of human misunderstandings in communication, sometimes with tragic results. The situation becomes poignantly moving when we realize that this failure to be understood has been typical of the dying man's entire life.

W. D. Snodgrass, *These Trees Stand . . .*, *page 1201–1202*

The poem reflects a modern poet's wry realization that his is a very limited art; yet clearly it gives him joy. In the midst of grandiose words and concepts like the "heavens," the "steep celestial gulf," and "civilizations," (even though they are coming down with "the curse,"), here is the poet, "walking through the universe"—and attention must be paid. The poem is full of echoes: Lucinda, the kind of name that poets for hundreds of years after Elizabeth I gave their lady loves, the allusion in "Lucinda's skirts" of Herrick's "Whenas in silks my Julia goes," of Eliot's "Wipe your hand across your mouth" ("Preludes" [759]). Snodgrass puts them all together in a moment of high good spirits, and announces that even if the world were to end right now, he is walking through the universe, and having a great time, and (by implication) everyone should do the same.

Cathy Song, *Lost Sister*, *pages 1202–1203*

The poem details the repressed and restrained life of a Chinese woman, with her feet traditionally bound (line 16), and contrasts her life with the physically freer life of a woman who emigrated to the United States. But the speaker finds a good deal to admire in those women who remained in China (line 22). By contrast the expatriate finds the loneliness of unfamiliar and threatening surroundings. None of the women leaves any "footprints" (line 61), i.e., no special marks of identity, whether in the homeland or in the new land, but the traditional woman at least has the identity of being part of a long line of women upheld by well-understood and honored traditions.

Gary Soto, *Oranges*, *pages 1203–1205*

"Oranges" is a short narrative poem about the tentative but inexorable process of growth. The speaker recalls an incident of his boyhood (he was twelve) and his first date with a girl. Trying to impress the girl, he takes her to a drugstore and offers to buy her candy. The chocolate the girl asks for costs a dime, but the speaker has only an orange and a nickel, which he offers to the "saleslady" as payment. We presume after line 43 that the saleslady has understood the speaker's need to impress the girl, and that she has accepted the nickel and given him the chocolate. At the poem's end, the girl is opening the chocolate while the speaker is peeling his orange. The concluding image of seeming to make "a fire in my hands" symbolically suggests the emergence of adolescent sexuality.

GARY SOTO, *Kearney Park,* *page 1205*

"Kearney Park" is a short narrative. The speaker describes his memory of dancing and happiness, and, by implication, he describes one of the experiences that go to make up his mind and poetic spirit. At sunset in a park, the speaker throws himself into a dance to the throbbing music of the accordion and the drums. His grandmother is there urging him on in Spanish, and with the noise and the shouting and the clapping, he and his partner, "who is a brilliant arc of smiles, / An armful of falling water," spin, dip, and laugh until they seem merged with the intensity of the dance.

WILLIAM STAFFORD, *Traveling Through the Dark,* *pages 1205–1206*

The subject of this poem is the loss and possible extinction of the natural world that result from the encroachment of people on the environment. Specifically, the topic is an incident in which a pregnant doe has been run over and killed on a highway. The speaker, coming upon it in the dark, describes his thoughts about saving the living but unborn fawn. The pathos is intensified by the fawn's being pictured as "alive, still, never to be born" (line 11). As the speaker decides what to do, it is as if the whole landscape listens. But his decision is fixed by his participation in mechanized society; the lights of his car are focused forward, and he examines the doe "by the glow of the tail light" (line 5), as if Nature has been forgotten and deserted by human civilization.

GERALD STERN, *Burying an Animal on the Way to New York,* *page 1206*

As with Stafford's poem, the subject is the killing of animals on highways. Here the speaker addresses a generalized listener-driver who feels regret at the sight of a dead animal being powdered and vaporized by the many passing cars. The speaker suggests that the cars passing over the body, and carrying traces of it along the highway, are in fact burying it. Consequently, not only the body but the animal's ghost is being spread along, and the driver is asked both to imagine the death and be alert to the "twittering" of the passing spirit. The situation is indescribably sad.

WALLACE STEVENS, *The Emperor of Ice-Cream,* *pages 1206–1207*

This poem is in the *carpe diem* tradition dressed in modern garb. It proceeds in images, which initially suggest sensual enjoyment: big cigars, muscularity, girl/boy flirtation, ice-cream, and concoctions made of "concupiscent curds" (lines 1–8). The contrast beginning with line 9 focuses on the impoverished life and death of a woman and the grotesque reality of her corpse. Thus, if *be* is the "finale of seem" (i.e., an honest attempt to understand life's realities as opposed to illusion), we recognize that death is the reality that none can avoid. In this circumstance, what can human beings do? The speaker's answer is perhaps an avoidance: Live for the moment, even though we know that the moment is fleeting and brief; follow the pleasure and sweetness of the "emperor of ice-cream." This leader's empire may melt away, but it gives pleasure while it exists.

MAY SWENSON, *Question,* *page 1207*

The speaker suggests that the body provides a horse (i.e., a means of movement) and a hound (something to find things for us), and wonders what she/he will do when they are gone, i.e., when they are dead. What will it be like to be without a body, and to "lie in the sky"? Even worse, with only clouds for clothes, how will the speaker hide? Amid questions about what death is like, the speaker also suggests that in life we can hide who we are, but once dead there is nothing left but truth.

JONATHAN SWIFT, *A Riddle (The Vowels),* *page 1207*

The poem is a short virtuoso piece which illustrates the vowels (*a* in *glass*, *e* in *jet*, *i* in *tin*, *o* in *box*, and *u* in *pursue*). The idea here is to demonstrate the immense range of topics to be found in poetry. The content of Strand's "The Remains," for example, is exceedingly paradoxical, difficult, and problematical. By contrast, Swift's intention here is to be as simple and unambiguous as possible—to offer the reader an easy puzzle, and to use his poem as a mnemonic guide by which children might learn one of the most basic details of civilization. For other poem-puzzles for comparison, see Sylvia Plath's "Metaphors" (724) and Emily Dickinson's "I Taste a Liquor Never Brewed" (982).

JAMES TATE, *The Blue Booby,* *page 1208*

On one level, the poem describes the mating ritual of the booby, whose silly name makes it easy for the reader to become relaxed and positive. The male booby, a simple, undemanding fellow, has found the courting behavior which has the perfect "magical effect" (line 31) on his mate. Thus the reader is prepared, at line 37, to understand their mating not as copulation but as lovemaking, and to perceive how distant stars are reflected in the foil lining their nest "like the eyes of a mild savior" (line 41). Their behavior becomes part of the scheme of things in the universe, which for this reason seems gentle, benevolent, and loving. The poem thus is an idyll, an Edenic vision of a desirable and enviably unfallen world.

Dylan Thomas, *A Refusal to Mourn the Death,* *page 1209*

The language here calls upon Biblical and theological tradition: "mankind making" (line 1), "Fathering" (line 3), "Zion" (line 8), and "synagogue" (line 9) all elevate the event of a dying child to a dignified and serious level. The initial statement about the refusal to mourn is perplexing and startling: How could a person not mourn so terrible a death, especially that of a child? But the speaker widens this individual case into a universal one, and determines that it is all death, any death, which is the issue, in all its stark tragedy. As is typical of Thomas, the music of the poem is stressed, with complex rhythms and rhymes. The announced refusal to mourn becomes a stately elegy, itself a form of mourning.

Chase Twichell, *Blurry Cow,* *page 1209*

This poem is like James Wright's "A Blessing" (647) inasmuch as it too considers a rural scene. Twichell's vista contains two cows and also a woman carrying laundry. Her language ranges from plain and direct ("two cows stand," "the hot sting of a deerfly") to metaphorical ("sudden slur," "mirage of laundry"). The "blurry cow" refers to how the animal appears to the observer in the moving train, not to the objective cow itself. The last two lines stand as a summary of the meaning of the rural images; one's life is built from such afterimages of many days on earth. The poet captures the connections between experience and character, on the one hand, and the sights that seem temporary but which register permanently on the mind, on the other.

John Updike, *Perfection Wasted,* *page 1210*

The poem arises from a dramatic situation, like Shakespeare's "Shall I Compare Thee to a Summer's Day?" (794) and Donne's "The Canonization" (946). The speaker begins the first line as part of a conversation that he has been having with someone; the subject has been the "regrettable" things about death. Although we do not discover what these regrettable things are, the speaker is going in a new direction in this poem, to offer another regrettable thing. In effect, he is summarizing what makes each life unique, what gives life "your own brand of magic." The actions he cites to illustrate each person's unique charm suggest the value and happiness of living. The last two lines are particularly poignant, for they indicate the finality of death—it is not just the stopping of the heart and other vital processes, but is the cessation of individuality, companionship, activity, memory, laughter, love. Once a life has been lived, it is over, for "Who will do it again? That's it: no one." Although the speaker mentions a second person *you* and your in the poem, and may be referring to his listener, is seems that he is making observations about himself and expecting assent not only from his listener but from all readers.

TINO VILLANUEVA, *Day-Long Day*, *pages 1210–11*

"Day-Long Day" is a poem of social protest. It describes the long, hot, arduous labor of picking cotton for migrant workers, and the "unbending dreams" (line 14) of a mother who wants her child freed from this misery. The mingling of Spanish and English presents the mixture of two cultures and two peoples. The demands of the harvest turn the family into "sinews and backs" (line 8), and their exhaustion at day's end and their powerlessness combine to damn the child to become part of the world they cannot escape. For comparison, see "In a Farmhouse," by Luis Omar Salinas (1193).

SHELLY WAGNER, *The Boxes*, *pages 1211–12*

The poem describes an unbearable human tragedy—the accidental loss of a child and the unending grief it brings to a parent. Focusing on the police search through every sort of box or place of concealment in which the child could have been caught or imprisoned, the poem leaves us with the one box, both coffin and earth, in which his body is now held. The mother's agony is expressed indirectly, as she imagines going to the graveside and urging the boy, with the sternness a mother might use to a naughty child, to come home to bed where he belongs. The description of the police search, now familiar because of on-the-spot TV news coverage, is chilling. Wagner renders the drowning and the mother's grief indirectly, presenting a kind of denial on the mother's part as shown in her desire to sit by the bedside of her "sleeping boys." The overwhelming concluding lines make her grief both immediate and crushingly poignant.

ALICE WALKER, *Revolutionary Petunias*, *pages 1212–13*

The poem presents a vivid picture of the African-American underclass in American society. Touched with a smattering of traditional culture (note the names of the woman's five children in lines 18–20), and probably unable to get justice from the white legal system, "Sammy Lou of Rue" revenges her husband's death with the tool at hand, a farmer's hoe. White society, by contrast, has more efficient machinery, and will dispatch her by the "electric chair" (line 23). Her final words give the dimensions of her world—the word of God and the demands of her garden (lines 21–26). What does the world gain by sending such a person to her death?

EDMUND WALLER, *Go, Lovely Rose,* *pages 1213–14*

This is a lovely and haunting poem. It establishes the image of the rose, a conventional comparison used by many poets of love lyrics, but it uses the flower as a metaphor of the beauty, fragility, and impermanence of life. It is a perennial favorite of readers, and has often been set to music (for example, by Roger Quilter). The situation of the poem is a dramatic one, in which the speaker addresses a rose which he is about to send to a lady. The brevity of life that is the common lot of both rose and woman suggests that the poem is more a philosophical reflection than the invitation to sensual experience which is the basis of *carpe diem* poetry.

ROBERT PENN WARREN, *Heart of Autumn,* *page 1214*

"Heart of Autumn," by the first of America's poet laureates, is in the tradition of pastoral poetry, in which the autumnal season has conventionally signaled the winding down of life. It is also a nature poem, and its details of hunting and shooting wild geese demonstrate strongly the device of onomatopoeia ("Some crumple," "Some stagger," "last glide," "far glint," "great wing-beat"). The dominant metaphor of the poem is that the destiny of the geese is like that of the speaker (and all persons), for all living things know "time and distance." The geese are in one respect more fortunate than human beings, for they "know / The path of pathlessness, with all the joy / Of destiny fulfilling its own name," while the speaker does not know why he "is here." Nevertheless, the poem's concluding lines, with their strong yearning, are uplifting and exalting. For comparison, see Oliver's "Wild Geese" (957) and Graham's "The Geese" (948).

BRUCE WEIGL, *Song of Napalm,* *pages 1215-16*

Students may need reminding that napalm is an incendiary substance, gelled gasoline, used in anti-personnel weapons. When it is exploded and when it burns, it sticks to the person it splashes on, creating horrible and painful burns, which are usually fatal. The narrator of "Song of Napalm" is apparently a Vietnam veteran who has returned home and is resuming a normal, peaceful life, but even though he is safe and is in love, he cannot forget the image of a child he saw who was killed by burning napalm, "Stuck to her dress like jelly." The vision is indelible, and no present or future happiness "can deny" the reality of the horror the speaker has experienced. For comparison, see Owen's "Dulce et Decorum Est" (810) and Dan Georgakas's "Hiroshima Crewman" (1154).

PHILLIS WHEATLEY, *On Being Brought from Africa to America*, *page 1216*

The speaker, who is visualized as a person displaced from his or her native Africa in the eighteenth century, accepts the supremacy of Colonial America and the Christian religion. In the speaker's white/black imagery, white equals the angelic and the saved, black the "sable race" (line 5), the benighted soul (because non-Christian), and God's judgment on Cain (line 7). Although the concluding lines exhort Christians not to condemn blacks, they do so only in the belief that blacks, once converted, become equal to whites. There are many poems in the anthology with which this poem may be contrasted.

WALT WHITMAN, *Full of Life Now*, *page 1216*

This poem is Whitman's letter to posterity, to us, celebrating the fact of vitality ("full of life now, compact, visible") at the time he writes. He regrets that future readers will be alive when his life is gone, but he wishes nevertheless to be with us. The concluding line is a wish for us to consider him still with us. It is also a celebration of poetry, because, although he is not with us in actuality, his poems—his ideas, the life he transmitted through his words, his power—are. The conclusion therefore makes this poem comparable with poems like Shakespeare's "Shall I Compare Thee to a Summer's Day?" (794) and similar poems on the imortality that art confers.

WALT WHITMAN, *Beat! Beat! Drums!*, *pages 1216–17*

Whitman wrote this poem at the beginning of the Civil War, the most destructive conflict in which the nation has ever been engaged. The image of the beating drums pervades the poem, touching all aspects of life. Nothing will be untouched by the terrible drums and the horror of war. Nothing peaceful can continue, not schools, not churches, not farmers, not sleepers, not businessmen, not lawyers—not anyone. The sound of the drums and the horrors of war invade every corner of the land, every activity, every person, every thought. Usually poems about war touch on atrocities and death. Here, however, the relentless sound of the drums, which is the brutal sound of war, is predominant.

WALT WHITMAN, *Dirge for Two Veterans,* *pages 1217–18*

The narrative of this poem, which Whitman wrote during the mid point of the Civil War, is that the speaker describes a sorrowful funeral procession in which a father and a son are to be buried. The "son is brought with the father" to a double grave. The moon is like an immense and silent phantom ascending the sky to provide a ghostly light. In the face of such inexorable and pervasive truth there is little consolation except the moon's light and the music of the bugles and the drums. The speaker gives what he can—his love. Nevertheless, death has won; people have not.

RICHARD WILBUR, *April 5, 1974,* *page 1218*

One of America's Poets Laureate, Wilbur is widely recognized not only as a major poet but also as a translator. This poem contains obvious echoes of Robert Frost, inasmuch as it is basedin an outdoor environment, in this poem, in early spring. The poem also echoes the opening verses of the Bible ("There was a subtle flood of steam / Moving upon the face of things," lines 13–14). The image relating the scene to a "set mind" in line 18 is something of a surprise, and it is also somewhat problematic ("blessed by doubt"). The conclusion is simply expressed, and perfectly appropriate granted the rural scene depicted in the poem. Flowers will of course come of it, as will the flowers of ideas develop from a "set mind" when it "relaxes into mother-wit."

WILLIAM CARLOS WILLIAMS, *The Red Wheelbarrow,* *pages 1218–19*

The red/white contrast of the mentioned objects bears the weight of the poem's only assertion, "so much depends ..." The wheelbarrow, the rain, and the white chickens are simple but essential to the life of the farmer and therefore to all life.

WILLIAM BUTLER YEATS, *The Wild Swans at Coole,* *page 1219*

In this meditative lyric of five stanzas the speaker considers the inevitable alterations that life brings, and the impermanence of life. The situation of "The Wild Swans at Coole" is that the speaker returns to a scene known in previous years—the same type of occasion that Wordsworth describes in the "Tintern Abbey" lines (1044). At Coole, the wild swans are the same as they were long ago; they have not changed and they will not change. The speaker describes the habits of the "brilliant creatures"—paddling, swimming, flying, drifting "on the still water." To the speaker the swans are constant; their hearts have not grown cold (implied is the idea that the hearts of others have grown cold). The swans bespeak a mysteriousness and beauty that the speaker is unable to define. His concluding thought is that "some day" he may awake "To find they have flown away." Although this concluding line indicates that the birds, too, will depart, like everything else, it is more likely that the speaker will be gone and will no longer be able to see them. A major image in the poem is in lines 9–12, in which the speaker describes the swans as mounting the sky in "great broken rings." This image suggests the gyre, that image of blending change that waxes and wanes as time progresses, of "The Second Coming" (961).

PAUL ZIMMER, *The Day Zimmer Lost Religion,* *page 1220*

The title is ironic. It should be "Zimmer's Coming of Age," for the poem describes the thoughts of a young speaker who, raised as an observant Catholic, chooses to miss Sunday mass. As a result, he speculates that a pugnacious and aggressive Jesus will "wade into" his "blasphemous gut" and knock him out, as though he is in a boxing match cheered on by the devil in a "reserved" seat roaring "until he got the hiccups" (line 7). The imagery of the poem abounds with holy objects of worship together with the symbolism of the boxing ring, such as facial "cuts and mice" (line 17), "drop me" (line 5), and "I was grown up and ready for Him now" (line 21). The principal mode of description is overstatement, producing the poem's irony and also its comedy (the metaphors are fresh, clever, and funny).

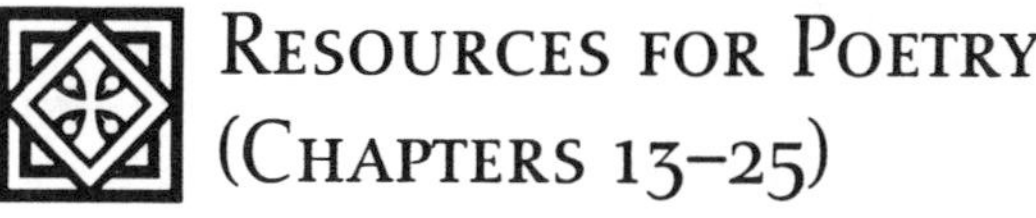

Resources for Poetry (Chapters 13–25)

Audiotape and CD Recordings of Poetry

❖ *Readings Mainly by the Poets Themselves, and also by Skilled Actors*

For decades, poets have been reading their poems to eager and curious audiences at colleges, universities, and poetry workshops. Often they introduce their poems briefly before they read them, and they often discuss poetry in general. Only rarely do they just read their poems without comment. Prior to the invention of the tape recorder, these readings were totally lost. In the last fifty years, however, many poetry readings have been taped, and it is now unusual if someone does not make a recording of the reading. Often these recordings are privately maintained in the English department or the College library, and they are not available to the larger public.

A great service for lovers of poetry is being accomplished by commercial recording companies, some of which are quite small and dedicated, who have arranged with many individual poets and actors to make studio recordings for wide distribution. The Academy of American Poets has launched a tapes program for the distribution of recorded readings at the Academy. In these ways, the voices of many contemporary poets have been preserved, along with the voices of many other major older poets such as Robert Frost, Dylan Thomas, T. S. Eliot, Ezra Pound, Wallace Stevens, and William Butler Yeats. Some of the sources of such recordings are these:

❖ Academy of American Poets Tapes Program (32 tapes)
584 Broadway, Suite 1208
New York City, New York 10012-3250

❖ Audio Bookshelf
174 Prescott Hill Road
Northport, Maine 04849

- Audio Partners
  Auburn, California 95604
- Caedmon Records (Caedmon [HC])
  Now controlled by HarperCollins.
- Dove Audio
  Beverly Hills, California 90210
  New York City, New York 10023
- HarperCollins
  10 East 53rd Street
  New York, New York 10022
  HarperCollins now controls Caedmon recordings.
- Highbridge Co.
  1000 Westgate Drive
  St. Paul, Minnesota 55114
- Spoken Arts
  8 Lawn Avenue
  New Rochelle, New York 10801

Recordings of many of the poets in the fifth edition of *Literature: An Introduction to Reading and Writing* are available from these sources. Many older tapings have been remastered, and their quality improved. The list below refers to these companies whenever it is known that a commercial audio cassette is available.

It is worth mentioning that a landmark four CD box is available entitled *A Century of Recorded Poetry*, issued in 1996 by Rhino Records, Inc., 10635 Santa Monica Blvd., Los Angeles, CA 90025-4900. The first CD contains the voice of a speaker who is probably Walt Whitman. Many other poets are also present on the entire four-CD set, including Cohen, Forché, Lee, Nemerov, Plath, Pound, Rich, Roethke, Sarton, Stafford, Wakoski, Wilbur, Yeats, and Zimmer,

In addition, a notable general collection of readings is the *Caedmon Treasury of Modern Poets Reading Their Own Poetry* (HarperCollins). Included on this three-cassette set, among other poets, are Auden, Eberhart, Eliot, Frost, MacLeish, MacNeice, Moore, Pound, Spender, Stevens, Thomas, Wilbur, William Carlos Williams, and Yeats.

Many recordings exist that are not available commercially. The Poets House in New York City contains an archival treasure—The Axe-Houghton Poetry Tape Archive—of recordings of many poets who have given readings at the Academy of American Poets (584 Broadway, Suite 1208, New York City 10012-3250), the Poets House itself (72 Spring Street, New York City 10012), and other nearby important poetry workshops and projects such as the Poetry Project at St Mark's Church in New York and the 92nd Street Y. These audiotapes, deposited in the Axe-Houghton Archive, are noted below with the designation "Poets House."

Following is a listing of seventy-six poets included in the anthology for whom tapes are A–available for purchase, as indicated by the publishing company that has issued them (including the Academy of American Poets), or B–on deposit in the Axe-Houghton Archive at Poets House.

A. R. Ammons

1. Poetry reading, Academy of American Poets, March, 1965. Poets House.
2. Interview, June, 1980. Poets House.
3. Conversations with A. R. Ammons, February, 1980, in the Academy of American Poets Conversations series. Poets House.

Maya Angelou

- ❖ *And Still I Rise*. Random House, 1996.

Margaret Atwood

1. Readings in the Caedmon *Voices in Time* series, 1977. Caedmon (HC).
2. *Margaret Atwood Reads*, HarperCollins

W. H. Auden

1. Readings in the Caedmon *Voices in Time* series, 1955.
2. Readings in the Spoken Arts Series, *Modern American Poets Reading Their Poems*. Spoken Arts.
3. Readings at the Academy of American Poets, January and March, 1966. Poets House.
4. *Selected Poems by W. H. Auden*. Spoken Arts.
5. *Tell Me the Truth about Love*. Random House.
6. Readings at the Guggenheim Museum, intro by Marianne Moore. Academy of American Poets.

Imamu Amiri Baraka

1. Reading, St. Marks Poetry Project, general series. Poets House.
2. Symposium at the St. Marks Poetry Project, May, 1985. Poets House.
3. Discussion of African American Oral Traditions, Poets House, March, 1990. Poets House.

Elizabeth Bishop

1. Readings in the Spoken Arts Series, *Modern American Poets Reading Their Poems*, 1985. Spoken Arts.
2. Private recording of a poetry reading, 1982. Poets House.
3. Reading at the Academy of American Poets, May, 1969. Poets House.
4. *Conversations with Elizabeth Bishop*. Academy of American Poets, November, 1977. Poets House.
5. Reading of Bishop's poems by Randall Jarrell. Academy of American Poets, 1964. Poets House.

William Blake

❖ William Blake: *Poems*. Highbridge.

Louise Bogan

1. Readings in the Spoken Arts Series, *Modern American Poets Reading Their Poems*, 1985. Spoken Arts.
2. Reading at the Academy of American Poets, intro by John Hall Wheelock. November, 1968. Poets House.

Gwendolyn Brooks

1. Reading at the Academy of American Poets, May, 1983. intro by Jane Flanders. Poets House. Academy of American Poets.
2. Readings in the Spoken Arts Series, *Modern American Poets Reading Their Poems*. Spoken Arts.
3. *Gwendolyn Brooks reading Her Poetry*, intro. by Don L. Lee, HarperCollins

Olga Broumas

1. Commercial recording, 1981, *If I Yes*, Watershed.
2. Reading at the St. Marks Poetry Project, October, 1986. Poets House.

Elizabeth and Robert Browning

❖ *How Do I Love Thee*. Audio Partners.

Lord Byron

❖ *Poetry of Byron*. Read by Tyrone Power. HarperCollins

Amy Clampitt

❖ Reading at the Academy of American Poets, 1987. intro. by Seamus Heaney. Academy of American Poets.

Lucille Clifton

1. Reading at the Academy of American Poets, May, 1983. Poets House. Academy of American Poets.
2. Reading in the Family Stories Series, Snug Harbor Cultural Center, June, 1990. Poets House.

Countée Cullen

❖ Readings in the Spoken Arts Series (with Richard Eberhart), *Modern American Poets Reading Their Poems*. Spoken Arts.

E. E. CUMMINGS

1. Readings in the Spoken Arts Series, *Modern American Poets Reading Their Poems*. Issued by Spoken Arts in 1985.
2. *E. E. Cummings Reads*. A selection of poems recorded in 1953. Issued in 1993 by Caedmon (HarperCollins).

James Dickey

❖ Readings in the Spoken Arts Series, *Modern American Poets Reading Their Poems*, 1985. Spoken Arts.

Emily Dickinson

1. A discussion of Emily Dickinson's poetry by May Swenson at the Academy of American Poets, April, 1984. Poets House.
2. A discussion of Emily Dickinson's poetry by Susan Howe in the "Passwords" Series, May, 1990. Poets House.
3. *Poems and Letters of Emily Dickinson,* read by Julie Harris, 1991. Caedmon (HC).
4. *Fifty Poems of Emily Dickinson* (2 CD's). Dove Audio.

John Donne

1. *A Treasury of John Donne,* read by Robert Speaight. Spoken Arts.
2. *The Love Poems of John Donne.* Read by Richard Burton. HarperCollins.

Richard Eberhart

1. Reading at the Academy of American Poets, December, 1969. Poets House.
2. Reading in the Spoken Arts Series (with Countee Cullen), *Modern American Poets Reading Their Poems,* 1985. Spoken Arts.

T. S. Eliot

1. Reading in the Spoken Arts Series, *Modern American Poets Reading Their Poems.* 1985, Spoken Arts.
2. Reading of Selected Poems, including "Macavity." Caedmon (HC), 1991.
3. *T. S. Eliot Reading "The Waste Land" and Other Poems.* HarperCollins.

❖ Many additional recordings.

Carolyn Forché

❖ Readings at the Academy of American Poets, 1994/1978. intro by Cyrus Cassells (1994) and Lauren Shakely (1978). Poets House. Academy of American Poets.

Robert Frost

1. A private recording of a public reading, 1950. Poets House.
2. A private recording of a public reading, 1952. Poets House.
3. Reading in the Spoken Arts Series, *Modern American Poets Reading Their Poems*. Issued in 1985 by Spoken Arts.
4. *Robert Frost in Recital*. Recordings made during readings in 1951, 1952, and 1953. Issued by Caedmon (HC), 1992. HarperCollins
5. *Robert Frost Reads*. HarperCollins

Allen Ginsberg

1. Reading in the Spoken Arts Series, *Modern American Poets Reading Their Poems*, 1985. Spoken Arts.
2. Reading, *The Lion for Real*, 1989, for Great Jones. Poets House.

Louise Glück

❖ Readings at the Academy of American Poets, 1992/1981. intro. by Thomas Lux (1992). Academy of American Poets.

Robert Graves

❖ *Robert Graves Reads*, a selection of poems recorded in 1957. Caedmon (HC), 1993.

John Haines

1. Reading and discussion with Sonia Sanchez at the NY/NJ Teachers Conference, April 1992. Poets House
2. Reading at the Academy of American Poets, March, 1980. Poets House

Donald Hall

1. "Names of Horses," 1985. Watershed.
2. Reading in the Spoken Arts Series, *Modern American Poets Reading Their Poems*, 1985. Spoken Arts.
3. *Donald Hall: Prose and Poetry*. Audio Bookshelf.

Robert Hayden

- ❖ Reading at the Academy of Amerian Poets, 1976. intro. by William Meredith. Academy of American Poets

Seamus Heaney

1. Reading at the Academy of American Poets, the "Education of the Poet" Series, March, 1987. Poets House.
2. *Stepping Stones*. Penguin Audio.

William Heyen

1. Three readings in 1991 issued by Time Being Books
2. Reading of poems from *Erika* and *Pterodactyl Rose.* Poets House

John Hollander

1. Reading in the Spoken Arts Series, *Modern American Poets Reading Their Poems*, 1985. Spoken Arts.
2. Reading at the Academy of American Poets, 1992. intro. by Richard Howard. Academy of American Poets.

Langston Hughes

1. *Langston Hughes Reads and Talks About His Poems.* Issued by Spoken Arts in 1985.
2. *Langston Hughes Reads,* poems recorded for the BBC in 1962 and 1964. Issued by Caedmon (HC) in 1992. HarperCollins.

Randall Jarrell

1. Reading at the Academy of American Poets (also including the reading of poems by Elizabeth Bishop), 1964. intro. by Robert Lowell. Poets House. Academy of American Poets.
2. Reading in the Spoken Arts Series, *Modern American Poets Reading Their Poems*, 1985. Spoken Arts.

Robinson Jeffers

- ❖ Reading in the Spoken Arts Series, *Modern American Poets Reading Their Poems*, 1985. Spoken Arts.

Donald Justice

- ❖ Reading at the Academy of American Poets, March 1975. Poets House.

John Keats

- ❖ *The Poetry of Keats*. Read by Ralph Richardson. HarperCollins.

Carolyn Kizer

1. Reading at the Academy of American Poets, March, 1986. Poets House.
2. Reading at the Academy of American Poets, 1995 (with David Wagoner). intro. by Stanley Kunitz. Academy of American Poets.

Maxine Kumin

- ❖ Reading at the Academy of American Poets, 1979. intro. by Jane Shore. Academy of American Poets.

Philip Levine

- ❖ Readings at the Academy of American Poets, 1978/1991. intro. by Stanley Plumly (1978). Academy of American Poets.

Audre Lorde

1. Reading at the Academy of American Poets, March, 1977. Poets House.
2. Reading at the St. Marks Poetry Project, April, 1976. Poets House.

Archibald MacLeish

- ❖ Reading in the Spoken Arts Series, *Modern American Poets Reading Their Poems*, 1985. Spoken Arts.

Heather McHugh

- ❖ Reading at the Great Neck Library, 1979. Privately recorded. Poets House.

W. S. Merwin

- ❖ Reading at the Academy of American Poets, 1966. intro. by Robert Lowell. Academy of American Poets.

Ogden Nash

- ❖ Reading in the Spoken Arts Series, *Modern American Poets Reading Their Poems*, 1985. Spoken Arts.

Howard Nemerov

- ❖ Reading at the Academy of American Poets, 1989. intro. by Helen Vendler. Academy of American Poets.

Naomi Shihab Nye

- ❖ Reading in the Poets House Festival Series. "Southwest Poetry," a joint appearance with Joy Harjo, March, 1991. Poets House.

Sharon Olds

- ❖ Reading and discussion at the NY/NJ Teachers Conference, 1987. Poets House Education Series. Poets House.

Linda Pastan

1. Reading at the Great Neck Library, 1975. Privately recorded. Poets House.
2. Reading in the "Family Stories" Series at the Snug Harbor Cultural Center, May, 1990. Poets House.

Sylvia Plath

1. Reading in the Spoken Arts Series, *Modern American Poets Reading Their Poems*, 1985. Spoken Arts.
2. *Sylvia Plath Reads*. HarperCollins.

Ezra Pound

1. Reading in the Spoken Arts Series, *Modern American Poets Reading Their Poems*, 1985. Spoken Arts.
2. *Ezra Pound Reads*, a selection of poems recorded in 1960. Issued by Caedmon (HC) in 1993. HarperCollins.

John Crowe Ransom

- ❖ Reading in the Spoken Arts Series, *Modern American Poets Reading Their Poems*, 1985. Spoken Arts.

Theodore Roethke

- Reading in the Spoken Arts Series, *Modern American Poets Reading Their Poems*, 1985. Spoken Arts.

Muriel Rukuyser

1. Reading at the Academy of American Poets, December, 1976. Poets House.
2. Reading at the Great Neck Library, 1975, privately recorded. Poets House.

Sonia Sanchez

- Reading and Discussion at the NY/NJ Teachers Conference, Education Series, April, 1992, with John Haines. Poets House.

Carl Sandberg

1. Reading in the Spoken Arts Series, *Modern American Poets Reading Their Poems*, 1985. Spoken Arts.
2. *Carl Sandberg Reads*, a selection of poems recorded in 1951 and 1952. Issued by Caedmon (HC) in 1992. HarperCollins.

May Sarton

- *May Sarton Reading Her Poetry*. HarperCollins.

Anne Sexton

1. Reading in the Spoken Arts Series, *Modern American Poets Reading Their Poems*, 1985. Spoken Arts.
2. Readings in the "Voices in Time" Series, 1974. Caedmon (HC).
3. *Anne Sexton reads*. HarperCollins, 1993.

William Shakespeare

- A Selection of Shakespeare's Sonnets read by Sir John Gielgud, recorded in 1963 and 1988. Two cassettes, issued by Caedmon (HC).

Percy Bysshe Shelley

- ❖ *Poetry of Shelley*. Read by Vincent Price. HarperCollins.

Leslie Marmon Silko

- ❖ Reading at the Academy of American Poets, April, 1987 (Writers/Readers Series). Poets House.

W. D. Snodgrass

- ❖ Reading in the Spoken Arts Series, *Modern American Poets Reading Their Poems*, 1985. Spoken Arts.

William E. Stafford

- ❖ Reading at the Academy of American Poets, 1974. intro. by Frederick Morgan. Academy of American Poets.

Wallace Stevens

1. Reading in the Spoken Arts Series, *Modern American Poets Reading Their Poems*, 1985. Spoken Arts.
2. *Wallace Stevens Reads*, a selection of poems recorded in 1956. Issued in 1993 by Caedmon. HarperCollins.

Mark Strand

1. Reading in the Spoken Arts Series, *Modern American Poets Reading Their Poems*, 1985. Spoken Arts.
2. Reading at the Academy of American Poets, 1978. intro. by Gregory Orr. Academy of American Poets.

May Swenson

1. Reading in the Education/Poet Series at the Academy of American Poets, November, 1978. Poets House.
2. Reading at the Academy of American Poets, 1985. intro. by Howard Moss. Academy of American Poets.

Dylan Thomas

1. Reading of May, 1952, private recording. Poets House.
2. *Dylan Thomas Reads*, a selection of works recorded in the early 1950s. Issued by Caedmon (HC) in 1993.

Mona Van Duyn

- ❖ Reading at the Academy of American Poets, 1991. intro. by Anthony Hecht. Academy of American Poets.

David Wagoner

- ❖ Reading in the Spoken Arts Series, *Modern American Poets Reading Their Poems*, 1985. Spoken Arts.

Diane Wakoski

- ❖ Reading at the Academy of American Poets, January, 1970. Poets House.

Robert Penn Warren

1. Reading in the Spoken Arts Series, *Modern American Poets Reading Their Poems*, 1985. Spoken Arts.
2. Reading at the Academy of American Poets, 1977. intro. by Stanley Kunitz. Academy of American Poets.

Richard Wilbur

1. Reading at the Academy of American Poets, April, 1969. Poets House.
2. Reading at the Academy of American Poets, 1989. intro. by James Merrill. Academy of American Poets.

William Carlos Williams

- ❖ *William Carlos Williams Reads*, a selection of poems recorded in 1958. Issued by Caedmon, 1993. HarperCollins.

William Wordsworth

- ❖ *A Treasury of William Wordsworth*, a selection of poems read by Robert Speaight. Spoken Arts.

James Wright

1. Reading in the Spoken Arts Series, *Modern American Poets Reading Their Poems*, 1985. Spoken Arts.
2. Reading in the Academy of American Poets Poetry Series, "The Music of Poetry," March 1967. Poets House.

3. Conversations with James Wright at the Academy of American Poets, March, 1977. Poets House.
4. Reading at the Academy of American Poets, 1964/1978. intro. by Mark Strand (1978). Academy of American Poets.

William Butler Yeats

- *The Poems of W. B. Yeats,* readings by various readers, including Yeats himself. Spoken Arts.

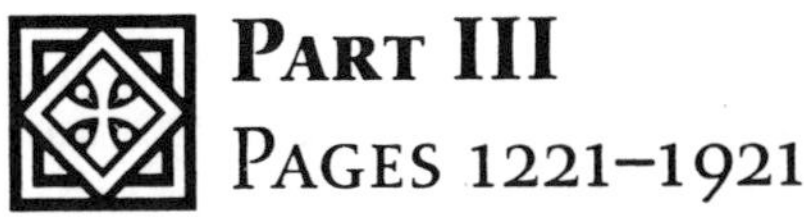

PART III
PAGES 1221–1921

Reading and Writing about Drama

Coverage of the Manual

The plays included in the text feature introductions, explanatory glosses and notes, study questions, and writing topics. Because this material is relatively extensive, we have limited coverage in the manual to discussions of some of the more vexing study questions and suggestions about teaching. Where possible, we suggest filmed or videotaped versions of the plays that you might use to supplement the texts.

Organization of the Drama Section

Unlike the other major sections of the text, the drama section is not organized according to discrete elements. Rather, the elements of drama are introduced and discussed in the first part of Chapter 26. This material is followed by four shorter plays, any one of which can be used for classroom illustration. Chapters that focus on tragedy, comedy, and realism in drama follow this introductory chapter, together with a brief chapter on film and a concluding chapter on the career of Henrik Ibsen (Chapter 31). While the elements of drama remain important considerations throughout the drama section, these later chapters focus on the distinctive qualities of the mode (i.e., tragedy, comedy, realism, nonrealism, film).

Organization of Each Drama Chapter

Each chapter follows the general plan pursued throughout the book: introductory material followed by a selection of plays. The plays are accompanied by extensive apparatus, including introductions, notes, glosses, questions for study and classroom use, and "General Questions" for writing and further discussion. Each chapter concludes with a section on writing, which comprises discussions of strategies for writing about specific aspects of drama, sample essays, commentary, and special writing topics for studying the subject of the chapter. The sample student essays take up elements or aspects of one of the plays included in the chapter; they can be used for your own writing assignments or for supplementary reading.

Suggestions for Teaching Drama

We do not expect that you will use all the plays during an introductory course (unless the course is focused on drama). The broad scope of the selections provides for variation and flexibility. We do recommend, however, that you begin with the elements of drama in Chapter 26. Any one of the plays in the chapter will illustrate various aspects of the elements, and some plays will highlight specifics. Kauffmann's *The More the Merrier* illustrates the nature of dramatic involvement and also the qualities of comedy and farce. Glaspell's *Trifles* is ideal for demonstrating dramatic responses between characters on stage together, and also showing the changes and developments of their characters. Keller's *Tea Party* is brief enough to be read and discussed in one meeting of class, and it may be used to show the power and compactness of dramatic dialogue. O'Neill's *Before Breakfast* is a virtuoso piece illustrating how dramatic interest may be centered upon just one major character on stage. Though the plays show great variety of topic and treatment, any or all of them may be used as examples for most of the elements of drama.

For the remainder of your course, you may pick and choose as your interests dictate. You might concentrate on a specific mode of drama, or offer your students a wide variety, combining, for example, tragedy with comedy. You might also explore the possibility of a thematic orientation here, focusing on plays that deal with topics such as love, marriage, the family, and society.

In teaching drama to students with little or no background, you will need to be sure that they understand how plays work on the stage so that they can build imaginative theaters in their minds. To this end, we have discussed aspects of production at some length. We recommend that you encourage students to go to whatever live theater may be easily available. We also suggest that you screen a film or videotape of at least one play or film you are teaching, if time permits. Some instructors find that using class time for complete viewings may preempt valuable instruction time. One solution to the problem is to show only selected parts of the videotape in class; another is to set aside larger blocks of time outside of class for complete viewing.

Many other strategies can be used in the classroom to make plays come alive. One of these is an open-book reading of an entire short play, as we have suggested for Keller's *Tea Party*. The time taken for readings will of course vary, but plays like Glaspell's *Trifles* and Chekhov's *The Bear* should take no more than thirty-five to forty minutes. While you cannot expect your students to give polished readings, the spoken words will often carry more impact than the words alone on the page. Another approach, particularly for longer plays, is to have students enact specific and crucial scenes, such as the play-within-the-play in *A Midsummer Night's Dream,* some of the soliloquies of Hamlet, or the confrontation of Biff and Willy Loman in Miller's *Death of a Salesman.* The scenes from the Wells/Mankiewicz *Citizen Kane* and Laurents's *The Turning Point* are made to order for brief classroom enactment. This sort of pointed work might involve out-of-class preparation, but the results can be impressive, particularly if student-actors and the class at large can discuss why individual readings were made, why vocal inflections were done, how another reading might have created a different effect, and so on.

Also, to bring theater alive for your students, you might look into the possibility of using some of the expertise available in your college's theater department. Given this possibility, another broad range of options is available. You might, for example, arrange for a group of theater students to stage one of the text's short plays for your class (either a memorized or an open-book reading). At some larger schools, a significant number of literature classes might study the same play at the same time. In this situation, a drama department, given enough lead time, might be willing to plan a full-scale production of one of the plays in the text. Sometimes, individual classroom drama instructors might stage a brief "open-book" production as an exam for their students, with your students invited as audience. Keep in mind that theater students are eagerly looking for audiences; such projects can be mutually constructive.

In teaching an individual play, your approach will be determined by the available time and the level of preparation. If there is not much time, you can deal only with the play's major features: what happens, why it happens, the major characters, the subjects, and major themes. Even this sort of overview can teach students much. If you have more time, you can have your students examine conflicts, structure, irony, and language, because a close look at these aspects will help them to become more disciplined readers of drama. In any event, your approach should always be geared to the needs and abilities of students. A close analysis of the "flower imagery" in *Hamlet* or the Ovidian elements in *A Midsummer Night's Dream,* for example, is rarely as useful as a study of Hamlet's character or the structural importance of Bottom and his crew of "hempen homespuns."

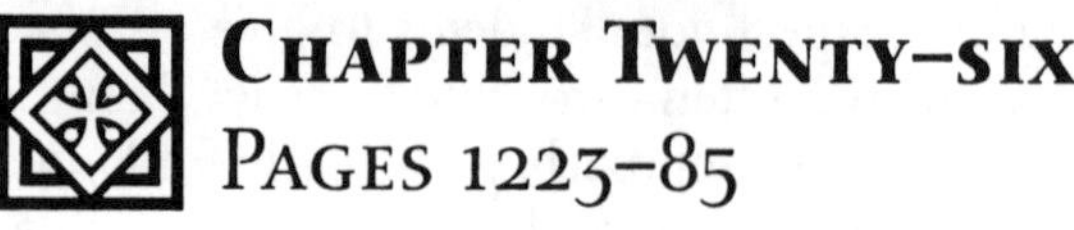

Chapter Twenty-six
Pages 1223–85

The Dramatic Vision: An Overview

The introductory material provides a definition and description of drama (1223), an extensive discussion of drama as literature (1223–31) and as performance (1231–34), and a survey and brief history of types of drama (1234–41). Most of these topics can be assigned as outside reading, but the discussions of drama as literature and performance would benefit from classroom review, and this can be combined with study of specific plays. The section on "Reading Plays" (1241–42) will help students come to grips with this experience.

Anonymous, *The Visit to the Sepulchre (Visitatio Sepulchri)*, *pages 1237–38*

The *Quem Quaeritis Trope* has the virtue of being extremely short, thus making it possible to read and discuss almost simultaneously. Students unfamiliar with the mass and the movable feast days of the medieval Catholic Church may need more explanation than the text provides. Usually, students express great interest in seeing the entire play, brief as it is, and in discussing ways in which the play could evoke great dramatic excitement, perhaps too much excitement, in a church ritual.

Suggestions for Discussing the Study Questions, page 1238

(1) The dramatic characteristics are the action of the three Marys in walking to the sepulchre, their meeting the Angel, and his informing them that "He is not here. He has been resurrected, as was predicted." The most dramatic part of the play is the rejoicing by the Angel and the three Marys as they leave the scene, together with their cries of "Alleluia." One may imagine the powerful effect of these simple dramatic actions and speeches on an audience of churchgoers.

(2) The dramatic actions might be imagined as beginning with the three Marys entering and demonstrating their grief. After this, anyone's guess about further action is as good as anyone else's,

because there are no specific directions in the remaining texts of the trope. However, let us suppose that the angel holds up the shroud to show the three Marys, and then that he shows the shroud to the spectators. The effect might well have been overwhelming, for the empty tomb is the initiating and also the most powerful symbol of Christianity. The scene direction included within brackets on page 1237 suggests some additional properties that might have been used by those acting the various parts.

(3) Suggestions for this question have already been made. It is difficult to assume that any believing audience would have remained silent through the exit of the actors, however. It is possible that responses would have been great: Some would have knelt and prayed; others would have shouted allelulia, along with the actors. Students might enjoy speculating further on audience responses.

WRITING TOPICS. The biblical basis of the *Visitatio Sepulchri*. The possible dramatic actions in the trope. How would the trope have created an interest in further biblical enactments?

WORKS FOR COMPARISON WITH "THE VISIT TO THE SEPULCHRE"

Crashaw, *Our Crucified Lord*, 758
Herbert, *Easter Wings*, 907
St. Luke, *The Parable of the Prodigal Son*, 445

SUSAN GLASPELL, *Trifles*, *pages 1244–54*

This play examines the agony and desperation that often occur in life (good pieces for comparison are O'Neill's *Before Breakfast* and Keller's *Tea Party*). It also explores traditional male attitudes toward women, together with the expression of female responses to these attitudes. The key irony in the play, of course, is that the two women characters do what the men cannot do; they solve the problem of motive based on the evidence of "trifles," and they pass judgment on the murderer based on both the crime and the context.

Although the play is set on a farm and concerns a family murder, it is really about marriage, society, and the relationship between men and women. These thematic concerns are repeated on three levels: the history of the Wrights' marriage, the traditional repression of women, and the conflict between the men and women in the Wrights' kitchen. In each case (and in general), woman is protagonist and man antagonist. In the context of the play, we find resolution in the women's decision to suppress the evidence against Minnie Wright. In a our larger society, however, the conflict remains unresolved.

Suggestions for Discussing the Study Questions, page 1254

(1) The men enter first in a group and move directly across the stage to the stove. The two women follow; they move "slowly," "look fearfully about," and remain "near the door." The two groupings and the differences in movement establish traditional hierarchies and suggest very different attitudes toward the murder investigation. The preserves have frozen and almost all the jars have broken. The men are not concerned about this fact, but all the women are concerned (including Mrs. Wright, in jail). This difference is further evidence of the restrictions blinding the men and the freedom of the women to see things as they are and to draw conclusions accordingly.

(2) Hale reports that he found Mrs. Wright in the kitchen, rocking back and forth and pleating her apron, and also finding Mr. Wright strangled in his bed upstairs. Hale is observant, and his testimony is accurate as far as it goes. He doesn't notice signs of disturbance in the kitchen, and he doesn't make much of Mrs. Wright's "laugh" or her "scared look."

(3) The authorities need a motive. The sheriff is convinced there is "nothing" in the kitchen that will establish motive. Because the women deduce the motive from looking at "kitchen things," we may conclude that the men are restricted by traditional thinking about men and women.

(4) The badly stitched square suggests to the women that Mrs. Wright was upset ("didn't know what she was about"). Mrs. Hale re-sews the square. She may suspect Mrs. Wright at this point, but her action is presented as instinctive rather than as a conscious suppression of evidence.

(5) Mrs. Hale reveals that Minnie Foster had been a pretty but frail young woman who liked to sing. Her childless marriage removed her from social contact, and also isolated her on the farm with Wright, a dour and hard man who was "like a raw wind that gets to the bone" (speech 103). This background, scattered throughout, lays the groundwork for motive, but it also begins the justification of Mrs. Wright's actions.

(6, 7) The broken cage and the strangled bird provide evidence of the motive for the murder. The women look at each other with "growing comprehension" and "horror" at this point. This is the crisis; the women have proof of motive and must decide what to do with it. The cage symbolizes the Wrights' marriage or Minnie's status in it (it also parallels the jail, visually). The fact that the cage is broken reflects the current status of the marriage and Minnie's desperate act to escape. The bird with its "neck wrung" is a visual parallel to the strangulation of Mr. Wright, but symbolizes the cruelty that Wright had inflicted on his wife (she had been "like a bird herself" in her youth [speech 107]). It seems clear, from this point on, that the knot used to strangle Wright was one of Minnie's quilting knots.

(8) At first, the women have different reactions to the evidence and their developing interpretation of it. Mrs. Peters is torn; she understands the situation, but she is conventionally fixed on the idea that "the law has got to punish crime." Mrs. Hale blames herself for not helping Minnie, and believes that the murder was justified. Finally, however, they tacitly agree to cover up the crime; both try to hide the box containing the dead bird. Mrs. Peters cannot do it, so Mrs. Hale puts it in the pocket of her coat (page 1160, speech 146.1, S.D.).

(9) Mrs. Hale feels partly responsible because she did not provide human contact and support for Minnie: "Oh, I wish I'd come over here once in a while! That was a crime!" (speech 133). She knew how wretched Minnie was, but she didn't visit. Her guilt is justified only insofar as society as a whole is responsible for the conditions and conventions that led to Minnie's desperation and isolation. Nevertheless, Mrs. Hale feels personally at fault, and this contributes to her final decision.

Suggestions for Discussing the General Questions, pages 1254–55

(1) The title and the word "trifles" refer to domestic matters or concerns that the men consider insignificant and funny. Ironically, these trifles have a profound impact on life, death, and judgment in the play. They reveal the shape of the pathetic life of the Wrights, and also the events leading up to the murder. The men's mocking attitude and the women's sensitivity to trifles underscore the basic distinctions in the play.

(2) It is important to the play that the male characters be flat, static, and representative. Puffed up as they are with their own importance and sense of superiority and competence, their minds work in narrow and conventional patterns, and they are thus condescending toward the women who worry about "kitchen things." They therefore miss the significance of the trifles of the kitchen, and also miss the women's agitation.

(3) By contrast with the men, Mrs. Hale is strong, assertive, and sympathetic. From her role as a subservient wife, she grows during the play, and is therefore round. She quietly makes light of the men and their work, wishing they would be quick about getting

evidence. She picks up on the significance of the trifles, and understands the crime without difficulty. She feels a sisterly responsibility for Minnie, and thus blames herself for Minnie's solitude and isolation. The high point of her growth is the decision she makes, along with Mrs. Peters, to hide the evidence.

(4) Students may agree or disagree, so long as they present a good argument. Glaspell keeps Minnie offstage so as not to prejudice the judgment of readers: We must decide about justice without seeing the criminal/victim. In addition, keeping Minnie offstage helps to make her an everywoman figure.

(5) The symbolism of the cage and bird suggest, first, the status of Minnie Wright on the Wright farm. Her nature and her freedom have been lost because she has been almost literally caged. Beyond that, there is a general value in the symbol, suggesting that traditional marriage (women used to vow that they would obey their husbands) is a cage. The word "knot" links the quilting (a "womanly" occupation and thus an amusing trifle to the men) to the rope which was knotted about Mr. Wright's neck.

WRITING TOPICS. The character of Minnie. The issue of legality vs. personal bonding in the story. The character of Martha Hale, or of Mrs. Peters. The play (*Trifles*) contrasted with the story (see page 202 for "A Jury of Her Peers").

Works for Comparison with *Trifles*

Anonymous, *Barbara Allan, 1119*
Whur, *The First-Rate Wife, 809*
Keats, *La Belle Dame Sans Merci, 954*
Williams, *Taking Care, 95*

STANLEY KAUFFMANN, *The More the Merrier,* *pages 1256–64*

This is a play that grows on one. It begins in apparent romantic farce, and ends that way, but in between it raises issues that are of particular interest to students, and, also, to all young (and older) people. In short, *The More the Merrier* brings smiles and laughs, but it also brings thought and the contemplation of one of the most important and vital aspects of life.

Suggestions for Discussing the Study Questions, pages 1264–65

(1) The two major characters are of course Emily and Raphael. Just immediately before the play opens, Raphael has proposed to Emily, and as the play opens she consents, so that the first word in the play is her "Yes." Theoretically, at least, both characters have an

idealistic view of love and marriage, believing that a married couple can create a new life with each other, severing all previous experiences and relationships. They make promises—he to give up cigars, she to give up lipstick—and, of course, they almost immediately break them. The problem is that unrealistic resolutions are doomed to fail.

(2) Simon Latchflake enters just when Emily and Raphael are most interested in exiting from their previous lives and in beginning their new life alone together. Simon, with the ugly sound of the doorbell, is interested in interrupting the two lovers on the ground that he wants to reestablish his previous relationship with Emily. Thus, the past intrudes on the lovers, especially when they least like to be reminded of it.

(3) Emily and Simon discuss the possibilities of reality vs. unreality in marriage. Emily is much more down-to-earth than she has previously revealed, speaking about Raphael quite objectively (e.g., "I encourage him in it [turning over a new leaf] because it makes him happy to think about it; but I don't really believe it." Speech 186). It would not be possible for her to speak this way with Raphael onstage, because her accepting him and billing and cooing with him are too recent for her to speak realistically and objectively in his presence. Emily's image of chewing gum in the hair is a good symbol of the inextricability of the past in a person's life (Speech 186).

(4) Vesta and Simon are similar in their attitudes toward marriage. Vesta, by saying "I'm sort of tired of the old life; I want to turn over a new leaf" (Speech 221) echoes Simon's statement "I'm sick of the old life" (Speech 175). They are thus both cuts from the same stalk.

(5) Emily and Raphael use many intimate statements of endearment, and, similarly, so do Vesta and Simon. The words, such as "dear," "honeybunch," "darling," "Sweetikins," and "Honey lamb," seem sentimental when they are used publicly. It might prove interesting, however, for students to discuss the sorts of language that couples in love use when they are totally private.

(6) The entry of Simon and Vesta are sufficient to remind both Emily and Raphael that there is no escaping the past, and that marriage is thus to be viewed more realistically than seems to be the case at the play's beginning. Emily states that she will marry the man she loves and who loves her (Speech 180), while Raphael states that he wants to marry Emily despite the past, or perhaps because of the past. Ultimately, Vesta coaxes Simon into an embrace for perhaps these same reasons.

(7) The speaker of the stage directions is somewhat amused by his characters. The directions serve a primary purpose of describing many of the play's actions, but they also establish rapport with readers. Direction 62.1, for example, is "Yes, they kiss again." This reminds readers that the speaker is as aware of the demonstrative excess of Emily and Raphael as the readers. The concluding direction also is directly aimed at readers: "They continue to chatter; but you have the idea." The use of "you" for the readers and audience is a way of promoting friendliness and intimacy.

(8) Virginia and Arthur are together at the end to suggest the continuity of the sort of relationship established by Emily and Raphael. They will keep talking and establishing their life together, and then two additional people will do the same thing, and so on ("you have the idea").

Suggestions for Discussing the General Questions, page 1265

(1) Students will generally agree with the statements of Simon and Emily that our lives are tied up with those of many other people. Presumably this idea will lead into a discussion of just what relationships can prevail in marriage. Ideally, a married couple may want to be "apart" from everyone else, but with the "chewing gum in the hair" idea (Speech 230), this kind of absolute separation seems impossible. A major problem of marriage emerges, then, in determining where the boundaries of public and private relationships should be set.

(2) Speeches 192 and 193 might be considered the heart of the play, dealing with the issue of happenstance as opposed to fate in the lives of people. The issue of determinism and free will comes up here. If one sees one's true love "across a crowded room," and then deliberately sets about to know and then marry that true love, is the ultimate cause of marriage luck or deliberation? What if people destined for each other never meet? How could deliberate action have any effect on this circumstance? Students will be quite interested in considering such questions.

(3) Although the play begins innocently enough, and seems at first to dramatize a silly relationship between relatively silly people, the introduction of Simon and then Vesta establish that Kauffmann is dealing with significant issues that affect most human beings. The idea of marriage making a world apart from everyone else is worth considering, just as is the idea of demonstrating the impossibility of a world apart. The introduction of a number of new persons and

couples toward the play's end also is a means of indicating that many, many people go through the same experiences and (probably) arrive at the same solutions as Emily and Raphael.

WRITING TOPICS. The importance of Simon the the development of the play's action and ideas. The question of what constitutes an ideal marriage. The importance of other people, other lives, in one's own life. The play's farcical actions.

Works for Comparison with *The More the Merrier*

Chekhov, *The Bear, 1625*
Colwin, *An Old-Fashioned Story, 67*
Lynn Emanuel, *Like God, 1151*
Ridler, *Nothing Is Lost, 830*
Rückert, *If You Love for the Sake of Beauty, 766*

BETTY KELLER, *Tea Party,* *pages 1266–69*

This brief play was originally designed as a teaching instrument for students actors. Its brevity therefore makes it perfect for an introduction to dramatic character, situation, setting, and meaning. The story is that two aged and desperately lonely sisters plan to entertain their paper boy on his collection day, but the boy snubs them and thus baffles their plan, leaving them as lonely and bereft as before. One's first response to the paperboy's snub is to claim that he is unkind, knowing that the sisters wish to take up his time and not wanting to have anything to do with them. On the other hand, the play makes it clear that he has spent such time with the ladies before, and now does not wish to get caught with them again. He does, in fact, have other papers to deliver and other customers from whom to collect. Thus, while life goes on busily outside the window of Alma and Hester's home, it remains stopped inside, and all the ladies have left is their silence and loneliness.

Suggestions for Discussing the Study Questions, page 1269

(1) The major conflict is the advancement of age, senility, illness, and death upon Alma and Hester. The minor conflict is their loneliness, their attempts to encourage visits, and the refusal of others, as represented by the paperboy, to tolerate the two ladies, thus highlighting their solitude. The two also have minor conflicts, as shown by their discussion about circumstances and dates of past events.

(2) The two sisters discuss their seating arrangements so that they might center the visiting boy between them and hold him, therefore, for a more extended conversation. We learn that they have

made these arrangements before because they mention a previous visit by "Charlie" (speech 14–17).

(3) Alma's use of the twenty-dollar bill (speech 45) shows that she is capable of manipulation, for she expects that the paperboy will not have change and will therefore need to return another time for his money. Obviously, the discussion about the $20.00 and the previous paperboy shows that the women know that they can work this subterfuge only a limited number of times.

(4) Alma is four years younger than Hester, who states that Alma was too young to have known whether the correct name of the ship was the *Bainbridge* or the *Heddingham*. We may conclude that Alma is remembering what others told her, whose memories may have grown dim, while Hester is remembering what she actually saw. Therefore both sisters are still in sound mind, even though they may be differing on a factual matter.

Suggestions for Discussing the General Questions, page 1270

(1) The setting is described precisely. If students make a scheme of the furniture arrangements, they will see that the plans for serving, sitting, and so on, are exact. Generally, the changes and developments of characters in a play are related directly to place, time, and circumstances on stage. In *Tea Party*, for example, the discussions about how to serve the paperboy indicate that the ladies have been engaged in their pathetic arrangements as hosts for relatively unwilling people for a long time, and that the only interludes from their loneliness will be to continue these arrangements. The setting in this short play therefore highlights the plight and the pathos of the major characters.

(2) The women are at the end of the so-called "golden years" of old age, and the future will present even more difficulty and disability. *Tea Party* dramatizes these difficulties in detail. One might cite the play in strengthening a sociological/political argument because it vividly illustrates, better than an extensive treatise with generalized commentary, the physical inability and the isolation of the aged.

WRITING TOPICS. The deteriorating characteristics of the two women. The importance of the sets in the development of the action. What will life be like for the two women in the future?

Works for Comparison with *Tea Party*

Kennedy, *Old Men Pitching Horseshoes*, 956
Porter, *The Jilting of Granny Weatherall*, 651

Ridler, *Nothing Is Lost, 830*
Whitman, *Full of Life Now, 1216*

Eugene O'Neill, *Before Breakfast,* *pages 1271–76*

O'Neill's play is a study in character and perspective, and it also provides a good actress with a virtuoso acting piece. Because Mrs. Rowland is on stage throughout, we focus on her, and might conclude that she is the sole cause of difficulties in her marriage. From what we may learn of Alfred through her speeches, however, we may conclude that he has not been without fault in the troubles the couple has experienced.

Suggestions for Discussing the Study Questions, pages 1276–77

(1) The setting implies that the Rowlands are poor, bohemian, and careless. The plants "dying of neglect" symbolize the decaying relationship between man and wife.

(2) O'Neill uses negative adjectives to convey the impression that Mrs. Rowland is careless and coarse. These are "slovenly," "drab," "formless," "shapeless," "shabby," "worn," "characterless," "nondescript," "pinched," "weak," and "spiteful." Her initial actions—putting on the apron, getting a drink—are equally negative. She moves "slowly," "wearily," and acts with "clumsy fingers." There is also a vindictive aspect to her; she "hastily" sneaks a drink, and then "stealthily" finds and reads Alfred's letter from Helen. These initial impressions are expanded in her speeches to Alfred throughout the play.

(3) Throughout the play, Mrs. Rowland treats Alfred with condescension and derision. She accuses him of being "lazy," "good-for-nothing," "silly," and of being a coward. Her taunts become especially sharp and vindictive when she speaks about Helen, just before Alfred cuts his throat.

(4) Mrs. Rowland became pregnant during the premarital affair. She did not wish to be bought off because she assumed that Alfred, being an heir, would eventually inherit a huge amount of money, much more than she would have been given for going away. This situation does not reflect favorably upon either Alfred or Mrs. Rowland.

(5) The crisis occurs after Alfred nicks himself when shaving and then begins to stare at himself and Mrs. Rowland. It is at this point that he probably thinks of suicide. Other signs of crisis include Alfred's growing "pale" and shaking "dreadfully." Mrs. Rowland's unsympathetic mockery of his relationship with the pregnant Helen

pushes Alfred to suicide and the play to its sudden catastrophe. The catastrophe is Alfred's slitting his throat and Mrs. Rowland's discovery and genuinely terrified response.

(6) Mrs. Rowland is defensive in her attitude toward Alfred's affair with Helen. She is unsympathetic to Helen's pregnancy, and claims that Helen is old enough to have known better. She also threatens Alfred's relationship with Helen by stating that she will refuse the divorce he needs so that he may remarry. She insults Helen, saying that she thinks of the other woman as being "no better than a common street-walker" (speech 29).

Suggestions for Discussing the General Questions, page 1277

(1) The setting shows the characters to be poor, careless, and negligent of themselves and their surroundings, suggesting the deterioration of character that results in neglect. Significant details are the size and location of the apartment, the dying plants, the clothing hung on pegs (no closets), and the clothesline. This tacky setting suggests the darker side of realism and verisimilitude.

(2) Mrs. Rowland is flat, static, and stereotyped. These choices, and the missing first name, suggest that she represents a type. She is not, however, without depth, as is indicated by the fact that she goes out to work, thus shouldering financial responsibility, and also that she has thought about the implications of Alfred's affair.

(3, 4) By keeping Alfred offstage (except for his hand), O'Neill presents the conflict completely from Mrs. Rowland's perspective. For this reason, the play is much like Browning's "My Last Duchess" (695). O'Neill gives Mrs. Rowland exclusive control of the stage, to show, through her speeches and attitudes, her anger and resentment at her situation. Had Alfred been brought on stage to speak with her, the focus and impact of her personality might have been diffused. In addition, we would have had to consider the real problems of Alfred's irresponsibility, drinking, and guilt. Mrs. Rowland's view of Alfred is distorted by her anger, limited mentality, and feelings of grievance. She does not value the things valued by Alfred, such as art, education, and poetry. Indeed, she terms poetry "silly." Her views about Alfred are not without some justification, but her personality renders it impossible to grant her more understanding and sympathy than that.

(5) By presenting the background out of order and in fragments, O'Neill creates tension and prolongs the revelation of Mrs. Rowland's

character. Chronologically, Alfred graduated from Harvard (why Harvard?), began writing poetry (why poetry?), and became involved with his future wife, who became pregnant (why does O'Neill make her father a grocer?). Alfred's father tried to buy Mrs. Rowland off; she refused; they married; and the father died with his fortune being claimed by creditors. Once this information is put back in order, Mrs. Rowland's interest in the Rowland money seems clear.

WRITING TOPICS. The deteriorating characteristics of the two women. The importance of the sets in the development of the action. What will life be like for the two women in the future?

WORKS FOR COMPARISON WITH "BEFORE BREAKFAST"

Broumas, *Circe*, 978
Browning, *My Last Duchess*, 695
Gilman, *The Yellow Wallpaper*, 617
Kizer, *Night Sounds*, 734

Writing About the Elements of Drama, *pages 1277–84*

This section helps students formulate ideas for essays about how significant elements work toward dramatic meaning and impact. The section may be assigned in conjunction with any play in the text; it is as relevant to tragedy or comedy as it is to the five plays in the chapter. Students can be directed to this discussion and the relevant cross references whenever they write about a particular element.

The topics for discovering ideas (1277–79) suggest the development of central ideas about specific aspects of a play, and also refers students to earlier relevant sections. The section also treats organization and provides a demonstrative essay on Glaspell's symbolism in *Trifles* (1281–83).

The most important point in teaching this introductory material on drama is selectivity. In an effort to fill pages as easily as possible, students often summarize dramatic events or else present random but disconnected observations. The solution is selectivity and focus; press the students to think about and deal with only one or two topics for any given play.

The boxed section, "Referring to Plays and Parts of Plays" (1280) contains answers to questions that many students have asked about how to refer to acts, scenes, lines, and speeches in plays. Be sure that your students know about the suggestions contained there.

Special Topics for Writing and Argument about the Elements of Drama, *pages 1284–85*

(1) The point about sentimentality is key to *Tea Party*. The most important consideration is that the sisters, despite their pathetic attempt to overcome their isolation and loneliness, and despite their vulnerability, exhibit individuality, determination, understanding, and a certain combativeness. These strengths keep the play away from the edge.

(2) The characters belong, basically, to the same relatively privileged class of society, and they are quite similar. Thus they can take their economic lives more or less for granted, unlile the characters in O'Neill's *Before Breakfast*, and rather they are free to concentrate on their own immediate problems of getting on in life and love. In "An Old-Fashioned Story" we are given a virtual life history of the major character, while in *The More the Merrier* we infer much about the lives of Emily and Raphael.

(3) This question is discussed in this manual in response to both the first specific and Suggestions for Discussing the General Questions for *Before Breakfast* (please use the text page guide in this manual for the locations of these discussions.

(4) A good case may be made that *Trifles* is about all the points except crime; Mrs. Wright is not a criminal. A good topic might also be bottled-up anger. It would of course be unthinkable today for anyone like Mrs. Hale and Mrs. Peters to poke around at the scene of a murder. The play as we have it could only have been set in a rural area during a past day, when law officers were comparatively unskilled in systematic and controlled investigations.

(5) This topic is potentially one of the most rewarding of the group of questions. Glaspell uses many of the same speeches and situations in both play and story, but it is clear that within the short-story framework she is free to sharpen her focus on Martha Hale and also to explain more of the thoughts and considerations of the characters. In the dramatic form, she is constrained to present only dialogue and action, whereas in the story form she fleshes out the dramatic materials. The story is hence more visual than it otherwise might have been, inasmuch as fiction often contains greater discussion and abstract explanations than drama.

(6) The list of topics might create an extensive essay. If students settle on a single aspect, however, and pinpoint specific actions and character traits in just a few plays, the essays might be kept within

manageable limits. If you use question 6 for a term paper, many more of the topics might be developed.

(7) The problem students will encounter in this essay, as in any essay entailing the consideration of a number of separate works, is to preserve thematic unity. The key to keeping things together is to utilize the topics as the basis of the discussion. Thus the topic of dialogue may be kept foremost while various plays are described and compared as they relate to this topic. The same applies to action, use of soliloquies and asides, stage directions, and so on.

(8) This library topic, like many others, is designed for students to go to the library and, knowing little or nothing about a topic, acquire a good deal of information. The reports envisaged here are to be short, for any of the topics could quickly grow unwieldy. It might be desirable to combine the library search with topic 7.

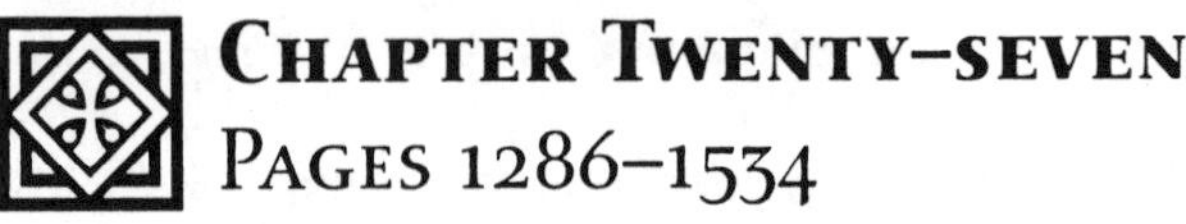

Chapter Twenty-seven
Pages 1286–1534

The Tragic Vision: Affirmation Through Loss

The goal of this chapter—by far the longest in the book—is to introduce students to the concept of tragedy and the special considerations for dealing with tragic drama. The introductory material on tragedy has been closely revised for the sixth edition (1286–1303). It is focused largely on ancient Athenian tragedy, but it also deals with general aspects of tragedy that are relevant for the later plays (1292–98). The photographs of the Theater of Epidauros and of an actual production at the theater, which were both in the fifth edition, are included in the sixth edition (1299, 1300). The caption on page 1300 is helpful in explaining the details of production, but students would benefit from your discussion of both photos. The chapter also includes extensive introductory material on each of the three tragedies included here.

If you assign one or all of the tragedies for your students, you can begin with a general discussion of the mode (i.e., tragedy) or you can develop a working definition based on the introductory material in conjunction with the play under consideration. In any event, class discussion of the mode will be helpful for students, especially since in modern usage the term *tragedy* is loosely applied to any unhappy or unfortunate event. (The development of the word and the genre is considered on page 1288).

Sophocles, *Oedipus the King,* *pages 1305–1343*

If you assign *Oedipus the King,* you should have the students read the introduction to Greek theater and the introduction to the play. Both explain many of the conventions of Greek drama that students may at first find odd or intrusive. In teaching the play, you may need to prepare arguments against the propositions that, realistically, Oedipus is a fool (why couldn't he see what we saw?) or, symbolically, as nothing much more than a representative figure illustrating that human beings are the pawns of fate and destiny, without any capacity to control their lives. Neither is an accurate assessment of

Oedipus. His circumstances are singular, and he is not a fool—at the beginning of his career he solved the riddle of the sphinx, and for twenty years he has ruled Thebes successfully.

Oedipus is like a murder mystery in which the reader (or viewer) already knows "who did it"; the interest and agony are produced as we follow the slow process of discovery. But *Oedipus* offers a twist; the detective discovers finally that he himself is the murderer. One of the play's central problems is whether Oedipus's tragic fall is a result of fate or character. Is he controlled by forces beyond his control, or by aspects of his character that have led to errors in judgment and action? A good teaching approach is to balance these two alternatives and present each side of the argument with equal force.

At least two productions of *Oedipus* are available for classroom use. A 45-minute film or videotape of a production done in masks in an ancient Greek theater is available from Films for the Humanities (Box 2053, Princeton, NJ 08540). A 1957 color film of Tyrone Guthrie's Stratford (Canada) production of Yeats's version of the play is available from Contemporary/McGraw-Hill Films (1221 Avenue of the Americas, New York, NY 10020). This version is done in papier-mâché masques and fine costuming; it thus gives an authentic sense of this aspect of ancient Greek productions of the play.

The following questions, answers, and comment can serve as a programmatic teaching guide to *Oedipus;* the material may be used to organize either class discussion or lecture.

I. PROLOGUE (LINES 1–150).

1. ***The first stage direction (S.D.) and Oedipus's opening speech (lines 1–13) provide exposition about the state.***

What does the first S.D. tell you about the city? About Oedipus?

Since the people are supplicants—praying to Oedipus for help—we know that something is seriously wrong. Since the prayers are addressed directly to Oedipus, he is identified as a significant power.

What do we learn about Thebes in Oedipus's first speech?

Prayers to Apollo and the cries of mourners weigh the city down; there is death and mourning.

What is Oedipus's attitude toward the people? Toward himself?

He calls the people *My Children*, suggesting dominance. He refers to himself as "I, Oedipus, a name that all men know." His greatness is based on defeating the Sphinx and on his own success as ruler for twenty years.

2. **The priest's answer (lines 14–57) provides exposition.**

What does the priest tell us about the city's current problem? About Oedipus?

Thebes is facing plague, sterility, famine, divine fire, and death. Oedipus once saved the city from the Sphinx; he holds the power here.

What attitude toward Oedipus is reflected in the priest's speech?

Respect, awe, the expectation that he will make everything right.

How do the people (chorus) put pressure on Oedipus throughout the play?

Their expectations; they assume he can fix whatever is wrong.

How are these expectations ironically right?

They are ironic because Oedipus unwittingly caused the problem in the first place. They are also ironic because making things better will require self-banishment.

3. **In answering the priest and supplicants (lines 58–78), Oedipus claims know about the suffering; he says that "not one of you [is] so sick as I" (line 61). How is this claim an instance of *foreshadowing* and *irony*?**

It is ironic because he will turn out to be sickened by his own life and he is the source of the plague that is destroying Thebes; in addition, Oedipus's assertion ironically foreshadows the catastrophe and resolution.

What steps has Oedipus already taken to correct the situation?

He has previously sent Creon, his brother-in-law, to the Oracle at Delphi to find out what must be done. Note: At this point you might want to describe and explain the Oracle at Delphi. You might also discuss the symbolic value of the oracle (as the voice of Apollo, it represents divine will) and the frequency with which this oracle influences the play's action.

4. **No sooner mentioned, than Creon arrives from Delphi (line 84 s.d.). This is an example of the compression of time in drama and of the kind of coincidences that often occur in this play. Creon returns and reports Apollo's message; we learn more background about Thebes and Oedipus.**

What happened long ago to Laius, the former king?

He was presumably killed by bandits, but in fact was killed by Oedipus. Nobody knows exactly who committed the murder, which is considered an unsolved case.

Why weren't the "murderers" tracked down at the time?

The Sphinx told the Thebans to turn away from obscure problems and instead try to learn things that "lay" at their "feet." (lines 130–131).

What must be done now?

Thebes must be purged, cleansed, purified. The murderer(s) of Laius must be punished by death or banishment.

What does Oedipus promise to do?

He will begin the search for the murderers again; "make it plain" for all to see.

What personal reason does Oedipus give to finding the killers?

"Whoever murdered him may also wish to punish me" (line 139). The personal reason is therefore self-preservation.

How is this entire speech ironic, given what we know about events?

His quest for justice and vengeance will lead him to himself. Laius's murderer could only kill Oedipus if he committed suicide.

How is Oedipus's promise to make everything plain consistent with his personality?

It reflects his need to know or discover hidden things.

II. (lines 151–220). *The chorus, on its first entrance, the parados, represents the voice of the people, reflecting standard values and attitudes. The parados is a prayer to the gods interrupted by a vivid description of the plague (lines 173–190). Thus, early in the play, the plague is linked directly to the power of the gods.*

On which gods does the chorus call? What do they want the gods to do? What is the chorus's attitude toward the gods and prophecy?

The gods are Zeus, Apollo, Athena, Artemis, and Bacchus. They want the gods to cure the city and destroy the murderer. Their attitude is respectful, awestruck, believing, reverent; this is the social and ethical standard—the public and traditional position.

III. EPISODE 1 (lines 221–467). *Oedipus responds to the prayers of the chorus and claims that Thebes will have relief if the citizens obey him. He demands any information about the murderer of Laius that the chorus might have (lines 221–228). Oedipus places a curse on both the murderer and anyone who knows about the murder and does not reveal the information.*

What curse is placed on the murderer and those who have knowledge of him?

Ostracism and a prohibition from religious rites.

How does Oedipus ironically turn this curse on himself?

He curses himself if he has knowledge of the murderer (lines 254–256).

Why is Oedipus's claim that he will fight for Laius "as if for my own father" (line 269) ironic?

Laius is his father; we know it but he does not.

What second way of getting information about the murder does the Choragos suggest?

The prophet and seer, Tiresias.

What is the significance of Tiresias's blindness?

The importance is to accent the ironic reversal: Tiresias is blind but can see the truth; Oedipus has sight but is blind. The blindness also foreshadows Oedipus's self-blinding at the catastrophe.

2. **Tiresias arrives at line 301 S.D. Oedipus explains the whole problem—the plague and the defilement—and asks for help (lines 305–20). This is, of course, a method of reviewing the situation.**

What is Tiresias's first response? Why does he react this way?

He does not want to say anything; he wants to leave: "Let me go home" (line 325). He reacts this way because he knows the truth and he anticipates the agony that revelation will produce.

How does Oedipus respond to Tiresias's refusal to speak? What does this show us about Oedipus?

He flies into a rage, becomes abusive, and accuses Tiresias of traitorousness. Oedipus is a king and is accustomed to being obeyed immediately. He wants answers quickly and suspects those who seem evasive. When his will is thwarted, he intimidates those who are crossing him.

What other instances of rage are significant in Oedipus's life?

He rages at the feast in Corinth, at Delphi, at the place where three roads meet, in conversation with Creon, and at the catastrophe.

3. **Tiresias tells Oedipus the whole truth: "you are the vile polluter" (line 358); "You are the murderer" (line 367); "You live . . . in the greatest shame" (line 372). Because we know these allegations are true, our interest is not in the revelation, but rather in Oedipus's rage on hearing them.**

How does Oedipus respond?

He calls Tiresias blind and a liar, accusing him of plotting usurpation with Creon; he belittles seers and prophecy.

How does the Choragos react?

The Choragos suggests that both men have spoken in anger (line 410). The chorus embodies moderation and calmness.

What does Oedipus's rage and accusation drive Tiresias to do?

Deliver a prophecy (lines 417–433) and tell truth in an indirect riddle (454–467).

What does Tiresias prophesy for Oedipus?

Blindness and wretchedness.

What does Tiresias imply will be revealed?

Truth about Oedipus's birth.

On what aspects of Oedipus's life does the riddle touch?

His birth in Thebes, future blindness, incestuous marriage, and parricide.

Why doesn't Oedipus recognize the truth?

(1) His thinking is clouded with rage. (2) He thinks that Polybus and Merope are his parents. (3) He sees no connection between himself and the bandits who murdered Laius.

IV. STASIMON 1 (lines 468–517). *The stasimon embodies the choral reaction; each stanza takes up a different aspect of the chorus's feelings and responses to what has just happened between Oedipus and Tiresias.*

What is discussed in each stanza?

Strophe 1 considers the power of Apollo over the murderer. Antistrophe 1 discusses the killer and his doom. Strophe 2 expresses fear and confusion. The chorus also reaffirms its faith in Oedipus and in his power to solve the problem.

V. EPISODE 2 (lines 518–867).

1. The debate between Oedipus and Creon.

About what is Creon upset?

Creon is upset by Oedipus's charge of treason and usurpation.

How does the Choragos explain Oedipus's words?

The Choragos states that Oedipus spoke in anger.

Of what crimes does Oedipus accuse Creon? What proof does he have?

Oedipus accuses Creon of murdering Laius, stealing the throne, and plotting treason with Tiresias. He has no proof at all; Creon calls it unsupported speculation (line 613).

What emotion(s) dominate Oedipus during this debate? Does he ever really hear Creon?

Rage or mindless willfulness prevents Oedipus from hearing. This rage is an important aspect of Oedipus's personality.

How does Creon defend himself and refute the charges?

Creon bases his defense on reason and religion. He correctly points out that he has all the power and influence of kingship without the anxieties (lines 588–607). Also he tells Oedipus to check with the Oracle (line 608); he condemns (curses) himself to death if he has lied (line 612).

Characterize Creon. How is he different from Oedipus?

Creon is rational, calm, careful, prudent, not hasty. Some of his representative statements are these: "I never talk when I am ignorant" (line 574); "think about this rationally, as I do" (line 588); "a prudent man is never traitorous" (line 605).

2. Jocasta appears for the first time at line 638.1 S.D.; she is upset with Oedipus and Creon for stirring up private troubles during Thebes's sickness.

What does Jocasta want the men to do?

She wants them to stop arguing and go inside.

How does the chorus echo Jocasta?

They want Oedipus to defer to Creon.

Why does Oedipus view this as a him or me situation?

Absolving Creon indicates that Tiresias was right; Oedipus will face exile or death.

What is Creon's view of Oedipus's character?

Creon sees Oedipus as sullen, angry, and unreasonable. Creon states that "Natures like yours are hardest on themselves" (line 679).

3. The conversation between Jocasta and Oedipus (lines 682–867). Jocasta's questions about the argument provide an opportunity for more background. Oedipus explains Tiresias's accusations and discusses his own history.

What is Jocasta's attitude toward prophesies? What accounts for this attitude? What proof does she offer?

Jocasta rejects the prophesies: "no mortal is ever given skill in prophecy" (lines 713–4). Her proof is that a major prophecy has not come true, for she believes her child dead and also that Laius was killed by foreign robbers.

How is this proof ironic?

Oedipus is the child; neither knows it.

Why does Oedipus begin to suspect that he may have killed Laius?

He remembers killing some men at Phocis—a place where three roads meet.

How does Oedipus push for additional information at this point? Why?

He asks about Laius's appearance and the size of the traveling party. He wants the one survivor called so that he can be questioned. Oedipus's drive toward truth is a function of his character and also a result of his initial vow. It parallels his quest to learn about his parents.

What occurred at the feast?

"A man denied I was my father's son."

How did Oedipus react?

He could barely control his depression, and he was driven to find out the truth: "It kept grinding into me" (line 790).

Where did Oedipus go to discover the truth about his parents?

To discover the truth about his parents, he went to Delphi consult the oracle in the temple there.

What prophecy was delivered?

The oracle declared that Oedipus would murder his father, marry his mother, and be the father of children by his incestuous relationship (lines 796–798).

What was Oedipus's response? How is his reaction characteristic?

He fled; his reaction is hasty and irrational because he gained no real information about his parents.

What happened at the place where three roads meet?

Oedipus killed a group of men, including his [unknown] father, who tried to push him off the road: "I killed them all" (lines 805–818).

What was the psychic trigger of Laius's death?

Oedipus's rage at being struck (his father struck out at him). The past is parallel to the present; Oedipus has not changed.

What is Oedipus on the verge of knowing?

That he killed Laius, not that he killed his father; he does not yet suspect that Laius was his father.

Why does Oedipus want to interview the lone survivor; what is his last shred of hope?

He wants to know if it was robbers or one man (line 849).

What conflicts have emerged up to this point in the play? Which are emerging as central?

The conflicts are these: Oedipus–Tiresias; Oedipus–Creon; Oedipus–plague; Oedipus–gods/fate; Oedipus–himself (his rage, depression, haste, drive, demand to know the truth). The last two emerge as central; the others reflect these.

VI. STASIMON 2 (lines 868–915). *Significantly, the chorus separates itself from Oedipus for the first time.*

What point does the chorus make about itself in Strophe 1?

It claims reverence, orthodoxy, and obedience to the laws of the gods.

What point is made about tyrants in Antistrophe 1?

Tyrants are ruled by pride (*hubris*) and fall through impiety.

What sins are discussed in Strophe 2?

Haughtiness, pride, sacrilege, unholiness, and injustice. These are implicitly linked to Oedipus.

What does the chorus say about the state of religion in Antistrophe 2?

Prophecy is ignored, Apollo is abandoned; religion slips away (line 915).

VII. EPISODE 3 (lines 916–1090). *The information of the first messenger (shepherd). We see Jocasta going to pray; she speaks to the chorus.*

How does Jocasta describe Oedipus's state of mind?

Jocasta says that Oedipus is excited and irrational.

What news does the messenger from Corinth bring? Why is it good news?

Polybus is dead and Oedipus will be made king of Corinth. The news apparently frees Oedipus from the horror of the oracle delivered at Delphi.

What attitude toward prophecy and oracles do Oedipus and Jocasta express?

Both Oedipus and Jocasta reject oracles completely. Jocasta asks, "Oracles of the gods! / Where are you now?" (lines 951–952). Oedipus asks "why should we look to Pytho's vapors?" (line 969).

How is this good news about Polybus ironically reversed?

Polybus was not Oedipus's father; the baby was given to Polybus by the Messenger, who got the baby from another shepherd, who worked for Laius.

What does Jocasta know at this point that Oedipus does not know?

She has put all the clues together and discovered the full horror of the truth; she knows that Oedipus, her son, murdered his father and married his mother.

Contrast the attitudes of Jocasta and Oedipus toward pursuing the investigation to its end.

Jocasta wants Oedipus to stop: "Pay no attention . . . give up this search . . . please don't do this thing." Oedipus is driven; he cannot give up with "clues like this within my grasp." See lines 1061–1077.

What does Jocasta intend when she enters the palace? How do you know?

Suicide is indicated by her promise never to address Oedipus by any name other than man of misery and by the Choragos's reference to savage grief.

VII. STASIMON 3 (lines 1091–1114). *This stasimon provides a fleeting sense of anticipation and possible joy that Oedipus's origins may be explained to his credit.*

What is the chorus anticipating about Mount Cithaeron?

That Cithaeron, "at tomorrow's full moon," will be shown to have been the home country of Oedipus.

Why does the chorus ask "who was your mother, son?"

The chorus anticipates an answer that will provide a satisfactory outcome of Oedipus's uncertainty.

VIII. EPISODE 4 (lines 1115–1190). *Catastrophe, peripeteia, anagnorisis. The interview with the shepherd who gave the baby to the Corinthian and who survived the murder of Laius leads to the revelation of truth.*

Why won't the old herdsman look at Oedipus; what does he know about him?

He recognizes Oedipus as the murderer of Laius; he does not realize the full truth, however, because he does not link the man with the child.

Discuss the coincidence that this shepherd (a) saved the infant Oedipus, (b) was with Laius at the crossroads and was the lone survivor, and (c) will now be the agent of revelation.

Such coincidence suggests divine will; it also implies that a person cannot escape his or her fate.

How is Oedipus's behavior with the herdsman (threatening torture) consistent with his character?

He knows that he is about to hear the dreaded truth, but he is driven on by his compulsion for full disclosure.

What does Oedipus discover about himself?

See lines 1187–1190. Oedipus realizes the full truth of the prophecies about his birth, marriage, and murder. This is the moment of anagnorisis; it is also the catastrophe.

X. STASIMON 4 (lines 1191–1232). *Here, and later, the chorus draws a moral about Oedipus's life and provides a final reaction to him.*

What moral does the chorus see in Oedipus's life?

The chorus concludes that human beings must appraise their lives as worthless and that no mortal can be judged fortunate (lines 1191–1201). In the last lines, they assert that no man can be considered happy until "he has crossed the border of his life without pain" (line 1543). In other words, they assert that no one can be judged fortunate until he or she is dead.

How are Antistrophe 1 and Strophe 2 a summary of Oedipus's life?

The first reviews Oedipus's rise; the second reviews his wretched fall.

What are the chorus's feelings toward Oedipus now?

Pity and fear; they wish that they had never seen him.

XI. EXODOS (lines 1233–END). *Resolution, dénouement, tying up loose ends.*

What does the second messenger report about Jocasta? About Oedipus?

Jocasta has hanged herself. Oedipus has blinded himself by stabbing his eyes with the gold pins from her dress. The pins symbolize both (a) the goad with which Laius tried to kill Oedipus, and (b) Oedipus's crime of incest. Symbolically, that Oedipus puts out his own eyes indicates his recognition of his guilt and also shows that he can no longer bear the sight of his moral violations.

What does the messenger say that Oedipus wants now? What does Oedipus want from the Chorus?

He wants to be exposed to the people as Thebes's pollution and then banished (line 1300). He wants the chorus to lead him out of Thebes.

Whom does Oedipus blame for his tragic life and fall?

He blames Apollo (lines 1339–41).

What is Creon like as the new king? What acts indicate his carefulness, reverence, political wisdom, and kindness?

Creon treats Oedipus with cool compassion and calculation; he wants to consult the gods and have sure knowledge before he acts. He displays kindness in having Oedipus's daughters, Ismene and Antigone, brought to him and in grasping Oedipus's hand. His political acumen and careful statesmanship are evident in his assertion that "I never promise when . . . I'm ignorant."

Suggestions for Discussing the General Questions, page 1344

(1) The play follows a regular five-stage pattern, but exposition is distributed throughout because so much of the story has already happened when the play begins. Exposition occurs in the opening dialogue, where we learn of the plague afflicting Thebes because of the hidden murderer. Complication builds as Tiresias accuses Oedipus of the crimes and Creon delivers the message of the Oracle at Delphi. The crisis occurs when Oedipus vows to find

the murderer, no matter what the search entails. The keys to the crisis are haste and anger; these lead Oedipus down the path to his downfall. The *peripeteia, catastrophe,* and *anagnorisis* all occur at the same instant when Oedipus discovers the truth of his parentage. These revelations affect Jocasta and Oedipus most immediately; she commits suicide and he blinds himself. The resolution involves the passing of power to Creon and the consideration of Oedipus's future (he will be banished).

(2) Oedipus was the only son of Laius, king of Thebes, who was warned that his son would kill him and marry Jocasta. The baby's feet were pierced and he was given to a shepherd to expose on Mount Cithaeron. The shepherd relented and gave the baby to another, who gave the child to Polybus and Merope, the childless king and queen of Corinth. They named him *Oedipus* because of his injured feet and raised him as theirs. (*See page 1304 for additional details about the legend of Oedipus.*)

Years later, Oedipus was told that Polybus and Merope were not his parents. Deeply troubled, he asked Polybus and Merope, who insisted that he was theirs. But Oedipus could not rest; he consulted the Oracle at Delphi. The Oracle refused to answer his question, but told him that he would murder his father and have children by his mother. Horrified, Oedipus fled Corinth, vowing not to return until Polybus and Merope were dead.

While traveling toward Thebes, Oedipus came to the junction of three roads. There, he met a nobleman (Laius) who ordered him off the road. The man struck Oedipus with a goad; Oedipus became enraged and killed the noble and all but one of the servants accompanying him.

When Oedipus arrived at Thebes, he found the city terrorized by the Sphinx; she ate Thebans who couldn't answer her riddle. At the same time, Laius's body was discovered. Creon offered the crown and hand of Jocasta to anyone who could free the city. Oedipus solved the riddle—causing the Sphinx to commit suicide—was crowned, and married Jocasta. The lone survivor of Laius's retinue returned, and after finding that Oedipus had become king, asked to become a shepherd in a distant region.

Oedipus ruled for twenty years, and he and Jocasta had two sons and two daughters. At the end of these twenty years, Thebes is afflicted by a plague (the play begins at this point); Oedipus sends Creon to Delphi to discover the cause. Creon learns that the murderer of Laius defiles the city by living unpunished.

Oedipus begins the investigation; he swears to find and banish the murderer. Tiresias is consulted; he accuses Oedipus, who flies into a rage. The shepherd who gave the baby to Polybus is consulted. The survivor of Laius's group is consulted; he is the man who was ordered to kill the baby. Finally, the truth is revealed. Horror abounds; Jocasta commits suicide and Oedipus blinds himself (he will be exiled from Thebes).

Sophocles's arrangement of the elements of the story produces a highly focused and effective theatrical moment. Pieces of the past are revealed only as they are needed to tighten the web around Oedipus. Keeping the play in the present maintains pressure on Oedipus throughout. Such an arrangement also raises the level of dramatic irony. The audience knows the whole story, while the play itself begins at the very end, on the very last day of Oedipus's reign.

(3) The central conflict is either Oedipus against the gods (fate) or against himself (anger, haste, irrationality). There is no right answer; a decision depends on one's view of the genesis of the play's tragic fall.

(4) Reporting (rather than staging) violence is a convention of Greek and Roman drama. The result of reporting is the absence of violent action. Incidentally, reporting became a characteristic of French drama, while action and spectacle became prominent in English and (later) American drama. There are advantages to reporting rather than action: The playwright can focus on character and on the reaction to violence, rather than the violent act itself. Moreover, the spectators and readers can imagine violence in more horrid detail than staging can present (such, of course, is not the case with contemporary film and the full range of special effects available to directors).

(5) Coincidence is best embodied in the single character who reappears at every crucial moment on Oedipus's life. This is the herdsman who took the infant to Mount Cithaeron, accompanied Laius on his fatal journey, survived Oedipus's attack, and reveals all at the close of the play. Although coincidence is common in drama, this much suggests the operation of fate or the gods. Coincidence is a prime factor in arguing for a tragedy based on fate.

(6) Virtually everything Oedipus says and does in the play is ironic because we know so much more than he does. His vow to hunt down the murderer, his claim that the murderer may try to kill him, his treatment of Tiresias and Creon, and his joy at Polybus's death, are all ironic.

(7) *Oedipus,* like *Hamlet,* is a tragedy in which individual fortunes rebound on the state. Initially, Oedipus's undisclosed guilt leads to plague and famine in Thebes. In the end, his fall leads to a shift in the kingship and possible questions about succession (where do Oedipus's two sons fit into the future of the crown?). These imply an unstable future for Thebes.

(8) The Chorus and Choragos (*Koryphaios*) represent the Theban public; they embody moderation, reason, and reverence for the gods. They also communicate the choral reaction to the events and conflicts in the play. Stasimon 1, for example, expresses the chorus's reaction to the news about the murderer and the accusations of Tiresias. Similarly, the Choragos is a voice of reason and a mediator. He reminds Creon, for instance, that Oedipus often speaks in anger, without thinking. At the close of the play, the chorus draws its own moral from the fall of Oedipus; their conviction that no person can be considered happy until dead underscores the instability of power and glory.

(9) Oedipus's quest for the murderer quickly becomes a quest for the truth of his own past. The nature of the quest changes when Oedipus realizes that he may have murdered Laius. From that point on, he is driven toward a discovery of his own past and recognition of the present horror.

■ Renaissance Drama and Shakespeare's Theater, *pages 1344–49*

This section has been revised to reflect recent archaeological discoveries in the theater district of Shakespeare's day, provides a detailed introduction to the physical conditions and stage conventions of the Elizabethan public theater, particularly the Globe. Also included are photos of the New Globe Theater (1346) and the New Globe stage (*insert*), which have been reconstructed in accordance with best judgments of what Shakespeare's actual Globe was like. It is important for students to develop a knowledge of theater conditions during Shakespeare's day because many aspects of his plays were determined by the conditions and conventions of his stage and the expectations of his audiences. Material about the Globe beginning on page 1345 can be assigned in conjunction with *Hamlet* and/or *A Midsummer Night's Dream* in Chapter 28. The material will help clarify the less realistic aspects of either play.

WILLIAM SHAKESPEARE, *Hamlet*, *pages 1350–1451*

Hamlet is a touchstone of Western civilization. Your students will be enriched by studying and understanding it, although comprehension at any level will require care and attentiveness. Shakespeare's language, although different in many respects from Modern English, is comprehensible. At times, however, the syntax may need unraveling, and also the issues and interests of Shakespeare's characters may need explaining. The glosses, notes, and questions should help. As much classroom instruction and discussion as you can provide should help more.

When you begin the play, you will need to establish priorities about what to stress. We suggest the following: (1) What's happening—the story, the plot, the pattern of the plot. (2) Who is Hamlet, the protagonist, and what is he about—his personality, dilemma, motives, growth? Who is Claudius and what are his situation and motives? (3) Why should we read about a dead Danish prince, anyway—the universal ideas about human responsibility, choices between responsibility and desire, justice, and revenge that the play explores?

Students' appreciation and comprehension of *Hamlet* can be significantly enhanced by watching a production after they have read the text. In 1990, a new film production, featuring Mel Gibson, received wide circulation. In 1996 another film version featured Kenneth Branagh (now available on videotape). In 2000 a filmed "modernized" version, in which the setting in Denmark is changed to a modern corporation with Hamlet being played by Ethan Hawke, has been likened to a computer "nerd." As yet, the Ethan Hawke version has not reached the public in videotape or DVD. Many of your students, however, may have seen at least one or perhaps all of these. In addition, the following videotapes and audiotapes are available:

- Videotape (1948), 153 minutes, directed by Laurence Olivier. Starring Laurence Olivier, Basil Sydney, and Jean Simmons. Audio-Brandon Films, 34 MacQuesten Parkway South, Mount Vernon, NY 10550.
- Videotape (1969), 114 minutes, directed by Tony Richardson. Starring Nicol Williamson, Sir Anthony Hopkins, and Judy Parfitt. Audio-Brandon.
- Videotape (1980), 222 minutes, starring Derek Jacoby. Time-Life Video, Box 644, Paramus, NY 07652.

- Videotape (1990), 135 minutes, directed by Franco Zeffirelli. Starring Mel Gibson, Alan Bates, Glenn Close, and Helena Bonham Carter. Available in most video outlets.
- Videotape (1990), 175 minutes, directed by Kevin Kline and Kirk Browning. A Joseph Papp/Great Performances Production in modern dress (Thirteen/WNBT). Starring Kevin Kline and Diane Venora.
- Audiotape (1979), directed by Howard Sackler. Starring Paul Scofield. Issued by Caedmon (CP232), 1995 Broadway, New York City, NY 10023. Caedmon releases have been acquired by Harper Collins.
- Audiotape (1992), 210 minutes, four cassettes. Starring Kenneth Branagh. A BBC Radio Production, issued by Bantam Doubleday Dell.

Please note that productions available on film are likely to be available on videotape in the near future. These films or tapes, and numerous other productions of *Hamlet*, are available from many other film distribution companies as well. The BBC/Time-Life production (1980) has obviously cut the least from the text.

Programmatic Guide to Hamlet

The following programmatic guide to *Hamlet* is mostly a series of questions that can be used to shape class discussion or lectures. A significant number of answers, lecture points, and points for review are also included. The guide follows the play scene-by-scene. Questions are printed in italic and answers follow immediately, indented, in regular type. To conserve space, at times we provide only a line reference as an answer, thus pointing our question directly into the text of the play. Rosencrantz and Guildenstern are abbreviated as "R&G" throughout. The guide includes all the study questions listed at the end of the play.

Act I. Exposition: *The establishment of character, situation, conflict.*

I.1: The watch on the battlements, Horatio, the Ghost.

This scene establishes that there is something wrong (rotten) in Denmark; what tells us that things are not right?

(1) The nervousness of the watch; the first words are "Who's there,"

establishing a tense and questioning tone. (2) The appearance of the Ghost. (3) The preparations for war (lines 70–79). (4) The problem with young Fortinbras (lines 95–107). Shakespeare thus uses minor characters here to introduce us to deeply troubled and chaotic circumstances.

Whom is Horatio going to tell about the Ghost? Why?

Horatio recognizes that it is his duty to tell Hamlet, on the grounds that the spirit, dumb to them, "will speak to him" (lines 169–173).

The most important character we meet in I.1 is Horatio; what is he like? How is he different from Barnardo and Marcellus?

Horatio is educated and a rationalist; at first, he thinks the Watchmen have imagined the Ghost. He understands the grave significance of the Ghost and recognizes his duty to inform Hamlet about the appearance.

Note: A broader approach to the scene can be achieved with three questions: (1) What is the function of the scene? (2) What mood is established in the scene? (3) What do we discover about Denmark in the scene?

I.2 The Court: Claudius, Gertrude, Hamlet, Laertes, Polonius, etc.

This scene establishes initial images of Claudius, Hamlet, Gertrude, Polonius, Ophelia, and Laertes. It also contrasts with the first scene because it shows normal court life. The king is speaking to his subjects and hearing their concerns. The scene illustrates the way in which a Renaissance court would actually have operated, with the king at the center and with the courtiers in attendance. The King's job is to make declarations, listen to petitions and either grant them or not, and give advice.

What is the first impression of Claudius as king and speaker?

Claudius is in control. He controls the attention of the courtiers, and the first scene is structured so that he is seen dealing with business and with the petitions of his subjects.

What problem concerns young Fortinbras? How does Claudius deal with it?

Fortinbras is planning to invade Denmark with a Norwegian army. Claudius resolves to send Cornelius and Voltimand to the uncle of Fortinbras, so that the uncle may quash the invasion plans (lines 17–42).

What business does Laertes raise? How does Claudius deal with it?

Laertes wants to return to Paris; Claudius asks Polonius, Laertes's father, if the matter has been settled within the family. When Polonius indicates his blessing, Claudius approves (lines 43–63).

The next piece of business is Hamlet and his behavior. What is the problem with Hamlet?

Hamlet is still mourning the death of his father; the clouds still hang upon him.

What sets Hamlet apart? How is his clothing different?

He is the only one dressed in black mourning clothes. In arranging the tableau of the scene, most directors keep him well away from all other characters, ignoring the activities of the court. He is depressed and unsettled.

What thematic point is introduced in Hamlet's "Seems, madam" speech (lines 76–86)?

Appearance vs. reality (*see the demonstrative student essay, page 1532*).

How do Claudius and Gertrude try to deal with Hamlet's sadness?

Both assert that death is natural and inevitable, and that now that the mourning period is over, Hamlet should cheer up and take up normal life as he had been living it before King Hamlet's death (lines 87–117). The argument is especially ironic in light of old Hamlet's unnatural death.

What does Hamlet's first soliloquy (lines 129–159) tell us about him?

He is depressed, suicidal, and bitter; he is bothered by his father's death, his mother's remarriage, and the fact that he is not king.

What do we find out about Horatio in his conversation with Hamlet (lines 160–258)?

He is Hamlet's friend and fellow student. Hamlet wants them to be equals (friend instead of servant); he likes and trusts Horatio.

What does Horatio tell Hamlet? What does Hamlet decide to do? Why?

Horatio tells Hamlet about the Ghost. Hamlet decides to see for himself, and arranges to meet the guard upon the platform between eleven and twelve o'clock in the evening. He is uneasy about the spirit, believing that there may be "some foul play" (line 257) that it is his duty to uncover.

I.3: Exposition of subplot. We meet Laertes, Ophelia, Polonius.

The scene occurs in three conversations: Laertes-Ophelia (lines 1–51); Polonius-Laertes (lines 51–88); Polonius-Ophelia (lines 88–136).

What do we find out about the relationship between Hamlet and Ophelia? What is Laertes's attitude toward the two?

Hamlet is courting Ophelia. Laertes thinks Hamlet is trifling and advises Ophelia to stay away from the prince. He is worried about her chastity and the family's (especially his own) reputation. Ophelia's last remark suggests that Laertes is better at giving advice than following it.

What advice does Polonius give Laertes? Is the advice good? Original? What does it show about the character of Polonius?

Polonius gives Laertes the advice that most fathers might like to give sons who are leaving home and going out on their own (e.g., be careful, don't let money interfere with friendship, listen to advice, don't be overly conspicuous in dress, be true to your character). Some critics claim that the advice is trite and hackneyed, and some productions of the play have both Laertes and Ophelia laugh at Polonius behind his back (*see particularly the*

Laurence Olivier movie version of 1948). Polonius, however, has been a trusted royal adviser and, though he is getting old, his advice is well meant, and he speaks with great concern and affection. Without doubt he has said many of the same things before, but most parents give advice to their children as long as they live. One must emphasize that Polonius is an upper-class father, and that in Shakespeare's time the father, as the *paterfamilias*, had absolute family authority. Polonius is thus using his position to give advice, and in the remainder of the play, until his death, his primary concern is to advance his family. Thus, by showing concern for Laertes, he is thinking about family honor. By controlling Ophelia, he is trying to preserve her for an advantageous marriage. This would be the highest honor and prestige he could bring to his family.

What is Polonius's attitude toward Ophelia's love of Hamlet? What reasons does he give for this attitude? Is he more concerned with Ophelia or himself? What does he tell Ophelia to do regarding Hamlet?

He holds the same (but stronger) opinion as Laertes. He is afraid that Hamlet just wants sex, and he warns Ophelia to stay away, because if Ophelia falls, her fall would hurt his family's reputation and ruin her chances for an advantageous marriage. Hamlet would, of course, make the perfect husband for Ophelia, but Ophelia and the family would benefit only if Hamlet and Ophelia marry. In any event, it is unlikely that Polonius understands the depths of Ophelia's feelings.

What is Ophelia like? How does she respond to Laertes and Polonius? To what extent does she or does she not behave according to her own will?

Although much of this depends on how Ophelia is played, the text suggests that she is compliant, obedient, perhaps too dutiful, and easily controlled. These qualities, together with her love for Hamlet, will prove to be her emotional undoing as she loses her sanity later in the play.

I.4: Hamlet, Horatio, and the Watch meet the Ghost.

A key question for Hamlet is what kind of ghost he faces. What are the two possibilities? Why is the question important? How does the problem affect Hamlet's subsequent action?

The two possibilities are that the ghost may be real, or a manifestation of the devil ("Spirit of health or goblin damned" [lines 40–42]). The possibility of the latter produces doubt and causes Hamlet to seek proof.

I.5: Hamlet and the Ghost

What does the Ghost tell Hamlet about who caused his death? What does the Ghost want Hamlet to do? What special instructions does the Ghost give Hamlet about Gertrude?

He explains that his brother Claudius, now king, killed him by pouring poison into his ear when he was sleeping. The Ghost wants Hamlet to revenge "his foul and most unnatural murder" (line 25). In other words, the ghost wants Hamlet to kill Claudius, but to leave Gertrude's punishment "to heaven" (lines 84–88).

Why does Hamlet swear the watch to secrecy?

He wants to watch Claudius secretly.

Why does Hamlet decide to pretend insanity—put on an "antic disposition"? Why can't Hamlet act against Claudius at this point?

Feigned madness will protect him (i.e., people will explain strange behavior as a result of his mental disturbance, without seeking other motives) while he is trying to get the necessary proof of the Ghost's honesty. Hamlet cannot carry out any act of revenge at this point because he simply has no concrete proof of any crime. The word of the Ghost would not go far in any inquiry into a vengeful act.

What is Hamlet's reaction to the Ghost's demands?

At first, he swears immediate action (lines 93–112), but at the end of the scene he expresses reluctance and unwillingness about his new role, and he indicates that the "spite" of murder is "cursed" (lines 188–189).

Act I Review: Act I establishes the character, conflicts, and situations. It reveals that much is wrong. The Ghost tells Hamlet about murder and usurpation. By the end of Act I, Hamlet believes that he knows what he must do: He must confirm the Ghost's accusations, and must defend himself from Claudius while doing so. Act I also establishes the major characters. Hamlet is melancholic, upset about his mother, introspective, and traumatized by the Ghost. Claudius is smooth, politic, efficient, murderous, lustful, and evil (if we believe the Ghost). Polonius is past his prime, and is unable to wield a great deal of power. Ophelia is obedient and dutiful, but there are strong forces in her that may cause her trouble. Laertes is a concerned brother, and Horatio is a scholar and rationalist who is trusted by Hamlet.

The central problem here and throughout is delay. Why doesn't Hamlet kill Claudius immediately? This is not really a problem (*see the demonstrative essay, page 1527*). The problem is rather how Shakespeare justifies Hamlet's delay and makes it credible. One answer is the difficulty of confirming the Ghost's story. The Ghost might be a devil; Hamlet needs more evidence. Once he thinks he has it, he kills—and kills the wrong man (Polonius). This causes more delay. A second answer—the problem of character. Hamlet is introspective and contemplative. His introspective nature accounts for the soliloquies in which he accuses himself of delay despite the reasonableness of delaying. If this delay could not be justified, according to the codes of revenge, then it would be a character flaw. If it is not justified, then it is not a flaw.

Act II. Complication: *Three Main Lines of Development*

1. Hamlet's quest for proof; 2. Hamlet's introspection and self-accusation in soliloquies; 3. Claudius's defensive actions through Rosencrantz, Guildenstern, and Polonius.

II.1: *Focus on Polonius and Reynaldo, then Ophelia*

What does Polonius want Reynaldo to do in Paris? What does this show us about Polonius?

Polonius wants to keep track of what Laertes is doing in Paris, and asks Reynaldo to learn whatever he can, even if doing so means dropping hints that Laertes is carousing and misbehaving (a "bait of falsehood" [line 60]), so that such action may be confirmed or denied. The action shows the extreme to which Polonius will go in insuring the reputation of his family. He fears that Laertes might do something that might cause embarrassment or disgrace, and he is willing to use people in the service of his suspicions. It would seem that his interest is in maintaining the level of family respectability so that a potential match of Ophelia and Hamlet would not be compromised.

What does Ophelia report about Hamlet?

She reports that Hamlet came to her greatly disordered and disturbed, seemingly out of his senses (lines 74–81, 85–97).

What conclusions about Hamlet does Polonius draw?

He concludes that Hamlet is mad for love: "The very ecstasy of love" (line 99).

What will Polonius do with this information? What does this tell us?

"I will go seek the king" (line 98). Polonius has earlier suspected Hamlet of just toying with Ophelia. This new information makes him believe he was wrong. His action and behavior show his belief and hope that Hamlet might be brought to marry Ophelia (and overcome the "madness"), and thus to elevate the family beyond his greatest expectations. By reporting to the King, he probably hopes to persuade the King to his way of thinking, and to see that Hamlet should marry Ophelia.

II.2.a (lines 1–40): *Claudius and Gertrude greet R&G*

Why are R&G in Denmark? How does Claudius plan to use them?

Claudius wants R&G to watch Hamlet, and find out what is troubling him ("aught to us unknown" [line 17]).

To what extent do R&G cooperate with Claudius? To what extent does their cooperation justify their deaths later in the play?

Hamlet claims that they courted power and paid the price; they clearly agree to be used for profit. It seems clear, at the start, however, that R&G believe that they really might be helping Hamlet.

II.2.b (lines 40–85): *Resolution of the Fortinbras problem*

How has the threat to Denmark posed by young Fortinbras been resolved? What does he plan to do with his army?

The king of Norway dissuaded him; Fortinbras plans to attack Poland instead, and seeks permission to cross Denmark. He and his army have a long march ahead of them.

II.2.c (lines 85–170): *Polonius's explanation of Hamlet's madness*

Describe Polonius's language. What does it show us about him?

It is extremely wordy. It shows that he is nervous, for he is trying to lead the King and Queen to consent to a marriage of Hamlet and Ophelia. He cannot openly suggest such a marriage because a proposal must come from the royal family. His confusion, and his false starts, are thus amusing.

What does he report about Hamlet? How does he prove it?

He claims that Hamlet is mad for love, and cites Hamlet's letter and behavior.

How does Claudius react?

He is interested but doubtful, and asks, "How may we try it further?" (line 159).

What plan does Polonius come up with?

To use Ophelia and to spy on the meeting: "I'll loose my daughter to him. Be you and I behind an arras" (lines 162–163). This plan shows his assumption that his will as a father takes precedence over Ophelia's own feelings and involvement in promoting a possible marriage with Hamlet.

II.2.d (lines 170–220): *The confrontation of Hamlet and Polonius*

How does Hamlet act? On what things does Hamlet focus in his pretended insanity? How is there method in his madness?

Hamlet pretends to be mad; he focuses on Polonius as whoremaster, and also on daughters, death, graves, and the emptiness of language. All these are relevant to Hamlet's situation.

II.2.e (lines 221–430): *Hamlet meets R&G.*

What do R&G try to find out from Hamlet? How successful are they?

They want to learn the cause of his behavior. They do not.

What does Hamlet want to know from R&G? Why is this important? How does R&G's confession that they were sent for affect the way Hamlet deals with them?

Hamlet wants to know if they were sent for (lines 265, 269, 275, 281, 284). When they admit it, he recognizes them as Claudius's tools, but confesses that he (Hamlet) is "but mad north-north-west; when the wind is southerly, / I know a hawk from a handsaw" (lines 361–362). The scene is ironic. Hamlet thinks he knows the reasons for R&G's inquiries; R&G do not.

What news do R&G bring Hamlet? Who is on the way to the court?

They report the approach of a traveling company of actors. Polonius brings the same news almost immediately. When with Polonius, Hamlet resumes his feigned madness.

II.2.f (lines 430–END): *Hamlet and the actors, the closing soliloquy*

Hamlet wants to hear the speech about Hecuba and the Fall of Troy. How is this relevant to the problems of Hamlet?

Hecuba was a loyal queen; Priam was killed through treachery. These are parallels to Denmark's situation and to Hamlet's concerns.

What play does Hamlet arrange for? Why? When will it be acted?

Hamlet arranges for the actors to present "The Murder of Gonzago." The action of the play closely parallels the crimes that the Ghost has accused Claudius of committing. Hamlet will use the play "to catch the conscience of the king" (line 580).

Of what does Hamlet accuse himself in the soliloquy (lines 523–62)? Are the accusations accurate?

He calls himself a dull rogue, coward, and villain for not feeling or taking action. He is, of course, taking action, so his accusations are not literally true.

What point does Hamlet make again about the Ghost in his soliloquy?

The Ghost may be a devil trying to damn Hamlet (lines 574–79).

Act II Review: Act II advances the conflicts of the play and focuses the action; it can be reviewed with six questions: 1. How is the characterization of Hamlet advanced? 2. What do his soliloquies show us? 3. How has Hamlet moved closer to the confirmation of the Ghost's accusations? 4. What defensive or protective actions has Claudius initiated? 5. What role does Polonius play in Act II? 6. How does our opinion of Polonius change?

Act III. Crisis and Confrontation: *Hamlet's Act and His Use of Actors*

III.1.a (lines 1–28): *Claudius and R&G*

What do R&G report to Claudius? How successful are they as spies?

They have been unable to discover anything; Hamlet will not answer them.

III.1.b (lines 29–55): *Claudius, Polonius, and Ophelia: the Test of Love*

What do Claudius and Polonius set up for Hamlet using Ophelia?

They set up the chance encounter that will test whether Hamlet's madness is derived from love. The scene is ironic. Claudius wants to know if Hamlet's behavior really results from love or from suspicion, while Polonius believes that if the behavior is from love he may become the father-in-law of the future King of Denmark.

How is this confrontation like the play-within-the-play that Hamlet uses later in Act III to test Claudius's guilt?

Both are staged actions; both involve audiences; both are designed to test information through reactions.

To what extent does Ophelia's role in this test change or confirm our opinion of her?

Ever pliant and obedient, Ophelia allows herself to be the tool of Polonius and Claudius. To the extent that she is playing out their instructions, she is an actress, even though she does not fully understand the role she is playing. Hamlet, who knows that Claudius and Polonius are trying to manipulate him, and may also believe that Ophelia is in on the plan, therefore takes out all his anger and suspicion on her. This misconception explains why Hamlet brutally accuses her of face painting, fraud, and deceit.

III.1.c (lines 56–88): *Hamlet's "To Be or Not to Be" soliloquy*

What is Hamlet contemplating? Is he actually suicidal? Is his contemplation personal or abstract?

Hamlet's depression leads him to contemplate death ("not to be") and suicide in an abstract and impersonal manner, but he concludes that fear of "something after death" dissuades him from suicide ("Thus conscience doth make cowards of us all," 83).

III.1.d (lines 89–149): *Hamlet and Ophelia in the Lobby*

What does Ophelia try to give to Hamlet? Why? What does Hamlet say about his feelings toward Ophelia?

She tries to return favors as part of the test; he refuses them. At this point, Hamlet is playing with Ophelia; he claims that he loved her once and then denies it (lines 115, 118).

How does Hamlet treat Ophelia? Does his treatment (and attitude) change? If so, how and when? Why does he ask Ophelia about Polonius (line 130)? Does he know (or discover) that he is being watched?

Hamlet begins by toying with Ophelia and ends up in a rage. The change occurs at line 130 when he asks about Polonius. Since the text does not account for the shift, many directors stage the scene so that Hamlet spots movements by Claudius and Polonius behind the arras. If staged this way, Hamlet's following rage reflects his return to feigned madness and his real disappointment with Ophelia.

What does Hamlet stress in his tirade against Ophelia? How is this relevant?

Hamlet stresses honesty in women, the falsity of using makeup, and the manipulative roles that he believes women take against men. He may be speaking in anger against her; he may also be inveighing against the King and the Queen and Polonius; and he may be reflecting on his own needs for playing a role to acquire more information about the truth of the Ghost's information. Hamlet is a complex character, and the situation clearly causes him to become distrustful and easily angered.

III.1.e (lines 150–188): *Reactions to Hamlet's behavior*

What is Ophelia's reaction to Hamlet? What is Claudius's?

She thinks he is mad. He is suspicious; he concludes that the source of Hamlet's behavior is not love, but something more sinister and threatening to him (lines 162–166).

How does Claudius plan to deal with Hamlet?

Claudius proposes to send him "with speed to England," ostensibly to serve as an ambassador to secure tribute from the English, to take his mind off his melancholy and therefore to get him back to normal.

What is Polonius's reaction to the confrontation?

He still thinks love caused the madness; he cannot give up his hope that Hamlet might yet marry Ophelia and thus benefit him.

What new plan to find Hamlet out does Polonius offer?

He proposes that Gertrude speak to Hamlet and that he eavesdrop (lines 181–187).

III.2: *The Crisis of the Play.* *Before a close reading, ask your students what and where the crisis is. The crisis is Claudius's reaction to the play-within-the-play. It sets Hamlet and Claudius on a collision course; each knows the truth about the other at this point.*

III.2.a (lines 1–126): *Hamlet's instructions and preparations*

What does Hamlet tell the actors about acting and drama?

He does not want the actors to over-act or ad-lib. Drama (playing) is defined as holding "the mirror up to nature" (line 20).

How does Hamlet explain his relationship to Horatio? What does Hamlet want Horatio to do during "Gonzago"?

Hamlet likes and trusts Horatio because the latter is well-balanced, honest, and controlled. The "pipe" (recorder, oboe, or flute) metaphor here (lines 65–66) indicates that Horatio cannot be manipulated and is a true friend. Hamlet trusts Horatio, and wants him to observe Claudius during the murder scene in *The Murder of Gonzago* to see if his guilt will show itself.

Hamlet (line 85) says "I must be idle." What course of action does this involve? How does Hamlet sustain his antic disposition?

Idle here means foolish or insane. Hamlet sustains the illusion of madness by speaking pointed nonsense and punning suggestively.

III.2.b (lines 126–246): *The Dumb Show and* The Murder of Gonzago

What is a dumb show*? What happens in this dumb show? How is it relevant? Why doesn't Claudius react to it?*

It is a pantomime enactment of the entire play, including the murder. Claudius's failure to react is inexplicable unless we assume he isn't watching the actors. The text does not provide an answer here. In performance, however, many directors choose to have Claudius busy chatting with others and with Gertrude at this point.

Summarize the plot of Gonzago*. How is it relevant to Hamlet? What are the parallels between the characters in Hamlet and "Gonzago"? Why is* Gonzago *an effective test of the Ghost's accusations?*

Gonzago includes all Claudius's major sins: murder, lust, usurpation, and an unsavory marriage. The player King is Old Hamlet, the Player Queen is Gertrude, and Lucianus is Claudius. The parallels make the play an ideal test of Claudius's guilt.

How does Claudius react to the staged murder?

He is deeply disturbed; frantically, he orders the play to stop, asks for light, and rushes out (lines 252–255).

Why is this the crisis of the play? What does Hamlet learn about Claudius at this point? What does Claudius learn about Hamlet?

Until this point, both Hamlet and Claudius have avoided confrontation and direct action. Now, both will try to act: Hamlet to kill the eavesdropper in III.4. and Claudius to send Hamlet to be executed in England.

III.2.c (lines 246–364): *Reactions to the play and events*

How has Hamlet's position changed?

"I'll take the ghost's word for a thousand pound" (lines 271–2); he is convinced of Claudius's guilt.

What do R&G report to Hamlet? Whose interests do they represent? How does Hamlet treat them? Explain the metaphor of the recorder.

They represent Claudius's interests and report his rage as well as Gertrude's desire to speak with Hamlet. Hamlet treats them with scorn and anger; he accuses them of trying to play him as they would a recorder.

III.2.d (lines 365–407): *Hamlet's soliloquy*

What is Hamlet's frame of mind? What is he ready to do? How does his language and imagery reflect his attitude?

He is ready to revenge (drink hot blood); images like "witching time of night" and "Hell itself breathes out contagion" suggest his commitment to bloody (and evil) deeds.

What is Hamlet's attitude toward his mother in this scene?

He is going to her room to speak with her, and is angry with her because of her closeness to Claudius. Does he suspect her of conspiracy with Claudius against his father? He resolves not to kill her, but to speak daggers to her to get her to part from Claudius. His expectation is of course preposterous in view of Gertrude's commitment to Claudius.

III.3: *Claudius at prayer and Hamlet's avoidance of revenge*

What does Claudius have planned for Hamlet?

Claudius goes through with his plan to send Hamlet to England (to be killed), and asks R&G to accompany the Prince (lines 1–7).

What is Rosencrantz's vision of the state and the death of a king? Why is this vision ironic in connection with Claudius?

A king's death produces universal sadness and chaos because of the disorder in the cosmos. This is ironic because Claudius as a usurper has already produced cosmic disorder.

What does Claudius reveal in his soliloquy? How does his speech affect your evaluation?

The soliloquy reveals that Claudius is guilty and that he feels guilt; it humanizes him by showing that he is not pure evil.

What reasons does Hamlet give for not killing Claudius at his prayers? Are they convincing? Are they within Hamlet's character? What else is on his mind at this point? Why is Hamlet's decision here ironic? To what extent does this scene support either Hamlet's own sense that he is guilty of delay or the nineteenth-century argument that Hamlet's tragic flaw is his inability to act?

This moment is hotly debated by critics. Hamlet says that he avoids stabbing Claudius because he would send Claudius's soul to heaven, and sending him to heaven would not be revenge but reward. Instead, Hamlet states that he wants to kill Claudius when he will be damned, just as Hamlet's father was killed with his sins on his head, without the ministrations of a priest. Some critics are struck by the uncharacteristic bloodthirstiness and bad theology here. Ironically, Claudius cannot pray (*see lines* 97–98). In any event, Hamlet clearly has his mother, whom he is going to meet, on his mind (line 95). Since Hamlet acts with speed in III.4, this moment of delay should not carry too much weight.

III.4.a (lines 1–24): *The death of Polonius*

What is Polonius doing in Gertrude's chamber?

Polonius, who is still trying to test Hamlet's behavior and who therefore hides during the confrontation, advises Gertrude to tell Hamlet that she has been protecting him and that he should straighten out (lines 1–7).

How does Hamlet treat Gertrude? What frightens Polonius? How is Polonius killed? Why is he killed? Whom did Hamlet hope he was killing? Hamlet calls Polonius a "wretched, rash, intruding fool" (line 31); is this judgment accurate? To what extent is Polonius responsible for his own death? What does this act show us about Hamlet?

Hamlet verbally attacks Gertrude; she becomes afraid and calls for help (lines 20–21). Polonius also calls out from behind the arras, and Hamlet runs him through, believing that the person in hiding might be Claudius (line 26). The killing shows that Hamlet can act impetuously and with speed when the occasion demands. Polonius has been intervening in royal affairs since the play's opening, even though his motivations have been his own and his family's advancement. He has not understood what is going on, and thus he has been an "intruding fool." Because he is hiding, and could be a threat as far as Hamlet is concerned, Polonius brings about his own death, even though he intends Hamlet no harm.

III.4.b (lines 35–217): *Hamlet's lecture and the Ghost's return*

What two men does Hamlet compare? What points does he make about Claudius? About Gertrude's behavior? What disturbs Hamlet most here? What effect does his lecture have on Gertrude?

Hamlet compares old Hamlet to Claudius (in production, he often holds miniature portraits of both men up to Gertrude. He is wearing the miniature of old Hamlet; she wears the miniature of Claudius). He accuses Gertrude of lustfully shifting from the godlike grace of the senior Hamlet to become attached to a murderer, villain, and usurper. He seems far more upset by Gertrude's remarriage than by his father's murder. Later, he tells Gertrude to avoid Claudius's bed.

Why does the Ghost return?

Hamlet assumes the Ghost returns to criticize his delay (tardy son). The Ghost says that he has come "to whet thy almost blunted purpose" (line 111). Thematically, the return of the Ghost brings to mind the details of Act 1 and the accusations of murder against Claudius. In addition, the Ghost is scary and mysterious, and his presence deepens the mood of anger, depression, and death.

What is Gertrude's opinion of Hamlet's mental state? What does he tell her? What does she promise?

She thinks he has gone mad. He explains that he is feigning madness and warns her not to tell Claudius. She promises to keep silent.

What does Hamlet know about R&G and the impending trip to England? What does he plan to do about the problem?

He knows they cannot be trusted and are leading him to knavery. He plans to destroy them through their own devices (see lines 200–210).

Act III Review and Introduction to Act IV: Act III has focused on Hamlet: (1) His effort to confirm the Ghost's accusations; (2) his avoidance of revenge during the praying scene; (3) his accidental killing of Polonius; (4) his interview with his mother. The death of Polonius, however, puts Hamlet into a defensive position and gives Claudius the upper hand. Thus, in Act IV, the focus shifts away from Hamlet (who goes to England) to Claudius. While Act III focuses on Hamlet's attempts to gain vengeance, Act IV focuses on Claudius's attempts to eliminate Hamlet. Act IV begins with Claudius's first plan of attack—to have Hamlet murdered in England. It ends with his second plan: the rigged fencing match.

Act IV. The Tightening Web: *Claudius's counter-moves*

IV.1: *Claudius and Gertrude*

What does Gertrude report to Claudius? What does Claudius realize about Hamlet's killing of Polonius? What does he plan to do with Hamlet?

She reports Hamlet's madness and murder of Polonius. Claudius realizes it was meant for him (line 13); he plans to send Hamlet to England at dawn, now as a way of ostensibly getting Hamlet out of court so that the crime may be forgotten. (lines 40–45).

IV.2: *Hamlet and R&G*

What is Hamlet's attitude toward R&G?

He scorns them as sponges who soak up Claudius's orders, rewards, and authority. They have become mere extensions.

IV.3: *Claudius and Hamlet*

How does Hamlet act with Claudius when questioned about Polonius?

He maintains the appearance of madness but drops hints to trouble Claudius.

What has Claudius planned for Hamlet in England?

Claudius plans to have Hamlet killed in England. He has now let R&G into his confidence, and hints at rewards for them if they will accompany Hamlet and see to it that the orders are carried out (lines 51–65).

Why does Claudius plan to have Hamlet killed?

There are two reasons: Hamlet's popularity with the people and Gertrude's love. Claudius wants Hamlet dead, but he wants no one to know his responsibility. This plan is consistent with Claudius's readiness to use people for his own ends. He uses Polonius, Ophelia, R&G, and Laertes, and most of these people willingly serve him out of duty or the hope of advancement.

IV.4: *Hamlet on the way to the seacoast and England*

Where are Fortinbras and his army going? What does Hamlet learn about the land that will be fought over? How does this meeting influence Hamlet's thinking (soliloquy, lines 32–66)? Of what does Hamlet accuse himself?

They are going to fight over a barren plot of land in Poland worth nothing but honor. Hamlet sees this instance as a rebuke of his own tardiness and lack of passion. He argues that he has far greater cause to act than Fortinbras and yet lets all sleep. The charges are not an accurate reflection of the situation; at this moment, Hamlet is powerless to act.

IV.5.a (lines 1–70): *Ophelia's insanity*

What is Ophelia's condition? How does her language convey her madness? How is her madness different from Hamlet's?

Ophelia's madness—the real thing—is conveyed in fragmented grammar, nonsense, bawdy songs, and oblique allusions to Polonius's death. There is no apparent method in her madness, but her speeches show what has unhinged her. They also show her kindness and vulnerability.

Why is Ophelia mad? How is madness consistent with her character?

Her madness evolves from her father's death, Hamlet's treatment of her, and a sense of betrayal of her affections for Hamlet. Throughout the play, she has been guided by Polonius or her brother; now she has no one. The madness is consistent with her obedience, sense of duty, and selflessness. In a structural sense, her madness symbolizes the effects of the original murder of King Hamlet by Claudius. Evil, in short, begins with one action, which spreads out to destroy everyone in its swath.

IV.5.b (lines 71–151): *The return of Laertes*

What is Laertes's attitude on returning to Denmark? What does he want? How is he comparable to Hamlet? Is he more or less justified than Hamlet?

Laertes is enraged over Polonius's death and secret burial; he blames Claudius and wants revenge (lines 133–134). As a son whose father has been murdered, Laertes is an exact parallel to Hamlet; his desires are equally motivated. This twist of the plot ironically makes Hamlet parallel to Claudius and reveals the moral corruption inherent in vengeance.

IV.5.c (lines 152–214): *Laertes and Ophelia, Laertes and Claudius*

How does Ophelia behave with Laertes? What is the focus of her madness? What is Laertes's reaction?

Ophelia's madness continues; she dwells on images that suggest Polonius's death. Laertes's desire for revenge grows.

What does Claudius offer Laertes?

Claudius offers "satisfaction" (line 204); that is, that Hamlet will be eliminated. Laertes asks that no honors be given to Hamlet after death (lines 197–214).

IV.6: *Horatio and the Sailors*

What does Hamlet's letter reveal?

The letter reveals that Hamlet will return to Denmark while R&G go on to England.

IV.7: *Claudius and Laertes hatch a plot*

What had Claudius proven to Laertes about Polonius's death? What news does he expect from England? What news does he get?

He convinces Laertes that Hamlet killed Polonius while trying to kill him. He expects to hear that Hamlet has been executed; instead, he hears of Hamlet's safe return.

How do Claudius and Laertes plan to murder Hamlet? To what extent is Laertes manipulated by Claudius? To what extent is Laertes the author of this plan? How is Laertes's commitment to revenge different from Hamlet's?

They plan to murder Hamlet by trickery during a fencing match. Claudius invents the plan, but Laertes adds the detail of the poison (lines 139–147). He manipulates Laertes into doing his dirty work, but Laertes's own commitment is absolute.

What do we find out about Ophelia in this scene?

Ophelia has drowned herself in a nearby stream. Gertrude explains the death as an accident (she fell off a bough, and the weight of her clothing dragged her under the water; lines 164–183). We may conclude that Ophelia simply threw herself into the water and was thus drowned.

Act IV Review and Introduction to Act V. Just as Act III was mostly Hamlet's act, so Act IV is mostly Claudius's. Having killed Polonius in Act III, Hamlet is on the defensive. In Act IV Claudius is on the offensive. The Act contains Claudius's two plans for getting rid of Hamlet: the English execution and the rigged fencing match. The re-introduction of Laertes as a secondary revenger (and a parallel to Hamlet) complicates the play's neatly unfolding structure, but Laertes is quickly co-opted and absorbed by Claudius; Laertes becomes a willing tool for Claudius. By the end of Act IV, then, the two central thrusts of motive-action are clearly established: Hamlet's desire to eliminate Claudius and Claudius's desire to eliminate Hamlet. These two forces meet head on in Act V, where the resolution is death.

Act V: Vengeance, Catastrophe, and Resolution

V.1.a (lines 1–55): *The Clowns (Gravediggers)*

What is the subject of the clowns' conversation? How is this subject relevant to the play? To what extent is the conversation amusing?

The general topic is death and decay. Death permeates *Hamlet*, and this scene provides another focus on this central fact, but does so comically.

Death is of course heavy material for comic relief, but the treatment is successful. The intention of comic relief is to divert the emotional pressure that a play builds up through conflict and tension. Rather than have the audience laugh at the wrong point in the action, Shakespeare provides a legitimate outlet for laughter. The result is that when the concluding dueling, poisoning, and dying are over at the end of the play, an inappropriate response of laughter has been left behind, and the audience is left free to focus on the deaths and to respond sympathetically.

V.1.b (lines 56–201): *Hamlet and the Clown*

To what extent is this conversation also comic? What do the skulls make Hamlet think about? How is this subject relevant to Hamlet's earlier thought? How does Shakespeare's comic relief work thematically?

The conversation is made comic primarily because of the gravedigger's word play and matter-of-fact attitude toward death. The skulls, like so much else in the play, remind Hamlet of death, but they bring the physical reality of death directly to his thinking. In addition, the references to Alexander the Great and Caesar suggest death's universal and leveling power. These realizations bring him to readiness for the inevitable outcome. Thus the comic scene is not wasted, for it reflects a major concern of the play and it prompts Hamlet to advance his thinking about death and his involvement in the tightening chain of circumstances.

V.1.c (lines 201–282): *Ophelia's funeral*

How does Laertes act? What point does Hamlet make about his own feelings for Ophelia? About Laertes?

Laertes acts with conventional grief. Jumping into a grave may seem overly demonstrative, but it is not unusual in some cultures. To most audiences today, however, Laertes seems to be carrying things too far. Hamlet claims that he can overmatch Laertes since his feelings are greater.

V.2.a (lines 1–80): *The fate of R&G*

What orders were R&G carrying? What did Hamlet do to R&G? To what extent is their fate just? What is Hamlet's attitude toward their fate?

R&G had orders from Claudius for Hamlet's immediate execution (lines 18–25); Hamlet altered the orders so that R&G would be killed upon arrival in England (lines 38–47). Hamlet thinks they deserved to die (lines 57–62) because he assumes that they were in league with Claudius.

V.2.b (lines 81–179): *Hamlet and Osric*

What is Osric like? Why does Hamlet call him a "water-fly"? What is his language like? How is he like Polonius? How does Hamlet mock Osric? What is Osric's business with Hamlet?

Osric is an overdressed dandy who is a cause of humor. Hamlet's reference to him as a "water-fly" reflects his pretentious clothing and manners. Osric has the courtier's manner of speaking in indirection and circumlocution. Hamlet mocks his manners with the bonnet, and mocks his overly courtly doubletalk by feeding it back to him (lines 109–119). Osric's task is to deliver Laertes's challenge; his effect is to create another comic scene before the final resolution in death.

V.2.c (lines 179–206): *Hamlet and Horatio*

What is Hamlet's attitude toward the fencing match?

He thinks he will win (line 194), but is suspicious (lines 194–201).

What has Hamlet learned by this point in the play?

Hamlet has learned the virtues of patience, acceptance, and readiness (see lines 202–6). He accepts the providence of all things and believes that the readiness is all. Ironically, these lessons will neither help nor save him, because he will be forced to act suddenly when he finally acts.

V.2.d (lines 207–344): *The fencing match; the catastrophe*

How do Hamlet and Laertes act toward each other before the match? Which is sincere?

The men exchange pardons and love; only Hamlet is sincere.

Who wins the first two bouts? What is Laertes's problem? How does he solve it?

Hamlet wins both; Laertes cannot get a legitimate hit with the poisoned foil, so he stabs Hamlet between bouts. This violation of the rules of fair play underscores Laertes's corruption and his commitment to vengeance.

How is Gertrude killed? Laertes? Claudius? In what way are all three deaths ironic?

Gertrude is killed with the poisoned wine that Claudius prepares for Hamlet. Laertes dies from his own unbaited and poisoned foil, and confesses that "I am justly killed with mine own treachery" (line 290) while naming Claudius as the guilty one. Hamlet, learning this fact and having almost no time left to live, kills Claudius with both the poisoned sword and the poisoned wine. Ironically, he therefore revenges himself not so much for his father's death but for his mother's and his own. The deaths of both Claudius and Laertes are ironic because they are killed with their own weapons. Gertrude's death is ironic because the poisoned wine was not for her.

Why does Hamlet want Horatio to stay alive? What is Hamlet's final concern?

He wants Horatio to remain alive to tell his story (lines 326–332). Thus, up to the very last, Hamlet is concerned about his reputation and about the real reasons for his action. One might add that in the telling, it would make great sense for Horatio to be able to state that Hamlet killed Claudius because of the death of Gertrude and the conspiracy against Hamlet by both Laertes and Claudius.

V.2.e (lines 345–386): *Resolution; tying up of loose ends*

Who will be the next king of Denmark?

Fortinbras will be the next ruler (line 339).

What does Horatio plan to explain to the unknowing world?

He will tell the story of "how these things came about"; i.e., murders, arbitrary judgments, unpremeditated slaughter, treachery, and self-ruin (lines 362–369).

What is Fortinbras's attitude toward Hamlet?

Fortinbras has returned from war in Poland to speak the last words over the dead bodies on stage. We must conclude that a good deal of time has elapsed since he received permission to cross Denmark on the way to Poland. Fortinbras treats Hamlet with honor and respect; he calls him most royal and has the body honored with a soldier's procession. Thus, Fortinbras implicitly accepts the justice of Hamlet's cause.

Suggestions for Discussing the General Questions, page 1453

(1–4) All these topics focus on character. Claudius, Horatio, R&G, and Polonius are discussed at length above. Of the women, Ophelia is the more fully developed. We see Gertrude mostly from Hamlet's perspective, and he considers her morally weak. We learn that she is a loving person and that she thinks well of her son. That she married with undue haste after the funeral is a fact, but she may have been thinking more of the continuity of the state and her role in the succession than about her own feelings. She is totally committed to Claudius and to helping him in his rule. There is never any suspicion that Gertrude knew that Claudius killed King Hamlet or that she learns about the killing as the play progresses. Hence, her second marriage is more an indication that she appreciates her role as queen, with all its powers and privileges, than an indication of evil or even weakness.

Ophelia, as noted above in discussions of I.3 and IV.5, is controlled by the men in her life: Polonius, Laertes, and Hamlet. In her dutiful cooperation with Claudius and Polonius, she is used in a situation she does not understand, and the treatment she receives from Hamlet, indicating to her that she is scorned rather than loved, is one of the situations bringing her down. We may conclude that the murder of her father causes her deep grief, and also that her death is a suicide brought about by all the evil circumstances of the court.

Revenge is a major influence on character in the play: Hamlet, Laertes, and Fortinbras are all parallel revengers. Fortinbras wants to avenge his father's defeat and death at the hands of old Hamlet. He seeks to do so through military action against Denmark. Although deflected from Denmark to Poland by his uncle, he ultimately claims the Danish throne and gains the dying Hamlet's approval.

Hamlet's quest for vengeance is complicated by his need to prove the Ghost's accusations, his fixation on his mother's incestuous relationship with Claudius, and his own guilt about what he sees as delay. These combine to postpone his killing of Claudius until it is too late to escape death. Hamlet's is perhaps the most thoughtful but least effective quest.

Laertes commits himself more directly to vengeance, but also allies himself with evil. He is not interested in corroborating evidence or finding truth; his is thus the most corrupt quest for revenge.

(5) There are at least two ways of looking at conflicts in *Hamlet.* If one views Hamlet as a man incapacitated by his own character and responsibilities, the conflict is internal. If one considers the play in terms of action and political dynamics, the central conflict is between Hamlet as protagonist and Claudius as antagonist. From this perspective, Hamlet's conflicts with R&G, Polonius, and Laertes are all secondary, because all these characters serve as (witting or unwitting) extensions of Claudius. In either event, resolution occurs in the catastrophe.

(6) The crisis occurs in III.2 (*see above*), during the play-within-the-play. Claudius's guilty reaction fixes Hamlet's subsequent course of action, as it does those of Claudius, and the outcome is then inevitable.

(7) In terms of immediate action, Claudius murders only one person (Old Hamlet), cooperates in the murder of another (Hamlet), and accidentally kills a third (Gertrude). The rest are killed by Hamlet (directly or indirectly). From a broader perspective, however, Claudius is responsible for all the carnage. His original murder of an anointed king, combined with his taking over the throne along with the queen, upsets cosmic order and introduces destructive chaos into the world of the play. The first destructive act thus causes a chain reaction of suspicion, accusation, plotting, counter-plotting, plans for elimination, depression, suicidal thoughts, and uncontrollable anger that finally result in all the deaths.

(8) When *Hamlet* begins, the state is already diseased and disordered; the first scene suggests unnatural and chaotic events. The close of the play holds the promise of order and control; Fortinbras makes a valid claim to the throne, and Horatio suggests it will be

upheld. Nevertheless, Denmark has lost both a good king and a prince with great potential. Order returns with the death of Claudius and the emergence of Fortinbras as a strong leader, but the price is monumental.

■ Tragedy from Shakespeare to Arthur Miller, *pages 1453–54*

This discussion provides an introduction to the modern theater and many aspects of contemporary drama and staging. It could also be usefully assigned in conjunction with Tennessee Williams's *The Glass Menagerie* (beginning on page 1579).

ARTHUR MILLER, *Death of a Salesman*, *pages 1457–1522*

Miller's American masterpiece illustrates the evolution of modern tragedy. The introduction to the play (1454-57) briefly surveys the stage history, the concept of the common man as tragic hero, and the critique of the American Dream that parallels the fall of Willy Loman.

The play, like Williams's *The Glass Menagerie*, represents a midpoint between the pictorial and schematic realism of Henrik Ibsen and the imaginative and reconstructive realism, or non-realism, of Thornton Wilder. And like *Oedipus* or *An Enemy of the People*, it embodies the end of a much longer story. Here, however, this longer story is brought into the present through dramatized fragments of memory. These scenes of past action come out of Willy's head; they are consequently subjective and distorted visions of the past rather than accurate recreations. Psychologically, they suggest that the past is always in the present, shaping our thoughts, actions, fears, and dreams.

There are two crises in the play. Both occur on stage and within Willy's mind; students will have to decide which is the primary one. The first is Biff's discovery of Willy's adultery (Act II. Speeches 674-729); this single moment shapes the future of both Willy and Biff (i.e., the present action of the play). It also accounts for the ongoing alienation between father and son, Biff's self-destructiveness, and Willy's guilt. The second crisis is Willy's decision, while in conversation with Ben, to commit suicide; it shapes the catastrophe, which follows closely when Willy drives off to his death (Act II. Speech 930.1), and the resolution of the play (the Requiem). Willy and Biff each experience a partial recognition. Willy realizes that he has run out of lies, dreams, and illusions (Act II. Speech 522) and that Biff loves him (Act II. Speeches 889–894) Biff recognizes that he does not want Willy's version of the American Dream (Act II. Speeches 882–888).

In teaching *Death of a Salesman,* you might focus mostly on character and theme. The chief character for discussion is Willy. Students will perceive him as a good deal less heroic than Oedipus or Hamlet, but his problems are equally consuming and fatal. A key question: What makes Willy heroic? Thematically, the play explores ideas about individual dignity, the impact of a single trauma on subsequent life, and the corruption of the American Dream. All these points can lead to effective discussion.

The play was first produced on Broadway in 1949 with Lee J. Cobb as Willy Loman. Cobb was a large man; Miller had to revise parts of his original script to accommodate Cobb's enactment. The present text—the one Miller published in his complete works—reflects these changes. In 1984 the play was revived on Broadway with Dustin Hoffman in the lead. This production was filmed for television, and was broadcast in 1985. Hoffman plays Willy as a small and nervous man always on the edge of collapse. In many respects, his performance is closer to Miller's original conception than the 1949 production with Cobb. Most recently, the play was revived on Broadway (1999) with Brian Dennehy in the starring role. In this production, the changes in time and place were effected by revolving sets. The entire production was characterized by relatively harsh lighting. Even in happy scenes, the lighting kept things from looking too sanguine; there was always the expectation of impending difficulty and embarrassing confrontations.

Suggestions for Discussing the Study Questions, page 1522

(1) The first stage direction suggests that Willy's world is fragile and dreamlike. We are presented with a setting that is only partly real (or realistic). Willy himself is described as exhausted; the large sample cases represent his burdens. Every move combines weariness and anxiety. In addition, there are clues early in the play that Willy is losing touch with reality. One is his inability to drive (Act I. Speech 12). The other is his assertion that he "opened the windshield" of the car (Act I. Speech 22). It is clear of course that Willy could not have opened the windshield of his post-war Studebaker (the windshield did not open), and it is also clear that he is thinking about the car he owned in 1928. Willy's confusion is even more evident when he slips completely into memory for the first time

(Act I. Speech 195.1). Here, a number of events that occurred in 1928 merge into one memory sequence. Willy, in short, is "losing it" in the course of the play.

(2) Stealing is a motif that runs throughout the play. In the past, Willy encouraged (or at least tolerated) the boys' thievery from construction sites (the very apartment houses that now hem him in). Biff has a long and sorry history of stealing: the football, the sporting goods, a suit, Oliver's pen. Much of his post-1928 thievery is self-destructive. Happy steals in another way; he takes women from other men simply to prove to himself that he can do it. Willy himself cheated on his wife when on his selling trips. Willy's toleration of stealing suggests a link between this sort of dishonesty and the emphasis he places on appearances (smiling, being well liked) and selling (one's product, one's self).

(3) Willy's claim never to have told Biff anything but decent things reflects the degree to which Willy deludes himself. At least by example, Willy has shown Biff that dishonesty is acceptable and that appearances matter more than substance. He continues to stress appearances in the present, maintaining the illusion of his pay check and insisting that Biff look and act just so (sell himself) in his interview with Oliver. In effect, this line is directly contradicted by Biff's claim that "we never told the truth for ten minutes in this house" (Act II. Speech 867).

(4) Throughout the play, Willy cannot (or will not) deal effectively with machines. He continually wrecks his car, the refrigerator is always in need of repair, and the wire recorder (a precursor of tape and cassette recorders) in Howard's office terrifies him. These machines represent the (1949) present—the world that Willy can no longer deal with adequately. For Willy, the present time, dominated increasingly by machinery, is contrasted with the past of Dave Singleman, 1928, Uncle Ben, and Willy's childhood memories of his father.

(5) Willy is asking Bernard about the secret to success, achievement, dignity, and recognition—fulfillment of the American Dream. He clearly understands, at least part of the time, that he and his sons have tried to be successful, but that somehow they have failed to reach the heights of success. Charley and Bernard illustrate the truth that there is no secret beyond hard work and a concentration on substance rather than style (early in the play, Willy observes that Charley is liked, but not well liked). Looked at another way, the secret might be that Willy has lived according to a false system of values, and has imbued his sons with the same values.

(6) This is a complex and disturbing moment in the play—it brings together all of Willy's desperation, confusion, and agony. On the one hand, the garden represents the past: a time before the house was hemmed in by brutal and impersonal apartment houses and before The Woman in Boston—a time when Willy was still idolized as a heroic figure by his sons. Willy's need to plant a garden reflects his desire to return to this state of innocence. On the other hand, having "things in the ground" or growing can be taken to represent success, achievement, and security. Willy's desperation reflects his knowledge that his life is empty and fruitless. In addition, he understands that his sons (who are, of course, other kinds of growing things) are not thriving in the "soil" in which he has planted them.

(7) Biff's line (Act II. Speech 867) indicates his realization that the Loman men have consistently deluded themselves with half-truths and unrealistic dreams. To some extent, this continues to be true to the end of the play. Only Biff realistically assesses his own life and abilities; he understands that he will be more content on the land. Willy remains partly self-deluded right to the end; he assumes that his funeral will be well attended and he imagines that the insurance money will make Biff a success. Happy's last lines indicate that he remains trapped in Willy's deluded visions of success.

(8) Linda's final line is open to various interpretations; give students free rein with this one. It might imply that the Lomans are free of hot air and self-delusion. If so, the assertion is not true, at least for Happy. The line might also suggest that the Lomans are free from the false values and standards of Willy's American Dream. Again, this is not true for Happy. It could also mean that, with the house free and clear, the family is free to grow and expand without the constant, nagging worry of making payments and the pressure of living from paycheck to paycheck to keep from being dispossessed. This meaning is true, except that neither Linda nor Willy ever had any idea of what to do with freedom if it came to them. That may be the greatest tragedy of all.

Suggestions for Discussing the General Questions, pages 1522-23

(1) The degeneration in the setting (the house, the surrounding scrim) reflects the degeneration of Willy over the years. The past (of 1928 and before) is indicated by green light, the shadow of leaves, blocking that moves characters through the wall-lines of the house, and Ben's flute music. The present is reflected in the angry orange glow of the apartment houses and the realistic blocking in which the

wall-lines of the house are observed. The staging of present action is mostly realistic, while the staging of memory sequences reflects the nonrealistic nature of dreaming and memory.

(2) Generally, detailed stage directions are designed to help the reader understand the play and experience it fully. In this case, however, Miller's lengthy stage directions suggest that he wrote with readers (rather than actors or viewers) in mind. Stage directions that cannot be played on the stage clearly indicate the double audience (spectators and readers) that modern playwrights address.

(3) Willy's suicide is foreshadowed at the very beginning of the play when Linda asks if he smashed up the car (Act I. Speech 5). Later in the first Act, Linda tells her sons that "all these accidents in the past year weren't—weren't accidents" (Act I. Speeches 648–663). These comments directly anticipate Willy's vehicular suicide at the close of Act II. Suicide is also foreshadowed and symbolized in the rubber pipe and "the new little nipple on the gas pipe" that Willy has apparently installed in the basement (Act I. Speeches 667–672).

(4) All the characters in the present are real and realistic (the 1949 version of the Lomans, Charley and Bernard, Howard, Jennie, and the people in the bar). These characters act and speak realistically. The hallucinatory characters that emerge from Willy's memory include the 1928 Lomans, Charley and Bernard, Uncle Ben, and The Woman. These figures are a good deal less developed or realistic; they have been flattened out and stripped of inessential characteristics through the subjective filter of memory and guilt. Their stage movement is often nonrealistic; their language is formulaic and repetitive.

(5) The four central symbolic characters of the play are Willy, Dave Singleman, Uncle Ben, and The Woman (Howard, Charley, and Bernard are secondary symbols). Willy, the low man, embodies failure and false values. Dave Singleman (present only by reference) symbolizes the single (or singular) man; he is Willy's personal symbol of success. Uncle Ben represents another version of the American Dream; he is the self-reliant pioneer/exploiter who opens new territories and carves wealth out of the land. Willy's father is a much less well-developed version of this same symbol. It is this romanticized and sentimentalized dream to which Biff is drawn at the end of the play. The Woman symbolizes guilt and trauma (as well as past pleasure) for Willy and for Biff; the sound of her laugh or a knock on the door catapults Willy back to the horror of that moment of discovery.

(6) Willy is heroic in his struggle for dignity, his willingness to go back on the road; he simply will not accept defeat. He even

(mistakenly) sees his death as a heroic victory that will make people appreciate him and give Biff a new start in life. His central failing is self-delusion (lies, dreams, hot air), which blinds him to the realities of his own life and his sons' lack of ability. It can be argued that Willy's failure comes from within, from the lies and illusions he has fostered all his life. Conversely, students might argue that Willy's values reflect those imposed by a corrupt society; he measures himself against a misguided version of the American Dream. From this perspective, Willy's failure is society's failure.

(7) Willy says to Charley, "you never told him [Bernard] what to do . . . you never took any interest in him." Charley replies, "My salvation is that I never took any interest in anything" (Act II. Speech 341). The exchange epitomizes the differences between the two father-son relationships. Willy took an interest; he passed on his own values and delusions to his sons. Charley apparently let Bernard shape his own values and life, guiding only by example. To put it another way, Willy invested too much of his own life in his sons. Moreover, he willingly set himself up as a heroic ideal—an ideal that is destroyed for Biff in a single moment of revelation. Charley never fostered illusions of heroism in Bernard; there were no heroic ideals to be exposed as fake.

(8) Linda is completely supportive of Willy; she accepts his lies and exaggerations (even when she knows they are false), and she fights for him against Biff and Happy. Linda is both an admirable and a culpable character (let the students decide which predominates); her support is both essential and destructive. It creates a reasonably strong marriage, but it also allows Willy to sustain his illusions far too long.

(9) Happy is an exaggerated and degenerated version of Willy. He embodies all the faults of Willy's dreams and delusions: the emphasis on externals and on being well liked, lies about achievement. He continues to pursue the same corrupt dream, "to come out number-one man" in the world of selling. His obsessive conquests of other men's women suggests a continual need to compete and prove himself to himself in the only arena in which he can still be successful. Happy is not happy, and probably never can be.

In contrast, it can be argued that his brother Biff changes—that he has the most significant and beneficial *anagnorisis,* or recognition, in the play. Such knowledge suggests the potential for a better life in the future. If students accept that Biff's return to the land embodies a viable alternative to Willy's dreams, then Biff's recognition implies hope. Looking at the play from this perspective, with Biff as the educated protagonist, creates a radical shift; it changes the focus from Willy's fall to Biff's redemption. One problem with this perspective is that Miller forces readers to be suspicious of Ben's version of the American Dream and of Biff's ability.

(10) Willy's assertions about being "well liked" are symptomatic of his commitment to dreams, illusion, and style rather than substance. He preaches this dogma to his sons, but it has not worked for him and will not work for them. Miller gives the explicit refutation of this philosophy to Charley (Act II. Speeches 366–368). Moreover, Charley and Bernard are living refutations of Willy's belief in style over substance.

(11) For Willy, 1928 was the last really good year, the year of promises, the year of "a hundred and seventy dollars a week in commissions" (Act II. Speeches 144–146). It was the year that Frank Wagner (may have) promised him a position in the home office, Biff played the championship game, and Ben last visited. It was also the year in which Willy's adultery was discovered by Biff—the end of the boy's hero worship of Willy. For the nation, 1928 was the last year of optimism and prosperity, for the great depression began in 1929. These two patterns come together for Willy. For him, 1928 was the end of hope and innocence.

Writing About Tragedy, *pages 1523–33*

This section discusses and illustrates ways to plan and write essays about tragic drama. While the discussion does not focus specifically on the elements introduced in Chapter 27, you can easily assign such an essay in connection with *Oedipus the King, Hamlet,* or *Death of a Salesman.* All three plays lend themselves to investigations of plot, structure, conflict, setting, character, tone, language, and theme. *Oedipus the King* and *Hamlet* offer excellent opportunities for writing about irony, and *Death of a Salesman* is especially rich in symbolism. Because approaches to these topics are covered in Chapter 26, we introduce two new types of essay in this chapter. The first is an essay about a problem (1524–29). Here, we discuss ways of formulating and writing about a problem in literature. The sample student essay takes up the problem of delay in *Hamlet.*

The second type is an essay on a close reading of a passage from a play (1530–33). In this example, the close reading focuses on content (rather than style) and relates the passage to a theme of the play. The demonstrative essay focuses on a key passage from

Hamlet and links it to the theme of appearance versus reality. Both of these essay types can be valuable and useful not only for discussing tragedy but also for dealing with the other genres.

Special Topics for Writing and Argument about Tragedy, *pages 1533–34*

(1) Topic 1 suggests an in-depth treatment of the importance of vision and understanding in *Oedipus the King*. Some of the ideas for such a paper are included in this manual in the discussions of the questions for that play. A full treatment, however, should include most of the topics detailed in question 1 here.

(2) Topic 2, also on *Oedipus*, deals with the issues of free will and character. The topics are difficult, and students will not create definitive answers to the problems in their essays, but it is important for them to consider as they study tragedy.

(3) Topic 3, on the subject of the women in Hamlet, might seem offensive to some of your students. They may need reminding that it is *Hamlet* who makes the assertion, and that it is their task to consider the rightness of the remark. Quite important in this consideration is the status of both women, and their niche in the society of the Renaissance as Shakespeare reflects it in the play.

(4) Topic 4, about the three young men in *Hamlet*, requires the technique of comparison-contrast (see Chapter 35). It is reasonable to request that students use details about Fortinbras and Laertes, who are minor characters, to highlight qualities about Hamlet himself.

(5) Topic 5 will require as much knowledge of sociology and other cultures as students possess. Obviously, the play succeeds in various periods and cultures because the characters, conflicts, and themes remain as relevant today as they were more than forty years ago. Willy is a universal figure, the low man instead of every man. His dreams and delusions are universal in type if not in detail. All cultures produce value systems and standards that individuals either follow or reject as they seek success and dignity. The details of Willy's fall are of course peculiarly American, but the pattern of his struggle is transcendent.

(6) Topic 6 might be easier for students than the fifth. *Death of a Salesman* attacks a specific version of the American Dream that is based on style, competition, and wealth. This dream and these values are championed by Willy and Happy; Biff realizes that it is no longer valid for him. Howard represents success in this mode, and

he comes across as self-absorbed, heartless, and petty. Charley and Bernard represent a different (and more viable) American Dream—success through hard work, realism, and intelligence.

(7) Topic 7 is a searching one; it would be most appropriate as a longer assignment in which extended comparison-contrast is the means of supporting the assertions about tragedy that students will be making. (See Chapter 35).

(8) Topic 8 is an open-ended research direction for students to learn as much as they can from using the library's catalogue. You might wish to confine their searches to one specific topic. Or, if there is time, students might go their own ways and then make classroom reports on what they have discovered.

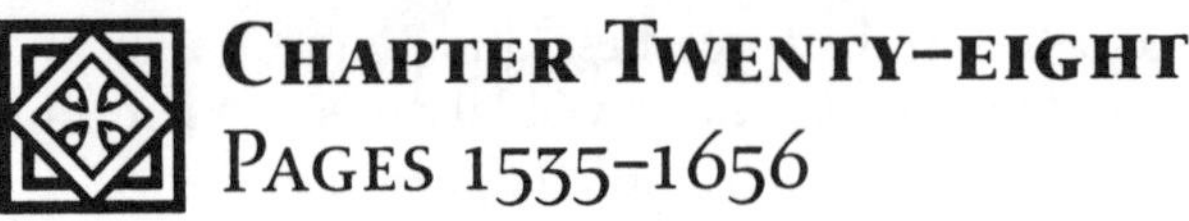

Chapter Twenty-Eight
Pages 1535–1656

The Comic Vision: Restoring the Balance

This chapter introduces the major aspects of comic drama. To that end, it begins with introductory material that discusses the history, nature, and pattern of comedy, as well as comic characters, language, and types of comedy (1535–43). In reviewing this material with your students, you might emphasize the distinction between *comic* and *funny*. Like the terms *tragic* and *tragedy*, the terms *comic* and *comedy* are used colloquially with a far broader application than is useful for understanding drama. In plays, the terms refer not only to a tone or attitude, but also to a reasonably well-defined pattern of action that usually (but not always) leads to a resolution that is affirmative and regenerative. In satiric comedy such as Molière's *Love Is the Doctor*, this regenerative impulse can be transferred from the play to the audience, the readers, and the world at large.

Key points in discussing comedy include the distinctions between *high* and *low* as well as *romantic* and *satiric*. The chapter is designed to illustrate these distinctions with reference to three superb examples of comic drama. Shakespeare's *A Midsummer Night's Dream* combines high and low comedy. Molière's *Love Is the Doctor* and Chekhov's *The Bear* contain low comedy and farce throughout, and Henley's *Am I Blue* mixes low comedy with some aspects of normal comedy. All the plays contain varying degrees of romantic comedy. *The Bear* amusingly portrays a relationship growing from hatred to infatuated love, *Am I Blue* presents details about the possibilities of a developing relationship, while *Love Is the Doctor* contains no such details at all and *A Midsummer Night's Dream* treats the romantic developments and conflicts through a haze of magic. Of the four plays, the strongest satire is found in *Love Is the Doctor*.

If you have the time to include videotapes or audiotapes for use in your class, Shakespeare's *A Midsummer Night's Dream* is available in a number of commercial productions, including a ballet version:

- VIDEOTAPE, black-and-white, 1935 (117 minutes). Directed by *Max Reinhardt,* STARRING *Olivia de Haviland, Mickey Rooney, Dick Powell, Victor Jory,* and *James Cagney.* United Artists.
- VIDEOTAPE, color, undated. Directed by *Joseph Papp,* New York Shakespeare Festival. Films for the Humanities.
- VIDEOTAPE and DVD, 1999 (116 minutes). Directed by *Michael Hoffman.* Starring *Kevin Kline, Michelle Pfeiffer, Rupert Everett, Stanley Tucci, Anna Friel,* and *Callista Flockhart.* 20th Century Fox.
- VIDEOTAPE, color, 1996. Directed by *Adrian Noble. Royal Shakespeare Company.* Starring *Desmond Barrit, Finbar Lynch, Monica Dolan, Emily Raymond, Kevin Doyle,* and *Daniel Evans.* Buena Vista Home Video.
- VIDEOTAPE ballet, 1966 (95 minutes). A "fantasy" of *A Midsummer Night's Dream* by the *New York City Ballet Company.* Directed by *Dan Eriksen.* Starring *Suzanne Farrell and Edward Villella.*
- VIDEOTAPE, color, 1968 (124 minutes). Directed by *Peter Hall. A Royal Shakespeare Company Production,* starring *Diana Rigg, David Warner, Ian Richardson, Bill Travers,* and *Helen Mirren.* Audio-Brandon Films.
- VIDEOTAPE, color, 1982 (120 minutes). Starring *Helen Mirren* and *Peter McEnery.* Time-Life Video.
- AUDIOTAPE (49 minutes). Starring *Eithne Dunne* and *Eve Watkinson.* Spoken Arts.

These films and/or tapes are also available from other distributors. It is a good idea to delay showing a film until after the students have read the plays and begun class discussion. Too often, students come to believe that watching a film (or tape) can replace reading the play. In addition, the characterizations and interpretations created by actors and the director may affect the students' own reading of the play.

WILLIAM SHAKESPEARE, *A Midsummer Night's Dream,* *pages 1544–98*

This is one of Shakespeare's funniest and most accessible comedies. If you teach it without (or before) doing *Hamlet,* it might be helpful to assign the introduction to Shakespeare's theater and life (1344–50). The first of these will help students understand many of the important conventions of Elizabethan theater. The introduction to *A Midsummer Night's Dream* (1544–45) provides a survey of plots, characters, and themes.

Teaching this play is a delight. It provides an opportunity to deal with a number of dramatic elements at the same time. The three that can be most successfully emphasized in teaching are plot, character, and theme. Language (especially the different types of poetry) can be explored if time permits. The central plot (the four lovers) illustrates the New Comedy pattern of blocked and then triumphant love. This plot is recapitulated (with a pseudo-pathetic ending) in "Pyramus and Thisby," the play-within-the-play. The characters in the central plot are flat and conventional types that exemplify the dangers of irrational love, infatuation, and uncontrolled doting. In this plot and in the fairy plot, Puck serves as a jester, trouble-maker, and bizarre version of Cupid.

Thematically, the play explores at least two interconnected subjects: love and imagination. The absurdities and dangers of infatuation are illustrated in the plight of the four lovers, the conflict produced by Titania's wish to keep her changeling child, her subsequent adoration of Bottom, and the pathetic deaths of Pyramus and Thisby. The power of imagination (and the intersection of imagination, perception, art, love, and dreams) is explored through the rehearsal process, the play-within-the-play, Theseus's commentary, and the device of love-in-idleness (the flower whose juice produces boundless infatuation).

Another approach to teaching structure and theme in this play is to contrast it (and "Pyramus") with *Romeo and Juliet* (written at about the same time). All three follow similar plots and offer related examination of blind love. *Romeo and Juliet* is often taught in tenth or eleventh grade; if your students are familiar with it, you can use the play as a parallel to both the comedy of *A Midsummer Night's Dream* and the pathos of "Pyramus." In such an approach, Lysander parallels Pyramus and Romeo; Hermia parallels Thisby and Juliet. The blocking agents are similarly parallel: 1–Egeus and the old Athenian law; 2–the wall; 3–the Montague-Capulet feud. In all three cases, the attempt to circumvent the obstructions involves moving outside the normal constraints of law or society (into the night, woods, Ninus's Tomb, a secret marriage, away from Verona).

Suggestions for Discussing the Study Questions, pages 1598–99

❖ ACT I

(1) Lines 1–19 supply exposition and characterization. Theseus and Hippolyta are to be married in four days; this provides the general time-frame of the play. In the past, Theseus fought a war against

Hippolyta (Queen of the Amazons) and captured her (lines 16–19). Their relationship, once characterized by the irrationality and passion of war, has evolved into a rational and harmonious dynastic alliance. However, they have very different attitudes toward the approaching marriage. Theseus is typically anxious and impatient. For him, time moves slowly, and the moon is a blocking agent delaying the fulfillment of his desires (lines 2–6). For Hippolyta, time is moving quickly and the moon (a silver bow) symbolizes Diana, goddess of chastity and the hunt (lines 7–11). Theseus and Hippolyta (along with Athens itself) represent absolute order, rationality, law, and authority. Indeed, Theseus will learn in the play that the rigor of the law must be relaxed in acknowledgment of the higher authority of love.

(2) Hermia and Lysander are conventional and typical lovers; their problems are explained in Act I, Scene 1, lines 20–127. Egeus wants Hermia to marry Demetrius; she wants to wed Lysander. Egeus accuses Lysander of bewitching Hermia by moonlight (linking love, moonlight, magic, and irrationality). He invokes the ancient law of Athens which requires that Hermia obey Egeus, die, or become a nun at Diana's temple (since comedy is typically concerned with sexual and social regeneration, the third choice is, in comedy, a fate worse than death). Theseus gives Hermia four days (until his own wedding and the new moon) to choose. We also learn that Hermia and Lysander are desperately in love, that Egeus favors Demetrius, that Demetrius and Lysander are identical as far as wealth and status are concerned, and that Demetrius has previously courted Helena. The ensuing conversation (lines 128–79) reveals the depths of young love (perhaps infatuation). Lysander plots an escape from Athens (lines 156–68) by running off to a rich aunt's house (no financial sacrifice here) and Hermia agrees.

(3) Helena is love-sick for Demetrius, jealous of Hermia's power to attract men, and extremely self-deprecating. Her low self-esteem is the result of Demetrius's scorn. Although the world considers her fair, she sees herself through Demetrius's eyes. Hermia and Lysander tell their plans to Helena to make her feel better. She, in turn, will tell Demetrius all to gain a moment of attention. Helena's soliloquy about love (discussed below in the "General Questions") is a central thematic statement that provides a definition of the kind of blind and irrational love examined in the play.

(4) The hempen homespuns meet to assign roles for "The most lamentable comedy, and most cruel death of Pyramus and Thisby." They hope to present the play at court to celebrate Theseus's mar-

riage and thus earn a pension (see IV.2.14–15). The casting of Flute as Thisby comically duplicates Elizabethan stage practices. Bottom's eagerness, energy, and conceit are reflected in his desire to demonstrate his acting skill and to play every role. He shows his limited education through his misuse of words. Here, he misuses *generally* (line 2), *aggravated* (line 69), and *obscenely* (line 91).

❖ ACT II

(5) The action of Act II, scene 1, lines 1–145 is expository, introducing Puck, Titania, Oberon, and the conflict over the changeling. The fairy's lyric verse (lines 2–13) is a characteristic mode of poetry for the spirits; it contrasts with Theseus's blank verse and the lovers' rhymed couplets. Puck is identified as Oberon's jester, a roguish trickster, and a trouble-maker (lines 32–58). His love of trickery and confusion becomes important later when he is trying to deal with the four lovers.

(6) The conflict between Oberon and Titania over the changeling is introduced by Puck (II.1.18–31) and explained more fully by Oberon and Titania (lines 60–145). Titania is infatuated with the child; she spends all her time with him and ignores Oberon. Oberon is jealous, but he also has the right of command (as husband and King) over Titania. Her involvement with the child disrupts her normal relationship with Oberon. This conflict is further complicated by Oberon's previous relationship with Hippolyta and Titania's with Theseus (lines 64–80). As the ruling spirits of nature, Oberon and Titania are linked to cycles of time and season. Their discord disrupts these cycles (lines 81–117). Oberon claims that the chaos can be made orderly if Titania hands over the child. She refuses, claiming that the boy was given to her by his dying mother.

(7) Oberon plans to humiliate and cure Titania by using love-in-idleness to put her madly in love with something monstrous. This shift of affection will make it possible for him to get the changeling. Oberon explains the source of the flower's magical power (lines 155–72); the flower symbolizes the kind of blind and hasty love that Helena described in the first soliloquy. Oberon enchants Titania (II.2.1–34) by squeezing the juice from love-in-idleness on her eyes and reciting the appropriate lyric incantation; he hopes that she will wake when "some vile thing is near."

(8) When Demetrius and Helena appear in the woods, he is chasing Hermia and Lysander, planning to seize one and kill the other. She is pursuing Demetrius, seeking any attention at all (even

abuse, see II.1.202–10). He runs off, threatening Helena with injury if she follows. She pursues, claiming that she will "die upon the hand I love so well." Oberon, who announces that he is invisible, overhears the exchange and decides to correct the situation by using love-in-idleness to change Demetrius's affections. As a being accustomed to command, Oberon orders Puck to take care of things, and Puck does what he is told except that he makes the innocent mistake of squeezing the juice in Lysander's eyes (II.2). When Helena awakens Lysander, he instantly falls madly in love with her (see II.2.103–22). Helena assumes that this adoration is mockery (lines 123–34). With the enchantment of Lysander, the love relationships among the four lovers move to the second stage—a perfect round-robin in which no love is reciprocated.

❖ ACT III

(9) In III.1, Puck disrupts the rehearsal and transforms Bottom. He gives Bottom an ass's-head for at least three reasons: 1–it is a good joke and consistent with Puck's love of trickery; 2–it is appropriate since Bottom (with a pun on the name) is already an ass; 3–it provides a suitably vile object of affection for Titania. When Bottom awakens Titania with his singing (III.1.115), she falls madly in love with him. Bottom's reaction is significant; he asserts that she has no reason to love him, but that "reason and love keep little company together now-a-days" (III.3.128–32). The speech, a key thematic statement, is ironic because Bottom (the fool) can see what none of the more noble or educated characters can understand.

(10) In III.2, Puck reports to Oberon about the transformation of Bottom, Titania's love, the harassment of the mechanicals, and the anointing of the Athenian's eyes. When Demetrius and Hermia arrive, the fairies realize that an error has occurred. Demetrius is pleading his own love; Hermia is seeking Lysander. Oberon accuses Puck of intentionally anointing the wrong man's eyes to cause trouble; he sends Puck off to get Helena and he puts the flower juice in Demetrius's eyes. While Puck did not intentionally produce this chaos, he enjoys it immensely (see III.2.110–21); he realizes that two men will now woo Helena, and he finds such mortal foolishness highly amusing.

(11) When Demetrius awakens under the influence of love-in-idleness (line 137) and spots Helena, he falls madly in love with her. This situation (stage three of the love relationships) exactly reverses the one that began the play; now both men love Helena and

loathe Hermia. Because Helena's self-image is so badly damaged, she assumes that both men are mocking her. When Hermia joins in the fray (lines 177), Helena assumes that Hermia is part of this confederacy of mockery.

(12) Once the four lovers are together in the woods (III.2.177), things become progressively more chaotic and dangerous. The men decide to fight a duel over Helena (lines 254–255), and the women begin to fight (at first verbally and then physically). The potential for disaster here is real (although we never believe it because Oberon and Puck remain in attendance). The men could kill each other; the women could be abandoned to wild animals (compare "Pyramus"). Oberon takes control of the situation at line 345, and orders Puck to abort the duel, mislead the lovers through the night, and use the herbal antidote (Dian's bud) on Lysander, thus restoring his love for Hermia. The play begins to reverse direction and return toward order, daylight, and Athens. Puck uses trickery to mislead the young men, prevent the duel, collect the lovers in one place, and put them to sleep. By using Dian's bud on Lysander, he moves the love relationships into the fourth stage (as realized in IV.1.): two reciprocally loving couples.

❖ ACT IV

(13) Resolution begins in IV.1. with the rapprochement between Oberon and Titania. Oberon uses Dian's bud (IV.1.70) to release Titania from her infatuation partly because he has begun to pity her (IV.1.46) and partly because she has surrendered the changeling (IV.1.52–62). Oberon also orders Puck to restore Bottom to his original shape so that he can awaken and return to Athens; the events of the night will become an inexplicable dream for him. When Titania awakens, she is restored to harmony and amity with Oberon. This restoration is visually symbolized on stage by music and dancing (IV.1.82–92), traditional symbols of harmony and order. This rapprochement is significant because it restores cosmic order and it suggests that order will be similarly restored at every other level of action.

(14) The play reverses direction when the fairies exit and the rulers enter (IV.1.101), shifting from night to day, gods to human beings, and nature to society. Theseus and Hippolyta are hunting on the morning of their wedding day. Theseus spots the lovers, has them awakened, and asks for an explanation of their presence together. The explanations reflect the dreamlike confusion that the lovers have experienced. Lysander begins to tell how he and Hermia ar-

rived in the wood (lines 145–152), but Egeus interrupts, demanding legal action. Egeus has not changed; he has not gone through the long night of passion and confusion which has purged the minds and cleared the eyes of the lovers. Demetrius best expresses the changes that have occurred (lines 159–175). He admits that fury and fancy (both irrational passions) drove him and Helena to the wood, but that his infatuation with Hermia now seems childish. Hermia and Helena do not speak. The conflict resolves into two reciprocally loving couples. Given this situation, Theseus overrules Egeus and abrogates the Athenian law. This reversal of Theseus's earlier position, possible because Demetrius no longer wants to marry Hermia, represents a moderation of Theseus's earlier rigidity and an acknowledgment that there are powers above the law.

(15) Comedies often end in marriage, and this one has been headed toward a royal wedding since the opening. Yet this wedding and two others occur offstage and are reported by Snug (IV.2.13–15). Why didn't Shakespeare stage the weddings? One answer is found in the dynamics of the play; one line of action ("Pyramus") remains incomplete. Staging the weddings would provide premature formal closure. This, in turn, opens the question of why "Pyramus" is treated as a co-equally important line of action.

❖ ACT V

(16) Pyramus and Thisby are young lovers separated by a wall because their families have a long-standing feud. They plan to overcome these obstructions by leaving the city and meeting at night at Ninus's tomb. The plan leads to disaster because of irrational haste. Thisby arrives at the tomb first, is frightened by a lion, and drops her cape, which the lion bloodies. Pyramus, finding the bloodstained cape by moonlight, assumes that Thisby is dead and kills himself. Thisby returns to the tomb, finds Pyramus's body, and also commits suicide. The parallels between this story and Romeo and Juliet are numerous.

(17, 18) The fairy masque combines a number of traditional symbols of harmony and order to bless the marriages (it thus replaces the wedding as the formal ritual of order and closure that ends the play). It also embodies a fusion of the two worlds of the play; the kingdom of night, the supernatural, magic, and dreaming flows into the world of daylight, order, and rationality. In the epilogue, Puck suggests that we should consider the play a dream that we experienced while slumbering. The statement neatly puts us on a par with Bottom and the lovers. It also links fantasy and imagination with drama and art (illusion) and thus reinforces the connection among poets, lovers, and madmen advanced by Theseus (V.1.4–22).

Suggestions for Discussing the General Questions, page 1600

(1, 2) Most of the characters are flat, conventional, and representative; some are symbolic. Theseus and Hippolyta represent law, order, and rationality. Theseus changes to the extent that he learns to moderate the rigor of the law. Egeus is the conventional angry and irrational father who obstructs love. He neither learns nor changes. The four lovers are equally conventional and flat, but they are educated and purged of love madness through their long night of chaos and passion in the woods. When they awaken, their relationships and feelings have become regenerative and reciprocal love. Oberon and Titania symbolize the power and cycles of nature. In addition, they represent chaos and passion (at first) just as Theseus and Hippolyta represent order. They change to the extent that their relationship returns to harmony and accord. The mechanicals, also conventional, represent the lower class. Although the play is set in ancient Athens, they are clearly based on Elizabethan rather than Greek or mythological figures.

(3) Each group of characters has a distinctive mode of language. Theseus and Hippolyta speak blank verse, as befits their status and dignity as rulers. The four lovers speak mostly in less dignified and more amusing rhymed couplets. When not playing roles in "Pyramus," the mechanicals speak in conversational prose, consistent with their low status. The fairies speak in both blank verse and in rhymed couplets, but they are also the only characters to speak in lyric poetry (variously rhymed lines of iambic tetrameter and additional meters). This verse sets them apart from the rest of the characters and suggests their separation from the human beings.

(4, 5) The two-place structure, its symbolic import, and its relationship to the dramatic structure of the play are discussed in the demonstrative essay (1653–54). Both the world of the forest and the world of the city change for the better. The woods, initially disordered (as is all of nature, see II.1.81–117), become ordered with the resolution of the conflict between Oberon and Titania. Similarly the city, which initially embodied overly rigid law and order, is modified by Theseus's decision to overrule Egeus and permit the marriage of Hermia and Lysander. Most of the characters who make the round-trip from city to woods to city undergo a learning or altering experience which improves them. The lovers suffer the dream-like chaos of Oberon's manipulation, and emerge more rational and mature. The rulers (especially Theseus) learn that law must be tempered by judgment and higher authority. The mechanicals neither learn nor change; they go to the woods to rehearse, and their round-trip simply heightens the confusion.

(6) Helena's soliloquy is a key thematic statement of the characteristics of irrational love. This kind of love distorts perception and evaluation (I.1.232–233); it is blind, rash, immature, changeable, and lacking in judgment (lines 234–241). Many of the relationships in the play illustrate this type of love. Chief among these is the shift in passion produced among the four lovers by love-in-idleness. The most extreme instance of this type of love is Titania's blind infatuation with Bottom. In some ways, the lovers are educated and transformed during their long night in the woods; they emerge into the daylight world on the day of Theseus's wedding with a stronger and more regenerative love.

(7, 8) *A Midsummer Night's Dream* explores the nature of drama and the links between drama (illusion, art) and imagination (passion, madness, dreaming, and love) in three ways: 1–through the mechanicals' production of "Pyramus"; 2–through the internal audience's reaction to "Pyramus"; and 3–through thematic statements (such as that by Theseus in V.1.4–22). The mechanicals have no understanding of drama as a mimetic art. Their concerns over lion, sword, moonshine, and wall (III.1) and the solutions they come up with indicate that they make no distinction between illusion (drama, art) and reality. In addition, they assume that their audience will make no distinction; the difference never occurs to them. The internal audience for "Pyramus"—the nobility and the four lovers—are more concerned with their own wittiness than with the play. For the lovers, the play-within-the-play recapitulates lessons that they have just experienced, but they do not perceive this connection. Shakespeare expects us to be a better audience, seeing both the connection between the main plot and the "Pyramus" plot, and judging the lovers on their failure to see it. In opposition to all this failure, the play includes a thematic line that argues for a linkage of passion, imagination, dreaming, illusion, art, and love. This connection is articulated (negatively) by Theseus at the beginning of Act V and underscored in Puck's epilogue.

(9) Both plays-within-plays parallel the main plots of the plays of which they are a part. In *Hamlet*, the drama is made to be an

exact parallel of the murder of King Hamlet by Claudius. Thus, *The Murder of Gonzago,* with some parts putatively interpolated by Hamlet himself, is used as an ongoing part of the plot whereby Hamlet tries to secure confirmation of the initial accusations of the Ghost against Claudius. In addition, *Gonzago* occurs midway in the play, and it is a crisis and climax in which the future actions of both Hamlet and Claudius are set. "Pyramus and Thisby," by contrast, is a part of the sub-plot concerning the rude mechanicals, but coming at the end as it does, it also serves as an alternative ending and as a commentary on the action. Therefore, it serves two purposes: a- to show the realistic, true-to-the-world fact that confusions such as those dramatized in the main plot can produce disastrous outcomes, and also b- to tie together the upper and lower groups of people presented in the play, demonstrating the qualities of each and the comparative understandings of each. "Pyramus," while a commentary, is also a part of the resolution of the plot and a return to the world as it was before the confusions of the play.

■ The Theater of Molière, *pages 1600–1604*

Molière, *Love Is the Doctor (L'Amour Médecin),* *pages 1605–1621*

This play is one of Molière's typical farcical comedies. He put it together rapidly, within a five-day period, in 1665, and it was well received at the Court of Louis XIV at Versailles. It demonstrates to the highest degree the plot of intrigue—so much so that it would serve as a prototype for many such plays that followed it in the seventeenth century, and also for romantic-intrigue novels in the eighteenth. The major flaw in *Love Is the Doctor* is the introduction of the detail about the traveling druggist or Mountebank who is selling "Orviétan." This allusion is totally lost on a modern audience, and Molière, after the brief scene between Sganarelle and the Mountebank, drops this thread of the plot entirely. For us to read the play successfully, we must take the Mountebank episode, thematically, as an example of the gullibility that leads Sganarelle to be fleeced of his fortune in the concluding scenes.

Suggestions for Studying the Study Questions, pages 1621–22

❖ ACT I

(1) We learn in the first scene that Sganarelle is wealthy and that he has self-seeking relatives and friends. He is a widower and he has only one daughter, who has symptoms of an undisclosed

illness. He shows a willingness to listen to suggestions, but he also shows shrewdness in exposing the motivations of those who try to use his openness to make money for themselves. He is, in effect, a traditional *satirist* figure; that is, he is the character in a satire who makes satiric commentaries (as at the end of the scene), who serves to bring out the negative qualities of others, and who himself exhibits qualities that the author is satirizing.

(2) The relationship on Sganarelle's part is one of paternal dominance, and on Lucinda's part is one of assumed deference. Sganarelle speaks to Lucinda as though to a tiny girl, not to a young woman. He is concerned about her, but is unable to understand her. The relationship is shown to be exaggerated and comic because the play is a comedy, and a disobedient daughter like, for example, Juliet in *Romeo and Juliet* would set a tone not of comedy but of tragedy.

(3) It is important structurally to learn that a young man has shown interest in Lucinda, and that he has made overtures to her, because it is this young man (Clitander) who intrigues with Lisette to win her in marriage in the last scenes of the play. His later appearance is hence not illogical, for, though the audience has not seen him, both Lisette and Lucinda have.

(4) Lisette is the *soubrette*, the maidservant who is secure in the home and gets the plot moving. She is a figure out of the *Commedia dell'Arte*—essentially flat, exhibiting great independence, and very little humility or deference toward her master. She is an intimate of Lucinda because Lucinda's mother is dead, and a maidservant would have been a greater friend and intimate anyway (cf. the Nurse in *Romeo and Juliet*).

(5) Sganarelle does not want his daughter married (I.5) because he wants to keep all his money for himself, and does not want to give his daughter and her husband a marriage settlement. This strain of selfishness and his clear disapproval of his daughter's hopes of married happiness make him a deserving gull at the end. If he had granted consent, he would not have forced Lucinda and Clitander into the intrigue, and everyone would have been happy about the relationship, including Sganarelle himself.

❖ ACT II

(6) In III.1, Dr. Fillpocket speaks extensively of how doctors hoodwink gullible people and thereby fill their pockets. Sganarelle is one of the gullible ones of whom Fillpocket speaks. Furthermore, this quality of gullibility is essential as a trait if Clitander is to be successful

when he masquerades as a famous doctor and whisks Lucinda away right under Sganarelle's nose. Lisette's skepticism refutes Sganarelle's exaggerated faith, and it makes Molière's satire prominent.

(7) Dr. Slicer is positive about his knowledge of medical practice, and his authority is the word of the ancient Hippocrates. Lisette, by contrast, speaks from her knowledge of reality. The person is dead, and no ancient medical authority can contradict that. The contrasting views, with Lisette deflating Dr. Slicer's pomposity, makes the scene comic.

(8) Pantomime action is an important part of the staging of a play, particularly of this play. Students might imagine the sorts of responses that people can make when receiving a large sum of money. Some students who have a background in dance or theater might even create movement that would illustrate Molière's point about the greediness of the doctors.

(9) By having the doctors discuss their mules and horses, together with the controversy in which a sensible doctor is censured by a stupid doctor who outranks him, Molière demonstrates the venality and lack of professional integrity of the doctors.

(10) Slicer recommends bleeding; De Pits, purgation through vomiting; Gouger, laxatives and also, apparently, emetics; Golfer recommends both purging and bleeding (probably until the patient dies). The doctors Slicer and De Pits are truthful because they each attack the proposed remedies of the other. The scenes of the prescriptions are comic because the doctors are demonstrating their witlessness and their combativeness.

(11) Sganarelle is alternately amused and befuddled by the jargon of the doctors. His attempt to find medical truth causes him to seek out a charlatan of another sort. By the time Clitander appears in the final act, Sganarelle is a sitting duck for any medical quack who comes along.

❖ ACT III

(12) Ostensibly, Dr. Fillpocket is telling his colleagues to present a united front of knowledge to the world. In practice, however, his logic is that the reason for unity is to keep up public confidence in doctors, or else the profession will lose its privileges and its wealth. The speech is comic because the audience only is overhearing it, and the audience is not a part of the play's world. Thus the doctor may express truths that otherwise would never be uttered by anyone in the medical profession. The questions about seriousness and the

degrees of truth will best be left to students for their discussion and/or writing.

(13) The stratagem is that Clitander will masquerade as a famous doctor who cures patients by unusual means such as "words, sounds, letters, signs, and mystical rings" (III.5.5). That Sganarelle has already shown great faith in doctors is assurance that he will trust a doctor that Lisette recommends (after all, she has shown skepticism about doctors, and her enthusiasm must therefore seem to him like the highest recommendation possible).

(14, 15) The irony is that Clitander is speaking directly and honestly to Lucinda, while Sganarelle believes that he, as a "doctor," is deceiving her in order to cure her. Sganarelle's joining in on the deception, and signing away the twenty million, is of course the deception being practiced on him even though he believes that he is the one doing the deceiving. The final scene is kept comic and light by the singing and dancing. A dark production could keep Sganarelle disgruntled, but more likely is that Sganarelle joins the concluding dance. His last words indicate anger, but they could also suggest that he simply gives up and participates in the merriment.

Suggestions for Discussing the General Questions, page 1622

(1) Because Sganarelle is the figure in constant focus in the play, he is the protagonist. This role is complicated by the fact that the antagonism is the love of Lucinda and Clitander, and by the comic plot that makes them triumphant at the end. Conflicts develop between Sganarelle and A–his friends and relatives, B–his daughter, C–Lisette, and finally D–the scheme of Clitander and Lucinda to marry despite his opposition, and to wheedle him out of a fortune. There are also amusing conflicts between Lisette and the doctors, and among the doctors themselves. The satiric conflict is that of quackery and ignorance within the medical profession.

(2) The "biter bitten" comic twist is a common one in humor. Shakespeare, for example, uses it in *Twelfth Night* (Malvolio), and Jonson uses it in *Volpone*. Sganarelle is the bitten one in *Love Is the Doctor*, for his unwillingness to consent to a marriage for his daughter produces the plot that enables Lucinda and Clitander to win the twenty million away from him. Humor is a complicated topic. Henri Bergson draws attention to the idea that the inability to adjust is the primary cause of humor. Certainly this inability is present in Sganarelle, who is the rigid and unyielding *paterfamilias*. Another view of humor is presented by Hobbes, who holds that laughter

develops from superiority over a comic object or butt of humor. Sganarelle, like Malvolio, is such an object. The topic of laughter is interesting, and it makes for both informative and amusing classroom discussion.

(3) To deal with Professor Knutson's assertions, students should focus on the doctor scenes: II.2–5, and especially III.1.

(4) Of the funny physicians, Dr. Slicer stands out by supporting a senior doctor who killed a patient (II.3.8) and by his insistence on medical procedures even though patients are dying. Dr. Gouger is funny in recommending a treatment, reassuring Sganarelle that if Lucinda dies, the death will have happened "in accordance with proper procedures" (II.5.9). Obviously, the most fully developed doctor is Fillpocket, who shows a good deal of self-awareness and also cleverness in his speech to the contending doctors. The "rabbit" and the "turtle" are funny, while not, of course, real. In fact the doctors are all lively and memorable. Probably the issue of roundness and dynamism is not relevant to the group as a whole as Molière presents them to us. Because they are satiric figures, they are necessarily flat and representative, even though they also are the cause of explosive laughter.

■ Comedy from Molière to the Present, *pages 1623–24*

This is a brief review of comedy and aims at no more than a small number of highlights for those students who have had no previous experience with comedy. The emphasis is on English and American comic dramatists, and also on the tradition of comic opera and musical comedy. Students who have seen plays, either on stage or on the movie screen, will be able to provide additional materials for discussion.

ANTON CHEKHOV, *The Bear, pages 1625–33*

Most comic in this play is the swiftness with which antagonism between Mrs. Popov and Smirnov changes to love. Students may deny the realism of the play because of this speed. However, while there is no need to claim fidelity to real life for *The Bear,* it is true that Chekhov points out that the self-dramatizing major characters are both romantic and impulsive, and that their love is credible enough even if the comic circumstances in which they fall in love are not.

Though the play is short, it contains a number of major and minor conflicts. The major one is between Smirnov and Mrs. Popov. Also, it is clear that both major characters bear their own inner conflicts, such as the rage that Mrs. Popov exhibits at the cruelty and infidelity of her dead husband, and the anger that Smirnov bears toward women as a result of his misfortunes in love. There is a servant-master conflict between Mrs. Popov and Luka, and also between Smirnov and his offstage groom Semyon (Speech 45). There is also a conflict over the extent of the loyalty that the living owe to the dead, not to mention the general battle between the sexes out of which Mrs. Popov and Smirnov find love.

Suggestions for Discussing the Study Questions, pages 1633–34

(1) At the opening Mrs. Popov is in mourning for her husband, who has been dead for seven months. She indicates, however, that her life had been difficult with her husband inasmuch as he had been unfaithful and had also been mean and cruel (Speeches 4, 72). Even though she is trying to be a model of faithfulness to his memory, she is also angry at him. At the play's opening, Luka's practical advice and his directness show that her behavior is overdrawn, sentimental, and just plain silly (particularly because of her deep feelings).

(2) Smirnov has come to collect a debt owed by the dead husband (Speech 21). He is gruff, loud, and outspoken. He tells Mrs. Popov that he has had his fill of love, having been jilted nine times and having jilted women twelve times (Speech 69).

(3) Luka is important because he is the first one to speak with Mrs. Popov, and on occasion he is also alone with Smirnov. As a character, he is outspoken but not very brave or strong. His reactions (exclamations, handwringing, signs of developing anguish, rushing offstage to get help, etc.) to the actions and emotions of Smirnov and Mrs. Popov underscore their anger and make their eventual embraces seem especially unlikely and therefore funny.

(4) Smirnov's repeated and angry requests for money occasion Mrs. Popov's asking him to leave. When he refuses and becomes more angry, she calls him a bear, a brute, a monster (Speeches 101, 103, 111). As the anger and insults mount, Smirnov challenges her to a duel (Speech 112).

(5) Toby is the horse who had been the favorite of Mrs. Popov's husband. He symbolizes the shifting of her emotions, because at the start she orders an extra bag of oats for him, but at the end, when she has fallen for Popov, she withdraws the request, indicating that her vigil for her dead husband is over (Speeches 8, 154).

Suggestions for Discussing the General Questions, page 1634

(1) Laughter is unpredictable, but some likely spots at the start

are Luka's observations about his dead wife, about living like spiders, and about the waving of the fanny. The play takes off from there. Certainly Smirnov is quite comic, for he says outrageous things, imitates his offstage groom, criticizes his handling of the horse, spits out water (probably), breaks chairs, and clearly indicates his increasing desire for Mrs. Popov. Students will, let us hope, find other parts that they think are comic.

(2) All of the things cited in the question point out the extravagance in language and action characteristic of farce. Normal feelings and responses are inflated, stage business (such as the breaking of chairs) is exaggerated, and speeches are loud and out of proportion. The novelist Henry Fielding, in an early play (*The Author's Farce*, 1730/1734), said that the aim of farce is nothing more than "to make you laugh." The primary goal is laughter, and in farce, everything is directed toward that end.

(3) From the shortness of their acquaintance and the increasing hostility of their speeches to each other, one could never predict that Smirnov and Mrs. Popov would be falling in love at the play's end. But because both are portrayed as being committed to love (Mrs. Popov's dedication to mourning for her dead husband, Smirnov's many affairs), their falling in love is sudden but not surprising, granted that their relationship takes place in the heightened emotional atmosphere of their argument and name-calling.

(4) Each of the ideas listed here could result in extensive discussion, or else in an essay-length treatment. "The Difficulty of Keeping Resolutions," for example, might involve introducing the declarations about life of both Mrs. Popov and Smirnov, and then considering the circumstances of their lives that make the resolutions unlikely. A discussion of this topic need not consider their meeting and falling suddenly in love, but rather might treat the general directions in which their characters and circumstances would point them, the idea being that decisions made at one time may not necessarily apply later.

BETH HENLEY, *Am I Blue*, *pages 1634–49*

Suggestions for Discussing the Study Questions, pages 1649–50

(1) Ashbe's actions and speeches set her out as an unusual person, to say the least. Ordinarily, people do not hide under other people's raincoats, nor do they crawl under tables (when sober) to escape the gaze of waitresses. Ashbe's speech demonstrates that she

is streetwise and brash, and her comparison of herself with Robin Hood suggests a vivid imagination together with the brashness to carry out her pose. In a real sense, Ashbe is resorting to her poses and her inhibition-free speech in an attempt to find herself and establish her character.

(2) Ashbe's family is in ruins, and this aspect of her life should be taken seriously. Her father is frequently gone, perhaps on business, but it seems that he has become a drunkard and does little to assist her beyond maintaining the dreary and messy apartment to which he occasionally returns. Ashbe's mother has gone entirely, and is now living in Atlanta and is staying with a woman named Martine (Speech 339). The implication is that Ashbe is completely on her own. She must therefore carry on without any of the supports that normally should be provided by the family.

(3) Ashbe may be fabricating what she says about G. G., but she does succeed in tearing down the woman whom John Polk has a ticket to see. Her motive is not clear, since she has just met John Polk, but it would seem that she immediately likes him and does what she can to forestall his going to the house, first by denigrating Myrtle, and then by indicating the danger at the house ("Only two murders and a knifing in its whole history," Speech 49). This speech, together with her description of the type of fancy dress ball she would prefer to attend, suggests her aversion to the life which she is being forced to live and her yearning for something better.

(4) John Polk is a person cut adrift, just like Ashbe. Under pressure to conform in all the areas of his life, he is frustrated and uncertain. He thinks negatively of both going to college and spending his life in the family soybean business. His uncertainty is shown in the fact that he has felt drawn to the ministerial profession. He is, however, uncertain about his theological beliefs, and therefore there does not seem to be a sense of call or vocation there. To help himself socially, he has joined a fraternity, but he dislikes the boisterousness of the fraternity activities, and he believes that the birthday appointment that his frat brothers gave him with the prostitute is casting him in a role he does not wish to take. Ashbe notes his qualities of acquiescence and passivity by calling him a "sheep" (Speech 257), and he soon recognizes the aptness of her remarks.

(5, 6) For people who have not known each other more than a few minutes, Ashbe and John Polk begin arguing and taunting each other quickly. Rather than dividing them, however, the arguments bring them together. When John Polk offers to leave after she calls him a sheep, she urges him to stay, and describes her words as "friendly criticism" (Speech 265). It seems that Ashbe uses her arguments to encourage John Polk to describe his circumstances and feelings. Ashbe, by contrast, volunteers much information about herself in her taunts. John Polk turns Ashbe down in her offer to make love because he says that he likes her—the implication being that he respects her as an individual and not as a sexual object. His suggestion that they dance all night shows that they recognize each other as kindred spirits, who together find some of the security they have been seeking.

Suggestions for Discussing the General Questions, page 1650

(1) The plot of *Am I Blue* develops from the conflicts of both Ashbe and John Polk against the circumstances of their lives and families. Both are fighting against loneliness and alienation. The crisis and climax of the plot is the phone call that Ashbe receives from her father (Speech 267). We conclude from her conversation that her father is drunk again, and that for some reason he is trying to use her to make contact with her mother. After Ashbe hangs up, her vulnerability shows clearly: (She looks at him blankly, her mind far away). From this point the two become more clearly drawn to each other, as though together they may contend more strongly against the situation and attitudes that have been suppressing them. The resolution of the plot is the immediate security of their friendship.

(2) There are a number of separate techniques in Henley's verbal comedy. The major one is Ashbe's selection of topic material. When she mentions a butcher and a silver pirate, for example, she exhibits a flamboyant and unusual imagination which produces laughter. The technique of understatement also evident, as in the description of Myrtle's acne (Speech 71) and the reference to the two murders and a knifing (Speech 49). There is also the reversal of what is expected, as in the question of what soft drink to include in rum (Speech 148). Throughout, Henley maintains a surface easiness and humor, even though the seriousness of the plight of Ashbe and John Polk is also constantly emerging.

(3) Both Ashbe and John Polk are appealing because they are vulnerable, pleasant, questing characters. John Polk is more realistically presented than Ashbe, whose oddities would make her out of place in most circumstances. Both are more articulate than young people in their positions would probably be normally. They develop as characters because they quickly see the benefits to be gained from

continuing their friendship. (John Polk, for example, speaks about the need for being able to speak to a girl the next day.) Both characters may also be seen symbolically or typologically, for both are in the stage of the quest and initiation. John Polk, however, rejects his initiation in favor of continuing his quest for identity with Ashbe.

(4) The play's major theme concerns the difficulty that young people find when they have not been able to establish certainty in their lives or when they are alienated from the roles they are expected to take. The immediate effect of the comic mode is to create a surface diversion from the seriousness of the theme, but the language also exposes the uneasiness and uncertainty of the major characters. In fact, the dialogue, together with the change of scene to Ashbe's home, finally focuses on the plight of the characters, and hence stresses the thematic point that friendship and communication can help people to face and begin to surmount their difficulties.

(5) Although the French Quarter of New Orleans is frequently an exotic setting suggesting leisurely and pleasant days and ways, in *Am I Blue,* which takes place in some of the less savory parts of the French Quarter at night during a rain in November, the district and its clientèle symbolize the dangers that Ashbe and John Polk are facing. The two murders and the knifing (Speech 48), though they are mentioned only briefly and comically, indicate the menace and brutality that people may escape only when they are certain about themselves and are able to direct themselves elsewhere. The interactions of John Polk and Ashbe with the street folk indicate a certain knowledge of the streets as long as there are no threats. The drunken man vomiting in the street may symbolize how low people sink if they never put their lives together (perhaps like Ashbe's father, who is an alcoholic).

Writing About Comedy, *pages 1650–55*

Unlike the discussion of writing in the previous chapter, this material does not introduce any new types of essay. Rather, the section on questions for discovering ideas returns to a focus on the traditional elements of drama. Students are referred to the relevant section of Chapter 26 for additional review of these elements. We recommend that you encourage them to read (or reread) this material before they begin to plan and write. In these pages, we discuss specific aspects of plot, structure, character, and language that can be especially appropriate for comedy. Keep in mind, however, that the comedies in this chapter lend themselves to almost any kind of writing assignment.

The demonstrative essay on *A Midsummer Night's Dream* illustrates how setting, symbolism, and comic structure may be explored at the same time. The essay thus links and considers three separate elements. In making writing assignments, you may want to consider topics that ask students to deal with one, two, or even three elements that are related and that work toward a single effect. Once again we suggest that you warn students about the necessity of focus, development of a few key ideas, and selectivity. As with most other writing projects, students will frequently employ the scatter method, introducing numerous observations about many elements in a disorganized manner. You should strive to encourage a selective focus.

Special Topics for Writing and Argument about Comedy, *pages 1655–56*

(1) Topic 1 contains enough questions to enable students to develop a fairly complete essay if they do no more than answer them. The problem, of course, is in organizing all the answers and ideas into a coherent whole.

(2) Topic 2 is a good one because it forces the consideration of the differences between the tragic and comic modes. Students might use examples from other works to reinforce their points about Molière's comic methods. In *Hamlet*, for instance, Ophelia is in a position like Molière's Lucinda. Her father, Polonius, tries to influence her, and her inability to resist, as Lucinda does, finally drives her to madness and suicide (there are, of course, other disastrous influences acting on Ophelia). Similarly, Mabel Pervin of Lawrence's "The Horse Dealer's Daughter" (500) has been driven to the point of suicide after losing first her mother and then her father. With examples like these for contrast, students might be able to work out more clearly the nature of Molière's comic resolution of the effects of the Sganarelle–Lucinda relationship.

(3) Although many of the circumstances of the characters in *Am I Blue* are serious, the play nevertheless is a comedy. The actions of John Polk and the strangeness of Ashbe, such as her use of Kool Ade, would provoke laughter in an audience. Students will of course describe their own reactions, but the serious underpinning of the comic development makes the play worthy of serious consideration. The use of additional Henley plays to be found in *Beth Henley: Four Plays* would add dimension to this topic.

(4) This topic requires the reading of an additional Chekhov play, and enough alertness to see points of similarity and difference. All the mentioned plays are popular, but none of them has the boisterous good humor which has made *The Bear* an enduring favorite.

(5) The fifth question is a big one, most appropriate for a long investigative essay after a term's work, particularly if some of the suggested books are added to the subject. Some of the answers that students may find may be that comic material does not need to be light, that a comic resolution might easily become tragic under the wrong circumstances, that jokes are funny but not essential to comedy, that farce is also not essential and that too much of it might interfere with the seriousness of what happens in comedy. The "edges" between comedy and tragedy can be dealt with only if students introduce comparisons with tragedies, such as *Hamlet*, where many of the situations could turn out well for the characters if there were not such destructive forces at work. If students turn to this problem, the essay will become even more extensive than if the three comedies alone are treated. The edge between farce and comedy is more readily dealt with within the scope of the plays included in this chapter. The answer is probably one of emphasis; a certain amount of farce and business enhances the happiness and hope that one looks for in comedy. Too much clowning action, on the other hand, will turn anything into a farce.

(6) Suggestions for how to handle this assignment may be found on pages 1537 and 1542, where the types of intrigue plot related to the *Commedia dell'Arte* are described. The pattern of lovers being blocked and overcoming the blockers is the type to be explained, and students may bring out important contrasts while explaining the similarities of the situations in the two plays.

(7) Topic 7 is designed to give students some of the joy of writing creatively. They might believe that they need to write jokes, and will need assurance that writing jokes and one-liners is not necessary for this assignment. (They are not, indeed, planning to become comic dramatists.) The essential thing about the assignment is to concentrate on the situation, and to imagine what characters in particular situations and with certain interests might say under the circumstances that the students create. Again, as with all the creative-writing assignments, the critical essays of self-analysis are quite important, so that students may articulate the discoveries they have made about the principles of good comic writing.

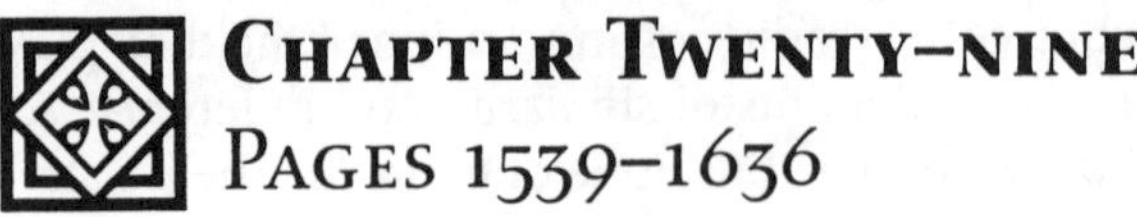

Chapter Twenty-Nine
Pages 1539–1636

Visions of Dramatic Reality And Nonreality: Varying the Idea of Drama as Imitation

This chapter examines the differences between realism and nonrealism in drama. Unless you begin teaching drama with plays from this chapter, these concepts should not be totally new for students. Because all dramatic conventions are nonrealistic, students should be familiar with some nonrealistic devices and techniques before they read this material. Most of the plays in Chapter 26, for example, are fairly realistic, whereas *Oedipus the King* and *Death of a Salesman,* both in the *Tragedy* chapter, demonstrate much that renders them unrealistic as opposed to realistic. In this chapter, the plays show varying degrees of realism. Hughes's Mulatto is as close to reality as it is possible for a play to get, while Wilder's *The Happy Journey to Trenton and Camden* is unreal in some respects and totally real in others (as unreal as riding in a car that isn't there; as real as a hot dog). Tennessee Williams's *The Glass Menagerie* is also mixed, with qualities of both realism and nonrealism.

Another way of approaching realistic and nonrealistic drama in class is to discuss the extent to which a play acknowledges or ignores its own fictiveness and the presence of an audience (or reader). Because realistic plays attempt to imitate life as closely as possible, they do not contain devices that call attention to their own existence as plays, nor do they create any direct links with the audience (even though living actors always respond to the reactions they are getting). The ideal realistic play exists in isolation, and we as an audience are the unacknowledged spies watching through the missing "fourth wall." In contrast, nonrealistic plays usually contain devices that emphasize both the theatricality of the moment and the presence of spectators (or readers).

A 1950 filmed version of *The Glass Menagerie* (107 minutes, B/W, starring Jane Wyman, Gertrude Lawrence, Kirk Douglas, and Arthur

Kennedy) is available for classroom use. The films may be obtained from many distributors, including Films Inc. (1144 Wilmette Ave., Wilmette, IL 60091). If you use films or videotapes to help students appreciate the plays, you might remind them that movies are very different from staged plays. In film, directors gain a much broader canvas and the ability to use cinematic effects such as close-ups and quick cuts; these are impossible on the stage. Conversely, film loses live theater's sense of the entire stage action and scenery, and also the intimacy that connects the actors with the audience. See also Chapter 30, on Film.

Langston Hughes, *Mulatto*, *pages 1663–88*

Mulatto is above all a realistic play. The interior is real and the references to the outside world are real. What happens on the outside, in fact, creates the oppressive reality of the inside. The prevailing social structure of the American South of the 1930s is really the antagonist of Robert, the son, and to a lesser degree of Colonel Norwood, the father. The massively condemnatory social structure of white supremacy uses all its force to suppress Robert. His fast driving of the Ford, his affront to the woman at the post office, the posse chasing him in the areas near the house, and his suicide at the end of the chase—all these are features of the play's predominant realism.

In light of Hughes's desire to dramatize the real circumstances of African Americans in the deep South during the 1930s, the play, indeed, had to be realistic. Anything unrealistic and impressionistic would have lessened the impact of his critique of white supremacy and his dedication to changing the system. His characters are therefore real, and their inner conflicts and their resistance to change are real. The characterizations are real, from the rebellious Robert to the more subservient Billy and Sam. The most realistic of the characters is Cora, who has patiently tried to make the best of things. The final element of realism in this realistic play is Talbot's slapping Cora at the play's end. It is a symbol of suppression, although Cora bears it with the stoic patience she has always possessed. Hughes's implication is that it will be the Coras who will ultimately prevail.

Suggestions for Discussing the Study Questions, pages 1688–89

❖ ACT I

1. To say that the children belong to anyone but Cora would be to acknowledge Colonel Norwood's paternity openly. At one point it is stated that all African American children are considered the

children of their mothers only, thereby asserting perhaps covertly that all African American women are promiscuous.

2. The Colonel does not permit Sallie's bags to be carried out the front door because to do so would put her on an equal footing with him. The use of the front door is therefore unthinkable for him.

3. Robert's idea is that he has a right to claim both Norwood's paternity and name, and that in the future he could inherit Norwood's property. Higgins and Norwood find such an attitude impossible and unacceptable because Robert is a "yellow" mulatto and has no rights at all.

4. Colonel Norwood wants no schooling available to the African Americans in his area or on his plantation. His thought is clearly that education would be a means by which blacks could justify claiming equal rights with whites. He therefore advises Sallie to develop her cooking and cleaning skills, and to forget about education.

5. Talbot, representing the brute power by which Norwood rules, is the overseer who assumes the unpleasant task of keeping the blacks on the plantation in line. He is, of course frequently involved in the corporal punishment of blacks. Because he does not enter until late in the play his presence is an offstage threat, but the delay of his being in the action also enables the domestic drama in the Norwood household to develop in intensity.

6. Higgins reports on Robert's insistence on being treated with the same fairness a white would be, i.e., to have his money returned, to make those behind him wait while he returns the broken package, etc. Robert, by his assertiveness, frightens the white clerk and then resists being thrown out of the post office. Higgins also says that Robert drives in a way which does not show sufficient deference to white drivers and pedestrians.

7. Higgins adopts the apparent attitude of white men of his class and place toward women of color, namely that these women exist for the sexual pleasure of white men and for the bearing of "yellow" children. In no way does Higgins ever believe that women of color are the equals of white women, who alone are to be treated with respect and who are the only ones fit to become the wives of white men.

8. Colonel Norwood's previous kindness toward Robert ceased once the child called him "papa" in public, and he probably wouldn't have accepted such an action privately either. The beating causes resentment in Robert, but it does not frighten him enough to cause him to be publicly cautious.

9. The Colonel has apparently decided not to continue Robert's education but to put him to work in the fields. Cora's general fear is that the Colonel will punish all the people of color on the plantation, and she fears that the Colonel will refuse to permit Sallie to go back to school.

❖ ACT II. Scene 1.

10. For Colonel Norwood, the issue is control. As a man who has "never had trouble" with his "colored folks," he doesn't want to lose that authority. He expects gratitude for all he's done for those whom he terms "Cora's children," and he refuses to be pushed by Robert into acknowledging paternity for Robert or any other child. Yet the Colonel is being lenient to some degree, for he is willing to let Robert leave the plantation instead of being put to work in the fields. For Robert the issues are his determination to be acknowledged as Norwood's son and to be treated and allowed to act like any normal man, with all legally guaranteed rights and privileges. In addition, he resents Norwood's attitude toward Cora.

11. As the Colonel explains it (Speech 35), Robert's dilemma is that he is acknowledged and respected by neither whites nor African Americans. He belongs to neither group, and as a result he dislikes both groups. Because of this confrontation, the Colonel orders Robert off the plantation and even out of the state.

12. Robert believes that Norwood will not use the gun, and that beneath his white hostility of blacks Norwood believes he has obligations toward his mulatto children. There is both irony and pathos in the disparity between Norwood's verbal aggressiveness and dismissiveness toward Robert and the history of care (for that time and place) he has shown and continues to show by not carrying through on all his threats.

13. Talbot and the storekeeper immediately organize a hunt for Robert, with the obvious intention of lynching him if they find him. Robert realizes that he has virtually no chance to escape. Perhaps the fact that he refuses to run out the back (where he would not be seen by the whites) indicates his recognition of the fact that the only outcome of the situation, later if not sooner, is that he will be captured.

14. Cora's long speech gives us a sense of the life of a woman of color living in her circumstances in the South of her time. Her long sexual servitude to Norwood, and her own mother's apparent welcoming of her daughter's protected position, makes clear that

supplying sexual services and household care was the only way for such women to survive. Clearly she has labored and schemed to protect her children, to get them educated and away from the South. Although such plans have doomed her to an old age without her children near her, the sacrifice was worth it to her. With Norwood's death and her son's imminent tragedy her servitude has ended, but she breaks emotionally and delivers the speech in a state of apparent dissociation which echoes the double life she has had to live. In such a state she makes her long pain and suffering clear as she could not have done had she remained fully lucid and in touch with reality.

❖ ACT II. Scene 2.

15. The undertaker and his companion return us brutally to the real world after the glimpse of Cora's broken state. Their insensitivity to Cora and their obvious enjoyment of their planned lynching deepen Hughes's rendering of the tragedy of African-American life in the South during the time of the play.

16. The old ways of the South constituted virtual slavery for African Americans despite their alleged freedom after the Civil War. Clearly all African American women had to be sexually available to any white man who wanted them, and there was no redress for any person of color, black or white, after any kind of wrong.

17. Cora's second monologue tells us more about Colonel Norwood, making it clear that although he followed the "old ways" overtly, there was a side to him which found them repulsive. But clearly he was not strong enough to go against the mores of his time and place, and, quite possibly, had he done so he would have lost everything he had and become as much of an outsider as Robert was.

18. Robert kills himself in Cora's room. There are a number of reasons for which Talbot slaps Cora. First, he is frustrated because she has helped her son elude the rope. Second, his blow is a brutal way of showing her that she and Robert have not scored a victory by foiling the mob's intentions. Third, the slap symbolically represents the continuation of white supremacy over blacks.

Suggestions for Discussing the General Questions, pages 1689–90

1. The play contains may details about the plantations and the customs of the South because those details are peculiar to that time and place. Even though such conditions continued well up to the civil rights movement, some twenty-five or thirty years later, they

are generally unknown to a new generation of Americans. The richness of detail here helps base the play in reality, and keeps its meanings accessible to any reader or audience.

2. The front door symbolizes the importance of those who use it and the insignificance and subservience of those who cannot. The incident in the post office shows how the caste system worked outside of Norwood's house, just as the front door shows how it worked inside that house. By insisting on equal treatment, and by inconveniencing whites standing in line behind him, Robert was violating all the customs of the state. And in driving the Ford fast and refusing to yield to white drivers and pedestrians, once again, he was displaying his insistence that he be treated as an equal.

3. Norwood is a pathetic figure to the degree that he cannot be who and what he really is. He observes the customs of his time and place openly, but in the privacy of his own home he breaks them in many ways. Participating in a lynching, but being sick afterward and killing the dogs which had hunted human prey; having both a white wife and an African American mistress (perfectly acceptable), but then installing the mistress as the only woman in his house for all the years after the death of his wife (not acceptable); fathering mulatto children, but then educating them. In all these ways Norwood is unusual and, perhaps, doomed. Clearly, beneath his authoritarian and often verbally threatening exterior, there is far more fondness for his children and a far greater moral sensibility than his status enables him to acknowledge.

4. Robert is clearly very like his father in that he is assertive and willing to use his obvious good looks and intelligence to demand what he wants from the world. But he displays a tragic (and perhaps youthful) idealism which makes him blind to the realities which have bred him but from which he has been away. In great measure he brings about his own destruction—a destruction that is inevitable, granted the depths of self hatred he expresses.

5. Cora is a pathetic figure, for she has been powerless all her life except for whatever power her sexual appeal to Norwood has given her. Using that power has clearly necessitated that she sacrifice any individual desires she herself may have had, but her careful use of her position has enabled her to give her children all the advantages that could have been available to children of mixed race in America of the 1930s. She seems aware that Norwood is a man of greater kindness that he often displays, and is fond of him despite their master-slave relationship. But in her two speeches we get both a

picture of her life and of his, of her personality and of his, and we see, as she dissociates herself from reality, that the life-long stilling of her own emotional needs has quite suddenly, under the terrible shock of Norwood's death and the impending death of her son, driven her into a final emotional state in which painful reality has no further hold on her.

6. Granted the time and the place and the personalities of the persons involved, it appears unlikely that the play could have ended any way but tragically. The conclusion shows Hughes' intention: to expose and attack the racial tragedy which America was living and which was headed to burst onto the stage of history and remain there for many decades. W.E.B. DuBois's comment that the major issue of the twentieth century in America would be the issue of color is clearly demonstrated by Hughes' play.

Thornton Wilder, *The Happy Journey to Trenton and Camden,* pages 1690–1701

Suggestions for Discussing the Study Questions, pages 1701–1702

❖ Preparation for the Journey

(1–5) The opening stage directions present us with a bare stage and the absence of properties except for "a few dusty flats" that perhaps are "leaning against the brick wall at the back of the stage" (assuming the stage wall is composed of bricks). We are asked to imagine all the common stage properties that ordinarily occupy our eyes at the beginning of a play. The major characters also appear during the opening. We see a family of four, dressed in ordinary garb, and find nothing unusual about the people (this, of course, is what Wilder wants us to conclude about the family). As the preparation for the journey progresses, we learn more about the family, but not much more. Arthur is a little kid who likes to play marbles. Caroline has recently entered high school, and is trying to act grown-up by applying facial makeup in preparation for going on the trip—to her mother's horror. Ma is friendly to everyone, and speaks too loudly about family affairs, to the embarrassment of her children. Elmer Kirby is not on stage immediately, but when he comes on we learn that he is a conscientious father and husband, whose concern before a long trip is to make sure that the car has been serviced. He deferential to Ma, and is described as one who is "always even-voiced and always looking out a little anxiously through his spectacles." We learn that the Kirby family speaks English with the usual mistakes of people who have not studied grammar or heeded it carefully. The family is going to take a trip to see their eldest daughter Beulah, who lives in Camden, New Jersey, close to Philadelphia. The daughter has recently been "downright sick," and we may suppose that the family is traveling to see her to offer her their love and support. This may be ominous. We also learn that the family possesses a cat, and that the relationships among neighbors are good enough for one family to entrust not only their cat but their home to the care of another family when they leave town for a time. All in all, the Kirbys are designed by Wilder to be representative of the typical American family.

❖ The Journey

(6) The family reads the billboard advertisements along the road (a) to indicate some of the things that were well-known and popular in the United States at the time, and (b) to indicate the passage of space and time in their "journey" to Trenton and Camden.

(7) Ma reacts soberly to the funeral, and starts thinking about death and her own death. She observes that the dead person was a "lodge-brother" of Elmer's. She also is reminded of the death of "our good Harold," who, we assume, was her older brother or Elmer's older brother, who died when in the service, presumably during World War I.

(8) She gets along well with the garage attendant in her own garrulous manner, first by asking the way to Camden and their destination to the home of their daughter, Beulah (Loolie). Caroline is embarrassed by this chattiness and pokes her mother to stop talking. The attendant, we learn, can give her no information about the YMCA in Camden or anywhere else because he is "Knights of Columbus" (i.e., Roman Catholic). We learn from this interchange that Ma is an ingratiating person whose friendliness enables her to get along well with strangers.

(9) Ma forgives Arthur for his earlier remarks about her religiosity. She comforts him when he begins to cry, and is also affected when Caroline, too, cries.

(10) Ma is impressed with Washington, now that they are going through Revolutionary War country, because he "never told a lie," of course referring to the anecdote about Washington's boyhood confession to having chopped down the cherry tree. Her opinion is significant because she uses the occasion to make a point of parental advice to her children, who are "duly cast down" as her idea sinks in.

(11) Ma spots the signpost to Camden first, and Elmer then turns the car around to go the right way. The significance of Ma's finding is that it stresses her central role in the family as a guide and guardian on whom everyone relies.

❖ The Arrival

(12) Ma never loses a chance to provide parental advice. Her reaction to Caroline's observation about the "richer" location of Beulah's home is therefore to stress once again the importance of family strength: "I live in the best street in the world because my husband and children live there." Ma is a person of great conviction and has the insight to express herself on points of morality and behavior whenever anything happens that might challenge her. You have to give her credit.

(13) We infer, correctly, that Beulah has had a stillbirth and that she spent a certain amount of time in the hospital after her delivery. To Beulah, the experience was truly "awful. It was awful. She didn't even live a few minutes, mama" (Speech 179). Ma's strongest quality emerges here to enable her to comfort Beulah: "We don't understand why. We just go on, honey, doin' our business" (Speech 180). The name *Beulah* means "married" in Hebrew, and the symbolic value of the name is involved in the history of ancient Judah and the optimism of reconnecting the dispersed Jews, after the Babylonian captivity, with God and with a new time of fertility. Hence the significance of the name is one of optimism, for it suggests that Beulah will have other children to compensate her for the loss of her stillborn daughter.

(14) The significance of the hymn is that Ma is a person of simple faith, whose principal function in life is to keep people from straying too far. Her treatment of her children bears out this role. She is a person of great strength, a genuine glue that holds everyone together. The hymn, popular as it was at the time of the play, also underscores her belief in the guiding power of God. The play is not a sermon, but it does emphasize the need for families to be held together by a person of great conviction and great influence over family members.

Suggestions for Discussing the General Questions, page 1702

(1) The effect of having the stage manager do all the small parts and remain on stage during the entire action emphasizes the artificiality of the play as a play. Despite this apparent artificiality, however, the play presents a series of probable and strong characters, and their story is worthy of telling.

(2) The play unfolds straightforwardly in the order of exposition to final resolution. The crisis is the meeting with Beulah and the need for getting her over her great sorrow at having had the stillborn daughter. Because Ma has been so dominant and vital a character throughout the previous part of the play, she is the one character who is able to discuss the situation with Beulah, provide the comfort of her religious faith, and begin taking care of the house while Beulah rests. The catastrophe and the resolution are therefore the forestalling of a breakdown of Beulah and the assumption of household duties by Ma.

(3) The play's protagonist is Ma and her simple values. The antagonist is not any one character, but the problems of bringing up younger children and keeping them worthy, and also of assuaging the grief of the older child. In some respects, Ma is the protagonist and the difficulties of living are the antagonist.

(4–6) Ma is in many respects a stereotype. She is conventional in her ideas of family, history, child-rearing, and religion. Nothing she says indicates any great weight of mind on her part, and one might claim that being around such a person for long might be a total bore. One would wait a long time for elevating ideas from such a person. But she does indeed have a sense of humor, and she cares profoundly about those around her. She takes herself seriously and she seems totally unself-conscious. She is friendly with everyone, but maintains her position as the center about which her family turns. These are certainly compensating virtues. She has the ability to hold firm to her beliefs when they are assaulted by the derogative remarks about her religion by Arthur, and also when they are challenged by the deeply grievous experience of Beulah. One might say that she is "too good to be true" and that she is a fundamentally sentimentalized character, but it is a fact that many characters in life perform exactly the same function within families as Ma does. The reality of her life and the courage she shows keep her from going entirely over the edge into sentimentality. She is, essentially, a real person—not brainy, but real.

(7) "Happy" probably means here that the family takes what comes and adjusts to it. Thus Caroline accepts her mother's objections to her use of cosmetics (although nothing is said about her removing her makeup after Ma has voiced her opinion). Arthur is able to apologize for having offended Ma. The family is able to watch the funeral with appropriate thoughts about respect for the dead and remembrance of a departed loved one. When Elmer takes a

wrong turn, Ma points out the mistake, and Elmer simply gets back on the right road. When Ma speaks to Beulah she is able to deal with the sorrow of the loss, and then to console Beulah while continuing with the everyday needs of the family. In short, the family gets on with things. Being happy of course has differing meanings for different people, but the relationship of the word to things that "happen" suggests the importance of adjustment and carrying on with life as perhaps the most significant ingredients of happiness. Wilder's choice of the word "happy" in the title directs us to accept such a definition—not an unreal indulgence in pleasure, but rather a facing of life and handling the problems that happen to us.

TENNESSEE WILLIAMS, *The Glass Menagerie,* *pages 1703–1754*

This play combines realistic and nonrealistic techniques in a fairly even balance to produce a highly effective portrait of the Wingfield family. Many of the play's nonrealistic devices are discussed by Williams in the production notes (1705-1706). Classroom discussion should be focused on each of these elements. All of Williams's nonrealistic devices heighten the fact that the play is a work of art, a construction. This, of course, is in keeping with the idea of a memory play.

The other primary focus for class discussion is the characters. They live in fantasy worlds or pursue dreams that are doomed to fail. Amanda seeks release in her romanticized memories of Blue Mountain. She plans marriage or a business career for a daughter who is so reclusive that she can barely speak to strangers, let alone function effectively in the world at large. Laura takes shelter in a fantasy world built on old phonograph records and a collection of glass figurines. Tom, the would-be poet, dreams of a life of adventure based on the movies—his mode of escape from the apartment and the warehouse. Even Jim, "the most realistic character in the play," embodies failure. He has not fulfilled the promise he showed in high school, and it is clear that his dream of jumping from the warehouse to an executive position by way of night courses in public speaking and radio engineering is overly optimistic.

The Glass Menagerie is produced often by both professional and amateur groups. A 1973 color production first done for TV is available commercially (100 minutes), directed by Anthony Harvey and starring Katharine Hepburn, Sam Waterston, Joanna Miles, and Michael Moriarty. The virtue of this production is that it was specially adapted for TV by Williams himself; in addition, the production marked the first time that Hepburn had acted on TV. There is another notable color version (1987) directed by Paul Newman and starring Joanne Woodward, John Malkovich, Karen Allen, and James Naughton. A 1950 version starring Jane Wyman is also available.

Suggestions for Discussing the Study Questions, pages 1754–55

(1) The setting defines a world of poverty, deprivation, and desperation. Key adjectives are *warty, overcrowded, lower middle-class, dark, grim, narrow*, and *sinister.* The alleys symbolize dead ends, confusion, and entrapment—the world that Tom wants to escape. The fire escape represents both the squalor of the Wingfields and also a way out.

(2) The fifth character—the missing father—is present in his often illuminated photograph, dressed in his military uniform. This absentee figure parallels Tom's appearance on stage in the uniform of a merchant sailor. The father and son both attempt to escape by abandoning the family. Amanda remarks that Tom's attitudes and behavior are similar to those of his father (Scene 4, Speech 63). Tom also compares himself to his father, claiming that he is following in his father's footsteps (Scene 7, Speech 323).

(3) Amanda describes her genteel past in Blue Mountain, and her success with Gentlemen Callers, in scene 1 (Speeches 14, 16, and 29, pages 1709, 1710). These memories come up several times in the play (Scene 5, Speech 101; Scene 6, Speech 19), contrasting with the decay and poverty of life in Saint Louis. Amanda's habitual retreat to the past and her repetition of these memories is indicated by the way Tom and Laura react to the story; they have heard it all many times before, but Laura insists that Tom "let her tell it" because "she loves to tell it" (Scene 1, Speeches 18, 20).

(4, 5) Laura was unable to deal with her own fear, shyness, and insecurity at Rubicam's. She became ill during the first typing test and stopped going to class thereafter (Scene 2, Speech 16). Laura's failure provokes a crisis for Amanda and leads to the central crisis of the play. Amanda refuses to face the reality of Laura's incapacity; she sees two possible futures for Laura—business or marriage. Either would make Laura secure and save her from becoming the barely tolerated maiden lady that burdens many families. Because Laura fails at business, Amanda turns her attention and energy to getting a Gentleman Caller. This evokes the image of Jim, the one boy that Laura admired (from afar) in high school. This image and memory of Jim foreshadows his visit in the last scene. Amanda's plan to marry off Laura is impractical because of Laura's insecurity, withdrawal, and inability to deal with social situations.

(6) The argument in Scene 3 highlights the central concerns of the two characters. Amanda is worried about the survival of her family and, more particularly, Laura's future; she accuses Tom of being self-centered and trying to run away from his responsibilities. Tom considers himself self-sacrificing. He is disgusted with his life at home and at the warehouse and he wants to escape from the apartment and the Continental Shoemakers and go in search of adventure. He claims that he has given up all his dreams to support the family. Laura is spotlighted throughout the argument (scene 3, Speech 3.3 S.D.) because Williams wants to emphasize the impact of this conflict on her feelings and future. Amanda's concerns and Tom's ultimate decision to leave both have a pronounced effect on Laura.

(8) Scene 5 contains the announcement (annunciation) of the impending visit of Jim, the Gentleman Caller. Amanda sees Jim as a potential husband for Laura; she goes to extraordinary lengths to present Laura and the family in the best light. Her expectations are unreasonable and unrealistic; she cannot or will not see Laura's limitations. Tom is a good deal more realistic; he observes that "lots of fellows meet girls whom they don't marry" (Scene 5, Speech 82) and he is aware that Laura is crippled, different, and peculiar: "She lives in a world of her own—a world of little glass ornaments" (Scene 5, Speech 132). Laura is terrified by the idea of a Gentleman Caller. Moreover, she becomes almost totally incapacitated when she discovers that the Caller is Jim O'Connor; she refuses to answer the door or sit at the table, and she seeks refuge in her old phonograph records (Scene 6, Speech 59). She behaves this way partly because of her shyness and inability to function with people and partly because Jim, since high school, has embodied her secret fantasy of having a boy friend.

(9) The unicorn symbolizes Laura (as does the whole glass menagerie). Like Laura, the unicorn is unique, isolated, peculiar, different, fragile, unreal. The broken unicorn (missing its horn) is ironically more normal; Laura observes that the "horn was removed to make him feel less—freakish. Now he will feel more at home with the other horses" (Scene 7, Speech 262). This may symbolize Laura's momentary emergence from fantasy to reality and her normal interaction with Jim. Laura's giving Jim the broken unicorn as a souvenir represents the end of Laura's hopes. In both a real and symbolic sense, Jim carries Laura's potential for a normal life away with him. After she gives him the souvenir, she crouches beside the Victrola to *wind it up.*

(10, 11) Tom, as narrator in the present, indicates that he escaped from the apartment and the warehouse, and "traveled around a great deal" (Scene 7, Speech 323). He has not, however, escaped from memory, guilt, or Laura. Laura and Amanda face a bleak existence in Saint Louis. Although Amanda ends the play comforting Laura, the extinguished candles suggest the end of hope.

Suggestions for Discussing the General Questions, page 1755

(1) The nonrealistic aspects of this play include the setting, lighting, music, screen devices, use of a narrator, direct address to the audience, and the idea of the play as memory. Each of these will lend itself well to class discussion and/or writing assignments. There is, of course, no "right" answer to which is the most effective; all contribute to the total impact and meaning of the play. Williams incorporates the screen device to provide thematic focus for scenes or parts of scenes. It focuses our attention on the major idea or event that is taking place at the moment—the sights along with the sounds that define the period and culture of the Wingfields.

(2) Amanda, as protagonist, battles against poverty and abandonment in a vain (and heroic?) attempt to sustain genteel values, hold the family together, and provide for Laura's future. Tom, as protagonist, struggles for artistic expression and escape from his tedious and troubled life in the apartment and the warehouse. Laura, as the most passive character, is also the most difficult to cast as protagonist. One might argue, however, that her scene with Jim, the climax of the play, embodies her struggle to gain a normal life.

Unfortunately, all the central characters fail. Amanda and Laura are abandoned by Tom and Jim. Tom finds that he cannot escape the past. Tom is the only character who learns or gains self-knowledge in the play. In a larger context, both religion and the American Dream of adventure (Tom) or upward mobility (Jim) fail. Tom travels, but he achieves neither the artistic fulfillment nor the Hollywood-inspired adventure that he craves. Jim's failure to live up to his high-school potential suggests that he, too, is destined to remain trapped (in the warehouse, the past, marriage, unfulfilled dreams). The religious imagery of the play ironically highlights the failures; Tom is not reborn; Amanda fails as a mother; the annunciation leads to a disaster instead of a miracle; Laura blows the candles out.

To deal with the harshness of life as they face it, Amanda escapes into her memories of an idealized Southern past of plantations and genteel society. Laura seeks refuge in her fantasy world of the glass menagerie and the father's phonograph records. Tom escapes by going to the movies where he can have vicarious adventures.

(3) This distinction is discussed in the demonstrative essay (1758). Tom as character strives for escape, adventure, and self-expression. Tom as narrator understands that one can never escape from guilt, memories, and the past.

(4) Laura's crippled foot is a visual representation of her crippled spirit. This, in turn, accounts for her shyness, withdrawal, and inability to cope with the world at large. Williams uses Laura's high-school memories, the episode at Rubicam's, and her initial reaction to Jim's arrival to illustrate her limitations. The glass menagerie is part of her fantasy world; she constantly retreats to this world of old records and glass figurines. The fragility of the glass also symbolizes her fragility.

(5) In using *The Glass Menagerie* as a writing assignment, you might ask students to focus on either Amanda's laughable or her admirable qualities. For a longer essay, have students deal with both. Amanda's pretensions toward gentility, her idealization of the past, and her unrealistic assessment of Laura. These are pitiable and laughable. Her fierce attempts to provide for Laura's future, however, are heroic and admirable. Williams seems to want to leave us with the latter image at the close of the play. When Amanda silently comforts Laura, *her silliness is gone and she has dignity and tragic beauty* (Scene 7, Speech 322.3 S.D.).

(6) Jim is realistic in the sense that he is the most nearly normal person in the play, "an emissary from the world of reality." He is an optimistic and energetic would-be achiever who is concerned mostly with himself. Jim's goals (an executive position, a perfect marriage) reflect the American Dream of upward mobility; they are more normal (acceptable) than Tom's dreams of artistic expression and escape. Even so, they are almost as unreachable as Tom's. Jim's momentary interest in Laura grows out of the fact that she remembers his high-school glory days. His realism is qualified by the fact that Tom (Williams) uses him as a symbol of "the long-delayed but always expected something that we live for."

(7) Tom focuses on the geopolitical and economic social background of the dramatized events twice (see scene 1, Speech 1; scene 5, Speech 10). In each instance, the relative calm and ignorance of the United States is contrasted with the growing chaos in Europe. The contrast—and Tom's retrospective awareness of it—might suggest a number of considerations for discussion or writing: A–the self-absorption of the Wingfields parallels national blindness; B–Laura's

fantasy world parallels the national fantasy of approaching peace and prosperity; c–Tom's memories of St. Louis represent a mid-point between Amanda's idealized Southern past and the impending disaster of World War II.

(8) Like Ibsen's *A Dollhouse*, this play contains a wealth of symbolism. Writing assignments can be geared to a specific type or specific line of symbolism. The two symbolic characters are Jim and Malvolio the Magician (Scene 4, Speech 9). Symbolic places include the alley, fire escape, Guernica, Blue Mountain, the Paradise Dance Hall, and the warehouse. Symbolic actions include Laura's polishing the glass figurines, playing the Victrola, and the two instances in which glass figures are broken (scene 3, Speech 38.1, and scene 7, Speech 249.1). Symbolic objects and images include the photograph, blue roses, the unicorn and the glass menagerie, movies, and the coffin. The diffuse line of religious imagery and symbolism relates to all three central figures. Malvolio's escape from the coffin suggests resurrection or an escape from death (Lazarus); both are linked to Tom's desire to escape. The *Ave Maria* ironically celebrates Amanda as a mother. The Paradise Dance Hall—across the alley from the apartment—embodies a false heaven (reflecting the national blindness) in contrast to the hellish life of the Wingfields. The *annunciation* and the candles give Laura a religious aura that heightens her pathos and isolation.

Writing About Realistic and Nonrealistic Drama, *pages 1756–61*

This section discusses the planning and writing of essays about realistic and/or nonrealistic aspects of plays. The primary focus is on the relative realism or nonrealism of the element and the degree to which this, in turn, affects the impact and meaning of the play.

In developing (or having students develop) a writing project that engages the issue of realism or nonrealism, you have the option of calling for a relatively simple or a somewhat more complex essay. At the simplest level, you might ask students to select an aspect or element of a play and support an assertion that it is realistic (or nonrealistic). Such an essay might demonstrate the realism of one of Ibsen's characters or the nonrealism of the lighting in *The Glass Menagerie*. At a more complex level, you can ask students to discuss both the realism (or nonrealism) of a specific element and the effect thus produced. This is the more difficult but more rewarding assignment; it will help students learn much about the play at hand.

Special Topics for Writing and Argument about Dramatic Reality and Nonreality, *page 1761*

(1) Only the family of the Kirbys represents what could be called a model of family stability. At the beginning of *A Dollhouse*, the Helmers seem at first stable, and the husband-wife-children pattern seems in order, but things disintegrate quickly once the couple starts discussing the truth with each other. The Wingfield family in *The Glass Menagerie* is of course split apart and is in the process of splitting even more apart, for this family is presented as a network of contradictory desires and hopes, which are embodied in the ongoing conflict between Tom and Amanda. From Tom's perspective, family is also a trap. Poverty complicates the dynamics of the family considerably; it motivates Amanda's desperate efforts to secure Laura's future and it keeps Tom trapped in the warehouse. Personality is shaped by the past (Amanda's memories, Jim's high-school achievements, Tom's memories), dreams, and physical form (Laura's crippled foot). Colonel Norwood of *Mulatto* is at heart not a bad sort, and he has been Robert's childhood idol. The Colonel is prevented from normal family relationships, however, because of his social, economic, and racial position.

Normality of course implies a judgment based on what is happening today, in which families split apart in great numbers. By such a standard, the normal family is the Helmers, the Wingfields, and Norwood and his offspring. Ironically, the Kirbys, because of their strong family ties and their ability to bring things out into the open for discussion, are abnormal.

(2) The question of comparable settings will require the technique of comparison-contrast (Chapter 35). Students will need to analyze the stage-setting descriptions, and they should also consider how the settings figure into the action of the play, such as the lighting, the projected images, the voiceover backstage, the stage hand, the groups of invisible children, etc. Of great interest would be the statements that students might make about the effects of staging on audience perceptions. Is photographically realistic staging necessary? Can a play work well if it is set on a bare stage? To what degree does the eye yield to the dramatic action, once a play begins?

(3) Topic 3 is considered in this manual in question 1 of the study questions and question 1 of the general questions.

(4) For beginning an essay on symbolism in *Mulatto*, please see the discussion of general question 2 on the play.

(5) Economics and the need for feminine independence are applicable to all the plays in the chapter to at least some degree. Cora is totally dependent on the generosity of Colonel Norwood. Ma, as independent as she is, is also a dependent on the industry of her husband, although such matters are only hinted at toward the play's end. Amanda is in a position of distress. She tries to get along, but she constantly labors under the financial difficulties her household is experiencing.

(6) Topic 6 is a full-blown research assignment, especially if students add to the list of works by consulting the bibliographies in the works they find in the library. Usually the difficulty of such a research undertaking is the limitation imposed by collections in smaller college libraries.

(7) Students may pick their own topics in addition to the ones suggested in topic 7. What is important is that they create scenes of different levels of reality. It would be satisfactory for many of the same speeches to be duplicated in either version, so long as the realistic or unrealistic context is maintained.

Chapter Thirty
Pages 1763–86

Dramatic Vision and the Motion Picture Camera: Drama on the Silver (and Television) Screen

This chapter was added in the third edition at the request of a number of instructors who have used films in their courses. At the present time the seeing of films has been totally revolutionized by the existence of videotapes and DVD. Virtually the entire corpus of films, right from the very beginning to the last six months, is available for classroom use. The problem in studying films is hence not so much availability but rather being able to choose from the plethora of existing films. One needs only to enter a typical videotape rental outlet to conclude that the problems of teaching films today did not exist as recently as ten years ago.

In teaching film you may go as far as time may allow. The "Thumbnail History" of film (1763–64) is intended as no more than a hasty outline which includes only the most essential details. You might carry this as far as you class's interests will allow. More to the point of a course in literature including film, the discussions of *Stage Plays and Film, The Aesthetics of Film,* and *The Techniques of Film* (1765–70) are of major interest, especially the sections on visual, action, and sound techniques.

Since a discussion of movies is designed to increase understanding of film literature and techniques, it is appropriate to stress what students should look for in a film. Here you might rely on those students who have had experience in taking photographs. Almost everyone has snapped a picture, but few have ever done so in accordance with artistic principles. A discussion might raise the question of what can be achieved by a closeup, or by a longshot. Why take one or the other? Which type do students prefer? What is the effect of a longshot in which the entire body is included? What is the effect of a photograph of a person standing underneath a tree, with the tree dwarfing that person? Is it good or bad to have an object, say a tree branch, in the foreground of a picture? With a discussion developing from questions like these, you can make a number of points about photographic technique.

Invariably you will find that some of your students will have used either motion picture or (more likely) videotape cameras. They might thus be able to describe the differences between stationary and motion photography. How much time should be devoted to photographing a single person? Why should a running camera be shifted from one point to another slowly rather than rapidly? How should a zoom lens be used? Perhaps a description might be made (and illustrated, if possible) of a home movie—usually taken with appalling technique—and this description might be contrasted with the description of a professionally photographed film. Such contrasts are effective in helping students recognize basic problems, and solutions, of motion-picture photography.

There are many other aspects of film technique, and you may devote as much or as little time to them as you wish. Probably the most important additional element to stress, however, is *montage* or editing. Students knowing about the possible results of editing can see a film with confidence and develop informed responses to it.

Orson Welles and Herman J. Mankiewicz:

Shot 71 from the shooting script of ***Citizen Kane,*** *pages 1770–74*

Students would of course benefit from discussing this passage after having seen the entire film. A videocassette copy of *Citizen Kane* is readily available for use if your department or your audiovisual service has any budget at all for rentals. The updated and revised fiftieth anniversary edition of the film has been released in videocassette and is available for rental at most video stores (Turner Home Entertainment. Catalogue No. 6261).

Suggestions for Discussing the Study Questions, page 1774

(1) The scene follows Kane's political loss in the gubernatorial election. Jedediah enters with the obvious purpose of declaring that he wishes to end his immediate associations with Kane. In effect, the scene is a major showdown between the two men, although there is a final one later when Kane rewrites Jedediah's damnatory review of the operatic performance given by Kane's wife. The opening words indicate that the two men have been the closest of friends, for Kane says "I thought I heard somebody knock" (Speech 2). This is a criti-

cism of Jedediah's formality, for we may assume that he never had to knock before to see Kane. Jedediah's speeches show the cause of his unhappiness: Kane cannot accept objective criticism and advice, because he takes everything personally. Jedediah is frustrated with this situation, and asks for a transfer, which Kane reluctantly grants, while corroborating Jedediah's judgment in the scene's last speech (Speech 31).

(2) The reason for the title might be debated. Kane certainly is an American tycoon, and his self-indulgence with his own money ultimately leads all his friends and associates to desert him, thus illustrating the perils of wealth. The reason for the choice of *Citizen* as the title, however, may be taken as an ironic commentary on Kane's life. This scene demonstrates how Kane conceptualizes his role as a citizen: If he can't control things, he will either lose or not participate. This is not the position most citizens are in; hence the irony.

(3) If one is accustomed to straight-on, eye-level photography, the camera angles from below exaggerate the height and distance of the characters' heads, thus emphasizing both their size and suggesting their general significance as symbols as well as characters. The use of light and shadow suggests that even in open conversation (light) there is still an immense amount of thought, feeling, and motivation that are obscured (shadow). The theme of the movie is that Kane is a riddle and an enigma, and the development consists of the attempt to explain him. Thus, the use of camera and light in this scene fits right into the story and structure of the film.

ARTHUR LAURENTS, *A Scene from* ***The Turning Point,*** *pages 1775–80*

There are two major films which have succeeded because of their use of ballet. One is *The Red Shoes* (1948), in which the ballet ultimately becomes the heroine's story. The other is *The Turning Point,* in which the ballet scenes are included as aspects of the developing story. The feature dances are by Michael Baryshnikov and Leslie Browne. The concluding credit unit, in which Leslie Browne dances to the music of a Chopin Etude, is one of the most entrancing ballet sequences ever to have been put on film.

Suggestions for Discussing the Study Questions, page 1780

(1) The argument between Emma and Deedee, boiling over as the women whack each other, indicates that their friendship is stronger than the pent-up resentments and jealousies they have allowed to fester over the years. Emma makes the confession that she "had to

have" the ballet years before (Speech 80), and therefore she would have said anything to get it, including giving false advice to Deedee about her marriage. Once this admission is made, Deedee can put away all her self doubts, because Emma has in effect recognized that Deedee was a superb dancer.

(2) The last ten speeches add nothing to the conflict and reconciliation that has just occurred between the two women. In fact the conclusion suggests, as they "walk in opposite directions," that the reconciliation may not be complete. In the finished film, the scene ends logically, without including what is in effect an anti-climax.

(3) If the scene had remained in the bar, it would have made the purse-whacking impossible, for presumably someone nearby would have tried to stop the two women. By moving outside to the plaza Emma and Deedee have the privacy to shout at each other loudly and vent their anger completely. This kind of fidelity to realism would be impossible on stage, unless, of course, the stage scene were established as the open, empty, darkened plaza. Obviously, the movie form, with its many scenes and shots, provides for many possibilities that stage plays cannot possess.

(4) There are a number of changes from script to film. The elevator becomes a stairway, and afterward there is a second hallway along which the two women walk. The plaza is the same, but the images of the women are first taken from above, at a distance, as they argue and throw things at each other. When their battle-scene develops, they are seen closely, and at the fountain they are filmed from the waist up. In this way the visual presentation complements their emotional reconciliation. When the whacking ends in the film, it is laughter and not exhaustion that ends it, and thereby the reconciliation takes place within a mood of emotional release and merriment. Students may be able to suggest additional changes, but a major one is that a number of verbal variations may be noted, which may have been introduced directly by the actresses, Shirley MacLaine and Anne Bancroft. Students might wish to discuss the freedoms that film actors possess.

Writing About Film, *pages 1780–85*

A major decision here is for students to select a suitable topic. The easiest path to follow is to focus on normal literary topics like character development, a major idea, structure, and so on. As long as students rely on references to film action and dialogue, they will be on safe ground for whatever conclusions they make. References to non-literary techniques like facial expression, camera angles, and lighting and shading are much harder for students to interpret with confidence. Even so, they should try to approach the topic. Obviously, as students spend more time studying film techniques, the more reliable will be their references. If students are experienced with film, they might concentrate on purely cinematic as opposed to literary matters, but many students—and instructors—will feel more secure if they emphasize the literary.

A common problem for students writing about a film is shortness of memory. Use of a videocassette or DVD, and the re-running of a particular scene, can help in this regard. Also, however, a well-kept journal is essential here, for once a student begins writing there may be no further opportunity to verify details in the film.

As a preliminary, students may benefit from a number of exercises to help them in their understanding of film. Here are some useful hints:

a. For a film or TV show, determine how your understanding of a particular character is influenced by cinematic techniques (camera angles and views, lighting, setting), acting techniques (facial expressions, tones of voice, actions, "body language"), and costumes and makeup.

b. Observe a chase scene in a film or TV show, and determine the effects of camera techniques on your responses to the chase. (There is a hilarious chase scene in *What's Up, Doc?* [1972], in which Barbra Streisand and Ryan O'Neill are pursued through the streets and steps of San Francisco.)

c. For any film or TV show, record all unusual or noteworthy uses of camera or lighting. If any scene especially affects you, try to determine those elements that contribute to the effect.

d. Consider the uses of silence, sound effects, and music in a scene or series of scenes. What is the relationship between the dramatic situations and sound? Does sound help make a happy scene happier? A tense one more tense? A dangerous one more dangerous? A threatening one sinister? A scary one frightening? etc.

Special Topics for Writing and Argument about Film, *pages 1785–86*

(1) In selecting a single technique for analysis, students might find the study of montage to be a good start. In discussing montage, students would not find it necessary to discuss all the details in a movie, but might find their analysis effective if they follow the technique through two or three sequences of action. The same would apply if students were to discuss camera technique, the use of closeups or longshots, and so on.

(2) Topic 2 requires the full examination of just about everything that goes into the assemblage of a particular scene. The scene itself, therefore, will not need to be long, because the problem students encounter here will be coming to a stop.

(3) Although this is a creative-writing topic, it would be appropriate only after students have already spent a little time in analyzing and discussing film techniques and the relationship of dramatic to film presentations. The perspective that students should bring to the assignment is that of the director, giving directions to actors in order to realize a conception of a particular scene. Topics abound in the daily papers, and even more topics might be found in the weekly tabloids that contaminate the racks near grocery checkout counters.

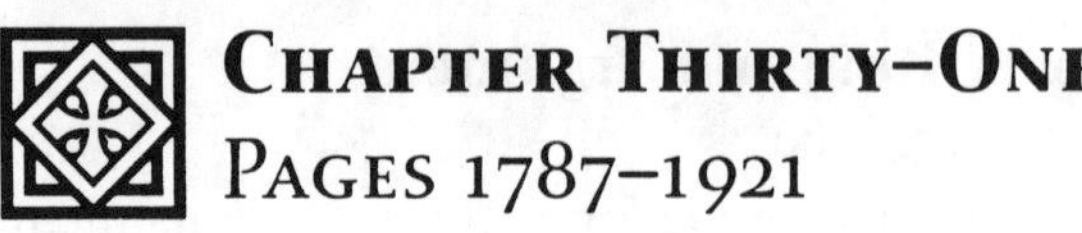

Chapter Thirty-One
Pages 1787–1921

A Career in Drama: Two Major Plays of Henrik Ibsen

This chapter was first included for the first time in the fifth edition in order to match the career chapters in the sections on fiction and poetry (Chapters 11 and 24). Obviously one cannot hope to include a number of plays in this career chapter to match the numbers of short stories and poems in the other career chapters. Thus the two plays included here take up 130 pages in the anthology, far more than the other two chapters. You will find in these two plays, however, an abundance of material for study, discussion, and writing. Those who are interested in special critical approaches to literature will find that Ibsen is amenable to interpretations based on the feminist, economic, moral/intellectual, topical/historical, and new critical/formalist approaches. In addition, *A Dollhouse* and *An Enemy of the People* can be studied for comparisons of character, plot, and structure, not to mention symbolism, tone, and setting.

A Dollhouse, *pages 1793–1842*

Time has not dated *A Dollhouse* or made it irrelevant. On the contrary, Ibsen anticipates modern concerns with identity crises, role playing, the rights of women, and the fulfillment of human potential. In class there is a tendency to focus on the themes at the expense of other elements. Ibsen's ideas are important and attractive; they inform every aspect of the play. At the same time, character, language, structure, and symbolism are also worthy of classroom discussion.

The play is carefully structured to build up to the climactic confrontation between Nora and Torvald (Act III. Speech 222–END). Anxiety about money permeates the entire drama. With the appearance of Krogstad, tension increases considerably, and continues to rise until the catastrophe. Nora faces a rising flurry of dilemmas: Will Torvald find out about the loan and the forgery? What will happen when he finds out? What will happen to the marriage? Torvald's self-centered diatribe (Act III. Speech 222–42) and the subsequent discussion answer these questions and comprise the catastrophe and resolution.

It is tempting to claim that the only puppet figure in the story is Nora, the doll living in her dollhouse. Certainly the doll-like role playing and make believe that she assumes is imposed by everything that society can bring to bear on a woman. The close of Ibsen's play makes it clear, however, that Nora is not the only doll. Torvald is as badly in need of education and self-fulfillment as Nora. Their role playing has failed to create for them the adult characters that could make them complete human beings. Interestingly, the play closes just as this educational phase of their lives is about to start (or should be about to start).

A Dollhouse, which has been extensively produced since the 1960s, is available in two 1973 films, both in color. One (106 minutes, available on videotape) was directed by Joseph Losey and stars Jane Fonda and Trevor Howard. The other (105 minutes) was directed by Patrick Garland and stars Claire Bloom and Sir Anthony Hopkins. More recently, Juliet Stephenson has done the starring role in a performance that was aired on public television in 1993. In 1997 Janet McTeer was featured in a critically praised Broadway production. Word has it that she is working on a film adaptation of this production; we hope it will appear sooner rather than later.

Suggestions for Discussing the Study Questions, pages 1842–43

❖ ACT I

(1) The opening stage direction indicates that the Helmer family is middle-class and reasonably well-off. Adjectives like *comfortably* and *tastefully* as well as the specific pieces of furniture names contribute to this impression. The stage direction also indicates that it is winter. Throughout the play, the warmth inside the apartment contrasts with the cold of the Norwegian winter outside.

(2) Ibsen sets the tone and nature of the relationship early in the play when Nora sneaks a macaroon and then lies about sweets to Torvald (Act II. Speech 63). The pattern of behavior is more appropriate for a parent-child relationship than for a husband and wife. Torvald often acts out the parental role. In Act II, he tells Nora that she can make as much noise as she pleases since he will not hear her in the study (Act II, Speech 139). Nora understands the dynamics of the relationship; she tells Rank that "being with Torvald is a

little like being with papa" (Act II. Speech 239). Torvald's paternalistic and superior attitude toward Nora is reflected in the terms of endearment he uses: *my little lark, my little squirrel, my little spendthrift.* Such phrases diminish and dehumanize Nora, and remind her of her inferior position. The repetition of *my* suggests that Torvald has objectified Nora and turned her into his possession—a common enough assumption of many men who accept a male-dominated view of the world. The repetition of *little* similarly indicates Torvald's perception of Nora as an object of no real significance. Nora's reference to herself as *we skylarks and squirrels* (Act I. Speech 49) and her flattery of Torvald's male ego (*some clever man,* Act I. Speech 287) suggests that she is aware of the situation, has come to terms with it, and is able to function within it.

(3) Torvald's pompous statements about borrowing (Act I. Speeches 16, 22) indicate his tendency to moralize and to assume conventionally proper and acceptable positions that will make him appear good and responsible. Other instances of such posturing are found in his attitude toward unsavory cases (Act II. Speeches 111–13), fear of losing face (Act II. Speech 115), working with Krogstad (Act I. Speech 478), and even Nora's decorating the Christmas tree (Act I. Speech 73). Torvald's moral posturing reflects his sexist and paternalistic attitudes, his concern with appearances, the degree to which he is trapped by background and society, and the role that he and society have successfully imposed on Nora. He is, in fact, pompous and sententious.

(4) The Helmers have spent years struggling to maintain appearances with too little money. Torvald has doled out the household funds carefully; Nora has scrimped in order to maintain a middle-class home and surreptitiously pay off her debt to Krogstad. Money is thus an abiding concern, especially for Nora. As the play opens, she sees a change in their financial situation (and a release from the burden of the debt) through Torvald's new job and big salary as director of the bank. She thinks that their "hard times are over" and that Torvald is "going to have a big salary and earn lots and lots of money" (Act I. Speech 13).

(5) Christine Linde's arrival (Act I. Speech 85.1 S.D.) is the first complication of the play. Christine is a striking contrast to Nora. She made an unhappy marriage for money and has had difficulty supporting herself since her husband's death. In contrast, Nora's life seems comfortable and her marriage loving. We discover, however, that Nora has her own burdens—the loan and the need to save and

earn secretly to pay it back. In the course of the play, Nora moves progressively closer to Mrs. Linde's initial status. Ironically, Mrs. Linde moves in the other direction, toward an honest and equal union with Krogstad. At the end, the women have almost exchanged positions. Christine will find stability and security with Krogstad, while Nora will struggle alone to become a whole person. Nora's success in getting Christine a position at the bank ironically places her in jeopardy. Torvald gives her Krogstad's position. Krogstad, in turn, pressures Nora with threats of exposure to get him a better position.

(6) Ibsen uses stage directions (movement, expression, tone) and dialogue to indicate that Krogstad (the second complication) is a threat to Nora (Act I. Speeches 213–23). Mrs. Linde starts, trembles, and turns away. Nora steps toward him and speaks in a strained, low voice. At this point in the play, Krogstad is symbolically linked with winter, sickness, and cold; when he goes into the study, Nora quickly stirs up the fire in the stove (warmth against coldness).

(7) The children's scene (Act I. Speeches 309–13) is significant for three reasons: (1) it shows us the happy domestic world of game playing that is threatened by Nora's crime, Krogstad's knowledge, and Torvald's conventional attitudes; (2) it identifies Nora as another child as she talks and plays hide-and-seek with her children; (3) it significantly expands the image of the Dollhouse and stands as a metaphor for life in the Helmer household. Nora's games with her children are metaphorically parallel to the roles and games that Nora and Torvald play in their marriage.

(8) Nora's secret "crime" is that she saved Torvald's life by borrowing the money to pay for the year in Italy. Nora tells Christine Linde this to show that she has known troubles (Act I. Speech 180). Ibsen also hints at the crime here when Christine points out that "a wife cannot borrow without her husband's consent." The crime is forgery; Nora forged her father's signature on the bond with Krogstad (Act I. Speech 401). Ironically, Nora's crime duplicates the crime that ruined Krogstad originally. Nora's motives transcend law; she forged the name in order to spare her father and save her husband (Act I. Speech 416) Krogstad points out that "the law cares nothing about motives" (Act I. Speech 413). At the close of Act 1, Nora is facing the horror that Krogstad will reveal the forgery and the loan—Nora's secret joy and pride—to Torvald.

❖ ACT II

(9) In Act 1, the Christmas tree is placed in the middle of the room and decorated with candles, flowers, and other ornaments (Act I.

Speech 429). At the opening of Act II (the next day), the tree is stripped of its ornaments and has burnt-down candle-ends on its disheveled branches (Act II. 0.1 S.D.); it has also been shoved into the corner by the piano. The stripped tree and its displacement from the center of the room symbolize the erosion of Nora's happiness, the growth of anxiety, and the mounting threats to her carefully patterned life.

(10) Here, as elsewhere, Nora's references to herself as *your little squirrel* and *your skylark* (Act I. Speech 49) indicate that she is consciously playing a role for Torvald. Nora offers to play her role to the hilt ("I will sing for you, dance for you") if Torvald will let Krogstad keep his post in the bank. Nora's awareness of the role that Torvald expects her to enact leads her to attempt to manipulate him. For additional discussion of role playing, see question 2 above and question 4 in the "General Questions."

(11, 14) Torvald's claim that he is "man enough to take everything on himself" (Act II. Speech 135) conforms to Nora's hope for a wonderful thing. Nora anticipates with both dread and longing that Torvald will assume full responsibility for the loan and the forgery. She asks Christine to witness that the act was solely hers in the event that "someone . . . wanted to take all the responsibility, all the blame" (Act II. Speech 337). At the close of Act II, Nora is waiting for this wonderful thing (Act II. Speech 423). The thought of such an act of self-sacrifice never occurs to Torvald. Nora explains her hope for this wonderful thing in detail after Torvald's failure to measure up to her heroic ideal (Act III. Speeches 340–48).

(12) While Torvald is Nora's husband-lover-father figure, Dr. Rank is her companion and friend. She talks to Rank about things that she never mentions to Torvald. The flirtation (touching Rank, showing him the stockings) is motivated partly by Nora's desire to control him and partly by her need for money; she almost asks him for the necessary cash (Act II. Speech 209). Nora feels safe playing with Rank; she considers herself his equal (or perhaps his superior). When Rank admits his love for Nora (Act II. Speech 214), he changes the basis of the relationship and makes it impossible for Nora to go on. She can accept Rank's love and maintain her own sense of conventional morality so long as he does not tell her about it, but once the profession of love has been made, Nora has no choice but to reject it, along with him.

(13) The tarantella occurs at the close of Act II, after Krogstad has made his threats and left the letter in the mailbox. The wild abandon of the dance symbolizes Nora's mounting desperation. Torvald sug-

gests that she is dancing as if her life depended on it and she replies, "So it does." The dance, linked to the poisonous bite of the tarantula, suggests that the poison of fear and deceit is eating away at Nora's life. Ironically Rank, who plays the piano for the dance, is also being destroyed by hidden internal poisons.

❖ ACT III

(15, 16) Christine rejected Krogstad about ten years earlier out of a sense of duty to her helpless mother and two younger brothers (Act III. Speech 21). Krogstad's prospects seemed hopeless, and Christine had to marry for money. She suggests a union with Krogstad at this point as a mutual redemption; she has faith in his real character and she needs something to work for (Act III. Speech 47). Unlike the Helmers' marriage, this will be a union of equals based on mutual need, understanding, honesty, and self-knowledge. Christine eventually decides that this same honesty and knowledge is necessary for the Helmers. Although she had originally wanted Krogstad to recall his letter, she decides that is must be read by Torvald so that the unhappy secret will be disclosed and the Helmers can have a complete understanding with each other (Act III. Speech 77).

(17) Neither Torvald nor Nora is significantly moved by Rank's imminent death. Nora, who already knew about it, is preoccupied with Krogstad's letter and her hope/fear that Torvald will save her. Torvald's lack of concern reflects his consistent focus on himself and his own needs. At this moment, he is far more interested in making love with Nora than he is in hearing about Rank.

(18) Torvald reacts to Krogstad's letter with rage, indignation, and fear for his own position. He condemns Nora and accuses her of destroying his happiness and future. His concern is completely focused on himself, his own reputation, appearance, and standing in the community (notice Torvald's frequent use of first-person pronouns here). Far from acting with the love and selfless heroism that Nora had imagined, Torvald plans to appease Krogstad and maintain appearances (Act III. Speech 242). Nora begins to see Torvald and her marriage clearly for the first time. The stage directions here (*steadily, questioningly*) indicate Nora's progressively greater understanding of Torvald and alienation from him.

(19) As a result of the experience, Nora has fully recognized that her life with Torvald has been without substance, communication, or meaning (Act III. Speeches 274–80). She realizes that she has been Torvald's doll-wife (Act III. Speech 286, the speech that explains the

title) rather than a fulfilled individual. She understands that she must try to educate herself, to comprehend the world, to learn what she can about God and religion, to get to the "bottom" of things, and to fulfill her duties to herself despite the demands of husband, family, and social conventions and restrictions. She also sees that Torvald is an incomplete person who needs to establish knowledge about himself.

Suggestions for Discussing the General Questions, pages 1843–44

(1, 2) Almost all the elements are realistic. One of the less realistic aspects that deserves discussion is Ibsen's use of coincidence. Perhaps the least realistic element is Ibsen's symbolism. The Christmas tree and the tarantella are discussed above (questions 9 and 13). Rank symbolizes hereditary corruption and death. The macaroons are symbolic of Nora's doll-like relationship with Torvald. The children's presents (sword, doll, horse) symbolize the perpetuation of traditional and conventional sex-linked roles. The locked mailbox serves as an emblem of Nora's (and women's) second-class status in society and marriage. Nora's clothing is also employed symbolically. The fisher-girl costume evokes the south, Italy, freedom, and Nora's saving of Torvald. When she wraps this costume in black (Act III. Speech 83.1 S.D.), this "southern energy" is transformed into a symbol of death. The final change of costume (from party clothes to severe daytime dress) and the slamming of the door make concrete Nora's emotional and conceptual shift away from Torvald, marriage, family, and convention, and toward self-fulfillment. You might also ask students to consider Ibsen's symbolic use of time. The play moves inexorably toward midnight. Act I occurs during the day; Act II begins in daylight, but it grows dark during Nora's conversation with Rank. Act III begins at night and ends near midnight.

(3) Ibsen wants us to judge Nora as a victim, protagonist, and heroine, rather than a villain. He creates a situation in which Nora is trapped by convention, law, and custom. (Who is the villain or antagonist of the play? It seems to be Krogstad at first. Can we finally conclude that Torvald is the antagonist? Society?) Nora's abandonment of husband and children in the light of her duties to herself is intended to be taken as necessary, if not admirable. Audiences and students have not always seen it this way; traditional values can lead many to view Nora's departure as scandalous. Indeed, Ibsen was forced to write an alternative ending to forestall unauthorized tampering with the play. In this alternative version, Torvald

forces Nora to look upon her sleeping children and she collapses in tears, agreeing to remain in the home as a wife and mother. Ibsen considered this ending a disgusting travesty and advised theatrical producers not to use it. As a spur to class discussion, you can tell students about this alternative ending and ask them which they prefer. In order to elicit the best discussion, you should press students to explain and defend their choices.

(4) Role playing is linked to the idea of the dollhouse and the doll-like existence of the characters. In the beginning Nora seems to be childish and empty-headed, for she has accepted the role of doll-child and doll-wife that her father, Torvald, and society have cast her in. The servants keep the dollhouse running smoothly; Nora contends that they know how to run things better than she does. But we soon learn that Nora is a strong adult who is aware of the conflict between her expected role as an object for display and her real role as the bulwark of the family. In this real role she secretly borrows money to save Torvald's life, and we learn that the financial responsibilities make her anxious and fearful because this necessary action is incompatible with her role as doll. At the play's close, her adult self emerges, and she articulates her knowledge that her home has been a playroom, that she has been a doll-wife, and that her children have been little more than her own dolls (Act III. Speech 286). Torvald is perhaps the most interesting doll, partly because he has no awareness of the role imposed on him by background, heredity, and society. Unlike Nora, Torvald had no sense that he is acting the role he has been conditioned to play. Nevertheless, Nora concludes that his life is as incomplete and doll-like as hers; he unconsciously follows a set of rules and roles as constricting and dehumanizing as those that have controlled Nora.

(5) Torvald is concerned with appearances and reputation rather than substance. This is evident throughout the play every time he opens his mouth. Examples are his version of the public image of the family, his own self-importance, his patronizing attitudes toward Nora, his inability to abide even the slightest hint of venality in others, and his holier-than-thou refusal to accept Krogstad back at the bank. Particularly telling in the discovery scene is that he does not ask Nora for any explanations, but immediately fulminates against her and renounces her as the mother of their children. His weakness and hypocrisy are shown in his sudden delight when he learns that Krogstad will not expose Nora's crime, and also in his pompous forgiveness of her.

(6) Inherited or hereditary corruption (disease, evil, immorality) is an idea that fascinated Ibsen; he explored it at length in other plays, most notably in *Ghosts.* In *A Dollhouse,* the idea is applied to Nora, Krogstad, and Rank. Torvald asserts that Nora inherited her corruption and amorality from her father and might pass it on to her children (see Act I. Speech 50, Act III. Speech 236). Both Rank and Torvald contend that Krogstad is morally corrupted and that he may be infecting his own sons (Act I. Speeches 251 and 478). Rank is the most explicit symbol of corrupted blood; he is dying of the diseases he inherited from his morally and physically corrupted father (Act II. Speech 38).

(7) Ibsen's ideas about marriage, growth, and self-fulfillment are expressed partly by Christine in conversation with Krogstad, but mostly by Nora at the close of the play. Christine has achieved self-knowledge; she seeks fulfillment with Krogstad. Nora grows to realize that her own education and development as a complete person are more important than husband, marriage, children, law, religion, or convention. At the same time, she begins to question the validity of forces such as religion and law that have guided her life. Although Nora is the only character who acts in a radically untraditional manner on the basis of these realizations, Ibsen makes clear that all the characters locked into the system need to develop as human beings. Nora, for example, claims that Torvald needs to reshape his view of their lives as individuals, just as she is hoping to do. Her final words concern the idea of changing, and she seems to be hoping at the end for real changes to occur that would turn their "life together" into "real wedlock" (Act III. Speech 380). Thus, in terms of the play's themes and structure, Nora's decision to leave and seek self-fulfillment is a move for the better, but her final exit still shocks some people because of her abandonment of marriage and children. The question may not be resolved in class discussion, but it should provoke heated argument.

(8) The three concluding essay subjects are designed to encourage students to take a position and then develop it and defend it with reference to the text of *A Dollhouse.* Probably students will take the position that the play is "something in between." A good argument can be made that the characters change for the better. And the conclusion may be interpreted as affirmative, largely because all the major characters come to recognize their situations clearly whereas they do not possess that vision when the play opens.

An Enemy of the People, *pages 1844–99*

A brief word about the translation seems in order. As any person who has ever attempted to translate a work in a foreign tongue into English knows, fidelity to the original and the quality of the English are the elements on which a translation should be judged. I hope that the version of *An Enemy of the People* contained here will meet this test.

Although the present text is faithful to the original, it reflects a great many decisions. First of all, this is a translation for students. Ibsen's play is timely and prophetic, and I have tried to make my language as accessible as possible. In a few cases this has meant a slight shortening, without changing the basic ideas, of some of Ibsen's more prolix speeches. An example is in Act IV. Speech 158 (1885), where Dr. Stockmann mentions a controversy he and Mrs. Stockmann have had about the frequency of housecleaning. The passage is inessential in the original, and it has seemed unnecessary to include it here.

In just a few other instances, in consideration of the fact that this is a text for students, I have used translation as an opportunity for explanation. When Dr. Stockmann, for example, uses the image of Methuselah as a comparison for the age of ideas, I have made the sentence "truths don't live for 969 years, like Methuselah" (Act IV. Speech 124, [1883]). Ibsen assumed that his audience knew Methuselah's age, and therefore did not mention the number of years, but it seemed appropriate to add the detail for students who may be unfamiliar with biblical details.

There are a few other minor modifications. In Act IV, for example, I have numbered the various citizens (e.g., *1 Citizen*), to indicate the many speaking parts that Ibsen includes there, and I have also given some of the citizens the names that Ibsen himself designates. Also in this scene, I have made Stockmann's public meeting conform more nearly to rules of order than are apparent in Ibsen's text. On the details of the local problems of bacteriology and pollution, I have used some recent words as the proper translations, on the assumption that Ibsen would have used them had they been available to him.

Another feature of this translation may be illustrated by Dr. Stockmann's concluding speech: "... the strongest *person* in the world *is the one* who stands most alone." Ibsen's original reads ". . . *den stærkeste mand* i verden, *det er han,* som står mest alene" ("the strongest *man* in the world, that is *he* who stands most alone"). I have made such renderings throughout, on the assumption that any current translator of Ibsen should treat him as a dramatist who was, above all, conscious of the implications of language.

A particularly important translation is part of Dr. Stockmann's key speech in Act IV (Speech 115, [1882]): "Yes, the damned, solid, popular majority!" The original here is "Ja, den forbandede, kompakte, liberale majoritet." All the other translations I have consulted render this as "Yes, the damned, compact, liberal majority," because the words come across easily this way. However, *An Enemy of the People* has nothing to do with liberalism as a philosophy, but more properly concerns Ibsen's quarrel with politicians who build their strength on majority rule and public opinion, and therefore minimize intelligence and truthful analysis. As a result, I believe that "liberal" is an inaccurate translation here, and that "popular" more accurately renders Ibsen's idea. In addition, the word "liberal" is a word that has been misused and demeaned in the political climate of today's America. To include it in Ibsen's text, regardless of earlier translations, would not clarify *An Enemy of the People* but would make it more problematic.

Filmed versions of *An Enemy of the People* are rare, as are stage productions. There is a videotape of the Arthur Miller version (1977) featuring Steve McQueen, Charles Durning, and Bibi Andersson. The play was revised to make it applicable to modern-day Bengal and was issued in 1989, featuring Soumitra Chatterjee, Dhritiman Chatterjee, and Ruma Guhathakurta. In 1992 Miller's version was televised in a production featuring John Glover, but this filming is not commercially available.

Suggestions for Discussing the Study Questions, pages 1899–1901

❖ ACT I

(1, 2) By introducing The Mayor before Dr. Stockmann, Ibsen illustrates The Mayor's side of their (lifelong) brotherly antagonism. The disapproval that The Mayor shows about the family's waste of food and money, for example, will later be amplified to his opposition against Thomas's conclusions and recommendations about the Town Spa. In conversations with Hovstad and then with Dr. Stockmann, The Mayor is supercilious and is unable to accept criticism. He sees things personally, not abstractly, and his version of events is locked into his own personal sense of his role and duty. He uses his considerable intelligence, therefore, to defend his own actions, not to seek constructive solutions. These qualities of his character determine the antagonism that Dr. Stockmann, the protagonist, will face throughout the play.

(3) Dr. Stockmann holds back his paper initially because he has sought laboratory confirmation about his conclusion that the Spa waters are dangerous. His hesitation is evidence that scientifically he is a careful and responsible person.

(4) As a realistic feature of *An Enemy of the People*, Ibsen includes these scenes to show normal conversations during a gathering of people and their guests. After Dr. Stockmann leaves, for example, enough time must elapse to enable him to read the letter Petra has just brought him, and therefore the people onstage continue talking. Before Petra enters, we learn much about Dr. Stockmann's earlier isolation "up north." Life has been hard for him, and it is better now. (When he is later threatened with dismissal, therefore, we know that he has much to lose.) We also learn about Horster's occupation, and about Dr. Stockmann's connection with the *Messenger*. During the interval before Dr. Stockmann returns with the results of his letter, we learn about Petra's independence and frustration, and the interest that Horster has for her. We also learn about the indiscreetness of both Billing (*Billig* in Norwegian means "cheap") and Hovstad. Billing, particularly, precedes almost all his utterances with an oath, even though impressionable children are present.

(5) Dr. Stockmann's discovery (*oppdagelse*, or *opdagelse*, a word he uses constantly in the play) is that the waters of the Town Spa are being polluted by the runoff of the nearby tanneries at the town of Mølledal. He naively believes that the town authorities will accept his report and hasten to correct it. He does not recognize that making the necessary improvements will be enormously expensive. He is intelligent but politically naive.

❖ ACT II

(6) Morton Kiil is Katrina's step-father. Dr. Stockmann therefore addresses him as "father," though he also refers to him as the old "badger" when he is not around. Kiil is totally ignorant of science. He mispronounces *oxygen* later on (*sure stoffet* for *surstof* in Act V. Speech 149), for example, and has no concept of microbial life whatever. He therefore takes Dr. Stockmann's important discovery both as a joke and as an attempt to hoodwink the local authorities. His reducing the amounts he promises to give to the poor demonstrates his hypocrisy, and he is therefore funny in his own blunt and insensitive way.

(7) During the discussion with Dr. Stockmann at the beginning

of Act II, Hovstad states that the problem with the water pollution is only symptomatic of the general failure of the town's administration. He therefore declares his intention to offer the *Messenger's* support in a general campaign for reform. In other words, he indicates his intention to use Dr. Stockmann's discovery in his political cause. All of this is important later on because in Act IV Dr. Stockmann espouses and amplifies Hovstad's ideas in his attempt to expose official incompetence in the town, including, especially, the incompetence of his brother The Mayor.

(8) Aslaksen is the printer and publisher of the *Messenger*. His insistence on moderation is so constant that of course it becomes a cause of laughter. Aslaksen is one of the town's pillars of society, being involved in the local homeowners association and, naturally, in the temperance movement. He is not, however, a fool, and his self defense in Act III (Speeches 70–84) indicates that he understands the need for discussion and cooperation in political matters, particularly with the people who have political clout. He is a defender of the need for the curtailment of public expenditure, and, for this reason, he becomes the ally of The Mayor when the play's principal antagonisms develop.

(9) The scene develops out of The Mayor's professed skepticism about Dr. Stockmann's discovery. We know, however, that The Mayor's opposition is also linked heavily to his personal pride and also to his belief that the town cannot afford to make further expenditures to purify the Spa waters. His case against Dr. Stockmann is therefore well reasoned, and his offer to correct the situation is not without merit. He is by no means a straw man set up for the Doctor to knock over.

(10) The Act II speeches from 200 through 225 represent the last chance in the play for reason and cooperation to prevail over the opposition of the two brothers. Dr. Stockmann's declaration in Speech 212 may be the final nail in the coffin, for after this the men begin defending their own rights and methods. They threaten each other, and their conversation descends to the level of a shouting match. Nothing constructive can come out of this, and nothing does.

❖ ACT III

(11) The opening metaphors of pugilism and warfare provide a theme because almost everyone in the act is involved in antagonism in one way or another. Hovstad and Billing, though they work together, are at odds. Aslaksen is pursuing his own interests, and

puts both Hovstad and Billing in their places. Petra disavows the attentions of Hovstad. Finally, The Mayor secures the alliance of all three men—Aslaksen, Hovstad, and Billing—against Dr. Stockmann. By the end of Act III, the simmering warfare between the brothers erupts, and the consequences of this warfare are the subject of the remainder of the play.

(12) Dr. Stockmann first believes that the problem with the Spa is confined only to the issue of polluted water. As he speaks with his brother he comes to the conclusion that the problem is with the Mayor and the town officials who put finances above public health. He becomes, in short, a political person.

(13) There is agreement among the men that Dr. Stockmann is a good ally in the cause of purifying the Town Spa, but all the men have reservations about him for more general causes because they think he is impetuous and impolitic (they are right). Whereas earlier, in Act II, the men have declared him the people's friend, they will soon declare him (in Act IV) an enemy of the people. Ibsen is showing that all three men, despite their intellectual and theoretical pretensions, are serving their own interests first.

(14) Petra returns Hovstad's story without translating it because to her it represents an overly optimistic and sentimental view of the world. As she returns it, she still believes in Hovstad's idealism. Hovstad's explanation for wanting the story—that it could serve as a "hook" to get people reading the paper so that they could absorb his political ideas—disappoints or even disillusions her. Hovstad's clumsy declarations of love destroy her faith in him. She believes that Hovstad is not only trying to use her, but that he has been using and therefore betraying her father.

(15) The Mayor undermines the Doctor's report by asserting that following the recommendations will bankrupt the local taxpayers. His attack on Dr. Stockmann is not necessary, except that it serves as a reinforcement of his position. The Mayor knows that the men have been wavering against him, and demeaning Dr. Stockmann's character will cement their new alliance. He is the one with power. Dr. Stockmann has no power at all.

(16) Katrina's entrance does four things. First, it angers Dr. Stockmann and hardens his resolve to pursue his cause in purifying the town's water supply. Second, it threatens his own position and authority to make scientific decisions. Third, it makes him vulnerable in the eyes of The Mayor, Aslaksen, Hovstad, and Billing. Later on they will use his family against him, claiming that his action is a

major threat to his wife and children. Finally, his wife's being there makes him believe that he may be becoming more isolated in his position and in his recommendations, because she too asks him to desist out of consideration for the children. His speech using her as an example of weak old women (Act III. Speech 337) is brutal. Her response in his support, however, shows that despite what he has just said, she is on his side.

(17) The first act makes clear that there has always been tension between the two brothers. Act II accentuates the tension, particularly because The Mayor accuses Dr. Stockmann of ingratitude for all the past help and political favor that The Mayor has given. This tension breaks out into vehement antagonism in the third act, not so much as a new element in the relationship, but as a development of long-standing antagonisms brought to a head by the conflict over the polluted water. Act III brings Hovstad and Aslaksen into alliance with The Mayor, and he therefore feels both the political strength and justification to push his antagonism to the point of threatening and breaking with his brother.

❖ ACT IV

(18) Horster is a minor character throughout the play, but is a constant friend and protector of Dr. Stockmann and his family. He is in love with Petra, but, unlike Hovstad, he does not say so in the play (although the implication is clear). That he is not political makes him totally unlike Hovstad, and makes him a kind and loyal friend (and, after the meeting, a bodyguard) in Dr. Stockmann's life. He explains his offer of his house because he is usually away from home, but we may reasonably conclude that he wants the family nearby so that he may also be near Petra whenever he is home.

(19) The pretense for taking over the meeting is that there might be controversy, and that a chair will be needed to keep the meeting orderly (Act IV. Speech 39). The "spontaneous" acceptance of Aslaksen as the chair has been prepared for by the speech of the "6 Citizen" to follow the lead of Aslaksen (Act IV. Speech 16). In short, the crowd is being manipulated, and under these circumstances Ibsen shows how a popular majority may be misused. The implication of this act and the entire play is that it is always so misused.

(20 The Mayor and Aslaksen attack Dr. Stockmann's integrity by claiming that he is interested not in solving the Spa problem but in leading a revolution against the town government. Dr. Stockmann overcomes their attempt to squelch him by claiming that he is going to speak about "something different" (Act IV. Speech 80).

(21) Dr. Stockmann's speeches are extensive. They stem from his "discovery" that the great enemy of society is the popular majority (Act IV. Speech 115). He first attacks local officials because they "inhibit freedom" and therefore should be exterminated. He then attacks the popular majority on the grounds that most people are stupid and that their decisions as a majority are therefore stupid and misguided. The political power they wield represents the worst that humankind has to offer. Also, their formation into political parties brings out not the best in people but the worst, for the party becomes an extension of the lowest common denominator.

Although some of Dr. Stockmann's ideas are related to Hovstad's reform position in Act II, many of the ideas are new in the fourth and fifth acts. The attack on the way the "stupid" control "the intelligent," for example (Act IV, Speech 120), is new, as is the Doctor's image about the inherent intelligent of the thoroughbred few among humankind (Act IV. Speech 143). Particularly new is the scorn he heaps upon the idea that the masses and the people are the best hope for the future. The people, he claims, are dangerous because they reject truth while accepting lies and deceit (Act IV, Speech 158).

Dr. Stockmann includes The Mayor in his attack because (a) he is angry, (b) he believes that The Mayor has been leading the opposition to him, and (c) he sees The Mayor as a representative of the lies and deceit he associates with the popular majority.

(22) The actions of Pettersen offer a suitable object for the release of audience tension. The situation is deadly serious, but Pettersen's drunken outbursts offer perspective. The crowd's disapproving and increasing hostile responses are necessary because by the end of Act IV the meeting will declare Dr. Stockmann the people's enemy. Without their early hostility, their vote would have a weak foundation.

(23) Dr. Stockmann asserts that truths can live for no more than eighteen to twenty years (i.e., a generation) because as time progresses situations change and therefore solutions (truths) must also change. His concept is that a static society is also a moribund society. If progress and growth are to occur, the assumptions of government must constantly be reevaluated and new solutions must be proposed and instituted.

(24) The two Biblical passages refer to (a) what the Disciples should do when they have been rejected in a community, and (b) Christ's words when on the Cross. Although the quotations are apt, they suggest that Dr. Stockmann's views may show an overly developed vision of himself. Part of the strength of *An Enemy of the People*

is its lifelike ambiguity. The good people are not saints, and the evil people are not devils. Rather they are people who sometimes get carried away with themselves and allow their own personal concerns to overbalance the more compelling needs for consensus, accommodation, and constructive discourse. The conclusion of Act IV brings out this point.

❖ ACT V

(25) Dr. Stockmann's study is in shambles because the previous night, after the town meeting, the mob of people threw stones through his windows.

(26) In Act V, the pattern "didn't dare not to," after the outbursts of Act IV, becomes a cause of laughter. The pattern, however, does not evoke hilarity, because in the context it is ironic. The popular majority has the power to boycott and make a pariah out of anyone who stands in its way.

(27) The Mayor introduces an entirely new element in Act V, and this is that the boys, Eilif and Morten, will inherit Kiil's money. When Dr. Stockmann makes a misstatement that may be construed to mean that he has carried out the attack because he wanted to be named in "that revengeful old man's will" (Act V. Speech 140), The Mayor seizes the chance to impugn Dr. Stockmann's motives. At this point the older brother leaves, declaring that their relationship is at an end.

(28) In Act V, Both Hovstad and Aslaksen demonstrate a new degree of cynicism and self-interest. Most disturbing is that they assume that Dr. Stockmann is also guilty of the same corruptibility because of Morton Kiil's buying of Spa shares. Their understanding of the process by which the public may be manipulated and cheated shows that all their previous claims of integrity, purpose, and ideology have been hypocritical (Act V. Speeches 212, 213, 222, and 236).

(29) Morton Kiil expects that Dr. Stockmann will recant his previous claims about the Spa pollution. In the wake of Stockmann's pronouncement, Kiil expects the price of shares to rebound and make him wealthy, and in the process he also expects his reputation to rise. Kiil's threat, however, is that if Dr. Stockmann doesn't make the pronouncement he, Kiil, will disinherit Katrina and the children. After deliberation, Dr. Stockmann denies Kiil's request. In this way he maintains the integrity he has established throughout the play, particularly the choice he makes in Act III, when the welfare of the

family is threatened because of his bringing out the report on the water pollution.

(30) Dr. Stockmann is devoted to science and truth. Therefore it is fitting that the play should end on one of his discoveries. This one, that the strongest person in the world is the one who is most alone, grows out of his elevation of the individual and his attack on the popular majority in his diatribes at the meeting in Act IV.

Suggestions for Discussing the General Questions, page 1901

(1) In most respects, Ibsen presents *An Enemy of the People* as a play representative of the Norway of 1882, the time of the play. The settings and costumes reflect the period, and the situations and circumstances are real. Little was known at the time about bacteriologically caused disease and the mechanisms of water pollution, but Ibsen's description of the process is nevertheless accurate. The degree of knowledge, and the difficulty of engaging in research on a personal level, is indicated by the fact that Dr. Stockmann has had to send samples to the university to verify his suspicions about the nature of the local water.

The social and political structure shows us a time when women could not vote, and when the power within a town (unnamed in the play) was wielded by the taxpayers. Hence Aslaksen, as leader of such a group, would have had a good deal of power. The Mayor, Peter Stockmann, held an appointive rather than an elective office. His title was that of "*fogd*," meaning chief magistrate, although "Mayor" does describe his executive position and responsibilities. A strong magistrate like Peter Stockmann, who could ally himself with the various important civic associations in a locality, would possess enormous political power, since appointment to the various local offices would go only to people whose loyalty would be unquestioned. Billing's seeking the office of secretary of the judicial bench—and the uncertainty of his being granted it—indicates the precarious life of an outsider within the political system.

Within this framework, *An Enemy of the People* dramatizes a plausible situation and creates the sorts of conflicts that would have arisen out of it. Some of the events in the play are of course heightened for theatrical effects. On a number of occasions Dr. Stockmann seems to waver in his cause as he ponders the consequences of what he is doing. Thus his leaving the stage at the end of the Act III is a dramatic *coup*, and so also is his mimicry of his brother in the third act. The citizens voting to brand him an enemy of the people is another startling event, as is the milling mob leaving the stage at the end of the fourth act. The news about Morten Kiil's will which The Mayor takes to Dr. Stockmann is evidence that has not previously been important, but in Act V it becomes the killing blow to any chances the brothers might have had for reconciliation. Dr. Stockmann's violent expulsion of Aslaksen and Hovstad stretches realism, and the event may be hence be considered theatrical rather than dramatic. On the whole, however, *An Enemy of the People* is a play that conforms to the concept of stage realism.

(2) The theme of the friend of the people is introduced in the first act, and continues into the second, when it appears that Aslaksen and Hovstad are lending their support to Dr. Stockmann's campaign to preserve the water quality and also the town's reputation for honesty and integrity. In Act II, however, the theme of the enemy of the people is introduced by The Mayor when he tries to dissuade Dr. Stockmann from pursuing his campaign for clean water. In the third act the *enemy* theme is predominant as the printer and editor desert Dr. Stockmann, whose campaign becomes more isolated and personal. In Act IV the *enemy* theme is made public, and the broken windows and the notice to vacate in Act V indicate how Dr. Stockmann's role has been publicly perceived. At the play's end, his decision to undertake his own private school can be defended as his attempt to reform society, even just a little bit of it, and therefore we may regard him as a friend of the people, as he has been all along, though the people definitely do not consider him friendly.

(3) There is no part of the play that does not focus in one way or another on Dr. Stockmann. A full answer to the question therefore could involve a detailed examination of the entire work. Some of his traits, however, are these: idealism, dedication to research and truth, stubbornness, quickness of temper, slowness to judge the character of others, impetuosity, love of family, impracticality, the willingness to allow a cause to overbalance his own self-interest and the interest of his family, satisfaction in material things, a capacity for laughter and conviviality and joy. In his marriage he clearly loves his wife, but demeans her publicly without recognizing how his words have wounded her. His difficulties with his brother may indicate a degree of immaturity, for surely the problems of childhood should not spill over into adulthood, although they often do, and not just in this play.

(4) Dr. Stockmann's attack on the popular majority consists of two phases. The first is an attack on those politicians and public

people, such as The Mayor and Editor Hovstad, who bend public opinion to their own interests. It may be that this phase is the major one that Ibsen explores in the play. But he also expresses a theoretical objection to the very concept of popular sovereignty. His comparison of people to mongrels and thoroughbreds, for example (Act IV, Speech 143), is an attack based more on Plato than Thomas Jefferson. In addition, his attack on political parties is governed by his objections to the "fatheads and meatheads" among the party faithful (*"grødhoder og kødhoder,"* Act V. Speech 74), although he also implies that party power is exerted by pressure that is, somewhere, being originated and manipulated.

(5) Students undertaking to answer this question must first decide for themselves what the rights of a minority are within a political system governed by the majority. Dr. Stockmann's position is that the minority always has right and morality on its side, while the position of Hovstad and Billing is that the majority makes right. These are opposing views that, if pursued rigorously, would lead to large-scale disaffection and even revolt. An answer to the question then is that if the majority tolerates the views of the minority the system can undergo change and growth, because a majority open to analysis and criticism has within itself the ability to adapt to new circumstances. The two problems in *An Enemy of the People* are that the power structure is unyielding and also that Dr. Stockmann, himself, seems unwilling to work within the structure. The attack against the cynical control over public opinion in the interests of preserving majority power is a major theme once Ibsen introduces it in Act II.

(6) The tanneries at Mølledal are a major symbol of how polluted ideas pervert the public good by causing people to pursue their own interests regardless of the consequences. Ibsen emphasizes this symbolism through Dr. Stockmann in Act IV. Speeches 113 and 158.

(7) The primary shortcoming of Dr. Stockmann's speeches is that he does not come to grips with the need for advancing ideas within the fabric that exists. The results of his efforts to improve the town come to nothing, not because he does not have merit, but because he antagonizes the people with whom he has to work. (His brother The Mayor tells him this in Act II. Speech 243.) It is then the angry tone of his speeches, certainly resulting dramatically from his frustration, that constitutes his greatest weakness. We may also look, perhaps with superiority, on his comparison of the breeding of

people and animals, for this analysis is somewhat unsophisticated. So also is his analysis of the relationship of housecleaning to the abundance of oxygen needed for good mental health. What is important about Dr. Stockmann's speeches, however, is not that they demonstrate shortcomings, but that they are so consistent with the circumstances of the play, and that they are hence so dramatically powerful.

(8) The play has a number of comic situations and speeches. Dr. Stockmann's claim that he is now making almost as much as his family spends is funny, as is his admission that he and his brother are descendants of an old Pomeranian pirate. His stress on the theme of "they didn't dare" is repetitively funny in Act V, and a bit of farce is introduced in Act V when he throws out Aslaksen and Hovstad. There is a bit of drunken horseplay and business that in Act IV also causes humor, and, of course, Aslaksen's presentation of himself as a man of moderation is another source of laughter. Because the situation of the play, including many of Dr. Stockmann's speeches, are so serious, and because they are in effect political diatribes, such comic elements are essential to keep the play within its confines as a drama. Students may find other comic and laughable elements.

(9) Almost all the characters come to life on the stage, with the strongest realizations being of course Dr. Stockmann, The Mayor, and Aslaksen. Some of the major characteristics that examination should bring out are these:

DR. THOMAS STOCKMANN: See study questions 5, 10, 16, 21, 23, and 24.

MAYOR PETER STOCKMANN: Strong consciousness of his own self-importance. Insecurity when challenged. Use of his great intelligence in self-defense.

ASLAKSEN: A careful man, whose self-image is that of a person of moderation. Sacrifices principle for expediency.

HOVSTAD: A professed idealist who wilts under pressure. A coward and renegade at heart.

BILLING: Dramatizes himself as a freethinker and a person of independent views, but really a straw in the political wind. A profane man.

CAPTAIN HORSTER: A person of loyalty and friendliness, having great courage. Will stand up for his friends, although he himself professes no great convictions.

PETRA: A person of strong and consistent dedication to truth and her father. Frustrated with the role she plays, which requires her to make public avowals with which she disagrees.

MRS. KATRINA STOCKMANN: A strong woman in defense of her family. Possesses a strong recognition of the limitations of a woman at a time when there was no women's suffrage.

MORTEN KIIL: Totally devoted to his own interests. Not a well-educated man. Angry at real and perceived slights. Willing to hurt those who don't follow his interests.

Edited Selections from Criticism of Ibsen's Drama, *pages 1902–1921*

Like the selections from criticism of Poe and Dickinson (567 ff., 1079 ff.) the selections from criticism of Ibsen are intended collectively as a brief "casebook," with an emphasis on the two plays included here. (As one would expect, there are also discussions of other Ibsen dramas.) Writing topics may be drawn from the list on pages 1901–1902, to which you are free to add your own topics and modifications. The selections will readily serve students as the basis for short research essays. The marginal page numbers provide the opportunity to use original pagination, and therefore the selections can give students experience with documenting research essays. For a detailed discussion of research, see Chapter 32, especially pages 1930 ff.

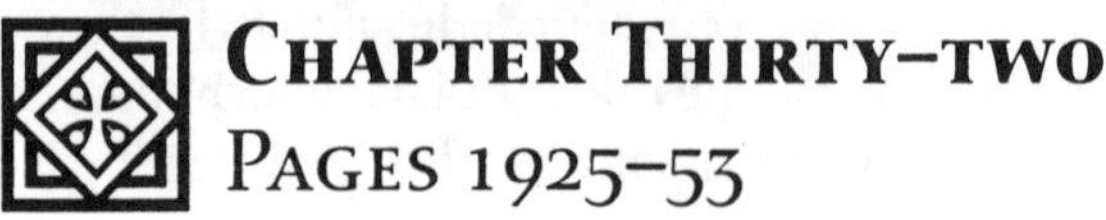

Chapter Thirty-two
Pages 1925–53

Writing and Documenting the Research Essay

The greatest problem that students encounter when doing research is to use their own words even though in a research essay they are often relying on the language of expert critics and scholars. For this reason it is important to emphasize the section on taking notes (1930–37). Students need to know that recognition must be constantly made to their sources. They also should recognize the ways in which they may be original even though they are relying on sources (1937–39).

Because of the pitfalls that writers of research essays encounter, it is most important that your students be given specific essay topics. These should not be repeated from semester to semester, but must be changed to eliminate temptations to appropriate a version of the topic that an unknown student (or professional) has completed in an earlier semester (and often on another campus).

The section on online library services (1928–30) is offered as a method of research that augments the standard use of the library catalogue system. It is important, however, to get students into the library and to get them to use books and journals. An online service is only as good as the material that has been put into it by someone interested in the process, whereas a library collection has been assembled over many years, by professional acquisitions librarians, in the best interests of learning and scholarship.

Throughout the book, at the ends of chapters, the "Special Topics for Writing and Argument" questions include various research activities. Some of these may be used as exercises in advance of the assignment of a research essay.

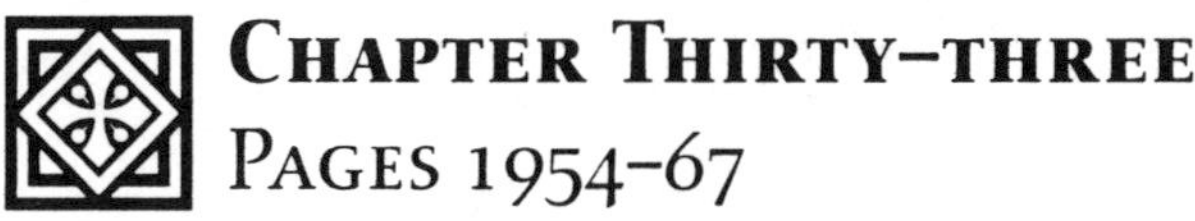

Chapter Thirty-three
Pages 1954–67

Critical Approaches Important in the Study of Literature

Needless to say, pursuing the subject of critical study is an occupation in itself. The materials in this chapter are designed to do no more than introduce students to the existence of the various critical approaches. You may therefore wish to augment the chapter with a detailed set of materials for their consideration. A good place to start is the second edition of Charles E. Bressler's *Literary Criticism: An Introduction to Theory and Practice* (Upper Saddle River: Prentice Hall, 1999). This book goes over all the ground in great detail. It is highly recommended. Especially significant about Bressler's book are the twenty pages of bibliography, beginning on page 279, which is extensive, well detailed, and up to date. The bibliography lists more than 350 books, an overwhelming number for any student getting interested in literary approaches. Among the works on which Bressler bases his illustrative discussions are three works that are also included in the sixth edition of *Literature: An Introduction to Reading and Writing*. These are Glaspell's *Trifles*, Keats's "To Autumn," and Shakespeare's *Hamlet*.

As an abbreviated bibliography, the following books, most of which Bressler lists, might be useful.

- ❖ Bloom, Harold, and Paul de Man, Jacques Derrida, Geoffrey H. Hartman, and J. Hillis Miller, *Deconstruction and Criticism* (New York: Continuum, 1988).
- ❖ Brooks, Cleanth, and Robert Penn Warren. *Understanding Poetry*. New York: Holt, 1928.
- ❖ Calahan, James M. and David B. Downing. *Practicing Theory in Introductory Literature Courses*. Urbana: National Council of teachers of English, 1991.
- ❖ Donovan, Josephine, ed., *Feminist Literary Criticism: Explorations in Theory*. Lexington: Kentucky UP, 1975.

- Hirsch, David H., *The Deconstruction of Literature: Criticism After Auschwitz*. Hanover: Brown UP, 1991.
- Richards, I. A., *Practical Criticism*. New York: Harcourt, 1929.
- Scholes, Robert. *Structuralism in Literature: An Introduction*. New Haven: Yale UP, 1974.
- Tompkins, Jane P., ed., *Reader-Response Criticism From Formalism to Post-Structuralism*. Baltimore: Johns Hopkins UP, 1980.

Many of the "Special Topics for Writing and Argument" sections ending the chapters throughout *Literature: An Introduction to Reading and Writing* include questions that bring in a number of the various critical approaches. These may be used as exercises for this chapter.

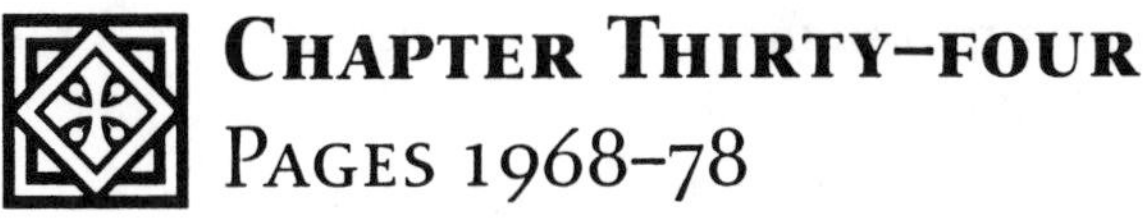

Chapter Thirty-four
Pages 1968–78

Taking Examinations on Literature

Students have been taking tests as long as they have gone to school, but even so, many of them do not prepare adequately for tests.. The most common habit they should correct is reading and cramming and then trusting to luck at exam time. They need to know that good writing, even on an exam, is always organized and well developed, and that these qualities *must be preceded by planning.*

Students should therefore be advised that practice writing should be indispensable in their preparation for examinations. Practice writing is always better than no writing, and the practice helps students in a number of ways. First, it reinforces their knowledge of the work being studied. Second, it gives them experience in structuring at least some of their ideas about the work. Third, on the principle that it is easier to do something a second time, practice writing helps students develop confidence about their ability to adapt their knowledge to whatever questions may appear on the exam.

The second objection is that it is difficult for students to know what questions to practice on. There are two answers to this objection. First, it is really more important to practice on *any* question about a work than to do no practice at all. Practice gives experience in structuring thoughts about the work, and it is this structuring that is important. Whether a student can anticipate exam questions is irrelevant to the total educational experience that the exam should generate. Second—and a kind of assurance—students may use their notes as the basis of their practice questions. The text demonstrates how sclassroom note may be turned into questions.

Students might profit from the following exercises for taking tests.

1. Using passages from classroom notes, phrase five questions, using the substance of your notes. In a brief paragraph, identify the principal issues of the questions. Try to see how a person could go astray in answering your

questions, and reword the questions, if necessary, to forestall any tangential answers.

2. For each of five identification questions, which you may develop on your own, create a three-part answer: (a) show the author and name of the work, (b) show how and where the thing being identified fits into the work, and (c) describe the general significance of the thing being identified.
3. As you read a work, write at least two questions of your own about it. Exchange these questions with a fellow student. Outline and write answers to your fellow student's set of questions.

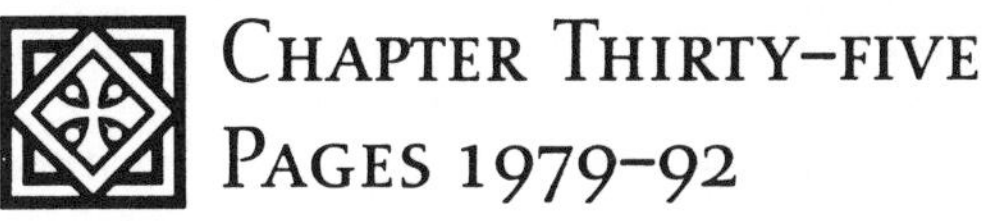

CHAPTER THIRTY-FIVE
PAGES 1979–92

Comparison-Contrast and Extended Comparison-Contrast: Learning by Seeing Literary Works Together

The comparison-contrast essay is one of the most satisfying assignments for students and instructor alike. Its value is that it breaks the pattern of single-structures that are inevitably promoted by the typical semester-in, semester-out college curriculum. The comparison-contrast method forces students to recognize that works of the mind are interrelated, and that education should promote wholeness and entirety, not compartmentalization.

In planning a comparison-contrast essay, most students experience greatest difficulty in finding a common ground of comparison (1980–81). To counter this difficulty, you might formulate their topic yourself, or else make the assignment on works that are patently similar in topic or theme (the topics for comparison in this manual are designed with such assignments in mind). Your doing so will simplify the writing tasks for your students.

Students need reminding that two works should be considered together, not separately (1981–82). What sometimes happens is that students *de facto* write two separate essays for a comparison-contrast assignment. One part is a page-and-a-half on, say, "Love in Colwin's 'An Old-Fashioned Story'" and the other is an equally long section on "Love in Butler's 'Snow'" whereas the product should have been three pages on a topic like "The Sympathetic Treatment of Love in Colwin and Butler." Such a division of subject results from the failure to comprehend the nature of comparison. The two works must be kept prominently together on the basis of the common grounds of comparison. Once the student says that "Falling in love draws out the good qualities of the major characters," then both works must be drawn upon as evidence for this assertion, and similarities must be explored. If students need a blanket rule, they might be encouraged to mention both works an equal number of times in each of their paragraphs.

The same idea also applies to extended comparison-contrast essays. A topic like that of the second demonstrative essay (1988), on the conflicts between private and public life, could easily become a dozen separate essays if not managed properly. To prevent such disintegration, the commentary on the essay (1990–91) can prove helpful, for it makes plain that the stress in the essay is on constant comparison and contrast. If students study the demonstrative essay and use the commentary as a guide, they should be able to write good extended comparison-contrast essays on their own.

The goal of the extended comparison-contrast essay is to provide you with a strong control in courses where a long paper is required but where you are unable, for whatever reason, to assign a full-blown research essay. It should not prove difficult to develop a common ground of comparison for this assignment. The thematic table of contents provides you with twenty-two possible topics. In addition, some courses are organized according to principles like "individualism vs. the state," "the quest for individual identity," "treatments of the family," " the differing interests of parents and children," "the meaning of love," or "the quest for faith," "the possibilities of renewal," "the role of women in society," "the difficulties of racial harmony," and "the presence of death." Often, common themes develop as you move from work to work in your course. One of these topics could serve as the subject of an extended comparison-contrast essay.

Some possible exercises for the comparison-contrast essay:

1. Write a paragraph comparing two major characters in a story (or play), making sure to refer to each character an equal number of times within your paragraph.
2. Compare the use of a common theme, place, incident, or idea in two (or more) works, such as the view of London in "A Description of the Morning" (832), Blake's "London" (695), and Wordsworth's "Composed upon Westminster Bridge" (1057).
3. For as many as five works, define a common element, such as "considerations of race" or "the view of women," and outline several paragraphs as though you were preparing an extended comparison-contrast essay.

Special Topics for Writing and Argument about Comparison and Contrast, *page 1992*

(1) The speakers in these two poems are in somewhat similar situations, for both are making observations about natural and cultural scenes. Both are speaking in the present tense, although Wordsworth's speaker is addressing no one in particular except his unseen readers, while Arnold's speaker is addressing a listener, presumably a woman. W finds beauty in the scene of London at rest. A detects a certain loneliness and symbolic intellectual isolation in the extinguishing of lights on the dark and distant coast of France.

(2) All the poems make a point of fidelity to love. K speaks of yearning and pillowing his head on his loved one's breast. S speaks of a more desperate love that must be loved "well" because of hastening death. A points out that lovers must be true to each other because the world does not offer much else. L seems to indicate that love must continue and a happy life must be sacrificed when a loved one dies.

(3) The women in *The Bear* and "The Necklace" are dependent on their husbands, even when a husband is dead, as with C. M's husband is supportive of his wife even when she loses a valuable piece of jewelry, and there does not seem to be any question that man and wife will stay together. In C the wife (Mrs. Popov) is disgusted with her husband now that he is dead, but she remained with him as long as he was alive and treasures his dead memory. She so values the married state that she does not resist falling in love with Smirnov, regardless of how problematic a husband Smirnov will probably be.

In G, the women exercise a good deal of independence in making their decision to hide the evidence about Minnie's murder of Wright. Minnie has been a specimen doormat for most of her married life, but under the duress of her husband's killing the canary, she snaps and tightens a rope around Wright's neck when he is sleeping. These women are all in a position of dependence, but they nevertheless have not abandoned their individuality. In R, the speaker is lost in memory of a vanished loved one, and she is therefore dependent even beyond death, as C's Mrs. Popov is at the beginning of *The Bear*.

(4)The point about descriptive scenery in all these works is that the settings are essential. With the exception of L, in which the setting provides a background and a place in which the speaker is walking, the settings of the other three works are totally integrated in their respective stories. H is dreamlike, but essential to the action. P could not have the story at all as it is without the dreary but plausible Montresor catacombs through which the two major characters walk. The story of Farquhar by B is dependent on the circumstances of the railroad bridge from which Farquhar falls. After the drop, the setting is realistic at first but then becomes increasingly dreamlike.

(5) The link between H and F in these two poems is one of disapproval. In H the disapproval is the loudness of the guns; in F the disapproval is the vast and impersonal distance of space which, fearful as it is, is less fearful to the speaker than the deserted places within his own soul. A contrast is that H is more clearly political than F, who is more personal and philosophical.

(6) In R the emphasis is on the personal sorrow at the loss of past love. In W the loss is that of a child, and the emphasis is on the irony and the agony of the loss, which is still immediate for the speaker. Longing is the mood of R. Anguish and heartbreak are the moods for W.

(7) This topic is entirely in your hands and in the hands of your students.